Praise f

'Marina Warner is one of our most erudite and morally serious writers.... interested in the ways that the really big furniture of our minds—religious as well as secular worldviews—came to be there. *Phantasmagoria* is her most ambitious book, an intellectually dazzling struggle with how the modern world (beginning roughly in the Renaissance) has imagined the stuff of souls, the nature of the psyche, the "mysterious, elusive, and ethereal" thing that somehow distinguishes the truly dead from the living and makes us what we are.' Thomas Laqueur, *The Nation*

'As always Warner's scholarship, eclecticism and inventiveness dazzle.' Ben Mooney, *The Times*

'Her subject is the metaphors that have been used to clothe the ideas of soul and spirit since the Enlightenment, from religious art to gory death-masks, and from the fairy photographs that fooled Sir Arthur Conan Doyle in the 1920s to the avatars in today's "massively multi-player online role-playing games". As one would expect from some of Ms Warner's earlier surveys, which have included books on monsters, fairy tales, heroism and the veneration of the Virgin Mary, the result is a wonderful cabinet of keenly observed curiosities.' Anthony Gottlieb, *The Economist*

'Frighteningly literate and well-informed' Roz Kaveney, *Time Out*

'Marina Warner is particularly well-equipped to conduct this investigation... She is exquisitely alive not just to ideas and arguments, but also to the jag and whiff and tang of things.... *Phantasmagoria* is a cabinet of familiar wonders: a jetting, generous, humane spree of thought, richly quickened by the life it finds within us and abroad, in our media and machineries of mind.' Stephen Connor, *The Independent*

'*Phantasmagoria* is a fascinating history of spirited bodies and haunted machines, but a reminder too of why the metaphors still get under our skin' Brian Dillon, *Daily Telegraph*

'This book's enquiries are wide-ranging, pertinent and up-to- date. All Marina Warner's material is freshly and enticingly presented.... This book is a powerful statement.' Hilary Mantel, *The Guardian*

'The general effect is rather like that of reading through a first-class encyclopedia.' Nigel Barley, *Times Higher Education Supplement*

<u>Jacket illustration</u>: Known as *Petit Fantôme* (Little Ghost), this agate belonged to the philosopher, writer, and Surrealist Roger Caillois, who made a collection of such images, the spontaneous work of Natura Pictrix (Nature the Painter). Musée National d'Histoire Naturelle, N°188.117. Photographer: Karin Maucotel, Paris-Musées.

Phantasmagoria

Spirit Visions, Metaphors, and Media
into the Twenty-first Century

MARINA WARNER

OXFORD
UNIVERSITY PRESS

OXFORD

UNIVERSITY PRESS

Great Clarendon Street, Oxford OX2 6DP

Oxford University Press is a department of the University of Oxford.
It furthers the University's objective of excellence in research, scholarship,
and education by publishing worldwide in

Oxford New York

Auckland Cape Town Dar es Salaam Hong Kong Karachi
Kuala Lumpur Madrid Melbourne Mexico City Nairobi
New Delhi Shanghai Taipei Toronto

With offices in

Argentina Austria Brazil Chile Czech Republic France Greece
Guatemala Hungary Italy Japan Poland Portugal Singapore
South Korea Switzerland Thailand Turkey Ukraine Vietnam

Oxford is a registered trade mark of Oxford University Press
in the UK and in certain other countries

Published in the United States
by Oxford University Press Inc., New York

British Library Cataloguing in Publication Data
Data available

Library of Congress Cataloging in Publication Data
Data available

Typeset by SPI Publisher Services, Pondicherry, India
Printed in Great Britain
on acid-free paper by
Clays Ltd., St Ives plc

ISBN   978-0-19-923923-8

I

For Graeme

'Hang there like fruit, my soul,
Till the tree die!'

Acknowledgements

This book has evolved through many conversations and encounters; it draws on work undertaken alongside friends, family, and colleagues in different ways, and I have been helped and inspired by them throughout. My profound thanks go to Peter Hulme, who has given my work invaluable encouragement and support over the years, and who read this book in draft. Jacqueline Rose has given me most generously of her interest, questioning, and discernment. Hermione Lee's judgement and incisiveness have provided me with bearings to steer by; Roy Foster's interest, questions, and wide knowledge have been invaluable, as always; Mark Haworth-Booth kindly read some work in progress, and from his expert knowledge rescued me from errors. Victoria Nelson offered me much wise counsel after reading chapters in draft, and directed me towards a host of fascinating sources. I am aware how very fortunate I am in their support and their friendship: I wish I could express better my gratitude to them.

At the very start of the research, Ann Sutherland Harris brought me to the University of Pittsburgh, where students at my seminar brought fresh material to bear on the theme. I was also awarded, by Trinity College, Cambridge, an invaluable year to read and write when I was a Visiting Fellow Commoner in 1997–98; their resources in relevant materials enrich the book, and my special thanks go to Anne Barton, Adrian Poole, Jean Khalfa, Sashiko Kusukawa, and the late Jeremy Maule. Towards the end of the writing, in 2003, I was a visiting fellow at the Italian Academy, Columbia University, New York, and was able to bring the book nearly to completion there, where the Fellows offered the opportunity for helpful discussion, and the director David Freedberg gave me generously of his thoughts and encouragement. In 2006, I returned to Columbia for a symposium on 'What Is Enchantment?', and I am most grateful to Akeel Bilgrami and the Heyman Centre of the Humanities for the stimulus of this gathering. Since 2004, I have been fortunate indeed in the company of my colleagues at the University of Essex, and have been greatly helped by their discussion of parts of this book. To all, very much thanks.

During the making of *Phantasmagoria*, I have had invaluable opportunities to exchange ideas with colleagues who have invited me to give talks in different institutions, including Penn State University; the Getty Research Institute; the University of St Andrews; the University of East Anglia; the

Museum of Photography, Film, and Television in Bradford; the DIA foundation, New York; Stanford University; Northwestern University, Evanston, Illinois; Paris VII and Paris XIII; the University of Auckland, where I gave the Robb lectures; and the universities of Bologna, Salerno, and Palermo. My warmest thanks to all my hosts, especially to Claudia Swan, at Northwestern, whose conference 'Interior Temptation' provided much wonderful food for thought, Giuliana Bruno at the Institute of Visual Arts, Harvard, and to Mariet Westermann at the Institute of Fine Arts, New York; their knowledge and judgement have always provided me with a compass. Also many thanks to Russell Roberts, Sally Alexander, Linda Colley, Julia Kristeva, Vita Fortunati, and Daniela Corona. I am especially grateful to the Tanner Foundation, which sponsored the lectures I gave at Yale in 1992, where my host Peter Brooks was unstintingly kind, and provided me with stimulating respondents—Terry Castle and Esther Da Costa Meyer. Duncan Salkeld convened a lively conference, 'The Soul in Western History and Culture', at the Chichester Institute of Higher Education, 1998, where I learned much from Jill Kraye and Myles Burnyeat amongst others. Ivor Indyk, editor of *Heat* magazine, Sydney, and the Sydney Grammar School were most generous hosts in Australia; as were Michael Neill and Joanne Wilkes in New Zealand. I was honoured by the invitation to speak at the Warburghaus, Hamburg, and I thank Wolfgang Kemp and Marianne Pieper for their hospitality, and Catherina Berents for her translation of my work for publication. The editors and staff of *Raritan*—Richard Poirier and Suzanne Hymans, and since 2003, Jackson Lears and Stephanie Volmer—have been most perceptive as well as encouraging in publishing various parts in progress. The late Edward Said first put me in contact with the journal when he invited me to the Heyman Institute of the Humanities, Columbia, as a Visiting Fellow, and for this, among many other acts of support, I will always remember his energy and his spirit.

Others who have contributed in many other crucial ways, whom I would also like to thank, include Roger Malbert, with whom I worked on related exhibitions (*The Inner Eye* and *Eyes, Lies and Illusions*); Jacqueline Burckhardt and Bice Curiger, editors of *Parkett* magazine; Sina Najafi and his team at *Cabinet* magazine; Alan Jenkins and others at the *Times Literary Supplement*; Irène Andreae, Lisa Appignanesi, John and Gillian Beer, Roger Cardinal, Terence Cave, William Christian, Jr., Steven Connor, Lorraine Daston, Bob Davis, Rudolf Dekker, Wendy Doniger, Mark Dorrian, John Forrester, Rob Irving, Mary Jacobus, Sir Geoffrey Lloyd, Roger Luckhurst, Patrick Parrinder, Pam Thurschwell, Bart Verschaffel, Kim Reynolds, Michèle Roberts, John Beebe, Stefan Andriopoulos, and, as always, Mary Douglas. At the Warburg Institute, Elizabeth McGrath, Paul Taylor, and Jill Kraye have offered inspiring guidance. My search has been wonderfully enriched by David Scrase, at the Fitzwilliam, Cambridge, and his discernment and huge knowledge.

It hardly needs saying that I must take responsibility for what is published here, in spite of the benefit I've received from their keen-eyed and perceptive comments, suggestions, and conversation.

Lavinia Greenlaw read the book in draft, and I benefited greatly from her discriminating and careful comments; Alison Samuel also saw an early version, and her response led to shaping it in its present from—my thanks to them both. My agents, Binky Urban in New York and Gill Coleridge in London, were unswerving in their support for my work: I owe them a great deal for their faith.

Several contemporary artists have also helped me draw out the ideas in the book: I am especially aware of the loss of Helen Chadwick, who involved me early on in the unique quest for embodied imagination. Among the staff of the libraries and collections I've used, I'd like to thank Ken Arnold and Sarah Bakewell at the Wellcome Institute, and the staff in the Library there as well; many have helped the book on its way at the London Library, the Warburg Institute, and the British Library. Alan Wesencraft (formerly of the Harry Price Library, Senate House), Julia Walworth (formerly at Senate House, in Special Collections); at the Bill Douglas Centre, University of Exeter, Hester Higton and formerly, Richard Crangle, and Rob White, formerly at the British Film Institute, also helped me with specific materials. In the Prints and Drawings department of the British Museum, I have depended on the incomparable knowledge and generosity of Anthony Griffiths and Sheila O'Connell and their staff.

I would also like to acknowledge the help of Susan Acland-Hood, then at Trinity College, Cambridge, with research into the SPR materials and the correspondence of Henry Sidgwick and F. W. H. Myers in the Wren Library; Helena Ivins, Imogen Cornwall-Jones, Beatrice Dillon, Philip Oltermann, and above all, Tom Fisher, have all helped me in different ways, and I thank them all for their work.

Above all, I wish to express my profound thanks to Oxford University Press, and to Andrew McNeillie, my editor, who responded with curiosity, infinite generosity, and trust: his interest in the book's themes and his inspiring belief in my writing made possible a final draft, and I owe him and his team the emergence of my work in this volume—special thanks to Tom Perridge and Jean van Altena. Pippa Lewis, long-time collaborator and friend, was wonderfully perservering in tracking down images and permissions.

For permission to reproduce the images, I acknowledge with especial gratitude the Syndics of the Fitzwilliam Museum, Cambridge; the Master and Fellows of Trinity College, Cambridge; the Trustees of the British

Museum; the Society for Psychical Research; the Getty Museum; the Imperial War Museum; Pierre Huyghe and the Marian Goodman Gallery, Paris; The British Library; the Arnold Schoenberg Centre, Vienna; The Pitt-Rivers Museum, Oxford; The British Film Institute; The Victoria and Albert Museum, London; The Sterling and Francine Clark Institute, Williamstown, Mass.; The Cleveland Museum of Art; the Keith de Lellis Gallery, New York; Laurent Mannoni.

I would also like to thank Susan Stewart for permission to quote from 'Sung from the generation of AIR,' (*Columbarium* (2003)), and Richard Crangle for references to the *Magic Lantern Journal*. Lines from 'Mapping the Genome' and 'Attempts on Your Life' from *Corpus* by Michael Symmons Roberts, published by Jonathan Cape, are reprinted by permission of the Random House Group Ltd. "Angel Surrounded by Paysans", from *The Collected Poems of Wallace Stevens* by Wallace Stevens, copyright 1954 by Wallace Stevens and renewed 1982 by Holly Stevens. Used by permission of Alfred A. Knopf, a division of Random House, Inc. Although every effort has been made to establish copyright and contact copyright holders prior to printing this has not always been possible. The publishers would be pleased to rectify any omissions or errors brought to their notice at the earliest opportunity.

During my work on the book, my son Conrad Shawcross founded the IBLS (Investigative Bureau into the Location of the Soul), with its team of soul-catchers, including Bruce Springshaw, whose Ford Capri, fully rigged with rods and fishing nets, was long parked outside the house. The project—which became a series of works, an installation, and an ongoing history—accompanied my analogous quest in my study upstairs; Conrad's curiosity and response have been a crucial stimulus, always. To other dear friends and family, I also owe more than this dry print can express.

Contents

List of Illustrations

Cover

Known as *Petit Fantôme* (Little Ghost), this pictured stone is an agate from the collection of Roger Caillois, writer and scientist, now in the Galerie de Minéralogie, Musée nationale d'histoire naturelle, Paris. Reproduced in *Trajectoires du rêve*, exhibition catalogue (Paris, 2003). Ancienne collection Roger Caillois, Inv. MNHN 188–117. Photo: Paris-Musées/Karin Maucotel.

Colour plates

Black and white illustrations

List of Abbreviations

AB	*Art Bulletin*
AMH	*Annals of Medical History*
AMO	Ashmolean Museum, Oxford
Bodley	Bodleian Library, Oxford
BDC	The Bill Douglas Centre for the History of Cinema and Popular Culture, University of Exeter
BFI	British Film Institute
BJHS	*British Journal for the History of Science*
BJPR	*The British Journal of Psychical Research*
BL	British Library
BM	British Museum
CI	*Critical Inquiry*
CUL	Cambridge University Library
DNB	*Dictionary of National Biography*; <http://www.oxforddnb.com/
FMC	Fitzwilliam Museum, Cambridge
HGL	Hayward Gallery, London
HPL	Harry Price Library, Senate House, University of London
HRCANU	Humanities Research Centre, Australian National University, Canberra
IBLS	Investigative Bureau into the Location of the Soul
JAI	*Journal of the Anthropological Institute*
JHI	*Journal of the History of Ideas*
JJC	John Johnson Collection, Bodley
JSPR	*Journal of the Society for Psychical Research*
JWCI	*Journal of the Warburg and Courtauld Institutes*
IWM	Imperial War Museum, London
LC	Library of Congress, Washington, DC
LRB	*London Review of Books*
MAMVP	Le Musée d'Art Moderne de la Ville de Paris
MassMOCA	Massachussetts Museum of Contemporary Art
MMA	Metropolitan Museum of Art, New York

NCE	*New Catholic Encyclopaedia* (Washington, DC, 1967–79)
NGAL	National Gallery of Art, London
NGAW	National Gallery of Art, Washington, DC
NGS	National Gallery of Scotland
NMLJ	*New Magic Lantern Journal*
NMPFT	National Museum of Photography, Film, and Television, Bradford
NYRB	*New York Review of Books*
OLJ	*Optical Lantern Journal*
PASPR	*Proceedings of the American Society for Psychical Research*
PISA	*Proceedings of the International Shakespeare Association*
PMLA	*Proceedings of the Modern Language Association*
PQ	*Psycholanalytic Quarterly*
PRM	Pitt-Rivers Museum, Oxford
PSPR	*Proceedings of the Society for Psychical Research*
RS	*The Riverside Shakespeare* (Boston, 1974)
SBT	South Bank Touring exhibition, HGL
SPR	Society for Psychical Research
SPRA	SPR Archive
TGL	Tate Gallery, London
TLS	*Times Literary Supplement*
VAM	Victoria and Albert Museum, London
WIC	Wellcome Iconographic Collections, WL
WL	Wellcome Library, University of London
WLTCC	Wren Library, Trinity College, Cambridge
WMS	Whipple Museum of Science, Cambridge
WNC	Werner Nekes Collection

Every Angel is terrible.

Rainer Maria Rilke, *The Duino Elegies*

You are on a mission to discover
why the human heart still slows
when divers break the surface,
why mermaids still swim in our dreams.

Michael Symmons Roberts, 'Mapping the Genome'

(Some things must be believed to be seen.)

Andrew McNeillie, 'Homage to Patagonia', *Slower*

Saint Caterina de' Vigri, who died in 1463, sits up in
her mummified body in her shrine in the church of
Corpus Domini, Bologna, waiting like a wise virgin for
the last day.

Prologue

Probably no images are utterly silent.

Roger Caillois, *Writing of Stones*

I.

Nobody in the street knew where the mummified saint was, and I had left my guidebook in the hotel room. Bologna is a city famed for free thinking in science and politics, so my request for directions to the body of Santa Caterina de' Vigri, preserved entire in a reliquary chapel since the fifteenth century, met with embarrassment and, sometimes, incredulous laughter. It was a very hot day, quite unseasonably hot for June, and only a holy fool—or an Englishwoman—would pursue such a quest down one side street after another. But I had seen a photograph of the effigy, and female saints and Catholic magic have always held a spell over me, so I persevered.

Eventually, past the barrier on a side street in the process of excavation, there stood the church of Corpus Domini. Inside, through a bare ante-chamber, and in the very depths of the convent buildings beyond, I found la Santa, in a reliquary chamber of her own, oval in shape, musty, shadowy, glinting with silver and gold ornament, crystal and velvet; there are no windows, and the walls are all richly encrusted with dusty *ex votos* in the shape of flaming hearts and other body parts. The whole room is her reliquary. Caterina died in 1463 at the age of 50, and is sitting up in the middle of the shrine quite straight in a glass box, looking younger than her age. She is wearing the white wimple, black veil, and brown habit of her order, the Poor Clares, with the knotted cord of her vows. Her eyes are shut as if in concentration; her face has developed a brick-red complexion, while the rest of the flesh that is visible has blackened till her thin fingers and bare toes look like a small monkey's, with touches of rouge on the toenails. She is wearing a narrow ring on her wedding finger (as a bride of Christ), and all around her, on the circular walls of the reliquary shrine where she keeps vigil, there are bones among the offerings, resting on faded silk cushions in crystal caskets.

She liked to pay the viol, and her instrument lies in one cabinet to her left, very small and looking very mute as well. On her right, in another cabinet, the manuscript of the book of meditations she wrote is on display. Called *Le sette armi spirituali*—the seven weapons of the spirit—it belongs to the late medieval movement for private prayer which was radical for its time.[1] Her script is very fine, regular, and shapely, and I took the language at first to be Byzantine Greek, though she in fact wrote in her own Italian dialect—again a rather modern gesture presaging the Reformation. These personal things are full of her, more so than her effigy. Her musical instrument echoes one that has come unstrung, held by the statue of the angel kneeling beside the body. Caterina also painted in a rather old-fashioned iconic style, and her work hangs among the *ex votos* in her shrine—a fallen Christ under the cross, a Madonna with the bambino, a crucified Christ bloodied all over and fountaining jets of more blood and lymph from his wounds.

She is sitting surrounded by these memorials to her earthly existence, preserved in her embalmed body, because she appeared to her sisters in the convent in a vision soon after her death, and told them she wanted to keep them company.

As happens with special saints, her body was miraculously still pliant (and fragrant) when her tomb was opened fifteen days after her death, but as soon as the Abbess ordered her 'to sit down under obedience', she 'sat down submissively'. Only then did rigor mortis set in.[2]

According to Catholic belief, a holy person, especially a virgin, will remain incorrupt in death while awaiting the reunification of body and soul on the Last Day. In Catholic cult, this belief—this hope—inspires effigies of the body of the deceased saint, displayed in their miraculous entire and imperishable state. Such corpses testify to their owners' spiritual wholeness—'immaculate' meaning unmarked literally and metaphorically—and any visitor to Italy or Spain will have seen such figures, lying under an altar in their 'urna', or casket. They are almost always recumbent, sleeping as they wait for the Last Day and the resurrection of the flesh. Sometimes the visible parts of the body are crinkled and blackened with age (Santa Chiara in Assisi), but mostly they have been embalmed, using wax as the most visible element: Santa Fina, who died in San Gimignano in 1253 at the age of 15, is brought out twice a year in procession; also in Bologna, in the university church of San Sigismondo, a wax effigy of Imelda Lambertini, who died at the age of 12 in 1338 and was beatified in 1862, lies in her glass coffin beside her bones. She is crowned with a chaplet of white flowers, her face's lifelikeness has been enhanced by real eyelashes, and on her feet she wears a modern schoolgirl's cotton socks. Santa Vittoria, a virgin martyr, is preserved in her glass coffin in full view in S. Maria della Vittoria, Rome—in the same church as Bernini's *Ecstasy of St Teresa*. In her case, the wax sculpture sheathing her skeleton has cracked, and the bones of her fingers poke through.[3]

Any travels in Catholic territory will lead to more discoveries of such effigies, many of them of more recent date, lying on cushions in glass cases under altars, sleeping the sleep of the just before the last trump. But Santa Caterina de' Vigri is sitting up, a wise virgin.

Her shrine was later all frilled and furbelowed by the team of baroque stuccoists, painters, and carvers who worked on the church interior, and it survived the bombing raids of 1943 which smashed the rest of the decorations.[4] La Santa's living likeness, this life-in-death effigy of her kippered corpse, is much too grisly for most of us now, even those of us who have been brought up Catholic, and who, like me, are curious about the religion's magic rites, its play with the flesh and the spirit. When I came into the side chapel, my eyes were fastened on Santa Caterina sitting there so still, and the presence of a woman kneeling at a prie-dieu behind me barely registered, or rather, I took her still form to be another statue, so, when she moved, it was so unexpected in that charnel chamber that, all of sudden coming to life, she made me jump out of my skin. I had entered the shrine and thought nobody else was there, and I was awed and not a little scared of the mummy enthroned in front of me. But like the twitching eyelids of a corpse in a horror film, the woman getting up from the prie-dieu gave me a shock, for she introduced life into the frozen atmosphere. I had expected death to hold everything in that chamber in its grip.

Then, with a harsh scraping on its metal grooves, a small shutter slid across an invisible aperture, and the face of a nun appeared; she shushed, and wagged a finger at my camera, 'Vietato' (forbidden), she whispered. Later, I followed this sister into her vestibule, where she sold rosaries and souvenirs, votive masses and candles, and some literature about la Santa; she was young and round, and bundled up in an old-fashioned habit, the kind you no longer see nuns wearing. I had to pass my euros tightly rolled up to get them through the lattice of the grille behind which she officiated, which went from the counter up to the ceiling.

In Santa Caterina's presence, I felt I had entered the ambiguous, terrible, and enthralling borderland between animation and lifelessness. The effigy of Santa Caterina gave me a vivid experience of the uncanny, the mixed-up feeling famously discussed by Freud in 1919 (see below, Chapter 1).[5] A lifelike effigy like Santa Caterina's throws the question of spirit into sharp relief: it excites inquisitiveness, to plumb the mystery of its lack.

II.

When I came out of the shrine into the main body of the church, I found a trace of the search for that principle. In an open side chapel across the nave, an inscription on a large marble monument read simply 'Galvani': it was the tomb of the great physiologist who was a professor of medicine at the University of Bologna, where he died.

Luigi Galvani (1737–98) probed the effects of electricity on dead matter, and in 1786 wrote up the famous experiments he made when he caused the corpse of a frog to twitch and kick.[6] His experiments recast divine relations to life itself, and Galvanist theories implied such foundations to animate being that I was surprised to find him buried inside a church, in a side chapel of his own with such a fine, proud monument. For after his work, a different metaphor was needed to convey God's activity, that divine effect on human clay that Michelangelo had conceived, for example, in the much overused image of the Creation of Adam. There, God the Father touches his creation with his finger as if running a current through him. Electricity and vitality were indeed mysteriously interwoven, and far beyond anything Galvani analysed: in cloning experiments today, a spark kick-starts the process of cell division and thus development of the embryo. In some senses, Dolly the sheep, first clone to live, was 'galvanized' into life.[7]

Galvani's surmises about the nervous system and electrical charges were soon to be challenged and were eventually overtaken by a better understanding of electricity,[8] and his experiments were enthusiastically taken up as a form of pseudo-scientific entertainment. Giovanni Aldini, Galvani's nephew and assistant, pressed the implications farther, and performed with corpses of animals much larger and more sympathetic than frogs, from species with whom audiences could identify; he even administered electric shocks to parts of human cadavers and to severed heads to make their facial expressions alter as if they were moving and responding. It was Aldini who inaugurated shock therapy for mental illness, a method still in use in some parts of the world today, though it remains incompletely understood. After him, Franz Mesmer deduced from his own theories about electricity and its relation to vitality another form of spiritual cure which in the late eighteenth century gained an even more enthusiastic society following than Galvanism.

These apparent trespasses across the border of life/death contributed to Mary Shelley's nightmare vision of her scientist, Dr Frankenstein. After an evening discussing Galvanism in the Villa Diodati on that famous stormy night in the summer of 1816, Mary Shelley produced, from her own dream of reason, the most mythic monster of modern times. As she wrote in the preface, 'The event on which this fiction is founded has been supposed . . . as not of impossible occurrence'.[9] Her cursed protagonist Frankenstein acquires 'the capacity of bestowing animation'; from exhumed body parts gathered from charnel houses and burial grounds, he prepares 'a frame for the reception of it, with all its intricacies of fibres, muscles, and veins'. In his excitement he believes, 'Life and death appeared to me ideal bounds, which I should first break through, and pour a torrent of light into our dark world . . . if I could bestow animation upon lifeless matter, I might in process of time . . . renew life where death had apparently devoted the body to corruption.'[10] At last, Frankenstein, progenitor of a thousand mad scientists in fiction and cinema, 'infuse[s] a spark of being into the lifeless thing that lay at my feet', and the creature he has made opens one 'dull yellow eye'.[11]

As I say, it surprised me to emerge from the hushed and fervid atmosphere in Santa Caterina's shrine and find Galvani memorialized there as well. But somehow the two great citizens of the place balance each other in the business of understanding the relation of body to spirit, embodied identity and remembered individuality. Caterina de' Vigri, a hallowed figure of the Catholic faith, remains present in her body, incorrupt on account of her virtue, because divine privilege has prevented mortality from claiming her. Such a marvel proves that sanctity thwarts nature and time and miraculously overturns their laws. Meanwhile, Galvani showed that a frog which had been killed could kick its legs and respond to stimuli as if it were still alive.

In her glass box, Santa Caterina looks like the embalmed effigy of Jeremy Bentham, who left his body to University College, London, to be displayed as an 'auto-icon'. Like her, he is also sitting, displayed in the main corridor of the college seated in a wooden box with folding doors which are opened for viewing the figure. But Bentham's mummy preserves his identity for posterity precisely because, according to his principles, the body is the seat of the person and there is nothing beyond it. He also desired, he said, to keep his friends company at dinner on the anniversary of his death, and he is still brought out to take his place at the table at the annual gathering of the Bentham Society. But he was a sceptic, and he was bidding posterity to accept his mortal remains as vacant matter, no different from any other inanimate thing.[12] While la Santa is sacred, a hallowed recipient of suppliants and adorers, the rationalist philosopher Bentham was claiming the freedom to be profane and let his corpse remain in the world. He has not quite succeeded: his preserved and clothed body does not settle into the invisibility of the other statues in the College corridors: he still spooks me, however often I see him sitting there, alert and kind of smiling.

Caterina's prolonged presence refuses time, as measured by mortality and physical decay: she is waiting for the day of judgement in the body she will reassume in a perfected and radiant form at the promised resurrection of the flesh. As for Luigi Galvani and his fantasy shadow, Dr Frankenstein, they threaten to quicken the dead. Jeremy Bentham also communicates his continuing presence through his preserved and seated body, looking for all the world the very thing, and in his case, he maintained that this is all there is. His fleshly envelope is him and yet not him. In some elusive way, Santa Caterina and Jeremy Bentham in death both manifest the people they were, across time.

By a profound paradox, which will continue to surface in what follows, the Christian, religious effigy and the sceptical philosopher's auto-icon are solid, present, corporeal, and material, whereas the force that the scientist Galvani detected and applied is immaterial—or, more precisely, it inheres in the material world but is mysterious, elusive, and ethereal. The proximity of these different figures of the dead, and the inversion of religious and scientific approaches they communicate, describe an arc in the story I am trying to tell.

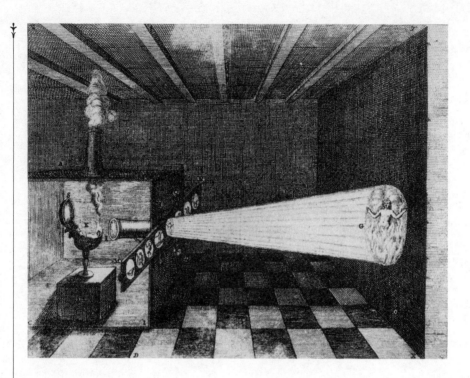

The first magic lanterns projected fantasies of the
supernatural: visions of angels and devils, ghosts and
skeletons, as in this slide of a soul in purgatory from
Athanasius Kircher, *Ars Magna Lucis et Umbrae*, 1671.

Introduction: The Logic of the Imaginary

> Words are too awful an instrument for good and evil to be trifled with:
> they hold above all external powers a dominion over thoughts.
>
> William Wordsworth, 'Essays upon Epitaphs'

I.

The Catholic catechism, which as a child I knew by heart, puts the question: 'How is your soul like to God?' To which the answer is: 'My soul is like to God because it is a spirit, and is immortal.'[1] Though I no longer believe in a God-given soul, the concept 'soul' survives strongly in my experience. Since I began listening out for the word, I hear it every day, and rarely couched in religious belief. 'Soul' overlaps with spirit in these comments or exchanges, and both soul and spirit still brim with meaning. 'Soul' is larger than 'mind', conveying the whole of a person's imponderable organizing principle, including the parts that remain mysterious. It evokes personal truthfulness to feelings (soul music), the authentic homeland (soul food), while 'spirit' continues to evoke the vital spark even when we are not certain what the principle of life consists of.[2] Mind–body dualism has been discounted (as in Gilbert Ryle's famous, scornful phrase 'the ghost in the machine')—for many reasons and after many long arguments—but it is still difficult to turn one's back on the deep hinterland behind the principle of animation: the difference between life and death depends on an *animus* or *anima* imagined to lurk within embodied personality. Even when we profess agnosticism if not unbelief in a supernatural order, we are the inheritors of much classical cosmology and medieval philosophy about spirit and soul—in unconscious ways and in common parlance.

The oddity of spirit's material and secular usage is not made easier by the overlap between the terms 'soul' and 'spirit'. René Descartes's theory about animal spirits flowing from the brain exercised a profound influence, which leaves its traces on ideas about someone's disposition or state of mind: to be in 'low spirits', for example.[3] Surprisingly, in what has been considered the era of secularism and rationality, immaterial aspects of human experiences have multiplied alongside the extraordinary discoveries of science, long after Isaac Newton speculated about empty space, Anton Mesmer proclaimed the existence of 'vital spirits', and Luigi Galvani wandered in the electromagnetic field.

In relation to the character of the 'life-giving principle' in general (what is the stuff of the soul?) and in particular (what is *my* psyche?), all kinds of empirical, even forensic methods have been brought to bear, as this book will later explore. Yet the opposition set up between Enlightenment and 'Counter-Enlightenment' does not hold in the history of thought about the life force at one level, or individuality at another: Sigmund Freud's powerful influence as well as the most recent studies of consciousness (by Roger Penrose, for example) navigate by rational methods to arrive at new working models for the mysteries of spirit—the unconscious, the 'shadows of the mind'—in accordance with what has become in some quarters of contemporary culture a still evolving form of material mysticism.[4]

At the end of the eighteenth century, S. T. Coleridge's poetry and commentaries began to absorb and alter such reflections on the nature of spirit in relation to his own, Romantic, era's changed view of the psyche, consciousness, and inspiration. The term 'spirit' can be used with exclusively psychological meaning in a secular context: it applies to the distinctiveness of a friend's character as well as to that *élan vital*, the energy that distinguishes them from an effigy or a corpse. More widely, it is used to evoke the special feel of a place, or of a time, or the temper of a meeting, or of the mood in a room, the feeling among a group of friends. Apart from expressions in popular speech, the gossip circuits of unofficial knowledge give the mental skyscape of the twenty-first century the wild heterogeneity of the Hellenistic world, as residues from different eras have adhered to form a sticky, bristling deposit. Judaeo-Cabbalistic angels, Gnostic energumens, phantasms, and succubi; Neoplatonist daimons; Middle Eastern ghouls and genies; Romantic vampires and revenants; African, Caribbean, and Native American zombies and spectres—all these various spirits and more besides flock and throng the entertainment ether and the world-wide Web. Some of them will appear in what follows.

Phantasmagoria: Spirit Visions, Metaphors, and Media into the Twenty-first Century springs from this paradox: that modernity did not by any means put an end to the quest for spirit and the desire to explain its mystery; curiosity about spirits of every sort (to adapt Oberon's phrase) and the ideas and imagery which communicate their nature have flourished more vigorously than ever since the seventeenth century, when the modern fusion of scientific inquiry, psychology, and metaphysics began.

II.

The French art historian Henri Focillon, in *The Life of Forms in Art* (1934), proposed that forms have a life of their own, and forms in art both derive from and generate other forms, autonomously, according to their own internal principles, both organic and abstract. He argues that no amount of explanation of the historical, social, economic, or personal circumstances in which the Gothic develops will ever give you the particular shape of the Gothic arch: 'The time that gives support to a work of art does not give definition either to its principle or to its specific form.'[5] He also insists that forms exist independently of signification, so that while the Gothic arch might symbolize aspiration, divinity, and ethereal lightness, it does not intrinsically do so, and could attract other meanings. Wallace Stevens was much taken with Focillon's thinking, which helped form in turn his own theory of active imagination, through which 'form makes things happen, rather than embodying them', as Angela Leighton has commented. 'It is an event of art, not an art object.'[6]

I would not go as far as Focillon in uncoupling aesthetic forms from history and society, but his argument strikingly offers a path out of a certain impasse in the study of signs and symbols; it frees them from the fixity inflicted by ideas of the collective unconscious, on the one hand, and on the other, from the relativism of historicism that denies any intrinsic properties to materials or bodies of any form. The cultural object, in Focillon's perspective, possesses a dynamic autonomy that interacts with experience and modifies it. Motifs are simultaneously subject to continuous metamorphoses, and yet preserve a certain integrity: they are not altogether empty signifiers waiting to be filled, but take up their polymorphous being autonomously, and then attract a host of meanings which interplay with them and continue to generate new forms. '[Form] prolongs and diffuses itself,' writes Focillon, 'throughout our dreams and fancies: we regard it, as it were, as a kind of fissure through which crowds of images aspiring to birth may be introduced into some indefinite realm—a realm which is neither that of physical extent nor that of pure thought.'[7]

Expressions of the subtle body—the form of spirit—pour through this fissure. Compounded of recurring ingredients—wax, air, light, ether—and mingling with a crowd of analogous spirit forms and materials—with blots and smudges, clouds and haloes—the larval ghosts who have their being in the conventional language of the supernatural appear to float free of historical circumstances. But such a ghost also arrives at definition and distinctiveness according to specific temporal circumstances—individual quests, mass fads. This book tells the story of this interaction, between the life of spirit forms, their habitual vehicles, and their vicissitudes in modernity. Through ten different vehicles—from wax to film—this book attempts to handle materials through which spirit and spirits have paradoxically taken form in the world; taking Focillon's perspective, *Phantasmagoria* treats the subject of spirit forms as a work of art continuing over time, similar to a cathedral or another grand and sacred artefact.

Focillon's radical theory of forms strikes several echoes in the writing of the surrealist and polymath Roger Caillois (d. 1978), student of the 'sacred in ordinary life'. In an inspired essay, Caillois took up Mallarmé's concept that the imagination possesses its own logic, and speculated that there might exist a language of forms inherent in the universe, a 'universal syntax': 'Philosophers have not hesitated to identify the real and the rational. I am persuaded that a different bold step . . . would lead to discover the grid of basic analogies and hidden connections which constitute the logic of the imaginary.'[8] This 'logic of the imaginary' structures the return of those metaphors—wax, breath, cloud, light, shadow, ether—when spirits are in question; the intrinsic physical properties of these substances have structured the axioms of our shared languages of the spirit.[9] Such substances form a cluster, almost bound like a molecule, in the repertory of linguistic vehicles for soul and spirit, and they persist into modernity, and came to be refashioned in the light of the new technologies, from the first public wax-works displays to contemporary video games and digitized film. As the vast array of modern inventions began to change our experience of the world— from the telescope and the microscope onwards—their advent interacted with imagery from antiquity and theology which had dominated thought about the stuff of the spirit.

Verbal and visual, these languages share with the language of demons the capacity to institute forms, meaning, and experience.[10] They have a syntax, grammar, vocabulary, a complicated history, and a changing development over time. The intelligibility of their elements depends partly on handed-down expressions, on habitual ways of envisioning, on codes known, assembled, and disassembled in cognitive patterns that have been learned and passed on. But in their frequent unintelligibility, in their blur and fum-ble, they grasp at shared characters and figures in the effort to communicate. The apprehension of mysteries, within the natural and outside it, is as rooted in the mind's freight of empirically acquired patterns of data and thought as is the mastery of a new skill. And among these manifestations, crucial yet oddly overlooked, are the figures of the inner world, unavailable to the senses. Nobody, except perhaps a child seeing a baroque angel for the first time, finds it strange that a naked boy could hurl himself *sotto-in-sù* from heaven's ceiling on a swan's white pinions, or that lost loved ones should return with arms stiffly held by their sides and wrapped head to foot in the shroud in which they were buried.

Yet these are conventions which govern 'the logic of the imaginary'; they authorize belief, and the story of their development can be told, as I shall try to do later.

Unseen phenomena—spirits like angels and cherubs, shades of the dead, ethereal or astral bodies, subtle matter—have been visualized and communicated so effectively that the conventions they rely on and adapt have themselves become invisible. The metaphors that enflesh them introduce them into reality. But that reality can be expressed only through metaphor.

Because the logic of the imaginary streams back into these strata of deep time, the story the book tells will carry us back into the past—to the cloud-compelling gods of the Greeks who summoned mists and clouds in which to wrap themselves and their protégés to keep them from harm, to classical and Renaissance theories of the inner eye and fantasy, to Newton's fiery luminiferous ether. These different elements contributed to the language of spirit which remains dynamic in our culture.

In rather the same way as a land surveyor takes a core of earth to see the foundations and the ongoing settlement of a building, the search in *Phantasmagoria* has involved creating an archaeology of spirits today by making sections taking the reader back through time. With areas of long and crowded human settlement, however (Jerusalem, Rome), the strata get turned over and jumbled up: a pediment from a Greek temple taken for a threshold here, a pillar laid down in a carriageway there. This creative topsy-turvy has overtaken ideas about spirits: vampires, cradle-snatching demons, and monsters from antiquity and the Middle Ages have returned in the aliens, child-snatchers, and bogeys of popular horror stories and games, for example, while ideas about the transmigration of souls that return to Pythagorean cosmology circulate through New Age cults and literary fiction.

III.

New technologies for seeing, recording, and picturing have reconfigured the traditional materials from which soul and spirit have been formed by imagination, and so, alongside the constellation of spirit metaphors, I take up the story of 'haunted media', in the fine phrase of Jeffrey Sconce, and follow some of the ways in which modern technologies communicate the imagination's make-believe, its desires and terrors, and shape them through the latest telecommunications and imaging techniques. *Phantasmagoria* opens with the uncanny public entertainment of the waxworks displays, founded on the ritual death mask (Chapters 1–3). After this section on 'Wax', *Phantasmagoria* moves to explore 'Air' and the principle of animation, which no portrait or effigy, however like its subject, can command (Chapters 4 and 5). Clouds have affinities with air, and provide the habitat of gods, angels, and souls in bliss (Chapter 6). At this point in the book, I revolve the angle of view to consider the necessary dynamic between the seer and the seen, the role of the perceiving subject's imagination in spirit visions, and the anxiety about fantasy that accompanied them.[11] Vision is never far from illusion—in some sense the fears which the Doctors of the Church expressed about the status of appearances and apparitions can still alert us to the problems of perception and cognition; the status of phantasms in 'the optical unconscious', in the term Walter Benjamin uses, remains a live question.[12]

A vast and enlightened body of theology and philosophy—not least the opposition to witch-hunters—has warned against relying on the products of *fantasia*, for anything more solid or indeed truthful than the subjective reflections of a person's mind. Yet heavenly visions—castles in the air—have also habitually been received as signs, and interpreted because they signified something—or did so for their wishful observers. The metaphor of clouds and cloudiness returns to communicate the elusive, changeable, internal material of someone's mind: it can serve to signify the spirit indwelling the person. Meteorology offers, as I shall describe, a prime vehicle for inward experiences inaccessible to bodily vision, and clouds dominate imagery of personal, imaginative experience: they provide a subjective correlate to wax's objective impression of someone's unique, outward appearance. The history of imaginative projection is itself packed with prodigies—with castles in the air and faces in the clouds (Chapters 7 and 8).

Introducing the crucial role of subjective perception, decipherment, and intelligence carries my story to various speculative models of the mind, with emphasis on early modern ideas about the different souls in the mind, and about the third or inner eye, and 'eidetic' images—that is, pictures seen with hallucinatory vividness by imagination alone. When the Jesuit Athanasius Kircher began making painted slides and projecting them with a 'magic lantern' in Rome in the 1640s, he pictured devils and visions that could not be seen with the eyes of the body (Figure 2, p. 8; Chapters 9 and 10). In tracking the idea of the mind's eye and the development of tools for broadcasting its phantasms into the exterior world, I hope to show how optical devices did not concentrate solely on extending the faculty of sight as an organ of sense, but developed concurrently as instruments of imagination. Media that expanded the faculties, such as microscopes and telescopes, and drawing aids such as the Claude glass and the camera lucida, made possible visions that bodily eyes could not gain unassisted, and immeasurably increased empirical observation. As visual prostheses, they opened up hitherto unimagined universes. But subsequent interpretation did not remain at all stable or objective: the first drops of water put under the microscope excited diabolical chimaerae, and conjurors delightedly adopted the latest devices to perform magic illusions. The so-called magic lantern—an ingenious prototype slide projector—reveals by its very name the lack of distinction between revelation and illusion; sometimes also called the camera obscura, this device and other ingenious proto-cinematic machines actually brought into being models of interior thought, and conjured all kinds of things that do not and cannot exist except in that enchanted condition: the enigma of appearances.[13]

So, after the telescope and the microscope, bold optical technologies turned to communicating the inner workings of the mind, not retinal pictures or observations of the world. The magic lantern, dark chamber or camera obscura, mirrored the melancholic mind, and its early adepts used it to project imagined interior processes and their characteristic products. The technical means introduced to create mental pictures was not determined by them, nor did it shape them; their interaction depends rather on the necessary limits of imagination itself, which cannot imagine itself outside its own boundaries. The first proto-cinematic spectacles that followed from these experiments continued to conjure ghosts and spectres, fantasies and nightmares—indeed, the brilliant inventor Etienne-Gaspard Robertson called his popular Gothic horror show, in Paris in the 1790s, the Phantasmagoria, which has given me the title for this book (Chapter 11). Spirits and science were deeply interwoven in these early spectacular enterprises, and the dancers of the modern *danse macabre* stepped out to the measure of the latest, cleverest discoveries and devices. Unlike waxworks, phantasmagorias gave an impression of vitality. The images flickered and fluttered, and so created an illusion of possessing that quality of conscious life: animation. As Robertson boasted, he could 'raise the dead!'

After sections on 'Wax', 'Air', 'Clouds', and 'Light', Part V, 'Shadow', introduces the discussion of photography in the book, exploring the origin of 'writing-in-light' as a form of shadow play, the legends gathering around this form of portraiture (Chapter 12), the dangers of reproduction reverberating in such myths as the story of Narcissus (Chapter 13) and the figure of the doppelgänger (Chapter 14). The shade (*psyche* in Greek, *umbra* in Latin) evokes a person after death, a ghost, in our culture; *eidolon* conveyed the concept of a figment like Pandora when she was first created by the gods before they breathed life into her, or the phantom of Helen of Troy for whom the Greeks fought, mistaking her image for flesh-and-blood in Euripides' play *Helen*. The camera's early shadow play appeared to communicate just such ghostly semblances from our Western traditions, and the belief spread that the camera had the power to steal the soul (Chapter 15). Why and how did this myth develop? Primitive people ran away, many travellers reported. But I propose another line of approach, and argue that magnificent portraits taken in early encounters show Native Americans, Chinese, Tierra Del Fuegans, and many others from around the world facing the lens without a trace of discomposure. So the fear might rather have been projected by the photographers on to their subjects, and express some quality of the process that was true—or that at least was felt to be true—by the photographers because of ideas about spirit inherent in their (our) belief systems.

The pioneering portraitist Julia Margaret Cameron declared that she wanted to capture the soul of her sitters, who were friends, family, idols, heroes, protégés, and favourites. In Chapter 16, Cameron and her contemporary Clementina Hawarden represent photography as a medium of imagination, through which the mind projects its poetic inner visions. The camera's role as a recorder, as the indexical guarantor of reality or supreme documentary instrument, has occupied much space and interest in criticism, so here I emphasize its function as another kind of magic lantern and invoke some of the other pioneers—such as Charles Dodgson the photographer, who, in his other persona of Lewis Carroll, turned habitual modes of photographic representation—mirror inversion, miniaturization, suspension of time—into the conditions of Wonderland and Looking-Glass country.

Lewis Carroll was interested in fairyland and other worlds to a serious degree, as were many of his contemporaries, artistic and scientific, and in the same decade as *Alice in Wonderland* was published, the first photographs of ghosts were taken. Chapter 17, 'Spectral Rappers, Psychic Photographers', describes how, depending on the beliefs of the sitters, new media captured evidence of life after death or other emanations, the 'spiritual body' in its modern variants—astral bodies, auras, visitors, and 'spirit controls'.

The camera documenting the apparition of such spiritual bodies seems a contradiction in terms: the medium of record furnishing proof of spirits, and what spirits! Wrapped in sheets, or swathed in cotton wool, these revenants from the land of the dead will not convince many viewers now. But they did then, for reasons that require entering the history of Victorian physics and innovatory scientific speculation.

Photographs did not satisfy the curiosity or the scientific standards of nineteenth-century questors after the nature and meaning of spirits, and their further inquiries became even more tightly wound into the remarkable burst of inventiveness of the late Victorian era. Chapter 18 then takes up the most unexpected discovery that I made in the course of writing this book, that Victorian science applied rigorous laboratory methods to the proving of ghosts and a spirit force: the brilliant William Crookes, for example, used spring-balances to measure psychic phenomena, and Cornelius Varley applied cable-testing devices to monitor the medium Florence Cook. This approach lay at the industrious heart of the Society for Psychical Research, founded in 1882 by many distinguished men and women, including Henry and Eleanor Sidgwick. As Richard Noakes has argued, to the Victorian researcher 'epistemic differences between electrical and spiritual telegraphs, spectra and spectres and between radiometer and psychic forces seemed to be very hazy.'[14]

Part VIII, 'Ether', focuses on media and mediums, on the new forms of communication over distances through space and time, such as the radio and the telephone, and introduces some of the women who acted as conduits in the seances conducted by researchers to make contact with ethereal inhabitants of spirit worlds. The word 'medium' was extended to include individuals in 1854, a telling date, since the Spiritualist movement had begun around ten years before that.

Alongside photography, the acoustic inventions communicated spirit presences: ether, the classical philosophers' airy element, was refreshed, as the new media redrew the possibilities for action at a distance (Chapter 19). The wireless, the telegraph, the telephone, television, and the movies, began to move voices and images through the air and to displace them in time as well as space (Chapters 20 and 21). In seances, spirits made themselves heard as well as seen, and they also began to impinge in the material world, leaving palpable traces—sometimes flowers, sometimes thumbprints, sometimes ectoplasms (Chapter 22). The great materializing mediums, Eusapia Paladino and Eva C., of the late nineteenth and early twentieth centuries persuaded many acclaimed scientific minds (Chapter 23).

New instruments have taken human vision to places the eyes themselves could never reach, and the images they bring have become part of our intellectual furniture as well as means of bodily survival. At the same time they have revealed to us the sensory boundaries which we inhabit. Our cognitive range exists perpetually in play between these powers and these limits, and what we can understand from this experiential instability is that we see and understand what we see according to what we already know.[15] The brain baulks at non-meaning; meaninglessness, like formlessness, becomes the dominant scandal against reason, and reason, seeking to abolish it, generates fantasies (Goya comes to mind, for his iconic image of himself, with its magnificent warning, 'The dream of reason produces monsters'). The power of imaginary projection emerges as the prime activity of personal consciousness, the mark of the thinking self in action and relation to the world in the thought of Neoplatonists like Fichte and Schelling, and the Romantics who read them, like Wordsworth and Coleridge. Since them, in the nineteenth and twentieth centuries, clinical psychology and psychoanalysis, on the one hand, and literary and artistic Surrealism, on the other, established the faculty of projective or constitutive imagination as a crucial function of the psyche and the distinctive mark of the self. The Rorschach test, for example, which offers patients blots to decipher, precisely demands just such subjective projections, and was used as a diagnostic tool for personality from the 1920s in Zurich (Plate 7; Chapter 24).[16] Rorschachs still stand as a prime modern example of the shift away from external portraiture to internal imaging and the corresponding rise in the value of the mind's vagaries in the search for what it means to be somebody.

Animation, that crucial property of living beings, had eluded reproduction by even the most cunning fabricators, until it entered the world of images through the invention of film. So in Part X, 'Film', the book's last section, *Phantasmagoria* returns to the question which underlies the uncanny presence of the waxwork, and takes up the cinema's peculiar properties of moving representation and the phantoms whom they have brought into being. A critic commented after the first public show of the Lumière Brothers' films, 'when everyone can photograph their dear one no longer in a motionless form in their movement, their activity, their familiar gestures, with words on their lips, death will have ceased to be absolute.'[17]

Belonging to the same metaphorical constellation as breath, the quality of animation demarcated the living from the dead, the real from the artefact. Waxworks could not quite attain it, even when equipped with clockwork mechanisms, neither could photography. In myths and legends, gods and goddesses, artists and scientists, could sometimes achieve it: Hephaistos forged golden hand-maidens to attend him in his subterranean kingdoms. They looked like real-life girls, but were automata, 'living dolls', a kind of *eidolon*, or phantom. In Ovid's *Metamorphoses*, Pygmalion managed to breathe life into the statue he carved of Galatea, and Dr Frankenstein acted like a 'New Prometheus' and quickened his Creature with electricity. But in the movies, images live and move exactly as they did when they were alive: the copy here has become somehow more than a copy. It partakes of the living nature of its original, and continues to be present and animate when they are not there, and indeed, to survive long after they are dead.

How this filmic order of living likeness powerfully shapes the present culture of apocalypse, in politics and entertainment alike, is the sharp question explored in Chapter 26. The book then closes with a short genealogy of zombies (Chapter 27), the comic, tragic, alluring, repellent creatures born of global encounters, close cousins of the vampire, but different in effects revealing of modern existence. Among the many types of the undead who haunt culture world-wide through the movies and computer-generated images, zombies are still lively—for reasons to do with changing ideas about what a person's spirit means, and what it means to lose your soul.

In the Conclusion, I take up one of the symbols which have been denatured: first chemical warfare, then the atomic bomb, and increasing atmospheric pollution have cast their shadow over the glowing, spiralling clouds that once carried saints to heaven, and signified their translation from flesh to spirit. The metaphors of spirit are changing. I then suggest some of the tendencies that are shaping the ways in which bodies, souls, and spirits take form in contemporary stories and other works of art, fictional and otherwise.

At times the task I had set myself in *Phantasmagoria* here reminded me of a parable I also know from my Catholic childhood: St Augustine was walking on the beach of Civitavecchia near Rome and pondering the mystery of the Trinity, when he came across a little child pouring sea water into buckets. When challenged as to what he was doing, the little boy answered that he was measuring the sea. When the saint showed scepticism as to the outcome, the Child—for it was the infant Christ—countered that Augustine was one to talk.

Different ideas of what a person might be have developed in relation to contemporary media and the potential and virtual universes they have created. This contemporary self, this new protagonist, belongs in the history of thought about individuals and consciousness. The faculties of what used to be called soul—fantasy, memory, sensations, emotions—now exist in symbiosis with televisual communications, and with the laws that organize them and the loops and warps in the manifold planes and volumes of space-time that they have brought into play. One of the consequences of this enfolding image-world is that materialism's long history has rendered matter itself insubstantial: physics has brought a new metaphysics into being. This has the profoundly unsettling consequence of closing the gap between phenomena that do not possess corporeality or substance or mass or gravity and entities that do. To some extent contemporary conditions have returned us to pre-modern psychology: for Lucretius, a dream, a thought, a hallucination, could affect the experience of reality. 'The imagination is the power that enables us', wrote Wallace Stevens, 'to perceive the normal in the abnormal, the opposite of chaos in chaos. It does this every day in arts and letters.'[18] *Phantasmagoria* presents an aspect of this chaos; this book tries to explore some of the work of imagination in envisioning the invisible and giving form to the impalpable.

Part I

Wax

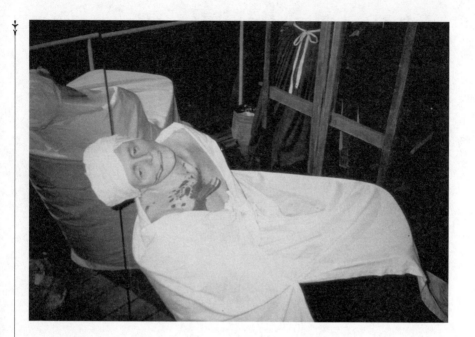

Marie Gresholtz, later Madame Tussaud, made a death
mask of Jean-Paul Marat soon after he was assassinated
in 1793; the waxwork copy on display at Madame
Tussaud's, Baker Street, London, descends directly
from this portrait.

I
Living Likenesses; Death Masks

> [O]ne need no more ask whether body and soul are one than whether the wax and the impression it receives are one.
>
> Aristotle, *De Anima*

Wax takes such an exact impression that it has been used as a stamp of authenticity since the beginning of written documents; set to a personal sign in the form of a seal, or a thumbprint, or a hair, it hardens, and cannot be undone; it can only be broken, and then reveal tampering. This binds it to testimony and to truth, and, as with a life mask or a death mask, it fortifies conviction as well as faith. It belongs in the embalmer's pharmocopeia; working with wax is a forensic skill. Waxen artefacts, even when removed from the practical ground of their origin and their legal and medical uses are no longer apparent, retain their challenge to the stuff of life, their antithetical connection with bodies and embodiment. Wax has been used for *ex voto* plaques reproducing limbs and organs from Neolithic times to the present day—excavations at the shrine of a goddess in Cyprus, for example, yielded miniatures of breasts and bones alongside votive statuettes to entreat her help or to give thanks for help received.[1] In Portugal recently, in a shop selling religious articles, I saw wax emblems for sale—babies, breasts, limbs, lungs, and eyes—to offer at the shrine of the appropriate local Madonna or saint. At the same time, however, wax gives rise to thoughts of mortality: it melts, it burns down, it suggests the vanity of the world, the weak candle flame of hope, the deliquescence of flesh. The material implies organic change.[2] Like many symbols, it packs and binds opposite meanings within its range. The folk etymology given for the word 'sincere', that it comes from 'sine cera'—without wax—and alludes to potters' practice of filling flaws in their handiwork with wax, is not historically correct, but it does reveal the paradoxical properties of the stuff. Wax cheats death; it simulates life; it proves true and false.

The word 'mummy', applied to bodies embalmed according to Egyptian burial rites, derives from 'moum', the word for wax or tallow; since those remote times, wax has been the principal material used in preserving the dead so as to make them look as if they are still alive. Wax was also mingled with pigment to form 'encaustic', and laid on to the cartonnage or mummy mask to give the painted face the semblance of real flesh and skin. Organic, malleable, animal, this unique storage and building material of the bees has the added property of soaking up light, like alabaster, rather than deflecting it, and in consequence it glistens as well as glows subtly as if from within.[3] The resemblance of its surface appearance to skin, especially to a fair, luminous, warm, and slightly moist complexion, lent it to the simulation of flesh, and a market in waxen erotica flourished. Marie Tussaud's teacher— and official uncle—Philippe Curtius, furnished private clients with curiosities in this tradition.[4]

Wax's multiple natural qualities forestall the corruption of the flesh both literally and figuratively, and as a result, the substance has also provided supple and enduring metaphors for life, for truth, for art. Aristotle, discussing the soul as substance, 'in the sense of being the form of a natural body, which potentially has life', resorted to the metaphor of a wax impression to develop his crucial definition, quoted above: 'one need no more ask whether body and soul are one than whether the wax and the impression it receives are one.'[5]

Death masks, and their popular offshoot, waxworks, keep active the metaphor Aristotle used in relation to a person's unique body–soul compact: the essential distinctiveness of feature moulds the generic enfleshed body that one particular subject shares with other humans and makes the mask unique. Death masks do not incorporate the corpse itself into the matter of the representation or effigy, as in the case of a mummy or an incorrupt Catholic saint, but they do derive their potency from their contact with the actual deceased, with his or her flesh. The important difference between a portrait painted from life and a mask moulded in death is not the difference in reliable resemblance—in this a painting can be the better portrait, and many artists have pointed out that the stilled moment when the mould is taken and, in the case of a life mask, the necessary stiffness and closed eyes of the subject make for an inert, blank, unspeaking likeness.[6] The eloquent funerary portraits from Fayum, Egypt, were painted before death, so that the painters could seize their living likeness, or so it has been persuasively argued by James Fenton.[7] These artists' skills enhanced the appearance of vitality: they invented, for example, the flecks of white highlight to give life to their large, soulful, staring eyes. However, while a Fayum portrait looks as if the sitter were still alive, the crucial character of the death mask depends on its status as a relic, as the nearest remnant that can be preserved of a body before its disintegration or embalming.

The death mask is a psychological precursor of photography, as well as being connected aesthetically to photography's tradition of realism. Pliny describes the making of such a portrait by the Greek sculptor Lysistratus of Sikyon, and his book was known to Renaissance artists, like Leonardo.[8]

The ritual purposes to which such masks were put anticipate present-day uses of photographs in commemoration, sentimental, nostalgic, religious, and social. The interval between life departing and the forces of corruption asserting themselves creates a threshold of solemnity and serenity, in which the habitus of a person's face is distilled. 'With a death mask, the dead face is profanely resurrected as image.'[9]

The *encyclopédiste* Denis Diderot singled out for praise the vivid semblances of encaustic portraiture: 'The ancients thus made for their statues themselves an epidermis of wax with which they countered the damage of air. Every year we regularly tear the skin from our statues with sponges laden with a hard gritty liquid. On the days of that cruel operation I flee the Tuileries Gardens, just as one leaves a public place on the day of an execution.'[10] So, on the eve of the first waxworks shows for public entertainment, Diderot was binding living flesh and statues together through the metaphor of a waxen epidermis, significantly shadowed by the threat of summary death.

Ritual use of death masks began at least in the Middle Ages, when the kings and queens of England were paraded in effigy at their funerals: the figures were composed of jointed limbs, and a groove on their brows allowed the crowns to fit snugly and stay on. Facial idiosyncrasies were cast and then reproduced faithfully: the results of a stroke—a drooping mouth and flattened left cheek—have been rendered in the case of Edward III, who died in 1377; Anne of Denmark, James I's queen, has a large mole on her left cheek. The eyes were painted and the figures or busts were fully dressed in wigs and robes of state and regalia, and were carried with the bier or set up beside it.

After 1660, the chosen medium of the royal effigy was wax, and the surviving statues of Charles II and his mistress, the powerful and clever duchess of Richmond and Lennox, belie their sacred function, looking just like the gaudiest waxworks in a hall of fame. They are both dressed in the clothes they actually wore—the oldest surviving set of robes of the Order of the Garter, with a fantastic lace jabot and prodigious lace cuffs in the king's case; in her case, she wears the full dress robes in which she attended the coronation of Queen Anne, and carries her pet parrot—the oldest stuffed bird in the British Isles.

These waxworks are housed and displayed in Westminster Abbey, the seat of coronations and other royal ceremonies: they would look at home at Madame Tussaud's, but here they are sacred objects, rather than *objets d'art*. It is interesting that the great historian of science Joseph Needham argues in his study of Chinese civilization that sacred and ritual interests act as the spur to invention: reading and writing begin on oracle bones, not business letters, for example; gunpowder for fireworks, not guns. For the extraordinary capacities of wax, as a lifelike medium of precise, vivid detail, were first exploited for ritual use, in these sacred statues.

Statues which are particular objects of pilgrimage are robed and adorned and groomed as if they were living. One of the most venerated crucifixes in Naples, for instance, which once miraculously nodded its head to avoid a stray bullet, has a long hank of real hair which is said to be still growing from under his crown of thorns.[11] Such artefacts cease to be sculptures, objects of high art, and become fetishes, effigies to focus passions. Indeed, the presence of unmediated accessories, reproduced in their proper and material nature rather than translated through the metaphorical processes of an artistic language of imitation, can often provide an index of a sculpture's popular power in the religious scale; the more elaborate the wig, the costume, the jewels, and the more human matter is included in the figure, the more intense the fervour surrounding the cult. Realism paradoxically reinforces the supernatural presence of the departed; a fairy-tale does not produce the same shiver as the banal, and imaginary figments in the realm of art do not make themselves felt: the reality effect is needed to produce the *frisson* of the uncanny, and the theatrical density of Catholic rites, conjuring experience through arousing every sense, aims at breaking down the border between this life and another.

One line drawn between fine art and religious imagery also distinguishes between spectators and participants: a painting or fresco is used as an object of contemplation, a stimulus to prayer, a door to mysteries, but it does not invite handling, stroking, combing, adorning, robing or disrobing, touching and kissing, as relics do. An icon that is the object of a cult, or a magical image in any medium, becomes part of a process, is treated like a doll, as the principal of a cast of characters in an unfolding game of make-believe.

Figures of the Christ-child, for instance, made in wax, were and still are enshrined in decorated cribs on Christmas Day in Germany and in Italy; St Francis of Assisi introduced the devotion into his fellow monks' ceremonies in the thirteenth century, and it continues to be performed in family homes on Christmas Eve in many Catholic families as a domestic coda to Midnight Mass. It has also been a favourite practice in convents. In Bologna, for example, Santa Caterina de' Vigri made a swaddled baby Jesus, embroidered and painted his face, and studded the figure with jewels and gold lace. In the early twentieth century, Saint Thérèse of Lisieux described in her memoirs how in their Carmelite convent she and her sisters lovingly swaddled and cared for the baby in his manger. Interestingly, the Augustinian monks at Monte Oliveto Maggiore in Italy have reversed the sexes of this particular sacred game of pretend with their cult of La Santissima Bambina—not the Christ-child, but Mary as an infant. On the feast-day of her nativity, this resplendently bejewelled idol is taken from her glass case on the altar and processed by the all-male, celibate community through the grounds of the monastery before she is returned to her shrine with perhaps a little more paint and a few more jewels. It is a highly uncommon cult of a girl baby.

Devotion to the Holy Child inspired different costumes for different aspects of his power—he appears as the Good Shepherd in an eighteenth-century wax figure from Bavaria, for example. The Christ-child of the S. Maria in Ara Caeli, Rome, has been worshipped since the fifteenth century—an idol entirely swaddled in gold and gems, with a doll's face and hands, modelled with sensitivity on a real child's pudginess by some forgotten artist—it is characteristic of sacred icons that, as relics, they should be thought to be 'acheiropoeiton' (made without hands), communicated miraculously from heaven to earth. In Seville, the statue of the Madonna known as La Macarena, after the poor quarter of the city where her shrine stands, has an immense wardrobe of different embroidered and jewelled costumes for the different liturgical seasons, real eyelashes implanted, glass teardrops on her cheeks—as well as a finely modelled expression of grief. The object of a passionate cult all year round, she appears on the customary holy pictures on sale to pilgrims, and these are also dressed and jewelled, embroidered and encrusted, to give palpable, tactile substance to her holy presence, in real glitter glued to the surface and real thread stitched to clothes, crown, and halo.

The authenticity of the paraphernalia, its non-metaphorical state, lends authority and truth to the image, bringing it back to the plane of the actual and the living. The waxwork, as secular reliquary of the hero's body, has another, even more eloquently Mediterranean progenitor: the *ex voto* effigy.

Wax life casts of limbs and organs—breasts, kidneys, lungs, hearts—bought by petitioners sometimes line the walls and ceilings of miracle-working shrines in Catholic Europe, as many visitors will have seen. But in a few very special pilgrimage centres, these thanksgiving offerings take the form of life-size portraits of the lucky recipient of Mary's grace. In S. Maria dei Miracoli, near Mantua, for example, the entire walls of the nave are barnacled in wax images of organs cured by the intercession of the Madonna venerated there; but above these are rows of fully clothed, life-size polychrome figures: these thankful votaries escaped sudden death in one way or another, and tradition suggested that they have themselves portrayed at the moment when the miracle took place. One wears the suit of armour in which he providentially escaped death on the battlefield; another shows himself in the rags he was wearing when he went to the gallows and the rope broke; and another in his work clothes beside the well into which he fell headlong but was providentially spared from drowning. They form a dusty phalanx of human stories—of *faits divers* from the local newspaper—that happened 500 years ago. There also hangs in the nave a large stuffed crocodile found in the nearby river; its capture and death, achieved through the Virgin's intercession, ended the plague from which the city was suffering. (The creature had probably escaped from the Duke of Mantua's menagerie, one of the first of its kind.)

Like a waxwork, which can be cast from the original mould many times over, the substance of the image does not have to be permanent; but the image itself must incorporate a memory of contact with the subject's form. The authenticity derives above all from the incidentals, the trimmings, the supplements. Cult statues of this kind share with waxworks a common aesthetic: unlike other forms of statuary, they both depend on illusions in vivid polychrome to support their claim to truth telling and direct contact with their original.

Only later was wax adapted to create the remarkably exact anatomical models of the seventeenth and eighteenth centuries, models of the Enlightenment's hunger to know, and still in use for teaching medical students the organs of the body and their placing and function (see next chapter). The same artists who had created the effigies for sacred purposes were employed to model simulacra of bodies, after nature, as literal a copy as could be made without actually stuffing the body or preserving it through taxidermy.

The powerful closing scene of *The Winter's Tale* displays Hermione, Leontes' wife, whom he supposes dead, in the form of a masterpiece of realistic statuary such as might have stood in a pilgrimage church. Paulina, as mistress of ceremonies, revealingly attributes Hermione's effigy to 'Julio Romano', a contemporary of Shakespeare, and a painter, rather than a sculptor, celebrated for his rich polychromatic use of oils. She invites Leontes to gaze upon the statue:

> 'Here it is; prepare
> To see the life as lively mock'd as ever
> Still sleep mock'd death.'

She draws the curtain, and Leontes, astonished, exclaims,

> 'Her natural posture! . . .
> Would you not deem it breath'd? And that those veins
> Did verily bear blood?'

To which the reply comes, from one onlooker:

> 'Masterly done:
> The very life seems warm upon her lip.'
>
> (*The Winter's Tale*, V. iii)

Paulina stages Hermione's resurrection, a moment of high, poignant drama; for the scene, with its enigmatic shifts between illusion and reality, dream and act, fulfils a more general longing that effigies, be they funeral portraits or *ex voto* figures, will somehow come back to life. Both Leontes and Hermione are poised in different ways between sleep and waking states; as the statue moves to Paulina's command, Leontes still thinks it might be an illusion, as in a dream. 'O, she's warm!', he exclaims in surprise when he embraces the statue: a most heart-stopping effect in the performance of the play.

Though some Renaissance portrait busts, carved by contemporaries of Giulio Romano, are made of variegated marbles, the use of pigments in statuary on the whole degrades the artefact to cult object or souvenir, especially after the seventeenth century. Colour becomes linked to popularity, even to vulgarity: busts of great men, for example, turn white; the effigies of George Washington and Napoleon alike are carved in smooth, unblemished Carrara marble. Henry Weekes, a Royal Academician, in his Lectures on Art in 1880, commented on the sculptor John Gibson's *Tinted Venus* (1851–6), a neo-classical nude with slightly enhanced complexion and gilded elements, after the statue had caused a scandal.[12] Weekes admitted that the Greeks had painted their sculpture in the brightest colours, as Diderot had pointed out, and he gave the reason for it: 'Their colossal coloured statues stood or sat in the midst of the temples . . . There was a crowd of ignorant devotees to be impressed with wonder, to be made to conceive a real presence, and to feel awe at its power.'[13]

Weekes could just about countenance coloured surfaces in the Greek past, but he came out strongly for colourlessness in the present:

That a too literal rendering of Nature renders a work of Sculpture commonplace, if not still more offensive, I need not urge to you . . .

The absence of Colour in a statue is, in short, one of the peculiarities that remove it so entirely from common Nature that the most vulgarly constituted mind may contemplate it without its causing any feeling of a sensuous kind.[14]

He thus banished from the canon of high art the whole Catholic effort to awaken exactly those feelings; but popular art forms—waxworks and dioramas—would take over and make their own that sensory panoply which the Church understood so well.

The responsiveness of wax to impression, its ductility and smoothness of texture, lent it to forensic use in medical modelling, an art that reached an apogee of hallucinatory skill in northern Italy before it spread through Europe, beyond the universities and into the cabinets of princes and patrons, as a badge of their scholarship and enlightenment.

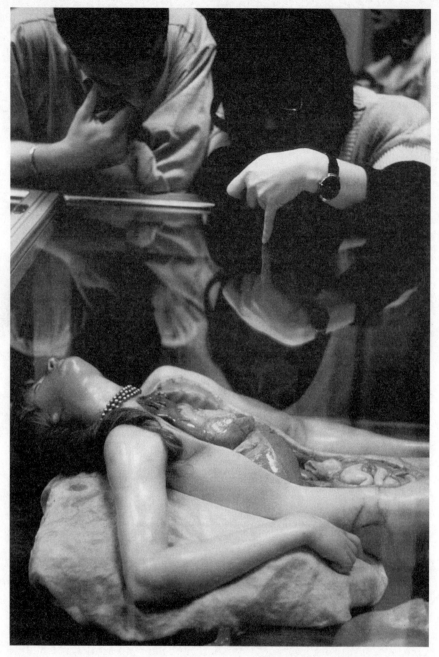

Skilful forensic waxworks were pioneered in Italian medical schools, and continue to be consulted, as by this group of trainee nurses studying 'La Venerina' by Clemente Susini. Bologna, 18th century.

2

Anatomies and Heroes: Madame Tussaud's

[T]hat rare Italian master, Julio Romano . . . would beguile Nature
of her custom, so perfectly is he her ape: he so near to Hermione hath
done Hermione, that they say one would speak to her and stand in
hope of an answer.

Shakespeare, *The Winter's Tale*

The Sicilian artist and abbot Giulio Gaetano Zumbo (1655–1701) was a
hell-fire preacher such as later tormented James Joyce, and to communicate
his warnings, he made finely crafted, morbid miniature tableaux of death
and doom, dwelling on 'The Judgement of the Damned' and 'Time and
Death', and depicting souls in torment, screaming as the red-painted wax
flames burn them. His favoured medium—wax—implied vanity, transitoriness, and mortality.[1] Zumbo is a typical example of an early modeller in
wax, not only because he indulged a taste for queasy Catholic symbolism,
but because he simultaneously worked in Italy and France as an anatomical
model-maker. In Bologna and Florence, two of Zumbo's staging posts,
medical museums still display the remarkably accurate figurines made for
the study of the body and its organs. Waxwork makers in the formative era
in the medium's secular history, working towards other ends—commem-
orative portraiture or edifying monuments—were following in the immediate footsteps of forensic science even while obeying broad principles of
sacred representation. Paradoxically, the more scientific the approach, the
deeper the marvellous character of the work becomes, synthesizing sacred
and profane bodily image making.

The earliest of the European cabinets displaying anatomical waxes was
created in Bologna, in the first half of the eighteenth century, when the
scientific and cultural patron Pope Benedict XIV commissioned the anatomical wax sculptor Ercole Lelli to create a study collection for the
Medical Faculty of Bologna University.[2] Lelli cast directly from bodies
and from body parts, and built the results on to actual skeletons. These
preparations illustrated stages of medical dissection as practised in the
anatomy theatre, with the difference that flesh and blood were transformed
into their own living likeness but no longer possessed any of the
deliquescent qualities of matter that made medical studies so physically

repugnant. He posed the bodies in similar tableaux as the great anatomists' engraved pictures, but surpassed his predecessors with his faithful, literal, three-dimensional realism. Disturbing as these anatomical waxes still are, they placed scientific distance between the real condition of the human body in death and observing it to explore its workings.

More medical models of body parts, cast in awe-inspiring detail, theatricality, and fidelity were later made in Bologna by Giovanni Manzolini and his wife, Anna Morandi, and are now displayed as part of the university's remarkable historical collections.[3] Manzolini and Morandi made self-portrait busts, half-length and clothed in their own clothes, like waxworks, with the objects of their skill prepared as specimens in front of them. Morandi portrayed herself in her crinolines, without gloves, handling a skull, with a flap of the scalp lifted to expose the brain to view. She survived her husband and opened her own museum of anatomy; after her death in 1774, the Institute of Science acquired her collection. In the present arrangement, Galvani's instruments occupy another room, with a fine dramatic painting of his experiments on a dead frog.[4]

The anatomical waxworks collection specialized in obstetrics, and these careful models of different foetal presentations are still used by students, as were the full-scale model figures illustrating the workings of the muscles, the nerves, the circulation of the blood, and so forth. When I first visited the collection, I joined a party of student nurses who were being instructed in the medical value of the exhibits by a doctor in a white coat, and we were all very quiet, indeed aghast, as we gazed at the then unfamiliar virtuoso models (*pièces montées*) showing foetal presentation and liver malfunction (Figure 4, p. 30).

Lelli and his successors worked in the high Renaissance tradition of sculpture when they modelled standing nudes exposing the flesh under the skin. A graceful statue of Eve at the start of the sequence stands like a tall and slender classical goddess, except that she is wearing a wig of long hair. But the next figures in the series—*écorchés*, or flayed—display the inner workings of the body, the musculature, the nervous and lymphatic systems, with remarkable precision and delicacy. The methods which the wax casters and sculptors applied are not fully understood, but they involved complex preserving and embalming techniques. The intention was to replace cadavers with wax replicas in medical studies, for several reasons. Instinctive repugnance (exacerbated by the hot climate) on the part of students figured alongside Catholic reverence for the body. But above all, cadavers for study were not easy to obtain.

The only bodies available were criminals from the gallows or suicides fished out of rivers—and their supplying the dissecting table continued the punishment due to their misdeeds: Hogarth's hero from *The Rake's*

Progress ends up foully disembowelled in full view of the crowd assembled in the operating theatre, while a dog laps up his intestines from a bucket. Alternatively, the bodies were illegally dug up by body snatchers—as Mary Shelley describes Dr Frankenstein's proceedings. Or, in the examples of anthropological museum displays which have provoked international scandal in recent times, stuffed specimens of individuals, or preserved parts and organs, were mounted to display racial characteristics. In Vienna, for example, after he died in 1796, Angelo Soliman, a slave who was born in Nigeria, and joined the court of Emperor Franz II, was flayed, given a wax head, and placed on show in the emperor's cabinet of curiosities.[5] At the Hunterian Museum in London, a pigmy woman who was brought to England to be exhibited, and then died in childbirth, is preserved—or rather a half-section of her.[6] The case of the Hottentot Venus, whose genitals were removed and bottled and exhibited separately in the Musée de l'Homme in Paris, has inspired widespread protest.

That pioneering reforming Pope, Benedict XIV, authorized investigation of the body in the enthusiasm of the Enlightenment for learning: he evinced no superstition about putting cadavers to use and preserving their simulacra. Yet, because of the anxiety that surrounded dissecting the dead, one of the purposes of the modellers' verisimilitude was to obviate the need for medical students to have direct contact with corpses. The good intention was frustrated, however, for the production of exquisite replicas, destined to replace real specimens, exacted a flow of bodies that taxed the supply: Lelli used fifty corpses for the *écorchés* on display in Bologna,[7] and in Florence, later, during the work for the anatomical cabinet La Specola, a porter is on record protesting bitterly at the horror of his work as he had to cart so many corpses from the hospital to the laboratories through the hot streets in order to meet the needs of the anatomists.[8]

The Gothic romance would be born later the same century, soon followed by Mary Shelley's magnificent invention *Frankenstein*, as mentioned before, in which she compacted all the horror, dismay, and fear felt at the hubristic overreach of science in its quest for the vital principle. But by an acute paradox, Pope Benedict XIV and his supporters could deem that the soul had safely departed the bodies of the dead. To uncover the exquisite tracery of veins, the miracle of nervature, and so on, did not strike them as profaning divine creation, but, on the contrary, honouring its complexity.

Medical researchers of the sixteenth century did not flinch at many processes that conflict with contemporary ideas about the sanctity of mortal remains: the network of veins and arteries, for instance, was probably reproduced by injecting the real body with wax and then making a mould, exactly as if casting a bronze statue. The flesh, once the soul had departed, could be treated with dispassionate and unbridled curiosity, and though particularities of different bodies were of some interest—the Bologna collection includes a liver which has been distorted by corsets to become shaped like a figure of eight—on the whole the generality of the universal characteristics of the human body were stressed, and each body's evidence could be applied to all. Nothing resisted investigation, nothing provoked horror or pity. When I asked the doctor who was taking us round if anyone had ever fainted at the sights, he looked at me in dismay and said, 'Why should anyone feel shocked?' He then cried out, 'This is knowledge, this is the Enlightenment!'

The sensibilities of our forebears did not draw away from the grisliest assemblages: an Italian anatomist presented Napoleon III with his master-piece, a variegated marble top composed of bone sections, vertebrae, severed ears, and a whole human foot, the pattern against a background stained crimson with blood.[9]

The uniqueness of the person was located firmly elsewhere; nothing of this record-taking could desecrate that departed essence. Hence the anonymity of the subjects in medical cabinets, the nudes of universal man in the corridor leading to the inner cabinet—Adam—and universal woman—Eve. The bodies left behind are seen as an empty husk. They might be awaiting the resurrection, but this in effect promised the reassembly of their bodily parts. It was precisely because the Pope believed, as a good Catholic, in the immortality of the soul, once the mortal coil was shuffled off, that he could encourage such scientific experiments into the bodily remains.

Bologna represents the apogee of a heroic attempt to pluck out the heart of the mystery of life in the *siècle des lumières*. It pioneered the form, but several other cabinets followed suit, most spectacularly the collection of the Florentine School of Anatomy, which became the Museo della Specola around 1770 under the patronage of the Grand Duke of Lorraine, successor to the Medici in Tuscany. Clemente Susini was chief modeller there, and his preparations surpass Lelli's in their hyperbaroque displays of viscera, veins, and often abnormalities. These centres gave a lead to various showmen, often self-proclaimed doctors, who met the inquisitive desires of the public far beyond the confines of medical instruction. Throughout the eighteenth century, great cities like London and Paris exhibited specimens, often in the same settings as menageries, freak shows, and fairgrounds, and always solemnly disguised as education. In 1783 in London, Rackstrow's Museum advertised a new entertainment showing 'That curious Figure of a Woman, six months gone with child, representing, by liquors flowing thro' glass tubes imitating arteries, and veins, the circulation of the blood, actions of the heart and lungs, and shewing how the child is nourished in the womb'. The same show also included 'a preparation of a boy, fourteen years of age, in which the blood vessels are seen innumerable'.[10] In the *Prelude*, Wordsworth remembers similar weird delights; Dickens' *Old Curiosity Shop* itself catches their flavour, the unique, funny-peculiar Victorian mixture of prurience, knowledge, and pleasure in shock.

This new disregard for the integrity of the body after death gradually sharpened the value of its integrity and its liveliness in life. A new form of attention began to be paid to the details of features and individuals' specific differences, the way in which character might be read from the body. The very same skills which made it possible to anatomize the corpse without compunction, to dissect and then cast in wax the nerves which give expression to a person's face, or lay bare the convolutions of the brain, also made it possible to create an illusion of suspended time or of immortality in the images of the once-living individual: anatomies spurred the ambitions of new practitioners in physiognomy, phrenology, and portrait photography. It is significant that outward portraiture developed into passionate musing on inward characteristics.

From the end of the eighteenth century, the details of someone's outer physical presence became more and more invoked in the attempt to capture individual specialness: the you that makes you you. It is as if uniqueness, unable to find a habitation elsewhere in the body, had now fled to the surface: to the face, seat of particular personal identity. The French portrait sculptor Jean-Antoine Houdon, studying in Rome in the 1760s, was one of the first fine artists—not forensic anatomists—to learn from watching and performing dissections.[11] In this way, Houdon perfected his dazzling skill at sculptural verisimilitude and realist scrutiny.[12] He disfigured the idealized, glabrous tradition of the classical bust, and carved acne scars and coarse pores, scraggy torsos and chap-fallen limbs, when he rendered Great Men—Voltaire, Benjamin Franklin. Such unflinching verisimilitude foreshadows the precision lenses of photographers. A contemporary exclaimed at his 'extraordinary talent for giving a soul to his figures'. Houdon pioneered a trade in replicas, casting his coveted portraits of contemporary heroes in editions as souvenirs. He thus stands, alongside secular waxworks shows, at the very beginning of commodifying celebrity through disseminating simulacra of idols. Franklin, also in his own lifetime a subject of waxworks display, ordered a marble version of his head by Houdon—and four copies in plaster. Some of Houdon's sitters even bought as many as thirty.[13]

Around this time, Josiah Wedgwood also began mass-producing classical profile cameos on his pottery. Meanwhile scholars, patrons, and museum keepers were casting antiquities from 'life' in order to bring them home and create study collections of world art and architecture: as in the Victoria & Albert Museum in London, a self-styled centre of civilization could not do without its anthology of copies—the 'cast court'. Walter Benjamin's famous essay on 'Art in the Era of Mechanical Reproduction' does not push back nearly far enough the date of the era's beginnings, and also does not express a law of contemporary celebrity that replication, far from leaching aura from the original, magnifies it so richly that every copy grows numinous by contact with the original.[14]

Wax modelling was closeted for many centuries in the embalmer's laboratory and the forensic cabinet. But the exploding cities of modern times—Paris, London, Berlin—turned the streets into showcases for knowledge, and made knowledge itself a form of entertainment. The funeral effigy and the anatomical model became the travelling showman's stock-in-trade, attracting the new, mobile, curious public of city-dwellers and artisans to unfamiliar wonders. Taboos surrounding sacred bodies were not exactly lifted: they added to the excitement of the spectacle.

When the biological sciences of the Enlightenment converge with the quest to grasp knowledge of the secret of life, we find a new emphasis on the face as the repository of individuality. The immortal soul may have fled once life has ceased, but that which made the person himself or herself remains behind in the flesh, in the image that the body has become. This will lead eventually to realistic photography becoming the most convincing available record of the soul, and ultimately the usurper of other material relics. The distinctiveness of the countenance was established as the seat of the individual; the person's image, and especially their portrait, summons their particular memory in the mind of the living.

Waxwork makers began to incorporate the subject's own hair, as in the effigy of a saint, as well as articles of dress which had belonged to their subjects. Marie Tussaud's grandson even attributes the idea to no less a personage than the leading Revolutionary, Robespierre, who volunteered to give his portraitist a suitable outfit from his own wardrobe to clothe his waxwork. Glass eyes, taken over from optical science, were introduced from the beginning of the nineteenth century in Vienna,[15] but on the whole, organic substances were preferred to anything counterfeit or illusory. Again, the earlier context in which the artists strove for this fullness of naturalism, including actual hair and clothes, lace, ribbons, jewels, and objects, was religious cult.[16]

Philippe Curtius (1737–1794) was a Swiss physician before he took up wax sculpture as a pastime and found he was so successful at this new *métier* that he abandoned medicine. His art was patronized by a very varied clientèle, whose portraits he made. His original French patron, the Prince de Conti, invited him to Paris in 1766; later his subjects included freethinkers and radicals like the artist David, as well as the revolutionaries Marat and Robespierre, who gathered at his table. When Curtius left for Paris, he took his sister with him and the 6-year-old Marie Grosholtz, who was either his niece or possibly his own daughter.[17] He soon apprenticed Marie, the future

Madame Tussaud, to his studio, where he began teaching her his art of waxworks, then called with a flourish of learning, ceroplastics.

Curtius was also one of the earliest entrepreneurs in the business of commercial, popular visual display. In 1770 he opened the first of two W*underkämmerei* to the public. Le Cabinet de Cire ('The Wax Cabinet') exhibited contemporary celebrities in the Palais Royal; this cabinet was soon followed by another in the Boulevard du Temple, which included large tableaux of the royal family, including one showing them dining in public at Versailles after Mass on Sunday as was their custom. In this surprisingly modern arrangement, the curious populace, who could not take the coach to Versailles to see them in person, could enjoy that same sight in waxworks. In 1783, Curtius added the Caverne des Grands Voleurs ('The Cave of the Great Thieves'), a prototype of the Chamber of Horrors, with re-creations of scenes of the crime and portraits of famous villains. The lessons could go both ways, to praise as well as to blame, and a life-size death effigy of Voltaire was exhibited as 'The Dying Socrates': it is significant that impersonation of the great by the great was considered awe-inspiring. The classics also gave French politics an exalted, mythical identity.

The entrepreneur's own politics were fluid. Marie Tussaud recalled in her autobiography that she was summoned to Versailles to attend the king's sister Madame Elisabeth, and to make wax posies of flowers, medallion profiles from the life and other ladylike pursuits at court.[18] But when the Revolution started, she was in Paris, in the thick of things: Curtius took part in the storming of the Bastille, and he later signed documents adding after his name 'Vainqueur de la Bastille'.

The family skills in wax were very much in demand from the Revolutionaries. Two days before the fall of the Bastille, when Philippe d'Orléans and Necker fell from power, there was an immediate protest in the streets of Paris at the removal of these popular champions, and in one phase of the riot, the crowd rushed on Curtius' Wax Cabinet: the busts of the two heroes were seized, veiled in mourning crêpe, and paraded through the streets. When the demonstration met a detachment of soldiers, these set upon the wax effigies and their defenders. There were one or two casualties—the very first of the Revolution—including Necker's wax portrait.

The outburst seems to have been spontaneous: the waxworks of the heroes were treated by the crowd in exactly the same way as the reliquary busts or cult statues of miracle-working saints, which are carried in effigy on their feast-days in stations, so that the energy of their holy power will be renewed to flow through the place which claims their protection.[19] Later Jacobin pageantry and ceremonial, as spectacularly represented by the public fêtes—de la Liberté, de la Raison, and so forth—consciously adapted the Catholic Church's brilliant strategy of crowd control in order to mobilize a new faith—in the Revolution. But Curtius' waxworks inaugurated a novel medium for the relation between politics and imagery, between impresarios, money, the people, and representation.

The connection was soon tightened, by design. The Jacobins' brilliant feeling for crowd management inspired the National Assembly to commission Marie Tussaud to portray the Revolution and its triumphs. At their orders, she made the death masks of the Revolutionary leaders Hébert, Robespierre, and Carrier, as well as of the severed heads of Louis XVI and Marie Antoinette. The portraits, taken in this direct way as a print from the beheaded victims, are still displayed impaled on staves in the Chamber of Horrors in London.

Their bad wigs are a little time-worn, but the blood, still vivid crimson where Marie Tussaud painted it so scrupulously, leaks from their mouths and nostrils. With historical precision, the blood splashes *up* their necks. During the years of the Terror, Marie Tussaud continued to receive heads straight from the guillotine, and modelled more and more portraits of its victims—many of them Jacobins who, like Robespierre, had sat for her at the height of influence, as well as many noblemen and women whom she had known at court before the Revolution.

Wax casting allows for copies: intrinsically a reproductive process, it can continue *ad infinitum*, in theory. Like bronze portrait heads or medallic effigies, they proceed from an original to a sequence of replicas, each of which partakes of the essence of the progenitor or model. That original contact with the subject's vanished physical being intensifies the hallucinatory effect of presence in absence, of ubiquity and deathlessness in the waxwork—as process and artefact.

Of all the heroes and villains, stars and scenes, the waxwork that remains the most bizarre and immediate link with the past through Tussaud's career and craft remains the tableau of Citoyen Marat in his bath at the moment after Charlotte Corday has stabbed him to death (Figure 3, p. 22). Marat, one of the hardliners of the Revolution, architect of the Terror, had destroyed the milder Girondins; Corday, who was 25, gave her allegiance to the Girondins, and was no less ardent and idealistic in her vision of Revolutionary allegiance; she went to the guillotine that year.

Marat was much loved, called 'L'Ami du peuple', and after his assassination, at the request of the painter Jacques-Louis David, Madame Tussaud was given permission to take a death mask from Marat's corpse: 'I was ordered to come at once,' she remembered, 'and to take with me what appliances I needed to make an impression of his features. The cadaverous aspect of the fiend made me feel desperately ill, but they stood over me and forced me to perform the task.'[20] Yet, however cadaverous Marat might have been moments after death, however desperately ill Marie Tussaud felt, she continued in her unusual task throughout the Terror, making numerous death masks of its victims.[21]

Curtius and Marie worked together to incorporate the death mask of Marat into a valedictory memorial tableau, showing Marat (labelled 'I am the Rage of the People') sitting in his hip bath where he would compose letters as he tried to soothe the painful itchiness of his psoriasis. The *mise-en-scène* was opened to the public soon after the murder to demonstrations of great grief and commotion—with Robespierre adding his own personal laments to the general clamour.

David was composing his key work of Revolutionary *pietà*, Marat as the dead Christ at the same time, and the two scenes echo each other. David may have used Tussaud's mask. He had worked for three days with the corpse as model; meanwhile, Madame Tussaud followed David's ideas for a pictorial composition, as well as her own experience of the scene of the crime, to create the wax tableau. When the hot weather (it was July 1793) required the burial of Marat's body, David then substituted Tussaud's wax-work as a model for the painting, a studio custom in which he was following Poussin.[22] David's famous icon also annexes Catholic ritual for the purposes of Revolutionary not religious metaphysics, and the waxwork to this day converts Catholic ritual exposure of the dead into a secular effigy; citizen Marat recalls the Passion Week figures of the dead Christ on his bier, showing his wounds to stir the pity and repentance of the onlooker.

In 1802, when the waxworks first toured in Britain, Marat in his bath was included.[23] Today's tableaux, in both Madame Tussaud's and the Musée Grévin, are third- or fourth-generation casts from the original death mask—though only Paris has Marat's actual bathtub.

After Curtius died in 1794, Marie continued the work on her own. In London, a tableau of unsparing grue shows Marie Tussaud hunting through the morgue piles of the executed in order to locate the head of Marie Antoinette, while opposite, the blade of the guillotine is on display as well, with a label announcing that it is 'the one that beheaded Marie-Antoinette in 1793. It was purchased from the executioner's family.' Marie Tussaud brought it with her to London, as part of her founding touring show, and the shop in the waxworks show she founded now sells a replica, but in cuddly soft toy form.[24]

Although Madame Tussaud was summoned before the Committee for Public Safety, she survived her interrogation and took up her uncle's legacy on her own, leaving for England in 1802, with a collection of waxworks and memorabilia. Several other waxworks portraitists had already found fortune; it was a *carrière ouverte aux talents*, especially female. 'Ceroplasty', alongside quill-rolling and flower wreaths, seems to be an overlooked corner of work for busy female hands. Patience Wright, an American in London, was known as 'the Promethean modeller' for her uncanny living likenesses of celebrities, including King George III; she exhibited in her own 'House of Fame' from 1772 until her enthusiasm for the American revolutionaries lost her her English clientèle. A certain Mrs Salmon also showed her wax-works figures not far from Baker Street. A Mrs Jarley of Portland, Maine, showed her 'Wax-Work figures in theatrical poses'. The tradition continued, on an upwardly mobile trend: in 1893, the grandly named Panopticon Museum in Leicester Square, London, boasted showing 'various living delusions . . . executed by young ladies'.[25]

Some of the beheaded aristocrats and former Revolutionary favourites whom Marie Tussaud depicted, as well as Marat's assassin, Charlotte Corday, have been lost over the years of tours, accidents, and fires. But, amazingly, the original standing portraits of the King Louis XVI and Marie Antoinette and their children, made when they were alive, are still displayed. The direct link across time to the victims' bodies, through death masks taken from their features so soon after death, brings them very close. One of the awestruck journalists, seeing Madame Tussaud's exhibition in Liverpool around 1820, was moved to quote that very scene in The Winter's Tale when Hermione is unveiled by Paulina as if she were a statue ('Would you not deem it breath'd? And that those veins | Did verily bear blood?').

Madame Tussaud understood the *frisson* of personal effects, pursuing humdrum items associated with her heroes and villains with a modern fan's enthusiasm and the even-handedness of curiosity—or, rather, the omnivorousness of prurience. She acquired Napoleon's coach from Waterloo, and his cloak from Marengo; and with various other articles, these were arranged in 'The Shrine, or Golden Chamber' of 'the Relics of the Emperor Napoleon (admission sixpence)'. Memorabilia could turn very morbid: the chewed toffee from the pram of a murdered baby used to be on view.[26]

The descendants of Madame Tussaud in England took pains to disinfect their founder of her Jacobin associations, and when they toured Britain from 1802 until 1833, the waxworks were presented as exemplary and horrifying testimonials to the atrocities of the French. That year she estab-lished her permanent show in the Bazaar, Portman Square, near the museum's present site in Baker Street, where it attracts crowds of over two million a year.

Public waxworks extend the function of memorial portraiture: as with portrait heads and busts, the face and head are the vital seats of identity, the core of resemblance and personality, where truth-to-life above all must be grounded in order to convince the spectator. Madame Tussaud's acknowledges the affinity, for Victorian busts of great men by the official monumentalist Francis Chantrey stand on pillars in the entrance hall. The custom spread far and wide: the death mask of the outlaw Ned Kelly is still on display in Old Melbourne Gaol in Australia, where he was executed. Ned Kelly, like some of the Jacobins whom Madame Tussaud immortalized, epitomizes the doubled message of such a memento: both trophy of the victory of law and order, and an eternal memory of the heroic individual's continuing power.

The first showmen who took anatomical waxworks on tour sometimes advertised them 'For Gentlemen only', while others offered separate ladies' days, and even suitable chaperones. But the once salacious and near clandestine character of these forensic simulacra continued to weaken during Victoria's reign. Today, anatomical waxworks have taken their place in the contemporary aesthetics of shock, and belong in a more public iconographic language than they have ever inhabited before. A series of influential exhibitions has presented the meticulous waxen preparations of functions, illnesses, and abnormalities as an aesthetic process, a form of visual narrative drama, thus lifting them out of their medical uses, and focusing attention on the anatomists' artistic skills. These were heightened by the powerful principle of teaching from monstrous aberration, rather than from normal health, so that the subjects are often harrowing in their disfigurement and their degeneration (the cavern of a rotted mouth, the eruptions of cruel erispelas on the skin, the lunar eclipse of a blind eye, ears leaking blood), but always rendered, by some unholy irony, with the most jewel-like scrupulousness of detail and ornament. The wax artists obeyed the hyperrealist conventions of their craft, far beyond any medical necessity, and painted disembowelled cadavers with made-up faces and added wigs of real human hair to the underside of skulls they had split to display the section.

These conflicts between instruction and aesthetics, between human empathy and artistic ambition, turn forensic verisimilitude utterly monstrous. In a literal sense, anatomical waxworks embody departures from the norm, and these monstrosities are presented as wonders, exquisitely tooled and crafted—freak productions of nature as connoisseurs' playthings. Contemporary photographers such as Saulo Bambi, in his Taschen Icons book on the waxes of La Specola in Florence, have used baroque angles and special cropping to obscure the models' historical context, in medicine and biology, and instead linger lubriciously on the bodies' hyperbolic morbidity. Their images subscribe rapturously to horror and the grotesque as a pleasurable aesthetic of bodily representations for our time.[27] Meanwhile, scholarly explorations across several disciplines keeps growing.[28] Above all, the realist aesthetic of medical art and its embalming and taxidermic processes have profoundly imbued the uses of the body and its images in contemporary art, while the spectacular tradition combining popular entertainment, grisly tableaux, the embalmers' and ceroplasts' craft, and anatomical inquiry now shapes hard-core pornography.

In the last decade of the twentieth century and the beginning of this new millennium, anatomical sculpture has received much attention from art historians and artists, most notably from Jean Clair in his frontier-crossing and encyclopaedic exhibition *L'Âme au corps*, which opened at the Grand Palais in Paris in 1993 (a cruel roof leak closed it down all too soon).[29] On a reduced scale, the show later travelled to Venice for the Biennale, and the highly original, imaginative, and scholarly catalogue influenced the development of a new fascination with medical arts and a new acceptance. Four years later, the artist Deanna Petherbridge selected a touring exhibition, *The Quick and the Dead*, with an incisive and empathetic eye. Jean Clair was absorbed in philosophical questions of being and in scientific theories about the principle of life, whereas Petherbridge watched intently for the dynamic conversation between medicine and fine art, especially draughtsmanship. The blockbuster exhibition *Spectacular Bodies* at the Hayward Gallery, London, selected by Martin Kemp in 1999, developed these approaches and brought several of the preternaturally skilful Italian waxworks by the Florentine master Clemente Susini and others before a different and much larger public, who were largely dumbfounded by the morbid intensity of these objects. The translation of this startling epistemological adventure from the laboratory bench to the gallery vitrine continued with the travelling show *Körperwelten*, or *Body Worlds*, the creation of a pathologist called Gunther von Hagens. It provoked condemnation from clerics, both Protestant and Catholic, when it first opened in Mannheim, Austria, in 1997, but the crowds still flocked to the display of bodies and hundreds of body parts, some of them whole, some of them excoriated, strung, drawn and quartered, some of them in wafer-thin slices, preserved according to a new embalming technique, 'Plastination', that, like the master ceroplasts of Italy, incorporates real tissue in the preparations.

The extreme realist style of anatomies and waxworks has clearly directed contemporary artists towards literal specimens, as in Damien Hirst's taxidermy. But it also shapes dramatic *mises-en-scène* by artists in which the accent falls on the inherently disturbing potential of artifice and verisimilitude. From American Pop Art in the Sixties to the contemporary uncanny and perverse Chapman Brothers today, waxwork likenesses have presented an opportunity for mordant social observation, as in Ed Kienholz's lurid scene of teenagers' heavy petting in a car at a drive-in movie, and George Segal's spectral reproduction of the photograph of marines planting the Stars & Stripes in Vietnam. A recent sculpture by the Italian Maurizio Cattelan, 'La Nona Ora', catches the storytelling conventions of history, fame, and spectacle in commercial effigies. 'The Ninth Hour' represents a bolt out of the blue: Pope John Paul II lying in his papal raiment pinned under a meteorite. When it was shown in the Royal Academy, London, shards of wood and of glass from a shattered rooflight in the resplendent classical ceiling above were scattered around the prostrated prelate, whose features were scrunched up in convincing agony.[30] At closer inspection, the Pope was a little rosy and plump for maximum resemblance, and the raiment turned out to be cheap cloth, and the papal slippers slip-ons over white socks. The title, referring to the last hour of Christ on the cross, when he cried out, 'My God, my God, why hast thou forsaken me?', could be taken as a pious reminder of the divine judgment we must all face, or a high camp tabloid twist on divine providence. To some, the installation was blasphemous; to others, reverent (though this is a little puzzling).

'La Nona Ora' shows a strong sense of the absurd, and an enjoyable canniness about the histrionic appetite for catastrophe that surrounds fame and delights in punishing celebrities for that fame.[31] Cattelan's piece captures another aspect of morbidity, as embodied by the tradition: waxworks stage the mortal death of their subjects but take pleasure in their destruction, deserved or undeserved. The Pope's plight under the huge lump of rock come out of the blue just for him encapsulates the axiomatic greed for fatality that underlies the relations between the public and the subjects of celebrity cult icons, be they saints, kings, or rock stars—we are back to the *danse macabre*. But the wax sculpture gained in impact because it splintered time and seized a single moment to depict: on the whole, waxworks perpetuate infinite stasis, time standing still, as with La Santa in Bologna, the Venuses of the anatomists, and the casts of Madame Tussaud's idols and villains.

Developments in technique have also transformed artistic practice, and pleasure in exact representation has not weakened, even under photographic regimes. In his *Poetics*, Aristotle remarks from the very start how fascinating the human mind finds repulsive things, as long as they are drawn or otherwise represented: 'though a thing itself is disagreeable to look at, we enjoy contemplating the most accurate representations of it—for instance, figures of the most despicable animals, or of human corpses.'[32] Indeed, the pervasiveness of photography around us today has sharpened hunger for such experiences through images. Illusions of real presence, solid, tactile, and in the round, skilfully and exactly summoned by new processes and materials continue the aesthetic of the waxwork, its funerary function and its uncanny symbiosis with memory.

Something diabolical clings to the new techniques of reproduction and representation, as numerous early witnesses reveal. The superb Art Nouveau central hall of the Musée Grévin in Paris is decorated with *singeries*, light-hearted scenes of monkeys dressing up, looking at themselves in mirrors, generally mocking humans by their clever and mischievous imitations. In a less credulous spirit, they nevertheless recall the medieval conceit that the devil is the ape of God; monkeys (*singes*), are also the masters of signs (*signes*), which can illuminate or deceive.[33] With this fascinating opening scene, the Musée Grevin introduces the visitor to the perplexing involutions of meaning, as one copy follows another, and the status of the real, of the true, of the living, becomes unsettled. Waxworks create such an eerie feeling of presence that the archivist at Madame Tussaud's in London told me that if she stayed late and walked out through the galleries after everyone had gone, she still felt—after twenty years' familiarity—chillingly spooked by the standing, motionless effigies in the silent rooms.[34]

The success of waxworks inspired another branch of popular public entertainment: the diorama, created by Louis Daguerre in Paris in 1825. This novel spectacle combined the craft skills of anatomists and model-makers, the detailed, haptic reality effects of religious statuary and waxworks, and the staging of a fictional space. Furthermore, the diorama leads directly to the coming of photography, since Louis Daguerre segued instinctively from his work with three-dimensional illusions to experiments with photography, and wrote a book about his two great inventions. The earliest daguerreotype shows the view from the roof of the diorama in the Boulevard du Temple. It is an eerie scene, for the length of the exposure caused everyone in the street below disappear—with the exception of a customer's truncated boots and legs on a shoeshine's box.[35] It was made in early January 1839, barely a month before Fox Talbot demonstrated his own successes in fixing an image—by a different method—to the Royal Society in London.[36]

Movement eluded waxworks and the new photography alike, but animating a living likeness remained the deepest ambition of artists seeking to capture an image of life itself.

Philippe Curtius, who opened the first wax cabinet in
Paris and taught Madame Tussaud, created this 'Sleeping
Beauty' (1765), giving her a clockwork mechanism so
that she seemed to breathe.

3

On the Threshold: Sleeping Beauties

The oldest surviving waxwork in Madame Tussaud's in London is called 'The Sleeping Beauty': a female figure lying down, in the kind of pose often called abandoned; as if spellbound rather than asleep, she seems suspended for all eternity like an effigy on a tomb awaiting the resurrection, her relaxed, even languorous slumber a wishful fiction about death's defeat. The figure's face is hard to see, unless you go around her to look at her upside down—and then the upturned angle offers her throat and breast to the spectator's attention before anything else. This is indeed the most spectacular aspect of her: her breast rises and falls to her breathing. She looks alive. She looks real. She looks as if she has overcome time and death; she creates an illusion of life to strike wonder in the beholder (Figure 5, p. 46).

Thomas Aquinas singled out *animation* as the defining quality of soul, calling the soul 'the starting point of all motion in things which live' and continuing, with a reference to Aristotle, ' "The soul *is indeed, as it were, a life-giving principle in animate things*." '[1] Waxworks may offer living likenesses, but unlike the statue of Hermione in *The Winter's Tale*, they cannot cross the river between the quick and the dead. A waxwork only *looks* alive; its creepy inertia calls our attention to that missing ingredient: consciousness. Alongside animation, inwardness is the quality that waxworks intrinsically and conspicuously lack.

The figure called 'The Sleeping Beauty' was modelled by Philippe Curtius himself in 1765, and, according to the museum's tradition, portrays Madame Du Barry, the mistress of Louis XV, who would then have been 22.[2] At the turn of the century her clockwork breast was electrified. Until recently, she lay under a canopy in a four-poster bed, with several attendant waxworks gazing at her: a Victorian gentleman and lady, and at the foot of the bed, her page, an eighteenth-century 'blackamoor', keeping vigil.[3] The waxwork image of this sleeping woman, automated to look as if she were alive, was presented as the vehicle for communal dreams, aroused and shared in public, and a site of and stimulus to wonder.

Marie Tussaud's legacy to her waxworks museum in London included two more 'Sleeping Beauties', besides Du Barry, both of them also victims of the guillotine whose heads she modelled straight off the scaffold. They included the Princesse de Lamballe: she was the superintendent of the

Queen's household, and her favourite, also rumoured to be her lover.[4] Only one had sat in life for her portrait: Madame Du Barry, thirty years before she met her death. In the other two cases of the recumbent figures, Curtius or Marie modelled their likenesses from their severed heads: a contemporary who claimed to be an eyewitness described how in the cemetery of La Madeleine, Curtius rearranged Du Barry's rictus with a deft pinch of his finger and thumb: 'Il maquilla cette face d'un sourire posthume, la fit belle et agréable' ('He made up the face with a posthumous smile, rendered her beautiful and charming'—Du Barry was one of the few victims who had gone to her death protesting violently). He then poured a layer of wax straight on to the turf at the side of the grave, and rolled the severed head in it to take an impression of her features.[5]

By the time the earliest catalogues of Madame Tussaud's were drawn up in the 1830s, only one of these reclining figures survived—the one currently on view—and she cannot be the portrait made of Du Barry at the time of her death, when she was in her fifties. So in order to keep the gory toll of the Terror before the eyes of the public, the 'Sleeping Beauty' on show was provided with a different, spine-chilling story. She was re-identified with unabashed—and highly inventive—royalist loyalty as Madame de Saint Amaranthe, who was much younger than Du Barry at the time of her death:[6] 'She was one of the most lovely women in France, and Robespierre endeavoured to persuade her to become his mistress; but being as virtuous as she was beautiful, she rejected his solicitations with indignation. Robespierre, who never wanted a pretext for destroying anyone who had given him offence, brought Mme St Amaranthe before the Revolutionary Tribunal and, at the age of twenty-two, this victim to virtue was hurried into eternity.'[7]

The victim to virtue, sometimes dressed in black, lay on a couch, while the waxwork of Madame Tussaud (her own self-portrait), stood at the head of it, in poke bonnet and specs, resembling a little old loving governess at the side of one of Freud's hysterical patients—or perhaps, to use another image, a Catholic praying for the intercession of an ecstatic saint with access to magic, invisible powers.

But the 'Sleeping Beauty' at Madame Tussaud's has turned aside these historical circumstances, and the fairy-tale character has taken precedence. A notorious courtesan—or a minor aristocrat—who died at the guillotine has become an innocent love object from the French fairy-tale first written down by Charles Perrault in 1697.

The Tussaud 'Sleeping Beauty' bears a close and disturbing resemblance to the so-called Venuses of anatomical cabinets. The 'Venerina', or 'Little Venus', displayed in Bologna, for example, was made by the Florentine ceroplast Clemente Susini (1754–1814), who modelled her with a three-month-old foetus in her womb, adding hair and pearls to her outer form (Figure 4, p. 30).[8] The bodies of medical female subjects were strangely presented in the language of erotic art, lain languorous on velvet cushions, bedecked with jewels, and named after the goddess of love. Their secondary sexual characteristics were stressed, their abdomens revealed and interiors opened up to show the archaeology of innards in removable parts. By contrast, anatomical models of male bodies are usually depicted standing up, and illustrate the circulation of the blood or the apparatus of muscles—coded to correspond to manly qualities like strength and reason. The sleeping Venuses, on the other hand, document the nervous system and reproduction—affect and eros.[9]

Of a 'Parisian Venus' displayed in London in the early nineteenth century, for example, a black letter broadsheet declared, 'The figure is a beautiful Caucasian Variety of Mankind', and went on to draw attention to the mysterious borderland between life and death that such sculptures occupied in the view of medical science of the day: 'For the sake of convenience part of the Cranium is removed, and the Membranes which cover and protect the Brain brought under observation; these on their own are seen drawn aside, and the Brain itself, "The dome of thought, the image of the soul" with all its external convolutions, strikingly and correctly displayed.'[10]

The Bologna Venus is smaller than life-size, and though the museum offers the explanation that the original woman, who donated her body to science, suffered from a hole in the heart and, in consequence, did not grow to full womanly size and died in pregnancy, this seems unlikely. Other examples in Florence, by Giuseppe Ferrini as well as Susini, were also modelled at the same time as Curtius and his niece were working in France.[11] The alleged Madame Du Barry may have begun life as a medical model, and her body cavity, where clockwork swells her breast, may once have held detachable replica organs.

A waxwork like the Tussaud 'Sleeping Beauty' lies in timeless defiance; visitors hang back from her with more awe and solicitude than from other standing waxworks—she is not only uncanny, but also intimate, and the pressure on desire she exercises invites a closed door and a moment or two alone. Such a sculpture conveys a seductive vision of erotic, feminine catalepsy, which the peculiar translucence and slight sweatiness of the wax medium suit so creepily.

The sculpture's impact is not erotic only, or even necrophiliac, whatever its origins in the murky convergence of eighteenth-century science and libertinism. The museum display, taking a sleeping figure out of bed, has interestingly shifted the emphasis from the fairy-tale and the awaited prince. The waxwork embodies a growing theme in contemporary iconography, and invests the image of a dreaming woman with hope—not of possessing her, but of identifying with her, of knowing her, even of becoming her. She is available for psychic entry. The spectator looks at the Sleeping Beauty, and while the expectation of a prince's kiss interrupting the eternity of sleep dominates the familiar plot, the museum spectacle draws the spectator into wonder about her inner life.

Does she solicit imaginative empathy alone? One of the most frequently reproduced and purchased images throughout the Victorian era was Henry Fuseli's painting *The Nightmare* (1781),[12] in which another Sleeping Beauty, flung voluptuously in figure-clinging classical drapes on a bed, her head back, her body arcing as if in passion, is trodden by a hideous hobgoblin: here the curiosity excited by the spectacle of a dreaming woman summons a succubus in the likeness of one of the witch-hunter's lustful imps, to create an extravagant icon of female sexuality. The original paintings—for there are several versions—reveal the artist in his most lugubrious and scandalous mood drawing on classical dream theories as well as witchcraft fantasies. Besides the many versions by Fuseli's hand, supposedly, numerous engravings, reductions, imitations, and parodies exist, and you can still buy the image—as an Old Master reproduction in oil on canvas—from the web.

The Tussaud tableau of the 'Sleeping Beauty' reverberates with another universally familiar fairy-tale character: Snow White, who also falls into a long, enchanted sleep after being poisoned and yet wakes up. But in Snow White's case, her sleep is not presented as a likeness of death, but death itself—except that she does not decay, and her beauty does not fade.

Waxen effigies, like Santa Caterina de' Vigri and the many other saints immortally preserved in Catholic shrines, capture their subjects and then preserve them eternally, imitating the blessed state of a soul in heaven, out of time, beyond the reach of the laws of this world. Images of sleep, dream, and trance communicate this state, which lies in the zone neither of life nor of death, but somewhere else. The word 'trance' itself derives from the Latin *transitus*, a passing over, as in the theological concept of the translation of a saint from this world to the next. *Transitus* specifically describes the bodily passage of the Virgin Mary at her death, because her body was assumed into heaven without committal to the grave; in her special case she was spared the effects of mortality altogether and thus remains the perfect type of spiritual body, the pattern for the transition which the faithful yearn to make: to preserve undiminished the mind–body compact that guarantees personal identity, but to preserve it in some ideal state. *Transitus* implies some kind of change for the better. The entranced body has prevailed against the laws of death.

Yet it also presents an enigmatic picture of sleep, when the self has also let go of conscious control, but in a very different way. The absent state of the *transi* might figure a condition of receptivity, like trance. Waxen verisimilitude lends itself naturally to depicting the transitional state, suspended in the no-time and elsewhere place between life and death.[13]

It is difficult to find good photographs of these predecessors of Snow White in their glass coffins, because they are considered sacred relics, still venerated, beyond blasphemous handling and investigation. According to the beliefs which invest them with this numen, they are furthermore natural wonders, bodies suspended in time; hence they cannot be defined as *objets d'art* because they prolong the material presence of real people. So such effigies have not made their way into the art history books—even into the most scholarly accounts of the history of wax, as far as I can see.

The illusion of permanent sleep is invoked to deny the reality of death; with her rising and falling breast, 'The Sleeping Beauty' functions as an anti-*memento mori*, positioned in the antechamber of the Great Hall where the images of great men (and a few women) appear to have conquered death through glory and fame. Sleep is a refuge from death; a deception which can cheat death itself. 'The Sleeping Beauty's' false flesh offers a lens to the visitors through which to look at the waxworks to come. While these serve as eerie reminders that all flesh is grass (unless it be wax), and that even the most accurate and lifelike simulacra can never possess vitality itself, she promises immortality as the suspension of time.

Hypnos, the god of sleep, was depicted winged; he offered imaginative flight; his presence evoked a journey to an elsewhere beyond the moment and the place. In this sense the 'Sleeping Beauty' waxwork is a vehicle of fantasy into which visitors step in order to travel to wonderland. More particularly, the sculpture was made during the rise in interest in states of unconsciousness, in suspended animation, neither sleep nor waking nor indeed coma, as under hypnosis. The theorist, magician, and healer Anton Mesmer enjoyed huge social esteem at the time, and when a commission was set up to investigate his theory and practice of mesmerism, no less a figure than Benjamin Franklin chaired it. The commission reported in 1784 that there was no foundation to Mesmer's theory of animal magnetism, but it allowed that therapeutic benefits could be achieved through the powers of the imagination. (Coincidentally, Franklin was one of the many Great Men who sat for Curtius for his portrait in wax.)

The hypnotists who came after Mesmer in the late nineteenth century took the word over from the Greek word for sleep because they perceived a similarity between sleep and the form of suspended consciousness which their subjects experienced. The mind lowered its guard and became both suggestible and guileless; sensitivity to pain decreased, or even disappeared. A photograph, taken in 1845, shows a travelling hypnotist at work on four subjects sitting in states of trance.[14] Saint Bernadette was tested by doctors during her visions in 1854: she was pricked with pins and burned with candles and felt no hurt—to the wonder of the attendant crowd. Somnambulism figures vividly in the stories of Edgar Allan Poe and in films inspired by them; hypnotic trance became a popular theme at the turn of the century, in George du Maurier's bestseller *Trilby* (1894), and in the Gothic film *The Cabinet of Dr Caligari*, made in 1919 (more on this in Chapter 9).

The writer Lewis Carroll gave the concept of Wonderland far more serious thought than his readers imagine. Considering ways of entering such other worlds, he defined three psychic states: first, ordinary consciousness; secondly, an 'Eerie' condition in which the subject is conscious but aware of the presence of fairies; and thirdly, a trance in which the immaterial body—the spirit or soul—of the subject migrates elsewhere, either to places in this world, or to fairyland, but without causing death or permanent damage to the body from which it is parted. He proposed these possibilities in the preface to *Sylvie and Bruno Concluded* in 1891, but there are traces of it in much earlier writings of the 1860s. The Wonderland which Carroll invented for Alice was not a mere idle fancy to him (see Chapter 16).

The figures of entranced, Sleeping Beauties are usually women or children, and sometimes both combined, as in the case of the Blessed Imelda Lambertini, 12-year-old preserved in a casket in Bologna, as described in the Prologue. It would of course be absurd to suggest that all cult statues, all Mesmer's clients, all hysterical mediums and patients, were or are female. But, as Benjamin Franklin's commission on Mesmer noted, women were in the majority among his following, as they were among Freud's and Breuer's pioneering patients and analysands. Josephine Hilgard, in a study of hypnosis, has linked susceptibility to hypnotism with the imaginative capacity to lose oneself in a book, a film, or a soap opera, and has drawn attention to the mingling of fantasy and reality, the readiness to play pretend and make-believe games, of a subject in hypnosis—malleable, impression-able, and ductile, like wax. She connects this to the state of childhood, and, historically, perceptions of women and children have been tightly inter-twined.[15] Virgin martyrs—from Santa Fina to Bernadette—are frequently children, and their posthumous cults preserve them on the child-like threshold where death does not mark them.

Through her femaleness and her infantile smallness, the 'Sleeping Beauty' at Madame Tussaud's conveys with especial aptness this liminal state, which is in a sense the desired condition of the reader and viewer who begins to voyage by means of imagery, as Jane Eyre does when she looks at Bewick's engravings and other picture-books and imagines realms far beyond her circumstances.[16] The sleeper solicits us to return to the imagined percep-tions of childhood, an entranced floating out of range of all co-ordinates and moorings, a liminal openness, like a proverbial woman buried in a romantic novel, like a patient on the couch accessing the unconscious, or like the medium of wax before it takes shape and identity.

The artist Cornelia Parker has worked powerfully with things as links across time and space, with the connective tissue of former possessions, with nostalgic memorabilia, and has developed a new genre of visual pleasure that nevertheless casts Marie Tussaud as an unlikely foremother of contemporary art. In a memorable show at the Serpentine Gallery, London, in 1995, Parker assembled objects with all kinds of direct associations, some quirky, some poignant, some absurdist (a strand of hair from Freud's couch). But the centrepiece was called 'The Maybe', and it called the bluff of the waxwork effigy: here was a Sleeping Beauty—for real. The actress Tilda Swinton lay sleeping in a glass case all day, and we the visitors could watch her for as long as we liked. She wore ordinary day clothes, without adornment, without covers, with her spectacles by her side within reach. She moved, she breathed, she stirred, but she didn't wake or get up, and she remained on the other side of the glass, out of our reach.[17]

This was a sight to provoke sighs of wonder and pleasure, truly. It recalled the secrecy and intimacy and peace of watching another sleep—a loved one, a child. It gave permission to do something in this case forbidden, to be close to a stranger who is a great beauty and watch her while she was absent, mind-voyaging in her sleep and maybe her dreams. The glass box turned her into an exhibit, and it excited anxiety that she might suffocate and lose that connection to life that made her presence at an art exhibition so peculiarly thrilling. All this sharpened the experience. The title of the piece, 'The Maybe', captured its ambiguity as a perfect example of the uncanny, replicating in its undecidable status as art the mysterious, undecidable character of consciousness in sleep and of relations between self and sleeper. What was she in this living sculpture? Did she become a work of art, even though she was not in any sense fabricated? Can Duchamp's challenge (the urinal as pure form) and Magritte's echoing paradox ('Ceci n'est pas une pipe') be applied to a living being who is just happening to sleep in public? (After all, lots of tired commuters can be watched doing this daily.) The questions linger, and their resistance to solution throws a slanted light on relations of 'The Maybe' with the uncanny nature of the effigy and the waxwork.

With a famous essay, Freud has planted the idea of 'the uncanny' in the very ground of contemporary discussion of art and representation.[18] Freud begins his thoughts on the *unheimlich*, or 'unhomely', with the suggestion, made earlier by E. Jentsch, that the disquiet stirred by waxworks or automata arises from their ever protracted undecided state, between life and not-life. They appear to be alive, yet are not. But Freud is interested in the *heimlich*, or homely, aspect of the feeling, and develops the idea that the feeling arises when a figure or an image stirs a memory of something familiar that has been mislaid, or lost—hence the shivery or uncanny feel of *déjà vu*, or the prickly sensation excited by feeling that someone is in the room when there turns out to be nobody there.

Dissatisfied with Jentsch's emphasis on ambiguous animation, Freud turned to E. T. A. Hoffmann's tale of 'The Sandman', and produced one of his greatest imaginative *tours de force* in literary criticism, as he explores the story's bizarre and complex array of metaphors dramatizing the sinister Dr Coppelius who creates life-size dolls, the lovely singing automaton Olympia, and the doomed student Nathaniel. The essay is central to the Freud's insistence on the castration complex, and has been hugely influential, admired and torn to shreds in equal measure; but it has certainly instituted 'the uncanny' alongside the sublime or the absurd as the generic effect of a certain kind of art in any medium.

The undoubted *frisson* provoked by waxworks, robots, dolls, animatronics, and digital imaging, connects at the deepest level to the enigma of individual life itself, itself necessarily bound up with sexuality. But the analysis of magic and illusion carefully wrought by Christian thinkers, especially in the Renaissance and early modern period, can still help most effectively to illuminate this response, which is both emotional and intellectual. For the devil's power lay in conjuring phenomena that were delusions: Mephistopheles in *Doctor Faustus* summons the pageant of the Seven Deadly Sins, and then the beguiling phantom Helen of Troy. According to theological principles, these seemingly natural, living, moving figures are spectral, mere images, uncanny because illusory. The uncanny is an effect of doubling, as Jentsch indicated, when the subject represented does not exist. Such images or effigies consequently appear to supplant reality or take over from it when no prior referent remains in existence (the Seven Deadly Sins are allegories, Helen is long gone). The uncanny is an effect of reflection without referent, or of creation *ex nihilo*. In other words, it rises from a false impression that soul, in all its imprecision and mystery, is breathing in something; but these intimations of soul presence begin to stir only to be withheld. Living likenesses strive to guarantee and perpetuate presence, but ultimately underline the vanished and absent subject; creepily, they resemble someone or something who is not there, as in a mirror reflection with no subject. Modern optical media have greatly elaborated the scope of illusion since the audience of Athanasius Kircher's magic lantern shows in Rome in the mid-seventeenth century worried about the 'enchantments of the reverend father' (see Chapter 9).

In an essay about playing with dolls, the poet Rainer Maria Rilke describes the way imagination stirs to fill a void, to stop the love for a doll expiring on the blank slate of its response. Rilke often throws an oblique light on Freud, as if engaged in a distant conversation with him (as in the case of his poems on Narcissus), and he also illuminates the uncanny when he describes the power of make-believe in children. He writes:

I know, I know it was necessary for us to have things of this kind, which acquiesced in everything. The simplest love relationships were quite beyond our comprehension, we could not possibly have lived and had dealings with a person who *was* something; at most, we could only have entered into such a person and have lost ourselves there. With the doll we were forced to assert ourselves, for, had we surrendered ourselves to it, there would then have been no one there at all. . . . it was so abysmally devoid of phantasy, that our imagination became inexaustible in dealing with it.[19]

In waxworks, similar powers of projection invest the stubborn, inanimate, horrible thing with life, with soul. Through dressing up, adorning, handling, addressing—and destroying—the objects of play are crammed and heaped in visual and tactile specificities, and subjected to a fugue of passions. Among contemporary artists working in this vein, Ron Mueck creates effigies unsurpassed for their meticulous illusionism. His sculptures are composed of plastics and resins, are entirely factitious, yet provoke all the mixed feelings, anxiety, and awe of perfect imitations: the spectacle he offers baffles and puzzles by its exact replication, its *enargeia*, or vividness of presence. He pricks in eyelashes, body down, pubic hair, strand by strand; glistening gums, the blueish subcutaneous delta of veins, as well as moles, freckles, and smears, add pungent accents of exactitude that deepen the eerie impression of physical reality. These imitations of bodies shiver on the very verge of life, it seems.

The son of Australian toymakers, and himself a model-maker for cinema and television, Mueck has adopted the illusions of scale that film commands, and makes spatial shifts away from lifelike proportion; the resulting incongruities disclose with some unnerving subtlety that the figures have been made—made up—not cast or stuffed or embalmed. *Dead Dad*, the portrait of a naked older man, inspires its particular uncanny shiver because his perfectly rendered corpse is tiny—feet, hands, genitals, all miniaturized, and the more tender and ghostly for this shrinkage. *Big Baby*, which was displayed in the Millennium Dome, was gargantuan, by contrast. As with *Dead Dad*, the proportions communicated the psychological space the two subjects take up—death reduces someone to almost nothing, new life balloons the flesh with its huge energies. Another figure, a portrait of a gangly adolescent girl, was elongated beyond human dimensions, and given strangely greying hair, so that she existed not only stretched in space but also correspondingly extended in time. She is called *Ghost*, and Mueck's title here announces the contradiction at the core of his astonishing deceptions: there is nobody there, nor any body of anyone who ever was.

The artist's 2003 exhibition at the National Gallery, London, the result of a year's residency, included new works, three of them inspired by the theme of the Madonna, but carrying the icon into new zones of representation. Mueck's pregnant woman, a *Madonna del Parto* for our times, stood 12 feet high, stark naked; his smaller than life-size *Mother and Child* showed the naked baby crouched in foetal curl on the naked mother's tummy, before the delivery of the placenta, so the umbilical cord still attached them to each other. Mueck's figures often give the impression of startling themselves: they hang back from their own enfleshment in art, loiter uneasily or stand amazed, or lie stunned at their own paradoxical coming-into-being as image, as fabricated auto-icons. The sculptures packed all Mueck's earlier powers of uncanny imitation, but with a deeper tenderness and awe for the difference between life and image: the stillness of these last descendants of the fine art wax sculpture tradition draw attention to the utter elusiveness of whatever it is, that thing called spirit, the spark of life.[20]

A new generation of figures at Madame Tussaud's move and speak, sing and dance: in Kylie Minogue's case, her voice seems to issue from her famous *derrière*. These automata are so much hugged and kissed by visitors, especially for souvenir snapshots, that they have to be regularly replaced: both the to-the-life exactness of the simulacra and the wear-and-tear they suffer feature prominently on the attraction's posters—they proclaim the success of the deception.

The waxworks' state of suspended animation stirs all kinds of thoughts about that inner life that has fled them. Imitating sleep, such waxworks, like dolls, invite the beholder to speculate about that person's interior life, to supply inner processes: the more scrupulous the simulacrum of their exterior, the more the observer is persuaded that it might be possible to penetrate beyond it. Like 'The Sleeping Beauty', these likenesses invite us to enter into their minds and think about their dreams.

But faced with the illusion of life, we can only intuit the distinctiveness of that person's consciousness. For this reason, the next chapters will take leave of objective portraiture of an individual's likeness to explore approaches to understanding subjectivity: the spirit within. Wax reproduced bodies as an observer sees them, and in the novel public spectacle of the waxworks hall of fame translated an antique and hallowed ritual into the modern entertainment industry. Analogous materials—impressionable, inchoate stuff like vapour, air, breath, and cloud—also developed from the metaphorical usages of antiquity to become prime metaphors for communicating the elusive, changeable, internal contents of someone's being. Only God—or the mysterious life force—could animate the inanimate. The next chapter will look at the deep imprint that the presence of breath—*spiritus* in Latin, *pneuma* in Greek, and Hebrew *rūach*—made on the tradition of thinking about spirit, ghosts, vitality, and individual quiddity. In order to penetrate the developments that took place in the age of modern media, it is not possible to ignore the legacy that places air and angels at heart of ideas about the spirit dimension. Leontes marvelled at the lifelikeness of Hermione's statue, because, as he exclaims, 'There is an air comes from her. What fine chisel | Could ever yet cut breath?' (*The Winter's Tale*, v. iii. 78–9).

Part II

Air

The Holy Spirit joins the lips of Father and Son, the
living metaphor of their breath or of the kiss that unites
them, as it descends above the head of the Virgin Mary
in heaven, in the careful theological vision of the
Trinity by the Rubielos Master, *c*. 1400.

4
The Breath of Life

Yet air is the element most bearable   most bearable to every mortal thing.

Susan Stewart

When Lear at the close of the tragedy find Cordelia hanged and holds her lifeless body in his arms, he cries out in his anguish for a mirror to see if her breath mists it, though he knows that she is dead. Then he holds a feather to her lips, and fancies he see it stir. But when this hope is confounded, he rails:

> Why should a dog, a horse, a rat, have life,
> And thou no breath at all? Thou'lt come no more,
> Never, never, never, never, never.
> Pray you undo this button. Thank you, sir.
> Do you see this? Look on her! Look her lips,
> Look there, look there!

Lear, v. iii

With this refusal to accept that 'never', in the wan hope that Cordelia's lips still show the sign of life, Lear faints and, as Kent says, his ghost passes.

Air is the element where the imagining of spirit mixes with stuff of this world most richly and intimately. *Anima/animus*, Latin for 'soul' and 'spirit', depends on the metaphor of breath, principal token of living being. Breath partakes of the element in which heavenly creatures soar, the cherubim and seraphim and other orders of angels; it fills auras and rings with sweet airs or harmonies, inflates and shines with light and lightness, and, above all, in the band of upper air called aether or ether, provides the pure and luminous habitation for ethereal bodies. Spirit as breath (*rūach*) shapes the vision of the creator moving on the waters in Genesis, like some primordial breeze,[1] and as *pneuma*, figures the principle of life infused into clay by Prometheus and other creators of the first humans in various myths world-wide. It animates the concept of the Third Person of the Trinity, the Holy Ghost, who most commonly takes the form of a dove (see next chapter).

The images condensed into the word 'spirit' itself glow through the forms that spirits take: an airy physics passed from antiquity to early Christian thought, composed of breath, vapour, liquor, and cloud, governs the composition of beings imagined to exist beyond the apprehensible physical universe. In the second century the Gnostic mystic Valentinus composed a prayer called 'Summer', which set forth one view of their interrelationship:

> I see that all is suspended on spirit,
> I perceive that all is wafted upon spirit.
> Flesh is suspended on soul,
> And soul depends on the air,
> Air is suspended from ether,
> From the depths come forth fruits,
> From the womb comes forth a child.[2]

Metaphors clustering around spirit and spirits continue to pun and play on this range of axiomatic images. Breath itself gives 'spirit' from *spirare*, 'to breathe', in Latin, and a galaxy of words spanning the far horizon from life to death: among verbs invoking active agency ('inspire', 'conspire', 'inspirit') and physical states of many kinds ('perspire' and, finally, 'expire'); among nouns, it applies to concepts vast and tiny—the 'Earth Spirit', the 'Spirit of the Age' (the *Zeitgeist*); it also names the kind of fairy known as a 'sprite', as well as volatile essences of one kind and another.[3] No wonder that the history of medicine, since Galen at least, contends with divergent models of vitality, many of them involving the activity of spirit or spirits, fizzing away in the body.[4]

Descartes hypothesized that the information which the senses conveyed to the brain was suspended in and conducted by some invisible stuff he called 'animal spirits'—consciousness for him was material, but intangible, insubstantial, vaporous, and he chose the metaphor of spirits, which serve between the distinct worlds of mind and body in his model, as do clouds between earth and heaven.

That Greek word for air and breath, *pneuma*, does not specify physical breath but rather spirit as opposed to *physis*, or enfleshed nature. *Pneuma* carries us into another metaphorical zone, the pneumatic range of inflatable, cushiony stuff, foam and froth, surf, bubbles, balloons. All of these play their part in the imagery of spirit dimensions. *Homo bulla est* ('Man is a bubble'): the melancholy phrase about the vanity of human life compares it to a mere puff of air.[5]

The multiple and elusive metaphysics that airy metaphor struggles to convey has provoked such sharp quarrels that heretics have been done to death for millennia for apportioning flesh, spirit, and soul in heterodox quantities and relations. However, theology and history are not the focus of this book, but how the imagination has summoned up spirits—such as angels or ghosts.

The mystery of angelic nature had exercised the early Church Fathers, and they had not agreed. Augustine described angels as *corpus sed non caro*—body but not flesh, and the view that angels did not have bodies prevailed when Aquinas, writing with personal passion about angels, wrought the kind of meteorological metaphors that later suffuse the metaphysics of John Donne: 'Although air, as long as it is in a state of rarefaction', wrote Aquinas, 'has neither shape nor colour, when condensed it can both be shaped and coloured, as appears in the clouds. Just so the angels assume bodies of air, condensing it by divine power in so far as is needful for forming the assumed body.'[6]

This poetics of spirit stuff persists. In the lexicon of human fantasy, spirits still put on clothes of air and vapours, light and radiance, to make themselves manifest to human senses. (A working studio sketch after Raphael, attributed to Parmigianino, illustrates the problem that this airy nature presents to artists: in order to make a convincing study of an angelic foot stepping on a cloud, the artist drew from a model resting his foot on a twist of cloth—flesh and material standing in for the airy, unfleshed spirit and the insubstantial cloud.)[7]

In a rapturous sermon, Donne expands in some puzzlement on the incommensurate separation between material and immaterial being: 'that there are distinct orders of *Angels*, assuredly I beleeve; but what they are, I cannot tell. . . . They are Creatures, that have not so much of a body as *flesh* is, as *froth* is, as a *vapor* is, as a *sigh* is, and yet with a touch they shall molder a rocke into lesse Atomes, then the sand that it stands upon; and a milstone into smaller flower, then it grinds.'[8] In the love poem 'Air and Angels', he enters the problem from another angle, and evokes how thinking and imagining and feeling cannot work with nothing, but must grasp at the stuff of the world, just as an angel takes on airy substance:

> as an angel face and wings
> Of air, not pure as it, yet pure doth wear,
> So thy love may be my love's sphere . . .[9]

His love will put on the vesture of hers, as an angel wears a face and wings of pure air in a crude approximation of its true being. In this territory of the spirit, the metaphors can strive only inadequately towards their referent. But in magical thought—and this is where danger lies—thought can create forms, can turn image or word into substance and act: such is the performative nature of the spell.

Light, as both radiance and weightlessness, buoys the angelic body, an impossible body, incorporated but not enfleshed; light clothes it and renders it at once palpable and insubstantial: the lightness of being not so much unbearable as transcendent.

Ariel, Prospero's 'airy' and 'tricksy' spirit, can fly, shape-shift, and perform enchantments at the bidding of his master. In Shakespeare's original play of 'insubstantial pageants' and 'cloud capp'd towers' conjured by the magic of Prospero, the stage directions specify, three times, that Ariel enters 'invisible'. The actor—or actress—must perform to show forth Ariel's spirit nature. Alongside Puck and the mischievous fairies of *A Midsummer Night's Dream*, Ariel's nature is indeed fey, and he inhabits a kind of spirit body not bounded by human laws. As the Revd Robert Kirk described them in 1691, fairies are

'intelligent Studious Spirits, and light changeable bodies (like those called Astral) somewhat of the nature of a condens'd cloud, and best seen in twilight. These bodies be . . . so pliable thorough the subtilty of the spirits, that agitate them, that they can make them appear or disappear at pleasure. Some have bodies or vehicles so spungious, thin and defecate, that they are fed by only sucking into some fine spirituous liquor that pierce like pure air and oil.'[10]

Robert Kirk's elves, fauns, and fairies evaporate according to the axioms of metaphysical poetry and visionary Neoplatonism, but the twilight he invoked as the best condition for seeing the dwellers of subterranean fairyland later suffuses the Romantic ballet stage where Wilis (in *Gisèle*), sylphides, ghosts of wronged lovers in different, subtle shape, and many different kinds of fairies throng and flutter. When the inspired prima ballerina Marie Taglioni padded the toes of her ballet pumps in 1822, she pioneered the thistledown illusion of dancing *en pointe*: a light, changeable fairy body seemed to come to life through the new dancing before the audience's eyes.[11]

Another airy term, the related word 'aura', enfolds a triple image, being both an emanation of air, an effect of luminousness, and a sensation of presence, thus stimulating the senses of smell and touch as well as sight. Used in alchemical arcana, aura was adopted by the Theosophists and other modern spirit theorists to characterize the astral or spirit body, which enjoyed a long, international lineage before it became the tenet of New Age personal growth movements. Aura, the effect of soul visible in the body, functions as a modern pagan counterpart to the immortal soul of orthodox Christianity.

The energy that quickened human beings resembles these immortal figures of the spirit world. The first quality of animation, spirit's capacity for movement (motility), and the second, its shaping agency in relation to the manifest world, are both Aristotelian properties—according to Aristotle's long influential biology, the mother provided all the matter of a child, while the father's sperm formed it by the energy of its spirit. '[W]hat makes semen fertile is the spirit which is contained in the foamy body of the semen, and the nature in the spirit which is analogous to the element of the stars.'[12] So here the image of foam or froth—*aphros*—returns to qualify the character of spirit.

Aristotle also offered a rather more vivid domestic metaphor, writing that fertilization happened in the same way as rennet sets milk to make junket. This second property of spirit, the impressing power to form matter, associates spirit with active agency.[13] Galen grappled with the metaphors offered for spirit, and observed—with a touch of impatience—that 'If we are to declare the substance of the soul, we must say one of two things: either it is the shining and aethereal body, at which conclusion the Stoics and Aristotle must logically arrive, even if unwillingly; or that it is an incorporeal substance, and that this body is its first vehicle, through which mean the soul receives communication with other bodies.'[14] Unlike soul, spirit implies something inhabiting the corporeal even if not of it, a conduit between body and soul; in the struggles with definition in the sixteenth and seventeenth centuries, the ever-growing proximity of soul to spirit threatened to taint the thinker with Neoplatonism and heresy, for in Christian orthodoxy, soul cannot be material or corporeal.[15] 'Though we are told', wrote John Locke, 'that there are different degrees & species of angels & spirits, yet we know not how to frame district specific Ideas of them'.[16] In order to convey the character of such incorporeal beings, the logic of the imaginary annexed further qualities of airy matter: shining, diaphanousness, translucency, brilliance, evanescence, flux, extension, limitlessness, and weightlessness. In representations, light and lightness buoy the spiritual or etheric body, incorporated but not enfleshed, and renders it at once palpable and insubstantial.

The ambiguity of spirit's materiality continues in English, in which the word 'spirit' can mean a good malt at one end of the spectrum of meaning to an ectoplasmic apparition at the other. A spirit like Ariel in *The Tempest*, who flies and flames amazement in the topmasts of the shipwreck, partakes in that ethereal element that Galen points out must form either the substance of the soul or its medium. For many of us, this might not be very convincing as religion or philosophy, but the imagery of airiness communicates imaginative truth through the close-wrapped play of figures of speech.

Growing boldness in the natural sciences inspired a deeper probing for the secret of spirit in the sixteenth and seventeenth centuries, and ancient meteorological metaphors were reinvigorated to invoke the life force. It was not angels only that were clothed in air, but mortals were sustained by air and its spectral train of images, of wraiths and ghosts, and breath and cloud.[17]

In a lighter vein, John Dryden and William Davenant's intriguing and much performed revision of *The Tempest, The Enchanted Island*, written about sixty years after Shakespeare's play (1669), shows how closely breath and soul intermingled, as in this exchange between two of its beguiling ingénues:

> DORINDA. But I much wonder what it is to dye.
> HIPPOLITO. Sure 'tis to dream, a kind of breathless sleep.
>   When once the Soul's gone out.
> DOR. What is the Soul?
> HIP. A small blew thing that runs about within us.
> DOR. Then I have seen it in a frosty morning run
>   Smoaking from my mouth.
> HIP. But if my soul had gone, it should have walk'd upon
>   A Cloud just over you, and peep'd.[18]

Here her condensing breath figures her soul, while he imagines his, after death, walking on a cloud above her.

Within this volatile and subtle range of airy tropes, two aspects of spirit linger on, recalcitrant to Donne's angelic vesture. Light and lightness, airiness and ethereality, are qualities which can be rendered in paint or by other visual means, but until the invention of moving pictures, forms in motion eluded representation—except in stagecraft and the efforts of automatists (Curtius and his 'Sleeping Beauty'). Opera and drama developed techniques to conjure the illusions of Mephistopheles in Marlowe's play, and of Prospero's insubstantial pageants, Macbeth's spectral line of kings and Banquo's ghost, of Puck and the fairies, and Ariel's magic. But the essence of breathing: its *anima*tion resisted understanding. Motile and plastic, the live energy that communicates a breathing body, required a garment—the equivalent of that 'face and wings' that angels wear; the related power of spirit to shape or inform matter also necessitated metaphorical invention.

Just how this puff of air quickened the solid body inspired long and inconclusive experiment. In the first century, Pliny the Elder experimented to discover if bodies weighed more dead than alive, and claimed to have found that corpses were heavier, once the light part—the spirit—had fled. In 1646, Thomas Browne took up the long inquiry into the weight of the body after death, and disagreed with Pliny's result. He found that lesser animals rather became lighter dead: 'for exactly weighing and strangling a chicken in the Scales, upon an immediate ponderation, we could discover no sensible difference in weight, but suffering it to lye eight or ten howres, untill it grew perfectly cold, it weighed most sensibly lighter; the like we attempted, and verified in mice.' Browne's curiosity, however, was not satisfied: 'Now whereas some alledge that spirits are lighter substances, and naturally ascending do elevate and waft the body upward, whereof dead bodies being destitute contract a greater gravity; although we concede that spirits are light, comparatively unto the body, yet that they are absolutely so, or have no weight at all, wee cannot readily allow.' He then makes a distinction between spirit and soul: 'for since Philosophy affirmeth that spirits are middle substances between the soule and body, they must admit of some corporeity which supposeth weight or gravity.'[19]

This distinction does not always command attention, but when it does, it affects thinking about the mystery of life, human essence, and opens possibilities that are important in the context of spiritualism and psychic research in the nineteenth and twentieth centuries, during the quest to understand the imponderable and the invisible.

The unstable, in-between status of spirit continued to affect profoundly subsequent thinking about the mystery of life, human essence, the difference between the quick and the dead.[20] The quest to determine the nature of bodily existence continued well into the Victorian age, and took scientists in eccentric and frequently callous directions: during a famous case in the 1860s, Sarah Jacob, the 'Welsh Fasting Girl', claimed to live on spiritual food alone. Doctors placed her—and her parents—under close observation, and she died of starvation. At that date, the London medical establishment still felt it necessary to put her claims to the test in this shocking extreme, in order to prove the material foundation of life itself.[21] Experiments have continued to inspire attempts to ascertain the border between life and death: in 1905, a Dr Baurieux spoke to the severed head of a victim of the guillotine, crying his name and recording the response. Twice the eyes opened and looked at him. He calculated that after beheading, consciousness remained for twenty-five to thirty seconds.[22]

Baurieux's experiments constitute a nadir of Victorian-style positivism; today, questors after the phenomenon of spirit would mostly avoid the body as the object of medical experiment, and investigate instead the language that attempts to embody soul or spirit. As Henri Corbin wrote, 'Between the sensory and the intellectual world, [that] sages always have experienced an intermediate realm, [that is] one akin to what we call the imaginings of poets.'[23]

Harold Bloom quotes this in his book *Omens of Millennium*, where he explores the history of theological arguments about the nature of angels in the world's great religions. He introduces, for example, the opinion of Hayim Vital, a Jewish mystical follower of Moses Cordovero, and his disciple, Isaac Luria, in sixteenth-century Palestine, that 'every word that is uttered creates an angel'. This teacher also held that when Cabbalists read the Torah, 'not only the words but the letters and the spaces in between the letters and the words, and interpretations of these gaps also brought forth angels.'[24] Bloom expresses sympathy with this view, that it is indeed language that creates angels.

The word becomes flesh through art and imagery and metaphor. Paintings and poems do not represent phenomena waiting in invisible realms to be made apparent, but generate them, forge them, make them without external or prior referent. Mystical visions do not behold phenomena from another world, but realize them through linguistic tropes; the subjects of angelic visitations do not exist until they are made visible by the image. Bloom concludes: 'There is always a world to come, [but it is] not a world elsewhere, but one to be known here and now.'[25]

Unexpectedly, angels have not been banished by non-believers or sceptics, but are flourishing ever more strongly in contemporary society. Wallace Stevens, who himself returned again and again to the value of imagination in a collection of essays he entitled *The Necessary Angel*, fashioned a modern spirit body of the self in his poetry, as for example in 'Angel Surrounded by Paysans':

> Am I not,
> Myself, only half of a figure of a sort,
>
> A figure half seen, or seen for a moment, a man
> Of the mind, an apparition apparelled in
>
> Apparels of such lightest look that a turn
> Of my shoulder and quickly, too quickly, I am gone?[26]

The angels and spirits who now occupy modern fantasy descend from medieval and Renaissance art and poetry; they used to convey to us apparitions 'apparelled in | Apparels of such lightest look', and we are still able to see these evanescent 'men of the mind', these spirits who have been and are such necessary inhabitants of the 'intermediate realm' in terms established through time by language. Breath is, however, hard to enflesh in the mind's eye or on the page in material imagery ('What fine chisel | Could ever yet cut breath?'), and so the visible proof of spirit's insubstantial airiness shifted towards more palpable metaphors from nature, and imagination apparelled spirit bodies of air in recognizable attributes, with wings, voice, lightness, and translucency.

An enraptured Mary Magdalene is carried aloft in ecstasy by putti; in this drawing by Luca Cambiaso (d. 1585), her earthly flesh lifts weightlessly on their airy lightness.

5
Winged Spirits and Sweet Airs

It may be that universal history is the history of a handful of metaphors.

Jorge Luis Borges

The quality of lightness above all distinguishes the spirit element—lightness in both its luminous and its weightless aspects. As Titania says to Bottom, 'And I will purge thy mortal grossness so, | That thou shalt like an aery spirit go' (*A Midsummer Night's Dream*, iii. i). Spirits and souls take wing; they are made of light and of lightness; the gravity of the world and of flesh does not hold them in its grasp. In Plato's *Phaedrus*, Socrates invokes wings and wingedness as attributes of a soul in its perfection: 'The function of a wing is to take what is heavy and raise it up into the region above, where the gods dwell; of all things connected with the body, it has the greatest affinity with the divine.'[1] The spirit part of a living being comes clothed in metaphors of flight and light, of the upper air and ethereal ozone, of shining clouds and radiant auras. Italo Calvino opens his *Six Memos for the Next Millennium* with a meditation on the quality of *leggerezza*, and identifies this lightness with the flight of the poet's spirit and the trance journey of the shaman.[2]

Even when souls are condemned to the dismal greyness of the underworld, they have still shed the grossness—the weight—of matter. Virgil likens the shades of the dead flocking to the sound of Orpheus's music to birds sheltering from a storm:

> But, by his song aroused from Hell's nethermost basements,
> Flocked out the flimsy shades, the phantoms lost to light,
> In number like to the millions of birds that hide in the leaves
> When evening or winter rain from the hills has driven them.[3]

In the repertory of symbols in classical thought, the natural world offered embodied metaphors for the airy spirit: *psyche*, a word for 'soul', was used for butterfly or moth in Greek as well, and some images depict such a soul-insect fluttering from the tip of a penis, figuring the force that quickens matter into life and forms undifferentiated flesh into a person.[4] Sometimes the dead breathe out a sprite with transparent wings; sometimes it flies from the open wounds of a fallen warrior.

Spirit quickening, operated by the breath of the creator, occurs in language groups beyond Indo-European; the act attracts descriptions that connect the fabric of the imagination with the stuff and character of material existence. The ancient Egyptian hieroglyph *BA*, meaning soul, resembles a bird, and survived strongly in Hellenistic and Christian imagery, representing the departing spirit of the deceased (Figure 6a, p. 68). Classical sculptures of Leda and the swan, with Jupiter as a bird impregnating the mortal Leda, bear a surprising resemblance to early imagery of the Annunciation to Mary, and the affinity even helped the myth to survive and remain popular in the Christian Near East.[5]

When Plato wrote that the winged soul parts from the heavy, material body, he set out a distinction that runs through the history of spirit: unearthly beings—angels, cherubim, fairies, sprites—are winged, but those of us who inhabit a body of mortal flesh will not grow wings, not now, or ever: in imagination's geography, ghosts may be insubstantial, transparent, and flit and gibber; but they are somehow grounded, however disincarnate they have become.

Augustine had also said that angels were such by virtue of their office, not their nature; what they do characterizes them, more than what they are. *Angelos* (Greek) and *malek* (Hebrew) both mean messenger, and angels appear many times in the Old and New Testaments to give messages, sometimes in dreams, as in Jacob's vision of the ladder to heaven, and Joseph's, when he was warned of the massacre of the innocents; they proclaim events ('Hark the Herald angels sing!'); they perform embassies of other kinds, as when one is set to guard the gates of Eden with a fiery sword, and another to announce the birth of Christ to Mary. One of the most enduring and important embassies they perform involves mediating between this world and the other. Angels fly between worlds, able to inhabit the intermediate realm because they are themselves intermediaries, messengers from another realm, translating differences of earth and heaven, flesh and spirit. Just as spirit, however elusive a concept, belongs between soul and body, so angels move in the intermediate regions between enfleshment and immateriality, symbolized by the upper air.

Marking passages and passing messages, Christian angels borrowed, from around the fifth century, the features of several classical figures: winged Hermes or Mercury, the god of journeys, of crossroads, and the gods' own messenger, who wore a cap of invisibility and the first seven league boots of fairy-tale; Nike, the goddess of victory, who descends from the heights as in the famous Victory of Samothrace to crown the hero, and defines a precise moment in time when fortune changes, also lent many aspects of her bodily appearance to angels, though not, in Christian belief, her definitely feminine gender. In the seicento, baroque artists unequivocally adopted as their angelic model a divine Olympian: Eros, the god who has the distinction of appearing twice in Hesiod's *Theogony*, the most influential genealogy of the gods and goddesses. Significantly, before he enters the pantheon as the son of Aphrodite, the goddess of love, Eros appears—full-grown as it were—at the very beginning, at creation itself. There at the primordial origin, he brings chaos to order, the energy of love acting in the epic poem as the generative force of creation itself:

> Chaos was first of all, but next appeared
> Broad-bosomed Earth, sure standing-place for all
> The gods who live on snowy Olympus's peak
> And misty Tartarus, in a recess
> Of broad-pathed earth, and Love, most beautiful
> Of all the deathless gods.[6]

Later, in Hesiod's cosmic myth, when Aphrodite is born from the sea, 'Eros her companion' appears with her; while, according to numerous episodes in myth recounting the amorous adventures of the gods, Eros/Cupid becomes Venus' child by Mars, the god of war. *Aphros*, the word for froth, gives the goddess her name, and this foam, which is also surf churned by the waves, itself presents in metaphorical imagery the sperm of Ouranos' severed genitals, tossed on to the sea by his son, Kronos. Foam and sperm, as we saw in the last chapter, give two orientation points on the compass rose of metaphor that language assembles when it strives to capture spirit. Babies; froth; light, bouncy, flying natural forms, play around the elusive concept.

Sigmund Freud collected Greek angels of desire: in his last home in Hampstead, he arranged a fine group of terracotta figurines of *erotēs* behind him when he sat at his desk and opposite the couch; for him, the Greeks' envisioning of sexual passion in the form of a beautiful, smiling, winged youth effectively, even dazzlingly, materialized that virtual power within human consciousness that he called desire, and which Hesiod described:

> Love makes men weak
> He overpowers the clever mind, and tames
> The spirit in the breasts of men and gods.[7]

Freud also bought several examples of another, rare type of classical Eros, in which he takes the form of a child, neither cupid nor angel, but a mischievous, barely pubescent and puckish charmer, lifting his tunic to show his genitals with a complicit smile. Caravaggio's laughing darling, in *Amor Vincit Omnia* (1601–2), takes up a provocative pose in the same radiantly amoral spirit as the Hellenistic figurines; and, with his eagle's wings curving round to touch his thigh, plays the wanton, enfleshing the angelic form as if to mock it. He also, at the same time, embodies forcefully the peculiar, blithely pagan identification of erotic energy and angelic bodies in baroque art.

In both classical iconography and in Christian tradition, heaven swarmed with a lesser kind of angelic being—the *putto* or baby angel who throngs work after work that strives towards expressing heavenly rapture (Plate 2a). These *angiolini*, Cupid's kith and kin (not one of them a girl) altogether at home in the supernatural element, incarnate the energy of the animating principle. Yet they also figure a third species of flesh, neither dead nor alive in the human sense, but gravity-free, paradisically naked. Not altogether etherealized, they are often depicted as substantial and real enough to cast shadows themselves.

Such angels are also called *amorini*, or cupids, and they modulate classical ideas of pleasure and love; neither strictly Christian nor pagan, neither altogether personal subjects nor allegorical personifications, they people imaginary worlds sacred and profane as their most characteristic denizens. They embody a cluster of metaphors to express spirit, including the light-ness and mediating role already mentioned, but ranging beyond them in ways that illuminate the form of the beautiful boys who, at a later stage of development, represent angels. The *putti* of Italian art, those chubby cloud babies, are openly aligned with Cupid as their ancestor. Their presence underscores scenes of the Nativity or the Assumption, ascensions and apotheoses of saints, manifestations and visions of the divine. Like a musical motif playing in the background, *putti* imperceptibly fill the spaces of sky or the edges of the composition with their weightless, peachy bodies, their childlike innocent playfulness.

Though often thought of as cherubs, they do not conform to the cherubim who appeared to the prophet Ezekiel (1: 5–10), who have four faces, each of them whorled with four wings blazoned with eyes, and also have human hands, but at their lower extremities calves' hooves and feet of brass. Nor are baroque *putti* like the seraphim who stand above the throne of the Lord in the vision of Isaiah (6: 1–2), who are cocooned in six wings, two concealing their face, two for flying, and the other two covering their 'feet' (a euphemism to conceal the obvious difficulty about angelic parts). Seraphim and cherubim faithful to biblical description do occur, but they are eclipsed and outnumbered by the swarming, often bodiless heads of cherubs, with ruffs of wings, like corollae of petals.

Angels, especially infantile *angiolini* and *putti*, thus communicate Eros, in the classical god's double temporality, as both an irresistible youth and a naughty baby. In painted Heaven, Baroque *erotēs* materialize as a cloud of desire, frothing and foaming. They introduce accents of sinless and spontaneous carnality as they twist and bounce, presenting their plump and rosy rumps and their baby genitals to the spectator with unalloyed delight, replicated and even multiplied throughout the images like so many caresses made palpable. The indeterminate status of the *putto*, neither the individual, named angel, nor a general allegorical personification, enhances their effect in paintings, as visible vitality reproducing its own likenesses by sheer parthenogenetic energy: love breeding love, one kiss following another. *Putti* play a choric role, messengers giving expression to the passions that are passing between the protagonists.

When the Emperor Hadrian invoked blessings on his soul, he imagined it as a little child: '*animula vagula blandula . . . pallidula . . . nudula*' ('Dear little fleeting pleasing soul . . . pale little naked little thing'); the infant soul, kin to an innocent cherub, or a fluttering sprite, returns with variations in theological definitions, and in medieval art and poetry.[8] The wondrous and complex twelfth-century narrative of Creation in San Marco, Venice, shows the Creator as a much younger, indeed more Christ-like, deity than the usual bearded God the Father: he stands beside Adam and infuses his clay with soul. This principle of life appears to be a fluttering, fairy homunculus. Such a sprite with transparent wings picks up on Hellenic images of *psyche*, the soul as butterfly, but the San Marco mosaic is unusual, for on the whole, the miniature child-bodies that figure soul in the Christian tradition are seldom winged.

The most popular icons of Byzantium represent the soul at the hour of death as a tiny naked infant, issuing from the corpse, often swaddled like a baby. The convention was borrowed by the Roman Church and its artists, especially for images of the death and assumption of the Virgin Mary, and of the day of judgment—St Michael weighs miniature naked souls in the balance, and naked manikins rise from the lips of the dying in medieval miniatures.[9] A visionary painting like Joachim Patinir's sublime landscape of the underworld shows the last voyage of a dead man in an underworld borrowed from classical myth, with the startled soul figured as a child in a boat dwarfed by the looming cliffs and wide stream of the Styx.[10]

The story of spirit epiphanies becomes more complicated when angels—*putti, cherubini*, and *angiolini*—as well as spirits of another kind take the form of birds. Often synecdoche brings about the metamorphosis, through the wings such beings wear. Some artists of the seicento coupled flights of metaphorical imagination with intense observation, and introduced anatomical studies of real birds' wings for angels to wear: the pair of eagle's wings for Amor in Caravaggio's painting had been used by Orazio Gentileschi earlier, we know from studio account-books. Caravaggio also studied the humdrum pigeon for the dusky pinions of another seductive vision, the musical angel playing to the Holy Family in his painting, *The Rest on the Flight into Egypt.*[11] Not all artists managed to picture spirits' airy lightness. The convention only becomes visible when it runs the risk of collapse, as in a painting of around 1670, which shows an episode from the *Odyssey*: Gerard de Lairesse, a prominent theorist of art, did not manage to capture divine ethereal buoyancy, and the winged god Hermes looks dangerously close to crashing into the nymph Calypso as he seeks to deliver his message.[12]

When angels are sighted in America today, they usually come apparelled according to the conventions adopted by artists, mainly in Italy around 300 years ago, who developed these images from the classical repertory and its visions of the god of love and the messengers of Victory and Glory. These angels do not have short curls, or wear togas, as angels do on early Christian monuments, where they are also usually wingless. They do not put on deacons' liturgical vestments, nor are their wings blazoned with peacocks' eyes as in the mosaics and icons of Byzantium; the sweeping long tunics and rainbow plumage of quattrocento annunciations have been replaced by the accurately represented avian pinions and quills of baroque visionary realism. The baroque angel has come to epitomize, even delimit, the idea of angels.

Just as angels take the form of both winged youths and winged infants, spirits find form as winged creatures large and small, as moths or butterflies, as we saw in the last chapter. (In another of his famous extended similes, Virgil describes the souls flocking in the Elysian Fields as bees nuzzling flowers in a meadow in summer. Later, fairy creatures like Ariel in *The Tempest* also shape-shift into tiny insect forms: 'Where the bee sucks, there suck I,' sings Prospero's sprite, anticipating his liberty: 'In a cowslip's bell I lie; | There I couch when owls do cry. | On the bat's back I do fly . . . (v. i. 88–91).).[13]

But by far the most dominant and familiar spirit in the shape of a small winged animal remains the Third Person of the Trinity, the Holy Ghost, who conventionally appears as a white dove. This form that spirit takes is also, as with the cherubim, closely associated with desire and with love: doves come in pairs, and bill and coo, and were sacred to Aphrodite in the classical world, designated to draw her chariot through the skies. The later Christian application retains some of these overtones, expressing the bond of love between the three Persons of the Godhead. It has scriptural support from a single episode, when Matthew the evangelist describes the baptism of Christ in the Jordan by John the Baptist:

As soon as Jesus was baptised he came up from the water, and suddenly the heavens opened and he saw the Spirit of God descending like a dove and coming down on him. And a voice spoke from heaven, 'This is my son, the Beloved, my favour rests on him.' (Matt. 3: 16–17)[14]

The mystery of the Trinity made manifest here reverberates with divine love, the energy that flows between the deity and his creation, through the bird that in the Old Testament symbolizes the pact after the flood.[15] Artists introduced the same symbolic messenger into images of the Annunciation and Pentecost, when the Bible does not mention its appearance, in order to make visible the active word of God, conceived by Mary, and received by her and the apostles. When the Holy Spirit skims down a sunbeam in the form of a glowing dove in images of the Annunciation, tradition invests him with light, air, and fire to communicate his impalpable substance. This bird-spirit sometimes links God the Father and God the Son, the first two Persons of the Trinity, by hovering between their lips, like a kiss made flesh, breathed out between their lips in the form of a dove (Figure 6).[16] Theologically, 'spiration' illustrates the Latin doctrine of the Holy Ghost proceeding from the Father *and* the Son.[17] The dove hovers at the ear of Fathers of the Church, the sign of divine afflatus, or inspiration, as in paintings celebrating the renewed vigour of the Counter-Reformation Church: Carlo Saraceni's powerful work *Gregory the Great Writing his Gospel*,[18] and Guercino's wonderfully rich and dramatically elaborated papal commission, extolling the same Father of the Church with his spiritual sons, the missionaries St Ignatius and St Francis Xavier.[19]

The dove's flight echoes the winged hovering of angels and *putti*, and their somehow natural conjunction in the upper air of baroque art, whether religious or mythological, can help sharpen inquiry into their function. For in biblical Hebrew, the word used for the active intervention of the Godhead at the baptism of Christ and Pentecost, is *rūach*, which as we saw means breath, as in 'in*spir*ation'. But as spirits made visible, angels who breathe wisdom into chosen mediators do not shed that prime function of erotic energy: they enliven the seers who receive their messages, and their flight and soaring, their arabesques on the diagonal, and their acrobatics all reinforce the idea of a divine power that can miraculously move and shape and quicken matter on the lower plane. (James Joyce is burlesquing this whole mystical tradition when Buck Mulligan refers to the Holy Ghost as 'the gaseous invertebrate.')[20]

The resemblance between this Holy Spirit and the appearance of later spirit forms, in psychic photographs and seance phenomena, sometimes issuing from the mouths of entranced mediums, does not simply pun or rhyme within a tradition of supernatural, but arises from the core logic of the imaginary as constituted by language and metaphor. The continuity of certain attributes—whiteness, transparency, flimsiness, filminess—reveals how deeply the imagery works with cognition, providing a fantasy that leads to understanding, and then empirically, in order to support the suggestions of the fantasy. As bodies that soar, inhabiting the middle air, birds act as natural symbols of etherealized intermediaries. The winged and lightness of angelic spirits is bird-like; angels are also excellent and frequent singers. They carol at the Nativity and in numerous evocations of paradise: for Dante the spheres of heaven themselves ring in harmony to the sound of divine praises. Musician angels have scriptural support, but again, baroque artists introduce into celestial bands the strains of a pent-up blissfulness that differs profoundly from the decorous choruses evoked by Fra Angelico or by Piero della Francesca, for example. In a Ludovico Caracci painting of heaven, the members of a cloud-borne orchestra lean voluptuously towards one another, while the singers in the choir around them meld together in a golden summery afterglow around the score held high.[21]

The long philosophical tradition that moulded this fusion of breath, song, and the harmony of the heavens harked back to the Aristotelian view, expressed in *De Anima*, that voice above all is the physical, outer expression of the inner being: 'Voice is the sound produced by a creature possessing a soul.' He weaves voice into the very nature of consciousness and personal identity, writing: 'For, as we have said, not every sound made by a living creature is a voice (for one can make a sound even with the tongue, or as in coughing), but that which even causes the impact, must have a soul, and use some imagination; for the voice is a sound which means something.'[22] Birds, nature's only musicians in the perception of those days—even the keen-eyed, sharp-eared Aristotle had not noted the singing of dolphins or whales—belong in his taxonomy among the creatures who enjoy possession of a soul.

Child-angels and young androgyne angels singing and playing heavenly music sublimate the erotic, tap its energies to dematerialize the embodied anthropomorphic forms with which representational picturing has to work. The sight of singers, of flutes and trumpets, viols and pipes and organs, transports the onlooker into their acoustic range, into an elsewhere that is an ethereal, unearthly zone. It is not only singing children who grow wings; we are allowed to as well, as we look—to fly into those dizzy baroque spaces where there are no boundaries, not even between the sexes. The painted music of Counter-Reformation heaven does not gender the voice; it rather dissolves it into that mystical androgyny that makes male and female souls one with the Godhead, as in the enraptured piety of prayer in that era too.[23] A player on the viol in an exquisite draining of paradise by Agostino Ciampelli, for example, looks out at us invitingly; the viol da gamba player shows a single leg in the assymmetrical straddling position that characterizes the mobility of spirit, and embodies the kinetic and flickering energy of the baroque musical pulse.[24]

Combining ideas of spirit and song, these pneumatic bodies of baroque heavens are the vehicles of music and its image. This synaesthetic equivalence between air and music gives the words 'aria' and 'air', which began in the same period to describe tunes and songs of especial, emotive potency. Describing the enchanted surroundings where the shipwrecked crew find themselves in *The Tempest*, Caliban reassures them:

> . . . the isle is full of noises,
> Sounds, and sweet airs, that give delight and hurt not.

He then associates this magic and ethereal music with dreams, and with dreams descending specifically from the heavens:

> . . . And then in dreaming,
> The clouds, methought, would open, and show riches
> Ready to drop upon me, that when I waked,
> I cried to dream again.

To which Stephano, who aspires to courtly rank and power, replies:

> This will prove a brave kingdom for me,
> Where I shall have my music for nothing.
>
> *Tempest*, III. iii.

The clouds drop dreams on Caliban, and with the dreams, magic music—perhaps the music of the spheres. For the imagery of heaven includes a full angelic orchestra, sometimes including a harmonium, a wind section, a consort of viols, all supported on banks of cloud.

Robert Schumann, describing the *Lied* itself, said 'the child grew wings';[25] 'Oh for the wings of a dove,' sings the psalmist (Ps. 55), set by Mendelssohn in one of the most intense soprano arias and choral ascensions of English Christian liturgical music. The term 'soul music' catches this Christian past; torch singers and gospel choirs with 'soul' reverberate with the angelic choirs of a long tradition that grants voice a supreme place in the expression of inner life.

Conditions that obtain on earth cease in baroque realms of the spirit, and with the disappearance of weight and time from their celestial visions, painters worked against the intrinsic nature of their material practice to conjure illusions ('insubstantial pageants'); they rendered visible the invisible by operating a series of inversions; they turned air palpable, wrought illusions of motion and flight in dizzy vistas out of flatness and stasis, and attempted—also with success—to undo the silence of paint and make their pictures resound with the noises and sweet airs of enchantment.

Air, clouds, vapour, smoke, foam, froth, steam, and their spirituous, sublimed counterparts among airy and even gaseous substances (as Joyce noticed) have served to make manifest the invisible, supernatural, imponderable, and ineffable according to the promptings of belief and fantasy. Clouds and cloudiness, most natural and familiar forms of air and airiness, will fill the next part with their shape-shifting.

Part III

Clouds

According to Athanasius Kircher's visionary
cosmology, a labyrinth of fire forks through the
globe, connecting volcanoes which erupt into a
turbulent cloudwrack of fiery ether. From *Mundus
Subterraneus* (1665).

6
Clouds of Glory

In his Notebooks, Leonardo da Vinci suggested that, like angels and birds, clouds were useful in filling up the gaps around figures to situate them in space: 'The rest of the wall, up to the top, paint full of trees of a size that bears relation to the figures, or fill it with angels if these should be suitable to the story, or birds, or clouds or such subjects.'[1] This practical piece of advice on how to handle the notorious difficulty of picturing background assumes an equivalence between air and angels, empty space and clouds; it depends on spectators who have no reason to resist heaven as a metaphor and the sky as an image of the divine. Clouds are interfused with supernatural meaning, and this is by no means confined to the Judaeo-Christian tradition. Since classical times they have communicated mystical ideas of the highest heaven; they mark out the space of the world above, creating pontoons and bridges between the two spheres, human and divine; they have acted as vectors of other-worldly beings from heavenly realms; they pun, with dream word-play, on the nature of spirits; they materialize the invisible air.

Nebulousness has served to meet a need for expressing the bourne beyond which matter still materializes, but not as body, or, if within its bourne, the forms and shapes it takes. Clouds and cloudiness offer a magical passkey to the labyrinth of unknowable mysteries, outer and inner; they convey the condition of ineffability that the unknown and the divine inhabit.

Airy lack of substance joins the quality of motility in conferring a meta-morphic character on spirit: being *ipso facto* disembodied, it slips and shifts and fluctuates, and, as is evident from these metaphors, its linguistic habitat remains cloudy, vague, insubstantial. How to represent the invisible and the impalpable entails representing their effects: of the forms air takes, clouds offer material most apt to show these forth. Think of a cloud not as the figure, but as the ground: its form emerges under the force played upon it as a stencil outlines the gaps to produce the image. A moving cloud presents a picture of the air as a force in play around its shape, just as the human body is stamped out by spirit, according to that traditional biological model that, even while superseded, still inflects our shared imagination.

The chief of the gods usually dwells above, be he God the Father of Christianity, or Olympian Zeus. Zeus/Jupiter was a god of severe weathers, of storms and thunderbolts: his identifying epithets include the Thunderer, the Lord of the Black Cloud, the Cloud-Compeller, and the Cloud-Gatherer; in the *Iliad*, he conceals himself in the gentler disguise of 'perfumed mist' on the summit of Mount Ida, and in the *Metamorphoses*, Jupiter uses cloud as a cover for his wooing of Io. The ever-wary Juno

> Looked down on Argos: what could those clouds be doing
> In the bright light of day? They were not mists
> Rising from rivers or damp ground.

And so the goddess 'came gliding down from Heaven, stood on earth, | Broke up the clouds'. Jupiter changes Io into a white heifer to hide her from his wife, unsuccessfully. Juno finds her out, and sends a gadfly to drive the poor girl mad with its stings.[2]

Ovid tells Io's story in the first book of *Metamorphoses*, where he also describes the creation of the universe, and her story offers a parallel myth of origin, because Io becomes the founding ancestor of the Danaids, the Greeks' progenitors. When the sky is first divided from the earth, 'the fiery aether' fills the highest heaven, with the air where storms blow lying below it. Prometheus creates the first human being by taking earth, which 'being such a new precipitate | Of the etheric heaven | Cradled in its dust unearthly crystals'.[3] He then mixes this with rainwater. In the light of these lines, the subsequent story of Io's ravishing draws an analogy between genesis and rainfall, and casts the cloud's embrace as a dynamic fecundating principle, not simply an embrace; materializing the power of life in this vague, borderless shape, it rhymes with the story of another of Zeus' loves, Danae, who receives the god in a shower of gold.

In the early sixteenth century, Correggio painted both these profane Annunciations: Danae receives the god in her lap from another cloud, in this case amber-gold, more solid and compact, emitting a few golden drops that will inseminate her. When he painted the rape of Io, around 1532, he showed Io actually clasped close by Jupiter in the shape of a cloud, emerging from the soft indigo-grey massed mist as if he were consubstantial with cloud; his pointed, almost elfin face shimmers out of the miasma to kiss the nymph, and his right hand appears through a semi-transparent cocoon of cloud to embrace her (see Plate 1). This Io does not flee an unwanted assault, as she does in terror in Ovid's poem, but surrenders raptly to the enveloping fog, embracing its soft solidity with her left arm and curling toes; Correggio wonderfully communicates the haptic sense of Io's flesh brushed all over with some feather-light, shivery, close caresses. The art historian David Ekserdjian comments: 'The quality of the actual rendering of the skin and the lifeblood within it defies description.'[4]

The poet Mayakovsky claimed that he wrote 'A Cloud in Trousers'

(1914), a marvellous, reeling flight of fancy, because he wanted to combine lyricism with coarseness. His delirium pours out, a great tragic-comic blast of unrequited, savage erotic hunger and mad passionate blasphemies, addressed to a young woman he met in Odessa, and absolutely calculated to enrage the censor. The poem's English editors do not make the link with Jupiter on the rampage, but the king of the gods and of appetite is surely roving here:

> If you wish,
> I shall rage on raw meat
>   or, as the sky changes its hue,
>   if you wish,
>   I shall grow irreproachably tender:
>   not a man, but a cloud in trousers!

And could Correggio's picture itself flit behind the long poem's closing image?

> The universe sleeps
> Its huge paw curled
> Upon a star-infested ear.[5]

Mayakovsky's vertiginous fugue is irresistible: the brilliant, comic metonymy of trousers working here to speak of what the myth of Zeus' rapine does not say but is all about: the phallocracy superbly, deftly mocked.

Cloud-compelling is not an exclusive privilege of Zeus. Apollo intervenes on the Trojan side to put an end to Patroclus' triumphant rampage: wrapped 'in a thick mist', he deals the Greek hero such a blow between his shoulder blades that Patroclus, stunned, can no longer parry Hector's assault, and Hector is able to drive his bronze spear 'clean through' him; later, when his friend's death has roused Achilles to rejoin the battle, Apollo spirits away Hector from the assault, and Achilles finds himself lunging at 'empty mist'. Athena, for her part fighting for the Greeks, wraps Achilles in a golden mist and 'cause[s] his body to emit a blaze of light'; Achilles is also both enhanced and concealed by attributes of nebulousness[6]

In his essays, *Laocoön, Or The Limits of Painting and Poetry*, G. E. Lessing perceptively commented that later painters of divine deeds were faintly absurd when they took these phenomena literally, but he acknowledges how the metaphor has spread through visual conventions: 'The Homeric mist ... the painters have made their own not merely in the cases where Homer himself uses ... it—in actual invisibilities or vanishings—but everywhere when the beholder is to recognise something in the picture which the persons in it ... do not recognise ... the cloud is an arbitrary and unnatural sign with the painters; this arbitrary sign has not at all the positive significance which it might have had as such, for they use it as frequently to make the visible invisible as they do the reverse.'[7]

Clouds came ever more unquestioningly to figure the presence of the divine; as they cannot be seized or defined, they serve to convey the inexpressible realm of the supernatural, offering a metaphor for the veiled or hidden character of God: in the Old Testament, God wraps himself in a mist on the summit of Mount Sinai, and the smoke of sacrifice, rising from the inner sanctum of the Temple, obscures the rites—and their object—from view. The Shekinah, an aspect of divine wisdom, hovers over the Ark of the Covenant in a shining cloud: a veil concealing a further mystery. Clouds function as screens, as jalousies, as separation: in the medieval mystic image, divinity manifests itself through 'The Cloud of Unknowing'. God the Father's disembodied nature sometimes takes the form of a hand in glory, for example (the glory expressed by a little white puff of cloud such as sails sometimes into view on a perfect summer's day in a mosaic in the portal of St Mark's (1545)). At other times, God the Father floats, a legless torso only submerged in drifts of cloud, with trunkless heads of putti surrounding him in the stratosphere.

Hidden from sight, wrapped in cloud, unnamed and all the more longed for, the elusive divine element brought yet more lively curiosity into play: not sight alone, but other senses were brought to bear on the question. In Greek myth, the child of Zeus and Io was called Epaphus, a name related to the word for touch, because Io conceived at the *touch* of the god.[8] But this association of Io with tactility suggests several further variations on the efficacy of clouds as metaphors of spirit. Clouds develop in Christian iconography into the richest trope for the divine realm, and baroque artists in particular deploy them generously, extravagantly, and often unconsciously, for they embody most satisfyingly an impossible conundrum: ethereal materiality.

Renaissance clouds take on tactile, solid bodies; pillows, cushions, divans fill paradise. Correggio created exuberant, candyfloss seraglios in the *Assumption of the Virgin* in the dome of Parma Cathedral, where angels and saints swim, frolic, recline, and perch on reefs and banks of cumulus as if they were as buoyant as surf, and as docile as featherbeds (Plate 2a). His cloudiness has palpable substance—tactile, ductile, and plas-tic—strictly material qualities. It is a variety of voluminous foam with its own dependable organic structure; it persuades us of the essence of ethereality. Embodied in sensuous paint strong enough to support its emanations, *amorini* gambol in and out of the flossy fleece, and are, like the painter's Jupiter, apparently consubstantial with air and airiness. Experientially, the viewer is able to understand the angels' and saints' ethereal state precisely because they can recline so confidently on banks of mist and rise uplifted on banks of cherubim, as in Luca Cambiaso's drawing of Mary Magdalene in ecstasy (see Figure 7, p. 70). Nor do they disappear into cloud, as humans do when fog envelops them.

Although Correggio takes clouds to extremes of blissful presence that they had hardly enjoyed before, he is painting in a recognizable dialect of Christian iconography, not coining a new language.[9] Baroque artists expanded rhapsodically on these associations: Bartolomeo Schedoni, in a delicious *Coronation of the Virgin*, paints the *amorini* hugging clouds like giant whipped cream, and appearing to bob and swim through their incandescent puffs.[10] But do their bodies begin and end as bodies, or as this froth, this foam?

These painted clouds refract the nature of angels, for they too have become solid; they offer the inhabitants of the upper air dependable sofas and banks of pillows, daybeds of different bounce and spring on which to sit or recline, loll or dance. The baroque heaven tumesces with froth turned solid, and heavenly beings are intimate with these cloud swellings and hollows; again, they are embodied but not carnal, *corpus sed non caro*. Like Correggio's Jupiter, the turbulent dark cloudwracks and smoke columns of baroque heavens, evolve their metaphorical divine vesture from properties of matter.

Clouds are breath too, material and insubstantial at once, a variety of vapour or smoke, the exhalation of heaven. Thinkers in the seventeenth century—Leibniz, Harvey, Descartes—were inquiring into the nature of invisible forces, magnetism, the conducting of heat and cold, and the combustion of gases; these new ideas about physical but invisible forces charge the appearance of clouds and angels, and the painted illusions of their symbiotic substance. Ideas of spirit motion and energy excited baroque artists especially to push the metaphor of light and air into vision. Luca Giordano, in *Allegory of Divine Wisdom*,[11] and Giovanni Battista Gaulli, in *The Death of St Francis Xavier* in the church of Sant' Andrea al Quirinale in Rome, depict the interpenetration of the supernatural and the earthly in a vortex of cloud, flame, and rushing wind, achieving through this simulated turmoil a vivid sensation of kinetic energy. With every brushstroke and juxtaposition of elements and bodies, with every twist and fold, the baroque artists undo the stillness and the flatness of the painted plane in order to seize the commotion of spirit forces, physical and metaphysical. The turbulent fiery skies and torqued bodies of the baroque communicate the animate, spirited character of the supernatural; as painters and sculptors, these artists applied all their figural ingenuity to overcoming the stasis inherent in image making. In the illusionism of baroque art, angels and clouds are kinetic physical forces, possessed of disembodied bodies, incarnate and disincarnate at once. As Gilles Deleuze writes in his inspired meditation on seventeenth-century thought and art: 'In the Baroque the soul entertains a complex relation with the body. Forever indissociable from the body, [the soul] discovers a vertiginous animality that gets it tangled in the pleats of matter, but also an organic or cerebral humanity . . . that allows it to rise up, and that will make it ascend over all other folds.'[12]

These artists are rendering in paint or marble the poetics of spirit metaphors, for in such pneumatic and plastic extravaganzas, clouds work with the pun on spirit and breath as the embodied experience of vitality, with the power to mould matter into shape—not for the eyes alone, but for the full physical sensorium, not only in the three spatial dimensions, but also in extension through time.[13] The art historian Paul Hills connects this aesthetic instability with the search for transcendence: 'The idea of meta-morphosis, or of one material taking the form of or making an allusion to another, is common in anagogic meditation.'[14]

The ether, or highest heaven, the fiery band of air below the highest sphere of the fixed stars has acted as the prime medium of the sacred, the hyphen between matter and spirit, the fold that enfolds them. Isaac Newton suggested that the ether was composed of invisible, imponderable, flimsy, and fiery light vapours, and constituted the original protoplasm of the physical world, shaped by nature.[15] This 'luminiferous' air, the atmosphere of space ('the interstellar medium', as the emptiness between the stars is called today), exists in that empty space on the wall that Leonardo recommended could be filled by angels or clouds or birds. This vacancy has filled up with metaphors, visual and verbal: the word 'ether' gives 'ethereal', the adjective applied to the body after death, the ghostly double of the incarnate and living person. It is historically a form of the air, and the realm of cloud most closely linked to ideas about human spirits. Ethereal metaphors serve to communicate—to clothe in air—their subjects; but they also dominate the form of medium used in the attempt—from clouds in seventeenth-century painting to invisible rays and waves in nineteenth- and twentieth-century science and psychic experiments.

Newton's ethereal reflections of 1675 were, however, only published in 1744, with important and lingering consequences for psychic theories and representing invisible forces. After Newton and until Einstein, exquisitely imaginative etheric theories—about subtle matter, the elements of the universe, and the nature of light and fire, dating back to ancient Greeks and to early modern physics—continue to underlie the phenomena of Spiritualist experiments and psychic research, on the one hand, and the development of media communications, on the other. As the historian Logie Barrow remarks, 'Beginning in 1745 . . . all significant British electricians [i.e. physicists] postulated a special electrical matter identical with, or similar to, the springy, subtle, universal Newtonian aether.'[16]

The ether has now faded from scientific attention—but not from language or symbolism, where it has long offered a most potent and versatile vehicle for spirit. The smoky, fiery, and generative properties of the ether were much explored in classical philosophy and poetry, taking inspiration from a strand of classical physics. In Stoic thought, *pneuma*—the word for breath, spirit, as discussed in Chapter 4—was related to the ether and made up of light and fire. When the satyr Silenus sings a myth of creation in Virgil's sixth Eclogue, he describes:

> how seeds of earth and air,
> Of water and fluent fire were brought together and married
> In a vastness of empty space: how everything began
> From this, and what were gases condenses to form our globe.[17]

Those seeds of fluent fire return in Ovid's comparable, magnificent account of the origins of the world at the start of his *Metamorphoses*, as we saw, and when he describes how the sky was divided from the earth at the creation, he calls the uppermost air simply *ignis*, Latin for fire, a word that many translators expand to 'fiery aether', since otherwise the lines become almost incomprehensible to present-day readers:

> imminet his aer: qui, quantost pondere terrae
> pondus aquae levius, tantost onerosior *igni*.

('Over all these regions hangs the air, | as much heavier than the fiery aether as it is lighter than earth or water.')[18]

This upper heaven was also known as the empyrean, and the Judaeo-Christian God also dwelled there, in both his Old Testament and his apocalyptic manifestations.[19] The word 'empyrean', also encloses an imagery of fire, *pyros*, as in pyrotechnics, again interfusing fire, light, powers of generation, and divine sublimity.

In one of his wondrous books, the Jesuit Athanasius Kircher returns to this visionary physics. He relates how his *alter ego*, Theo-didactus, or 'Taught by God', was transported through the heavens, guided through the several spheres by an angel called Cosmiel. When they reach the upper air, or ether, Theodidactus finds he can no longer breathe, the atmosphere becomes so rarefied—'subtle'—and he asks, 'what is this vehement scent, sweeter than all amber and musk, which I now perceive, and by which I feel myself thoroughly recreated?' Cosmiel tells him that they have reached the planet Jupiter, and that what he senses is 'the health-giving exhalation and outpouring of that sphere of Jove, a clear sign that we are now close to its atmosphere'.[20] When Cosmiel comments in this way on the rarefied, intoxicating atmosphere of Jove's heavenly ambience, he reveals how the word 'ether' could expand to mean a commonly used twentieth-century anaesthetic, enshrined in the famous invitation from 'The Love Song of J. Alfred Prufrock':

> Let us go then, you and I,
> When the evening is spread out against the sky
> Like a patient etherised upon a table . . .[21]

Religious rituals aimed at inducing this state of swimming ecstasy, the light-headed high brought about by inhaling subtly modified air.[22] When the priests burned incense and sacrificed cereals and animals in the Holy of Holies in the Temple, they raised a pungent smokescreen. Similarly, when celebrants of Catholic liturgy waft smoking incense over the congregation, they are making manifest this special divine sphere, which both conceals the Godhead from mortal eyes, and makes the heads of worshippers spin with fragrance and confusion.[23] In these liturgies, the smokiness recalls the original sacrifice: for example, it was when God snuffed up the 'sweet savour' of Noah's burnt offerings that he decided to leave off cursing and smiting humankind (Gen. 8: 21). The burnt offerings to God, and the sacrifice of Jesus symbolically re-enacted in the Mass, dematerializes their material bodies: they are turned to smoke, which then ascends to heaven, joining matter and ether through the medium of fiery air.

In the same way as the word 'spirit' also describes a volatile essence—whisky, turps, surgical spirit, petrol, and even glue—so Jupiter's heavenly zone had the ethereal property of altering the mind.

Soon after the *Ecstatic Journey*, Kircher published his most beautifully illustrated volume of all, the *Mundus Subterraneus* (1665), a fantastical work about volcanoes and aquifers, underground lakes beneath the Andes and the 'Mountains of the Moon' in South Africa, about precious stones, rocks, whirlpools, geysers, tunnels through the centre of the Earth, caverns measureless to man, the dragons that live there, and salts and minerals and poisons. Part *illuminati* poetics, part dazzling scientific analysis, part alchemical and zodiac magic, part cabinet of curiosities, this magnificent piece of seventeenth-century book production contains some truly remarkable double-page illustrations. The all-encompassing airy space beyond the Earth, where he and the angel were transported, is designated 'Etheric Space' (Figure 8). Significantly, though Kircher's verbal accounts describe emptiness, the engraver working for him filled the space with charcoal grey puffballs of clouds, for otherwise, in visual terms it would have looked blank, inert, and meaningless. The perfection of this cosmological hydraulics mirrored for Kircher the human mind–body union in a classic model of microcosm–macrocosm: 'For as vital and animal spirits act in the Economy of the human body, so in the cosmic economy does the spirituous (*spirituosa*) or airy nature of the winds; and in the same way as man cannot live with these spirits fading, so with the winds taken away, it will come about that the geocosmos will necessarily perish.'[24]

Kircher was influenced by the Rosicrucian mystic Robert Fludd, and the sumptuous, sooty engravings in Fludd's book *Of This World and the Other* (1619) also imagined ethereal conflagration at the beginning. Shadow is a key concept in the history of the imagination; the Platonist idea of shadow has done heavy duty in conveying the character of thoughts that are not produced by direct sensory impressions or experience. And shadows' affinities in the shadowlands of the imagination lie with smoke, vapour, cloudiness: these phenomena can help summon the insubstantial character of spirit and the emergence of ideas. For Fludd, shadow is also original chaos from which form comes forth *ex nihilo*, or out of nothingness. In his book, two magnificent engravings illustrating the creation of the world show roiling clouds in a ring, embodying the first stage of emergence from darkness visible. They are then followed by rivers of fire. This apocalyptic murk will persist as the visual expression of the imagination's products.

This conjunction of elements departs from the vaporous and moist rain-making nature more normally ascribed to the stratosphere and its demarcating clouds. The greys and indigos and purples of metaphysical space, as represented by Kircher and Fludd's contemporaries in High Renaissance and baroque art, grasp this character, suggesting that the ethereal element is fire, not water, and shifting its vapours towards smoke, not mist. This will prove a step with potent consequences for the language of symbols, and eventually bear on theories of ethereal bodies and ectoplasm.

This vision of the beginning reached an audience beyond Jesuit circles: Kircher's truly wonderful hypotheses were translated into English by a fascinated vulcanologist. His abridged version came out in 1669 with the resplendent title, *The Vulcano's or, Burning and Fire-Vomiting Mountains, Famous in the World: With their Remarkables . . .* The author quotes Ovid to support Kircher's cosmological equivalence of air and fire:

> The Earth resolv'd is turned into streams;
> Water to Air; *the purer Air to flames.*
> From whence they back return; The fiery flakes
> Are turn'd to Air; The Air thickened takes
> The Liquid form of Water; that Earth makes.[25]

Alchemical thought inflects all these cosmic speculations: Athanasius Kircher was a keen adept. In alchemical thinking, the element of air figures as a fiery, fecundating principle equivalent to the ether. In another finely illustrated seventeenth-century work, the element of Air (*Aer*) is represented by the figure of Danae reclining on a daybed as Zeus descends on her in the form of a shower of gold and impregnates her with the future hero Perseus.[26] (It is a rather worldly mistake when painters shower Zeus's new love with gold coin—as does Titian in his famous painting of the subject.)

When Italian artists render the radiant heads of *putti* as swirling parts of celestial clouds, or depict Gabriel exploding through the wall of Mary's cell in Nazareth on turbulent plumes of smoke, they are borrowing for aesthetic impact early modern theories of the imponderable and invisible ether. Its winged denizens are emanations of light and fire: as we saw in Chapter 5, air clothes gods and angels; this air is properly ethereal, and its properties come under increasingly intense and imaginative scrutiny.

Titian's celebrated altar-piece of 1516 in the Frari in Venice, depicting the Virgin's Assumption into heaven, and, even more vividly, Nicolas Poussin's later vision of the same scene (in the National Gallery, Washington, DC) convey vividly the combustible nature of the ether (Plate 3). Symbolically, this world connects to the world above, the corporeal to the incorporeal, through the smoke of sacrifice. The Virgin rises with dark smoke spiralling around her ascending body as if the sarcophagus were an altar and she were wrapped in the smoke of sacrifice; *putti* support her airy flight in her swelling mantle, frolic in and out of the clouds, again apparently consubstantial with them, and direct her aloft through the gap opening up above her head.

Strictly speaking, the Mother of God should not 'go up in smoke', transmuted from flesh to spirit at the hour of her death, for uniquely she was assumed into heaven with her body, according to the Catholic belief which was proclaimed dogma in 1950. But, as in the case of saints, she looks as if she is being sublimed by alchemical process, especially in Counter-Reformation iconography depicting saints' translation to an unearthly state: the swelling clouds that carry up to heaven Ignatius or Aloysius or Teresa in paintings of apotheosis annex the classical scientific theories of fiery, cosmic, upper air to communicate their metamorphosis from body to spirit—the process of etherealization.[27] Murillo painted the ascension of the soul of Philip II—an apocalyptic tribute to the monarch—showing a vast towering tongue of flame soaring up towards a luminous opening in the clouds, as grandiloquent as a rocket blasted into outer space (see Plate 4).

Clouds that wrap such holy and translated beings rise up like smoke from the altar, like incense from the thurible, communicating the saints' ascension into heaven, their mutation from this element to another. Impassioned, fiery, ethereal swaddling functions as part of a sacred syntax, making visible within the limits of figuration a non-corporeal body that has become vaporized through salvation, sublimed from matter into air—into spirit. This is what Faustus is pleading for in Marlowe's play when at the point of death he begs the stars that presided at his birth to come to his aid, and then stirs a strange brew of cloudy vapours to describe how his soul might be hidden and saved—etherealized:

> Now draw up Faustus like a foggy mist,
> Into the entrails of yon lab'ring clouds,
> That, when you vomit forth into the air,
> My limbs may issue from your smoky mouths,
> So that my soul may but ascend to heaven![28]

This compacted meteorological metaphor casts Faustus' dying body as a vapour, drawn up by the heat of the stars to be swallowed up by clouds figured as women's wombs. In this Neoplatonist vision, the vast heavenly bodies of the stars rhyme with the microcosmic human form, and they too, in Marlowe's conceit, are embodied in human shape, endowed with mouths that can both breathe and spew. Faustus seems to be begging to be turned to a fine rain, that might issue from the clouds, but remain too misty, too light, and too subtle to fall to earth. He entreats that he might rise instead, like high cirrus to the upper heaven, and remain there, etherized.

Clouds formed the furniture of heaven and the enveloping mists of divine splendour, on the one hand; on the other, ethereal fire has provided a medium for divine manifestations. But the heavens and their mantling clouds have also acted as ethereal screens, or, in an image that anticipates later media, as 'airy films'[29] on which spirit visions appear, as in the case of many signs of divine work, and the unusual mirage known as *fata morgana*.

gia cœleſtia uiſa ſunt. Cerui eni inſignis ſpecies, pug...
utrinq́ magno impetu, atq́ clamoribus concurrentiũ, q́rum ſan-

guis inſtar pluuiæ in terrã decidit, ſol horrenda ſpecie, qui & tum

Vision or delusion, meteorological wonder or mass
hallucination? A stag appears in the sky with battling
armies in 1550, while cities, ships, palaces, and armies
appear in the depths of the sea, as in this engraving of an
occurrence of *fata morgana* in the 18th century in the
Straits of Messina, where the rare mirage sometimes
occurs.

7

Fata Morgana; or, Castles in the Air

> Here's another ballad of a fish that appeared upon the coast on
> Wednesday the fourscore of April, forty thousand fathom above water
> . . . The ballad is very pitiful, and as true.
>
> Shakespeare, *The Winter's Tale*

When the Normans became rulers of southern Italy, they carried with them
their cycle of Celtic legends in which Morgan Le Fay, the semi-mortal sister
of King Arthur, lures sailors into her palace under the sea by conjuring up
castles in the air.[1] In an alternative, Italian version of the legend, the fairy falls
in love with a mortal, gives him the gift of eternal life in return for her love,
and when he becomes bored and restless in his long captivity, summons up
fantastic spectacles to keep him entertained.[2]

The story—and the fairy's name in Italian, Fata Morgana—became
attached to a special meteorological wonder that sometimes occurs over the
Straits of Messina and elsewhere in extreme weather conditions such as
the dog-days of August, when layers of warm and colder air alternate near
the ground or on water. Such sights, it has been said, fill beholders with
inexpressible longings.

The Jesuit Athanasius Kircher described one instance in his book *The
Great Art of Light and Shadow* (1646), in response to a fellow Jesuit who
had written to him in raptures about a manifestation of *fata morgana* he had
witnessed himself in Sicily on 15 August 1643:

On the morning of the feast of the Assumption of the Most Blessed Virgin, standing
alone at my window, I saw so many things, and so many novelties that I shall never
be sated or tired to think on them again. It seems to me that the most holy Madonna
made appear . . . a trace of Paradise that day. . . . The sea that bathes Sicily swelled
up and became ten miles in length all round, like the crests of a black mountain,
and the [sea] of Calabria flattened out and appeared in a moment the clearest
crystal, transparent as a mirror . . . and in this mirror there suddenly appeared, in
chiaroscuro, a line of more than 10,000 columns of equal width and height, all
equidistant from one another . . . then a moment later, the columns halved their
height and arched over like certain aqueducts in Rome.

Kircher sternly reminded his colleague that, feast of the Assumption or not, the glimpse of paradise he had seen was a trick of the light, and he went on to denounce 'necromancers' who are quick to seize 'such marvels, produced without any work, as the mockery of demons'. Following in the steps of the Italian humanists, he will have no other miracle outside those attested in Scripture.

Kircher was born in Germany in 1602, and studied and wrote in Rome till his death in 1680. He was above all a scientist, interested in empirical study, a meteorologist and a mathematician, and, as was frequently the case with scientists in the seventeenth century, he was also an alchemist, an occultist, and a philosopher of optics, catoptrics (the science of mirrors), and magic. He was possessed of a voracious, wondering curiosity that sought in natural phenomena the handprint of divinity, but at the same time, he wanted to penetrate the mysteries of physics and of nature, to illuminate the secrets of God's ordering of the universe. Physics and metaphysics meet and mingle in his observations of light's behaviour.

The first careful observations by artists of *fata morgana* itself survive in engravings, for example by Gugliemo Fortuyn (1773), showing the fabulous trick of the light: ships projected into the clouds, cities floating deep down under water (see Figure 9b, p. 94). One of them illustrates a study of the illusion by a fellow Jesuit, Domenico Giardina, who was much exercised by popular superstition around him in Sicily: 'Until now, in a century of so little culture, the spectacle was a matter of great horror to the common people.'[3] His evocation of the *fata morgana* is both more analytical than his predecessor's and far more extravagantly rococo: Nature unveils 'grandi e maravigliosi treatri [sic] (great and marvellous theatres) without the enormous defects with which art is filled', he writes. He goes on to describe how he saw 'a city all floating in the air ... [so] measureless and [so] splendid, [so] adorned with magnificent buildings, all of which was found on a base of a luminous crystal, never beheld before'. This vision then transformed itself into a forest, and then into a garden, where the 'most capricious figures in the world' were arranged; another metamorphosis, and enormous armies in full battle array appeared, with mounted warriors, mountains, half-ruined towns, all disposed 'according to the canons of a perfect perspective' (Figure 9a, p. 94). Nature here is not only a supreme artist, but knows how to combine Albertian laws of architectural harmony and proportion with a Raphael-esque playfulness in capricious decoration. Some ascribe the wonder to enchantments, others to a divine miracle, he goes on; but he himself offers a chemical analysis of the minerals and salts in the region—talc, selenite, antimony, glass—which rise up in hot weather in vapours from the sea to form clouds, which then condense in the cooler upper air to become a *mobile specchio*, a moving, polyhedral mirror. He emphasizes the effects of fire and brimstone, which create the illusion of columns, arches, pyramids, and pinnacles in infinite recession, and distinguishes these from what he calls *l'iride fregiata*, the festooned rainbow. Giardina relates the spectacle to the *aurora borealis*, or Northern Lights. Giardina's secular, natural magic constitutes a response, even a protest, to credulity, with some surprising results. He retells a story about the mission in Peru, where the natives of Quito worshipped a god in a lakeside shrine, and crowds of phantom figures would appear in the mist rising off the water and bow down before his statue. With the help of a pocket mirror, the Jesuit missionaries were able to show the Indians that these celestial beings were simply their own reflections on the vapour—and thence to persuade them from their idolatry.[4]

There are many similar, mythic tales of conquerors' and proselytizers' superior knowledge carrying the hour (Columbus's foreknowledge of the total eclipse being the most famous). It remains a piquant irony that Christians went about demolishing wonders—or unweaving the rainbow—for their own religious purposes when it suited. Yet, giving another twist to these paradoxes, it is also the case that the Jesuits chose to explain an optical illusion by demonstrating another marvel—the mirror—and thus cast themselves as greater conjurors: the converts' allegiance is changed by an opportunistic wonder-working by the advocates of another faith.

However, Giardina does not dismiss all celestial apparitions as meteorological phenomena: he has to reserve the prodigies of the Bible as God's direct intervention. He is at pains to discriminate between *fata morgana* and miraculous signs from heaven in the Bible, such as the vision of horsemen in the clouds in the Second Book of Maccabees, for example, which he maintains devoutly as divine intervention.

Technically now known as a 'superior' or 'looming mirage', *fata morgana* appears above the horizon, often rising to great heights among the clouds. Layers of the atmosphere at different temperatures develop different densities, and the sun's rays, hitting the surface of the sea and the layers of air at a certain angle (45 degrees) turn them into an infinite recession of mirrors, multiplying and inverting reflections, diffracting and refracting the light so as to project images of far distant scenes and objects on to the clouds; these reflections, turned upside down and superimposed on one another, then mingle and change rapidly as the air layers move up and down from the observer's vantage-point.[5]

Real events and objects are reflected in this spectacular illusion, from unknown points on land and sea: a sailing ship somewhere far away appears in the mirror of the clouds, or a crowd of people waiting for a bus in a distant town materializes in the heat haze (as Werner Herzog recorded in his film *Fata Morgana* (1971), just as the ordinary and tantalizing mirage of an oasis glitters in the desert. But until the process was understood, the chimeras that the enchantress displayed were classed with heavenly signs and wonders, meteorological portents that used the heavens as divine manuscript, signalling warnings and—sometimes—blessings from on high.

Since classical times, the heavens have been scanned to discover the concealed signs of divine providence in meteorology and illusion, and *fata morgana* can be associated with many other signs and wonders of a meteorological nature in the Bible. The rainbow after the Flood, the pillar of cloud through the desert, the Shekinah hovering over the Ark of the Covenant, the writing on the wall at Belshazzar's feast, the darkness at noon at the Crucifixion, the cloud enveloping Christ's body at his ascension, and finally, the Second Coming in clouds of glory—give news of God's presence and changing mood. The incident from the Second Book of Maccabees, which Giardina invokes, describes how in the midst of the heroic resistance of the Jews to Roman oppression in the second century, an angelic host appeared:

As the fighting grew hot, the enemy saw in the sky five magnificent figures riding horses with golden bridles, who placed themselves at the head of the Jews, formed a circle around Maccabaeus, and kept him invulnerable under the protection of their armour. They launched arrows and thunderbolts at the enemy, who, confused and blinded, broke up in complete disorder. (2 Macc. 10: 29–31)

During the subsequent, bitter siege, another divine horseman appears in the sky, 'arrayed in white, brandishing his golden weapons', and again, this heavenly ally leads the Jews to victory, against the host of the enemy with his thousands of warriors, some of them mounted on elephants (2 Macc. 11: 8–12).

The visions which brought Judas Maccabaeus to triumph against the odds were famously echoed in 832 when the saltire appeared in the sky above the battle between the Picts and Anglo-Saxons, and, again, in Crusader history, when Saints George, Mercurius, and Demetrius appeared to the besieged at Antioch during the First Crusade.[6]

Some divine portents took the form of unusual phenomena: as well as comets, natural wonders such as St Elmo's fire, will-o'-the-wisps, fox fire or *ignis fatuus*, comets, waterspouts, and even rains of frogs or of fish (and sometimes saucepans) at one time inspired dread or thoughts of moral reform. A German doctor in the sixteenth century, Conrad Lycosthenes, made a superb compilation of heavenly portents throughout history. It includes numerous woodcuts of ships sailing through the heavens (Figure 9c,

103), warriors bleeding in the skies, and Christ on the cross, his blood streaming in the firmament, as well as the kind of anomalies that were sung in ballads (as Autolycus cries in *The Winter's Tale*), and later filled the freak shows like Ripley's 'Believe It Or Not!': three-legged cows, bearded ladies, a woman who laid eggs.[7] All the episodes given in Lycosthenes are dated and assessed for supernatural meaning; they often occur before crucial battles.[8] When private disasters occur, personal fancy becomes suggestible and perceives omens; when public crisis convulses a society, the apparitions come thick and fast, as during the Civil War in England and its fall-out. Numerous pamphlets were printed in the 1650s, 1660s, and 1670s giving news of 'Strange and Wonderful Sights Seen in the Air'.[9]

Lycosthenes' anthology influenced storytelling of this kind down the years, and the woodcuts he used to illustrate it circulated from one volume to another, sometimes applied to different incidents.[10] In 1560, another collector, Pierre Boaistuau, appealed to such precedents to support his evidence: 'I've protested many times that I won't fill my writings with anything fabulous, nor with any story which I don't verify through the authority of some famous author' (see Plate 2b).[11] The organs of today's occultists, such as the *Fortean Times*, continue to rely on this material, forging a slender catena of authorities back through time.

Apparitions were not always meteorological, but tricks of the light on a smaller scale: the face of Jesus in the bark of a tree, or of the Virgin Mary in a stain on a wall, gave rise to cult sites and holy images and pilgrimages. Albrecht Dürer carefully drew a vision of crosses in the sky on the day that his father died: the maid who had been with him on his deathbed had seen their shadows fall upon her blouse, and Dürer rendered the portent in his notebook for that day.[12]

Such signs and wonders used to fill those who saw them with confusion and fear, for it was hard to ascertain if they originated with providence or with the devil. Scripture itself warned of confusion with regard to marvels, St Matthew stating that false prophets can summon portents 'enough to deceive even the chosen' (Matt. 24: 24). The early modern historian Stuart Clark, exploring theology, psychology, and optics, takes up this central question that exercised believing Christians: 'whether vision is veridical'.[13] The controversy over the status of apparitions, their causes and origins, has an erratic pulse, and clearly grows quicker during periods of religious conflict. The 'politics of superstition' occupies different social spaces at different periods.[14] The debate grew fierce and malevolent during the Reformation and during the witch hunts of the early modern era, and it erupted again, in Catholic circles, during the papacy of John Paul II. A fervent devotee of the Virgin, he ascribed his providential escape from an assassin's bullet to the protection of Our Lady of Fatima (who appeared in

1915), while many of his own clergy and the faithful have attempted to draw away from such miraculous, popular approaches to the mysteries of salvation.

So it is difficult to put a date on the turn away from providential or diabolical explanation of portents; many religious thinkers of different creeds—Protestant and Orthodox as well as Catholic—upheld divine intervention and heavenly signs, while others combated superstition in the interests of scientific empiricism. The connection to imagination and to cognitive psychology was made much earlier, for example, than would normally be expected. That *fata morgana* might be the work of a wicked fairy was refuted in some quarters from the start of observations: the Paduan philosopher Pietro Pomponazzi (d. 1524), dismissed the claims of the great magus of antiquity, Apollonius of Tyana, that *fata morgana* was supernatural in origin, writing, 'since objects in the world below transmit their image into the ether and up to heaven and this returns it like a mirror in another mirror. And in this way objects can be seen from very far away.'[15] Pomponazzi also grasped the relationship between fantasies and optics: 'If one admits that apparitions can be produced in dreams, one must give credence to the possibility that they can also be produced in the atmosphere.'[16] Discussing a reported heavenly vision of Pope Celestine, around 1515 in the town of Aquila, Pomponazzi offered a natural explanation based on the theory of animal spirits: that they could be stirred into such turmoil and so heated in contact that they actually rose and mingled with clouds to form the saint's image in the sight of the excited crowd.[17] He went on to compare this mass psychology to maternal impression, 'just as when a woman imagines something during coitus she actually imprints that image on the foetus'.[18]

Heavenly wonders, benign and ominous, have not ceased in modern times: a phantom army was seen fighting in the sky above Verviers in Belgium in June 1815, a little before the Battle of Waterloo took place nearby, and in the most famous and most recent episode of all, in August 1914, 'The Angels of Mons' mustered in the clouds in support of the soldiers in the trenches, wrapped them in mist to give them cover, and even inflicted inexplicable *arrow* wounds on the Germans. The stories spread rapidly, first by word of mouth, and thereafter through press reports, psychic journals, purported eyewitness memoirs, and films, including Cecil B. de Mille's *Joan of Arc*, which opens with a scene set in the fields of Flanders, with angelic warriors including Joan overhead. The legend was in fact sparked by a tale written by Arthur Machen in a London newspaper, in which St George, called on by a English soldier, gallops to the rescue on a heavenly steed at the head of a battalion of angelic bowmen. Machen was a popular occultist, who, like many of his contemporaries, preferred rational explanations for weird occurrences. He tried to explain that he had made up the story, but his protestations were ignored.[19]

The meaning of *fata morgana* grows more and more apocalyptic over the twentieth century; it is used again and again to evoke ominous portents, especially during the rise of the Third Reich and during its aftermath.[20] In occupied France, André Breton called a long, delirious flight of poetry 'Fata Morgana', a hectic response to the catastrophe which had overtaken his country.[21]

The general category of cloud metaphor offers Breton a vast and hospitable field of analogies for inner states; the matter of cloudiness, its deep and long associations with storms, fate, power, and divinity, combined the ominous and the fantastical in ways that lent it to Breton's Surrealist purposes. The aleatory combinations that he advocated performed mimetically in verse a kind of ceaseless, cloud-like shape-shifting. In the preface to the volume in which the poem 'Fata Morgana' was published, Breton announces, in flamboyant manifesto mode, that the word he most abominates is 'donc' (therefore); by contrast, he hails 'comme' (like), the prime conjunction of comparison, and exalts it, asserting that the function of poetic analogy, both in simile and in metaphor (where 'like' is 'silenced') is to disclose what lies hidden: in Breton's gnomic (indeed cloudy) for-mulation, 'elle [poetic analogy] tend à faire entrevoir et valoir la vraie vie "absente" . . . et . . . elle ne songe un instant à faire tourner ses conquêtes à la gloire d'un quelconque "au-delà".'[22] ('[Poetic analogy] tends to make us glimpse and appreciate the value of the true life that is "absent" . . . and not for one moment does it dream of turning its conquests to the glory of some "beyond" or other.') Mirages are no longer charged metaphors for super-natural or mystical meanings, but direct the observer to the truly prodigious in the here and now—a fundamental Surrealist principle. The preface closes with a quote from Swedenborg, which would not have summoned quite the absurdist, Magritte-like vision here: 'Je vis des esprits rassemblés; ils avaient des chapeaux sur la tête.'[23] ('I saw spirits gathered together; they had hats on their heads.') By this image, Breton intends to bring *Fata Morgana* down to earth: *le banal merveilleux* ('marvellous banality').

Werner Herzog, one of the most original and turbulent film-makers in post-war Germany, was bent on inaugurating 'a new order of cinematic "reality" ', wrought from the active impress of imagination on experience; consequently, mirages attracted him, and he went on a quest to see them in the deepest Sahara in high summer. He and his crew were nearly driven insane by the extreme conditions. The hallucinatory, often Surrealist film *Fata Morgana*, made there in 1969, meditates in a kind of delirium on extremity and endings. The documentary footage he brought back conveys an enigmatic menace throughout: vast skies shiningly mirrored in mirages, remote and alien desert children with strange pets, and fine dust devils spinning across trackless dunes.[24] At one point in the film, Herzog and his crew approach a bus loading a long queue of passengers, all glinting and shimmering in the sun—but, as mentioned earlier, this is a true *fata morgana*: when they reach the spot, there is nothing there.

Such terrible disorienting illusions also arise in conditions of Arctic severity, and were known to the Norsemen, who called this kind of looming mirage a hillingar. Hillingars have been dramatically photographed and can be viewed on the Web: mysterious, gloomy cliffs of ice-blue-grey cloud towering high above the horizon, for all the world like a nightmare phantom swollen to colossal size. Sometimes, ships float in the clouds, as they did in sixteenth-century books of portents—ghost vessels of the *Flying Dutchman* (Figure 9c, p. 103). Even if you know it is nothing but an illusion, this knowledge cannot undo altogether the shivery eeriness of these colossal spectres looming in the cloudwrack.

The phenomenon has not faded altogether: legends of celestial apparitions persist. According to one of the most recent, highly popular instances, the Virgin Mary was found in a 'spontaneous photograph' taken around 1985 of the sky above the Monte Gargano, in Puglia, southern Italy, the shrine of Padre Pio. Padre Pio, a famous stigmatic, with bleeding hands in imitation of Christ's sufferings, was one of the many hundred saints canonized by Pope John Paul II; he has become a passionate focus of Catholic prayer, with whom the Virgin has a close association in the work of protecting her own. In another, the profile of a laughing devil appeared in wisps of smoke above the twin towers of the World Trade Center the day before their destruction.[25] Today, such images provoke disbelief and curiosity, in equal, competing measure.

Fata morgana may have begun as devil and spirit mischief, and then excited discussion among churchmen and scientists about its origins and agents—a fairy or divine providence?—but the effect became a rich arena for inquiry into the observer who perceives the sign and its meanings, and into the nature of phantasms in a person's mind. A natural phenomenon casts its own scintillating and dancing light on the story of the self, as the phenomenon changes character, shedding the divine portent to become a psychological mirror of the viewer's mind, and a Surrealist *foyer de songe*, a hearth for incubating inner fantasies. Changing ideas about cognition and subjectivity have profoundly altered the reception of *fata morgana* and associated special effects of light, in spite of continuing belief in signs of divine favour—or anger—in some quarters; this shift in turn reflects in crucial ways changing ideas of soul, its capacities and its limitations. The battle against divinatory significance provided the impetus from which a modern idea of the subject, an idea of radical personal vision, issued forth to replace supernatural causation, and the spirits who conjured the visions receded beside a growing inquiry into the spirit of the percipient, into where that lay, how it functioned, and what it was responsible for creating: celestial mirages might be the work of a fairy queen, but she needed the imaginations of others for her work to become intelligible.

The English artist Alexander Cozens encouraged his
students to follow chance and their own imaginations,
according to his 'New Method' of picturing landscapes
by blotting and crumpling the paper beforehand.

8

'Very Like a Whale'

One should not let this gigantic cinema play perpetually to an empty house.

Virginia Woolf

Natura Pictrix—Nature the Painter—was the phrase the Renaissance philosopher of art, Alberti, used to evoke the natural artistry of creation, and samples of spontaneous artefacts began to fill the cabinets of curiosities of princes and scholars during the Renaissance and more strongly afterwards. Wonder-struck at nature's aesthetics, collectors' displays framed assemblages of butterflies, for the eyes emblazoned on their wings, alongside ciphers in cut gems and hard stones (*pietre dure*). Athanasius Kircher created a famous *Wunderkämmer* in the Jesuit College in Rome—one of the first museums— where he exhibited ancient marbles, including stones and fossils that bore accidental marks in the shape of letters. He managed to complete a whole alphabet. He also had remarkably extensive examples of such spontaneous pictures: stones with images of the Madonna and child, the saints, the Crucifixion, and so forth.[1] These were *lusus naturae*: objects of the creator's playful imagination, and they still inspire a strand of antiquarianism (see endpapers, and tailpiece figures on pp. 6, 20, 57, 93, etc.).[2]

Phenomena such as the Brocken spectre, St Elmo's fire, will-o'-the-wisps, fox fire or *ignis fatuus*, and other natural *fata morganas* mentioned earlier enjoy an independent existence regardless of the observer—unlike faces in the fire or warnings in tea leaves and coffee grounds. Yet such processes of divination are linked to the ancient games of descrying shapes in the skies, faces in the clouds, or messages in stones; the pursuit presupposes that the effects of the weather or of time are plain for all to see, and does not attribute their appearance to the workings of human perception and imagination, requiring a seer's ability to read the enigmas. Another variation on the game, however, attributes the marks exclusively to the vagaries of individual reverie: you can see something in the clouds or the shadows which nobody else can.

These distinctions are not always clear-cut, as several of the words for such wonders attribute them to supernatural origins and reveal how it is in practice difficult to keep the experiences distinct, how subjective dreaming alters the experience of the natural event. As Nature abhors a vacuum, so does the mind resist meaninglessness, invent stories to explain haphazard incidents, provide reasons and origins; the amorphous, the inchoate, the formless, have beckoned irresistibly to the shaping powers of thought and imagination. Humans are polyglot creatures of language, and signs attract meanings, symbols stick to forms, verbal and visual. Pattern, design, system, significations—meaning—have accrued to every sort of natural phenomena.

One of Kircher's fellow Jesuits and contemporaries, the Cambridge Platonist Henry More, struggled to unlock the cryptic significances concealed in scriptural prophecy. Borrowing from Greek words meaning to depict, or figure, or make comparisons and conjectures, he introduced into English the little-known words, 'icasm' and 'icastic', referring to figurative expression. More stressed that the solution to Scripture's secrets lay in grasping 'the peculiar Icasms therein'.[3] This concept of the 'icasm' could be applied to figures appearing in the mind's eye. In the usage of More, phenomena are icastic when packed with secret significance that it takes a gifted scryer to grasp. He was looking for God's messages concealed in text, but in the twentieth century, the method pervades modern psychology: graphology, lie detection, Rorschach, and psychometrics. It grants precedence to the thinking eye of an individual, however unreliable, and thus illuminates changing ideas of person: perceived phenomena are indissolubly tied to the perceiver. Creative cognition becomes equivalent to a signature: it defines the beholder's uniqueness. A hundred and fifty years after Kircher published his research into tricks of the light, the study of the sky twists empirical observation into fantastical speculation, with the mystical strain making itself felt strongly in English Romanticism, especially Coleridge, who read deeply in Henry More.

The term *fata morgana* began to be applied to spectral illusions more generally, to hallucinations and eidetic images, and to fantasies formed in and by the mind's eye, in accordance with the general turn from the supernatural to the uncanny. (Thomas Carlyle said of the poet Samuel Taylor Coleridge that 'He [Coleridge] preferred to create logical fatamorganas for himself on this hither side.')[4] Both Sigmund Freud and C. G. Jung continued this divining practice in their discovery of unconscious symbols in dream imagery and art, including, most famously, Freud's interest in Leonardo's childhood dream of a vulture which he maintained appears unconsciously in the drapery that links the figures of the mother and daughter in *St Anne with the Madonna and Child*.[5] When the name of Allah is found inscribed in the heart of an aubergine, or Jesus' face in a burned tortilla, or pyramids on Mars, or the Virgin Mary in a tomato, or any such items beloved of organs such as the *National Inquirer*, and the world-wide web, we are not wandering very far afield from rather more respected methods of interpretation, surprising as it may seem.

The human desire to make such wonders legible did not abate; but they no longer testified to the activity of occult powers; instead, their oracles became decipherable by individual powers of cognition and projection. Whereas in times of faith, meanings discovered in this way revealed the hidden workings of divine providence, now the process tends to hold a mirror to the psyche of the subject. 'What we come to know orders and complements what we can actually see: we do not see what we think we see.'[6] And what we think we see can tell us something about who we are.

The art historian H. W. Janson distinguished between two ways of seeing: the first describes the artist discovering, within the stone or other material, the body inscribed there by nature—a procedure Michelangelo's *Slaves* most powerfully and eloquently embodies as they seem to struggle to free themselves from the stone. Janson associates this approach with mimesis, because the sculptor is trying to deliver something believed to be already there: the figure in the marble, the faces in the rock.[7]

Guzton Borglum, the sculptor of the looming colossi of Mount Rushmore, studied the range for days and nights until an image formed in the shapes and hollows of the rocks; he also borrowed Native American interpretations of landmarks, peaks, and other features. Borglum's projected Brobdingnagian portrait of General Lee, for example, was inspired by 'studying the formation of the rocks, watching the effects of light and shadow on the face of the cliff at various times of day. And on the third day, toward evening, when there was a pale young moon in the sky, he seemed to see the shades of a gray Confederate host, with Robert E. Lee, Stonewall Jackson, and Jefferson Davis, stealing across the great expanse of rock in gigantic proportions.' This memorial was never finished, but Borglum carried the idea on with him to Mount Rushmore. It could be said that his mammoth monuments represent the terminus and the nadir of the cloud-gazing method.[8] But the approach has also strongly influenced modern art—especially Surrealism, at the other end of the aesthetic spectrum from Borglum's official mythologies. Max Ernst meditated on patterns and knots in wood grain to develop the found *frottage* images of his book *Histoire naturelle* (1923), while Paul Klee traced his aesthetic origins to the marble table tops in his uncle's restaurant, which he would stare at as a child, 'obsessed' with drawing the grotesque creatures he discerned in the patterns.[9] Recent photographs published in England continue the esoteric tradition, discerning secret faces in the ancient megalithic circles and avenues of stones at Avebury.

The second way of making images, in Janson's classification, organizes them more directly through *fantasia*: seeing faces in clouds or images in rocks that Nature has *not* put there. The most patent and most ancient evidence of this arbitrary and mythopoeic faculty lies far beyond the province of art, in the enduring and wonderful ancient fantasies of star maps, which link up the random scattering of the skies into pictures and stories— and of course, portents. Different cultures have found different patterns, which have since been eclipsed by the global success of the Babylonian and Egyptian zodiac and constellations established in the Near East and adopted by European astronomers. Among the Amerindian people of Colombia, stars figured under such names as the Old Adze, Snake, Caterpillar Jaguar, Scorpion, Big Otter, Fish Rack, Foam Egret, Headless One, Armadillo, and the Corpse Bundle, while the Milky Way (still so called in our hemisphere after the infant Heracles spilling Hera's milk with his vigorous suckling) was known there as the Anaconda Path.[10]

Aetiological myths—Greek cosmologies, Ovid's *Metamorphoses*— similarly elaborate wonderful stories about mountains, rocks, trees, rivers, and other landmarks from their patterns, contours, and effects, reading figures into their forms. The very word 'chimera' evokes the fire-breathing monster who marauded a mountain in Lycia, taking off from the volcanic fox fire that dances from fumaroles on the slopes. Since then, 'chimera' has come to mean illusion, and the shift offers a key to understanding how this mythopoeic faculty of discerning figures in random marks began to describe the mindscape of a person, not the general cultural imaginary of a society. Chimerae turn into vagaries of individual fantasy—the *OED* gives 1514 for the first figurative use of the word meaning a kind of phantasm, and this change reflects Renaissance interest in the productive workings of imagination.[11]

Janson concludes that today 'we have at last resolved the ancient Greek dichotomy of *mimesis* and *fantasia* by assigning each of them to its own separate domain'.[12] But this contrast, while being helpfully orderly, seems to me too stark, for mimesis itself depends on a language of signs that is rooted in the work of the imagination with analogy, metaphor, and associations. In the struggle to represent the unseen, to figure spirit, men and women considered they were acting as imitators, turning the lens of empiricism on hidden forms, deciphering existing secrets and codes. But they were, rather, being led by their *fantasia*, and it in turn was shaped by diverse, buried codes of cognition and communication. (Sometimes both processes are engaged: the inspired individual working to become a unique instrument of cracking the divine secrets of icasms.)

Cloud-gazing is a game still played by many, and reading the sky's 'secret album of such nephographs'[13] has a very long history indeed, with no heavy religious freight. The comic playwright Aristophanes was already mocking superstitious uses with merciless glee in *The Clouds*, a satire on the arbitrariness and vagueness of his contemporaries and their philosophizing:

> STREPSIADES. Ah, but tell me then what is the reason
>   That if, as you say, they are Clouds, they today
>   As women appear to our view? . . .
> SOCRATES. Didst thou never espy a Cloud in the sky
>   Which a centaur or leopard might be,
>   Or a wolf, or a cow?
> STREPSIADES. Very often, I vow . . .
> SOCRATES. Why, I tell you that these become just what they please . . .[14]

For the plain-speaking, commonsensical Aristophanes all Socrates' talk about the invididual and perception was just so much hot air.

By contrast, the natural philosopher Lucretius wrote in a mood of lyrical wonder, well captured by Lucy Hutchinson (1620–81) in her translation of his *De Rerum Natura*:

> Who looks on Heaven, when without stormes
> Winds carrie on the clowds in various formes
> May there huge, craggie, bending hills behold
> And ayrie mountains, upon mountains rolld,
> May see the figures those vast bodies have.
> Like hanging rocks over a hollow cave . . .
> Like wild beasts, shut in dens.[15]

Perhaps taking his cue from Lucretius, the scholarly painter Andrea Mantegna shaped clouds into horsemen and giant faces in the background of his paintings. He does not seem to have wanted to convey any particular symbolic meaning, but was perhaps enjoying the game of imitating the procedure of *Natura Pictrix*, according to the humanist vision.[16] For it would be a mistaken reading of past ideas of the self, as I say, to overlook the emphasis on subjective vision long before the Romantics and the Surrealists made its workings paramount.

Vasari relates how Piero di Cosimo, an artist with a grotesque streak, saw things in the spit of the patients in a hospital where he was staying.[17] Leonardo refused any hint of madness and melancholia in such a process, and advocated studying blots and smears and stains as a crucial stimulus to making art. He cites Botticelli as an advocate of following the prompts and biddings of fantasia: 'Our Botticelli said, that [such] study [of landscape] was vain, because by merely throwing a sponge full of diverse colors at a wall, it left a stain on that wall, where a fine landscape was seen.'[18] And in another entry in his notebooks, also appearing in the edited *Treatise on Painting* in around 1550, Leonardo advocated the method as an 'aid to reflection', and said:

although it seems a small thing and almost laughable, nevertheless it is very useful in stimulating the mind to various discoveries. This is: look at walls splashed with a number of stains or stones of various mixed colours. If you have to invent some scene, you can see there resemblances to a number of landscapes, adorned in various ways with mountains, rivers, rocks, trees, great plains, valleys and hills. Moreover, you can see various battles, and rapid actions of figures, strange expressions on faces, costumes, and an infinite number of things, which you can reduce to good, integrated form.[19]

Interestingly, he then moved laterally to the method's acoustic equivalent, and likened it to hearing 'the sound of bells, in whose pealing you can find every name and every word you can imagine'. Such experiences, when occurring in the lives of a Joan of Arc who did indeed hear her voices sometimes in the carillon of her local church, are technically called 'locutions', and are attributed, like visions, to supernatural causes. But Leonardo was an empiricist, and imagination was a material organ. He then recommended especially the contemplation of 'the stains on walls, or the ashes of a fire, or clouds, or mud, or like things'. Later he writes: 'the mind is stimulated to new inventions by confused things, which are intrinsically meaningless and inscrutable but lend themselves for those very reasons to scrutiny'. They provide a 'way of nourishing and stirring up the "ingegnio" (mind) to various inventions': 'if you consider them well, you will find really marvellous ideas'.[20]

This form of projection turned clouds into extensions of the mind's vagaries, a move that Erasmus also makes, without sensing any obstacle, when he lavished praise on the German artist Dürer for capturing similar inchoate and confused objects, referring to Leonardo in passing: 'Nay, he even depicts that which cannot be depicted: fire, rays of light, thunder, sheet lightning, lightning, or, as they say, "the clouds on a wall" . . . something most similar to nothing or a dream.'[21]

This was the natural—not supernatural—play of fancy that Shakespeare refers to and in the famous exchange with Polonius in *Hamlet*, when Hamlet ribs him in a rather Aristophanic mood:

> HAMLET. Do you see yonder cloud that's almost in shape of a camel?
> POLONIUS. By th'mass, and 'tis like a camel indeed.
> HAMLET. Methinks it is like a weasel.
> POLONIUS. It is back'd like a weasel.
> HAMLET. Or like a whale?
> POLONIUS. Very like a whale.

Hamlet, III. ii. 375–82

By contrast, for Antony near his defeat, the fugitive clouds announce his own dissolution (*Antony and Cleopatra* IV. xii. 9–14).

While Hamlet and Antony were cloud-gazing, Italian and Dutch painters were picturing clouds as they had always been pictured, much to the later disgust of John Ruskin, who proclaimed that Old Masters' renderings had 'about the same relation to the clouds of nature, that a child's carving of a turnip has to the head of Apollo'.[22] Ruskin himself poured forth on the beauty of cloud formations, lavished praise on his fellow Englishmen Turner and Constable, who had properly observed cloud activity, and then set about leaving posterity guidelines, by making extraordinary technical drawings of cloud architecture that attempt to trap clouds in perspectival grids and projections.[23] Over two chapters, resoundingly entitled 'The Truth of Clouds', Ruskin continues to hurl his bolts against failures past and present, and singles out the little-known Gaspar Dughet for scorn—calling the two landscapes in the National Gallery, London, 'windy . . . abuses of nature and abortions of art'.

One of the exceptions to Ruskin's invective was Alexander Cozens, the Russian-born English watercolourist, draughtsman, and teacher of painting. Born in 1717, Cozens struggled through the 1770s and 1780s to capture the stir and flux of clouds on the page.[24] He was among the first artists to go 'skying'—painting clouds from observation, *en plein air*, and also making pencil drawings, in shades and tones of sepia, often on prepared bistre or buff wash backgrounds. His studies of the particularities of high cirrus, of thunderheads and storm clouds, and of moonlight and the sun's rays on their volumes have a breathtaking scrupulousness and intensity, creating rippling patterns of alternating figure and ground as he maps the play of light on nebulous contours, openings in the clouds, foreground drifts in shadow.[25]

Shape-shifting clouds offered a test case for an artist's representational skills, and Cozens struggled to number, annotate, and set out their forms on a grid for the benefit of his pupils. His idea was that by using the chart as an *aide-mémoire*, they could quickly revisit the volatile skyscape. At one time Cozens taught at Eton, and his private students also included the sugar millionaire and Orientalist fantasist William Beckford, author of the lurid Arabian romance *Vathek* (1786), and creator of the Gothic folly Fonthill Abbey. Beckford commented that Cozens was 'almost as full of Systems as the Universe'[26]—with his quasi-scientific tables, the artist was attempting to hammer his method of fantasia into a simple tool, a kind of spinning jenny or Davy lamp of landscape painting.

Yet Cozens's dedication to systematic empiricism still led him to wondrous invention. While he exhibits an Enlightenment passion to name and contain the prodigal polymorphousness of natural variety, the attempt took him deeper into a fresh, Romantic subjectivity. With *A New Method for Assisting the Invention of Drawing Original Compositions of Landscape* (1784–5), he recommended that his students crumple up paper and then dribble ink on it and fold it, then meditate on the marks to develop new compositions. 'Blots' were the way to enhance imagination and stimulate memory, and he made an instinctive identification of this practice with finding shapes in clouds, quoting on the title-page the passage from *Antony and Cleopatra*: 'Sometime we see a cloud that's dragonish . . .' He advised, 'Possess your mind strongly with a subject,' and then 'with the swiftest hand make all possible variety of shapes & strokes upon your paper'; letting the hand move unpremeditated and unguided and unconscious. He described how he stumbled across this practice when he pulled an old, 'soiled' scrap of paper from a pile to demonstrate something for a student, and found that the marks it bore helped crystallize his ideas. Asked about the influence of Leonardo, Cozens said he had not known the passage but was delighted with this corroboration, for his ideas aroused a great deal of ridicule, Aristophanes-style. 'This theory', declared Cozens, 'is in fact,' . . . '*the art of seeing properly*'.[27]

The opening page of an album of his sketches shows two pages of proposed schemata for 'Principles of Landskip': the third and fourth 'historical' tables, showing the Roman Age and the Modern Age, make no concession to the picturesque; they are diagrammatic, understated, spontaneous, and spare.[28] The examples of blots and the resulting landscapes that follow are vigorously painted, with impassioned mottlings and slashing strokes evoking mountain scenery or tangled undergrowth (see Figure 10).

Nobody coming across this work without prior knowledge would be able to date it to the late eighteenth century. His blots are vigorous, near-abstract splotches and streaks, tending ever more intensely to condensation and simplicity; the strokes of his brush arc and twitch with a vitality that announces the metaphysical abstraction of Wassily Kandinsky or the action painting of Jackson Pollock, while the very art of seeing properly, as Cozens practised it, was most energetically adopted by the Surrealists, in Max Ernst's *frottages* and *décalcomanies*, and more recently by artists such as Adam Dant and his 'Bureau for the Investigation of the Subliminal Image.'[29]

In Cozens' works we can feel the urgency of 'seeing properly': he was observing empirically, training fantasy not to be deluded, using the scrying faculty for scientifically and aesthetically harmonious purposes, so that rather than perceive castles in the air and phantom armies in the clouds as heavenly portents, fairy enchantments, or mental delusions, the artist becomes a master of vision and the disposer of its incoherent offerings, like drifts and assemblies of clouds. Cozens, while travelling further than any of his contemporaries into methods of mental picturing, was also set against—even defended himself against—the unruly procession of images in phantasmagorias and other optical effects.

Cozens was therefore advocating, as early as the late eighteenth century, that artists combine objective reproduction of observed natural randomness, ethereal flux, and the adventitious camouflage mottling of light and shade with an extraordinary attempt to probe such forms' potential for personal expression. The Platonic predicament of mortals in the cave, receiving experience in the partial, fragmentary, and deceptive form of flickering shadows was already resisted by both Botticelli and Leonardo when they placed heroic humanist confidence in the powers of imagination to winkle meaning from the most inauspicious hiding places—Cozens strengthened this approach.

The *New Method* that Cozens devised coincided with the first balloonists sailing up through the clouds and beyond, and artists roaming up fell and down dale to 'sky'[30]—to observe clouds directly. The metaphorical freight that the heavens carried began to lighten with the new appetite for empirical knowledge. Numerous experiments began to explore both the functioning of human perception and the imponderable and invisible contents of the physical world. David Brewster (d. 1868), S. P. Thompson (d. 1916), Peter Mark Roget (d. 1869), and Michael Faraday (d. 1867) were among the scientists who probed deep into the character of vision and the physical laws governing the universe and human beings within them: optical instruments such as the kaleidoscope, the stereoscope, and, in our times, moving LED (Light-Emitting Diode) displays now in use every-where, as well as numerous other ingenious devices, resulted from their analyses of the eye's way of seeing. Many of these were quickly translated into popular entertainment, as conjuring tricks at home and dazzling illusionism on-stage (vanishing ladies, materializing phantoms); they were the precursors of the cinema, as we shall see later. Their contemporaries also wanted to make the sky legible as well, to grasp the flux of the weather, to interpret the iconotexts of the clouds, to marshal even the vaporous, inchoate chaos of cloudscapes into reasonable order. The screens on which signs and wonders had played were to be clearly and objectively rendered from life.

While Benjamin Franklin probed the powers of lightning and electricity, other scientists—biologists, astronomers, and physicists sailed up into the new territories of the upper air in Montgolfier balloons, and wondered at the sublime view of cloudscapes. For the first time in human experience, men—and some women—saw the earth—and the clouds—from above. Erasmus Darwin wrote a marvelling rhapsody to the inventor about the experience from a balloon, in *The Loves of the Plants* (1789):

> So on the shoreless air the intrepid Gaul
> Launch'd the vast concave of his bouyant ball.—

Journeying on high, the silken castle glides
Bright as a meteor through the azure tides;
O'er towns and towers and temples wins its way,
Or mounts sublime, and gilds the vault of day . . .
—The calm Philosopher in ether sails,
Views broader stars and breathes in purer gales!
. . . —Rise, great Mongulfier! [*sic*][31]

The new knowledge demanded a proper, systematic record; modern meteorology was born around this time. In London, the pioneer of weather watching, Luke Howard, devised a lasting system to capture clouds. He called them 'the countenance of the sky', using an image that alludes to the new physiognomical and even phrenological systems of interpretation, and he gave them names according to type and shape: cumulus, cumulostratus, cirrus (after the Latin for a curl of hair).[32]

This was the period when 'skying' became a craze. Poets and painters—Coleridge, Wordsworth, Cornelius Varley—were climbing and wandering to find illusions and their causes. Coleridge sought out the Brocken spectre of the Harz mountains, but failed to observe it, and had to be content with the sight of a phosphorescent boar.[33] In Germany, the now venerable Goethe, hearing of Howard's work, became captivated: here was a fusion of natural science and metaphysical meditation. He hymned the Englishman and his classifications in a sequence of poems, entitled after each of Howard's cloud types. Howard was a devout Methodist; Goethe, the scientist-poet, accordingly exults in his demonstration that God's handiwork and intelligibility can be woven together with Enlightenment system, scientific nomenclature, and analysis. Constable's marvellous spontaneous studies of clouds, like Howard's, bear marginal notes of the time and place. Yet even in the midst of this keen scientific empiricism, the clouds continued to attract figurative meanings, and Goethe could not resist the pull of subjective fantasy:

Now our power of forming shapes begins to stir,
Creates precision from the imprecise,
Here a lion threatens, there rolls an elephant,
A camel's neck veers round to a dragon;
An army marches up, yet does not triumph
Since its power breaks on steep crags.

And he closes on a note of thanksgiving for Howard: 'Whenever a streak (of clouds) climbs, piles itself together, scatters, falls,' wrote Goethe, 'May the world gratefully remember you.'[34]

Constable, too, however assiduously he cast himself as a direct observer, found in the skies 'the key note, the standard of scale, and the chief organ of sentiment'.[35] He felt as he saw, and he expected to stir feelings in others through his cloud and sky paintings: it was not in practice possible to prevent projecting personal meanings on to the clouds.

Concurrently with these scientific struggles to seize bodies of cloud, the sublime cinema of meteorology offered a mirror of inner turmoil, especially about vision and illusion. James Hogg's *The Private Memoirs and Confessions of a Justified Sinner*, published in 1824, conveys the power of fantasy through a combination of weather portents, psychological delusion, *fata morganas*, and faces in the clouds. As I have discussed elsewhere the violent, hallucinatory link between the vision of the 'halo of glory' and the stricken protagonist's demonic double, I will not repeat my account here, except to emphasize how James Hogg refuses to distinguish between natural wonder and mental delusion: after his protagonist's terrifying vision of a spectral doppelgänger on Arthur's Seat, in Edinburgh, Hogg adds an airy, rather less hair-raising footnote that 'this terrestrial phenomenon of the early morn cannot be better delineated than by the name given of it by the shepherd boys, "The little wee ghost of the rainbow." '[36] Hogg had also sought out the effect of the Brocken spectre, so called after the mountain in Germany where a spectator's shadow looms vast and lowering across the cloud floor. Hogg wrote of such an apparition that it 'appeared to my affrighted imagination as the enemy of mankind'.[37]

The Scottish writer knew Coleridge's work well, and his diabolical delusion interestingly reclaims the phenomenon for a more profound psychological uncanny, than did the older poet's use of it. Hogg's extraordinary book veers in deep and gripping perplexity between a religious interpretation of the sinner's possessed state (the devil as its agent) and a psychological view (it is all in his mind), the novel epitomizing the ambivalence around the question of portents that still possessed a believer at the beginning of the nineteenth century. For even if the vision was all in the mind, the devil could be at work there; even if the vision were natural and physical, God was its originator, and if God was at work, his ape might be up to his mischief, again. For someone who rejects atheism, and cannot bear the tensions of agnosticism, the question of heavenly portents remains a painful conundrum. Since then, although the response now emphasizes personal psyche as the ground and origin of such states of mind, belief in the devil's existence has made a strong return, with fundamentalist forms of Protestantism related to the beliefs of the Covenanters, with which Hogg's novel grapples.

This propensity of the human mind to reject incoherence and decipher random marks and noises and shadows and patterns until they become intelligible as messages, signs, tales, and portents emerges in pride of place in theories of creativity from the late eighteenth century onwards, and develops in a newly valued view of human perception that begins with Renaissance theories of projective imagination, as we shall see in the next chapter. It marches with the dazzling invention of new prostheses to stretch our physical and mental capacities: the telescope, the microscope, even the full-length mirror, or 'psyché' (as a free-standing full-length glass was called in French). The unreliability of sensory perception and its intercommunication with the brain began to be understood more fully as a natural limit to cognition, not the work of supernatural (demonic) powers. Priority of concepts over percepts begins to emerge as a significant aspect of mental activity.[38]

This tendency grants precedence to the thinking eye of an individual, however unreliable, and thus illuminates changing ideas of person: perceived phenomena are indissolubly tied to the perceiver. Creative cognition and the capacity to descry 'potential images' become equivalent to a signature: they can act to define the beholder's uniqueness.

A clash about cloud-gazing between the painter Arshile Gorky and the sculptor Isamu Noguchi illustrates the place of human subjective vision in the contradictions of twentieth-century psychology and aesthetics. Noguchi was driving to California in 1941 with Gorky, who kept looking up at the huge skies of America and seeing shapes there, 'the tangled riders of Paolo Uccello. Lines like the lances in "The Battle of San Romano" connected one shape to another.' Noguchi expressed some scepticism, saying they were 'only clouds. . . . He'd be always seeing some peasant woman in the sky.' An ascetic formalist, Noguchi had recently been introduced, back in New York, to Gestalt psychology by Buckminster Fuller, and 'He took the view that to see the clouds as anything but clouds was wrong. There was nothing metaphorical about a cloud. One should not abuse clouds. They were clouds! Suddenly Gorky burst into a rage. "Stop the car," he cried. He'd had enough. He saw what he saw and that was that.'

In old age, however, Noguchi, telling this story to Gorky's biographer, Matthew Spender, revealed more respect for Gorky's 'capacity for reverie': he was forever 'weaving a lacework of imagery into whatever he saw', he said.[39] The quarrel between the two artists, over half a century ago, defines a fault line in formative attitudes to subjectivity and the imagination. Along one side of the divide are marshalled the Modernists and the Surrealists, with stream of consciousness, décalcomanie and frottage, accidental and automatic drawing; on the other side, the formalists, with their scientific analysis of intrinsic values of colour, form, and mass and their austere allusions to symbols. Gorky wished to act the part of the seer, who can conjure—and control—illusion. Noguchi, by contrast, accepted the more impersonal, withdrawn role of watcher rather than interpreter, of recipient observer rather than projective decoder. Noguchi was uncovering an aesthetic bound by natural laws regardless of his own viewpoint; Gorky was seeing what was not there. They were still playing out the conflict between *mimesis* and *fantasia*, in which *fantasia* gains the greater value to the constitution of the self. And yet, the signature of Noguchi on his artefacts—including that most ubiquitous item of modern design, his paper globe lampshade—is as strong and recognizable and individual as Gorky's tumescent, dripping, rhapsodic improvisations.

Part IV

Light

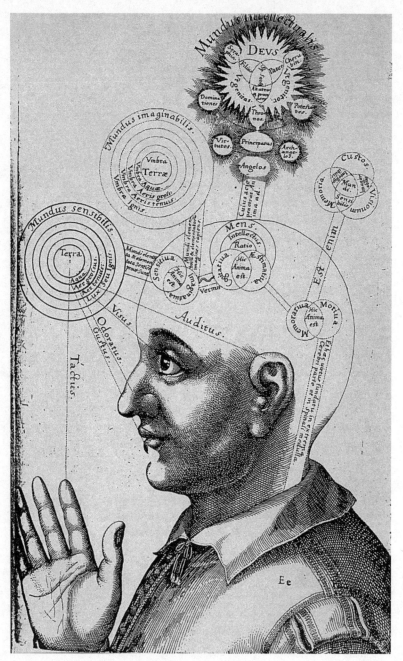

In the centre of the man's forehead, the imaginative
soul has its seat, and is linked to the five senses and to
other *animae:* Robert Fludd's 'Vision of the Triple Soul
within the Body', from *Utriusque Cosmi*, 1617–19.

9
The Eye of the Imagination

> '. . . I'll close my eyes,
> And in a melancholic thought I'll frame
> Her figure 'fore me. Now I ha' 't—how strong
> Imagination works! How she can frame
> Things which are not!'
>
> John Webster, *The White Devil*

'The soul never thinks without a mental image,' declared Aristotle in *De Anima*, his book on the soul, using the word *psyche* for 'soul' and *phantasma* for 'mental image': in contemporary idiom, the psyche does not think without phantasms.[1] How thought processes happen, where they take place in the mind, how the faculties are arranged, and what the character of mental images might be remain some of the most crucial puzzles about consciousness.[2] The replies which have been offered, at different times and in different ways, have played their part in the fashioning of experience, especially with regard to visual experiences and their meanings: among such phantasmata, dreams—and not just at night-time but day-dreams too—are the strongest example of volatile value, now treasured as prophetic soothsayings, now scorned and even feared as dangerous delusions, then emerging through Freudian psychoanalysis as the key indices to an individual's desires. The high value accorded to the visualizing faculty continued to influence models of mind, but the interrelationship between sense impressions, memory, imagination, and fantasy still generated competing and various schemes. Most famously of all, perhaps, the French philosopher René Descartes, in his meticulous examination of visual experience, decided that 'It is the soul that sees, not the eye . . . This is why maniacs and men asleep often see, or think they see, objects that are not before their eyes.'[3] He located the mind's eye in the pineal gland in the brain, the hyphen between body and spirit in his scheme, and illustrated the workings of this organ in several highly scientific-looking diagrams (Figure 11a, p. 129). Descartes also drew the figure of a blind man in order to illustrate how the brain makes pictures, not the eyes. Using two sticks to feel out the lie of the land around him, the blind man visualizes his situation. Seeing and visualizing bring personal consciousness into play, and demand active engagement, interpretation, and shaping, not passive receptivity.[4]

The imagination creates images as well as fantasies, but for many purposes the word 'image' is too broad a term for the imagination's products—and not fantastic enough, because memory also retains and communicates in images. The terms 'fantasy' and 'imagination' originate in Greek and Latin, respectively. *Phantasia*, in Plato, describes the world of appearances, with an emphasis on pictures in the mind's eye, so that the cognate *phantasmata*, Plato's word for images (including artists' pictures), refers to visions produced by sensory stimulus or in dreams. This usage has inspired a range of words in English strongly tinged with the supernatural and the psychological: phantasms, phantasmatic, phantasy itself, and phantasmagoria. 'Fantasy', the Latinized version of the Greek, has acquired a stream of distinct associations with the result that shades of difference now operate to distinguish imagination from fantasy in common usage, in ways that effloresce from definitions attempted by Renaissance philosophers. Pietro Pomponazzi (d. 1525) restricted fantasy to the sleeping mind alone, and granted imagination a connection with conscious perception. Imagination still carries these more positive, rational, even civic overtones: in common parlance, 'Use your imagination' does not mean the same as 'Go ahead, fantasize', but rather evokes conscious, responsible, and sympathetic behaviour, by contrast with 'You're fantasizing', which calls to inner realms of the unconscious and dream.

In Augustine's scheme, the power of phantasmata corresponded to the highest state of vision, which he termed 'intellectual'. In medieval thought, its power was active, itself radiating light; metaphor and act become interfused when, for example, the archbishop of Canterbury John Pecham (1240–92) extended the metaphor of the mirror or reflective surface to the eye itself: 'The eye is not merely the recipient of action but acts itself, just as shining bodies do. Therefore the eye must have a natural light to alter visible species and make them commensurate with visual power.'[5] This mind's eye was the faculty cultivated by Dante in his visionary poem *The Divine Comedy*, as well as the sovereign metaphor for the culminating bliss of *Paradiso*. The faculty here, ablaze with natural light, sways between figure and act: is it metaphorical (fire in the mind), or is it physical? Whichever way it falls, the very exaltedness of this inner eye and its creative intellectual power made any false use or devilish imitation all the more perfidious and dangerous.

One question concerns the relationship of imagination and fantasy, but another, lying deeper, places at issue the veridical status of vision itself. On the one hand, an array of metaphors for divinity and truth arises from optics: the very word 'illumination' encloses the idea of vision acting with light, and Dante cascades images of eyes, crystal, rays, haloes, and dazzle until the climax in Paradise when the poet experiences the very sight of God (the Beatific Vision).

By contrast, the much quoted passage from St Paul's First Letter to the Corinthians describes how on this earth we 'see through a glass darkly' (*in aenigmitate*). Only in the future shall we see 'face to face'—without riddling, reflections, shadows, or illusions. It is hard to escape the language of vision when discussing human understanding: the frontispiece of Athanasius Kircher's key work, *Ars Magna Lucis et Umbrae (The Great Art of Light and Shadow* (Rome, 1646)), shows the Saviour in the guise of a sun god, radiating light into the world, penetrating into the depths of a cave where a polished surface bounces the ray, as bright as ever. Seeing more sharply, more clearly, larger and better and further, promised a return to the illuminated state of humanity before the Fall, when Adam and Eve would have had telescopes and microscopes for eyes, and endowed with these powers, as yet undimmed by sin, would have named the beasts and all living things. Or so thought Robert Hooke, the great scientist of microscopy.[6] By the eighteenth century, the high-energy dynamics between optics and psychology spurred brilliant inventors to devise proto-cinematic devices: bristling with learned nomenclature, the new tools of the thinking eye projected a Leonardo-esque conception of dynamic vision, opening the way towards the camera and the photograph, the cinema and the virtual reality programme.

While light set a divine standard for intelligence and rationality (the 'Enlightenment', or *le siècle des lumières*, as these names for the epoch reveal, conveys the concept of reason through metaphors of lucidity and clarity), trust in vision was racked by doubt, and the working of eye and brain as human beings engaged with the world of appearances led into insecure zones where reality trembled. Concomitantly, the devil's medium was enigma, illusion, darkling sight. In medieval Christian tradition, he is a mimic, an actor, a performance artist, and he imitates the wonders of nature and the divine work of creation. But unlike God, St Augustine decided, the devil cannot perform real miracles or alter real phenomena. He is merely the ape of God, the master of lies, of imitating and simulating and pretending—impotent when it comes to really altering substance and matter (the waxwork, that perfect replica, remains inanimate). He can only conjure visions, as he did when he carried Jesus to a topmost crest of a hill and showed him the view and tempted him to dreams of power. Or when, in the person of Mephistopheles, he summoned the pageant of the Deadly Sins for Doctor Faustus and then seduced him with the bewitching appearance—the *eidolon*—of Helen of Troy. The devil summons images in the mind's eye, playing on desires and weaknesses. He *toys* with us, especially when creating spectacles that are not there, for the word 'illusion' itself comes from *ludere*, 'to play' in Latin. Conjurors mimic his tricks: the early Christian Hippolytus, in the midst of furiously denouncing magicians, gives a surprisingly vivid account of their stratagems, of the lamps and mirrors or basins of water they used, how they even conjured the stars by sticking fish scales or the skins of sea horses to the ceiling.[7]

The mind also produces illusions through dreams, which must inspire great wariness, for the devil plays tricks with the sleeping mind, enters the imagination in the form of a nightmare: the suffocating demons—the succubi, incubi, and 'ephialtes' of pagan mythology who were taken over into Christian belief.

One kind of mental image was described as 'eidetic', referring to optical experiences that are retained in the mind's eye with hallucinatory intensity. It comes from *eidos*, used by Aristotle for that which is seen, or 'form, shape, figure', both of something particular and of a generic kind of form, and it is related to *idein*, to see, and *eidolon*, a shape, image, spectre, or phantom, also an image in the mind, a vision or fancy. In Latin, the equivalent was *species*, confusingly, since this term's biological application has eclipsed the optical reference. For a long time, however, especially in seventeenth-century Neoplatonist circles, *species* meant the appearance of something or someone, even a phantom, or double.

When the German psychologist E. R. Jaensch later attempted a strict definition, he reached for an optical simile: 'They [eidetic images] may therefore be compared to the pictures produced by a magic lantern.'[8] This image, as a trope for the imagination at work, runs through Romantic and post-Romantic literature from De Quincey to Proust. Robert Louis Stevenson, for example, in an essay called 'A Chapter on Dreams', summoned optical metaphors to his aid in order to communicate mental picturing:

The past is all of one texture—whether feigned or suffered—whether acted out in three dimensions, or only witnessed in that small theatre of the brain which we keep brightly lighted all night long, after the jets are down, and darkness and sleep reign undisturbed in the remainder of the body . . . the past . . . is lost for ever: it is all gone, past conjuring. And yet conceive us robbed of it, conceive of that little thread of memory that we trail behind us broken at the pocket's edge; and in what naked nullity should we be left! For we only guide ourselves, and only know ourselves, by *these air-painted pictures of the past*. (Emphasis added)[9]

In the opening pages of *À la Recherche du temps perdu*, Proust's narrator invokes the magic lantern illuminations with which he played as a child as he embarks on the work of transmitting, as it were, his thought-pictures to ours.

Eidetic thus evokes vivid images that are seen by the mind's eye and arise from fantasy, reverie, reflection, and recollection. These faculties or processes combine with memory, but are not exclusively bound by referents to actual experience. The images they summon characteristically appear clothed in metaphors that communicate the conditions of supernatural other worlds and their creatures according to axioms embedded in religious iconography, in mythological visual narratives, and in speculation about the function and character of the imagination and of the senses. The eyes do not function as a mirror of nature, but as a mirror of mind. So the sharpest questions focus on that mind and its workings.

The need to distinguish between the imagination and judgement continued to inspire different models, and Platonist anxiety about fantasy and its mendacity persist, alongside the growing confidence in the brain's powers to generate fantasy. When Leonardo da Vinci dissected human brains in order to locate the faculties, he followed medieval physiology in the tradition of Aristotle and Galen and showed three cavities or ventricles in the core of the brain. A notebook drawing of around 1490, made for an unfinished study of the human body, shows the eye as a fold in the very membrane of the cortex, connected to the *imprensiva*, or sensory receiver of impressions, in the first chamber, or 'ventricle', and thence by means of a *vermis*, or worm-valve, to the next two ventricles. Whereas Aristotle had conceived of the imagination or animal soul as a stage on a kind of information assembly line, receiving data from the senses and passing it on to the mind, where it was ordered and assessed, Leonardo effectively departed from this Aristotelian hierarchy which gave mind or reason government of imagination. But then Leonardo also recommended—as we saw—staring at stains and clouds to stimulate the mind, and he explicitly went against Horace's classical aesthetics when he advised artists to cultivate the vagaries of fantasy, splicing and selecting from natural forms in order to create grotesque heads, creatures, and visions. Aristotle had, however, discussed the 'deliberative' powers of *phantasia logistikē*, and Leonardo continues this line of thought: the eye was the vehicle of imaginative thought itself.[10]

Leonardo offered one model of mind; there were many others, which arranged the faculties with certain differences. If the outer senses were unreliably subject to inner fantasy, it was crucial to determine their interaction. Soon after Leonardo's speculative drawings, an engraving of the *caput physicum*, or bodily head, attributed to Albrecht Dürer, tackled the issue of the imagination's role in thought. This image pairs *Fantasy* and *[Vis] Estimativa* or Judgement in a single ventricle of the brain, with *Memoria* behind the brain occupying a third chamber.[11] In this diagram *Imagination* is a faculty distinct from *Fantasia*, as it was in Thomas Aquinas's influential scheme: the former active in composing mental images, the latter in retaining them. So, although both Leonardo and Dürer conveyed their belief in the close workings of intellect and the imagination, Leonardo went further in affirming their interwoven character. Claudia Swan comments, 'for perhaps the first time, the mind's engine is the eye.'[12]

The zoologist, alchemist, philosopher, and polymath Conrad Gesner published a plan that differs yet again from both Leonardo's and Dürer's in his *De Anima* of 1586: he imagined the mind as a house, just such a house as a child might draw to represent home, with a front door through which sense impressions enter.[13] In one of the upper 'cells', he placed *Phantasia* and *Memoria* side by side but separate, according to the two aspects of the sensitive soul in the Aristotelian scheme. In this house of the mind, a humble two-storey dwelling, they occupy the first floor. Providing a roof over these equal and balanced faculties of fantasy and memory, Gesner designated *Ratio* (Reason) at the apex of the edifice, crowned by a star that irradiates with its light these lower cells. This star represents God, to whom, Gesner explains, all these faculties proceed. So Leonardo's claim for the imagination as part of the reasoning mind still did not cohere with German thinking over a century later.

At the beginning of the seventeenth century, an Englishman, Robert Fludd (*c*.1574–1637), published a highly esoteric but remarkable work of mystical philosophy, in which he set out his theory of imagination and memory. Besides being a polymath and a mystic, Fludd was an Oxford-educated physician, and an adept at chemistry, who won himself some reputation as a healer in London. He was also an ingenious *bricoleur* who created automata—a lyre that played by itself, a roaring dragon, and a bellowing bull. But his chief passion lay, as his writing shows, with questions of human consciousness, memory, and imagination, and their relationship to the macrocosm of divine creation.

His remarkable book *Utriusque Cosmi . . . historia* (*The History . . . of this World and the Other*), was published in two volumes (1617–18) by the celebrated master printer Theodore de Bry in Oppenheim in Germany. Fludd had wanted his work to appear in England, but the costs of his sumptuously designed and illustrated books were prohibitive. De Bry offered to publish them for free, after he had had the contents vetted by Catholic authorities. It is interesting that Fludd did not fall foul either of his fellow Protestants in his own country, where he was summoned to justify himself before the King, James I, and managed to do so. His work was not, however, generally well known in England, and his occult leanings and Rosicrucian enthusiasm show little trace of the religious paranoia and diabolism of his contemporaries. His thought made a greater impact on continental Europe than it did on his native country, but it travelled back to England through the work of admirers, including Athanasius Kircher, and its value and interest have grown.[14]

The author himself drafted the magnificent illustrations, which were engraved in de Bry's workshop; they communicate his thought far more eloquently today than does his abstruse Latin.[15] Influenced by humanist Neoplatonist ideas in Italy and Germany about the macrocosm and the microcosm, the beautiful plate entitled 'Vision of the Triple Soul in the Body' shows a man as an image of the universe. The faculties radiate in haloes around the profile of a man with suitably enlarged and sensitive external organs: a luminous single eye, a prominent ear, a hand raised to display the fingertips, swollen sensual lips (Figure 11, p. 120). The senses then radiate into a diagram of concentric circles labelled the 'sensible world' (*mundus sensibilis*), which is then linked to a constellation of *animae*, or souls, inside the cranium: in the forehead, the sensitive soul's circumference is interlaced with the imaginative soul's, just behind it. Another bridge leads upwards from this to another planetary system, the world of the imagination (*mundus imaginabilis*). '[This] soul', Fludd writes, '[is] called the imaginative soul, or fantasy or imagination itself; since it beholds not the true pictures of corporeal or sensory things, but their likenesses and as it were, their shadows.'[16] The concentric rings of the imaginative world are the phantasmic projections of the elements: at the centre, the *Umbra Terrae*, or shadow of the Earth, then radiating outwards, water, air, and fire (ether).

In Robert Fludd's vision, a wriggly little worm, labelled *vermis*, connects these interlooped worlds of imagination to the faculties of cognition and judgement (*aestimatio*) with their orbiting satellites—*ratio* (reason), *intellectus* (intelligence), and *mens* (mind). These rise toward the angels and the Trinity, in full glory above. At the back of the head, two more souls appear, designated *Memorativa* and *Motiva*—Memory and Motive Force, the latter controlling bodily movement, for Fludd explains that the motive soul controls involuntary motion. These are dependent aspects of memory that interact with the sensible world—that remember and safeguard its features. *Visionum*, or the capacity to envisage, appears here, as part of memory. None of these differently labelled aspects of mind is at all stable, however, even in Fludd's own vocabulary, let alone transhistorically.

Later, another remarkable illustration, in the concluding and most famous part of Fludd's book on 'The Art of Memory', shows the same section through the man in profile, but in this one, Fludd's interest focuses on the visualizing faculty, or imagination itself (Figure 12a, p. 130).[17] An eye appears in the forehead, in the exact position of the imaginative soul in the earlier diagram, and the images he is seeing appear on the *imprensiva*, or receptor of the eye's data, which takes the form of a screen behind him. Though he is discussing memory, in the course of a lengthy commendation of mnemonic devices, Fludd is concentrating here on the mind's power to summon up pictures, through the *oculus imaginationis*. His 'eye of the imagination' radiates a tableau of images: a tower (of Babel?), a guardian angel showing the way—or perhaps Tobias and his guide—and an obelisk, a two-masted ship on a high sea, and the Last Judgement with Christ in glory on a rainbow among trumpeting angels while the dead rise with supplicating hands.

These images belong to various orders of representation or imagination: the ship and the obelisk might be remembered from a traveller's first-order experience, or might be visualized from a browser's previously beheld representations. Alternatively, they may be conjured in the mind's eye from verbal description—or conceivably, from tactile or acoustic information. Others are generated from imagery that is itself fantastic, whether conveyed in the first place verbally or visually, as in the instances of the conventional depiction of Doomsday and of angels. This inner eye in Fludd's Neoplatonist conception does not receive images: it projects them on to a screen that lies beyond the back of the head, floating in a space that does not exist except in fantasy.

The idea of the mind's eye is one of the most productive of these powerful metaphors, and continues to communicate the work of the imagination, for *imagining the imagination*, for making its image long after the anatomical or biological actuality of its existence has been set aside. In itself a highly mythopoeic metaphor, it pervades the language of poetry, philosophy, and storytelling. The notion of an inner eye proved durable, with John Locke himself offering 'the conception of the human mind as an inner space in which both pains and clear and distinct ideas passed in review before an Inner Eye. . . . The novelty was the notion of a single inner space in which bodily and perceptual sensations . . . were objects of quasi-observation.'[18]

The different models of our interior cinema have impinged with different force: Fludd is less well known than Descartes and Locke. Today, we are chiefly the inheritors of Shakespeare and the Romantics in their adaptations of the metaphor and their inquiries into imagination and dream states, which were richly inflected by classical philosophy. Samuel Taylor Coleridge famously distinguished between the lesser faculty of Fancy, as he called it, and Imagination, which he furthermore subdivided into two orders—primary and secondary. Profoundly influenced by his reading of Henry More, one of the 'Cambridge Platonists', on the one hand, and German Romantic metaphysics, on the other, Coleridge struggled in metaphysical coils in his notebooks, producing some famous, if cloudy definitions ('The primary IMAGINATION I hold to be the living Power and Agent of all human Perception'). The secondary was 'an echo of the former', but this lesser faculty was available to mortals, to poets and other artists, those 'Gods of Love who tame the Chaos'. Both orders formed for Coleridge 'that reconciling and mediating power, which incorporating the reason in images of the sense, gives birth to a system of symbols, harmonious in themselves and consubstantial with the truths of which they are the conductors'.[19] Coleridge's high claims for the imagination's power to generate the language of truth draw on Neoplatonist ideas, which have come into play again in contemporary discussion of the perceiver.

In France another poet, Charles Baudelaire, in his 1859 introduction to some of his translations of Edgar Allan Poe, drew an emphatic distinction between fantasy, sensitivity, and imagination, in order to give the last the palm as 'la reine des facultés', the queen of faculties. 'Imagination', he continued, 'is a quasi-divine faculty that above all perceives, outside philosophical methods, the intimate and secret relations between things, the correspondences and analogies.'[20] Fantasy, by contrast, was a poor thing, that struggled to link disparate elements without success.

The attempt to define fantasy in contrast to imagination often shows this kind of strain: lofty ideals are proclaimed on behalf of 'the queen of faculties', both aesthetically and morally, in order to distance it from troublingly low effects such as self-delusion and romancing. Thinkers of the Counter-Enlightenment stress the limitations of rational thought, and proclaim the values of fantasy in the search for truth while maintaining stout defences against superstition and crankery; when Goethe or Coleridge questioned the nature and purpose of the imagination, they were arguing with predecessors, for whom the issue was live.

Shakespeare's plays, above all, reveal vividly the painful perplexity that the status of fantasy and its products excited in the aftermath of the Reformation. The resemblance between witchcraft's summonings and phantoms in the mind's eye, and the difficulty over ascertaining origins, troubled many of his contemporaries; few showed Fludd's familiarity with the Other World as a penetrable and marvellous place, perfectly ordered by the creator. Around the same time as Shakespeare was writing *The Tempest*, Fludd shows far less anxiety than the playwright, who keeps revolving the question of magic and illusion, benign and malignant, in plays throughout his writing life in every one of the genres (history, tragedy, comedy, romance). Shakespeare worried at the issues of dream, fantasy, hallucination, enchanted simulations, and true visions in many of his plays. The insubstantial pageants of *The Tempest* occur with variations throughout his work, and they continue to shape our fantasies: in many ways our thoughts still find a local habitation and a name through Shakespearian imagery and argument. The next chapter will explore Shakespeare's castles in the air, his insubstantial pageants.

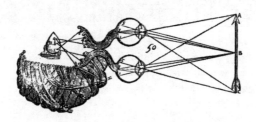

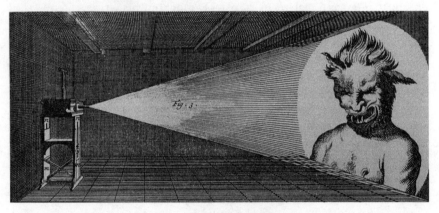

Pictures from the mind's eye: Robert Fludd's model of
the imagination, and a demonic apparition looms from
a magic lantern pictured in a Dutch mathematical
treatise, 1720–1.

10

Fancy's Images; Insubstantial Pageants

'tis the eye of childhood
That fears a painted devil . . .
Shakespeare, *Macbeth*, II. ii. 51–2

I. Painted Devils

When Macbeth quails from the visions brought to him by his inner demons,
Lady Macbeth taunts him, and dismisses his torments as fantasies; with
her image of painted devils, she shows her scorn for both the immaterial,
inward stuff that dreams are made on, and the material embodiment, made
by art.[1]

Both are figments, and she dismisses their power to issue warnings, calling
Macbeth 'brain-sickly' and a coward. In her scepticism and her chiding,
Lady Macbeth will be proved wrong-headed in this tragedy. But is she
adopting the view of a proto-rationalist, anticlerical, and enlightened philosopher when she deems the devil's illusions and such credulity childish?
She is declaring herself against images in the mind's eye, as they appear to
resemble pictures—implicitly, she is here rejecting the theory of the icon,
that an image partakes of the nature of its original. In so doing, she adopts,
interestingly enough, the more accepted cultural attitude to devils among a
London audience today, but not, it is likely, that of Jacobean England, where
image magic inspired real fear. Shakespeare shows her to be rash and proud
in her unbelief. Her hubris forms part of her transgressive unsexed desires,
which makes her place herself outside the limits of womanly as well as
creaturely humility.

Macbeth, interestingly, contains examples of both inner and outer vision:
both the male protagonist and Lady Macbeth are privately haunted by
their own, personal demons—the airy dagger, Banquo's ghost, the kings
stretching to the crack of doom—but in the play the oracular witches, who,
it is implied, have magicked themselves to their gathering, and will do so
again, are visible to everyone accompanying Macbeth.

In *Henry IV*, comparatively early in Shakespeare's dramatic career, the
challenge that Harry Hotspur issues to Owen Glendower casts doubts on

conjuring in a spirit of quick impatience: 'I can call spirits from the vasty deep,' boasts the Welsh magus; to which Harry replies, living up to his name:

> Why so can I, or so can any man,
> But will they come when you do call for them?
>
> *Henry IV*, III. i. 52–5

Shakespeare does not appear here to be disagreeing with the young hero.

But by *Macbeth* and the reign of James I, no such doubts are expressed; the poet now returning again and again to the status of the spirits who do come when they are bidden—and above all, when they are not. What is the status of Prospero's 'aery nothing'? Of his 'insubstantial pageants'? Like Paulina when she performs the resurrection of Hermione, Prospero acts like a conjuror in the double sense, a maker of magical illusions and an entertainer with magic.

This was treacherous terrain: Shakespeare saw the closing of the theatres, ostensibly on account of the plague, but the entertainment was also coming under attack from reforming zealots. Stagecraft was akin to magic, and warnings against its illusions rang throughout orthodox Christianity (for example, Celsus, an early scourge of credulity, vituperated belief in magicians 'who make things move as though they were alive although they are not really so, but only appear as such in the imagination').[2]

In some sense, devils cannot be otherwise than 'painted', in Lady Macbeth's scornful phrase, that is counterfeit, since they are mimics, not originals, and perform in disguise, and assume different forms—lovely temptresses, rich merchants—in order to beguile their victims.[3] The first performances of *Doctor Faustus* and of *Macbeth* may have used early magic lantern effects, projections on to smoke and through glass, to summon painted devils.[4] In Christopher Marlowe's *Doctor Faustus*, Faustus blazons the vision of Helen in celestial terms:

> Oh, thou art fairer than the evening air
> Clad in the beauty of a thousand stars;
> Brighter art thou than flaming Jupiter
> When he appear'd to hapless Semele;
> More lovely than the monarch of the sky
> In wanton Arethusa's azur'd arms.[5]

The comparisons here are featured not like a woman, but as vague, immense, dazzling portents—apparently flaring overhead, spread across the sky like a field of stars or the brightness of the planets and the Sun. Again, during his last despairing soliloquy, Faustus calls on Christ's mercy in visionary images that directly recall those signs and wonders in the heavens chronicled by Lycosthenes: 'See, see, where Christ's blood streams in the firmament!'[6]

Similarly, when Prospero talks of 'cloud capp'd towers', it is hard not to imagine stagecraft of an optical variety. Indeed, in his famous speech, he says, 'We are such stuff as dreams are made *on*,' and that 'on' suggests that dreams appear on something, perhaps on scrim as if on the internal screen of fantasy (*Tempest*, IV. i. 14 ff.).[7]

Theatre offers an analogy to the spectral conjurings of enchanters as well as to the phantasms of haunted minds. Its power to produce illusions lifts some of Shakespeare's most effective scenes to pure enchantment (indeed), as in Hermione's reawakening in *The Winter's Tale*. For in order to bring Hermione back into the unfolding story, Paulina demonstrates the power of illusion, as conveyed by stagecraft—that is, pretence. She performs equivalent arts of intervention, of painting, of performance, and in so doing, she appears to summon Hermione's eerie 'double'. The ambiguity about the status of 'image- or picture-flesh',[8] as in the case of a waxwork (as we saw), enhances the hallucinatory atmosphere of the play's closing scene. The paradoxes of ekphrasis—its material immateriality—relate to the illusions of presence in spectral conjuring.

Shakespeare plays with stagecraft, and then circles around theatre's powers of illusion, because, with his alertness to contemporary fears of witchcraft, he was all too aware of its connections with diabolical tricks and sorcery, and, within sorcery, with Catholic magic of transubstantiation, and to iconodulia, the forbidden worship of graven images. The condition of Shakespeare's apparitions is strictly uncanny: in Scottish demonology, the devil could conjure a spirit double, or fetch, sometimes called 'a reflex-man', a 'co-walker', and 'joint-eater'.[9] Like Helen of Troy, when she appears at the summoning of Mephistopheles in Marlowe's *Dr Faustus*, Banquo's ghost is both there and not there, Banquo but not Banquo, visible but not palpable.

Frank Kermode, in his edition of *The Tempest*, influentially distinguished between theurgy (good or natural magic) and goety (or sorcery)—the dark arts, and their foul deeds, called by the witch-hunters *maleficium*.[10] But, in *A Midsummer Night's Dream* and *The Tempest*, the two modes of supernatural manipulation are in practice confused, because the same persons perform both: Oberon and Prospero. Nor are ghosts and spectres raised only by adepts, sorcerers, or witches: Horatio recalls the portents that warned of Julius Caesar's death, after Hamlet's father has appeared to the watch, and that potent ghost of memory is seen—and debated—by several witnesses.

In *The Winter's Tale* Antigonus sets aside his scepticism about the truth of dreams, when visited by what he takes to be Hermione's ghost:

I have heard (but not believ'd) that the spirits of the dead
May walk again: if such thing be, thy mother
Appear'd to me last night; for ne'er was dream
So like a waking. . . .
                    In pure white robes,
Like very sanctity, she did approach . . .
                        . . . Affrighted much,
I did in time collect myself and thought
This was so, and no slumber. *Dreams are toys,*
Yet for this once, yea, superstitiously,
I will be squar'd by this.

The Winter's Tale, III. iii. 16–42; emphasis added

This ghost spouts tears and shrieks, and melts into air, a spectre from the underworld of Euripides and the Bible, after giving Antigonus fair warning of much of the later matter of the play; for, however closely Shakespeare presses sceptically on the question, an oracular time line and an atmosphere of spooky doings frequently add to the grip of the drama on the audience's imagination (in this case, Hermione herself, since she has not died, could have stolen in to visit Antigonus, but Shakespeare chooses the path of fancy and the supernatural).

Some of the same anxiety gathered around the nature of theatrical illusion as attended portents in the heavens and the spectacles conjured by *fata morgana*. A similar need to distinguish natural magic, the preternatural or even monstrous occurring in nature, from magic that is diabolical in origin, hung around the development of stagecraft.[11]

A further difficulty arises, however, that if Prospero and Ariel's spirit banquet arises from some wonderful properties of nature, not devilry, then the magic arts that conjure it become human powers; if human, are these materializations part of the natural world? In what sense can such wonderful and ephemeral materializations be in nature, unless materialism embraces a spiritual dimension, and a conjuror, such as Prospero, is breaking through the borders of the physical into the metaphysical? Shakespeare puzzles over the question of this border in his explorations of dreamed experiences; the immaterial materiality of dreams, their eidetic condition of being both real and not real, actual and not actual, there and not there, lived and not lived, offers an analogous zone to the natural magic that Prospero must command if he is not to be a diabolical sorcerer, like Medea. So, as Stuart Clark has deduced, the difference between natural and demonic magic resides ultimately in the character of the magician: hence the Church's—and the witch-hunters'—obsession with diagnosing the origin of the visionary's powers and the character of their faith, their morals, their life.[12]

Theatre realizes illusions, setting up a perceptual paradox about the play-world that cannot be resolved. The dramas that seem to resolve the problem of the supernatural, by breaking the spell and destroying, or at least limiting, the powers of ghosts and fairies, are the same plays in which Shakespeare meditates most obsessively on the debatable state of illusion itself and the power of fantasy. 'These are all actors,' Prospero tells his new son-in-law, Ferdinand, 'all spirits, and | Are melted into air, into thin air' (v. i. 149–50). The vision that Ferdinand has experienced since the ship-wreck stands on a 'baseless fabric'. The uncertainty this produces relates to the condition of the theatre itself, oscillating between event with con-sequences and an utterance or description as airy and ephemeral as the breath taken to speak. Shakespeare explores spoken language as event: he makes his poetry work to change experience: 'So long lives this, and this gives life to thee,' he concludes, sacramentally, at the end of the eighteenth sonnet.

In one of the crucial exchanges in Shakespeare's thinking about writing, Theseus and Hippolyta meditate on the interrelationship between fantasy and reality. When Theseus is discussing the lovers' madness, he comments, 'such tricks hath strong imagination. | How easy is a bush suppos'd a bear' (*A Midsummer Night's Dream*, v. i. 18, 22). His mind is still running on metamorphosis and illusion while watching the performance of 'Pyramus and Thisbe', when he says of the actors, 'The best in this kind are but shadows, and the worst are no worse, if imagination amend them' (v. i. 211–12). Fantasy supplies something more, when engaged with theatre, as it also does for dreamers and lovers—'imagination bodies forth | The forms of things unknown' (v. i. 14–15). This movement of the mind makes up for gaps and absence through invention. The poet's pen 'turns them to shapes'—that is to say, wields the magic power of metamorphosis and 'gives to aery nothing | A local habitation and a name' (v. i. 16–17). Hippolyta later counters the note of dismissal in this phrase 'aery nothing' when she rejoins with an awed quatrain:

> But all the story of the night told o'er
> And all their minds transfigured to together
> *More witnesseth than fancy's images*
> And grows to something of great constancy.
>
> *A Midsummer Night's Dream*, v. i; emphasis added

The convergence between the dream space of magical metamorphoses and the theatrical space of performance makes the one flow with and mingle into the other, both inside the plays and outside them. Inside the plays, Hamlet stages 'The Mouse Trap' to spring Claudius from his complacency—and succeeds. For Claudius, the events enacted on the stage prove too real to endure, and he calls for lights and storms out. The play that Hamlet has composed for the Players crosses the divide between insubstantial pageant and actual existence. So does Paulina's *coup de théâtre*. Life and art become mixed up: this is the dangerous magic of acted words; this is the basis for casting spells, as the weird sisters demonstrate with their oracles.

Magic is made by performative speech: its commands bring their contents into being, as in the priest officiating at a sacrament. 'With this ring I thee wed' accomplishes a marriage; Puck recites a love spell, as he administers the fatal juice dripped into her eyes, to make Titania fall in love with Bottom when she wakes. The words 'chant', 'incantation', 'cantrip' reveal the relationship of verbal music and song to spells and charm; such formulas do not record or describe, they produce events, they inaugurate change, they effect conversion and transformation. Then performative projection narrows the gap between act and illusion.

Shakespeare was puzzling over this all those years ago before the unconscious was discovered or cognitive psychologists pondered the structure of the visual cortex and attempted to analyse consciousness itself. More and more deeply entangled in the difficulties that the painted devils, fancy's images, and aery nothing of his own stagecraft raised for him, what can Shakespeare do, to elude the charge of conjuring in his own sense of himself and his own relation to spirit visions? The meshes of illusion's paradoxes set another, deeper snare. It is one that cannot be unsnarled here; for the question continues to hang, spectrally in thin air: how can language utter truth within the mendacious illusion of representation itself? It is not just the character of the visualization—the mental image—but the question around the origin of phantoms—that inclined the entertainments of early projection media to supernatural conjuring.

Curiosity and wonder bring into being a myriad devices that reveal worlds hidden from human eyes, to bring them closer and make them bigger, to penetrate to their innermost workings—the microscope, the telescope, and, later, X-rays and infra-red night sights. These instruments enhance the physical faculty of sight and expand human empirical under-standing. Optics developed tools that probed the unseen in an effort at rationality, and their use could be seen as a struggle to subdue the uncanny. But the character of the faculties involved was itself interwoven with imagery and symbolism, because the devices that amplified the mind's faculties were modelled on pre-existing ideas of the inner eye, the organ of envisioning, and they also reproduced mental imagery, and projected phantasms, dreams, and memories from the dark chamber of the mind into the light of day. Because it is a metaphor we have lived by, the inward eye has also proved a practical stimulus to technological invention, and, eventually, to optical media like the cinema, which reproduces the mind's capacity to form images with eyes closed, or with eyes open in the absence of empirical data of any kind.

II. The Enchantments of Athanasius Kircher

When Athanasius Kircher began experimenting with magic lantern slides and projecting them in Rome in the 1640s, a generation after Shakespeare's later plays, he chose fantastical and supernatural subjects, such as a soul in Purgatory (Figure 2, p. 8). After the telescope and the microscope, bold optical technologies turned to communicating the inner workings of the mind, not retinal pictures or observations of the world.

It is not known who invented the magic lantern, and for a long time Kircher was credited with its invention. He never made this claim, though, and many scientists and entertainers were involved in its development, including the brilliant Dutch horologist and astronomer Christiaan Huygens (1629–95). There are traces of its use in the Middle Ages, and by the mid-seventeenth century, a Danish magician, Thomas Walgenstein (1627–81), was touring and selling the equipment.[13] But the most vivid reports come from the experiments of Kircher at the Jesuit College where he lived and worked, and where he deployed smoking lamps, compound crystals, and various lenses and slides. He illuminated the inside of his projector, sometimes even introducing gems to refract the rays and casting coloured beams—to imitate divine light. He prepared glass slides with salts and chemicals which he had brought from Sicily and then heated up in the projector, then sprinkled with water to produce reactions, so that the colours playing on the wall changed. Kircher wrote: 'We in our college are accustomed to show in a dark chamber a large number of sufficiently bright and luminous pictures, to the greatest wonder of the spectators. The show is most worthy to see . . .'[14]

Kircher uses the phrase 'camera obscura', which might lead to confusion, as this term more properly describes the much more ancient method used to obtain a familiar, fascinating illusion, one that does not involve manufactured images at all—no 'painted devils', but only the light of day: through a pinhole pricked in the wall of a sealed darkened room, the 'real' image of the outside world will appear reflected upside down opposite the aperture, cast by the rays of the Sun moving in straight lines through the pinhole. The ancient Greeks, the Chinese, and the Japanese knew the phenomenon, and before the invention of the telescope, the astronomer Johannes Kepler used such a dark chamber in order to observe the spots on the Sun.

Magic lanterns imitated its powers of illusion, and in this sense, became the forerunners of entertainment media based on image projections, including the cinema. Camera obscuras were equipped with lenses in the pinhole, to focus the image, so the magic lantern Kircher was developing as an instrument of optical enchantments was the more ancient device's descendant; but he was not bringing the light from outside into the theatre, but creating his own illusions.

His *magnum opus* on optics, reflection, refraction, projection, and other possibilities of light, the *Ars magna lucis et umbrae*, includes many diagrams illustrating refraction, parataxis, reflection, and other optical effects, but the physics handled by this Jesuit magus has a pronounced allegorical tendency, and light and shadow resonate with all their moral and mystical meanings, as in that title-page engraving in which the divine rays of sunlight bounce off a mirror held by a personified figure of Shadow; they pierce through the roof of the cave on this Shadow side, and, as in Kepler's observatory, illuminate the dark. The blank surface of a mirror, the tool of shadow and enigma ('now I see through a glass darkly'), is a key instrument in Kircher's system of visual revelations. This image condenses brilliantly the mystical Neoplatonism of Jesuit Rome in the seventeenth century with the discoveries of the New Science. In the clouds, a sun god who bears the symbols of Jupiter also resembles the Christian Redeemer; he shoots his rays into a cave of shadows, where a mirror catches the beam and directs its light back through a lens towards the source. Plato's shadows in the cave flicker beneath the metaphor organizing this mental landscape. But Kircher does not appear to be lamenting this world below as a mere shadow: his optics celebrate the paradoxical illumination of darkness and the symbiosis of light and shade, casting Night as Juno consort of Jupiter, as the Moon to his Sun, also receiving his rays and returning them to the material realm below in a ray of light. Here God himself, seated in the sphere of Jupiter, the fiery empyrean, as the embodiment and source of all light, becomes the source of imagination's products, or of mental images of phenomena that cannot be seen with bodily eyes. Kircher does not even brush ethical matters or press darkness into service as the disguise of sin; instead, he uses optics to probe consciousness, and equates darkness with the mind's mysterious propensities to dream, to fantasticate, to see the invisible. Several of his most mathematical calculations of angles and distortions are illustrated with the figure of a devil, as if he were the natural projection of such optical wizardry.

In the second edition (1671), magic lanterns make an appearance in the book's remarkable illustrations—the earliest engravings of the instrument in action. The images have a striking feature in common: the projections are almost always supernatural creatures, with looming devils and dancing skeletons predominating. Such supernatural subject-matter was chosen, as if it went without saying, to illustrate the powers of the new machines of illusion. The subjects are fantastic: they cannot be seen with the eye of the body, except in representations by artists, and they give that *frisson* of the grotesque, designed to excite fear as well as pleasure. These are images that connote the visions of the mind's eye, and in order to do so, they draw on a supernatural lexicon. They depict beliefs about the supernatural—or what could be called hallucinations.

These illustrations of magic lantern images reveal an intrinsic, unexamined equivalence between the technology of illusion and supernatural phenomena: Kircher projected souls in hell, leering devils, the resurrection of Christ, and other products of imagination, not observation. There were antecedents for the magic lantern's diabolism: a medieval device to capture the flickering elusiveness of spirit visions—or demonic illusions.[15] Following Henry More's seventeenth-century coinage, it is possible to say that the paradox of darkness visible illuminates the peculiar icasms that are thought to belong to the mind's eye.

But it is hardly an accident that a naked soul burning in the flames of hell or purgatory, or Death as an animated skeleton with the scythe of the reaper and the hour-glass of Father Time should appear projected on to the wall (see Figure 2, p. 8).[16] Kircher was not alone in finding such scenes suited to the novel medium: a book published in Leiden in 1720–1 illustrates another early slide projector, and despite the learned and scientific title of the mathematical treatise in which it appears, it shows a huge, magnificent devil leering on the wall (see Figure 12b, p. 130).[17] The device thus reproduces the mind's capacity to fabricate in the mind's eye what the faculty of sight cannot see.

Athanasius Kircher's seances at the Jesuit College in Rome were attended by cardinals and grandees from all over the world, who gathered to witness 'what [were] known, in jest', writes his fellow Jesuit Giardina defensively, 'as the enchantments of the reverend father'.[18] But the later Jesuit's uneasiness is well grounded, for Kircher significantly chose to project supernatural images, and in this, he comes perilously close to the goety, or black magic, denounced by the Inquisition in his own time. One treatise published in 1641, during Kircher's heyday, gives a full inventory of the disruption and mayhem that the rebel angels create. In the midst of this terrifying and overheated litany of evil and catastrophe, the inquisitor instances metamorphoses of animal and human bodies. But these are not changed in their substance, 'sed aliam ex vaporibus extrinsecus circumponendo' ('but only by *investing them in another aspect, composed of extrinsic vapours*'; emphasis added).[19]

Kircher discusses many varieties of illusion in the second book of *Ars*

Magna, including *fata morgana*, as we saw, in order to demonstrate how many illusions arise as natural consequences of the properties of things. The play of sunlight on clouds or in mirrors produces unexpected wonders, including visions. His thinking continually collapses the imponderable—fantasy—with the physical conditions that obtain, and so his study of physical laws and of optics leads him to explore what he calls 'the radiation of the imagination'—the way the imagination forms objects where they do not exist and can shape and alter experience phantasmagorically. 'The efficient cause of such phenomena', he writes, is 'the material radiation of phantasy, apprehending external things through vehement imagination.' He discusses maternal impression, the idea then current that the mother's mental experiences can affect the development of a foetus: in the most coarse terms, that an expectant woman, startled by a goose or a horse, might imprint the creature's features on her child. He realizes that it has no basis in physiology. But he argues differently with regard to psychology.[20]

In the case of a man in the grip of melancholy, Kircher explains how this black stuff of the melancholic humour 'acts as a kind of mirror', a surface on which impressions are reflected—and transformed. Kircher develops specific metaphors for this operation of fantasy, and they will prove key images in later concepts of imagination: the dark chamber in which phantasms materialize, and the mirror of the mind which reflects them. 'Thus, as external colours', he writes, 'transmitted through a pierced aperture into the darkness, acquire an external existence, so extrinsic things, transmitted by a strong and vehement understanding . . . into the nebulous and vaporous medium of the brain . . . move the fantasy according to what they relate.' 'Melancholia', he continues, 'cooked by long meditation of the seething mind, and brought into the brain and adhering there, obstinately, pertinaciously, as in a mirror, reflects back the things brought to the fantasy, while the intellect and the dominion of reason are meanwhile bound by the turbulence and filth and dullness of the spirits.'[21] (Kircher was not alone in his time in linking the imagination's capacities with mental illness; Thomas Hobbes in *Leviathan* also attributes 'dreams and apparitions' to 'the distemper of some of the inward parts of the Body'.)[22]

In this account of the phantasmic powers of imagination, Kircher explores optical metaphors—a screen, a pinhole camera obscura—and then two dependent metaphors: first, the blackened surface of a mirror, and secondly, the smoky and boiling vapours in the brain of a person afflicted with melancholy. He borrowed the image of the mirror from optics, and the image of the inchoate and turbulent spirits from explanations of cosmic origin in hermetic physics, as represented in Fludd's work; it is not clear how metaphorically he intends their application to the mind.

Kircher then turns anecdotal, and instances the case of a man who suffered from the melancholy delusion that he had grown a pair of stag's horns. A doctor was able to cure him, Kircher tells us, by believing his story, and taking a knife and operating on the horns in a serious pantomime of make-believe: 'The horns cut away', writes Kircher, 'had the power at once to free the man from his madness.' To demonstrate the potency of the imagination, Kircher also set up a wonderful experiment (*mirabile experimentum*), using as his subject a hen (Figure 12c, p. 143). Even in birds of little brain, the shaping precedence of imagination over experience can be shown, he maintains. He proposed: 'Take a hen and tie her feet together and lay her down on the floor and hold her until she stops fluttering in protest; then loose her bonds, but draw, on the floor beside her, a picture of the cords that tied her.' 'The hen', Kircher declares, 'will lie quietly, utterly persuaded that she is still tied fast by the mere illusion of the cord, even if you attempt to stimulate her to fly away.'[23]

As in Fludd's model, the imagination is an active agent, with strong— indeed, even autonomous and ungovernable—powers not only to shape the fantastic lineaments of objects as they appear on the screen of the inner eye but also to change the person's own perception of self. Athanasius Kircher nevertheless concludes his speculations with a severe warning, founded in orthodox Christian teaching, that the soul cannot wander abroad on its own or leave a dreamer at night, nor can the imagination change the actual condition of matter; imagination is homeopathic, it works only on its like, on imagination itself, producing fantasy, not reality—he thus issues a palinode, denying the phenomenon of maternal impression except as a delusion.

To express the insubstantial pageants of the mind's eye, the novel device of projecting images, the camera obscura, lent itself as a rich metaphor of consciousness, transforming Plato's shadowy cave into a modern instrument. Leibniz imagined the human being as a house with the lower souls, animal and sensitive, in the downstairs rooms, and upstairs, the 'reasonable soul', as he called the thinking mind of a subject. Then, surprisingly, he embarks on a fully extended image of the curtained alcove of a camera obscura: 'It is the upper floor that has no windows,' writes Gilles Deleuze in his account of Leibniz's thought. 'It is a dark room or chamber decorated only with a stretched canvas "diversified by folds" as if it were a living dermis.' This skin, placed in the 'blind, closed' upper floor, vibrates with sounds emanating from below, as from a musical salon in Leibniz's simile, rather than images.[24] But it is nevertheless striking how for both Descartes and Leibniz, obscurity is necessary for conscious illumination.

The materials of the imaginative soul—the play of shadows, the opaque surface of a mirror, and vaporous swirling clouds—these three media for producing and rendering the operations of fantasy—return as palpable, physical instruments of projection in the first cinematic public entertainments, which happened to huge popular excitement 150 years after Kircher's magic lantern shows, and came to be known as the phantasmagoria (see next chapter).

The associations that Kircher made between the workings of the imagination and the possibilities of shadow play, between the disturbed mind and the bilious turbulence of the melancholic temperament, characterize the black box or dark chamber in which the images were conjured. Unspoken, unexamined associations coupled the new medium with the imaginary chamber in which the mind plays its own theatre, be they fantasized or recalled through memory. This equivalence, between the phantoms that a burning lamp, a series of mirrors and lenses, and a painted transparency can conjure up and the projections of the imagination, recurs in the development of optical devices that culminate in the cinema and in conventions of contemporary media (voice-overs, flashbacks, and dream sequences) and, eventually, the fantastic dimensions of virtual reality created by computer graphics. The creators of magic lantern shows chose scenes from myths and legends, and above all from their enactment in romances in the theatre, and from other performance arts (pantomime, ballet, opera), because the affinity between apparitions and projections was so patently close.

This novel instrument, which reproduced externally the internal visions of the mind, often excited thoughts of unruliness and gratification, pleasure and sin: such visions unsettlingly mimicked the devil's powers to conjure, and indeed scenes from Marlowe's *Dr Faustus*, where Mephistopheles brings forth the pageant of the Seven Deadly Sins, and then, famously, Helen of Troy, feature among popular topics of the magic lanternists. The pioneer Samuel Johannes Rhanaeus listed the slides he had made and used in his book of 1713. They included personifications of the three main vices of mankind rising out of hell as out of the underworld. A witness at the public spectacles later reported, 'when the projectionist decides, [they] return[ing] to their home while hell remains unmoved'[25]—as they do in *Doctor Faustus*. Portents and devils were the most popular figures: apocalyptic beasts rose from painted seas, and demons in hell administered 'satanic enemas' by means of clysters and bellows. William Hone, in *Ancient Mysteries Described* (1823) was struck by the return of dark jokes taken from medieval mystery plays, about devilish doings and divine retribution, as in 'Pull Devil, Pull Baker', about a baker who cheated and was taken to hell in his own basket. The earliest modern urban spectacles to win huge audiences quickly expanded their powers of illusion to please the growing public; interior obscurity begs rhyming subject-matter, it seems: infernal, ghastly, grotesque scenes, a supernatural full of eschatological menace. No snowdrops or daisies or daffodils, no sparkling seashores or sublime sunsets, no heroic long-legged horsemen or smiling full-lipped siren faces among the predecessors of cinema and other entertaining powers of illusion. The new instruments reproduced the perceived activity of the imagination itself; by imitating the motion of the spirit within, they cast on to the screen fantastic pictures of the supernatural.

Part V
Shadow

FANTASMAGORIE

DE ROBERT-SON,

Rue des Petits Champs, Cour des Capucines,
vis-à-vis la Place Vendôme.

APPARITIONS de spectres, fantômes et revenans tels qu'ils ont dû et pû apparoître dans tous les tems, dans tous les lieux et chez tous les peuples.

EXPÉRIENCES sur le fluide Galvanique, dont l'application rend non seulement le mouvement, mais encore les habitudes aux corps privés de la vie depuis plusieurs jours.

La salle où se réunit le public, en attendant les experiences de la Fantasmagorie, offre tous les prestiges de l'Optique imaginés jusqu'à présent pour tromper les yeux. Le spectateur voit successivement passer sous ses yeux, les lieux où se sont faites les apparitions chez les anciens.

On y entend l'Harmonica de Franklin, cet instrument précieux est touché par le premier virtuose de Paris.

L. séance a lieu tous les jours à 7 heures, Cour des Capucines.

The Phantasmagoria, spectacularly staged by Etienne-Gaspard Robertson in a disused convent in Paris in the aftermath of the Terror, became the earliest public entertainment in Gothic horror.

II

Darkness Visible: The Phantasmagoria

> All those large dreams by which men long live well
> Are magic-lanterned on the smoke of hell;
> This then is real, I have implied
> A painted, small, transparent slide.
>
> William Empson

In Paris soon after the Revolution, the showman and inventor Etienne-Gaspard Robertson staged a *son-et-lumière* Gothic moving picture show, under the name of 'Fantasmagorie'; coined from Greek, *phantasmagoria* means an 'assembly of phantasms'. Robertson used a projector, the Fantascope, dispensed with the conventional theatre's raised stage, the puppet show box, and the proscenium arch, and concentrated his lighting sources and effects in the projector itself by placing it behind a large flat screen like a theatrical scrim. He also mounted his newfangled magic lantern on rollers, so that when, concealed behind the screen, he pulled back from the audience, the image swelled and appeared to lunge forward into their ranks (see Figure 12b, p. 130). With a true impresario's flair for catching the mood of the public, Robertson deliberately excited screams and squeals. He—and his contemporary rivals and imitators—set the scene for the coming of the horror video, its ghouls, ghosts, and vampire-infested suburbs. The recent Terror furnished him with the inspiration for some deadly special effects: the severed head of Danton, adapted from his death mask, was projected on to smoke, and then gradually faded away, changing into a skull as did so. The show was even closed down by the police for a spell because the fear spread that Robertson could bring Louis XVI back to life.[1]

The phantasmagoria derived directly from the camera obscura and magic lantern shows, and many displays had been staged before Robertson's struck a chord with the public; but Robertson's Gothic horror spectacular, and its many brilliant twists and devices, turned any spectator from a cool observer into a willing, excitable victim. Whereas the dioramas and panoramas concentrated on battles, modern cityscapes, or exotic scenery, customs, and people—they are the forerunners of the wide-screen epic film—the phantasmagoria shadows forth great silent movies like F. W. Murnau's vampire movie *Nosferatu* (1919) and Robert Wiene's *The Cabinet of Dr*

Caligari (1919). The uncanny took a turn away from external, supernatural, and mysterious causes of fear and trembling, earthed to a common religious faith, and began to inhabit instead unstable, internal hallucinations, seething with personal, idiosyncratic monsters extruded from the overheated brain by the force of vehement imagination, or, as Goya would famously write on the opening *Capricho*, with monsters generated by the dream of reason.[2]

The intrinsic subject-matter of phantasmagoria turned to spectral illusion, morbid, frequently macabre, supernatural, fit to inspire terror and dread, those qualities of the sublime. It foreshadows the function of cinema as stimulant, and prepared the ground for the medium's entanglement with hauntings, possession, and spirit visions. Above all, phantasmagorias gave an impression of vitality far more beguiling than even the miniaturized intricacies of panoramas and peepshows; magic lantern slides, pricked trans-parencies, and other illusions flickered and fluttered in the candlelight, and conveyed a feeling of time passing—the daylight castle changed into a haunted ruin by the snuffing of a lamp—but the images projected by phantasmagorias swelled and shrunk, as well as shifting with tricks of the light, and so created an illusion that they possessed that quality of conscious life: animation.[3]

Robertson was born in 1763 in Liège, Belgium, and became a keen balloonist as well as a pioneering impresario. He refined many features of the popular magic lantern show when he used an Argand oil lamp for the first time; being so much brighter than candles, it allowed him to put on public shows to a crowded hall; in this way, he shifted the shared passion for religious festivals towards mass entertainment, and demonstrated the huge power of such spectacles and illusions over crowds. As well as moving the projector, he experimented with arrangements of lenses, and the play of shadows and the superimposition of one picture upon another to create certain special effects: ghosts rolling their eyes, the flickering flames of hell, a ghostly dance of witches. He introduced Benjamin Franklin's glass harmonica to create appropriately eerie and fairyland accompaniment, as well as a Chinese gong, which he struck at climactic moments. The apparition of a horrifying Medusa head, for example (a painted slide survives), wittily reproduced the petrifying effect of his spectacle on his audience. Robertson also realized that if the images were painted on black backgrounds, they would appear to float free in space. His screens were thin gauzes, saturated in wax, so that his phantoms were further dematerialized by the diaphanousness and translucency of the material on which they appeared. He was a skilful and sensitive painter as well, or employed artists who could interpret his ideas. Sometimes, he projected on to smoke.

For his most successful seances, Robertson rented an abandoned Gothic convent—the Couvent des Capucines—and dressed it in antique bric-à-brac and black drapes, painted it with hieroglyphs which, he wrote, seemed 'to announce the entrance to the mysteries of Isis', lit it weakly with 'a sepulchral lamp', and maintained before the spectacle began 'an absolute silence'. The show began with a speech: 'Citizens and gentlemen,' he declared, 'It is . . . a useful spectacle for a man to discover the bizarre effects of the imagination when it combines force and disorder; I wish to speak of the terror which shadows, symbols, spells, the occult works of magic inspire.' He then ended with a flourish: 'I have promised that I will raise the dead and I will raise them.'[4]

Teeming with devils, ghosts, witches, succubi, skeletons, mad women in white, bleeding nuns, and what he termed 'ambulant phantoms', Robertson's icastic repertoire offers a vivid census of the population deemed native to the imagination (Figure 13, p. 146). His sources reached back into pagan and heterodox mythologies of metamorphosis and metempsychosis, as well as contemporary sublime Gothic motifs. He showed the shades of the dead in the underworld, with Proserpina and Pluto presiding as judges, Orpheus losing Eurydice, Venus seducing a hermit, and the story of Cupid. Christianity supplied him with subject-matter of the forbidden and the transgressive, too: the temptation of St Antony by alluring hoydens, witches preparing for the Sabbath and flying off on broomsticks, while the Moon turned the colour of blood. One slide even depicted 'Mahomet', inscribed with the surprising words 'Pleasure is my Law'.

'The Bleeding Nuns', Death with his scythe, the 'Red Woman', as well as various recent agents and victims of the Terror—Robertson's characters rush at the spectators from the screen as if to grab them; Banquo's ghost and the three witches were summoned, among figures from contemporary artists like Henri Fuseli who had illustrated Shakespeare. 'The Dream or the Nightmare—A young woman dreams of fantastic pictures'—a tableau that owes a clear debt to Fuseli's famous painting—was provided by Robertson with a happy ending: the demon of jealousy first crushed her breast with an anvil, held a dagger over her heart, while above a hand of fate cut a cord with a pair of scissors. 'But Love then arrives and cures the wounds with rose leaves.'[5]

In his engaging memoirs, Robertson described his early attempts to conjure devils for real. After these failed, he wrote: 'I finally adopted a very wise policy: since the devil refused to communicate to me the science of creating prodigies, I would apply myself to creating devils, and I would have only to wave my wand, to force all the infernal cortège to be seen in the light. My habitation became a true *Pandemonium*.'[6]

The effect on the public of such spectacles was dramatic, and anticipates very closely the excitement—and panic—that greeted the first screenings of films proper, as in the famous case of the Lumière Brothers' advancing train. Robertson's spectacular assaults on his suggestible audience can be gauged from contemporaneous engravings: the phantoms loomed large and close, and swelled as the projectionist suddenly pulled the projector back from the screen, or manifested themselves wreathed in smoke and floating on clouds or even, as in the case of Death with his scythe, appeared to lunge head first, scythe at the ready, into the throng.

The phantasmagoria spread through Europe with travelling entertainers—or galanty men, named after the many Italians who toured(!). But when it adapted conventional imagery of spirits, it did so with a difference: it turned such scenes—and attendant beliefs—into secular entertainment.

One Londoner gave a lively account of 'The Red Woman of Berlin', who was summoned at the climax of the show put on by Paul de Philipsthal, known as Philidor, in 1825:

The effect was electrical, and scarcely not be imagined from the effect of a written description. I was myself one of an audience during the first week of its exhibition, when the hysterical scream of a few ladies in the first seats of the pit induced a cry of 'lights' from their immediate friends, which it not being possible *instantly* to comply with, increased into an universal panic, in which the male portion of the audience, who were ludicrously the most vociferous, were actually commencing a scrambling rush to reach the doors of the exit, when the operator, either not understanding the meaning of the cry, or mistaking the temper and feeling of an English audience, at this unlucky crisis once more dashed forward the *Red Woman*. The confusion was instantly at a height which was alarming to the stoutest; the indiscriminate rush to the doors was prevented only by the deplorable state of most of the ladies; the stage was scaled by an adventurous few, the *Red Woman*'s sanctuary violated, the unlucky operator's cavern of death profaned, and some of his machinery overturned, before light restored order and something like an harmonious understanding with the cause of alarm.[7]

Robertson, Philidor, and other lanternists toured during a period of brilliant innovation, when the latest scientific discoveries fuelled the business of amusing a public which was growing increasingly affluent and pleasure-loving. In an era of expanding urban pleasures, when waxworks were also transferred from the religious to the secular realm, and the diorama opened in Paris, the panorama was invented in Edinburgh by the Irish painter Robert Barker in 1785, giving a 360-degree command of the field of vision. Barker's view of the city was the first example of this particular optical device, and it inspired feats of heroic illusionism.[8] In 1821, for example, the Hull-born artist Thomas Hornor climbed to the apex of the cross on the pinnacle that crowns the Dome of St Paul's Cathedral, in London, and there he built himself a crow's-nest, a fantastic platform of lashed timbers with a cabin secured to it by overhead ropes, themselves tied to a tepee-like superstructure, and from this, where he lived for the time it took, he made a 360-degree picture of the city from above. He used a telescope to examine details, and calculated the perspective not only to unfold the vista on the curved walls of the panorama, but to position the viewer convincingly in the scene.[9]

This feat brings up the distinction between the sight and its image, for by this prodigious feat of daring, engineering, and survival, Hornor did indeed command a stable view of London unobtainable from the first Montgolfier balloons or, later, aeroplane; so his Olympian vantage-point did not unfold an illusion. The crow's-nest, the telescope, the geometry, enhanced the field of vision that lay around him. But the picture he made turned his experience into a rich illusion for his audience later, who flocked to this truly popular, classless wonder of Victorian ingenuity. Eighteenth- and nineteenth-century artist-showmen, like Robertson and Hornor, were moving on all fronts to expand the knowledge and scope of human faculties; with waxworks, they took spectators into anatomical theatres, to banquets in palaces, and to thrill at clandestine deeds of darkness; with models of the world, such as Hornor's *Panorama* or Wyld's *Monster Globe*, a relief map installed in a special rotunda in Leicester Square, where it drew vast crowds from 1851 until it was demolished in 1862, they opened up vistas of trade, discovery, and adventure. A great staircase led up to viewing platforms for the map's surface inside the sphere—the world was mapped on the inside, turned inside out to fit the convexity of the building.

The image produced by a pinhole aperture, also called 'camera obscura', had been applied principally for research purposes, as we saw: for examining sun spots, for example. But again, this illusion was transformed into spectacle, into a modern 'leisure activity': in mid-century Edinburgh, Maria Short, the daughter of an eye doctor, erected on Castle Hill the city's celebrated camera obscura, which captures moving scenes of the streets below, projected by light rays alone on a convex dish, and miniaturized. There the buildings materialize in every detail; tiny figures scurry, tiny buses grind silently over the cobbles. Still an astonishing effect, it brings into being, with no more magic than a series of angled lenses, ancient dreams of summoning absent sights—in the fairy-tale of 'Beauty and the Beast', for example, Beauty possesses a magic mirror in which she can see far beyond the Beast's ramparts, as far away as her own home where her father lies dying.

These early enterprises of optical researchers and instrument-makers and their users aimed at enhancing visual experience of the world as it offers itself to human eyes. But, as with Athanasius Kircher's magic slide shows, these spectacular entertainments often played into the second enterprise—expressing fantasy and communicating inward vision—wittingly or unwittingly. Haunted modernity was made by optics: Robertson's key predecessor in the enterprise is the artist-designer Philippe Jacques de Loutherbourg (1740–1812), the French-born Romantic painter who worked in England, and brought a Turneresque dedication to shipwrecks, waterspouts, and other storm-tossed scenes. He was a vigorous impresario of spectacular theatre over a very long London career, and a pioneer of animation techniques, a veritable model of Hoffman's figure of Dr Coppelius, the automatist.

In extravaganzas staged at Drury Lane, Loutherbourg plunged the audience into darkness for the first time, to intensify the impact of his spectacular magic shows, such as *A Christmas Tale* (1772), and later, the patriotic pageant *Omai*. He projected painted lantern slides in his productions, and in 1781 invented the 'Eidophusicon', which drew delighted crowds to see 'Various Imitations of Natural Phenomena, represented by Moving Pictures'.[10] A stage set furnished by banks of rollers turned by many hands, and numerous light sources, prickings, and cut-outs, raked the scene with shadows and dappled it with moiré effects and dancing firelight to show London bursting into flames in a tableau of the Great Fire, and to conjure Milton's 'darkness visible', with Satan and his minions 'on the Banks of the Fiery Lake' in the pit of hell.[11] At the end of his life, Loutherbourg acquired an extremely wealthy patron, the young aesthete William Beckford, and was commissioned by him to stage his notorious Christmas revels at Fonthill in 1782. Beckford later recalled

that strange, necromantic light which Loutherbourg had thrown over what absolutely appeared a realm of Fairy, or rather, perhaps, a Demon Temple deep beneath the earth set apart for tremendous mysteries . . . The glorious haze investing every object, the mystic look, the vastness, the intricacy of the vaulted labyrinth occasioned so bewildering an effect that it became impossible for anyone to define at the moment, where he stood, where he had been, or to whether he was wandering.[12]

The appetite for enchantments led far more sober characters than Beckford to create fantastic devices: the Scottish scientist David Brewster, friend of Walter Scott, invented the kaleidoscope (1819), which he named after the Greek word for beautiful. He also analysed binocularity, establishing its importance to human perception of depth, and accordingly applied it to another ingenious design—the stereopticon. It too became a hugely popular toy of the Victorian middle class, and helped popularize photography in the home.

Brewster was curious about legends of fairies, wonders, and superstitions, and collected examples in an anthropological spirit, publishing in 1832 an important series of public letters to Scott, engaging that great exponent of ballads and fairy-tales in a rational discussion of the supernatural. In these Brewster sets out, among other things, the double mirror trick later dubbed 'Dr Pepper's Ghost': by angling panes of glass under and above the stage, a spectre can be beamed to hover in the air as large as life.

David Brewster also attended phantasmagorias and gave highly detailed descriptions of the moving eyes and lips of the spectres, of the dissolves, fades, and other proto-cinematic effects; eyes rolling in an effigy's head gave the eerie impression that the head was turning with the gaze.[13]

Lewis Carroll, who was an indefatigable theatre-goer with a special taste for pantomime and spectacle, also dabbled in inventions, and was later inspired by these optical illusions to stage the transformation of the baby into a pig and the apparition of the Cheshire Cat. Alice protests:

'. . . I wish you wouldn't keep appearing and vanishing so suddenly: you make me feel quite giddy!'

'All right,' said the Cat; and this time it vanished quite slowly, beginning with the end of the tail, and ending with the grin, which remained some time after the rest of it had gone.[14]

With dissolves and fades and metamorphoses of this sort, Carroll the photographer introduced cinematic techniques into storytelling.

The characteristic material of the phantasmagoria thus occupies a transitional zone between the sublime and the Gothic, between the solemn and the comic, and between seriously intended fears and sly mockery of such beliefs. Although it bears a sharp flavour of its times, its aftertaste lingers, as mentioned earlier, in much of today's popular entertainment, with its cast of spectres and bogeys. Yet Robertson protested that his 'illusions were designed as an antidote to superstition and credulity', and claimed that he was staging a rational exhibition in order to expose the mechanism behind such spectres of the mind.[15] Hence the pseudo-learning displayed in the names of optical devices: Robertson's imitators and followers among showmen drew heavily on Greek terms to coin high-sounding words— 'Eidophysicon', 'Eidothaumata', 'Ergascopia', and 'Phantascopia'—to describe their instruments of uncanny illusion.

Philidor, the lanternist, also toured to great success all over Europe from 1801 onwards, becoming a friend of Madame Tussaud's. The Scottish writer James Hogg may have been present at his show in Edinburgh.[16] *The Private Confessions* certainly conjures the hauntings and doublings of the protagonists through optical metaphors that evoke the dark and looming shadow play of the phantasmagoria.[17] Meanwhile, the vogue for magic lantern shows grew strongly throughout Europe and the United States, where several showmen, including Robertson's sons as well as former assistants, enjoyed wide popular success from 1803 to around 1825 with their displays of optical illusions, ghosts, giants, and various apparitions. The sur-viving materials from this early cinema include exquisitely painted Gothic scenes, on two or sometimes three overlapping glass laminae, so that when the moon became overcast, lights came on in a turreted castle, and a phantom would appear on the battlements. The effects of gloom are in fact inkier than a slide projector can achieve, and certainly richer in depths than computer imaging.

James Hogg's demonic *alter ego* consciously harks back to Marlowe's Mephistopheles, and the conjurations of spectres and delusions in the novel also echo the damned enchantments of that play. Faust was a popular subject for phantasmagoria and magic shows, and when Goethe's version was per-formed, first in part in 1812, and then, in the first full production, in 1829 at Weimar, Goethe expressed special interest in conjuring effects with a magic lantern, and proposed that the Earth Spirit should appear in Faust's study like the dazzling microcosm (pentagram) in Rembrandt's engraving of the scholar in his study. Goethe made a sketch in which the portent was even more colossal. In 1812, he was frustrated in his plans, writing, 'How one might, perhaps with flaming hair and beard, to some extent approach the modern idea of the supernatural, on this we had come to no agreement.'[18] But a decade later, Goethe invoked the phantasmagoria as the model to be followed: 'that is, in a darkened theatre an illuminated head is projected from the rear upon a screen stretched across the background, first as a small image, then gradually increasing in size, so that it seems to be coming closer and closer. This artistic illusion was apparently conjured with a kind of *Lanterna Magica*. Could you please find out, as soon as possible, who constructs such an apparatus, how could WE obtain it, and what preparations must be made for it?'[19] Goethe made more drawings, suggesting that the devil's initial appearance in the form of a poodle and the vision of Helen of Troy should also be patterned on optical illusions, with two-way mirrors and changing lighting bringing her image suddenly into focus in the glass. For the spectacular staging of *Faust* put on in London in 1824, Mephistopheles carried Faustus through the air by means of a reflection projected into the air on the lines devised by Brewster and adapted, in the highly popular stage illusion, by Pepper's Ghost trick (or so the historian Frederick Burwick has deduced).[20]

This production of *Faust* in 1828 took place eleven years before Daguerre announced his fleeting silvered wraiths, but it announces vividly the possibilities that photographic projections would explore, that a fugitive moment could be stilled and the animated motion of living things captured, and both be repeated over and over. (Chapters 13 and 14 explore the seduc-tion and the menace of reflection as the prime vehicle of eerie presences and spectral doubles). Even supposedly natural wonders, rather than infernal hallucinations, take on a fantastic, haunted appearance in surviving Victorian magic lantern slides: icebergs, crags, volcanoes, geysers, alpine ranges loom and glow in the cabinets of the travelling showmen.[21] The linguistic and visual imagery that the new model applied, however, was very ancient: phantasmagorists were populating their entertainments from the baggage of past beliefs, and conjugating a series of symbolic equivalences between imagination and shadow play, mystery and darkness, suggestiveness and fear, evanescence and smoke that have their origins in Neoplatonism and its play with the metaphor of shadows.

The Royal Polytechnic Institute opened in London in 1838 to exhibit the latest technical inventions, and the magic lantern shows held there until 1876 enthralled a public with painted slides, dissolving views, iris lens effects, and kaleidoscopic fantasies; they also projected stories that drew on popular fairy stories, cautionary tales, old jokes, ghostly apparitions, all mixed up with recent reports of explorers' exploits and the latest news. At more than two feet wide, some of the slides were huge by modern standards. 'Aladdin's Lamp' was a favourite topic, since the medium of the magic lantern replicates the talismanic powers of the genie's lamp, which could transport its owner anywhere, collapse space and even time in the same manner as these first presages of cinema. In the Egyptian Hall, Piccadilly, London, from 1873 onwards, 'Maskelyne & Cooke the Royal Illusionists' put on their magic spectacles, with huge popular success. The 1880–2 season included, besides such perennial features as Psycho the fortune-teller, flying spirits and levitating furniture, tableaux of 'The Temptations of Good St Anthony', complete with an 'Imp with a Trumpet Snout'; while in the course of a 'Light and Dark Séance', the 'decapitation illusion' involved a tooth-chattering head of a skeleton floating out over the heads of the audience.[22] Toys for children obeyed the same principles: a fold-out paper model of a magic lantern, manufactured in the 1880s, offered different scenes from a haunted house for the children to project. One helpful informant, in a manual published in 1866 on the various lamps available to achieve the necessary effects, waggishly called his product 'The Magic Lantern, by a mere phantom'.[23]

The magic lantern mimicked the operations of the mind in another crucial way, besides its original affinity with interior phantasms: it attempted to represent movement. Significantly, it did not begin by showing moving objects as beheld in the world, but gorgeous kaleidoscopic geometries, achieved by ingenious slides and double or 'biunial' lenses. Slides with turning handles and 'rack and pinion' gearing entered the 'galanty' repertory. These proto-cinematic devices were given more imposing names: the Cycloidotrope projected whirling patterns etched on to layers of smoked glass; the Choreutoscope produced the illusion of the earlier flip books, and could make dead men dance or a ghost rise from the grave—or watch a girl taking off her clothes.[24]

The showmen operating the lantern were magicians, and they circulated through the same entertainment channels as conjurors and circus artistes; many of them came from that background, and like mediums, either adopted exotic names or were born with them. By the late nineteenth century, the lantern illuminated dreams and fantasies, not only supernatural, ghastly, and spectral, but naughty fulfilments of desire. The earliest 'trick' films borrow the seaside pier scripts, 'What the butler saw' jokes, and key-hole glimpses of girls undressing. For his ebullient series of optical illusions in his pioneering films of the 1890s, Georges Meliès conjured fairies, goblins, and demons, flew to the Moon, inflated his own head and blew it up, capered about in the guise of the devil, set a lighted fuse to himself, and so exploded on camera in full motion to the hilarity of all who were watching (cf. Figure 27 p. 318).

Special effects—from magically seeing through clothes to flying through the air—would become abiding passions in the cinema. But even more critically, the magic lantern shows revealed a link between the medium, images of desire, and the power of the artist who makes the fantasies visible.

Robertson and his peers were exploring shadow play to delight audiences with thrills and terrors. But the feelings that shadow play could prompt were also melancholy and reflective, and it happened that, at the same time as showmen were expanding their ingenuity in devising new illusions, artists were turning to shadow as a prime vehicle of ideas for absence, loss, and memory.

Dibutades, the daughter of a potter from Corinth,
traces the shadow of her lover cast on the wall in one of
many paintings of this classical legend. Joseph-Benoît
Suvée, *The Invention of Drawing. c.* 1791.

12

The Origin of Painting; or, The Corinthian Maid

Shadow is the stuff that art is made on, according to one legend about the origin of painting. The first portrait was created when 'the Corinthian maid', called Dibutades, saw the image formed of her young man in the shadow of his profile cast on the wall by a lamp; she then traced it, because he was going away on a journey and she wanted it for a memento during his absence. Her father, a potter, finding her drawing later, 'pressed clay on this and made a relief, which he hardened by exposure to fire with the rest of his pottery'.[1]

This story, as told in Pliny the Elder's widely enjoyed *Natural History*, was transmitted in manuals of painting that harked back to the antique, but comparable legends are found beyond classical culture and earlier. It is, however, Pliny's story that for a while—mainly in the seventeenth and eighteenth centuries—captivated Western artists' imagination,[2] and Dibutades' act of loving representation inspired several works known as 'The Origin of Painting': the French painter Joseph Suvée (Figure 14, p. 158) and the Scotsman David Allan both explored the story's potential for high drama in the single light source and the looming shadows thrown against the wall. In England, Joseph Wright of Derby further developed the romantic mood of the fantasy when he imagined the lover sleeping while his likeness was taken.[3] This aspect of the tale suited the era's taste for *sentimentalité*, and Dibutades inspired poems and songs in which she represents a faithful and true maiden who wished to recollect her beloved in tranquillity during his absence.

An odd thing about this legend is that of course it does not describe painting at all—the Corinthian Maid never touches pigment or brush, and a silhouette of its essence does not describe anything but outline. (Some artists noticed this inconsistency, and amended their titles to 'The Origin of Drawing'.) By contrast, Dibutades' father could be said to have invented bas-relief: Wright of Derby's picture was commissioned by Josiah Wedgwood, another potter, and the great producer of fired classical cameos, who consequently had strong reason to identify with the story. Cameo profiles are closely related to silhouettes: both play with inverted light and shade, relief and contour, and explore the inherent recognizability of an outline. The onlooker supplies features from memory, so that the act of looking and filling in the shadow activates his or her memories. The mind engages strongly with the 'unfinished thing': the aesthetic principle of *non finito*. Lord Kames in *Elements of Criticism* (1762) analysed three stages in this process: the first takes place in front of the object, the second when it is later called to mind ('recollected'), and the third when memory and imagination act in synthesis to inspire reflection, which he considered more potent psychologically. When John Ruskin returned to the theme, he emphasized how the power of imagination enhances aesthetic response through association. Interestingly, Ruskin called the faculty at work in this mental act of visualizing 'Second Sight'.[4]

The white marble bust and the black silhouette, in their aesthetic austerity, present a counterweight to the information overload of the polychrome and bedizened waxwork, yet the legend of Dibutades reveals the genealogy linking the death mask to the photograph: both copy directly from the real thing. For above all, the heroine of Pliny's story clearly came near to wielding 'the pencil of nature', as Fox Talbot called light in his famous account of the invention of photography in 1844. But of course in the story Dibutades did not think of coating the wall with light-sensitive chemicals; so she cannot be credited with precedence over the Victorian inventor.

From the mid-eighteenth century, a person's outer physical presence rendered in profuse naturalistic detail seemed to promise entry to their essence, their inner spirit, as discussed in relation to waxworks and the portraits of Houdon, for example (see Chapters 1–2). The distinctiveness of the countenance becomes established as the seat of the individual; the person's image, and especially their picture, summons their particular memory in the mind of the living. Photography hardly inaugurated this identification of image and person, but it did—and does—offer a ready new technology to continue and deepen the illusion of contact with an absent or dead subject that waxworks and other contact relics had offered before.

Realistic depiction of outer characteristics opened the way towards capturing individual quiddity. This at least was the highly rational ambition, expressed in scientific physiognomy, realist novels, and living likenesses in portraiture. Techniques such as mapping the idiosyncrasies of the skull as in phrenology, forensic approaches such as fingerprinting, taking copious measurements, and systematic analysis of criminal features, developed in the course of the century alongside photography. Early forms of photography were frequently involved in these now discredited attempts to pin down human variety: the Parisian police chief Alphonse Bertillon (1853–1914) created a special system of measuring features and skeletons, and then diagnosed criminal tendencies from this evidence;[5] a similar method was used by C. and F. W. Damman to classify 'Various Races of Man' (1875).[6]

Photography matched the new hunger for proof of personal distinctiveness, and its nineteenth-century users treated it as a scientific, analytical tool. Its powers of visual portraiture set the pace for literary realism and then surpassed literature's ambitious naturalism.

The idea of art as the play of light and shade was not itself new when Pliny told the legend of Dibutades. Plato's use of the image of flickering reflections in the cave is famous, and the Greek word *skiagraphia*, 'painting with shadow', recurs in his writing to express illusion, visual and intellectual. In the second century Philostratus, who was interested in the power of magic, challenged Plato's negative view, writing that even when an image is made only of *skia* (shadow) and *phos* (light), and has no colour or substance, it can still convey likeness, possess form, intelligence, and—interestingly—modesty and bravery. He went on to make the startlingly modern comment that 'the mimetic faculty' is needed when looking at pictures, and that *skiagraphia* plays upon this power: the beholder fleshes out the image in the light of personal knowledge and fantasy—akin to Ruskin's 'Second Sight'.[7]

This perception illuminates the growing presence of the love motif in Dibutades' story and the increasingly romantic appeal of the later retellings. The record of a face needs emotional engagement as a stimulus to a perception of accuracy, to resemblance leading to recognition. Some of the earliest ideas about portraiture assume that the relationship between the subject or model and the artist is intimate and loving, even erotic; the fantasy or memory of maker and beholder can later play on the gaps, and fill in what is missing—like colour. Such accounts of portraits often presuppose that the purpose of making such a likeness of a face, the most individual part of the human form, springs from personal attachment.

In at least one of the depictions inspired by Pliny, Dibutades' lover reaches out towards her, while she turns to his reflection on the wall. The very absences and inadequacies of the 'skiagram' create psychological space, where the experience of the image grows so intense as to surpass its subject. Dibutades was not the first person to discover that the living likeness of her beloved, however flat and monochrome a silhouette may be, spoke with surprising vividness to her feelings. Domestically, making silhouettes took off as a parlour game in society in both Europe and America, and played the part that photography would later fill. A shadow, preserved on paper, acted as an epitome of the subject's character. For all their schematic stillness, silhouettes can present the liveliest studies of family groups and friends (Figure 14a, p. 166). For example, the *Schattenreise* in the Beethoven House in Bonn truly capture the Beethoven family's gatherings, their pastimes, gestures, and demeanour, and entice the viewer into filling in the gaps.[8] The blackness, emptiness, and simplicity demand work, but as if by a miracle, the shadow figures appear to possess clear features: the shade summons the person. It is striking that this kind of informal, intimate, often affectionately comic portraiture, depicting children playing, young people at their music, older women sewing and reading, men at cards or other tasks, were made and framed in upper bourgeois and aristocratic households where busts also provided favourite interior décor and souvenirs. Indeed, silhouette profiles are often displayed as if they were cameos carved in relief in marble.

Drawing silhouettes also became a popular pastime as an amateur means of diagnosing character. Like phrenology and palmistry, and even short-lived fads for metoposcopy (reading the lines on the forehead), it offered a key to the inner man or woman through their outer features. In 1820, the influential physiognomist Johann Kaspar Lavater reproduced Dibutades' experiment in a rational rather than tender spirit. He placed himself on the other side of the screen from the light source, and analysed his subjects' characters from the silhouette: in one case he decided that his sitter was 'full of great goodness, with much fineness of character'.[9] He admitted that the silhouette did not reveal the gaiety of the original, as the nose dominated more, but it did convey more of her finesse.

In both domestic settings and public auditoria, these pre-photographic forms of portraiture played a part in building a new sense of equal distinctiveness and individuality for everybody. The urban working people who gathered in the Egyptian Hall, Piccadilly, and other venues up and down the country in the United States and Europe, had their profiles drawn, their bumps felt, and their palms read, and developed through these means heightened psychological self-awareness mediated through their physical differences.[10] And this modern sense of self, as an external being with unique traits operating in the world, grows in pace with the emancipation movements of the century.

'Photographic looking' existed before the appearance of the camera, as several critics have pointed out, and the new medium responded to desires which were articulated in other ways—to order, analyse, and store data, to measure and inventory phenomena, to make memorials of the past.[11] (It is interesting, I think, that the story of Dibutades, as a *topos* of art, faded in popularity after the 1840s, just as appearances began to be created and fixed by the new instrument of light, the camera.) At the same time, it responded to, and amplified, a growing realization that human vision was limited, discriminating, and linked to the vagaries of memory, and that a machine might be able to see more, more clearly.

Its muted colour palette helped stir associations with intimacy, even eroticism; the use of photography for sentimental record was enhanced by its early tonal range. The nostalgic potency of black-and-white imagery became even sharper after the general spread of colour photographs; indeed, monochrome became deeply identified with acts of memory. (Steven Spielberg using it for the 'documentary' scenes about the ghetto in *Schindler's List*.)

Absence of colour is linked to the absence of the subject who was there in colour before one's eyes when the image was made. It is as if black and white are the symbolic colours of loss, and hence of memory. Thus the era of melancholic romanticism set the stage for a new pictorial medium that intrinsically possessed the power to make permanent the crepuscular phantoms of imagination and of personal loss and historic elegy.

The legend of the Corinthian maid, with its emphasis on the shadow double as the site of resemblance, projects identity beyond the body: this living likeness does not only arise in flatness, obscurity, and lack of substance, but also exists as an external projection. Someone owns their shadow, as if it were an object: again, photography, and especially films, would fully realize this splitting of a person into a self-on-screen and a self-in-the-world, and lead inexorably on to the ghost realm of eternal celebrity.

Thomas De Quincey invoked the daguerreotype at the start of his essay 'Suspiria De Profundis' (1845). Eight years after its invention, he described it as 'light getting under harness as a slave for man', part of the 'continual development of vast physical agencies—steam in all its application, powers from heaven . . . powers from hell (as it might seem, but these also celestial)', which trouble, he wrote, 'the eye of the calmest observer'.[12] Daguerreotype images, imprinted on to highly polished silver-coated copper sheets, require tilting this way and that to bring the image in the surface into view, so the person in the image troublingly appears to hover and fade. This spectral effect, intrinsic to the medium, provoked *frissons* from its first appearance, so much so that many early examples are hand-tinted to give bloom to the sitter's cheeks and lips, or gilded to enliven a cushion, a fob, a pair of earrings.

Daguerre and his associates and followers chose to picture bas-reliefs and busts and other casts in some of the earliest photographic images ever made. They were exhibiting the fine-grained vision of the new process, its heightened powers of scrutiny (the buttons on the uniform of the microscopic guard standing to attention outside the Louvre in one image), its quiveringly alert sensitivity to different textural gleam and lustre (on marble, on plaster, on gilt, and on ormolu, on plants' foliage, on damask upholstery in an interior study).[13] But they were also proposing, subliminally, a kinship with peelings off life. The new medium possessed the accuracy of lost wax casting, combined with the illusory shadowy worlds of silhouette and reflections in mirrors, as we shall see. It is this deep relation that led Daguerre to move from dioramas to photography.

In 1841, the novelist Honoré de Balzac confided to the photographer Félix Nadar that he felt that 'each body in nature consists of a series of ghosts, in an infinity of superimposed layers, foliated in infinitesimal films, in all the directions in which optics perceive this body'. Balzac felt in consequence that every daguerreotype 'was . . . going to surprise, detach and retain one of the layers of the body on which it focused . . . from then onwards, and every time the operation was repeated, the subject in question evidently suffered the loss of one of its ghosts, that is to say, the very essence of which it was composed.'[14]

Balzac's fantasy echoes closely a once highly influential theory of vision, 'intromission', which was eloquently evoked by Lucretius and then developed by Roger Bacon in the thirteenth century; according to this model of perception, every object beams out images 'like a skin, or film, | Peeled from the body's surface . . . keep [ing] the look, the shape | Of what it held before its wandering . . . the way | Cicadas cast their brittle summer jackets'.[15] These eerie, flying sheddings from physical phenomena were called *eidola* in Greek, and *simulacrum* in Latin, and also known as 'radiant species'. Like a photograph made of light, they both retain the material substance of their origin but also reproduce it, as with an 'idol', an effigy, and a copy.[16]

This theory of vision survives with an uneven pulse in the history of science, and Balzac may be referring to it directly. But the anecdote captures more immediately the uncanny aura hanging around daguerreotypes from the very beginning, and which then began to emanate from photographs too. Images made of light and shadow cast by people, things, and places seem to preserve action at a distance: the transmission of the person through time. The metaphors adopted for the medium—including the word *pellicola*, little skin, for film itself in Italian—present a powerful instance of a figure of speech materializing into substance.

Later nineteenth-century printing processes made certain formal means available to the maker: scrupulous registry of subtle gradations of mono-chrome enhanced the detail in portraiture, and could bestow lifelikeness on the inanimate, often to an uncanny degree. Some early printing processes, such as calotype (1840 to c.1855), salted paper prints (1839 to c.1855 and the 1890s to 1900), and platinum prints (1873–c.1890), soak into the fabric of the paper, giving the image velvety depths. This bonding deepens the impression of presence immanent in the material; for this reason, con-temporary artists have revived these processes.[17] These early processes also widened the palette of shadows to indigo, maroon, saffron, and smoky grey. (The best books about these decades use colour reproduction for monochrome photographs.) By contrast, when the print medium is metal, paper, glass, or other shiny surface—such as created by the later emulsions pasted on to a coated surface—the materials themselves add more play with light and shadow, glistening and reflection (a problem, sometimes, in displaying photographs). This stuff of light and shade dissolves the substance in which the image is caught more convincingly than ever a stretched canvas or fresco wall dematerializes when painted. All these intrinsic properties of the photographic print made it peculiarly suited, as we shall see, to rendering the vivid products of the mind's eye.

Julia Margaret Cameron, making calotype portraits in the 1860s and 1870s, worked purposefully with the emotive range of *non finito* shadow play: she plunged her subjects into deep chiaroscuro, or posed them against the light to create a haloed head, or luminously outlined the edge of the profile. Her portrait of Thomas Carlyle looked like 'a rough block by Michelangelo', commented her friend—and subject—Herschel approvingly. Carlyle himself praised the 'high relief' of *The Mountain Nymph Sweet Liberty*.[18] Cameron also deliberately over-exposed the prints, so that the photographs look like silhouettes in reverse—white on black—as in numerous images posed by her favourite Mary Hillier, including the famous *Call, I Follow, I Follow, Let Me Die* and *The Angel at the Tomb* (see Figure 18, p. 204). Bowing to the aesthetic traditions of the preceding century, she also cut out a profile of Julia Jackson to create a kind of cameo.

Shadows can evoke likeness with startling acuteness even when the originals are not known to the viewer or are figures of fantasy. The brilliant silhouette-maker and puppeteer Lotte Reiniger, adapting the German tradition to the new art of the cinema and creating silhouette films, relied on the power of the audience's imagination to fill in depths and colour and emotion from the dazzling sleight of hand of her scissor art. Her master-piece, *The Adventures of Prince Achmed* (1926), a full-length Arabian Night fantasia composed entirely of cut-out silhouettes, conveys subtle nuance of humour and pathos as well as sharply drawn personalities and settings through illusions of light and shadow executed often in delicate filigree.[19] *Prince Achmed* has a dreamy mood with touches of melancholy, and some extended sinister passages bristling with demons and monsters, which the basic black of Reiniger's craft of course matches perfectly. But on the whole the film dances with delight, and does not plunge the viewer into the nocturnal range of early still photography.

The power of such images—the silhouette, and the black and white portrait photograph—arises from their origin in the light that once played on their subjects and formed their image. They are emanations, captured and stilled. Is that a figure of speech? They are copies of the originals, and in that sense, their character ceases to be metaphorical. It is here, on this edge where the figurative touches the actual and the image becomes reality, that shadow eerily communicates individual presence; this effect grows when a shadow becomes a shade, and that shade a reflection; then the projected image of a person brushes the condition of spirit.

Part VI

Mirror

Clementina Hawarden holds up the mirror of the
camera to her daughter, who in a photograph
taken around the same time as the second of Lewis
Carroll's *Alice* books, gazes at her double through
the looking-glass.

13
The Danger in the Mirror

> But the fairest will always remain inside
> But the fairest will always remain inside
> till through to the cheeks you are holding presses
> Narcissus, released and clarified.
>
> Rainer Maria Rilke, *Sonnets to Orpheus*

Narcissus, who looked at his own reflection, thought it the face of another, and fell in love with that 'mendacem . . . formam' (that lying form), excited in Ovid one of the most sustained and passionate complaints of his poem the *Metamorphoses*. Over thirty lines of rapture and anguish, Narcissus very slowly comes to realize the impossibility of his quest to reach this reflected self: 'spem sine corpore amat, corpus putat esse, quod umbra est . . . ([he] fell in love | With that unbodied hope, and found a substance | In what was only shadow).[1]

Ovid's dramatic treatment is the fullest and most eloquent source for this key myth, and it inaugurates a lasting enigma about self-knowledge. The poet's pent-up, anguished tale of error and transformation, which elicited from him all his feline powers of emotional observation (not untouched by irony), turns on the terrible seduction of a double and the dangers of mirroring. The episode has of course yielded most saliently a caution against self-love and its discontents, and has become a vivid site of contest in the history of psychology; but it also presents a rich parable for art's powers of self-creation and annihilation. In relation to this book, the tale of Narcissus illuminates the perplexing, alluring, and perilous status of a self that can appear in every way real and yet lacks embodiment: it tells a literal story about reflection in a way that bears on reflexivity, the foundation of selfhood. Narcissus and his double bring to light a form of spectre that has moved to the centre of consciousness today, when, as a product of post-eighteenth-century glazing techniques, as well as photographic media, we are fully familiar with our image—at many different stages of our lives.

Ovid opens the scene at the pool with an image of a sculpture when he first describes the reflection Narcissus sees: 'He [Narcissus] looks in wonder, charmed by himself, spell-bound, and no more moving | Than any marble statue.'[2] The classical poet reveals himself more concerned with the enigmatic border between art and life, between representation and death, than in Narcissus' personal psychology, and he touches on his persistent theme, that natural generation and death can be resisted through artistic creation and its reality, but that such an order of reality is still only illusion. In the water, as in a mirror, or in the lines of the poem and the virtual space it describes, life flickers and leaps, but only in semblance: this is the limit Ovid presses against, and the complex that Narcissus' story also explores, that the boy is in love with a picture.

In the famous note to 'Kubla Khan', Coleridge described how the vision of the poem came to him, and how, when he was interrupted, it fled just as an image reflected on the surface of a stream is shattered by a stone.[3] This way of imagining imagination itself owes something to water divination, and something to Narcissus.

Sigmund Freud produced his controversial 1914 paper on the psychology of narcissism the year after Rainer Maria Rilke wrote two of his many intense Narcissus poems.[4] The poet caught at Ovid's underlying aesthetic concerns, and identified himself with the doomed lover in several highly wrought meditations on love, autonomy, self-annihilation, and creativity. In one tight eight-line lyric of 1913 Rilke passionately describes Narcissus' beauty, and his absorption and final disappearance into the mirror of himself; in another, longer poem, his Narcissus imagines loving another or being loved by another, but rejects the possibility as damaging to the perfect unity of his twinned being for the making of beauty.[5] 'On Narcissism', Freud's paper, ostensibly counters the views of his former colleague and friend C. G. Jung, but it does seem to be replying, without acknowledgement, to Rilke's poetic manifesto, Freud laying out his damaging argument that both the ego and the libido are deeply entangled from infancy in self-love (primary narcissism); and prescribing that this energy be healthily cathected towards another object, most often a lover and, especially in the case of women, a child.[6] The paper, and the concept of narcissism which it has defined and spread, have eclipsed some of the threads in Ovid's fascinating, originary story about recognition and the self. Before Freud's essay placed the myth in the field of perverse sexuality, the motif of the imperilling mirror occurred widely, principally in tales defining primitives, savages: the instrument of revelation, a glass, could capture and subdue wild things and bring them within the compass of civility—usually disempowered.

The story of Narcissus puts the question, How can I know myself? The image in the glass offers me an image, but only by estranging me from my body: I see myself outside myself, as if someone else. Narcissus' error discloses the truth curled inside the paradox of representing self to self. (Jacques Lacan's 'mirror phase', identifying the child's realization that she or he is a person separate and distinct from the mother's body when the child recognizes her or his own face in the glass, places this severance in the kernel of self-consciousness.)[7] To Narcissus, the face in the mirror looks like someone else, an unfamiliar and unknown person; the experience destroys him.

Whereas in Ovid's poem the prophet Tiresias warns Narcissus' mother that he will live a long life only if he does not know himself ('si se non noverit'), in numerous other fables about self-recognition and reflexivity, mirrors operate above all as cultural talismans, symbols of society, art, human hierarchy, and values: to know yourself, as the oracle at Delphi recommended, was the goal of human nature (a long time before Descartes's *cogito*).

For example, one of the versions of the medieval story of Valentine and Orson describes how the twin brothers were parted at birth, when Orson was stolen by a she-bear and raised in the forest, and were at last reunited when Valentine, out hunting one day, captured his wild brother by showing him his face in a mirror. The sight so horrifies Orson that his huge strength ebbs away, and Valentine is able to lead him tamely to his palace in the city, where Orson learns to live as a human being again. This romance of recognition echoes another fable, also much retold in the Middle Ages. It prescribes a sure way to capture a tigress: the hunters should cast a mirror in the path of the animal, and the tigress, passing by, would see herself therein reflected in little, and, mistaking her reflection for her cub, would stop in her tracks to succour the nursling. The hunters would then be able to drop a net on her and capture her.

This unusual stratagem passed far and wide through the highly popular Bestiaries of antiquity onwards, and was illuminated in the many surviving manuscripts of such anthologies. In the imagination of storytellers for a very long time, mirrors thus act as instruments of taming, of dominion, of forcing a recognition that alters the beholders' nature; the reflection in the glass has a magical effect, it tames and civilizes its subjects. But another way of taking this plot motif would be to consider the response more revealing than ignorant: a mirror image is a kind of captivity, antithetical to freedom. The tigress does not understand that her reflection is herself; Orson does grasp this, and his image shocks him, because he does not know that he looks like that.

When Magellan set out to sail around the world for the first time, and provisioned the boat with all the necessary supplies for the long journey, he included, alongside jerky and biscuits and tallow and rope and knives and beads, hundreds of small pieces of mirror. They were destined to be gifts to the new peoples—the giants and amazons and wild folk—whom the travellers would encounter. In the full-scale replica of the boat which is moored on the Quadalquivir in Seville (or was when I was last there in 1996), boxes of tarnished mirror tiles are mysteriously stowed below deck without any explanation. As objects of exchange, these mirrors can perhaps reveal more than the patronizing trifles they seem. The traditional instrument of self-reflection, they could symbolize the idea of the self that the Portuguese circumnavigators were transporting around the globe: the looking-glass as self-portrait of its bearers. To behold oneself as one looks to others, in outward form: this is one story about self-consciousness told in the classical and Christian traditions. Faces can be read like a book (or not, of course). The word 'Speculum', meaning looking-glass, recurs in dozens of titles of books that pass on learning, wisdom, and rules for conduct and salvation: the *Speculum Humanae Vitae*, the *Mirror of Princes*, the *Mirror of Virtues*, and so forth. This metaphor of the looking-glass was gradually displaced, during the Renaissance, by the more medical 'Anatomy': limning the interior body conveyed more vividly after the seventeenth century the probing approach to self-knowledge. But the speculum remained one of the persistent fantasies about early encounters between cultures and continents and worlds in the voyages of discovery, that savages had to be discovered to themselves according to these principles; the delight they took in seeing their own reflections arose because they did not know themselves and were seeing themselves for the first time.

However, there is something not quite right about this interpretation—the Aztecs made obsidian mirrors, for example (one passed into the care of John Dee, the Elizabethan occultist, who used it for scrying and talking to his familiar spirits).[8] Water oracles are common features of many cultures, quite beside the ordinary occurrences of reflections in pools, in polished surfaces, and in the eyes and pupils of another person. (The word 'pupilla' comes from Latin *pupus* or *pupa* meaning small boy or girl, and thus recalls this ordinary observation that we see ourselves in miniature in someone's eyes.) The play between self-knowledge and self-image gives the mirror a role in identity long before Jacques Lacan defined the mirror phase. For example, in John Dryden's 'semi-opera' *King Arthur*, the heroine Emmeline is blind, but when her sight is miraculously restored in the course of the story, her nurse tells her: 'None sees themselves | But by Reflection.' She gives her a glass to look at herself for the first time. The young woman does not recognize her own face: 'The pretty thing is Dumb,' she exclaims. The Nurse approaches and they both appear, together, in the glass: 'Our Shadows, Madam', says the Nurse.

The ingénue responds, in a playful change on Narcissus:

> 'Mine is a prettier Shaddow far, then thine.
> I Love it; let me Kiss my to ther self.
>   Alas, I've kissed it Dead; the fine Thing's gone;
> Indeed it Kiss'd so Cold, as if 'twere Dying.' [*sic*, throughout][9]

Plate 1. Jupiter the cloud-compeller, the thunderer,
wraps himself in storm cloud to ravish Io.
From Correggio's series, *The Loves of Jupiter*, 1531–2.

Plates 2a and 2b. The heavens
manifest the realm of supernatural: signs and wonders
announce victory or disaster
in this miniature (below) of a
'Heavenly portent seen in 1553'.
From Pierre Boiastuau, *Histoires
Prodigieuses*, 1560. Cloud-matter
becomes consubstantial with
angels and the playground of
cherubim as living embodiments
of *pneuma* (breath).
Left: Correggio, detail from the
Assumption of the Virgin Mary,
Parma cathedral, 15.

Plate 3. Mary soars from her tomb on spiralling
clouds, like the smoke of sacrifice or incense from
an altar rising heavenwards.
Nicolas Poussin, *The Assumption of the Virgin*, c.1626.

Plate 4. The spirit, separated from the material body at death, appears to combust into fiery ether as it ascends to heaven.
Bartolomé Esteban Murillo, *Fray Juan's Vision of the Soul of King Philip II of Spain*, 1645–6.

Dryden here echoes Ovid, where Narcissus also laments that when he bends to the pool to kiss his beloved reflected there, he vanishes.

But mirrors are associated with enlightenment through their association with integration—the self as a bounded object in space—and, less obviously but by extension, with estrangement—the self as separate and elsewhere. It is a profound paradox that when I recognize myself in a mirror, I am seeing myself as an Other, as if seen by someone else (though I may not share or ever know others' response to what they see). Because the face, and most especially the eyes, cannot look at themselves except in reflection, reflections in the glass conflate self as subject and self as object into an insoluble enigma, as the myth of Narcissus so powerfully (and piteously) dramatizes. For while the self appears detached and bounded in the mirror, any move or gesture changes the image accordingly, through that indissoluble twinship that makes Ovid's Narcissus cry out in agony when he cannot reach his beloved *alter*. This extreme doubling turns the field of the visible into an extension of the beholder: a state akin to extreme delusion and mental disturbance.

It is possible perhaps for me to possess self-consciousness without summoning myself in my mind's eye as an object, without placing myself in space-time beyond the boundaries of my body as I inhabit and experience it, without appearing through the looking-glass in my mental world. Or is the mental world looking-glass country? It is certainly possible, as the medieval stories and the explorers' fantasy of barbarism reveal, to imagine living without knowing what I look like, and this would not necessarily entail that I do not know who I am or have no self to know with—or does it? The blind can tell us about this state, and have done so.[10] The motif of the savage and the mirror sketches the possibility that a wild child or a tigress has indeed realized something deeper than recognizing the outward semblance of self, that this exterior appearance does not match a sense of the self as held in interior consciousness.

For before the mirror became a commonplace item of every household, reflections were a cause of deep, widespread alarm: the story of Narcissus' death anticipates many later superstitions about doubles, or 'fetches', uncanny spectres who call the living into the land of the dead. A reflection, caught in a pool or a basin of water, could be fatal to the soul: as a premonition of impending disembodiment, and as a dispersal of bounded identity through a doubling of the self. Medusa, with the power to turn everything to stone by her gaze, is captured and beheaded when she beholds her own image in the polished shield that Perseus holds up. One of the ancient interpreters of dreams, Artemidorus, warns that dreaming of seeing one's own reflection in water is most unlucky, and probably announces one's death. The psychological 'narcissistic' interpretation of Narcissus' death and transformation, that he fell in love with his own reflection, may be an overdetermined reading, offered only comparatively late by Ovid, and obscuring the earlier magical meaning. But indeed the two could be related: to fall in love with one's own image is to lose that identity which is created in separation, in reciprocal interchange with others, in the difference of individuation—in this sense, at least, it entails death to the soul. Echo the nymph falls in love with Narcissus, and represents another variation of extinction: a voice which has lost integrity and distinctiveness, which exists only as reflection.

Precise evidence about the image endangering the soul is hard to pin down among the peoples to whom it has been so freely attributed. By contrast, it lies everywhere to hand in Western culture. The idea of the soul-stealer was already vividly present in the minds of the photographers and the collectors and the spectators of early photographs, for many reasons, and the stories they knew from classical and European tradition can help explain why the belief was reported so insistently of Others.

Significantly, J. G. Frazer closes his section on 'Perils to the Soul: The Soul as Shadow and Reflection', published in 1911, with a detailed account of European evidence. He discusses classical myths as well as legends and lore reported closer to his own time, giving a highly enjoyable tour of stories, some famous, some less familiar. All over Europe, Frazer continues, fears about mortality are still attached to images in water or other reflecting surfaces: in countries as distant as Scotland, Germany, and Italy, mirrors were—and still are—turned to the wall after a death, window panes draped in mourning cloths in case, first, the soul of the deceased might be trapped in the image and become unable to depart in peace; and secondly, so that the survivors might not see themselves reflected so soon after a death, because this too might capture their souls.[11] The Revd Robert Kirk, Scottish author of *The Secret Commonwealth* (1691), whom we have encountered before as an expert witness on fairies, lingers on the existence of doubles; it is possible, he learned from his parishioners, to have a fairy counterpart, 'they call this reflex-man a . . . co-walker, every way like the man as a twin-brother and companion, haunting him as his shadow and is oft seen and known among men (resembling the original) both before and after the original is dead. . . . This copy, Echo, or living picture, goes at last to his own herd. It accompanied that person so long and frequently, for ends best known to itself, whether to guard him from the secret assaults of some of its own folks, or only as a sportful ape to counterfeit all his actions.'[12] Kirk brings a harsh poetry to his prose, images grounded in the Highland scenery and its ruggedness, as in this evocation of the phantom double: 'a joint-eater or just-halver, feeding on the pith and quintessence of what the man eats, and that therefore he continues lean like a hawk or heron . . . Yet it would seem they convey that substance elsewhere, for these subterraneans eat but little in their dwellings, their food being exactly clean, and served up by pleasant children like enchanted puppets.'[13]

The thrill of this shadow double—a thrill bringing a shudder as well as the *frisson* of pleasure—sustains the hallucinatory plot of *The Private Memoirs*. James Hogg was a compatriot of Kirk, knew Kirk's writing through his friend and patron Sir Walter Scott,[14] and as a countryman (Hogg was nicknamed 'The Ettrick Shepherd' after his unlettered origins) would have come across the folklore directly. This strand of uncanny Celtic belief also provides the motif of the most famous doppelgänger tale of all, R. L. Stevenson's *The Strange Case of Dr Jekyll and Mr Hyde* (1886).

Although a reflection in a mirror or a pool is different from a shadow, and neither is identical with an embodied and independent double, such as possess the protagonists of Hogg's novel and Stevenson's novella, and while the relationship of a reflection or a shadow to image-making is not immediate (at least not until the invention of photography), the categories have been richly composted together in the widespread fears conveyed by superstitions and the stories they inspire. A shadow is similar to a reflection only when it is not a shadow but a shade, but then it shifts towards the nature of ghosts—Greek *psyche* covers both. An image in a pool or a glass is a reflection, an insubstantial, impalpable replication of the body, as Narcissus learned so painfully. It is not identical with a monochrome silhouette cast by an object or figure standing and blocking the light. But shadows and reflections are alike in one crucial aspect: both provide assurance by their presence of the existence of a body. They are united by a paradox, that their immaterial and insubstantial presence accompanies the being that casts them and gives evidence of that entity's materiality. Belief in the shadow's identity with its owner's corporeality can have a positive effect: in The Acts of the Apostles, for example, 'they used to bring the sick into the streets and lay them down on beds and pallets in the hope that even the shadow of Peter as he passed by might fall upon one of them . . . and heal of their infirmities' (Acts 5: 15–16).

Concomitantly, the absence of shadow or reflection gives shivery proof that something is wrong, that life is diminished, or simply lacking. Both are fundamental to representations of living being: Dante realizes that he is the only person in the underworld to cast a shadow (*Purgatorio*, III. 20–1), and, in another marvellously observed moment in *The Divine Comedy*, the dead souls notice the anomaly, and draw back in wonder (Purgatorio, XXVI. 10–24).

Doubled by a form that has no substance, we paradoxically possess a certificate of life. The attenuated darkness of our shadows and the illusion of our mirrored self hold within them the warrant of our existence in solid flesh—strange as it may seem. The shadow as reflection acts as a reminder of immortality—and hence of mortality, too—because it provides an image of the body that survives on the other side. A person's cast image acts proleptically to conjure that body's future condition as a spirit or shade; Homeric eschatology, for example, has left traces in Christian visions of the afterlife. *Psyche* was used, as mentioned earlier, for the spirit or shade in the underworld after death; similarly, those other words for shadow—*skia*, *umbra*—evoke, like the English 'shades of the dead', the ghosts of the deceased, as in the line from the *Odyssey* in which Circe describes Hades, where only Tiresias still possesses reason and the 'others flit about as shadows'. When Odysseus later encounters his mother among the dead, he tries to hold her:

> Three times I rushed toward her, desperate to hold her,
> three times she fluttered through my fingers, sifting away
> like a shadow, dissolving like a dream, and each time
> the grief but to the heart, sharper, yes, and I,
> I cried out to her . . .
> Mother—why not wait for me? How I long to hold you![15]

This anguished Homeric vision of the dead shapes the later underworlds of Virgil and, later still, of Dante. The darkness gathers in the myth of Orpheus, poignantly reimagined in the *Georgics*: Orpheus almost succeeds in bringing back his wife Eurydice, but when he breaks the prohibition and turns to look at her: 'at once from his sight, like a wisp of smoke | Thinned into air, was gone.'[16]

Biblical Sheol and Gehenna are places of darkness, too, and the endless night of the Christian hell is relieved only by the red flames of the devil's ovens. Dante's account of souls in Purgatory, before the resurrection of the dead, which conveys the knotted intricacies of Thomist doctrine about the soul after death, oddly looks forward to the phantom-like and mobile character of the photographed body, especially in the medium of film, since Dante's shades talk and appear in colour. To Dante's question in Purgatory about the souls' condition in the afterlife, the poet Statius explains how they take form before the resurrection of the flesh, and develops an intricate optics to explain how Dante can behold the ghosts at all. Drawing the properties of light, as in a rainbow and in flames, he says:

> e come l'aere, quand'è ben pïorno,
>   per l'altrui raggio che 'n se sì reflette,
>   di diversi color diventa adorno;
> così li'aere vicin quivi si mette
>   in quella forma che in lui suggella
>   virtüalmente l'alma che ristette;

e simigliante poi alla fiammella
che segue il foco là 'vunque si muta,
segue lo spirto sua forma novella.
Però che quindi ha poscia sua paruta,
è chiamata ombra . . .

(and as the air, when it is full of rain, becomes adorned with various colours through another's beams that are reflected in it, so the neighbouring air sets itself into that form which the soul that stopped there stamps upon it by its power, and then like the flame that follows the fire wherever its shifts, its new form follows the spirit. Since it has by this its semblance henceforth, it is called a shade . . .)[17]

Shadows and reflections overlap, too, in their coldness, their wraith-like nature, prophetic of the afterlife. Those who are neither living nor dead cannot project an image, either as mirror reflection or as shadow. Or the enchantment may alter the beholder, and rob him—or her—of the power to do so. In Jacobean England, a spell book recommended that a husband look into his wife's eyes: if you could not see your reflection in her pupil, then someone has bewitched her. In Transylvania, as we know well from Gothic vampire lore from the eighteenth century onwards, the undead cast no shadow and make no reflection: they have neither mortal bodies like human beings, nor souls like the living, and the proof of their terrifying and uncanny liminality is that their relation to light is negative: they have been drained of the light necessary to project an image, and their bodies do not displace light to make shadows. They have become shades in death, and the sign of being one is the loss or absence of shadow, of the power of projection. The uncanny folklore does not exist in sequestration from 'high art': the Romantics explored it in fiction, in narrative variations on the theme, written, painted, and sung.

The penniless hero Peter Schlemihl accepts the offer of
the mysterious Dr Scapinelli and sells him his shadow.
George Cruikshank illustrated the 1824 translation of
Adelbert von Chamisso's popular Faustian tale.

14

Double Vision

One is in danger of not being oneself when one lives at a reflective distance from oneself.

J. M. Coetzee

In 'The Lady of Shalott', the poem by Alfred Tennyson which is still learned by heart, the doomed heroine is a fairy lady who lives spellbound 'between four gray walls and four gray towers', forbidden to look at life outside except in the reflections of her magic mirror:

> And moving through a mirror clear
> That hangs before her all the year,
> Shadows of the world appear

The poet does not tell us why she lives under this enchantment, and the laws of magical stories lead us to accept it without question. From these shadows, she weaves into the tapestry on her loom images of the road and river winding down to Camelot, and of the passers-by travelling to and from the castle. One day, Sir Lancelot comes by. A fantastic description follows of his armour, his mount's 'gemmy bridle' with harness bells ringing merrily, and his handsome mien and 'his coal-black curls' flowing under his helmet. She sees this picture in the glass, but feels the temptation of the real, embodied Lancelot:

> 'I am half-sick of shadows,' said
> The Lady of Shalott.

She turns to the view instead of the image, in the most famous lines:

> She left the web, she left the loom,
> She made three paces through the room,
> She saw the water-lily bloom,
> She saw the helmet and the plume,
> She looked down to Camelot.

Quitting the shadow scene for the direct experience, the fairy lady breaks the enchantment that held her:

> Out flew the web and floated wide;
> The mirror cracked from side to side;

'The curse is come upon me,' cried
The Lady of Shalott.

After this explosive eruption of reality, the poem goes on to tell—bafflingly, inexplicably—how the Lady takes a boat, writes her name on the prow, and singing her last song, sets herself adrift down to Camelot. When she arrives there, Lancelot sees her—dead—for the only time:

> Lancelot mused a little space,
> He said, 'She has a lovely face;
> God in his mercy lend her grace,
> The Lady of Shalott.'[1]

Neither the Lady nor her enigmatic fate appear in Thomas Malory's *Morte d'Arthur*, Tennyson's prime source for his *Idylls*. But she does reprise Spenser's Britomart in *The Faerie Queene*, who was also enchanted by a magic glass wrought by Merlin:

> It vertue had to shew in perfect sight
> Whatever thing was in the world contaynd,
> . . .
> Forthy it round and hollow shaped was,
> Like to the world itselfe, and seemd a world of glas [*sic*].[2]

In this world of glass, this magic mirror, Britomart sees her true love, Artegall, as in a diviner's cup, and is smitten to the core of her being. There he flickers, 'only shade and semblant of a knight', and this shimmering sight brings her to a terrible languishing and pining:

> But wicked fortune mine, though minde be good,
> Can have no ende nor hope of my desire,
> *But feed on shadowes* whiles I die for food. (emphasis added)[3]

It is part of the spell that Tennyson's variation on this theme casts on its readers that the questions linger: what incurred the state in which the Lady of Shalott lives captive, what does it mean that she cannot look at the world except in a mirror, what does the mirror mean, why does nobody at Camelot know her, why has she never been seen?

There are no answers to these puzzles, in which the poem's life-blood flows, but there are some conjectures which can illuminate the shivery superstitions that shadows and reflections inspire in other myths beside faery lore. Interestingly, the poem inverts the belief as dramatized in tales and folklore about doubles and mirror images, for the Lady lives securely in the world of reflections and becomes endangered when she turns from it to gaze at reality instead. Tennyson's poetic figure from a make-believe age of chivalry personifies a crucial puzzle that still wraps imaginative responses to reflected reality. Appearing in print in 1842, at the very time when shadow play, cameras obscura, and other optical projections filled popular entertainment, when daguerreotypes had just appeared, the Lady of Shalott evokes the attractions and fears that the first photographic media excited. Her mysterious fate upholds the world of appearances as a safer zone of enchantment, compared to the world of firsthand experience. The real turns fatal for the fairy lady, just as contemporary society became repugnant to the Laureate, one of the first victims of modern celebrity, who desired only to live in seclusion with his private fancies and reflections. Yet, at the same time, the poem recognizes that in solitary seclusion in her tower, weaving images in her enchanted glass, she is in thrall to shadows, and they hold her in a state of captivity.[4] For all the poem's weird seduction, it is surprising to find in it a shrewd insight into the quandary of living only through images.

This twist on the theme of Narcissus preoccupied the German fantasy writer Adelbert von Chamisso, who in *The Wonderful History of Peter Schlemihl* (1814) tells the story of a penniless wretch who loses his soul all unknowingly when he sells his shadow. Chamisso gives the Faustian tale a realist and personal touch by telling it in the first person, as if in his own voice. A mysterious magician approaches the narrator and tells him how much he admires his 'beautiful, beautiful shadow in the sun, which with a certain noble contempt and perhaps without being aware of it, you threw off from your feet'. Willingly, Peter parts with it in return for fairy-tale riches: a purse that never dries, however much gold flows from it. Then his benefactor takes his prize: 'With wonderful dexterity I perceived him loosening my shadow from the ground from head to foot;—he lifted it up;—he rolled it together and folded it, and at last put in into his pocket.'[5]

This English translation was published ten years after the German, and was illustrated by the highly popular George Cruikshank (see Figure 16, p. 178). It was reprinted many times,[6] the story's growing popularity thus coinciding with—and keeping pace with—the spread of Victorian black-and-white portrait photography, both still and moving.

Chamisso's theme was taken up more obsessively by his friend, the German Romantic composer and writer of *Märchen*, or fairy-tales, E. T. A. Hoffmann (d. 1822). Hoffmann's fame, unlike Chamisso's, has not faded, for his *Tales* have inspired ballets, operas, and films, as well as Freud's famous essay, 'The Uncanny'. But Hoffmann has become more renowned as a source of fantasies rather than as a writer himself, because his ways of telling are tangled, and his sinister imaginings often make the reader feel queasy. (Michael Powell's filmed interpretation of 1951 of *Tales of Hoffmann* captures Hoffmann's perversity more closely than Offenbach's ebullient music.)

In several of his fairy-tales, Hoffmann took up the plot of the stolen shadow-soul, and in a highly bizarre, dark, and shivery mood, intensified the threat of insanity implied in the doppelgänger plot. He put his finger on one of the ideas circulating about the meaning of a person's reflection: that it is a true image, a *vera icon*, in which some essence of the person inheres. In one story, 'A New Year's Eve Adventure', 'The conversation limped along,' he writes, 'and in its course a fine young artist named Philipp was mentioned, together with a portrait of a princess painted with intense love and longing, which she must have inspired in him.' One of the characters listening then comments, 'More than just a likeness, a true image,' and the narrator replies, 'So completely true . . . that you could almost say it was stolen from a mirror.'[7]

As the eerie tale unfolds, there are *two* victims of the devil's appetite for reflections and shadows. The first comes into the bar heralded by the cry, 'Cover up your mirrors!' The sight of his missing image will drive the victim mad, it seems, and all others who witness his loss will become 'deathly pale, shrivelled, terrified'. A second story, embedded within the first in Hoffmann's preferred manner, then recounts how another man, a certain Erasmus Spikher, is inveigled out of his reflection by a young Italian beauty with whom he falls in love. When they have to part, she begs him, 'Leave me your reflection, my beloved; it will be mine and remain with me for ever.' 'How can you keep my reflection?', he responds, 'It springs out to meet me from every clear body of water or polished surface.' But he gives in, at her hot tears and even hotter kisses, and he sees 'his image step forward independent of his movements, glide into Giuletta's arms and disappear with her in a strange vapour'.[8] The translator uses 'dream-ego' for *Spiegelbild* (literally, 'mirror image'), the word for that part of his self that Erasmus has given away.

The story ends badly—as the reader might expect—but Erasmus does manage to resist the promptings of his wicked mistress to murder his wife and child, even though she is now in full possession of his inner being.

The threat to the self, as specifically conveyed by the optical illusion of mirror images, emerges in acute form in the first decades of the cinema, as Otto Rank quickly noticed in his study of the doppelgänger theme, *The Double* (1914): 'Perhaps it follows that filmic form, which reminds us of dream techniques in more ways than one, expresses certain psychological facts and relationships . . . in a distinct and manifest imagistic language.'[9] Rank was responding to an early German 'photo-play', *The Student of Prague*, written the year before by Hans Heinz Ewers, a popular writer of ghost and vampire stories in Germany who drew directly on Chamisso's earlier story. The implicit relationship between the story's treatment of reflections and shadows and the medium of photography reached fulfilment when Ewers's story inspired one of the most haunting and potent silent movies, which brilliantly harnessed the resources of film illusion. The shadow/reflection as an image of the soul became the centre of the plot in a medium which is itself shadow play.

The story was in fact filmed several times in the silent era, in 1913, 1921 (as *Der verlorene Schatten*, 'The Lost Shadow') and in 1926, and then, in sound, in 1936. But it is the first, 1913 version, directed by the Danish film-maker Stellan Rye, that is the classic.[10] The expressionist actor Paul Wegener co-directed, and it was his idea to use the illusions used in early 'trick' films to create the uncanny doubling of the hero; he appears in both roles: as Baldwin the student and as his reflection, which the credits revealingly call *Das zweite Ich* ('the Second I').

The film tells the story of a young rake—the best swordsman in Prague—who falls in love with a rich countess whom he happens to rescue from drowning after a riding accident. But his pennilessness and low social status debar him from wooing her. He tries gambling, and loses all his money, so, when the sinister, obsequious Dr Scapinelli appears, complete with Mephistophelian beard, hat, and cane in the style of a magus, and offers him a purse of inexhaustible gold, the student willingly signs over anything the doctor might want from his wretched lodgings. Scapinelli tells him he wants his *Spiegelbild*.

At this, in a compelling moment of early special effects, the student's reflection, his doppelgänger, steps out of the mirror and sidles out of the room beside the diabolically smiling doctor.

Baldwin merely shrugs at his shadow's disappearance. But he soon finds to his alarm that his shadow now enjoys an independent existence: like Hyde in Robert Louis Stevenson's earlier tale, who does things that Jekyll would not do. For example, when Baldwin has given his word to his opponent's family not to kill him in a duel, his image arrives early, and runs his opponent through. Like the multiple self in James Hogg's pioneering terrifying study in doubling, depravity, and possession (*The Private Memoirs*), Baldwin's shadow has a will of its own.[11]

The doppelgänger can be a symbol of a self from a lost past, but here, as in many such stories in the later nineteenth and twentieth centuries, the double is his shadow self, his secret, evil *alter ego*, his damned soul. Fairy-tales and ghost stories about such thefts do not insist verbally on the particular, recognizable, unique features of the stolen shadow—they assume the personal attachment to an individual's human essence. But visual representations, as in the films of *The Student of Prague,* of course stress the identity of personal appearance and shadow/reflection as a material presence, silently translating the shadow of the story into a mirror reflection.

Baldwin finds himself shunned by friends and strangers alike, and finally, in the final scene, he fires at his reflection in the glass in despair. We then see him clutch his own heart, for he has of course shot himself.

Interestingly, Oscar Wilde, writing in the fantasy tradition of the 'good crawler' that Stevenson also brought to high literary performance, stages a very similar scene at the end of *The Picture of Dorian Gray* (1881), which it is possible Ewers had read. Wilde also wrote a fairy-tale variation on the infernal pact in 'The Fisherman and his Soul'.

At an experimental phase, the cinema already played with the projections of an individual, and preparing the ground for the populace of replicants, doubles, phantoms, zombies, and other stolen souls who teem in mass entertainment now (see Part X and Conclusion). An actor like Wegener and a director like Rye relished the opportunity the medium offered to explore a self-reflexive metaphor of the cinema itself: a magic theatre of phantoms, of unstabling the idea of the self altogether through the doppelgänger of the film image of a person, with its disturbing potential of infinite reduplication.

Around 1911, the Austrian fantasy writer and great librettist Hugo von Hofmannsthal conceived a tale that he then began working into an opera libretto, *Die Frau ohne Schatten* ('The Woman without a Shadow'); he wrote it for the composer Richard Strauss, with whom he had often collaborated, and reworked it into a book-length prose-poem, an intense allegory of magical initiation, metamorphoses, and spiritual ascent. In this poetic fable, the shadow's journey as metaphor evolves from substanceless shade to a powerful symbol of embodied human identity.[12] The story is overwrought, sometimes grotesque, and throughout highly elaborate, symbolic, and some-times over-solemn; it is eclectically patched and pieced with Christian metaphysics, baroque Italian fabulism, and *The Arabian Nights*: Strauss him-self declared that he wanted to re-create *The Magic Flute* without Emanuel Schikaneder and Mozart's Freemasonry.[13] It takes the magical and suggest-ive theme of a body that casts no shadow, but its protagonist is a fairy queen called here 'the Empress', with consequent changes in the image's mean-ing. This young woman without a shadow is the daughter of a powerful prince of the spirits; with her crystalline form, she makes everything she passes more dazzling, more illuminated. In an open tribute to the story of Dibutades, her nurse takes a lamp to look at her as she sleeps, and then sees that she casts not the slightest shadow on the wall. In this fairy-tale, shadow symbolizes vitality, and its own shadow double, mortality; the power to cast it stands for the power to reproduce, which she does not possess: this heroine is barren.

She falls in love with a human, and, like mermaids who must exchange their immortality or their supernatural gifts (their siren voice) for access to the world of humans, the Empress has to acquire a shadow and conceive a child if she wants to remain on earth—and she cannot do one without the other. During the course of the allegory and of the opera, the Empress strives to achieve full humanity, that fallen, shadow state: she struggles through a ferocious sequence of ordeals to take possession of the shadow of a woman, the Dyer's Wife. This ordinary woman is a beauty in furious rebellion against the domestic drudgery of her existence, and she refuses to have the children for which her husband longs. A protracted struggle for a shadow takes place in the hovel of the Dyer, with shrouds and cloths dripping with colours hanging all around: in relation to the photograph as face-peeling, it is interesting to recall that the idea of *Die Frau ohne Schatten* came to Hofmannsthal during a trip in Morocco, when he was walking through the dyers' quarters and saw men working with skins.

Several times the Empress passes through a terrible ordeal, and finally, by an act of heroic renunciation, she gains a shadow without robbing someone else. In so doing, she releases her husband from the grip of a stony death and becomes able to conceive a child with him.[14]

The medium of photography, when it made images by fixing the cast image of a person or object, seemed to fulfil the prophetic collapse of distinction in such material between shadow and reflection. Hugo von Hofmannsthal's fable pleads that the mirror's answering image should open a magic casement, not close down the circuits of thought and exchange. Like the film *The Student of Prague, Die Frau ohne Schatten* is a story of the photographic age, and its author offered a possible approach to pl setting its immortal (sterile) replicant powers on one side, its fugit fantasy potential on the other. But moving film, by contrast to the still photograph, contributed an altogether different dimension—motion— which reproduced an intrinsic property of life, and so it fundamentally altered photography's relationship with death. 'The dream of the moving statue', in the title of Kenneth Gross' book, suffuses many stories of artists' ambitions, many legends of magic figures and living statues and pre-cinematic media of illusion. Waxworks artists who gave a Sleeping Beauty clockwork breath, the religious icon-makers who gilded their images to flicker in the light and added lambency to the figures' eyes, the kinetic silvery comings-and-goings of the daguerreotype, all strained to resemble animate life. But cinema fulfilled these dreams: reality not simulated but captured. The inventions of proto-cinema and then of the movies themselves brought about a revolution. Imagining what self-image was like before the family album is very hard today, but it is worth repeating that photography, still and moving, has fundamentally altered the grounds of self-knowledge. (Marcel Proust has continual recourse to photographic images in one form or another in his novel, *A la Recherche du temps perdu*, as he recovers lost time and past selves.)[15]

When J. M. Barrie created the famous story of Peter Pan, he may have been inspired directly by German Romantic tales. *Peter Pan,* first written as a play in 1904, then published as a novel for children in 1911, opens with a chapter called 'Peter Breaks Through': the boy who never grows up breaks through the window of Wendy's bedroom, into the Darling family house. But he also breaks through from the other side, from Neverland where the Lost Boys live—an image of paradise, or limbo, or at least of the beyond that exists outside terrestrial time.

When Peter Pan slips away again, he leaves his shadow caught in the window. Nana, the dog who acts as nanny to the Darling children, takes the shadow in her mouth and hangs it out of the window for Peter Pan to recover easily, but Mrs Darling rolls it up and puts it away in a drawer. Later, Peter Pan finds it with the help of Tinkerbell the fairy. 'If he thought at all,' writes Barrie, 'But I don't believe he ever thought, it was that he and his shadow, when brought near each other, would join like drops of water; and when they did not he was appalled. He tried to stick it on with soap from the bathroom, but that also failed. A shudder passed through Peter and he sat on the floor and cried.'[16] Wendy wakes up to find him sobbing, and she bossily takes him in hand and sews his shadow back on. 'Soon his shadow was behaving properly, though still a little creased.'[17]

In the next chapter of Barrie's classic, the Darling children are taught to fly by Peter: to fly, an image of dreams, of out of the body experience, of the other world, of the spirit. A boy who never grows up is free from time; a boy who loses his shadow, and survives it, who can fly and teach others to fly, is free from materiality. Neverland is a place where the dead live as if they are alive, and nobody grows up, and the laws of space-time are cancelled. This is what Hofmannsthal's fable and Strauss's opera resist: the shadow they seek to seize possesses substance, and with it, all the properties of vitality. Just as a shadow betokens the solid presence of a body, so spirit metaphors testify to the existence of material reality. But this presence shadowed forth by the image has a spectral power, expressed in the widespread belief that the camera steals the soul.

Running Deer, one braid unravelled, his quiff stiffened
with buffalo grease, faces the camera. Frank Jay Haynes
(1889–1900).

15
The Camera Steals the Soul

That camera is a portable tomb, you must remember that.

Tezcatlipoca, god of the smoking mirror, to Robert Smithson

When figures appear in your dreams, what are these thoughts made of? Can 'picture-flesh' be real? When someone kisses a face in a photograph, what kind of materiality does the loved one in the image possess? In what ways do a phantasm in the mind and an image made of light resemble each other? They exist on the obscure frontier of materiality and immateriality, but does this frontier correspond to the mysterious, ungraspable frontier between body and spirit, between physical individual forms and the animating character of persons? Some photographic images do indeed slip into this space, according to their makers' and subjects' beliefs: the exchange of light from a body to an image established a material connection far deeper and more weird than any painted image could do. The portrait photograph raises the dead on behalf of the summoners perhaps to allay *their* fears, not only to offer solace. It could also function as an apotropaic image, warding off the death of the onlooker. The myth that the camera steals the soul may turn out not to be a myth in the colloquial sense of delusion. It may be a myth in the sense of a deeper truth, a fiction with greater power to illuminate the workings of the psyche, however irrational its foundation.

Shadow-catchers, soul-stealers, face-takers, shadow men, photographers have been called, in different parts of the world, by various fearful names that exactly echo Balzac's image; in Canada, a local phrase translates as 'face-pullers'.[1] When Werner Herzog and his film crew were making *Fitzcarraldo* (1982) in the Peruvian Amazon, they were given the even more graphic description of 'face-peelers'. The images, taken from flaying, scalping, and, perhaps, printing, slide and slip between description and metaphor, as the shadow cast turns from a physical effect into a metaphysical concept, tinged with fear. The stories told about peoples who feared soul-theft do not explore the meanings of words for shadow in their languages, do not touch upon uses of metaphor in this domain of meaning; they simply expect that shadow and soul flow and mingle in others' belief systems as they do in imagery about ghosts in the classical legacy.[2] That 'savage thought'— magical thinking—fails to distinguish between metaphor and referent has become an axiom; but few commentators stop to inquire whether, even if this holds, such affinities exist between shadow, ghost, and spirit also in the classical European tradition.

The idea has become a commonplace, but the 'natives' in question change: the actor Rupert Everett in an interview mourned his inability to fall in love, and blamed it on his fame, on the unceasing replication of his face: 'You know,' he said, 'I really believe that Asian thing that the camera steals your soul.'[3] A New Yorker reported how he was told by his doctor that if he wanted to continue to be able to walk, he would have to have a serious operation on his spine. He took the subway home: 'Up to this point,' he writes, 'I had been in shock, but these thoughts jarred me out of it. All of a sudden my whole situation came crashing in on me, and I started to cry.' He felt himself to be alone—among strangers—but then someone approached him in the subway car and asked to take his photograph. 'The young man took his photos while I quietly wept.'

Though he had submitted—even consented—the writer describes how he was 'left with a strange empty feeling as though something had been taken from me. I thought of the primitive people who object to being photographed out of fear that it would steal their soul. I felt that had happened to me, that someone had sapped my inner reserves of strength at a time when I particularly needed them—and still do.'[4]

Could this repeated and unexamined hearsay, passed on down the decades about this culture and that people, match an uneasiness that arises elsewhere, not in the subject of the photograph but in its maker? Could the report of primitive fears reflect anxiety, perhaps shared by both the subject of the image and its maker, that the photographic image may be more than dead matter?

The belief marks the primitive mind in literary and ethnographical observers' reports. 'Indians' and 'savages'—as invoked with all-inclusive vagueness—are especially prey to such fancies. The chief instances of the belief's occurrence turn up in the anthropological literature of the mid to late nineteenth century, and it persists well into the twentieth. They extrapolate from myths and stories about the fear of reflections and shadows, as collected by the anthropologist J. G. Frazer, where he instances peoples all over the world who fear their own image in reflection and in reproduction, both past and present: Indians from the subcontinent, from the archipelagos of Indonesia, as well as from the Plains, the mountains, and the deserts of the Americas, Asians from China, Korea, and Tibet, Africans—'the Yaos, from near Lake Nyassa and, Esquimaux' in the far north.[5]

In the questionnaire Frazer sent out all over the British Empire to potential informants, he put the question, 'Does [the soul] resemble a shadow, a reflection, a breath, or what?'[6] His inquiry into 'the Customs, Beliefs, and Language of Savages' began circulating in the 1880s; the replies, from missionaries, surveyors, and others in the field, contributed to Frazer's salmagundi, assembled in Cambridge, and eventually shaping *The Golden Bough* (1890).

The belief, extended to photography as a new technical means of catching reflections, was ascribed to the Chinese in the first book of photographs taken in China by the enterprising Scotsman John Thomson in 1860–1. Thomson added a touch of lurid fancy to his role in the introduction: 'I . . . frequently enjoyed the reputation of being a dangerous geomancer, and my camera was held to be a dark mysterious instrument, which . . . gave me power . . . to pierce the very souls of the natives and to produce pictures by some black art, which at the same time bereft the individual depicted of so much of the principle of life as to render his death a certainty within a very short period.'[7] That single, fleeting 'frequently' at the opening of the sentence is doing heavy duty, covering up the inconsistencies in his disingenuous contrast between himself and his subjects. For Thomson's statement blithely ignores the familiar tradition of Chinese official scroll portraiture (emperors, statesmen face on, the gaze straight out), but it is also of course contradicted by the contents of his own book, which includes the earliest photographic portraits of Chinese individuals, from the ruling statesman Prince Kung to an assortment of vivid street vendors—none of whom look at all scared of losing their souls.

A generation later, in 1894, an explorer writing about the Sioux described how he set up his camera to photograph a village on the lower Yukon River. 'While he was focussing the instrument, the headman of the village came up and insisted on peeping under the cloth. Being allowed to do so, he gazed intently for a minute at the moving figures on the ground glass then suddenly withdrew his head and bawled at the top of his voice to the people, "He has all of your shades in this box." A panic ensued.'[8]

When such a reaction of awe or fear was not provoked, new arrivals can sound frustrated: a zoologist travelling in the Andaman Islands reported, 'I commenced to erect my photographic tent; but although this is a very remarkable object when erected, the natives scarcely took the trouble to look at it, and none expressed any surprise.'[9]

The note of pique betrays one purpose fulfilled by the fantasy: the pleasure of control. The explorer A. Simson, writing about the Jivaro people, recorded in 1880: 'we had great trouble to get [two Indians] to stand with us, as they have the idea that their soul is carried away in the picture; but they soon stopped and returned to us on our telling them that it was too late, since we had already secured their spirits.'[10] The photographer in this case did not deny the belief, but rather confirmed it in order to have his way.

Children photographed in 1879 in Tierra del Fuego huddle away from the apparatus held by F. North, a member of the surveying expedition; but, in a later image taken on the same British ship, the *H. M. S. Alert*, the same boys are facing the camera squarely, dressed in naval uniforms, no longer afraid. The change in their reactions may reveal that their initial distress arose not because they expected to lose their souls, but because they were apprehensive about the instrument pointed at them. Visitors often disclose that they assumed beforehand that their subject would take fright; some played to that fear to ensure their compliance. Maxime du Camp, Flaubert's friend and travelling companion in Egypt, told his boatman that if they did not obey him and hold still, the machine he was wielding was a cannon which would vomit a hail of shot.[11] As late as 1961, Jorgen Bisch, describing his travels in Borneo, invoked the same story as sufficient explanation for the animus of the tribespeople against him.[12]

Fear of the soul-stealing powers of reflection and doubling flourishes in Graeco-Christian mythology (see Chapters 13 and 14) as richly, if not more so, than it does among 'Indians', and the general belief was recognized—or imputed?—to Others from ideas about image and spirit well rooted in the thought of the photographer, and not in his or her subjects only. John Thomson's idea would have meshed with the preconceptions of his Victorian audience, and his claim illuminates the history of European ideas about soul and spirit, images and media, far more reliably than it does the ideas of his Chinese subjects.

There is no reason to suppose that any native/primitive/indigenous people would not have been frightened by the sight of a foreigner with strange mechanical equipment; they might well have taken to their heels to prevent its use on them. But it is the persistent Western interpretation of that fear, as arising from the interfusion of image and soul, that gives rise to questions. The repeated tale of the soul-stealer may correspond to a deeper desire of the incomers. It could function like cannibal stories, as a marker to docket and define the savage mind. Such a supposedly primitive concept became convenient shorthand for marking out indigenous peoples as superstitious, naïve, undeveloped. The display of technology proved the culture's power, and implied a superior relation to intelligence and to reason. In an anonymous photograph taken in Mexico in 1879, an unknown explorer is carrying a gun over his shoulder while his *eleven* native bearers are carrying the supplies for 'el patrón' (as the caption says) on his journey from Caraporta to Mayahamba-Loreta. One of them is carrying the camera.[13] When the Indian warrior chief Crazy Horse of the Oglala tribe did not allow himself to be photographed, saying that those who did lost the spirit of resistance, he was responding to the use of the camera alongside the gun.

But this commonsensical connection has been eclipsed by a more mythic —and derogatory—assumption: the reaction interpreted as a metaphysical fear, a superstition characteristic of the primitive mind.

The Sioux of the Plains recur in the literature of the Americas as the people who entertained the most vivid ideas and practices centring on the shadow as the vessel of the soul, of identity.[14] Yet there is a contradiction here, for the Sioux posed for some of the most memorable portraits made in America. By the Seventies and Eighties, the subjects performed in costume for the still portraitists, sometimes in the setting of the travelling shows, such as Buffalo Bill's circus. But such magnificent images of these chieftains and others, taken in the 1870s by Alexander Gardner, or of the warriors Red Cloud and Plenty Coups, taken around 1880 by Charles Milton Bell, or of the Apache Geronimo in 1904, define one of the camera's most compelling capacities, to scan and register the distinctiveness of an individual's face.

Many of Gardner's and Bell's subjects belong to the Plains nations, who feared the camera's soul-theft and practised magical protective rituals; some of them, like the Ghost Dance, developed during the Indian wars as particular defences in the crisis. Yet many, consenting subjects, hold the camera in their steady gaze: Bird Chief Arapaho, by either Gardner or Gurney, also taken in the early 1870s, or the Frank Jay Haynes portrait of Running Deer, of the Plains' Crow Tribe (Figure 17, p. 188). The leader of the Dakota and medicine man Sitting Bull was photographed several times; in one portrait made by David F. Barry in 1885, he faces the lens straight on, with tremendous, impressive uprightness. This was five years before his arrest and death before the Battle of Wounded Knee. These subjects do not communicate anything but heroic presence; it is hindsight that finds irony in their panoply of weapons, the defiant stance and the determined gaze of these resistants and combatants. The immobility of the chiefs' frozen pose, their deep, awe-inspiring silence, their gravity and authority, all contribute to the power of these images. Such dignified and powerful men are un-settlingly captured for the present, the tense of a perpetual and permanent now, and the uncanniness of that time zone to which the photograph has transported them is intensified because it seems that the immortal part of them has endured there, in the image, when the mortal remains have long disintegrated. Even the wrinkles on their faces, the marks of time's passage, have been arrested, partly smoothed out by the medium's own unwrinkled skin. These subjects remain present in their presence, crossing from the zone of the past into our time. This is not 'flat death', as Roland Barthes expressed it, but 'flat life', as Lucy Lippard has amended.[15]

Like these sitters, many indigenous subjects, in the very earliest decades of making fixed images, during the 1840s, showed absolutely no fear of the camera: the daguerreotypist Charles Guillain made powerful profile portraits of children, men, and women on a voyage to East Africa in 1846–8. 'Among the women who came aboard,' he wrote, 'one of them, who was a Warsangeli ... willingly agreed to have her portrait taken and seemed delighted that she had made the journey.'[16] The result shows a resolute, beautiful young woman, unbowed and proud.[17]

The interval between the invention of the daguerreotype and the widespread practice of the ambulant photographer marks the spread of the idea that the camera steals the soul. It travelled with the medium and its users, in the same way as fears of witchcraft travelled with witch-finders.[18] So it is possible that belief rose among photographers, above all, in contact with ideas about spirits, and became an expression of their power. This reversal offers another context for the idea of the soul-stealer, what it meant to the photographers and to the collectors and the viewers of these images (you and me) after the portraits were made, and it can throw light on the reasons for the repetition of the idea and its meaning for our culture, now.

For the indwelling, individual spirit of the subject (the personal soul, if you like) is of course not the same entity as the spirit presented in the invisible narrative, the historical and psychological allegory of Native American culture created by the photographer. With this important distinction in mind, these magnificent portraits then seem to offer two distinct aspects of the stolen soul and its meaning: first, the resemblance, materializing in its uncannily fixed form in the photograph, might contain some material residue of the person, transmitted with the light rays from his or her body. This is one idea of shadow-catching, and one possible version of the rationale underlying the belief that Indians are said to hold.

The memorable metaphor that Balzac used, that every photograph peeled a ghost from his being, brings our attention to a strong theme in the history of photography: soul-theft. This introduces the second variation on the theme. For the image of a warrior such as Sitting Bull or Running Deer happens to record the character of a culture at the time of its most agonistic trials; the subjects of the portraits are cast as actors in a drama of transience. And how different are those portraits from the record of Chief Big Foot stiffly half crouched in the snow where he fell and froze at Wounded Knee, like a clubbed seal.[19] Such men knew the threat to their way of life, and many of them, even as they sat with their weapons, understood that they were outgunned—even though the Sioux chieftains like Sitting Bull had succeeded in inflicting defeat at Little Big Horn in 1876, and, of all the tribes, theirs has not been wiped out. Yet several posed in full fig precisely because they knew their culture was changing irrevocably. The images even played a part in the dynamics of self-affirmation, of resistance, and became part of the history they were telling in dialogue with their conquerors. It provides a record which has kept vivid and alive their historical presence in excess of expectations on all sides.

Edward S. Curtis, one of the most majestically elegiac of the photographers of the West, working in the era after the Indian Wars, contributed consciously to this archive. He took no fewer than 40,000 images—for example, of He-Dog, one of Crazy Horse's friends, who surrendered with him on the day the chief died. He-Dog faces the camera in full war gear. Curtis 'always insisted that the Indians he photographed should be dressed like Indians, and if there was a background scene, it had to contain a vital part of their life or land'. He expressed sympathy and respect for his subjects and for the images that they wished to present to posterity.[20]

Yet the first image Curtis took of a Native American, he reported, was a 'Princess' he encountered working on the river bank in Seattle. She was not wearing tribal dress; nor was she especially distinct in appearance from another labourer. For Curtis, she embodied a culture in process of disappearance, not metamorphosis, and, as a result, the photograph remains exceptional as a result in Curtis' production. Thereafter he decided that 'the pictures should be made according to the best modern methods and of a size that the face might be studied as the Indians' own flesh. And above all none of these pictures would admit anything which betokened civilisation whether an article of dress of landscapes or objects on the ground. These pictures were to be transcriptions for future generations that they might behold the Indian as nearly lifelike as possible.'[21] His subjects thus perform an act of memory, part of a historical reconstruction not unlike the Buffalo Bill circus re-enactments that began touring in the 1880s.

Does Curtis' longing for 'a vital part' to be captured by the image express a wish, repressed but no less acute, to perform an act of sympathetic magic that would achieve precisely that? Is this desire to study the 'Indians' own flesh' in the images a version of scalping? Of bounty hunting? Of displaying trophies of conquest and its victims, however magnificent, grand, and proud the images? But even if their sitters did not approach the issue in the same spirit as the photographers, their images have become epitaphs. The studio props, the rocks, the trailing ivy, the blankets, the bonnets and stomachers, beads, feathers, bows, arrows, quivers, and full panoply of Red Indianness enshrine the subjects in their exotic and particular separateness, with the circumstantial, petrifying detail of waxworks.[22] Unlike the working princess, connected to the economy of Seattle's inhabitants, Curtis' imposing chiefs erase the story of interaction and of mutual if tense interdependence between indigenous inhabitant and incoming settler that had also occurred during the bitter decades of conflict.

The role of photography in making history was not confined to North America. A picture taken around 1895 in Marianhill in South Africa, shows a German monk arranging his subjects—Zulu warriors—to face his camera. The full ornaments and weaponry of the men posing for his photograph contrast dramatically with the informal simplicity of several other Zulus looking on as the image is taken; it reveals again the way in which photographers staged the presentation of their subjects, costumed them, groomed them, prepared them for self-representation for the purposes of posterity and their memory. The ornamentalism of such ethnographical records is a kind of Orientalism (as David Cannadine has punned in a recent book),[23] and it moves photography towards heritage spectacle, away from social and active belonging.

Edward Curtis also made a rich and invaluable archive of masked portraits of the different American nations, in which his sitters usually face the camera squarely, with the lighting dramatically arranged to reveal every item in the complex costume and to enhance its uncanny life. These images have been collected together, in an album called *Hidden Faces*, and they effectively make their subjects vanish. Meanwhile the ritual process of the original event also loses force. During the sitters' lifetimes, the masks formed part of a ceremony in relation to others, to dancers and audience. Now, the isolation of the sitter, the frequent disappearance of the person, the mask's dominance as subject, detach it from the society and history that gave it meaning, and turn it into a priceless and desired *objet d'art*.[24]

Displays of accoutrements and memorabilia take on the character of grave goods: placed in the tomb of the image for the passage to death, out of history, into the future timeless zone of elegy. One of Curtis's most famous photographs, which first appeared around 1904, is called 'Vanishing Race: Navajo', and shows a line of horsemen riding off into the mists, hunched and shrouded. The idea became a convention: photographs with titles like 'Sunset of a Dying Race' filled the albums of the early twentieth century,[25] and a careful edition of Curtis's work appeared in 2000 under the title *Visions of a Vanishing Race*.[26]

A different approach to the societies of the indigenous North Americans, coupled with a divergent political context as well as different working methods, produces a strikingly different impression, and reveals how the corpus of Curtis's legacy does literally entomb his subjects. Mary Schaffer (1893–1928) was a photographer who worked in Canada during the same period, but she travelled with her nomadic tribal subjects, principally the Stoney Indians from around Banff, befriended them, and made their portraits in groups as they lived their ordinary lives. Her pictures do not reject signs of the interaction of new, Canadian mores with traditional ways of life: her subjects wear mixtures of clothes, waistcoats and jeans (sometimes with the addition of a medal of Queen Victoria), and combine these with tribal elements; she shows them trading in the streets of Banff, and not only during the days when they put on displays of horsemanship and other skills. Above all, Schaffer added colour, hand-painting lantern slides for projection. One family group, the Beavers with their 4-year-old daughter Louise, sit together in a field of high grass in summer by their tepee; they are giving the camera broad, relaxed smiles, in an image of unprecedented affection and Indian coexistence with an individual from their territory's rulers.[27] Schaffer's work also reflects the losses of the encounter: she recorded scalps and necklaces of human bones, for instance. But she does not deal with them by raising an epitaph to a vanished race.

Edward Curtis was only one of dozens of photographers who went West, not to record the life of the Indians but their death. Their grand archival act of mourning was undertaken with the blessing of the President Teddy Roosevelt and financed by public subscription. Was this semblance of life endlessly prolonged a way of dealing death to its subjects? Does it make a show of remorse while presenting them as players in a finished story and so enshrining their culture's inevitable passing?

As Elizabeth Edwards has written, 'In many ways those people who fear the camera would steal their souls, would peel their faces were right. The camera was one of those instruments of appropriation, which recorded culture at the colonial periphery and removed it for analysis . . . in the metropolitan centres. Culture and histories became not what they were to the people themselves, but how they were defined and analysed externally.'[28]

Ethnographic image-makers frequently scoffed at their subjects' fear of the camera, but they may have imagined it, or at least attributed to it certain causes, because they themselves sensed its power. They may or may not have explored the views and feelings of the people they were photographing— but they were certainly acting in accordance with patterns in their own cultural tradition, which had increasingly come to identify a contact replica of outer form with the essence of a person. The prevalent idea that the camera steals the soul may at times express a sympathetic wish on the part of the image-makers that the subject will fade into the shadows.

This contemporary myth interestingly reveals enduring stratagems of the imagination when the self feels under threat of incomprehension, and their resulting wider cultural expression. The idea of soul-theft by image provokes a feeling of shame in those who hold it, however unconsciously, because it is not rational, it is not scientific. So it is ascribed to an Other who is primitive—noble and doomed; secondly, the idea is then borrowed and reiterated, in a kind of false tribute ('that Asian thing') to the eternal wisdom of those noble, doomed people; thirdly, those same peoples, who have not been altogether successfully exterminated, repossess the idea as an original defining belief of their culture, and in this act of appropriation reassert their authority; fourthly, this repossession then inspires the former colonial annexers to realize that they must take charge of their representations, too.

Contemporary photography has not abandoned the manners of this scientific mode of documentary presentation, but has made of it an aesthetic of high-pressure cool. Richard Avedon has paid conscious homage in his studies of types of the American West, and a portrait he made in 1994 of Moi, a Huaorani Indian from the Amazonian jungle of Ecuador, presents a most powerful example of the form. Moi offers his face and body to the lens, his left hand seeming to beseech the viewer, while the other tightly grips his upper arm.[29] It is also in keeping with the iconographic tradition that this kind of portrait accompanied an article about unregulated oil exploitation in the forest, which is polluting the rivers, destroying the vegetation, and gradually extinguishing the life of people like the Huaoroni. Moi, by protesting as far as Washington, had put his life in danger with his government at home. The article included the report that 'The word is that Moi is a dead man'. This sounds compassionate, but also lip-smacking. 'I found myself wondering', writes the journalist, 'if I would ever see him again.' This image we are asked to look at is Avedon's future memory of a dead man; who may indeed have become that in the time since the photograph was taken.[30] The living portrait made as a hedge against the mortality that threatens: the picture of a shade.

Photography has become a contemporary condition of existence, of communication and exchange, and a present and pervasive dimension of reality and experience. So the response can no longer be simple resistance or rejection of the image. Commanding the story it tells has provoked legal stratagems.

In the first decade of the twentieth century, a famous actor in Germany, Albert Bassermann, sued a photographer for taking his picture without telling him, expressing very strong misgivings altogether about the new medium, still and moving. In a telling legal formula, Bassermann claimed 'das Recht am eigenen Bild', the right to his own image. He was drawing on the jurist and historian Hugo Keyssner, who published legal arguments in 1896 for protecting the individual against 'the electrical light of publicity'. As Stefan Andriopoulos relates, Keyssner first drew an analogy with copyright (a person is the author, and hence owner, of his image), but then changed the basis of his argument to a human right: the person's image is an intrinsic and inalienable part of personhood, and cannot consequently be 'taken' by another without consent.[31] With a move that prepared the ground for Lacan's theory, that a child comes into consciousness of self through the looking-glass and the outside other beheld therein, Keyssner noticed that photography created a split between the me who is outside the mirror or the image, and the me reflected in it, the first a subject-ego, the second an object-ego, to which the subject lays claim. 'We are no longer affected by the scholastic scepticism', wrote another lawyer in response in 1903, 'that holds there can be no right to one's own personality, because the object of the right is lacking, because subject and object coincide.' Referring to Goethe's *Faust*, this commentator continued, 'For everybody knows that two souls inhabit our chest and that all the time one confronts one's own ego as a subject.'[32] The discussion was widely read and discussed, especially after Bassermann unexpectedly agreed to star in one of the current films exploring the theme of the doppelgänger—*Der Andere* (*The Other*, 1913).

Chieftains from the decimated tribes became one of the most popular types of spirit visitors to seances, and appear in numerous psychic photographs, channelled by different mediums in North America and in Europe. Warriors both historical and imaginary make their appearance in ectoplasmic masks or transmit their impressions.[33] These reproduce—borrow—photographic portraits: in effect, as we shall see in Chapters 17–21, spirits literally come back to haunt the living not in their bodies or in apparitions of their bodies, but in their semblance made for photographs.

Today, on the reservations and in the pueblos of Native Americans, photography is usually not allowed. In another part of the world, subcontinental India, tourists must not photograph bodies as they are cremated on the ghats by the banks of the Ganges (in Shusaku Endo's marvellous novel of cultural clash, *Deep River* (1994), a Japanese visitor—one of a group of international pilgrims—triggers a riot which culminates in murder when he wilfully flouts the taboo). Increasingly, local peoples charge tourists if they want snapshot souvenirs: it is not only need (and fairness) that inspire this. The transaction involves consent, and the 'fee', as the word's etymology hints, establishes a bond given in exchange, mitigating the bane of the image taken without agreement.[34] In Australia, the Aborigines have successfully obtained copyright on all portraits of Aborigines: these cannot be reproduced without permission of the subject or the subject's lineal descendants. In the USA, releases must be signed by the subjects of photographs before publication, and exclusive deals guarantee the appearance of a star's wedding photographs in one magazine only, with the selection overseen; at the other end of the income hierarchy, panhandlers and buskers (especially 'living statues') have followed suit. In Italy, the supermodel Carla Bruni sued a magazine when a writer gave free rein to his erotic fantasies about her, and printed photographs of her alongside. She won the case. In Britain, a clause was proposed to be added to the Copyright Act of 1988: 'A person who is the subject of a photograph which has been taken . . . without his knowledge or consent . . . has . . . the right not to have it shown or published.' The measure was not passed by Parliament. Since then, celebrities have used many different stratagems to defend themselves against paparazzi, under Data Protection Law as well as the Human Rights Convention. In 2004, Princess Caroline of Monaco successfully entered a plea, under the rubric of her right to a private life, at the Court of Human Rights in Strasbourg; this case extended the powers of stars, politicians, and other public figures to prevent their images being taken without their consent— 'the profession of the *paparazzo*', declared one lawyer, 'is in danger of becoming extinct'.[35]

Nobody would suggest, in a country where the principle of free speech exists as a right, that someone could not sketch a portrait. The material connection makes the photograph different, and it matters because this connection in turn has links with the deepest notions of uniqueness, presence, identity, existence, and the inalienable embodied individual.

As in the story of Dibutades, lovers exchange gifts of photographs, as do families and friends: when I travel, I like to have my loved ones with me, in the form of their images. When somebody sends a Christmas card with a picture taken that year, as is the custom in the United States, the image conveys that friend's closeness in spirit. When film stars sign fans' photographs, that too allows a little bit of themselves into their keeping. But without consent, the business of image-making and -taking contains threats that are stirring vigorous efforts at control. Rising commercial interests, growing out of the current pursuit of celebrity, indicate the profound psychological powers attached to photographs, as they float faces into the fantasy and memory of millions. But the effects of idolization, and its several shadows—stalking, look-alike beauty contests, pornography websites, karaoke—are fostered, and even incited, by the pervasiveness of photographic images disseminated, moving and still, through the pages of *Hello!* magazine and other public print, not to speak of television and the internet. So the desire to channel the flow arises not only from greed, or from a new twist on the idea of the self as commodity (your image is your property), but also from a deeper perturbation.[36]

Balzac's fear that the successive layers of his being would be lifted from him to inhere in the images made by the camera echoes through numerous fables on the photographic theme. Italo Calvino, in an acerbic short story of 1955 called 'The Adventure of a Photographer', creates a protagonist who refuses 'to live the present as a future memory', and feels contempt for his circle of friends who photograph their lives in order to conserve them. In the end, however, the same passion consumes him, and has hollowed out his life into a spectral series of endless images of images.[37] Michel Tournier picks up the theme in a gruesome tale in which a woman photographer consumes her (male) model by translating his substance into her photographs, like a forensic wax-modeller or taxidermist. Tournier deliberately names his sinister protagonist Véronique ('true icon'), after the weeping woman who wiped Christ's face and bore away its image on her veil. In his story, the model, Hector, runs away from Véronique, leaving a letter in which he protests: 'You have stolen my image 22,239 times. . . . 22,239 times some part of myself has been stolen from me and put into your little image trap, your "little night box", as you call it.' But Hector cannot escape that easily. She traps him again, and this time begins to take photographs directly from his body without mediation of the camera—exactly as if preserving him. The two processes become confused in Tournier's macabre fantasy, and at the end, Hector has been dissolved—into a vera icon, a true print, like the image in the 'shroud' of Christ in Turin, on the walls of Véronique's show of recent photographic works.[38]

The photograph has entered the rites of mourning and commemoration; it has become a traditional adjunct of the funeral all over the world, a visual elegy placed on the bier for the bereaved to kiss.[39] It is common to include portraits, rendered in enamel, on the tombs of the fallen in battle in Italian war memorials, for instance. All over Europe, family tombs now enshrine a photograph of the departed, printed on enamel; memorial chapels in Italy include banks of photographs of the fallen.[40] The religious use is echoed by civic monuments: in Bologna, a long wall of the main square is covered with hundreds of portraits of partisans who died in the struggle against fascism, often snapshots taken in happier times for other purposes; we pass by and stop to scan the faces, we are effectively enfolded in a powerful and moving ritual act of commemoration. In the demonstrations for the *desaparecidos*, the victims of the secret police in Argentina and other Latin American countries, photographs were carried as a reproach and a protest, a powerful testimony to those who had died but refused to go away.[41]

Roland Barthes meditates eloquently on mourning and melancholy in relation to the camera's images in his celebrated study *Camera Lucida*. Barthes concentrates on his struggle to find his dead mother through her photographs. Only one, of her as a little girl, 'achieved for me, utopically', he writes, 'the impossible science of the unique being'. Significantly, he does not reproduce this image.[42] But this relationship with the photograph of someone who is loved and absent may not be morbid, may not offer an icon of death; it may, rather, serve as a magical summons, aiming rather to enshrine identity, to create a memorial which pleads for deathlessness and issues a challenge to time—on behalf of someone.

The camera as weapon and its dependent metaphors (to 'shoot' a picture) is of course a topos richly explored by Susan Sontag in *On Photography* (1978);[43] in her last essay, *Regarding the Pain of Others* (2004), she returned to the theme, upholding images of atrocity and conflict as powerful vehicles for informed response to war today.[44] The knowledge of the consequences that war photographers send back home is vital to discussion of policy, democratic functioning, and responsibility; images of death can change the course of history, as she points out. So she withdraws part of her earlier criticism of the medium, defending the genre against imputations of complicity with violence and sensationalism, and against charges of voyeurism and numbing. She finds in its rapport with death a means of affirming life. In the words which Julia Margaret Cameron wrote on her portraits, the photograph is taken 'From Life', and it can preserve the vital energy of its long-vanished subjects.

Part VII

Ghost

Julia Margaret Cameron cast her family, friends,
and members of the household in imaginary roles,
using her camera to create the world in her mind's
eye. *The Angel at the Tomb*, 1869–70.

16

'Stay This Moment': Julia Margaret Cameron and Charles Dodgson

The most transitory of things, a shadow . . . may be fettered by the spells of our 'natural magic,' and may be fixed forever.

William Henry Fox Talbot

In Goethe's play, Faust makes a fatal bargain with Mephistopheles when, in the opening scene, he declares that if one of the devil's delights moves him so much that he cries out for time to stop, then and only then will he surrender his soul:

> Werd'ich zum Augenblicke sagen:
> Verweile doch! Du bist so schon!
>
> (Shall I say to the moment
> 'Stay a while! You are so beautiful!')[1]

These are the most celebrated lines in the play: his Faust will want to suspend time—a natural impossibility and hence a pinnacle of super-natural deception—if some moment (in German *Augenblick* means literally the blink of an eye) strikes him as so beautiful he cannot bear to part with it.

Saying to the moment, 'Stay . . . You are so beautiful', prophesies—even promises—the coming photographic age, and it is not incidental that the line appears in the scene when Faust makes his pact with Mephistopheles. It is connected to Goethe's ambitions for spectral effects, not because photography and projection are diabolical arts, but because these powers struck observers as inheriting diabolical powers of deception as defined in relation to optics and to the illusions of art.

In 1932, Virginia Woolf echoed Faust's bargain with Mephistopheles, writing in her diary: 'If one does not lie back & sum up & say to the moment, this very moment, stay you are so fair, what will be one's gain, dying? No: stay, this moment. O one ever says that enough. Always hurry. I am now going in, to see L[eonard] & say stay this moment.'[2] The feeling she expresses here so vividly replays the characteristic darting, alighting, pausing motion of her fiction, as it stays one moment and then another with bright illuminated epiphanies, and the phrase surfaces in *To the Lighthouse* (1927). Twice, Mrs Ramsay voices the same longing, saying, 'Life stand still here',[3] while towards the end, Lily Briscoe the painter is thinking about a memory becoming like a work of art, and she too picks up on Mrs Ramsay's saying.

Mrs Ramsay was closely fashioned after Woolf's memories of her mother, Julia Jackson (1846–95), the daughter of Julia Margaret Cameron's sister Mia, and also her god-daughter and favourite model—all Cameron's ardent family feeling and passionate erotic aestheticism crystallized in her contemplation of Julia's beauty. Cameron's avowed ambition was 'to arrest beauty', and it is possible that 'Life stand still here' was one of Julia Jackson's maxims.

Between 1864 and 1872, Julia sat for a magnificent and justly celebrated series of portraits, Cameron immortalizing elegiacally her grave, ethereal luminosity of countenance. The series shows her niece before her first marriage, then afterwards as a young mother, and, following the death of Herbert Duckworth, as a startlingly wraith-like widow, wreathed in ivy, her white face pale as a new moon against the blacks of her funereal clothes.[4] In 1870, Julia Jackson married Leslie Stephen, and her beautiful face, harrowed by so many deaths, eerily materialized again in their daughter Virginia. Julia Jackson wrote a brief entry on Julia Margaret Cameron for her husband's *magnum opus*, the *Dictionary of National Biography* (1886), one of the few articles about a woman in the volume, and Virginia devised family theatricals in her play *Freshwater* (1923/35), where her deft mockery shows her generation's anxiety to distance itself from its Victorian forebears. She gathers together several of the company around Lord Tennyson, but stages Mrs Cameron as a batty monomaniac.[5] In this way, Woolf suppressed the elective affinities that connect Cameron's dream photography with her own modernist ways of seizing 'moments of being' as they skim by or taking the pulse of the passage of time in order to 'stay this moment'.[6]

Photographs have realized a new relationship to physical co-ordinates— time and space—that has become so intrinsic to contemporary existence that it is no longer noticeable.

The Revd Charles Dodgson, mathematician, Anglican cleric, and author of the Alice books, was an inspired pioneering experimenter with the possibilities of photography in the earliest decades of its life.[7] In 1869, two years before the first of the Alice stories appeared, Carroll published a book of comic poems, called *Phantasmagoria*, in which the title-poem spoofs an apparition; he also composed, to the bouncy metre of *Hiawatha*, an earlier ebullient satire on the difficulties of portrait photography:

> Mystic, awful, was the process . . .
> Yet the picture failed entirely.[8]

Through the Looking Glass and What Alice Found There appeared in 1871, when Cameron was busy staying the moment on glass plates; Carroll's sequel to his first great classic is an early work of the photographic age. While Alice first found a disconcerting Wonderland down a rabbit hole in one of the city's meadows, in the second story of her adventures she climbs up on the mantelpiece and enters a double of this world on the other side of the mirror, a mirror which has become a window. In Looking-Glass country, the world behaves according to the optics of reflection; or, more precisely, it obeys the catoptrics of the dark plate inside the camera and the developing process, with its inversions of up and down, light and dark, and its contractions and distortions of scale. (*Through the Looking Glass* opens with Alice explaining to Kitty: 'there's the room you can see through the glass—that's just the same as our drawing-room, only the things go the other way . . . You can just see a little *peep* of the passage in Looking-glass House . . . and it's very like our passage . . . only you know it may be quite different on beyond.')[9]

Carroll developed many photographic narrative techniques more fully in the diptych of novels published in the 1880s, *Sylvie and Bruno* and *Sylvie and Bruno Concluded*, in which the child protagonists move out of the Here and Now into two other space-time universes, one call Elfland and the other called Outland. The transitions in space take place under Carroll's direction without comment, with swift, abrupt jump-cuts, involving transitions in time which increase the unstable sense of mirror worlds: the little girl Sylvie turns into the young woman Lady Muriel, from one sentence to another, just as if a wand had been waved over her. Further doublings involve the events themselves, not only the characters to whom they are happening. Carroll was especially fascinated by self-reflexive dream states in which you watch yourself, live through certain experiences more than once, and have the time over again to live it in a different way.[10] Miniaturization and magnification occur in fantasy storytelling before Carroll (*The Tale of Tom Thumb, Gulliver's Travels*), doppelgängers materialize in mirrors and mirages, and metamorphoses involving slow fades and dissolves describe the fate of Narcissus and others (Chapter 12). But Lewis Carroll annexed the tricks and illusions that he explored as the Revd Dodgson when taking and printing his photographs—which also starred children of course. The simultaneous existence of Sylvie as a child and as a young woman reproduces the effect of a photograph album, in which Alice Liddell and others from his huge circle of child friends and models are seen to grow up into young women. It is relevant, for instance, that Carroll fixed a round photograph of Alice Liddell at the end of a telescope so that you could look down it and see her—the real-life girl—as a dream image projected as it were into the stars,[11] just as he evokes at the end of *Through the Looking-Glass*:

Still she haunts me, phantom wise,
Alice moving under skies
Never seen by waking eyes.[12]

In a vast and dazzling range of imaginative literature, children are cast as natural and enviable sojourners in these dream worlds: George MacDonald wrote a series about his boy hero, Curdie, in which he enjoys special access to fairylands *At the Back of the North Wind* (1871), according to the title of one of his most successful stories. (He became a friend of Lewis Carroll after they met in a doctor's waiting-room where they were both hoping for a cure for their stammering.)

Dodgson also photographed Christina Rossetti, his friend, fellow campaigner against vivisection, and author of one of the strangest and most intense fancies about other worlds, her long narrative poem *Goblin Market*, written three years before his first *Alice* book. In this visionary and sometimes lurid ballad, Laura falls for the queer little goblin men and their enticing fruits running voluptuously with sap and juice, and like Persephone, after she ate the seven seeds of the pomegranate, Laura becomes spellbound, a psychological captive in the faery underworld and another entranced female subject (a sleeping beauty) of the late Romantic imagination. Her sister Lizzie then wrestles with the goblins and wins Laura's reprieve. The mysterious verses, tripping along in uneven nursery-rhyme rhythms, echo earlier visions of spellbound altered states of mind that also evoke an archaic, pagan past vulnerable to demons: Coleridge's 'Christabel' and Keats's 'La Belle Dame sans Merci'. Charles Kingsley's parallel universe, where the Water Babies dwell, inspired several titles for Julia Margaret Cameron's photographs of infants and young children. Plots set in a similar uncanny alternative space-time carry some of the touching stories of Frances Hodgson Burnett and of course, later, the ambitious allegories of C. S. Lewis and his *Narnia*, a country of the mind reached through a different kind of camera obscura, a wardrobe.

Ideas about the imagination from children's books written during the early phase of photography have flowered in the new mythology of their many followers (including Joan Aiken, Russell Hoban, Philip Pullman, and J. K. Rowling). In an era when the photographic media's omnipresence cannot be overestimated, children's fiction tackles the doubled, or multiple, worlds opened by mirrors and lenses. Will and Lyra, the boy and girl heroes of Philip Pullman's trilogy, *His Dark Materials*, access parallel worlds, including a mirror image of Oxford, by opening with 'a subtle knife' windows in the atmosphere of an ordinary day. Passing through to the other side of the material world means passing into something special, enchanted, illusory, sometimes alarming, always intensely vivid.

The history of photography and the uses to which it has been put over the centuries and decades have tightened the bond with memory, record, retrospection, and mourning. In an impassioned elegy for Roland Barthes, Jacques Derrida writes, 'Although it [the referent] is not longer *there* (present, living, real, etc.), it *having-been-there* [is] now part of the referential or intentional structure of my relationship to the photogramme, [and] the return of the referent indeed takes the form of a haunting. This is 'a return of the dead'.[13] Yet of all people Derrida was alert to the fluctuating interpretation of those visible referents by the beholder. The old saw, 'the camera never lies', is a feeble hope at best, as is widely acknowledged by now; but this does not entail the opposite thought, that the camera lies, but rather that it fantasizes.

While daguerreotypes and photographs do indeed preserve people, sights, and events with a totally engrossing precision and detail, they served from their beginnings to explore new, unknown experiences (countries, phenomena, flora), and to fill the minds of their beholders with things which they had not experienced or beheld before. This, a documentary pursuit for the photographers, turns into an exercise in imagining for the viewers. The medium has never been engaged solely with archiving; it institutes thought-pictures, most of which in a strict sense are not personal memories at all. Photographs can conjure memories that belong in fantasy, in eidetic recollection, and in some ontological reality, not in lived experience, The replicants in Philip K. Dick's visionary novel *Do Androids Dream of Electric Sheep?* (1968) are implanted with memories of imaginary past lives through made-up family snaps, because these can incorporate into someone's mind manifold perceptions far beyond her or his actual experience. (Most of the photographic material you or I come into contact with on a daily basis has no connection to your life or mine. When it enters my mind and becomes part of that experience, it is the photograph that I now store there, not its subject, and that is not a memory, at least not a memory of lived, direct experience. It is only through the ordinary activity of the imagination that it becomes alive, acquires warmth, scale, animation, and other qualities of reality.)

Also, from the earliest times, the making of photographs involved play-acting and illusion. What is captured by the apparatus does not always retain its own nature, or refer to itself. Indeed, that self may not be visible as such in the image: 'The Angel at the Tomb' by Julia Margaret Cameron (Figure 18, p. 204), refers to Mary Hillier, her servant who modelled for her, only if the viewer deliberately refuses the terms on which Cameron presented her subject's glowing and ethereal presence.[14] Alongside its pioneers' documentary uses, photography acts as a tool of constitutive imagination.

The camera could bring to visible life unearthly beings who come from outside, over there, as if they were real; the desire to do so spurred on the development of scientific devices. The relationship between subjects which appeared to the eye of the imagination, while remaining physically inaccessible to sensory perception, exercised profound fascination over many different types and social classes. Mesmerism, hypnotism, clairvoyance, and somnambulism continued to inspire street entertainment in the nineteenth-century city, as we have seen, as well as philosophical and religious inquiry.

For example, in 1824, Dr Samuel Hibbert published a book about ghosts, which included an elaborate fold-out chart about dream states, on which he set out a 'Formula of the various comparative Degrees of Faintness, Vividness, or Intensity, supposed to subsist between Sensations and Ideas'. He tabulated eight transitions in his full cycle, ranging from 'Perfect Sleep' to 'Somnambulism' by way of 'the common state of Watchfulness' to 'the tranquil state' to 'extreme mental excitement', and graded no fewer than fifteen different phases in each of them. They start from 'Degree of vividness at which consciousness begins', where it is still possible to impose the will on vision, to 'Intense excitements of the mind necessary for the production of spectres'.[15]

Dr Hibbert (1782–1848) was not a singular man of his time; his efforts reflect the passionate interest in the mind's workings throughout the period of the Romantics, with numerous counterparts in the literature of psychology, biology, medicine, and literature. His chart—a rather seductive graphic work in itself—imitates the elaborate taxonomies of his fellow scientists, but it also acquires an absurd charm as he becomes more and more entangled in definitions of his theme. Although he is himself pretty much forgotten today, his book created a stir because he went on to argue that stomach disorders were a chief source of hallucination, visions, *déjà vu*, nightmares, and even mental distress, and that this physical organ could overbear the mind to the point of altering a person's identity. In a still Christian age, such radical materialism was extreme, and a flurry of arguments for and against followed.[16]

'Seeing with eyes shut' (the title of an essay by the philosopher Charles H. Hinton, which appeared in 1862)[17] absorbed philosophers, scientists, and artists, who were inquiring into mental envisioning and its effects at the level of the individual and the species.[18] They were building on an earlier Romantic and Gothic fascination with reverie, dream, and states of inwardness, and the interaction between the inner eye and its images, the relationship of the mind to optical media in early monochrome photography became highly fertile. Acute difficulties still stirred around the status of illusions, as described in the last part: were they supernatural signs, inspired creations, or mad delusions?

In the 1780s, the inward turn of the uncanny had set in motion a new metaphysics of the psyche, and it was reflected in popular taste for spooky spectacles, like the phantasmagoria, and the lurid fantasies of Gothic tales. (As we saw, in relation to the Sleeping Beauty waxwork, one of the most frequently reproduced and purchased images throughout the era was Henry Fuseli's painting *The Nightmare* (1781).)[19] The type of entranced hero or heroine whom Coleridge had brought so vividly into his ballads 'Christabel' and 'The Rime of the Ancient Mariner' began to dominate entertainment.[20] The altered states of female subjects, especially of young women, enciphered sexual longings as well as states of possession. A short story by Samuel Warren, published in *Blackwood's Magazine* in 1831–2, describes the 'living death' of a victim of catalepsy, and adds copious notes about epilepsy, trance states, and 'attoniti'—women were specially prone, wrote the author, who thirty years later was 'Master in Lunacy' at Edinburgh.[21]

Hypnotized, sleep-walking, charmed, and possessed heroines haunted entertainment. At first they were subjects of medical experiment in theatrical settings: a century after Anton Mesmer's society success as a healer, Jean-Michel Charcot staged demonstrations at La Salpêtrière, Paris, in the 1880s, when he entranced his patients and then placed them on-stage and made them respond to his demands.[22] Freud was present, and was highly impressed by Charcot's revelations about the mind's power over the body; a famous engraving of the scene now hangs over the couch in his study in London.

Thomas De Quincey experimented consciously with his unconscious, actively welcoming, before opium—and stomach-aches—took such a grip on him, that 'dérèglement de tous les sens', proclaimed by Arthur Rimbaud later in the century. He transformed the *belles-lettres* essay form, especially in his 'Suspiria De Profundis', into a way of tracking his own thought processes, inaugurating imaginative self-portraiture in a stream of consciousness before its time, and announcing the automatic writing later undertaken by telepathic researchers, Surrealists, and experimenters like Henri Michaux. This attention to the mind's suggestibility absorbed very varied publics; it is the ground in which theories of the unconscious, as developed by Freud, and of the 'subliminal self', by F. W. H. Myers, were seeded and flourished.

Charismatic figures, often mysterious foreigners, put a spell on their subjects (mostly female) through ordinary, human magic—in a plethora of much-loved stories following Charcot's spectacular lectures; Charcot the modern physician merges with the fantasies around Cagliostro the magician in parables about the power and terror of sexuality. The novel *Trilby* (1894) by George du Maurier was a triumphant success; its fascinating mesmerist,

Dr Svengali, hypnotizes Trilby so that she can fulfil her dream of singing, and she reaches fame and fortune—and destruction. Svengali too has passed into the pantheon of mythic enchanters—a black enchanter of the early media age. Likewise, *The Cabinet of Dr Caligari*, Robert Wiene's Expressionist masterpiece of 1919, explores the borders between madness and a state of induced hallucination through the figure of its entranced protagonist. It focuses on murders committed by a sleep-walker, and then reveals that a hysterical female subject, who lives in a dream-like state, has produced the whole drama out of her own fantasy. She may not be as crazy as she seems, but rather the victim of Caligari's powers of suggestion. The film script leaves the question hanging, to considerable disturbing effect.

Alongside the girls and boys, youths and maids, of dream poetry and stories, many of the principal subjects of sleep and dream photographs were children or nubile women—again and again they appear, demonstrating the powers of dreaming, inviting the viewer to imagine their fantasies. In 1864, the photographer Henry Peach Robinson created his atmospheric tableau 'Sleep', with two children lying entangled in bed at an open casement, a wide vista of the open sea in uncanny proximity to their bed. The light catches a flutter of petals, or perhaps butterflies, in a vase by the window; if butterflies, the emblem illustrates a line in the Matthew Arnold poem inscribed beneath the photograph, and alludes to the soul, voyaging in sleep.[23]

Given Robinson's morbid tendency, 'sleep' here may be a queasy euphemism: the sharply focused and elaborate theatricality of the tableau draws attention to the dangers of petrification inherent in posing for the long exposure times then necessary, and Robinson, unlike Dodgson or Hawarden or Cameron, positively relished his affinity with the mortician's art (another of his well-known tableaux, 'Fading Away: She would not tell her love' shows a young girl expiring on a *chaise-longue*).

By contrast, when Lewis Carroll posed Alice Liddell as 'feigning sleep', for example, he made an implicit connection to the active dream voyages she undertakes as the heroine of his stories. He also photographed the MacDonald children in states of sleep or day-dream, and the *Sylvie and Bruno* books open with a short rhyming poem, asking the question: 'Is all our Life, then, but a dream?' These 'child-friends' are in transit between worlds in their minds. When *Sylvie and Bruno* move from one world to another physically, they open a door or pass through a wall.[24] In the preface, in the passage about mind-voyaging which I cited before (in Chapter 3), Lewis Carroll specifies the two kinds of dreaming in these stories: gazing at the fire in order fall into a 'brown study' at the sight of the glowing coals, and, more unusually, entering 'the Eerie state' of unconsciousness, which makes fairyland visible. In his later years, Lewis Carroll commented warmly on the powers of imagination to transport the mind–voyager elsewhere, and it is not at all clear that he intends his claims figuratively when he writes about travelling to fairyland.

Similarly, when Julia Margaret Cameron gazed through her camera at sleeping or day-dreaming children and young women, she depicts their mental activity as energy and concentration, sometimes puzzlement, sometimes rapture.[25] Several images direct the reader towards imagining the inner life of the child or the female subject, or to think of her as an invented character from a story or a poem. Frequently, Cameron presents their resemblance to heavenly creatures—taking her cue from Italian paintings, from ministering and angels annunciate, to Raphaelesque cherubim and Neoplatonist *erotēs* or cupids. The transition into the inner world of her own imagination needed go-betweens: children, girls and boys, as incarnate intermediary beings, offer themselves as its undisputed inhabitants.

Another contemporary, who took up the new art of photography around 1857, Clementina, Lady Hawarden, focused principally on her two elder daughters as *jeunes filles en fleur*. Hawarden (*née* Fleeming) brought a lyric sensuousness and frank admiration to her family pictures.[26] Young girls unmistakably on the threshold of womanhood, her models lie, eyes closed, daydreaming on sofas and *chaises-longues*, often clasping each other or lying intertwined, in enigmatic costumes gesturing towards romance and history. Their mother titled these images 'Study from life' or, even more simply, 'Photographic study', but for her, the medium opened on to the life of poetic fancy, not the physiognomic portrait. Hawarden staged her girls as portals—as 'charm'd magic casements'—into their inner make-believe world, staged in the privacy of their home in South Kensington, at their dressing-table, on their sofas, and on the terrace overlooking the new development of the museums there at the time. Hawarden's work contemplates the innermost reveries of women, and makes us feel admit private rituals and intimate feelings.[27]

So, while visitors at Madame Tussaud's in Baker Street were gazing at the waxen figure of 'The Sleeping Beauty' there, Hawarden's daughters were inviting the viewer across the threshold of their fantasies through the subtle caresses of their mother's lighting and her admiring gaze. In several other of her most exquisitely composed and lit photographs, Hawarden's daughters contemplate their reflections in mirrors (Figure 15, p. 168), and stand by the French windows of their London house, gazing at each other through the panes. She casts a subaqueous light over these interiors, floods gauze hangings with luminosity, and splashes highlights on the girls' silks and brocades; her aesthetic clearly revels at setting them up as mysterious twinnings, her flesh-and-blood daughters multiplied through different reflections and projections, as well as the image of the photograph itself.[28]

Hawarden exhibited in the Annual Exhibition of the Photographic Society of London, and Charles Dodgson bought five of the photographs shown in 1864, the year before *Alice in Wonderland* appeared, and seven years before *Through the Looking-Glass*. Carroll also took his friends George MacDonald's children to her for a sitting. It is not impossible that her vision of child contemporaries, dreaming in mirrors, sparked something in his own imagination; in one Hawarden image, her daughter is grappling with the reflection in the glass, and in several others, they converse through mirrors and glass with their reflections.

Their dressing-up belongs to the widespread contemporary love of charades and tableaux, much in evidence among early practitioners of popular, home photography: Lewis Carroll dressed Alice as a beggar girl, and Xie Kitchen as a Chinese mandarin, and so forth.[29] On the Isle of Wight, in the circle around Tennyson the Poet Laureate, the cult of fancy became pre-eminently social as well as poetical, and photography as a hobby—as an amateur art—made poetry into a fancy-dress game. Julia Margaret Cameron's titles continually allude to the literature of faerie and enchantment (rather than the Thackeray of *Vanity Fair* or the Dickens of *Pickwick Papers*).[30] Until she reached Ceylon at the end of her life, Cameron shows a marked flight from any allusion to the realities of the times, to the political or social circumstances, let alone her own precarious financial situation, especially where young women and children are at stake.[31] Carroll's celebrated image of Alice in bare feet and rags, with her hand cupped and outstretched, shares a Dickensian sentiment about children that has become repellent to us now, though much imitated by charity advertisements; however, as with such poster children, Carroll was aware of hardship, and later in his life campaigned on behalf of performing children to prevent their exploitation (economic and sexual).

All these various topoi direct the reader in varied ways towards imagining the child or the figure in the images as an idea in the mind, or a phantom or invented character from a story or a poem. Cameron saw herself engaged, like her great friend Tennyson, in a common enterprise of imaginative cognition, and wrote, for example, about her images for his Arthurian cycle *The Idylls of the King*: 'Tennyson 'is *the* Sun of the Earth and I am the Priestess of the Sun of the Heavens so that my works must sometimes even surpass his.'[32]

This boast—which she follows instantly with a disclaimer of all responsibility for her work and its qualities—still lets us glimpse how equivalent she felt their enterprise to be in representing images from the imagination and adopting the Renaissance principle underlying mythological storytelling in pictures, *ut pictura poesis*. Like her photographic peers, Hawarden and Dodgson, Cameron explored shades and degrees of reverie and dream throughout her photographic career, and her portraits solicit us to imagine the inward eye of her subjects, finely grading qualities and kinds of rapt absorption in children and adults.[33] She inquires into mental processes and inspiration, posing her models insistently to reflect, look down, or look away. Above all, in 'Vivien and Merlin' (1874), her husband Charles played the wizard, spellbound and struck blind by the raised arm of the enchantress. It is not difficult to imagine Julia Margaret Cameron enjoying herself when she staged this scene. The image sets humming all kinds of questions about vision, power, and desire: it shows a sighted younger woman—Vivien— wielding sovereignty over a venerable magician, and hence, over his mind; it asks, Who is the voyant now, the one who sees when Merlin cannot, or, perhaps, the one who sees all whom you—the viewer—do not see?[34]

Child and female models dominate the dreams in her photography, while great men crowd the named portraits. The camera permitted entry to the interior of the subject: the inner worlds that Cameron talks about capturing with her camera are her models' inner worlds, and she is making images 'From Life' (as she inscribes on several prints), taking an impression of exterior feature and lineament. These contrived and dreamy pictures reveal that some early photographers like her did not use the camera to observe the world as a set of percepts, but saw it as a magic mirror of private thoughts, shared between photographer and subject, where the world would be magically stilled, the moment made to stay. The time of the photograph abides out of time, in the *aevum*, or zone of art, a third order of time, as Frank Kermode has discussed.[35]

But why, specially, children as dream voyagers in the photographs of so many Victorians? Did they act as muses, as *alter egos*, as personifications of the spirit and its passions and states? The new child reader had appeared, fostered by Romantic ideals about childhood; these dreams were encoded in Romantic pedagogical idealism, on the one hand, and good commercial hard-headedness on the other. The stories of Wonderland and fairyland, Outland and Looking-Glass country, and even Tennyson's medieval and Celtic fancies were told with children in mind, to delight them and to enchant their minds. But the young who began to populate nineteenth-century photographs came trailing clouds of meaning from religious imagery, of *putti* and angels and heavenly spirits, as discussed earlier. The word 'angel', meaning messenger, suggests a go-between; the intermediate state of angels (bodies but not flesh) appeared to be written on a child's body in a dreamed absence of fallen human sex. Indeed, that very state of unfleshed embodiment requires that they not be sexed. Children's bodies could offer a this-worldly image of an imagined angelic being: the Revd Dodgson's little girls, some of them undressed, and the host of little boys and girls of Julia Margaret Cameron's circle represented an in-between state of identity, neither male nor female, a universal, ungendered being trailing clouds of a Christian androgynous godlikeness. Whatever the photographers' own impulses and desires—and Dodgson/Carroll's passion to photograph dozens, even hundreds, of little girls makes many viewers today deeply uncomfortable—his work and the work of Julia Margaret Cameron with children's nakedness and semi-nakedness share many contemporaries' dream investment in the young, with all the attendant psycho-sexual yearnings that alarm us today. And they appear exceptionally emotionally engaged only because they used the camera to pursue their fantasies.

To state such a connection between photography and fantasy seems to fly in the face of the evidence: Mrs Cameron was above all the supreme portrait photographer of her era, who created a unique gallery of Great Men of the Age. When she pointed out that her photographs were taken 'From Life', she was ensuring that viewers would recognize that, like the poet or the scientist, the angel or Madonna or blessed damozel or sprite in her photograph was a model of flesh and blood. Used in the 1860s, the phrase reveals the novelty that photographs made possible: a figment was at the same time real. But it also calls us to think ourselves back in time to the moment when that 'life' was present, was still alive. This is the referent at issue, and the fundamental, distinctive character of a photographic figment, as opposed to a painting or other art form.

Tableaux cast with real people, who then abide unchanged forever, seized in that moment, recapture lost time and bring it to a standstill; but these images have not necessarily taken place except through make-believe. As in Mephistopheles' conjurings for Faust, the camera stills figures in dreams of knowledge and power into lasting presences.

The approach adopted by Hawarden, Carroll, and Cameron casts photographs as dynamic in themselves, generating original images from a shared body of narrative, not passively copying actual events and relaying them to others as capturing what happened at a certain moment in time. Cameron in particular turned real-life friends and servants and their children into 'ideal subjects', swerving away from photography as documentary and forensic index. The formal and aesthetic manners of Cameron's art help capture, through a process of imitation, the imagination's ways of picturing, especially its fugitive and motile qualities. Her blurred images and different lengths of focus within one image consciously forestall that mortuary stillness of the daguerreotype portrait, which she specifically deplored. When Cameron wanted to depict the actual appearance of a historical person, appearing as himself (very few women sat in their own right for a portrait by her), she used light to delineate and bring out the features, and when she was framing an allegory or poesia, she altered the focus within the image itself, creating patches of suggestively dreamy vagueness and blur.[36]

She reveals rather than conceals her techniques: smudging, scratching, leaving fingerprints and other marks on the print, cropping, and combining in composite images; she spoils the camera's perfect smoothness, and in this way brings herself into the process, and diminishes the role of the machine.

The images quiver and dissolve in response to the flickering, evanescent indeterminacy of thought—the way in which images in memory lack definition, especially at the edges, how remembered faces or scenes move in and out of focus with gaps and lesions, how mental picturing possesses uncanny clarity and presence while simultaneously jumping and wobbling and eddying.

Cameron specifically acknowledged the influence of the photographer David Wilkie Wynfield, who may have taught her early on, for reproducing human vision and creating effects of movement and partial, fleeting glimpses.[37] Elaine Scarry, in *Dreaming by the Book*, a highly original study of the mental processes activated by phantasmata, or mental envisioning while reading, draws on the thesaurus evoking the essential filminess of mental imaging, on the images' gauziness and transparency, vagueness and indistinctness, spectrality and screen-like projected thinness. Writing about Proust's recapturing of memories, Scarry argues that they aim to duplicate the phenomenology of perception, and she comments, 'It is not hard to imagine a ghost successfully. What is hard is successfully to imagine an object, any object, that does *not* look like a ghost.'[38]

Cameron's out-of-focus blurriness, her smudges, wispy traces, and haloes, combine with early prints' fade at the edges towards etherealizing the bodies and faces unclothed for our gaze. Her repeated juxtapositions of faces in close and tender contact with each other and close up to our own vision also reproduce the processes of dream or reverie, in which relationships of scale are disturbed. The allegory of 'Arthur's Death', a much derided assemblage of costumed characters and cotton wool, represents its cast as actual size in relation to one another, and this aspect of lived reality fights the hallucinatory character of the poetic fiction; by contrast, in the haunting and justly iconic, 'The Whisper of the Muse', the faces of George Watts and his pair of youthful muses crowd the frame, making him loom, apparition-like; similarly, with others of her celebrated portrait heads. Scarry, again, points out this aspect of mental picturing, that it fills the field of vision, edge to edge: in dreams, when someone appears and is recognized, it is not uncommon for them to rise up in the mind's eye as the only subject of its concerns.

Those imposing portrait heads of Herschel and Tennyson and G. F. Watts, whom Cameron lion-hunted throughout the 1860s and 1870s, appear often crowned by ethereal fire, their profiles illuminated, their hair apparently aflame. Her use of *non finito* shadow play haloes them against the light in a kind of unearthly glow.[39] She also deliberately heightened the contrast, so that the photographs sometimes appear silhouettes in reverse—white on black—as in numerous images posed by her favourite Mary Hillier, including the lyrical 'Call, I Follow, I Follow, Let me Die' and 'The Angel at the Tomb' (Figure 18, p. 204). The aesthetic achievement of Cameron's photographs—both her fancies and her portraits—depends on their closeness to thought-images of a certain kind, to the fugitive, darting, glancing movement as the mind's eye tries to stay the moment.

Early on, G. F. Watts warned Cameron against her love of costume, but 'fancy dress was her undoing', wrote Claire Tomalin. 'Freddy as "Love-in-Idleness" with bow and quiver, is nauseous. So are all the tots with wings attached. It is vulgar to turn children into putti because it makes their beauty cute and false for adult amusement.'[40]

When Cameron offers too elaborate and precise an interpretation of legends and poetic fancies, and does not leave enough to the imagination, her images collapse into ridicule (a real bridle from a real harness can never possess all the gemminess that the phrase 'gemmy bridle' from 'The Lady of Shalott' stirs in imagination).

As Coleridge wrote, the imagination 'is essentially *vital*, even as all objects (*as* objects) are essentially fixed and dead.'[41] In other words, too much fixed precision of costumes and props can ruin fictional picturing. Such photographs of fantasies tend to become soppy-stern, even ludicrous, the farther they move from the slide and play of mental picturing towards the detail of material spectacle. Virginia Woolf's writings show how, when you stay the moment, it still flashes by, glimpsed, not frozen.[42] Photography, the great instrument of indexical veracity, must imitate the manners of the mind's eye and become vague and dreamy and imprecise if it is to communicate poetic fantasy or the realms of the inner eye. At her best, Cameron does this.

At the same time as Dodgson, Hawarden, and Cameron were making *tableaux vivants* of dream selves, photographers were beginning to capture ghosts and other spirit forms. Following a certain material logic, the two practices evolved side by side. And although spirit photography may appear an absurd, repugnant, and embarrassing episode in the medium's history, the close relation between image and fantasy offered a prototype. When Julia Margaret Cameron declared that she wanted to photograph the souls of her sitters, friends, relatives *et al.*, she revealed a continuum of thought about spirit, psyche, phantoms, and the material vehicles of the mind's eye.

William Crookes, the pioneering experimental
scientist, was persuaded by the spirit of Katie King,
summoned for him by the medium Florence Cook
and photographed with him here in 1874.

17
Spectral Rappers, Psychic Photographers

> We are not our bodies.
>
> Cromwell Varley

In 1848 two young girls, Kate Fox, aged 11, and Margaretta her sister, aged 15, began hearing signals in the form of knocks, or 'rappings', coming from the walls and under the floor of their new home in Hydesville in upstate New York. The Fox sisters were later joined by the eldest, Leah, when they began to tour and exhibit their powers; two years later, after a sensational—and controversial—impact on audiences in New York and farther afield, they founded Spiritualism as a church. The Fox sisters were the most celebrated and most influential 'wild talents', as the Victorian collector of esoterica Charles Fort described young girls and boys who were gifted with occult powers; he collected their feats for his immense archive of 'unexplained phenomena'.[1]

Like later heroines of fantasy literature and the angelic visions of Cameron's photography, these young seers acted as intermediaries between worlds: in the early 1850s, when the Fox sisters and others began rapping, the word 'medium' itself was extended to someone with paranormal powers. The medium of the messages—the light waves of the ether—and the interpreter became one and the same. The new technologies offered a model for understanding that was extended to mysteries beyond the reach of scientific empiricism. The sisters called themselves 'celestial telegraphers'.

Forces producing effects invisibly without contact over distance—magnetism, gravity, electromagnetic waves—are still keeping scientists hard at work, but since the end of the eighteenth century and the rise of public entertainment, communications, and the bourgeois city, their mysteriousness has inspired a plethora of theories about spirit and spirits, and these have spurred on the spread of technologies and their uses. Franz Mesmer won widespread fame and fortune for his cure—infusing his patients with 'animal spirits', a form of electrical current.[2] Psychic photographers harnessed the visible end of the electromagnetic spectrum and preserved light traces to offer proof of life everlasting to the faithful and consolation to the bereaved. Impresarios of seances claimed to reveal the imponderable powers governing the universe. But beneath the genuine epistemological ambitions and the myriad therapies, the chief quest still aimed at understanding the unknown field of spirit and spirits. Nineteenth-century scientific discoveries were popularly and influentially applied in the first place to explaining the paranormal and the supernatural.

In the same part of the country, near Rochester, New York, twenty-five years earlier, the most significant prophet in American history, Joseph Smith, saw the angel Moroni and was given tablets of gold inscribed with the Book of Mormon. Smith was then 17, and he went on to found the Church of Latter-day Saints. The area is also haunted by the unquiet spirits of Indians buried in sites after their lands were settled, and the terrain is consequently known—and much celebrated by the psychically inclined—as the Burnt-over District, where 'the God-haze may just be the echo of so much Protestant noise'.[3] The Fox sisters and Hydesville present a very American mix—teenagers, enterprise, self-expression, public entertainment, high-mindedness, Protestantism, and diabolism—the heartlands of Stephen King Gothic.

The Fox sisters did not name an angel as their visitor, nor at first a ghost of some departed loved one or even acquaintance, but identified a 'Mister Split-foot', as if their hidden communicator were Old Nick himself. They remained entirely cheerful at his advent. He was not an unexpected spirit, perhaps, given the territory. Their innovation—their inspired innovation—was to shed the trappings that Joseph Smith had gathered up—hoary stuff about radiant angels and golden tablets—and clothe their experiences in the language of new technology. The sounds that Mister Split-foot made with his cloven hoof they took to be enciphered, as if he were using telegraphic messaging or Morse code. This was cutting edge: in 1851, at the exact time when Spiritualists were gaining more and more believers, more than fifty companies were set up to send messages down the wire, by magnetic telegraph patented by Morse.[4]

Samuel Morse had chosen apocalyptic texts for the first messages: he dot-dashed the question 'What hath God wrought?' between Baltimore and Washington, DC, in 1844.[5] Thereafter rappings and seances and psychic research spread in step with the new uses of electricity and communication technologies. But if acoustic transmission modelled the spirits' way of contacting the living, visual media were crucial to guaranteeing that the spirits were real, not invented, and had been truly present. The camera could verify that something had really happened.

Soon after mid-century, photography was recording occurrences in the laboratory which the human eye could not see, and its evidence was increasingly relied on. But the invention of the medium coincides in time with the beginnings of Spiritualism, and this and later developments may not be quite as adventitious as has been assumed. The work on motion that

Étienne-Jules Marey and Eadweard Muybridge undertook in the 1880s and A. M. Worthington's experiments in 1908 with high-speed photography, capturing splashes and other events hitherto imperceptible to the human eye, continued to widen the horizon of vision.[6] The camera undid problems about human perception and fallibility—or so it was fervently believed. It could be trusted, because it did not have consciousness, and acted mechanically, objectively, and independently of the mind of its user.[7] In its supposed objective character, photography was brought to bear on psychic possibilities: as there was no ghost in this machine, it must be true when one appeared. This scientific conception of the medium had its limits, as I tried to show in the last chapter.

The various spirit forms of humans *sub specie aeternitatis*—spectres, phantoms, ghosts, apparitions, and shades—are not quite interchangeable, yet not easily distinguished either. Revenants from the land of the dead were deemed to be spirits, but 'of another sort' from angels, fairies, and the like, as Oberon says in *A Midsummer Night's Dream*, distinguishing immortals such as Titania and Puck from the insubstantial shades of the dead. Although ghosts often return from a place of darkness, they too clothe themselves in the imagery of time, in air and nebulousness, like more glorious intermediate beings—though wings are almost always forbidden to those who were once enfleshed. The period between death and the Last Judgement in Christian doctrine implies, however, an in-between condition when the body without a soul lies dead in this world, while the soul without a body lives immortal in eternity. St Paul's First Letter to the Corinthians on the resurrection of the dead offered the scriptural testament to this spirit double: 'It is sown a natural body; it is raised a spiritual body. There is a natural body, and there is a spiritual body' (1 Cor. 15: 44).

The camera could perhaps apprehend this spirit body in a way that fallible human eyes could not. Spirit phenomena might also lie below the threshold of vision and beyond the frequency at which the brain registers light. The camera began to make visible another, transcendental variety of invisible forms: photography and phantoms are joined by elective affinities within the limits of knowledge. The appearance of Victorian ghosts in psychic photography conforms to a late medieval turn in spectral portraiture, with frequent absurdities and unwitting comedy, especially when the image turns literal. Like many members of the supernatural population, the diaphanously sheathed revenant has become such a familiar figure that it seems just so, a given, the form as proper to its identity as the shape of an oak or a giraffe. But early illuminators were undecided about phantoms' appearance. Sometimes an artist will concentrate on reactions of awe or dismay on the part of the spectators and leave a void where the spirit stands.[8] In deathbed scenes the dying man or woman often exhales the soul in the form of a naked, androgynous sprite—a homunculus or version of themselves in miniature, as in the scene of Adam's creation in San Marco (see Chapter 5). Ghosts, however, never return in this shape in the iconography (or if they do, I have never seen one). It is essential for a ghost's purposes that the person he or she once was should be recognized by the living. Surprisingly, that cliché, the Hallowe'en spectre, a cadaver shrouded in a sheet, turns up for the first time in medieval illuminations of the later thirteenth century. The historian Jean-Claude Schmitt claims to have identified the earliest occurrences of this type of phantom. Concealed in a shroud of white from head to toe, eyes only peeping through holes, such a ghost announces the death of a child to his father in a vignette from a narrative series in a manuscript of around 1272.[9]

From their first photographic appearances, ghosts chose this guise: seekers and seers would otherwise not have known who or what they were. When seance sitters want to raise the dead, and psychic photographers summon lost loved ones, phantoms usually appear in the form of white, immaterial wraiths, borrowing on conventions about ghosts and spectres going back to the Middle Ages. Indeed, they would not have been convincing if they had departed from the tradition. Portraits of sitters, with their lost loved ones, adapt the formal ideas of the earliest optical devices for projecting spectres: the spirit of the unseen person summoned by the sitter appears shrouded yet insubstantial, or hovers in the air, like a wisp of smoke, the materialization of shades, as in Homer and Virgil's underworlds.

Around 1861, an American photographer, William H. Mumler, discovered a 'spirit extra' sitting on his knee in a self-portrait he had taken: the white blur was a little girl he recognized, a relative of his who had died twelve years before.[10] Even though Mumler was actually prosecuted eight years later for obtaining money by false pretences, and a cloud of fraudulence hung over his work and that of many other spirit photographers who also interpreted smudges, blots, and streaks as 'the blur of the otherworldly', the wave carrying photography to the forefront of psychic experiments had begun.[11]

In England, the brilliant experimental scientist William Crookes was captivated by a suggestion Faraday had made, about a possible 'fourth state of matter'. Energetic and versatile, Crookes was born in 1832 and died in 1919 after the First World War, and his long scientific career exemplifies the tumultuous inventions that brought the modern world into being.[12] His plural lines of inquiry led to many achievements in chemistry, particularly in relation to optics and spectroscopy; he also worked on ways of photographing stars and on light effects such as polarization; he invented a dry, far less messy collodion method than Julia Margaret Cameron had used; in 1854 he founded a journal of photography, destined to be one of several he was involved in, and in his eighties he was still at work on 'Crookes lenses'. His experiments radiate into many different aspects of today's world that we now take for granted but which were utterly unexpected and astounding to their contemporaries: radio, telegraphy, X-rays, neon lighting, and the cathode-ray tube that eventually made television possible. It is astonishing that he is not as well known as several of his peers, and the reason lies in his unwavering commitment to the reality of some kind of parallel world after assiduous encounters with spirits raised by a young woman, Florence Cook (1856–1904), over a two-year period from 1872 to 1874. She became his real-life, flesh-and-blood medium through whom he could access other worlds of experience: a harbinger of Alice, who in the same decade conducted Lewis Carroll (and his readers) to Wonderland and the 'Eerie' state.

Crookes astounded his colleagues and risked his considerable scientific standing by declaring that he believed Florence Cook's psychic exploits to be scientifically valid. He exulted, 'We have actually touched the borderland where Matter and Force seemed to merge into one another, the shadowy realm between the Known and the Unknown which for me has always held peculiar temptations. Here . . . lie Ultimate Realities, subtle, far-reaching, wonderful.'[13]

The very nature of spirituous, impalpable, and imponderable airy substances was changing under the scientific gaze, and in many minds, their new material constitution held a promise that the existence of a spirit dimension could be proved. Contemporaneous eagerness to magnify faculties of vision and hearing far beyond the human body's capacities led to a corresponding fascination with the limitlessness of the inapprehensible world. Seeing and hearing better, further, deeper, more, opened up intimations of yet more, elusive, and inapprehensible phenomena.

The Victorians' pursuit of spirits also coincides with the entrance of photography into the private space of the family as well as the studio: one (technical) medium in its early stages of social domestication interprets another (spiritual) medium's thoughts and experiences. The camera was becoming a domestic appliance, and it allowed Victorian women with far less social status than Cameron and Hawarden to distinguish themselves in the new medium.

This social connection of photography to the private, intimate spaces of women, both geographically and psychologically, illuminates the dynamics of the seance. Seances were often conducted in private houses through mediums; the photographers and the mediums themselves included some men, but women began to outnumber them very soon, and predominated in psychic circles by the end of the century. Spiritualism gave women equality and opportunity, even special value, while Spiritualism's agnostic doppelgängers, the sceptical 'psychic investigators', were also emancipated in this respect, in both Europe and the United States.[14] The seances themselves involved women directly and often intimately, and often young women. There were male mediums, many of whom moved through the networks of music-hall and variety shows with acts involving magic and clairvoyance; there were successful male spirit photographers too. But it was a *carrière ouverte aux talents* for women, both as researchers and as subjects in greater proportion than their numbers in related professions—the Church, the laboratory, medicine.

A man like Crookes would not have employed as lab assistants the young women who helped him with his psychic work; unconsciously, like many of his fellow Victorians, he valued their uneducated minds as truer vehicles. He first focused all his attention on Kate Fox, during a series of experiments that he believed were carefully controlled, and was delighted by the impenetrable nature of the sounds and effects she channelled. But his collaboration with Florence Cook over the course of those two years brought him even greater results. She had started as a medium at the age of 14, and had been dismissed from work in a school for poltergeist disturbances. Her phenomena principally featured apparitions of another girl, a wraith-like vision called 'Katie King' swathed in white (Figure 19, p. 220). Katie exchanged words, touches—even caresses—with Crookes. During an intensive week, this spirit visitor was photographed twenty-four times by Crookes. Afterwards, many thought that she rather resembled Florence Cook in build and age and other features, and the case produced acute controversy, exciting many scurrilous attacks on the man of science. He did not publish all the images he had taken, but he nevertheless stood his ground, and wrote, perhaps revealing more than he intended: 'I have reason to know that the power at work in these phenomena, like Love, laughs at locksmiths.'[15] As the classical scholar E. R. Dodds wrote to the philosopher C. D. Broad, a president of the Society for Psychical Research, it seems that 'Crookes was an honest man bemused by Eros'.[16]

During a seance, women were closely involved in the arrangements, in assuring the comfort and security and honesty of the seance conditions, as close inspections took place of the medium's clothes and person before a session—not unlike body searches today. A Berlin devotee reported that Florence Cook was 'each time searched thoroughly by two ladies, also to complete undressing. Then her whole body was fettered with cords very firmly. All double knots were secured by leaden seals.' At the end of this seance, which featured flying chairs, extended limbs, and invitations to caress the naked spirit's leg and foot, 'repeated telekinesis, voices in English, French, German . . . the medium cryed out loudly in the cab, after that vehement groaning and a long sobbing . . . Floating lightening phenomena . . . The medium was found every time utmost exhausted in deep trance, slowly waking, with staring eyes asking to be freed from the chains, who had caused deep cuts in her wrists and must be immediately cut open, the knots and seals always intact! The visitors were extremely satisfied and praised the modest proceedings and the plain, charming character of Mrs. Cook, who made a very sympathetic impression!' (*sic*, throughout).[17]

Florence Cook's spirit visitor, Katie King, who had also appeared in Spiritualist households in the USA, was identified as Annie Owen Morgan in real life, the daughter of 'John King', in turn the spirit form of a notorious buccaneer, the Jamaica governor Henry Owen Morgan, in the seventeenth century. His heroic adventures filled some of the most colourful pages of the most influential collections of pirate lore ever compiled, the source book for many a later tale of derring-do on the high seas: John Esquemeling's *Bucaniers of America* (1684), which exercised its charms over R. L. Stevenson and J. M. Barrie.[18] The spirit of the old sea-dog haunted several seances, making his first appearance in United States Spiritualist experiments and continuing very lively at the summonses of Madame Blavatsky. Among his other imaginary progeny could be numbered Long John Silver and Captain Hook, as well as his 'spirit child', Katie. As Roger Luckhurst writes, he returns as 'a powerful spirit control in a cultural practice itself considered unruly, marginal and semi-lawful'.[19]

Crookes built a special high-security room for experiments in his house; he also tested the consummate conjuror Daniel Dunglas Home, who in the presence of several other empirical scientists besides himself, made an accordion float in the air, gently playing by itself inside a cage, while his limbs were under strict control. The great physicist posited a 'psychic force', and wrote up the experiments for the Royal Society, which did not accept his paper for publication.

Bafflingly to our eyes now, Crookes was at the same time resolved to 'drive the worthless residuum of spiritualism into the unknown limbo of magic and necromancy'.[20] By proving the scientific basis of the apparitions, he would undo supernatural hocus-pocus. As a result, he was engaged with paranormal activities for thirty years, and was photographed, in 1916, with the apparition of his wife. Unlike some of his fellow investigators, Crookes held firm to the view that the spirits who visited were revenants, the spirits of the dead, but somehow material. His idea that a continuum existed between the rare earth elements he had identified and radioactivity also sparked theories in physics that younger colleagues in psychic research later applied to speculations about spirit matter, or ectoplasm, as we shall see. In many ways Crookes prophesied the world of mobile phones, satellites in orbit, dishes on houses, radio telescopes in outer space, and, generally, mass communications to come. 'Here is unfolded for us a new and astonishing world', he enthused, 'one which it is hard to conceive should contain no possibilities of transmitting or receiving intelligence. Rays of light will not pierce through a wall. . . . But the electrical vibrations of a yard or more in wave-length . . . will easily pierce such mediums . . . Here, then, is revealed the bewildering possibility of telegraphy without wires, posts, cables or any of our costly appliances.'[21] But he interpreted these physical discoveries in terms that no longer persuade, exulting in their psychic potential: 'In some parts of the human brain may lurk an organ capable of transmitting and receiving electrical rays of wave-lengths hitherto undetected by instrumental means. These may be instrumental in transmitting thought from one brain to another.'[22]

Spiritism or psychic science and domestic photography combined to bring Victorian women to the fore as active practitioners; the two very different activities overlap in the psychic photograph. Psychic photography can be divided into images on the one hand formed by telepathic or ghost communications, as explored by Crookes, and on the other, taken as records of seance phenomena. The mediums acted as photographer-telepathists in a burgeoning number of established studios during the last three decades of the nineteenth century and into the Twenties; they picked up on ideas circulated by scientists such as Crookes and the physiologist Charles Richet, and turned themselves into apparatus, a form of living camera, during the course of seances, as we shall see later.[23]

In 1882, Georgiana Houghton published *Chronicles of the Photographs of Spiritual Beings . . . Invisible to the Material Eye,* a beautifully produced volume. In the spirit of an earlier artist voyant, William Blake, Miss Houghton called herself 'The Sacred Symbolist', and acted under the guidance of archangels who revealed their names to her—Ezimor, Gliovus, Minax, Jarno, and so forth—all with precise meanings (the Searcher, the Clear-Seer, the Quiet).[24] She made paintings by free association, richly layered, abstract compositions, recalling those 'brushes of comet's hair' that Kipling invokes in his kitsch poem about heaven.[25] Wound in their clumsy shrouds and gesturing angelically, Miss Houghton's photographs of earnest 'unclad spirits' raise a smile today.[26] But in an era of rapid scientific change, such images anticipated a current of modernity; after the First World War they were to serve as a form of secular ministry to the bereaved.

Photography as impressions of mental powers, as translations of thoughts into images, as 'psychographs': this conception of the medium shaped the trust which Victorians placed in spirit photographs. Official, mainstream culture was not hermetically sealed against what would perhaps be seen now as the margins, where ghosts and the invisible forces were thriving. The camera reproduces spectral form in a manner that provided nineteenth-century metaphor for thought itself. Cromwell Varley, an experimental scientist who became a convinced Spiritualist, wrote that 'an iron wire to an electrician is simply a hole bored through a solid rock of air so that the electricity may pass freely . . . everything is solid in respect to something . . . therefore thought, which is power, may be in some sort solid'.[27] When Gabriel Tarde, one of the moving forces of sociology, a criminologist and the author of *The Laws of Imitation* (1890), wanted to invoke a crowd of people moving and behaving as one, he reached for an image for their thoughts and described the 'quasi-photographic reproduction of a cerebral image upon the sensitive plate of another brain'.[28] Eusapia Paladino, one of the most spectacular 'materializing mediums' of the late Victorian era, produced 'ideoplasts': these were low-relief prints of a face on wax—psychic masks, pressed out as if in the mould of the death mask to be the authentic likeness of the departed. But the images also resemble vague, swirling Symbolist portraits, as sculpted in wax by Medardo Rosso, Paladino's contemporary and compatriot.[29] It seems that spirits follow aesthetic trends with the same unconsciousness as popular culture, and their manifestations can be dated—from effects of style, in colour and composition.

One writer likened the process to photography: 'the mind "daguerre-otypes" the flash of thought—on the retina, or mirror of the eye, where it is recognized by the powers of perception.'[30] Paladino certainly claimed that she created these images by power of mental activity, beaming impalpable, imponderable, light and other immaterial forms on to matter. The chorus of corroboration continued well into the last century: F. W. Warrick, an irrepressible spirit questor and enthusiastic collector of such photographs, published his experiences with the popular psychic photographer Mrs Ada Deane in 1939 (a charwoman in north London, she took up photography after her brother began working as a high street photographer). Warrick made several albums of such ghostly *cartes de visite*, which he deposited on his death in 1953 with the SPR. Warrick considered that all psychic photos were ' "memory pictures exteriorised" & that in the future doctors will be able to *read* the brain in post mortems & thus "see" the individual's memories'.[31]

Vivid urban folklore still circulates about retinal images: that the face of the murderer can be read in the victim's eyes. For example, in 1868 Hans Christian Anderson in the story 'The Wood Nymph', writes, 'They say, too, that in the pupils of a dead man's eyes are photographed the last things he has seen.'[32] At the shrine of Guadelupe in Mexico, a double miracle of visionary optics occurred: the cloak of the visionary, Juan Diego, was imprinted miraculously with a true picture of the Madonna projected on to it when she appeared to him, and then, by a further miracle, his likeness was caught in the reflection in the iris of her eyes—this is the legend that has grown up, in modern times, around this passionate cult.[33]

Photography was above all the form of modern communications that dominated the concept of material thought, far more even than the new telegraphy or radio transmission. In many ways, the seance reproduces the camera obscura itself, and the relations with the invisible that it stages correspond to the relations between light and the photographic medium: spirits act like the equivalent of light, leaving a trace of their insubstantial passage in material form. Ghostly inhabitants of the other side, immaterial substances that informed the realm of the ether, impressed themselves on to the sensitive film of the here and now, through the lens of the medium seated inside a hooded and curtained alcove in a darkened chamber. Early camera obscuras were swathed in fabric with festoons and fringes of velvet and braid, and resemble very closely the draped cabinet of the seance, in which the medium was enclosed, and from which issued the 'phenomena'.[34] Only the lens of the camera obscura and the void in its interior had been replaced—by the woman sitting inside the box. She operated in the place of a camera itself or, later, in the place of the television cabinet itself.

Interestingly the means used to secure the medium follow styles of domestic technology: the medium Margery Crandon, visiting London from Boston in 1922, during the most intense forensic activity of investigators, was shut up inside a wooden box very like a large home apparatus or giant brownie camera. In the photograph that shows her under this constraint, she has become an instrument both receiving and transmitting, like a camera or a radio or a gramophone—a human Victrola. More precisely, she takes the place of the actual sensitive film inside a camera, ready to receive projections from the unseen realm, which in turn imprinted themselves on materials offered by the seance participants for their reception (wax, slates, paper).

This imitation of photography's processes was then itself authenticated by documentary images: psychic images taken with magnesium flares proved the prodigious character of the phenomena and the fleeting existence of ectoplasmic apparitions. These ways of generating spirit phenomena still cast the medium as a kind of camera, receiving and transmitting light's action upon matter.

The illusions that photographic processes at all stages from the camera to developing tray to print were capable of producing were zestfully exploited in both still and, later, moving pictures.[35] At first, lengthy exposure times turned passing figures into wraiths, child sitters into blurred wisps, and eerily emptied and stilled busy city streets; accidents in printing introduced unexpected presences, while flashes, streaks, and comet trails gave evidence of the medium's uncanny potential. The most practical productions of the age, far less marvellous than the new media, contributed to the rise of Gothic and spectral reality: even the manufacture of cotton wool, for example, played its part. Cotton wool was invented for dressing wounds in Birmingham by a doctor called Joseph Sampson Gamgee (d. 1888). It would become, alongside cheesecloth, the most used correlate of spirit substance, and shortly find a role in Christmas windows, angel outfits for school nativity plays, snowy mangers—and psychic photography.[36] In 1923, F. W. Warrick commented innocently, 'I am devoting much time to a study of the veiling and cotton wool surrounding the faces and I fancy I have discovered therein moulded forms which bring to mind the ectoplasmic creations of Eva C. and other continental mediums.'[37]

One kind of spirit photograph pictures phantoms of the dead: ghosts appear to the sitter through the eye of the camera, not to their own senses as in the hoped-for effects of a seance. Two shifts have taken place since the first projections of the camera obscura in the preceding century: the darkened chamber of the mind takes form in the darkened chamber of the seance setting, and produces one category of spirit photographs. These show effects that were visible to the sitters, even if so fleeting or so sudden as to be virtually invisible. But, concomitantly, the dark chamber materializes in the apparatus of photography itself, and then the ghosts are not visible to any physical or living witness, but only to the film or plate: in these circumstances, the sitter and photographer together have projected the presence of the desired spirit visitor. The distinction helps relate psychic photography's popular and widespread acceptance to the tradition of projective imagination—portraits of men and women facing the camera, with a revenant hovering above their head or diaphanously hanging over their breast or lap, were accepted as thought-prints, emanating from the subject in symbiosis with the photographer. The spirit photographer William Hope called his portraits 'psychographs';[38] the ghost of Arthur Conan Doyle (Figure 25, p. 298) was a great favourite, as the famous author had been an ardent supporter in his lifetime, and himself amassed a huge collection of such images.[39] Practitioners had the gift required, their numerous satisfied clients felt, to capture their losses and longings, which took the form of images in their mind's eye. Most often, the phantoms appear like thought-balloons above the subject's head, swathed in cotton wool or cheesecloth. The activity becomes twofold: first the sitter is able to thrust his or her object of desire and longing into the material world, where the camera, in the hands of a mediumistically gifted photographer, is able to perceive it; the camera plate then doubles its subject as in a mirror.

The magic lanternist who, hidden from view, flourished his fantastical images had transmuted into a very different kind of magical conjuror, and the differences in the use of bodies are indeed eloquent. The medium Eva C. created some of the most sensational effects in a long sequence of experiments conducted by Juliette Bisson, a wealthy widow and a sculptor, who promoted Eva's powers. Bisson acted as impresario, and brought in Baron Albert von Schrenck-Notzing as her co-producer. A Bavarian doctor with a practice in psychiatry, he lent scientific credibility to their endeavours through his profession; he also made records of the seances.

Schrenck-Notzing documented and photographed Eva C.'s phenomena, minuting exhaustively all times and details for a vast tome which appeared in Germany in 1913, and was translated into English in 1920 under the title *Phenomena of Materialisation*.[40] It made the type of seances he featured internationally famous, and spread their characteristics far and wide through psychic and Spiritualist circles (Figure 21, p. 252).

Eva C. was exposed to the camera, while she herself acted as a photographer: she produced many portraits of recognizable individuals. Grimacing, gritting her teeth, and screwing her eyes tight, she breathed out their image on muslins and veils from her ears, head, ears, navel, and breasts, exactly as if the thought-pictures in her mind were imprinting the image, like Christ's icon on the miraculous veil of Veronica, on to shapeless, cloudy stuff from the higher world. M. Bisson, Juliette's dear departed, appeared full-length, as well as the President of the United States Woodrow Wilson, and many others. They were identified from photo-gravures in magazines, but considered no less convincing for all that.

Photography also spread news of the wonders produced at a seance and sparked similar incidents almost immediately in many corners of the world—spirits appearing in photographs, entangled in veils and webs of diaphanous stuff, became the most coveted result of a seance from the turn of the century up till as late as the 1940s. One worried-sounding secretary, keeping minutes of such an occasion, reported, 'The mask-like appearance seen by several of the sitters and described by them as either hanging from or located beneath the medium's mouth was first noticed and examined by electric torch light at 7.30 pm, and the very divergent description of it given by Dr Wooler, Mr Dingwall and Mrs Salter seem to suggest an object of Protean changeability.'[41]

At the same time as ghosts were appearing on film and in person (as it were), fairies were also choosing the new medium for their mirror. Charles Dodgson reportedly bought a picture of a fairy and was delighted with it. As discussed before, the *Sylvie and Bruno* books adopt many photographic manners, and the miniaturization of the child protagonists when they pass into the 'Eerie' state picks up on native traditions about fairyland, but also enacts an intrinsic property of the photographic method. In 1900, the perceived magic of the medium even inspired Kodak to name its first fast camera the 'Brownie', evoking the family resemblance between the medium, its enchanted subjects, and, now, its child-sprite users who would make snapshots of themselves, their families, and little friends. These were images in which, like Peter Pan, they would never grow up or grow old. In the first advertisement for the new camera for the home, two diminutive brownies, the helpful little folk of native British lore, were depicted loading the film and dancing with glee.[42]

Jacques-Henri Lartigue, the most famous of child photographers, was given his first camera (not a Brownie) in 1901, and was soon making a wonderfully light-hearted series of spoof ghost pictures, with members of his family draped in great expanses of sheet and capering about on the verandah of their house in a genuinely funny exaggeration of spectres' general dress and behaviour: 'Zissou en fantôme' leaps in an imitation of a poltergeist's reputed limber antics.

By far the most notorious apparitions took place in 1917 when two cousins, Elsie Wright (16 at the time) and Frances Griffiths (six years younger), took photographs of fairies dancing in the dell below their house, where the girls often played and where Frances liked to go, saying she saw fairies there.[43] They showed the fairies flitting in the glen, taking a sun bath, and other kinds of dilly-dallying. The 'Cottingley Fairy Photographs' were a sensation. Published in the *Strand* magazine in December 1920, they were widely accepted as true—and even more astonishing, still are in some parts of the Web today.[44] But they would never have commanded public attention and persuaded people at all if spirit photography had not been so widely trusted against all its critics, and if children—especially little girls— had not enjoyed special access to wonderlands. The similarity in ages and family relations with the Fox sisters is worth noticing, bearing in mind the portrait of children in Victorian fantasy: the youth of the photographers lent sincerity and innocence to their report.

The girls were sent back to the dell three years later to repeat their feat, and succeeded with three more pictures. Sir Arthur Conan Doyle gave them his unequivocal endorsement. Coincidentally, Conan Doyle was the nephew of the fairy painter Richard 'Dicky' Doyle, who created the classic children's picture-book *In Fairyland* (1870); he was on close terms with fairies, however odd it might seem of the inventor of Sherlock Holmes and the deductive method.

Elsie and Frances' camera extended with lively imagination a Victorian nursery longing for cute, elvish, secret spirits, who also communicated, as in Richard Dadd's fairy paintings, a touch of sinister adult perversity as well. The series of photographs are playful and seductive, even though to present-day eyes, their concoction is so obvious (some figures were cut out of an advertisement for Price's *Night Lights*). Several of them are strange, especially the Blakean 'fairy birth . . . from a sort of cocoon'.[45] The pleasure they give is now shot through with ironic knowingness. This appears to be a deeply enjoyable state: two films have been made about the story, and several artists have revisited it and made more pictures in the girls' footsteps.[46]

The Cottingley Fairy Photographs reveal how Conan Doyle's scientific positivism compelled him to interpret the photograph as a document of an external reality, whereas the young girls themselves, one of whom worked in a photographer's shop retouching prints, understood the medium's deep relation to fantasy and other worlds, and made it the mirror of their dreams.

As sitters, monitors, stage managers, as well as mediums, women were also highly imaginative in new methods of contacting spirits and achieving their own desires, for the most part unconsciously and in good faith.[47] These obviously included self-expression and consolation, especially in social milieux of constriction and muteness. Throughout the decades after 1870 till the Second World War, advanced, intelligent women were active in psychic research and related experiments; their prominence skews easy assumptions that such interests arise among the poor and the ignorant, and presents an awkwardness for the social historian of women's emancipation.[48] It seems that women who were themselves spirited were strongly attracted to Spiritualism, trance, and telepathy: individuals at odds with Victorian domestic ideals, spinster educationalists, co-habiting couples who could not in a climate of deep inhibition admit to lesbianism, and single women of different social backgrounds, were all attracted to working in the movement. Harriet Hosmer (d. 1908), sculpting in Rome as an independent woman artist, and carving in white marble effigies of spirits in the form of winged babies, believed in her psychic powers, and was inspired by visions which came to her in sleep and waking; Hosmer acted as a medium for her friend the poet Elizabeth Barrett Browning.[49] The search for spirits appears to match a search for individuality outside prescribed borders, and while such beliefs now seem superstitious and embarrassing, it is important not to assume that they flourished among the deprived, uneducated, and resource-less.[50] The writer Radclyffe Hall (1883–1943) actively contacted spirits; most famously of all, two English gentlewomen, Charlotte Anne Moberly and Eleanor Jourdain, travelling together in France in 1901, saw the ghosts of Marie Antoinette and her retinue at Versailles. Later, living connubially in all but name, they became fellow tutors and eventually Principal and Vice-Principal at St Hugh's College, Oxford. In 1911, they collaborated on the story of their 'second sight' experience at Versailles: *An Adventure* was published pseudonymously and became a huge bestseller, inciting a vast secondary literature and faithful disciples to this day.[51]

From the sitting-rooms of the bourgeoisie, where the earliest table-turning and spirit visitations took place, the quest for spirit spread into the high streets and the public studio; seances were opened to interested parties. Spiritualists and their mediums were shadowed by spirit investigators who, like priests interrogating witches, sought to establish the nature, causes, and truth status of the psychic phenomena. In 1882, the Society for Psychical

Research was founded by a group of friends, philosophers and scientists; the philosopher Henry Sidgwick, the physician William Barrett, the psychologist Frederic Myers, the physicist Oliver Lodge, and others were determined to establish the status of spirits who were commanding the attention and energies of so many serious-minded contemporaries and to plumb the mysteries of 'unexplained phenomena'. They brought energy and assiduity to the task. As Frederic Myers wrote, 'We cannot simply admit the existence of disincarnate spirits as inert or subsidiary phenomena; we must expect to have to deal with them as agents on their own account—agents in unexpected ways, and with novel capacities.'[52]

In 1882, Henry Sidgwick, eminent philosopher at
Cambridge, founded the Society of Psychical Research
with a group of friends and colleagues who wished to
apply scientific principles to the investigation of
unexplained phenomena.

18

Phantoms to the Test: The Society for Psychical Research

> tomb shadow—
> no, divinely for not dead . . . change of mode of being, that is all
>
> Stéphane Mallarmé

The philosopher William James, a member of the SPR and its president from 1894 to 1895, put his finger on the similarity of the scientific and psychic experiments as perceived at the time, when he wrote that phenomena such as automatic writing were 'instruments of research, reagents like litmus paper or the galvanometer, for revealing what would otherwise be hidden'.[1] The enterprise of the psychic investigators—to weigh the imponderable, the measure the immeasurable—caught imaginations all over the world in the last decades of the nineteenth century. As James mused, '[there might be] in the universe a lot of diffuse soul-stuff, unable of itself to get into consistent personal form, or to take permanent possession of an organism, yet always craving to do so; it might get its head into the air, parasitically, so to speak, by profiting by weak spots in the armour of human minds, and slipping in and stirring up there the sleeping tendencies to personate.'[2]

The theories of the Society and its supporters proved as alluring and as contested in their time as alchemy had been before them, and they have become as haloed in doubt today (a lesson in a certain necessary heuristic humility for our time, too). The first scientists who became gripped by psychic research included believing Spiritualists, on the one hand, and on the other, a group of natural philosophers and other thinkers who wanted to address the deepest questions thrown up by the Darwinian revolution. Some of the pioneers did not belong to the traditional networks of authority (the Church of England, public schools, Oxford and Cambridge). William Crookes, William Barrett, and John Tyndall were Nonconformists in background, not Establishment insiders.[3] Their work placed them in conflict with orthodoxies of all kinds, regarding women, faith, and morals. For example, the physician William Barrett (1844–1925), one of the chief catalysts of the SPR, was the son of a Congregationalist minister who had left his flock in Jamaica in disagreement with the British policy towards labour on the island, which he considered a revival of slavery.[4]

The experiments with forces and phantoms and telepathy looked—and still look—to outsiders like 'right rum carryings-on'. Yet they enjoyed a huge success, and as the influence of Spiritualism and spiritism and psychic explorations grew among a great variety of publics—scientific experimenters, the growing number of believers in rapping and summonings and spirit photographers meeting clients' needs, the explorers and ethnographers reporting on other people's spiritual systems—a new, different group drawn from the next generation began monitoring and investigating the beliefs. Their research was conducted informally from 1874 onwards, and then formally, once the SPR was founded eight years later. The American branch, founded in Boston by William James, followed its English counterparts in 1884.

William Barrett apart, several founding members of the SPR were drawn from social groups that differed from the originators of Spiritualism and the first scientific pioneers. This second-generation wave of spirit researchers were eminent Victorians: Lytton Strachey indeed thought of turning his merciless attention to Henry Sidgwick (1838–1900), the first president of the Society (Figure 20, p. 236), but did not in the end include him. Sidgwick held the Knightsbridge Chair of Moral Philosophy at Cambridge; he specialized in ethics (*Methods of Ethics*, published in 1874, is still studied).[5] His wife Eleanor, herself a mathematician, who had been brought up with a strong sense of independence, was the sister of Arthur Balfour, who became Prime Minister from 1902 to 1904 and later pushed through the 'Balfour Declaration' of 1917. But they too were progressive: in 1871, Henry Sidgwick began the process of radical educational reform that eventually led to the establishment of Newnham, the first Cambridge college for women, where Eleanor went to study.[6]

The group's connections in the ranks of wealth and influence in late Victorian Britain ramified beyond politics: the physicist F. W. Strutt (later Lord Rayleigh) was married to Eleanor's sister Evelyn, while her brothers epitomized 'old school tie' alliances in action: Eleanor's second brother, Gerald, a gifted classicist, was one of the keenest advocates with the SPR for telepathy and automatic writing. (The Balfour clan were also connected by marriage to Gladstone: these were dynastic relations.) Thus the SPR eventually formed a constellation within Cambridge intellectual and national political aristocracy.

The original band of friends was also very close-knit by ties of friendship: Frederic Myers was Sidgwick's former student at Trinity College, Cambridge, and remained a beloved friend with his tutor, as did Edmund Gurney, another SPR founder. The society attracted a strong following:

the biologist Alfred Russel Wallace and, from the 1890s onwards, the distinguished physicist Oliver Lodge (1851–1940). In France, Charles Richet, who in 1913 would be given a Nobel Prize in Physiology for his research into sudden deaths, was an eager participant; so was Camille Flammarion the astronomer, an inspired popularizer of his subject and a pioneer science fiction writer. These men and women were well-to-do and well connected; they were also philanthropic and liberal, and their work unexpectedly sustained the original link between paranormal interests and social experiment which turned esoteric quests such as psychic research and Spiritualism into a nursery of emancipatory change in education, politics, women's status, and the approach and enterprise of scientific knowledge itself.

The members were not especially eccentric, but were responsive to the interests of the larger community. A dynamic convergence of ideas in late Victorian England inspired them to this incongruity: the application of strict laboratory standards to paranormal experiments. Early SPR members, like the Sidgwicks, were feeling out a scientific position in the years after Darwin, and grappling with some of the basic tenets of Christian theology— above all, the existence of the individual soul and its immortality. Rooted scepticism and unappeasable curiosity writhed in Sidgwick's energetic mind for four decades. In 1869, Sidgwick declared that he could not profess the Thirty-nine Articles of the Faith in the Anglican Church, as fellows of Trinity College, Cambridge, were required to do, and he resigned. This was an act of courageous honesty, but he was rewarded: the college responded immediately by creating a special lectureship in Moral Sciences for him, the first post in the university that did not require that the incumbent be a member of the Anglican Church. Sidgwick, as president of the SPR during most of its first decade until his death, lent the Society formidable *gravitas*. After he died, Eleanor continued to be highly active, becoming president in 1908–9.

His friend and fellow founder of the SPR, Frederic Myers (1843–1901), is the most original figure in the Society, a charming but contradictory character: a prize-winning classicist at Cambridge and a keen poet, also garlanded, though little read now (his fustian and overwrought diction a great contrast to his innovatory psychology).[7] Myers was found to have plagiarized parts of his medal-winning poems at Cambridge, and confidently defended himself on the grounds of prophetic inspiration, as with a sibyl or oracle. A man of highly wrought emotion and passionate yearning, he had a turbulent life—the philosopher C. D. Broad thought it likely that Myers was bisexual, though this was not acknowledged consciously by himself or by anyone else.[8] The pitch of his intensity can be felt in a letter he wrote to George Eliot after reading *Middlemarch*: 'Life has come to such a pass—now that there is no longer any God or any hereafter or anything in particular to aim at—that it is only by coming into contact with some other person that one can be oneself. . . . all that one can do is to feel the sparks fly from one for a moment when one strikes a kindred soul.'[9]

In 1869, Myers followed Sidgwick and resigned his fellowship at Trinity on the grounds that he could not profess the Christian faith any longer. He became an Inspector of Schools in Cambridge. Myers wrote keenly about the work of decipherment—almost deconstruction—that lay ahead: 'The old conception of the world's history as a collection of stories, each admitting of a complete and definitive recital, is giving way to a conception which would compare it rather with a series of imperfectly-read inscriptions, the sense of each of which is modified by the interpretations which we gradually find in its predecessors.'[10] A further paradox thus defines the early psychic researchers: they were pioneers in the secularization of the British Establishment.

From the 1870s onwards, Sidgwick and Myers travelled together up and down the country visiting mediums, attending seances, and assiduously exploring paranormal speculation; after they founded the SPR, they contributed indefatigably to the Society's work. The letters that they exchanged are deeply affectionate, and indeed, that degree and openness of affection could be expressed only if homosexuality were not at issue—not consciously.

In 1873, Myers fell profoundly in love with Annie Marshall, a married woman with five children. The feelings were mutual: they vowed deep attachment to each other—in entirely Platonic terms. Then three years later, Annie Marshall committed suicide, stabbing herself in her throat with a pair of scissors and then drowning herself in Derwentwater near her home. Her death was a devastating tragedy for Myers, and it suffuses his life's work and beliefs. It was not the only extraordinary and horrific calamity to overtake this otherwise charmed circle of clever, well-placed friends. Mary Catherine Lyttelton, the fiancée of Arthur Balfour, died of typhoid fever in 1875 during their engagement; her brother killed himself in 1876; and in 1882, F. M. Balfour, another brother and a golden boy of his generation, a pioneering embryologist at Cambridge, fell to his death in a mountaineering accident in the Alps. Their young ghosts haunted the bereaved, in the way that loved ones who die do, especially when those partings come unexpectedly, early, fatefully. But they haunted the SPR members with a difference: they became objects of study.

The Society proceeded with a form of early polling: by means of questionnaires, it canvassed evidence from hundreds of correspondents all over the world, relying on the efficient networks of the Victorian postal system and the diplomatic bag. For the Sidgwick Report on the

Census of Hallucinations, 17,000 answers were received, and the evidence of apparitions after death ran 440 times higher than chance, William James reported in his presidential address of 1894; he called the report 'that masterpiece of intelligent and thorough scientific work'.[11]

Eleanor diligently managed and edited the vast collection of records the Society amassed on the question of survival after death, apparitions, and psychic photography, and wrote copiously on everything from Theosophy to *déjà vu*.[12] (The keen automatist W. H. Salter commented that 'One of her diversions when young, was keeping elaborate housekeeping accounts. A very fine, gentle calm nature, with extraordinary powers of concentration and perspicacity.')[13] But Mrs Sidgwick's consistent scepticism about the results of these massive surveys, trenchantly expressed in numerous articles and reviews in the SPR's journal, profoundly annoyed many of the Society's members, including the distinguished biologist Alfred Russel Wallace. Wallace had written strongly in support of spirit photographs in his 1874 book *Miracles and Modern Spiritualism*, and believed that the objective evidence had only increased since then.[14] The quarrel within the SPR provides a huge and obsessive counterpart to tales of ghosts and apparitions, omens and marvels, in turn-of-the-century literature, and reveals those cross-currents of beliefs, visions, and fantasies that were stirred up by the British Empire's vast expanse: not only coffee, tea, and tobacco travelled from its dominions, but the shivers and thrills of spirits, and the knowledge of spectres too.

Myers helped Edmund Gurney (1847–88), another of the founders of the Society, classics scholar and star of Trinity College, Cambridge, to finish his immense book about ghosts, sightings, and telepathy, *Phantasms of the Living*, which was published after Gurney's early death.[15] Gurney argued against spirits' independence, and ascribed visions and presentiments to the hallucinative powers of the human mind. Frank Podmore, another member of the SPR, also contributed to bring the two-volume work to completion, though both he and Myers differed from Gurney's conclusions: they argued instead for the reality of spiritual existence in another dimension of reality.[16]

In 1882, the same year as the founding of the Society, Myers coined the word 'telepathy', to characterize thought transmission, as posited by Crookes, Charles Richet, and others. With this Hellenic neologism, the psychic researchers hoped to elevate 'second sight' from the disparaged domain of folk belief into a scientific concept. The prefix tele- was being used to form any number of new compounds to describe new discoveries— some established today as incontrovertibly physical, but others challenged by doubt, and worse: telegraph, telephone, telekinesis, teleportation, and, later, television. In the course of Myers' own *magnum opus*, *Human Personality and its Survival after Bodily Death* (published in 1903, after Myers' own death from illness), the philosopher developed a hugely ambitious syncretic theory of the self, drawing on Continental and Eastern thinkers and his own wide reading in classics and psychology.[17] He called this 'the subliminal self'. This self enjoys continuity over time and place, and unconsciously carries memories which preserve its integrity through eternity; these can be awakened or recalled through mediums and other supernatural means. Some individuals have more than one stream of consciousness, but even if experiencing several at one time, each person has only one psyche. This psyche enjoys different states, and moves through different zones in time and space.[18] As Rhodri Hayward puts it: 'Myers' subliminal self . . . operated as a kind of filter for the sacred, combining the extracarnate communication with the fragmentary memories and desires of the individual's own past. . . . The sacred was relocated within the field of memory.'[19]

Ideas of doubled and contradictory selves coexisting were increasingly coming under serious consideration (as we shall see more later): Myers' subliminal consciousness responds to Freud's theory of the unconscious, but places it in a metaphysical perspective, imbued with ideas about reincarnation. Nevertheless, the connections are there—almost at an unconscious level. Jacques Derrida, discussing how captivated Freud was in the 1920s by the possibility of thought transference, quotes Freud as saying, 'one could speak of a psychical counterpart to wireless telegraphy'. Derrida muses: 'Difficult to imagine a theory of what they still call the unconscious without a theory of telepathy.' He then allows himself to wonder, as most of us have done, how it is that someone telephones the very moment you have put your hand on the receiver to call them. For Derrida, modern media do not simply, uncannily, move the self over distances, but give 'the eerie feeling of replicating the movement of thought itself'.[20]

The two axes that structure the research of the SPR—rationalist inquiry into the supernatural, on the one hand, and the legacy of representation, on the other—intersect at the vertex of the new technologies, especially photography, itself a medium. Seance enthusiasts and psychic researchers— even the mystically inclined Myers—presented themselves as objective scientists applying methods of logical deduction, and proudly proclaimed their alertness to tricks and deception on the part of the mediums. In this respect, photography's nineteenth-century status as a truth-telling or indexical instrument was crucial to the growth of belief in spirit phenomena, and acted as the prime means of their credibility—and diffusion. So the photographs that were taken to verify the apparitions were not perceived as the phenomenon itself, or even a part of it, though the taking of them often provided the climax to the seance and its clearest aim; in this they differed from the psychic portraits channelled by Mumler, Houghton, William Hope, and Deane. Instead, they were adduced as proofs, outside the seance and separate from it; they seemed to offer crucial evidence of what had taken place, not interwoven into the process, or contiguous with the participants. The camera was accepted as the impartial witness, the mechanical eye that could not be suborned or deceived—though, of course, in some cases this claim was disingenuous. The camera was treated as if it were above all contingency. Schrenk-Notzing's book and Harry Price's later ghost-busting investigations applied photographic evidence in exactly the same way, but to opposing ends: to demonstrate irrefutably the absence of ruse, or to disclose its presence.[21]

Practical limitations also moulded seance processes, including their recording by the camera. At that stage in the medium's history, it heightened certain monochrome effects and erased other data from the record, and receivers of the images were not as accustomed as we are now to the faults of printing and the effects of accidental light. This relates to the second axis, the spirit photographs' connections with traditional symbolism.

The spirits' entrance and activities were also rendered persuasive through certain characteristics of the photographic medium: in black-and-white images taken during a seance, light traces appear phantasmic, conjuring the presence of wraiths, while other substances, the mysterious blobs and streaks that the mediums exuded, lose defining details of their appearance in the murk of the darkened chamber, illuminated only by a red bulb and the sudden dazzling flash of magnesium. They become, as it were, tran-substantiated. Thus the pseudo-scientific aims and claims of the investigators and performers collide with the phantasmagoric manipulations of sense impressions and data in the seance. Even more importantly, as discussed before, the camera catches the spectral form in a manner that provided a metaphor for thought itself. The psychic photograph analogously extended this process, making an image of the ectoplasmic form extruded by the spirit. F. W. H. Myers proclaimed the adept's ability to heal Western dualism and arrive at the wisdom of a monistic world-view that does not distinguish between spirit and matter. He wrote: 'the pervading unity of things remains incognisable [sic] to him save as an indwelling essence, which is the soul of his soul. . . . he has obtained an experimental insight into that "mind-stuff", whose existence we can only conjecture; he has half bridged over the gulf between objective and subjective, by actually learning to see his own thought, his own will.' He goes on to develops the metaphor of projection and photography: 'we are projected as images from the unmanifested unity of things.'[22]

The chief clients of spirit photographers were the bereaved, as perhaps goes without saying. The popularity of Spiritualism intensified, as is well known, in the aftermath of the First World War, when thousands of ghosts appeared to reassure their loved ones that they were well in the spirit world. Mrs Deane often encouraged her sitters to join in a hymn with her, as 'the vibrations caused by singing are helpful in the production of psychic phenomena'.[23] Her *Psychic Photographs*, taken from 1920 to 1923, show every kind of relationship: siblings who have lost a brother in the fighting, men who have lost a childhood friend, neighbours, wives, and sweethearts, and of course parents who have lost a child—a gallery of human grief and a moving picture of a modern mourning ritual. The albums also reveal the different bonds that held society together in an era when same-sex love was not defined exclusively in sexual terms: many of the ghosts are lost friends of the same sex, male and female.

The men and women whose adherence to Spiritualism confounds belief—that super-rationalist Conan Doyle, for instance—were in mourning. They had lost sons in the fighting, and the photographs of these lost loved ones look out from the frontispieces of many a tragic memoir. *Raymond, Or Life and Death* (1916), by the scientist Oliver Lodge, about his child who was killed early on in the war, touched a chord during the mounting death toll. Lodge followed this with a memorial to another casualty, Christopher Coombe-Tennant, who at the age of 19 also died on the Western Front. Lodge resisted the SPR's sceptical conclusions, and became one of the most resolute advocates of the truth of life after death and of spirits' presence all around us. In *Christopher*, he strongly recommended that those who face death should make a 'compact' with the living, to return, and then find the survivors happy, serene, waiting for their companionship to resume. He quoted his fellow psychic researcher F. W. H. Myers (Christopher's uncle by marriage): 'Not, then, with tears and lamentations should we think of the blessed dead. Rather we should rejoice with them in their enfranchisement, and know that they are still minded to keep us as sharers in their joy. . . . they guide us as with a cloudy pillar, but it is kindling into steadfast fire.'[24] The faith of Lodge and other Spiritualists that mortal death does not entail an end to 'com- munion' burns with hope against hope, at a pitch of wishful thinking that is painful to read now. Taking strength from this form of spiritual consola- tion diverts energy from attacking the cause of the young men's deaths, even in the midst of the most acute suffering. Christopher's mother tried to console herself in this way: 'And of the innumerable boys who have gone to the front and entered the repulsive complication of modern war, with no taste for it whatever but solely from a sense of duty, how great must be the happiness that necessarily follows so great a sacrifice! NO survivor should doubt for a moment the destiny in store for such as these. . . . There is a conservation of matter and of energy, there may be a conservation of life.'[25]

Geoff Dyer, in *The Missing of the Somme*, a reflection on the battlefields of the First World War, observes that photography itself altered the experience for contemporaries: 'The whole war was being remembered even as it was fought . . .'—in this sense it is the firstborn of photography, though photography itself was limited by technical limitations and by censorship. The faces of some of the thousands who died in the trenches survived in portraits taken before they went to fight: high street photography was a mass phenomenon, and this was the first generation of fighting men to have been photographed. They survived, they returned, they became revenants in the presence of the living, in elegies, memorials, and spirit photographs.[26]

Lodge believed strongly in the truth of the spirit photographer Mrs Deane, and became very excited by what he saw: 'The only normal explanation for this face is that it is an accidental one, but . . . it is far too perfect for that, and moreover it is surrounded concentrically by an ecto-plasmic veil (if that is the right name for these white appearances), such as would have had to be put on the plate by some non-optical means.' He conducted a session in his own laboratory, under 'very tight controls' with his own set of plates, marked and prepared six weeks earlier, etc., and reported: 'There was an "extra" [figure] on one of my plates, and on four or five of hers; which is a reasonable proportion . . . But the "extras" were not all of equal value. Still even an ectoplasmic smudge is not what you expect to get on a plate.' He continued: 'I shall be interested to hear what you think of two, viz., the one where two heads appear above mine . . . and secondly the one where the face appears to be in my lap, made out of the [crossed out] things belong [*sic*] to the sitters,—as is clear on magnification—and yet surrounded by the white stuff, and too clear in features to be regarded as accidental.'[27]

Spirit photographs have even more acute poignancy today because, with the advances in technique and our far greater familiarity with photographic illusion, doctoring, enhancement, they are so stagey, so comically, tragically absurd. A photograph survives of 'Peggy', the spirit who appeared regularly at the seances of Helen Duncan, a Scottish medium who became notorious when she was charged under the Witchcraft Act of 1753, found guilty and sentenced to nine months in prison in 1944. Duncan was the last of the materializing mediums, celebrated in her lifetime for her powers of clairvoyance and ectoplasmic production, as she sat in the spirit cabinet, groaning and shuddering in the grip of the trance state.[28]

Peggy was the spirit of a child, who, when she first appeared—anonym-ously—was piercingly recognized by her mother. After that, Peggy became a regular apparition, doing winsome routines, singing and dancing in the manner of Shirley Temple, the great child star of the period. But the photograph shows a ghastly crude mask, with huge white face and heavily daubed mouth wrapped in an old sheet, every inch a Hallowe'en bogey. That these ghosts could ever have persuaded anyone, that these makeshift clumsy apparitions could ever have been recognized as a lost loved child by the child's own mother, reveals the depths of people's need to reach some peace with the dead.

It also reveals, however, that photography itself has altered our relation to the past and the working of memory: if Peggy's mother had lived at a time when home videos were standard, it is unlikely that she would have been able to see in Helen Duncan's puppet the ghost of her daughter. Yet this context does not give a full explanation either of the trust placed in psychic phenomena. Helen Duncan continued to command a huge following until she died in 1956; spirit photographers were then still practising, in spite of numerous exposés and many pranksters, and any visit to the Web will disclose many continuing experiments—claims and counterclaims.

As with witchcraft itself, the history of psychic endeavour has been most richly chronicled by its fiercest attackers. At the end of the century and long into the twentieth, the most ferocious arose from the heartlands, not the periphery: the conjuror and escapologist Harry Houdini, a master of disguise and supreme lord of deception, was the scourge of charlatans, the hottest detective of duplicity, and the most implacable enemy in denouncing claims to supernatural powers. Many of the members of the SPR devoted their lives to challenging the beliefs they held or wanted to hold. The Sidgwicks remained the most persevering and the most obdurate. As a result, they have not returned as ghosts to instruct survivors in the other world, while several others—Myers above all—are still regular revenants.

What, if anything, can be taken from all these psychic ventures? Is there an alternative to shrugging or laughing at their oddness and folly, and instead showing sympathy with the quest for knowledge that genuinely drove them? In what ways do spirits speak, if not of themselves in any historical sense of the term, but of the constellation of knowledges that brought men and women to summon them, test them, believe in them, and attempt to define them? Yet the spectres who haunt someone or some time or some place tells us about what mattered then, to them, there.

There are some responses to offer within the scope of this book. First, serious men and women of the nineteenth century, within the limits of the knowledge they possessed then, were able to give their full attention to spirit manifestations as literal events, and to persist in their work even when they could not suspend their disbelief, as in the case of Crookes, the Sidgwicks,

Richet, and Lodge. Secondly, their discoveries, inquiries, speculations, and beliefs shaped a new way of being in the world for the individual, strongly conveyed in popular ghost and science fiction literature and in modernists' new insistence on the exquisite sensory apparatus of interconnected subjects.[29] Spirit theories fundamentally challenged the idea of the bounded person, and permeate the psychology of writers who flirted with the paranormal (Robert Louis Stevenson, Rudyard Kipling, Henry James). But several who were avowedly rational, and had no time for them (Virginia Woolf, Gertrude Stein), also adopted uncanny modes of transmission— receptivity through vibrations and waves between the characters in their fiction. Beside them, numerous occult fabulists and ghost storytellers flourished, and continue to do so.

Spirits who made their appearance were, crucially, no longer ghosts in the Christian sense of the term. The SPR members and other occultists and spiritists were industriously generating a vast and cloudy metaphysics basically premissed on the possibility of souls detachable from bodies and from time, and wandering from one period to another, one individual to another. This foundation in metempsychosis or the transmigration of souls, on the model of Greek and Indian and animist religious thought, reflects the classical training of many psychic researchers and their contacts, often through political and imperial employment, with India, Indonesia and Africa. When a medium in trance began speaking in tongues, and delivering messages in an altered voice, her 'spirit control' was in charge—her ultimate soul, as it were, the one that had taken up occupation of her body for this existence.

Frederic Myers defined these kinds of revenants as, first, 'projections of the double'—namely, the spirit of a person—and secondly, 'precipitations of the akās'—akās being a Hindu term borrowed by the Theosophists and designating the invisible energy that flows through and unites creation.[30] However, once these two forms are distinguished, it is clear that the spirits raised in seances or captured in photographs uneasily embody two contradictory concepts of the person and of the spirit's relation to that person: a ghost makes manifest an individual who has died, as does the psychic portrait. But the phenomena produced during a successful seance—apports of flowers or objects or musical instruments materializing by themselves and floating about, explosions of light and sudden noises, cool breezes blowing from nowhere, and, of course, tables and chairs leaping about in the air, ectoplasmic effluvia and pseudopods (more of these later)—do not body forth individual phantoms at all. They materialize, according to the sitters' theories, the enveloping presence of spirit forces. These spirit phenomena, which were sought so passionately by seance sitters and were so deeply satisfying to them afterwards, did not convey the medium's vital spirit; they sometimes emanated from their 'spirit control', whom the medium was channelling, but most of the time they were making manifest a cosmic force. The members of the SPR, with their scientific ambitions, invented the term 'IPA' (Incorporeal Personal Agent) to describe this kind of frequent spirit phenomenon.

According to this principle, as William James described when he proposed spirit stuff seeking a vehicle, a psychic photographer was picturing a spirit by channelling the spirit stuff of that person through his or her mind: this is not the same as Hamlet's father leaving purgatory to stride on the battlements of Elsinore and haunt the living; nor does it echo Gertrude when she cries out to Hamlet about the ghost of his father that he sees in her chamber, 'This is the very coinage of your brain.' Hamlet's mother sees his fevered mind as the origin of a delusion (*Hamlet*, III. iv. 137). By contrast, mediums actively put themselves in a state of mental *dérèglement* in order to access external forces that they and their co-sitters believed existed, independently and objectively.

Experiments with psychic phenomena also illuminate the development of technologies and its relationship with consciousness as the new mass communications appeared to demonstrate action at a distance: thoughts, words, pictures moved over huge expanses often at considerable speeds, and these exchanges criss-crossed the world in synchrony with the exploding trade and military might of Europeans. The Empire was already writing back, and had been since the start of Western empires. But in the late nineteenth and early twentieth centuries it was doing so ever more dynamically, with different, gripping stories to tell about the dead—and the living. As technologies shrank the globe, they brought people closer and closer— including people from the past, including their ghosts. Dealing with the new influences, in a fumbling, ignorant, often prurient fashion, cast up on the psychic shore a kind of colonial jetsam of fascination, desire, and guilt, as the next chapter will discuss. Female mediums, old and young, performed a series of knight's moves, stepping across time and either gender or race or all of them together, and grounded their mental adventures in an imagined history, not declared fantasy: imperial Gothic or psychic Orientalism persists in the mental landscapes of mediums and their clients.

Photographing ghosts, capturing souls, was a way of contacting the imponderable forces shaping the universe and ourselves as participants in its order; but visible evidence of light traces did not satisfy the cravings for proof felt by experimenters who had adopted a laboratory model for psychic research. To satisfy these standards, the photograph was not substantial or material enough; looked at from one angle, it was a mere trace or impression, and thus secondary to the phenomenon itself; looked at another way, it partook too deeply of its subjects' filmy spectrality to act as proof positive of spirit stuff. Further guarantees were wanting to prove the existence of spirits beyond the visible; to obtain them, questors began probing the ancient concept of the ether, and testing the possibility of ethereal matter.

Part VIII

Ether

The medium Eva C. performed in trance during
numerous seances diligently documented by the
physician Albert von Schrenck-Notzing, as in this
photograph taken 17 May 1912, in Munich.

19

Soul Vibrations; or, The Fluidic Invisible

> Clairvoyance, like so many other things in nature, is mainly a question
> of vibrations, and is in fact nothing but an extension of powers which
> we are all using every day of our lives.
>
> C. W. Leadbeater

From the beginning of the eighteenth century, when hydrogen was identified, the airy element grew ever more crowded, not only with light waves
and fiery atoms but with new varieties and properties of air—vapours and
gases, waves and vibrations, all of which enriched the concept of the ether
and contributed to the excitement of research into the invisible and the
nature of spirit forces. New instruments were devised to detect and inventory the components of air; their findings continually interplayed with
metaphysics, and were brought to bear on psychic as well as physical forces.

Not only light waves, captured by photography, but the unseen powers
of the electromagnetic field, on which Oliver Lodge spent his working life,
opened marvellous vistas where psychological theories and magical beliefs
sparked and fused. In the eighteenth century, for example, the craze for
mesmerism had ascribed the cure to a form of electricity, and in these public
displays of trance and therapy and 'magnetic spirits', the border between
psychology and physics was blurred. Public entertainers immediately
adopted the latest discoveries in this field, as they had in optics. Benjamin
Rackstrow, a most enterprising showman in Georgian London, staged 'The
Chair of Beatification', which involved irradiating a willing member of
the public with the kind of flaming amazement that Ariel conjured on the
shipwreck: 'a Glass Crown being placed on the Head of the Person who sits
in the Chair, immediately becomes filled with Aetherial Fire; and likewise a
Glass Sceptre, wherein is to be seen one continued stream of Electrical Fire,
of a beautiful Purple Colour.'[1]

The forces at work in the universe became instruments of revelation,
leading to new knowledge; developments in the natural sciences and
psychology, as well as in physics and communications, offered different
places for ethereal bodies to rise up: in 'radiant matter', in vibrations of the
ether, in the organic sparking of synapses, and in individual minds of mediums.
In 1855, the poet Gérard de Nerval rhapsodized on the connectedness of

matter: 'Everything lives, everything acts, everything corresponds: magnetic rays emanating from myself or from others cross without hindrance the infinite chain of created things; it is a transparent network which covers the world, and its loosened strands communicate as one neighbour to another with the planets and the stars. Captive at this moment on the earth, I converse with the choir of the heavenly bodies, who take part in my joys and in my sorrows.'[2]

The identification of radio waves, and the subsequent invention of the wireless, of the phonograph, of telegraphy, of the telephone, produced a fevered—and delighted—search to penetrate the unseen: the channels of communication through the ether presented themselves *in potentia* as deliriously numberless; they became intertwined with the physical possibility of moving objects at a distance by finding some vehicle analogous to radio waves through which thoughts could be transmitted. As the Theosophist C. W. Leadbeater put it, the problem of action at a distance required 'not so much the setting in motion of a current in astral matter, as the erection of a kind of temporary telephone through it'.[3]

In the course of the last decade of the nineteenth century, as we saw before, the prefix tele-, used in so many optical and acoustic devices, was also attached to 'telepathy' by Myers, and to other terms coined by the SPR, such as 'telekinesis' and 'teleplasm'. Crookes' explorations were dazzling but not exceptional in the history of Victorian innovation: research into communication at a distance moved on all fronts within interlinked disciplines, which unsettlingly included the occult. Oliver Lodge made a major contribution to the understanding of radio telegraphy with his experiments on wavelengths in 1888–98, and thereby paved the way not only to modern mass communications, but also to the theory of relativity; as we saw in Chapter 18, he was concurrently involved with psychic research, and an unwavering believer.

In many ways, the most brilliant of inventors in the Victorian age were at a loss to account for the marvels they made and were seeking ways to explain them, and many of them applied metaphors according to the logic of the imaginary, evolved during the course of a long history of speculation about spirits through concepts of ether, pneuma, light, immateriality, and so forth.

In the 1840s in Germany, Karl von Reichenbach proposed an analogous invisible and imponderable force to Mesmer's earlier animal magnetism. Reichenbach was no negligible scientist: ten years earlier he had discovered paraffin and creosote, and he retired with the proceeds to concentrate on electromagnetism, the most exciting mystery in physics in his time. Until his death in 1869, he experimented with subjects he called 'sensitives', who could detect invisible forces; these were almost all women, and through working with them, Reichenbach proposed a vital force he called the 'od', partly because he wanted a handy prefix or suffix, going on to name 'Somods' and 'odic' lights, and so forth. In a series of articles and experiments, he declared the od to be a different form of light, one transmitted by magnetic force, especially from crystals.[4] His theory was translated into English in 1846; Elizabeth Barrett Browning, for example, included the effect in her poetry.[5] Reichenbach saw—and took photographs of—odic lights and odic smoke in darkened rooms, as they radiated from magnets his collaborators held and energized—their touch providing the crucial contact between the empirical realm and the ethereal. How these effects came about cannot be discovered at this late date, and it is as improbable in his case as in Crookes' that he was setting out to deceive. Reichenbach speculated that the od was the principle that produced the aurora borealis, and he built a model of the Earth—a *terrelle*—which demonstrated that coloured lights grew far more intense at the poles, while 'odic smoke rose in abundance from the globe above the polar flames'.[6]

Dancing balls of radiance and flaring haloes around gifted mediums subsequently became a feature of early Spiritualism. New forms of visual record entered the evidence: spectroscopy made it possible to analyse previously inaccessible natural phenomena. By various brilliant experiments, new metals and elements were discovered—William Crookes finding thallium for the first time. Several different gases were also detected in this period of scientific excitement. Gas was given its name after Greek 'chaos' by the Dutch chemist J. B. van Helmont in a book published in 1652. It passed into English towards the end of the century, and was then defined as 'a Spirit that will not coagulate, or the Spirit of Life'.[7] Hydrogen had been analysed in 1700, as mentioned earlier; then, after a period when the combustible element of the air was termed 'phlogiston', Lavoisier isolated and defined oxygen in 1777; in 1810, Humphry Davy isolated the deadly and suffocating gas chlorine, as well as laughing gas—nitrous oxide. But in the 1890s, there came an astonishing flurry of new, invisible and virtually imperceptible inert gases: Sir William Ramsay and Lord Rayleigh discovered argon (1894), helium (1895), followed by neon, xenon, and crypton in 1898. Crookes was also involved in this research, and confirmed the finds.[8]

Furthermore, these inert gases were termed 'noble', and placed at the top of the Periodic Table of the Elements, above the volatile or combustible gases. In this way, they were aligned with the ascribed eternity and fixity of divinity, as against base matter, with its propensity for transformation or decay.

The atmosphere also seethed with noxious airborne particles: germs added to the sudden crowd jostling in the air waves, and it is perhaps startling to realize that the theory of infection was not established until Pasteur convinced his audience. Both Varley and Crookes were battling for acceptance of this analysis against conventional medical opinion; both were also hard at work on spiritual aspects of imponderables as well.

The discovery of X-rays, facilitated by Crookes' experiments with vacuums and established by Roentgen in 1895, seemed to give precious confirmation of the psychic believers' speculation that 'images invisible to the human eye can affect the sensitized plate' and that a ghost would radiate such imperceptible light.[9] The capacity to see through solid matter did not have the effect of disenchanting empiricism and turning such vision mundane, but the exact opposite: doctors now seemed endowed with supernatural powers. Around the same time, in Cambridge, new photographic techniques revealed hitherto invisible properties of air: the 'cloud chamber', built initially by the physicist C. T. R. Wilson in 1895 to establish the structure and components of clouds from water droplets, in fact enabled him to photograph the tracks of particles—images of pinpricks of light arcing through space that are indeed 'beautiful', as Ernest Rutherford said when endorsing the photographs' accuracy.[10]

During this period, poets and writers became entranced by the metaphorical riches of the new, complex air around us. Ruskin invoked Athena as a blast of fresh air;[11] Gerard Manley Hopkins wrote a prayer-poem, 'The Blessed Virgin Compared to the Air We Breathe', in which he blended the new ferment about the atmosphere with ancient physics, spinning a litany of praises to Mary as the life principle embodied in 'Wild air, world-mothering air'. He identifies Mary with blue, with 'this blue heaven' that softens and gentles the sun's 'blear and blinding ball'. Towards the end of this invocation of Mary's maternal mercy, he petitions, 'Be thou then, O thou dear | Mother, my atmosphere.'[12] Mary's blue heaven intervenes between the sun's ferocity and offers a life-giving supply of air, in the same way as she intercedes for sinners with the severe Judge of the Last Day. Implicitly, Hopkins' Marian meteorology observes the distinction between the fiery ether and the milder climes below it.

The distinction is borne out by Hopkins' wilder paean to the power of ether, 'That Nature is a Heraclitean Fire and of the Comfort of the Resurrection', written five years later, in 1888. Here, as in Athanasius Kircher's cosmological fantasies, the spectacle of the cloud layer delimits the space of a fiery, gaseous heaven which crackles and flares. The opening lines of the poem offers the most eloquent metaphor for the dynamics of nature's vital force:

> CLOUD-PUFFBALL, torn tufts, tossed pillows | flaunt forth, then
>   chevy on an air–
> built thoroughfare: heaven-roysterers, in gay-gangs | they throng;
>   they glitter in marches.

The fantastic word picture of the glittering cloudwrack swept by gusts continues to its effects on the earth, parching it and marking it, until a short finite sentence of the poem interrupts the fugue:

> Million-fuelèd, | nature's bonfire burns on.'

Hopkins then laments how the ethereal spark in human beings has died—drowned, blacked out, blotted out, and so forth. He then turns to God, and to salvation, and this reprieve is conveyed through an explicit contrast in metaphors of combustion: the 'world's wildfire' consumes its objects and 'leave[s] but ash', but the great conflagration at the end of the world will precipitate the poet into a new form, in an alchemical process of transubstantiation:

> In a flash, at a trumpet crash,
> I am all at once what Christ is, | since he was what I am, and
> This Jack, joke, poor potsherd, | patch, matchwood, immortal
>   diamond,
> Is immortal diamond.[13]

Almost 100 years afterwards, the oxymoronic energy packed by metaphors of dust and ashes inspired Jacques Derrida to metaphysical meditation. In his essay *Cinders* he presses the imagery to communicate concepts of soul, as he develops the distinction between ashes and smoke. Symbiotic doubles of religious sacrifice, they both symbolize transitoriness and mortality. But they are also packed with differences: 'I have the impression now that the best paradigm of the trace is not, as certain people have believed . . . the hunter's tracks, the furrow, the line in the sand, the wake in the sea, the love of the footstep for the footprint, but ash (that which remains without remaining from the holocaust, from the burned offering, the incense of the incendiary).'[14] Derrida's focus rests on the ash that stays behind—the terrestrial and material residue, and he sends his readers to a sonnet by Mallarmé, in which the poet plays on the ancient twinning of breath and soul through the metaphor of smoking a cigar:

> Toute l'âme résumée
> Quand lente nous l'expirons
> Dans plusieurs ronds de fumée . . .

('All the soul summed up | when slowly we breathe it out | in several rings of smoke . . .'.)

The soul leaves the body, he continues, holding to his semi-absurd conceit, as the ash falls from the glowing end:

> la cendre se sépare
> De son clair baiser de feu. . . .
>
> (the ash parts | from its bright kiss of fire . . .).[15]

These doubles—soul/body, smoke/ash—are not in tension, but part of a process which hyphenates body and soul through the metamorphosis of substances, as in smoking, or, one could add, in sacrifice. As flesh rises, winged and volatilized, from the altar, so 'base reality' ('le réel . . . vil') can be transubstantiated in poetry.[16]

Mallarmé's smoke, as it etherealizes its source, is necessarily heated, even fiery, chemically and physically distinct from breath, from the clement and merciful 'azurèd' air that Hopkins conjured as Mary's element. The difference was even more clearly marked in pre-modern physics than is understood today, but in these metaphorical modern appearances, ether still powerfully informs concepts of spirit, Newtonian fieriness taking on added intensity from the sparks and combustibility of the new, electric, and gas-fuelled cosmos.

At the end of the nineteenth century, when Mallarmé offered us a combustible soul in the image of a smoke ring, and Hopkins an alchemical precipitate of dust, they were writing against a background of unprecedented ferment about exploring the invisible, and they reached, as it were naturally at that time, for metaphors taken from combustion, condensation, and other ceaseless and invisible organic processes of change. Hopkins' paeans are also elegies, to the cosmology, physics, and meteorology of another age, for he was writing when the very structure of the atmosphere was undergoing metamorphosis.

Alongside the unseen properties of air, previously undetected acoustic phenomena also stirred huge excitement and led to inventions that have become the familiar furniture of our world today.[17] The revelation that there was so much more to empty air, that harmonic maps hummed beyond the reach of human senses, and that the universe was vibrating with imperceptible forces, stimulated wonderful ideas about other worlds, and reconfigured consciousness of the self, giving reflexivity new vehicles of memorable expression. As we saw in Chapter 18, the first mechanical communications technologies, such as Morse code and telegraphic signalling, disembodied persons in the world of the senses when they made it possible to broadcast human voices over the air waves and record them for playing back on a gramophone. They could move an individual through time and space—through the electromagnetic field—and the possibility has fundamentally shaped modes of storytelling, not only in literature and film stories, but in the way we tell our lives to ourselves.

In the absence of natural sensory means to verify the principle at work, a dependence on second-order technological proof of hidden energy arose, as in the photograph or the X-ray plate. So material impressions of the new media's work were in high demand. Many of the new media left the trace of their passage: indeed, their activity became legible only through such traces. Radio waves could not be grasped by the human senses, only the effects of the new methods of transmission, as the mark of a needle quivering on a drum as the taps came through, as the translated and disincarnate voices from the radio set and the phonograph. The new technologies offered a model for understanding that was extended to phenomena as yet beyond the reach of scientific empiricism. But the curious were not satisfied to leave it at that. By analogy, similar evidence was eagerly sought for other hypo-thetical forces, especially ethereal ones. Proof was needed, and the media—both the mechanisms and the individuals—had to be put to the test.

In Paris in the 1890s, the 'od', or vital force, postulated by Reichenbach inspired Doctor Hippolyte Baraduc (1850–1909) to tap psychic energies and record them in a series of *épreuves* (the French word carries a double sense of trial and proof). One of his many books, published in Paris in 1896, appeared in 1913 in an English version, *The Human Soul, Its Movements, Its Lights, and the Iconography of the Fluidic Invisible.*[18] It included an album of seventy remarkable photographs made without camera or lens. Instead, Baraduc laid the plate to the forehead or hand or other part of his 'sensitives' to draw out, by electrical magnetism, the 'nuée fluidique' ('the fluidic mist'). Many of these captured, he wrote, the somod or odic mist and particles (*pois*), sometimes extracted from the brow of a young man, at other times projected from a hand. Using infra-red light, the doctor then made exposures of a young boy in mourning for a dead pheasant, and showed the odic light of his sorrow lifting the curtain behind him; he also grasped 'L'Âme-Germe et son Corps fluidique' ('The Seed-Soul and [its] Fluidic Body') of dead friends. He meticulously categorized the images under different rubrics, calling some 'Psychicônes' ('Physicons'). He was certain he had captured, for the material world, the somods, or odic bodies of his subjects, living or dead.

Baraduc rhapsodizes on the object of his detection: 'There therefore exists in us a real physical and supramaterial soul, the fluidic double of the human body, whose intimate motion can be registered . . . this motion can inscribe (*graphier*) light at a distance on to a sensitive plate.' This material effect was the result of 'une force speciale, mode intelligentié de l'éther' ('a special force, the intelligent mode of the ether'), and it brought about the emanations that were recorded in his photographs: 'La force vitale est de l'intelligence en mouvement concrétant de la matière.'[19] ('The vital force is intelligence in movement rendering matter concrete.') Baraduc modified Reichenbach's analysis, and postulated an obverse of the od, which he termed the exhalation of soul force, by contrast to the od, its inhalation.

By the time his third book appeared in 1904, Baraduc was openly interested in hermetic mysticism and its therapeutic powers. *Les Vibrations de la vitalité humaine: Méthode biometrique appliqué aux sensitifs et aux névrosés* concentrated on picturing invisible vibrations in the universe and contains some marvellous horoscope-like diagrams and graphs, minutely schematizing the 'geometric form of the fluidic body' and predicting 'les temps nouveaux dits CHRISTIQUES' ('the new so-called Christic') time to come.[20] The images are tiny, sometimes only half an inch square, and several show only tiny streams of bubbles, like spray, or a pale wispy blur, or a starburst or cloud of light. *The Vibrations of Human Vitality* includes an image of a meteor shower depicting the odic impression of anger, as well as a lyrical mare's tail portraying 'the clockwise etheric vortex'.

'This photographic plate', writes Baraduc, 'was thus impressed in the dark without light or electricity by the placing of my right hand, without contact with the plate, motionless, after sorrow, during the night at 10 o'clock in the evening, in February 1895, a time of marked personality, the hour of etheric liberation.'[21] It is interesting to compare these images with the astronomer Camille Flammarion's prints of astronomical nebulae, in his work *Astronomie populaire*, published in 1900, and others.[22] Flammarion was an ardent subscriber to the activities of the SPR. At a macro scale, and a micro scale, the imagery of veils and mists exercises its tenacious influence.

Baraduc was by no means alone in experimenting with thought projection—Kircher's radiant imagination—direct on to the plate without benefit of lens or light. A compatriot and contemporary, Louis Darget (1847–1923), an army officer, took a more literal approach over a period of thirty years' attempts: he would rest his head against the back of his hand, which he applied to the wrapped photographic plate, and concentrate his mind. He tried mere staring, and other methods, and though he found the process 'capricious', he produced a handful of successful prints of mental objects.[23] His 'fluidic photographs' are inscribed 'The First Bottle' (Figure 21a, p. 263), 'The Walking Stick', and 'The Eagle', but in several cases, they are simply 'potential images', like Cozens's blots or Rorschach's diabolical faces.

Giving precise circumstantial details, both Baraduc and Darget show how deeply they considered their efforts scientific; today, however, their images of soul and thought are strange and captivating as acts of imagination and art. In their minimal non-figurative and gestural style, they have become unwitting examples of very early expressive abstraction.

In several ways, Baraduc's and Darget's images resemble the 'ideoplasts' of

Eusapia Paladino, except that she produced hers in group seances with the avowed intention of contacting spirits from the other world, not materializing her own moods. An enthusiastic observer explained the wonder,

Can we not imagine . . . that some objects may emit the usual light waves, long enough and slow enough to leave a picture, but that other objects may send waves which are short and step, and there made so swift an impression that it is not recorded? . . . the clairvoyant seems to be not a person with a better developed physical retina, but rather one who has the power to use that which corresponds with the retina in their own etheric bodies which are in harmony with etheric waves from outside.[24]

Experiments in 'thoughtographs' of this kind continued well into the twentieth century, and have not stopped: in the Sixties, a Chicago hotel worker called Ted Serios would concentrate on an image and then communicate it to Polaroid film, producing blurred, crooked, damaged prints. The process as observed by investigators cost him prolonged physical struggle, as in the trance states of the spiritualist mediums.[25]

The Parisian Doctor Baraduc's theories were deeply tinged with Hindu mysticism, reaching him through the Theosophists, and the general syncretic occultism of *fin-de-siècle* urban circles, in Paris, London, Dublin, and Berlin. In *L'Âme humaine*, Baraduc quotes from Zoroaster and Jacob Boehme, and he seems to have been in touch with Parisian occultists, like Eliphas-Lévi. 'The fluidic invisible . . . physical yet supra-material' concept of soul proposed by Baraduc owes much to ideas of the astral body, as developed in contact with Indian hermeticism by Annie Besant, founder of the movement, and its chief theorist, C. W. Leadbeater.

Leadbeater and Besant attempt to establish a system of natural values for colours, strokes, and shapes, through a series of influential booklets, still in print.[26] Theosophy proclaimed that every individual possesses a shifting, labile aura, which is the immaterial double of the body, a kind of mandorla of shining mist, such as sheathes the bodies of angels and deities, as we saw. By a form of psychological synaesthesia, Leadbeater keyed particular coloured auras to the passions—browny-red for avarice, red for lust, black for hatred. In figurative watercolour drawings of the body, he illustrated psychological and emotional states as floating shapes enveloping the subject; these auras were precisely matched to 'Vague pure affection', for example, as opposed to 'Vague selfish affection'; Shock of fear', in contrast to 'Shock of anger'. These graphic equivalences (flying barbs for jealous pangs, crescents exploding for fright) ring visual changes on clouds and light, concord and discord, tranquillity and syncopation. A most surprising tradition runs from Theosophy to the Bauhaus and the latter's system of abstract and universal elements of colour, form, stroke, line, and figure; for one of Leadbeater's auratic visions, 'Intense Anger', reveals close affinities with Kandinsky's experiments of the same period, when the artist was deliberately fashioning a new lexicon of line and form in his attempt to communicate inwardness beyond figuration (Plate 6).[27]

Around the same time, the composer Arnold Schoenberg was also struggling, through his music and his painting, to move beyond history-laden motifs and figures towards a new abstract expressiveness. This also led him into painting portraits of states of mind. In a sequence begun in 1908, Schoenberg moves away from depicting external physiognomy; when he stops reproducing his features and tries to communicate inner feelings, the paintings begin to swirl, and the subject depicted loses contour and inflates with turbulent scumbled fields of colour. In a painting called *Thinking*, the head occupies only a blurred area below a gleaming haze. In other studies, lambent spots appear through the cloudiness—burning red hollows of the eyes in *Red Gaze* of 1910 (Plate 5), while the paradoxically titled *Blue Gaze* pictures empty golden eyes and parted lips in profile, exhaling a fan-shaped breath of yellow and gold tints against a glowing fiery red. Amorphous, dematerialized, smeared, and diffuse, these personal icons fulfil Schoenberg's theory of synthetic portraiture: 'I never saw faces,' he explained afterwards, 'but, because I looked into people's eyes, only their "gazes". This is the reason why I can imitate the gaze of a person. A painter, however, grasps with one look the whole person—I, only his soul.'[28]

When Alfred Stieglitz made his famous, rapt sequence of cloud photographs (*c.*1924–5), he eliminated all external markers, such as the horizon, that would give a sense of scale, and treated them as abstract images of flux; significantly, he gave the images the title 'Equivalents', thus inviting the viewer to see them as pictures of feelings and inward processes. As with Schoenberg, the play and drift of vague and blurry shapes symbolize the psyche in Stieglitz's work.[29]

In the subsequent decade, experiments conducted by Semyon and Valentine Kirlian in the Soviet Union from 1939 onwards continued to search for aura. The Kirlians' photographs revealed fiery and mineral bright haloes surrounding people and objects; these nimbuses are ribbed, like luminous iron filings clustering on a magnet, and add the glow of the unearthly to the image. This electrographic method revealed something that the human eye could not see; it was interpreted as psychic aura, and several healers developed diagnostic theories connected to these emissions.[30]

As in the case of Reichenbach's odic effects and Baraduc's thought-pictures, Kirlian photographs result from an unexplained combination of electromagnetic phenomena reacting to moisture and other conditions. The images manage to communicate the vibrancy of vital energy inhering in things; aesthetically, they do not depict external appearance but delineate the subject within a radiating silhouette, which gives an illusion of flickering heat. Aesthetically, the images manage to overcome photography's double limitation, of coldness and stillness. Their look influenced Andy Warhol's icons of stars and powers, his Jackies and Marilyns, for in the period when fascination with Kirlian photography was filling the newspapers, he began building on accidents caused by printing out of register and emblazoning his subjects' outlines with Kirlian-style aureoles of different metallic hues.

All these differing attempts to create the image of soul and of soul states produced by ethereal forces—rays real or imagined—failed to capture one paramount aspect of their referents: their motion. Some kind of light energy made the pictures, but the essential animate vitality of that energy eluded them; animation, the defining principle of a living being, still resisted reproduction. By contrast, acoustic recording succeeded in ethereal materializations to a degree that static media could not achieve, as did the first moving images. Radio and cinema breached the barrier of time: they could stay passages of moments, not only single instances. They were to carry representation into the fourth dimension, opening up another horizon for psychic speculations.

Like Victorians assembled for a séance, the time
traveller's audience receives proof of his journey:
a flower from the future. From the 1960 film of
H.G. Wells' classic tale, *The Time Machine* [1899].

20
Time Travel and Other Selves

'Silently the Professor drew from his pocket a square gold watch, with six or eight hands, and held it out . . . "This," he began, "is an Outlandish Watch— . . . which has the peculiar property that, instead of its going with the time, the time goes with it."[1] Lewis Carroll, who appears to inhabit his creation, in *Sylvie and Bruno*, of a lovable dotty inventor, expands with evident pleasure on his magical device which can make time move with it— for a month. Within this period, it can reverse events and play them back differently: in this way, the hero prevents a fatal accident by rewinding the sequence that led to it and intervening to prevent the collision. Whereas in Looking-Glass country, motion is all mixed up spatially at times, with the Red Queen dragging Alice at top speed and ending up in the same place, here time runs backwards, and the effect Carroll describes captures exactly the earliest 'trick' films when they had fun reversing the footage, or the rewind function today on a video tape—though Carroll was writing about five years before the first movies were shown.

Science fiction, magical realist novels, and many movies have entertained the same dream of time-travelling: in such plots time becomes 'granulated'.[2] It breaks off into beads or grains moving at different rhythms which jostle up against other beads from other times. The independence and divisibility of time in this pre-Einsteinian world affects scale, as voyagers in fairyland had reported long before Carroll. Once through to the other side, Bruno, an ordinary-sized boy, changes scale, like Gulliver or Alice, and becomes so small that at one point in the book he uses a dead mouse for a sofa—a not entirely well-judged image perhaps for child readers.

The horizons widened; the new means for grasping and reproducing time's flow, bringing it from the past into the present through photography, have had, and still have, immeasurable consequences for human experience; the layering of memories through material records that followed has had immeasurable repercussions on consciousness itself, as well as on our ideas about the individual. The new simultaneity led to experiments in time, and these became intertwined with ideas about plural consciousness; the two axes met over the question of thought transmission. Telepathy was 'thought at a distance'. That distance could be geographical, and carry objects across space and between worlds, but before Einstein's theory of relativity, it was also often conceived in temporal terms, and inspired excited dreams of communications from one time to another between spirits and other, occult forces. To capture a hitherto imperceptible ethereal dimension to existence—supernatural or otherwise—filled the life's work of scientists, philosophers, and writers.

Freud's model of consciousness and Jung's theory of the collective unconscious are now well-established theories, even when not believed. But when those men were forming their ideas, they were part of a general wave of speculation, and several others who contributed to rethinking consciousness have not enjoyed the same stature, though their ideas were influential at the time and have continued to be so, though largely unacknowledged. Another theorist of memory and the unconscious—Samuel Butler (1835–1902), writer, photographer, and thinker—challenged the traditional view of the integrated and consistent compact of unique body and unique soul. He foreshadows the complexity of Proustian psychology when he argues, almost intemperately:

We regard our personality as a simple definite whole; as a plain, palpable, individual thing, which can be seen going about the streets or sitting indoors at home, which lasts us our lifetime, and about the confines of which no doubt can exist in the minds of reasonable people. But in truth this "we," which looks so simple and definite, is a nebulous and indefinable aggregation of many component parts which war not a little among themselves . . . There is nothing but "fusion and confusion" in that "hazy contradiction in terms of 'personal' identity".[3]

The year after, in 1878, Butler published *Unconscious Memory*, a further exploration of the issue, focusing on involuntary thought processes and multiple personae, and written with Butler's characteristic eclectic curiosity.

Butler did not join the SPR, perhaps because he belonged to the preceding generation, but it was around the same time that his younger contemporary, the enthusiastic SPR activist Frederic Myers, began formulating his theory of the 'subliminal self'; it has taken hold, appropriately through other channels besides himself, to permeate popular ideas of the personality. Myers's ideas caught trends in many different disciplines, religious and otherwise, and they have more in common with Freud's theory of the unconscious than Freud felt comfortable to admit.[4] But it was not only a dread of association with occult thought that led Freud to make light of any such influence, since on one side of this conflict, Jung has won wide acceptance. However, Myers insistently invoked spirit powers and projected his model on to a psychic and occult plane. The subliminal self transcended the limits of a life in one time and place: 'Each of us', he wrote, 'is in reality an abiding psychical entity far more extensive than he knows,—

an individuality which can never express itself completely through any corporeal manifestation. The self manifests itself through the organism, but there is always some part of the self unmanifested, and always, as it seems some power of organic expression in abeyance or reserve.'[5]

Myers also adopted the term 'stream of consciousness', thus conceiving of consciousness in spatial terms. In her perceptive study of these developments, Pamela Thurschwell defines the difference between Freud's biographical archaeology and Myers' feeling for expansiveness in spacetime: 'Myers' hope is for a human body and mind that would intimate immortality; Freud is looking for different things (the Oedipus complex, infantile sexuality, etc.), but both participate in versions of a late nineteenth-century hermeneutic project in which the subject is understood both as a text to be read and a space through which information flows.'[6] The psyche Myers postulated behaved like the properties of the ether, like a light wave and a gas, carrying traces of the past into the present with effect on the future, while invisible elements were at work in its processes, shaping its contours unbeknownst to the conscious mind. Telepathic communication was action at a distance, but that distance stretched into other, simultaneous worlds, inhabited by phantasms and spirits 'after bodily death'.

Seances thus both express and propel a very profound change in thinking about the human subject, and they frequently cast exotic foreigners as the spirits summoned by the mediums to channel reports from the other side (as we shall see more closely in the next chapter). During a seance, experiences were shared telepathically between sitters, identities mingled and merged, and individuals were taken over, possessed by other persons' presence, speaking in their voices and expressing their wishes. The theories about psychology and spirituality in which the idea developed lean on both pagan and Indian mysticism: Myers, as a classical scholar, wrote a long essay on prophetic dreaming and oracles in ancient Greece, and as a psychologist in his most ambitious work explored theories of wandering souls, trance, and possession.[7] Myers dismissed anecdotes about uncanny portents and sorcery, magic and miracles, and instead firmly placed beliefs in thought transmission within the mind and its powers. He invoked Socrates in his support, for Socrates conceived of 'a personal and spiritual relation between man and the unseen world, an oracle not without us, but within'. He upheld in the face of death, Myers argues, 'that the spirit who speaks within him is an agency which he cannot disavow'.[8]

The seance reproduces some of the characteristic features of oracles in antiquity: the sitters forming the ring are vital to the event, and to the success of the event; they gather as a solemn, ritual congregation, bonded together to follow prescribed steps in making contact with spiritual powers. But other similarities are more confusing. The medium's role is multi-layered—it might appear that Paladino or Carrière take the place of the sibyl, priestess, or priest, since they act as conductors of spirit. However, this role is complicated by the lack of identity between them and the spirit control and others, who could arrive in a number of guises—as a relation of one of the sitters, or, a famous figure of history. Myers' conception of subject or self, to which the work of the SPR contributed, imagines someone apt for occupation by another. Subjectivity becomes diffused, decentred, dislocated, and the long pact between soul and body is cracked—with immense consequences for psychology, for writing, and for visual modes of storytelling.

The concept of an entranced subject in these occult forays touches closely the latest medical—psychological—theories of the time, about multiple *alters* and psychopathic doubles. Authors drew strongly on these ideas: Charles Richet wrote a short story about split personality in 1889, three years after Stevenson also explored the idea in *The Strange Case of Dr Jekyll and Mr Hyde*; Richet published under the pseudonym Charles F. Epheyre.[9] Looking at the history of scientific approaches to telepathy, Ian Hacking has suggested that '[Richet] deserves a far larger place in histories of the origin of psychoanalysis than is commonly granted'.[10]

During its first decade, the SPR conducted six massive surveys—into telepathy, odic light, mesmerism, hauntings, materializing mediums, and general psychic episodes. The committee appointed to inquire into telepathy reported in favour over the course of years' research, attaching 1200 pages of evidence.[11] One of the Society's founders, William Barrett, had assisted John Tyndall, champion of the natural philosophical approach, at his celebrated displays at the Royal Society in 1863–7, when he demonstrated how tuning forks will vibrate in harmony at a distance, and flames dance into different shapes to different sounds from another room.[12] 'Similarly . . . for every thought there is a corresponding motion of the particles of the brain,' declared the SPR's first 'Report into Telepathy', 'and so pass under certain circumstances from one brain to another.'[13] These material analogies did not, however, demonstrate the cause of such transmission, and this exasperated the Spiritualists, who wanted to postulate a supernatural or spirit presence at work. From 1886 onwards, for this reason among others, the SPR and Victorian Spiritualism were never in harmony. In his presidential address of 1889, Sidgwick argued, 'before we introduce, in explanation of any phenomena, a cause unknown to science, we hold ourselves bound to try all that can be done in the way of explaining the phenomena by known causes'.[14] It was the spirit of scientific curiosity that spurred them on, they thought. But they were looking in the wrong place—as Freudian concepts of the unconscious, desire, and the psyche could have led them to see.

This new mobility in different time zones seemed to offer the chance of mind travel too, and for a long time, over the course of numerous experiments (continuing in some quarters to this day) telepathy seemed as possible scientifically as telegraphy or the telephone, or television, to be explored and tested and applied in ways analogous to X-rays or other light effects. Psychic research documents discuss beaming spirit messages from one world to another in terms of 'occult television'. In 1895, a Spiritualist called Carl du Prel wrote 'The Discovery of the Soul by Means of the Secret Sciences', in which he declared:

Natural science is already on the verge of providing a proof of the possibility of such an action at a distance, a proof based on the transmission of electricity through space without connecting wires. It is obvious that this works by means of the wave movements in the ether. For the fact that this wave motion gets through to its target in the case of human action at a distance, there is at the moment no other explanation than that the human agent is also capable of television.[15]

It is perhaps surprising that the most familiar and widespread domestic televisual device comes into action in the context of Spiritualist experiments, but Du Prel imagined this form of wireless broadcasting with electrical signals even before Marconi invented the telegraph, and for him, it promised the possibility that a *human agent* would also be able to beam images across time and space.[16] As the idea of the mind's eye becomes act with the magic lantern and the camera (Chapters 9–10), so the dream of telepathic 'action at a distance' infused the first transmissions of television; imagined psychic organs became physical.

The Crookes tube, described in his 1879 lecture on 'Radiant Matter', became crucial to the enterprise of 'image-writing' from 1906 onwards.[17] Many of the scientists working in the field conceived of their technological research as 'organ projection': the television was to take its place in society as the culminating mass medium of mind-voyaging in the modern era. This is not as far-fetched or crazy as it sounds, for television, once it began to broadcast world-wide, offers a magic glass in which the world in motion can be glimpsed at any one time however far away the scenes it conveys might be. However, in its present uses, television does not obey the command of the viewers, but conveys images summoned by others, who summon scenes in the manner of wizards—as in Prospero's banquet, Mephistopheles' masques, and the images that Beauty sees in her magic mirror in the fairy-tale. The association reveals the instrument's affinity with the enchantments of deception and with the promises of visual seduction. As Du Prel presciently foresaw, 'hypnotic suggestion' was never very far away. He himself relished the idea of this particular form of 'influence machine', for he lived during a time of enthusiastic practice of hypnotism. (Since television has become global, such eagerness strikes a false note. And in an age when the presidency of the greatest democratic power in the world hangs on a television debate between the candidates, the dark core of his message communicates an idea of mental influence that we have come to accept, if not overlook.)

A different experience of time began to be explored: in 1873, the versatile Flammarion wrote a curious Platonic dialogue about the possibilities of time-travel; in this early piece of science fiction, he personifies a comet called 'Lumen', and imagines travelling through the ether all the way back through that beam's history to the beginning of the world, via the Battle of Waterloo and other events.[18]

H. G. Wells' story *The Time Machine*, written in several versions from 1888 onwards, appeared in 1895. This famous fable develops another kind of time-traveller: this time an inventor on the saddle of a kind of bicycle, customized in a suburban workshop, part crystal radio set, part clockwork, part points-switching railway tracks, part camera—the first time machine of modernity. With this device, Wells created far more than a fascinating narrative vehicle for his views of human destiny, cosmic history, class warfare, the evolution of sex and leisure and labour, and much else; his story has lasted as one of the most popular ever written, one of the most imitated and influential to this day, because it reaches out beyond the related episodes and ostensible plot to give us an image of human consciousness *in potentia*. The time machine in some deep sense does perform as Wells' own imagination, vaulting into aeons of futurity. It translates a faculty of mind—projective imagination—into an actual piece of technology, and embodies it physically in time and space. It acts as a Delphic tripod (as he said himself), a crystal ball, a star-gazing lens, an I Ching trigram, but made to work in the age of the wireless, the cloud chamber, and the X-ray.

The cinema was just beginning when Wells was writing, and its first storytellers turned tricks they took from the circus and the music-hall: disappearing acts in puffs of smoke, cutting a lady in half, or making another vanish (such shows coincide quite purposefully with the women's emancipation movements then beginning to gather a strong following).[19]

In Hove, Sussex, the showman G. Albert Smith drew on this tradition, but at its most light-hearted.[20] In 1898, he began showing his pioneering films in the pleasure gardens he managed; each of them a minute long, with titles like 'The Mesmerist, or Body and Soul', 'Faust and Mephistopheles', 'Santa Claus'—and 'Photographing a Ghost'. Through a nimble use of double exposure, Smith's ghosts and spirits float, completely transparent; the same technique, also borrowed from stage effects, projected as similarly flimsy apparitions thoughts going on in their minds: the devil conjures for Faust the vision of Marguerite, while Cinderella dreams of going to the ball and dancing with the prince. Smith described his use of stop-motion: 'Suppose you want to make a man vanish. Well, just at the right moment you stop the handle [on the camera] . . . Wait till the man has walked off, and then go on. When the pictures are thrown on the screen, at the rate of sixteen a second, with no stoppage, the effect is as if the man simply ceased to exist. . . . This simple process is the key to all sort of fantastic jugglings.'[21]

Smith bought *Le Chateau hanté* ('The Haunted Castle', 1897), one of the trick films of the much better-known early film illusionist Georges Meliès in Paris, and so he knew Meliès's similar approach and themes. Meliès was an entertainer of exuberant good humour and a wonderfully droll and dry wit. He set his magic films of the 1890s in theatre sets, but relished the specific opportunities that moving pictures gave him: to fly to the moon, to resurrect Bluebeard's dead wives, and above all, to vamoose. When Wells devised *The Invisible Man*, published in 1897 and another of the writer's long-lasting popular successes, he described how his hero disappears 'between two radiating centres of a sort of ethereal vibration'.[22] But the invisible man's behaviour matches vanishing figures familiar from long-exposure photography and stop-action tricks from the new movies. Telling the story on the page turns his plight from an effect of the light into a realist narrative—Wells' brilliant way of pulling the fantastic down to earth, as when Martians land in suburban Surrey.

Movie illusion made a particular aspect of fantasy possible in unimaginable ways, far more consequentially than magic vanishing acts. Its victory over the stasis of the image meant that it could communicate time itself, and time out of time. Robert Paul was an inventor who read *The Time Machine* and visited Wells immediately to suggest telling the story in moving pictures. Paul was struck by the kind of effects that peepshows were using to amuse audiences, and was applying for a patent for an early kind of cinema which would give spectators 'the sensation of voyaging upon a machine through time' by simultaneously projecting pictures with several 'powerful lanterns'. They were to be viewed from different platforms, and the projectors mounted on trolleys and other devices to create dissolves and glides and fades and flashbacks and other, amazingly prescient ideas for effects of movement: 'It sought to liberate the spectator from the instant of Now.'[23] Paul did not manage to make his film of *The Time Machine*, but he had glimpsed the remarkable affinity of the story with the new entertainment.

When communications technologies altered the language of haunting and possession, they also unsettled notions of integrated personality in ways that have entered the mainstream of entertainment culture as well as psychology. Cinematic and acoustic media have keenly adopted SPR approaches to telling the self: telepathy, trance, amnesia, and possession pervade Hitchcock's thrillers, and have continued strongly in the ubiquitous movie plots centred today on replicants, Stepford Wives, and so forth.

Running through the myriad different approaches to spirits or psychic forces is a simple desire for connection, across time and space, within laws of mortality, separation, and even decorum. The medium at the seance in some senses vanishes like the vanishing lady in the conjuring trick, because what matters are the voices and presences coming through her, and they are not enfleshed. This disembodiment is the patent condition of spirit, and in some unspoken way, the deepest and most ambiguous desideratum of the long experiment with psychic research.

Whereas Henry James listened in to the whispers and intimations of his characters, watched for subliminal signals, and set them quivering in mutual attunement, some personalities found the newly populated airwaves and their communicating vessels very frightening. In Vienna in 1918, Victor Tausk gave a lecture to the Psychoanalytical Society, in which he invoked 'The Influence Machine', a device invented in 1706 by Francis Hauksbee, a student of Isaac Newton. It consisted of a globe which spun, crackling and sparking as it did so—in fact a form of the Crookes tube, as it happened. Taking the invention as a metaphor for a state of mind, Tausk discussed patients who believed that they were under the influence of some outside force, which they conceived of as a mechanical device, causing them to suffer from hallucinations, hear voices, and experience a despairing sense of losing control of their own being: 'The schizophrenic influencing machine', writes Tausk, 'is a machine of mystical nature. The patients are able to give only vague hints of its construction. It consists of boxes, cranks, levers, wheels, buttons, wires, batteries, and the like . . . It makes the patients see pictures . . . It produces, as well as removes, thoughts and feelings by means of waves or rays or mysterious forces . . . In such cases, the machine is often called a "suggestion-apparatus". The machine serves to persecute the patient and is operated by enemies.'[24]

The cases Tausk described were among the first of their kind to be analysed; the paper is a classic of psychoanalytical literature, alongside Daniel Paul Schreber's *Memoirs of My Nervous Illness* (1903), in which a High Court judge in Germany recalled his mental agony, breakdowns, and hospitalization over a period of some twenty years at the turn of the century. Schreber's long, minutely detailed, perfect simulacrum of a calmly rational memory act was cited enthusiastically by Freud, Jung, and, more recently, Gilles Deleuze, as the most remarkable personal testimony of derangement. Judge Schreber invokes waves and vibrations—the new mani-festations of the physical universe—to describe his mental states: 'Apart from normal human language', he wrote, 'there is also a kind of nerve-language . . . that is to say a human being causes his nerves to vibrate . . . in my case, however . . . my nerves have been set in motion from without incessantly and without any respite.'[25]

The stories of patients whose art was collected by another Zurich psychiatrist, Hans Prinzhorn, also calls on new technologies—photography, X-rays, radio, telegraphy—to account for experiences of double or triple personality, of voices, locutions, and messages overheard that direct the sufferer, of possession and trance.[26] In established religious practice, outside the boundaries of mental disturbance, similar metaphors are invoked when connecting to the divine: in Baptist ceremonies of glossolalia, otherwise known as speaking in tongues, for instance, God's messages come down the 'heavenly telephone'.

The messages came through sometimes obliquely: Henry James did not throw himself into psychic activities like his brother, the philosopher William James. But Henry's fiction is haunted, the high tension in *The Turn of the Screw* (1900) deliberately charged with ghostly speculation, and his characters interact with one another with nerves finely attuned to nuance and vibration, as in electrical transmitting and receiving.[27] Rudyard Kipling, perhaps surprisingly, began to think alongside experimental Modernists through the media of transmission and cinema in order to represent the processes of consciousness. One of his most virtuoso stories, 'Wireless' (first published in 1904) eerily dramatizes the channelling of Keats' poetry through a consumptive chemist with no conscious knowledge of the words coming through. In the same collection, Kipling created a tight, ambiguous, sailor's yarn, 'Mrs Bathurst', which features a distinctive modern ghost in the machine: the figure of a lost lover, Mrs Bathurst, returns from the past and from a distant country, apparently seeking the man who chanced upon this sighting of her in a newsreel, and feels compelled to return again and again to the scene of his haunting.[28]

The wireless had brought the acoustic presence of a person, living but impalpable, into everyday experience: His Master's Voice in the living room, as the famous 1933 image from the advertisement showed. The illusion was exciting, but it was also bewildering. Cinema could move someone back in time and space over and over again. One of the most haunting moments of the media age occurs in Robert Flaherty's documentary *Nanook of the North* (1922), when the Inuit Nanook, hearing his voice on a recording Flaherty has made and is playing back to him on a portable turntable, picks up the disc and puts it in his mouth—to see if it is made of matter at all. Nanook and Victor from His Master's Voice reveal the novelty and the weirdness of this disjunction. Techniques such as stream of consciousness in fiction and voice-over in film represented the perceived acoustic vitality of the ether. As in a photograph, somebody could be there and not there at the same time.

In 1901, when Frederic Myers himself joined the ghosts whom the

members yearned to contact, he became the principal spirit whom
mediums channelled. Characteristically, he left a carefully constructed
experiment behind, so that any sightings (or messages) received from someone in spirit form claiming to be Myers could be authenticated. He would
return, he promised, with the second half of the secret message taken from
literature, as a password from beyond the grave.[29] He did not disclose
what the message was, of course, but concealed the first half in a hiding place
which would be revealed by his ghost only to the mediums. This experiment in 'cross-correspondences' also involved double blinds: different
mediums worked in different places without contact with one another,
and then another matched the messages they received. This is telegraphy
mapped on to the spirit world across terrestrial and extraterrestrial frontiers.
Like the severed head of Orpheus, which goes on singing his elegy on the
death of Eurydice, the media of communication which were invented during the Victorian era—the telegraph, the telephone, and the radio—give a
major role to the voice as the prime indication of individual consciousness.
And just as the radio could broadcast voices over great distances, so spirits
began to leap barriers of time and space.

When the first newsreels began with the Kinetoscope, audiences experienced something that has now become so familiar as to be banal, but was
then prodigious: time past unfolding in time present, events that had
taken place beamed forward into the audience's space-time. It seemed that
Flammarion's fantasy was fulfilled: light carried the past and transported it
into the future. Images, beamed by the power of light, through the air waves,
are travelling on into space: it is one of the most eerie possibilities of our
time that a beam like 'Lumen', carrying a scene from a John Ford western or
a session with Oprah or a newscast from a city under siege or footage from a
terrorist attack, might voyage into cosmic emptiness until it encounters an
obstacle—which then becomes a screen where the images will appear and
look all those light-years into space as if the horses are still alive and riding
by, as if the talk show participants are still weeping or laughing, and the
explosions and flames and horror are taking place in the future now of our
then. Or Lara Croft, an eidolon or figment from a virtual reality computer
game, might be flickering for eternity at this moment on a distant star.

In the 1890s in Zurich, the medium Hélène Smith
described her multiple earlier existences and
illustrated them, including her life on Mars, its
inhabitants, flaming scenery, and domestic fauna.

21
Exotic Visitors, Multiple Lives

The seances that William Crookes conducted with Florence Cook created a pattern that returns throughout the history of spirit experiments, and it too involves power of one mind over another: messages transmitted through a younger woman to a distinguished professional, older man in a scientific setting persuade him of the truth of her manifestations. They tend to translate distance in time into distance in place, and bring home ghosts returning from a world conquered by military power and is no longer safely distant, but close and accessible through the new technologies. The star of the *fin-de-siècle* seance circuit, Eusapia Paladino, also conjured the spirit of John King, the former Jamaican buccaneer, whose daughter Katie had haunted Florence Cook. Mlle E. d'Espérance was visited, in 1897, by 'Elias Ben Ammand of Nazareth, who spent his life amongst the lepers in Palestine'.[1] The thought photographer Madge Donohoe channelled the pharaoh Amon who manifested himself in the shape of Golden Cloud, a Native American chief.[2] W. B. Yeats was inspired by the spirit of Leo Africanus, a Spanish-Arab scholar, traveller, and poet who became celebrated in sixteenth-century Italy.

The stories that the mediums told about their *alter egos*, their past lives, and their visiting spirit controls reveal a densely woven carpet where in figures of imperialist fantasy and guilt are plied with technological dreams and terrors, scientific discovery and speculations. Ideas of self, of body–soul integrity and personal stability, were remodelled in the violent and protracted encounter with the religious beliefs and rituals of cultures beyond the Empire-makers' original countries and generally Christian allegiance. Spiritualism was one of the developments profoundly influenced by ideas of soul survival and reincarnation, encountered principally in India, but several other strands are present in the magical thought of incipient modern times in the nineteenth and twentieth centuries, including divination, prophecy, trance, and metamorphic rituals practised in North and West Africa.

Eva C., for example, began her career as a medium in Algeria, in the French colonial community. After her fiancé, the son of a French general, died in the Congo, she began performing materializations for his mother, but was exposed as a fraud after a servant confessed that he played the spirit of Bien Boa, a heavily moustachioed and voluminously swathed spectre (the surviving images do not inspire confidence) who was summoned to the seance.[3] The young woman left Algiers and next surfaced in Munich, took the name of Eva C., and began exuding ectoplasms of a complexity and variety never before seen. These included the scrims imprinted with images, as discussed in Chapter 17. Eva C. was probably *au courant*, at least through her patrons, of the fabulous revelations of a trance medium, Hélène Smith, whose memories of her past lives, *Des Indes à la planète Mars: Étude sur un cas de Somnambulisme (From India to the Planet Mars)* had become one of the strongest sellers at the turn of the century, as related by Théodore Flournoy, a Swiss physician.[4]

'Hélène Smith' was the pseudonym of Catherine-Elise Muller, who began communicating in 1895 in a state of trance. Not strictly speaking his patient, but the subject of his eager unofficial researches, Flournoy experimented with her, and his assiduous curiosity, as well as his scientific and social status as a doctor, brought about rich results, though this aspect of their interaction (in Freudian terms, transference and counter-transference) was no more examined or even noticed then than it was in the relationship between Crookes and Florence Cook, or Sidgwick and Myers and the working-class female mediums they attended.

In the course of thirty sessions, the 30-year-old shop assistant from Geneva vividly described her experiences of other worlds through her familiar spirit, Léopold. Through Léopold, she had lived multiple previous existences, as 'Simandini', the daughter of an Arab sheik who was married to an Indian prince in the fifteenth century and threw herself on his pyre. Hélène Smith spoke in tongues ('glossolalia') while in trance, and Flournoy was sufficiently amazed by her proficiency in 'Hindu' that he called in experts from Geneva University—including Ferdinand de Saussure himself. Saussure did not mock the medium's utterances, startling as that may seem today, and even committed himself to saying that her Hindi vocabulary was made 'in some inexplicable manner . . . [but] was not necessarily false'.[5]

A further incarnation transported the medium into the body of Marie Antoinette, no less, when Léopold (now living in the body of Count Cagliostro) was the queen's lover. But a yet more fabulous incarnation took her to Mars, where Léopold yielded to a spirit called Esenale: Esenale had lived on the planet recently, and was thus able to interpret the Martian tongue for the entranced medium. There was a current craze for Mars, which Wells also responded to when he wrote *The War between the Worlds* almost coincidentally with the appearance of Flournoy's book.

Hélène Smith described the fiery red, purple, and violet landscape of Mars—'aucune verdure' (no greenery), recorded Flournoy, with a kind of relief that she had not mistaken her topic. She expanded on the activities of a Martian lord called Astané, who had a yellow complexion to match his native planet, and travelled by means of a flying machine, a hand-held flame-thrower something like a combination between a loud hailer and a child's toy girouette or windmill; he merely held it in his right hand as he flew. Hélène Smith spoke to Flournoy in fluent Martian; she wrote in Martian script, a fascinating ideographic notation resembling chemical, electrical, and zodiac ciphers; she painted scenes of life on the planet for him. In one, a little girl from Mars has a sci-fi mutant turnip head, but wears a little red skirt with braces like school uniform, and pats a shaggy animal with horns on upside down (Figure 23, p. 276).

The Martian cycle, or *roman* ('novel'), as Flournoy called it, reflects turn-of-the-century fascination with astrophysics and astronomy, which made it possible for Camille Flammarion, for example, to publish his 1900 study *L'Astronomie populaire* in a de luxe edition intended for a general public, with leather gold-tooled binding and magnificent steel engravings. These include many images that provided a template for spirit visions: galactic mists, solar flares, cellular structures under the microscope, resemble hypothetical psychic forms as captured by the photographs of Baraduc's odic prints, as we saw.

Flournoy's 1899 account of Hélène's prodigious feats went through edition after edition—the book was a pioneer of New Age publishing. His remarkable and very weird study does not describe an analysis or even therapy, in any sense understood today. During the seances, he took part in conversations with Smith's *alters*, disputed points with them, and tried to challenge their messages, and in short, collaborated. In his written account, by contrast, he placed the phenomenon within the medium's unconscious, and explained her fabulism as the product of her empathy with her listeners and her suggestible fantasy. His interpretation of Hélène Smith presents her as a 'medium à incarnations', who thereby revealed psychological possibilities of plural selves and a new form of psychic instability or self-contradictoriness. In other words, he psychologized her experiences of spirit travel.

She was outraged, since her spirit *alters* were historical realities for her and for the circle of sitters at the seances she regularly held, and where she continued to generate yet more existences—on the planet Uranus and on the Moon. She fought to regain rights of authorship over the book's material (with some justification, one might agree), but unsuccessfully, and it was translated into English immediately, and drew enormous, and indeed admiring attention to its subject, who became the idol of many thirsty Spiritualist adepts as well as a luminary in the Surrealist pantheon of automatists and visionaries. Jung read it, and reported how it 'made a great impression on me. I wrote to Flournoy that I wanted to translate it into German.' Flournoy had already appointed a translator, but the younger psychologist adopted him as his mentor after the break with Freud in 1912, as he was able to discuss with Flournoy his interests in 'somnambulism . . . parapsychology, and the psychology of religion. . . . I had long been interested in the connection of the fantasy products of schizophrenics, and Flournoy helped me to understand them better.'⁶

In the same decade as Freud's studies of the unconscious, and in the same country and medical community as Rorschach and Jung, the older Flournoy (he was born in 1854) was actively engaged in producing a new description of the psyche. The case of Hélène Smith unsettled ideas about the interaction between memory, fantasy, and identity. But her feats of displacement contribute in another way to thinking about media themselves in the third millennium. In trance, Hélène Smith performed acts of interpretation of the tongues she uttered and of the remote and unprecedented lives that her spirit had lived; Flournoy, cast in the role of interpreter and guardian of her messages (however unreliably) was working at two removes: the line of communication was stretched between Léopold or Esenale, Hélène, and himself. This draws exemplary attention, it seems to me, to the presence of the medium as a modifier and transformer. The medium is not a transparent or frictionless conduit at all; just as Hélène Smith acted in full paradoxical unconsciousness to translate herself, so other kinds of medium—technological as well—also perform operations on their transmissions and change them.

As in the case of Wells' story, science fiction was both fantasy and turning into something else besides. In the early part of the twentieth century, hauntings, possession, voices, entranced and spellbound personality, doubled or even multiple selves, had filled far-fetched supernatural fictions of Gothic outlandishness and extremes. By the end of the century, by contrast, doctors and scientists seriously exploring these pathological states paradoxically normalized them, or at least grounded them in real psychological possibilities, accessible to medical analysis and treatment.

W. B. Yeats read Flournoy in the English translation of 1911 made by Hereward Carrington, a vigorous exponent of Theosophist thought. From 1912 onwards and subsequently throughout his life, Yeats drew on the gifts of mediums to put him in touch with spirits. He sought the services of both men and women, but it was a young, well-brought up Englishwoman, Bessie Radcliffe, who succeeded best until Yeats' wife George Hyde Lees took over the task and surpassed her predecessors in unlocking for the poet in later life his creative—his projective—imagination. Since her teens, Bessie had performed automatic writing in several ancient and unknown languages conveyed to her by her 'spirit controls'. She eventually succeeded in summoning for the poet the exotic figure of Leo Africanus. The coming of Leo gave Yeats release from his writer's block, even though he conceded that this 'secondary personality' might be an impostor. 'The seances of 1912 and 1913', writes Roy Foster, 'helped inspire the most sustained burst of poetic activity for many years.'[7]

A friend reported Yeats' excitement at his spirit adventures:

Yeats was in most interesting mood: talked of his entrance into Spiritism fr. the magic of old days: this attendant spirit Leo Africanus, a man of the 14th century [sic] who converses in Italian: also the spirit of a policeman Emerson who drowned himself fr. Putney bridge [in] 1850, as he found in Somerset House records: also Louise Kirsch, the friend of Goethe, fr. whom he had messages. All this he absolutely believes.[8]

Yeats appears to be altogether conscious of the role that imagination played in the experiences, yet he still needed to believe in an external, impersonal, and disembodied actuality of the ghost visitors in order for the effect on his creative energies to happen. He related the process to ideas of self, for the same acquaintance goes on to recall: 'Then talked of Freud & Jung and the subconscious self, applying them to art; said the great thing is to reduce the conscious self to humility . . . leaving the unconscious free to work.'[9]

When Yeats struggled to write down his beliefs—and his doubts—he reveals how psychic forces and spiritist theories were not bound up for him with religious faith at all. He overlooks Christian teachings about the character of eternal life and the immortality of the soul, to distil instead faerie lore, pagan metempsychosis, and the new science and new psychology of multiple personality. In a dialogue with Leo Africanus in 1916, Yeats struggles with his position and asks:

Does in fact the human mind possess a power like that of the amoeba of multiplication by division? Perhaps every mind has originated at conception so, & the seance room but uses in a new way, a faculty necessary to nature, & thereby looses upon the world a new race of bodiless minds, who . . . continually seek a more solid and hard being [&] are in the end dependent not upon an individual body, but upon the body of the human race as a whole. The thought has some support from antiquity.[10]

The spirit of Leo then responds at length, reaffirming that 'all living minds are surrounded by shades, who are the contrary will which presents before the abstracted [?] mind & the mind of the sleeper ideal imerges [sic: images]'. The 'contrary will' Yeats calls elsewhere 'the other self, the anti-self or the antithetical self', and he held strongly that creativity was precipitated by the *coincidentia oppositorum*, an alchemical fusion of self and anti-self, or rather selves and anti-selves, murmuring from the vast storehouses of 'great memory'. As in his celebrated aphorism, he placed internal conflict, rooted in the plurality of the self, at the crux of creativity: 'We make out the quarrel with others, rhetoric, but of the quarrel with ourselves, poetry.'[11] These shades among whom Leo mingles are not ghostly revenants in the form of Hamlet's father or Banquo's ghost, risen to the world above from purgatory, but mental interlocutors whom Yeats also called, in Neoplatonist fashion, 'daemons', who fetch the dreamer back to hear the 'vast luminous sea' of time past.

One of Yeats' principal inspirations during this period was Henry More, the Cambridge Platonist who had earlier imbued Coleridge's imagination. But, as Roy Foster has mapped so lucidly, Yeats did not confine himself to books, but threw himself with equal hunger and openness into experimental science in order to resolve his quandary—were the spirits a product of his imagination, or did they possess autonomous actual being of some kind, and if so what was that being? These 'scientific' attempts strike a reader today as far more crackpot of course than the Neoplatonism and the metaphysics of Yeats's thinking.

Leo Africanus, and before him, John King a.k.a. the pirate Henry Morgan and his daughter Katie, tugged in their train a host of exotic visitors. Indian chiefs, as they were then known, were also popular: it is not irrelevant that in Neverland, the spirit world of the Lost Boys, Peter Pan and his crew do battle with Gentlemen of the Seas and Indian braves. In the 1920s, Madge Donohue (d. 1940), made a series of thought-images, in the tradition of Baraduc and Darget. She called them 'scotographs', and they show flaring weals and whorls in the photographic paper, vehement in temper. In order to transmit them, she channelled the pharoah Amon in the form of a Native American chief, as mentioned earlier—this spirit's name—Golden Cloud— oddly catches at 'the blur of the otherworldly' he imprinted through her.[12] Donohoe was an Australian journalist living in London at the time, and so she had experienced great distances at first hand; her psychic production shifts her own displacement on to an even more distant, esoteric horizon.

After the death of Frederic Myers, when his disciples in different quarters of the world began channelling voices in the hope of hearing him, they produced sheaves of automatic writings.[13] The results sprawl over huge quires of paper, as mediums transcribed ethereal fragments dictated from Greek, Latin, and other literatures, and hoped thereby that they would prove Myers' 'survival after bodily death'. The automatists change handwriting as well as languages, doodle pictograms and other ciphers, and these were then meticulously collated, tabulated, and cross-referenced until, like a photograph developing in the bath, or a face assembling in a rock or a cloud, significance materialized.

Some men took part in the experiment, but most of the dedicated mediums were women, including Margaret Verrall, the wife of A. W. Verrall (first King Edward VII Professor at Cambridge), and their daughter Helen Salter; several others, some remaining anonymous, also participated. Far afield, mediums listened in to the ether, including in India, a 'Mrs Holland', who was Alice Fleming, the sister of Rudyard Kipling. Eventually, an intricate puzzle, perseveringly attempted over an unbelievable period (the papers run from Myers' death in 1901 to the 1930s), eerily delineated a pattern, a story, a plot: the locutions tallied, the secret place of concealment was discovered, and from the other side of mortal existence, Frederic Myers had told in symbolic imagery the story of his undying love for Annie Marshall, enciphered under the sign of syringa.[14]

Are there echoes of these spirit communications in the overheard mutterings in T. S. Eliot's *The Waste Land*—including that cryptic phrase, 'They call me the hyacinth girl'? Tracking messages in imperceptible air waves deeply influenced the characterization of protagonists in more experimental writing than Kipling or Henry James. The Orphic turn that the Modernists took, when they gave expression to voices of disincarnate characters which then resonate directly from the page, also reverberate with the experiments of these years: *The Waves* by Virginia Woolf and, above all, Samuel Beckett's *Krapp's Last Tape*.[15]

The emblematic protagonist of paranormal experience no longer took the form of a poet conjuring Renaissance Africans; the visionary and susceptible Yeats is not ultimately exemplary of his era's scientific positivism. Nor is John Dee scrying his obsidian glass for angels, or Athanasius Kircher making damned souls dance in hell-fire on the walls of the Jesuit college in Rome. Alongside the quivering sensibilities of the Modernists, the modern psychic adept is not a figure from the annals of the occult at all. No, it is the foolproof empiricist, cool and hard, inventor of the deductive method of reasoning: Sir Arthur Conan Doyle. Conan Doyle never gave an inch over his belief in the etheric body. A person gifted with clairvoyance, he argued in 1921, is 'not a person with a better developed physical retina, but rather one who has the power to use that which corresponds with the retina in their own etheric bodies which are in harmony with etheric waves from outside'[16] The ether continued to communicate messages from distant worlds and times, but they were affirmed as scientific, not supernatural or miraculous. Oliver Lodge, Sir Arthur Conan Doyle's colleague in the SPR, and its president from 1904 to 1905, also never abandoned his beliefs in the results of seances, trance messages, and psychic photographs. He published a book called *Ether & Reality* as late as 1925. Sir Oliver, as he had by then become, having contributed significantly to the development of radio and television by his scientific research, became the Principal of the new Birmingham University.[17]

This exemplary modern man gamely persevered in the Einsteinian world with his theory of the Ether, a word which he always capitalizes. It was 'the tertium quid, the essential intermediary' between mind and matter. Ether itself was not 'what we ordinarily speak of as matter', but was nevertheless 'a very substantial substance, far more substantial than any form of matter'; 'a physical thing . . . the vehicle of both matter and spirit . . . it is manifestly the vehicle or substratum underlying electricity and magnetism and light and gravitation and cohesion'. He concluded, rapturously: 'It is the primary instrument of Mind, the vehicle of Soul, the habitation of Spirit. Truly, it may be called the living garment of God.' As he explained, one of the Ether's functions was 'to transmit vibrations from one piece of matter to another'; and it was because the Ether vibrated at a different frequency from matter that, he continued to believe, in certain very carefully constructed experiments it would reveal itself—fleetingly, ethereally—in the form of ectoplasm, a new kind of modern precipitate of the highest heaven.[18]

Plate 5. The composer Arnold Schoenberg
struggled to move beyond representing external
features to depict the inner state or 'soul' of his
subjects, including himself: *Red Gaze*, 1910.

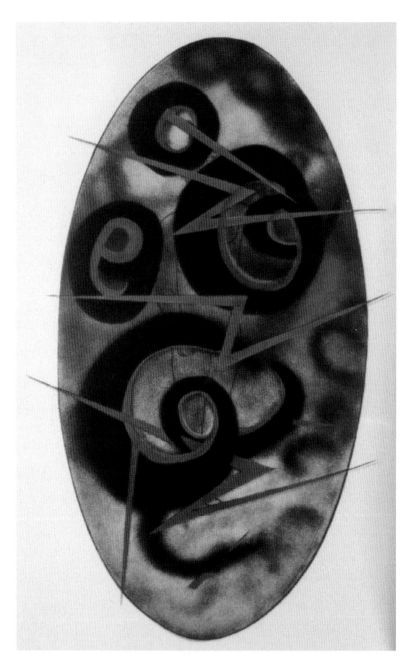

Plate 6. C. W. Leadbeater, Theosophist and collaborator of Annie Besant, coded states of the psyche by colour, form, and stroke, and influenced artists like Kandinsky, as can be seen from this image, *Intense Anger,* from *Man, Visible and Invisible,* 1925.

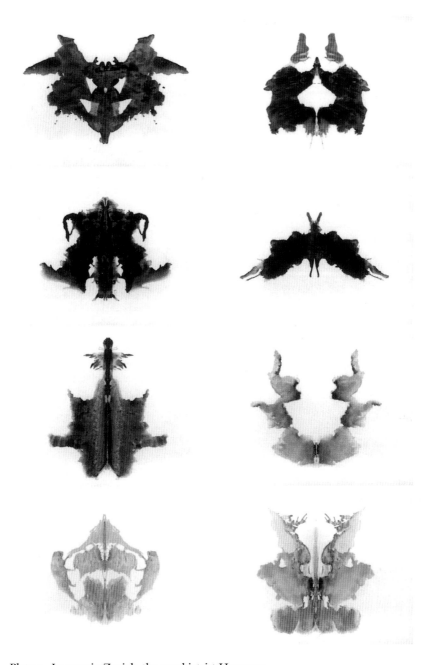

Plate 7. In 1920 in Zurich, the psychiatrist Hermann
Rorschach drew up a set of diagnostic Test Cards by
making inkblots on folded paper and inviting patients
to interpret them; this divinatory method remained in
widespread use in clinical practice.

Plate 8. One of Edgar Allan Poe's hallucinatory tales
inspired Magritte to paint a series of variations on the
idea of 'earth-angels'—forces at work mysteriously
shaping the world, like this eagle-mountain with eggs.
René Magritte, *The Domain of Arnheim*, 1944.

Part IX

Ectoplasm

Ectoplasm could appear and, like a ghost, pass through
obstacles: the medium Stanislawa P. exhales some
through a veil at a 1923 séance. From Albert von
Schrenck-Notzing, *Materialisations Phaenomene*, 1923

22

Touching the Unknown

Saliva is the deposit of the soul; spittle is the soul in movement.

Marcel Griaule

The poet Elizabeth Barrett Browning became keenly interested in spirits after meeting a circle of experimenters in Rome, and generally believed the truth of the phenomena conjured by mediums; during a seance in Ealing with the Scottish-born American medium Daniel Dunglas Home, she was visibly delighted when a wreath of clematis lifted into the air and wafted over and settled on her head—'whether naturally or by spirit hands I do not remember', wrote Home later. Her husband Robert Browning, by contrast, viciously satirized such activity in one of his most excoriating dramatic monologues, 'Mr Sludge, "The Medium"'. The poem was conceived in 1859–60, after the Brownings had attended one of Home's seances in Ealing.

The magician had dazzled his aficionados for years, successfully resisting all tests to expose him for fraud. As we saw, Crookes conducted experiments with him, and remained baffled when Home levitated an accordion inside an iron cage, where it played by itself. The medium was later pursued above all by the ghost buster *extraordinaire*, Harry Houdini, but even Houdini, who usually managed to copy a medium's feats and thus expose any claims to supernatural agency could not replicate Dunglas Home's most legendary exploit: in 1868, in daylight, in front of assembled witnesses, he floated head first out of one third-floor window and came in at another feet first, his body held rigid throughout his flight.

With broad satire, Robert Browning sets Sludge's seance in the United States, in the house of Mr Hiram H. Horsefall, a Boston millionaire, and among his targets are the vanity of patrons as well as the venality and opportunism of the psychic. Home had not pleased Browning, or persuaded him, and the poet stages him as a chippy, ingratiating, yet truculent rascal, who races through his arguments in bouncy pentameters with exclamatory, button-holing hail-fellow-well-met breeziness. But Browning also shows insight into the class hatred that drives Sludge to dupe his rich patrons and into their collusion with the results. The medium's loquacious self-vindication opens after the medium has conjured the spirit of his pat-ron's 'sainted mother', but has been caught cheating; he whines: 'Now, don't sir! Don't expose me! Just this once!'[1]

Later, Sludge describes the collusion between medium and seance parti-cipants, as he demonstrates the difference between 'cheating' and the real thing:

> Just an experiment first, for candour's sake!
> I'll try and cheat you, Judge! The table tilts:
> Is it I that move it? Write! I'll press your hand:
> Cry when I push, or guide your pencil, Judge!
> Sludge still triumphant! 'That a rap, indeed?
> That, the real writing? Very like a whale! . . .'[2]

The poet hints at the sexual implications of women's presence and proximity, both as sitters and as mediums in table-turning and spirit rapping sessions: Home, as a male spirit medium, was in the minority among mediums; yet this aspect of Victorian psychic experiments does indeed colour their his-tory, and in some ways, Sludge's loathsome abjection and desire for revenge reverberate with a subordinate's sense of injustice. Browning may not have shown the poem to his wife, since she had already expressed distress at the scepticism and contempt he declared towards Home soon after the seances.[3]

No ectoplasm appears as such, and the poem was written earlier than the valiant period of ectoplasmic production at seances; however, his egregious medium's name, Mr Sludge, does anticipate cruelly the spirit stuff that became the chief ambition of seance participants from the 1880s, when inquiries into spirit existences in the late nineteenth century moved decisively away from visual and acoustic illusions alone, from spectral apparitions and dematerialized sounds. The researchers now wanted to establish the reality of experiences. The difference between Myers and Gurney was repeated throughout the movement: were spectres and other phenomena an effect of imagination? Was the psychic psychological? And if so, was it a delusion? Or a true apprehension?

Psychic researchers worried at the issue, and tried to settle it by con-centrating on achieving a haptic experience of actual matter. Visible verifi-cation, as in photographs or seances, began to yield pride of place to other empirical warranties of presence—especially haptic. Many members of the SPR had a background in scientific naturalism and natural magic; they were often materialists and even positivists, and they spear-led an emphasis on objective analysis requiring tangible proofs. Images could be illusory, vision was not dependable. They demanded real objects, actual matter. How the imponderable and ethereal could be made palpable, weighed and verified, by touch above all, but also by smell and hearing, occupied some of the best minds of the last century, even as they postulated the possibility of paranormal phenomena.

Unexpectedly, Aristotle actually singles out the sense of touch in *De Anima* as the supreme mark of human intelligence:

in the other senses he (man) is behind many kinds of animal, but in touch he is much more discriminating than the other animals. This is why he is of all living creatures the most intelligent. Proof of this lies in the fact that among the human race men are well or poorly endowed with intelligence in proportion to their sense of touch, and no other sense.[4]

This is a startling endorsement from a philosopher more usually associated with the sovereignty of vision, and it throws light on the primacy of touch in the verifying methods used during the quest for ectoplasm in the late nineteenth and early twentieth centuries. Numerous scientific experimenters, including Spiritualists, were not to be satisfied with the risen Christ's injunction to Mary Magdalene, 'Noli me tangere'; they were doubting Thomases, one and all, and wanted to push their fingers into the wounds in the spirit body's side, to palpate the stuff of the other side, to feel its temperature and texture. Touch became the guarantor of the paradoxical presence of spirit.

The roster of eminent Victorians who attended seances and who wanted more than spirit photographs is truly impressive, and their hunger for manifestations inspired an extraordinary variety of tangible effects that stretched all previous concepts of ethereal bodies. In Manchester, for example, 'Mlle E. d'Espérance' materialized 'apports'—the most exquisite potted plants, ferns, strawberries, etc. Some flowers materialized before the sitters' eyes in a glass of water held in their hand, and were given their botanical names with Victorian scrupulousness. 'Ixora Crocata' was 'produced for Mr. William Oxley of Manchester at a seance held 4 August 1880'. A more precise spiritually symbolical apport, 'The Golden Lily', appeared in June 1890, lasted a week, then 'dissolved and disappeared'.[5] Another medium who enjoyed acclaim at the time, Mrs Guppy, ate her productions—which one of her spiritualist colleagues considered a mistake ('a great weakness').[6]

Victorian scientists, followed by some eminent moderns, endeavoured to apply innovatory techniques to probing interior mysteries, to making the impalpable palpable, and the leaders of the SPR persevered in attempting to obtain tangible proofs of extra-sensory phenomena—not only photographs, but real objects, actual matter proving the existence of spirit forces. Some of these have stood the scientific test: radio waves, gamma rays. But others that were ardently advocated and exploited—and wholly believed—have

to the echoes of embarrassed titters: animal spirits, odic (mag-
·adiant matter.

The concept of ectoplasm grew out of Victorian physics and cognitive
sciences and the post-Darwinian challenge to traditional faith. Ectoplasmic
phenomena figured generic stuff of the spirit, not unique ghosts of dead
souls. Ectoplasm did not *haunt* its believers: it offered a solution to the
problem of imponderables, and embodied a postulated *prima materia*. From
its first appearances in psychic experiments in the 1880s, ectoplasm was
intensely pursued by scientifically minded researchers, who did not always
believe in spirits as ghosts of the dead, and did not declare themselves to be
Spiritualists. They were questing to know the structure of the universe.

The word 'ectoplasm', from the Greek *ektos*, 'outside', and *plasma*,
'something that can be formed or moulded', as in 'plastic', first enters the
discourse of Spiritualism in Germany and France in the 1880s, though
Crookes's adventures with mediums, and the earliest spirit photographs,
taken first in America, pre-date this by some twenty years.[7] The word was
borrowed from biological usage: the *OED* gives as its first citation a quota-
tion from 1883 which discloses vividly the operating metaphor: 'Its [the
amoeba's] jelly-like body becomes faintly parcelled out into an outer form
(ectoplasm) and an inner soft (endoplasm) layer.' It is further defined there
as 'a viscous substance which is supposed to emanate from the body of a
spiritualistic medium, and to develop into a human form or face'. It is 'the
substance from which spirits make themselves visible forms . . . alive, sensitive to touch and light . . . cold to the touch, slightly luminous and having a
characteristic smell'.[8]

Ectoplasm thus materialized phenomena from the world beyond the
senses for its hopeful believers. It is 'the substance from which spirits make
themselves visible forms',[9] but in itself it is shapeless, 'informe', a kind of
primordial paste—and to show itself as this, it borrows the metaphors of
shapelessness, as with clouds and air and spirit bodies, as discussed earlier.
Cotton wool haloes and smudges, aureoles of flimsy white stuff enveloping
spirit visitors, borrow from the concept of aura. The physical attributes of
ectoplasm depend on a long tradition of making visible the invisible, of
rendering material the immaterial. It also bodies forth the etheric or astral
body, an idea about the spiritual dimension of human personality that was
expounded in Theosophical thought and twists and turns through the history of the occult. This new supernatural stuff approximated, awkwardly, to
the *hylē* of matter in Aristotelian thought; it receives the stamp of the spirit
conjured by the medium, and is extruded as form.

Darkness was essential for the phenomena to appear: light, almost everyone agreed, was highly destructive to their organism. William Crookes preferred moonlight, and reported excellent results by this pale illumination;

the French doctor Gustave Geley hankered after the light emitted by certain animals, vegetables, and microbes, reporting wistfully that highly successful seances had been held in Brazil by the light of glow-worms, but that this was very difficult in practice to realize.[10] But given a darkened room, willing, supportive sitters, the 'substance' might appear.

Spirit apparitions and ectoplasmic manifestations, during seances, took two predominant forms: luminous, veiled, phantom-like beings; or nameless, amorphous parts of such beings, called pseudopods, strings and veils and folds of gooey, smelly, haptic ectoplasm which flowed or dribbled from the medium's mouth or ear or even other orifices.[11] The seances at which they appeared were happenings, evolving over time and involving evidence of ectoplasm's vitality, in its power of movement as well as its ductility.

Dr Geley, a tireless chronicler of manifestations, described the stuff in detail: 'The colour white is the most frequent. . . . On touch . . . it can seem soft and a bit elastic when it spreads; hard, knotty or fibrous when it forms strings. . . . Sometimes it gives the sensation of a spider's web fluttering over the observer's hand.' He also emphasizes its motility: 'The substance is mobile. At one moment it evolves slowly, rises, falls, wanders over the medium, her shoulders, her breast, her knees, with a creeping motion that recalls that of a reptile.'[12]

Ectoplasms were not the only material products of experiment: Franek Kluski, one of the few successful male materializing mediums, specialized in the sheerest gloves and socks, extruded in paraffin wax under the imprinting power of spirit visitors.[13] These spectral casts echo the guarantee of authenticity that waxworks and death masks offer.

The perseverance of men of science had strong implications for the course of psychic research. When Sidgwick and Myers set up their tireless series of seances, they worried about paying the women: will it corrupt them? Will the mediums' husbands start exploiting the situation? Then they worry about *not paying* them, for they realize that the women are needy. The two philosophers evince no powers of self-scrutiny as to their own motives, however. Astonishingly naïve letters pass between them, about whether the kisses they received in seances were given by materialized lips. They continued in the enterprise for nearly half a century, and they were not alone.

Dr Charles Richet held seances in his villa on the island of Roubaud in the south of France during the summer of 1894, and later in his chateau on the mainland, near Toulon, and his apartments in Paris. He invited an international group of eminent philosophers and scientists, including Camille Flammarion and, from England, the leading members of the SPR. They included Henry Sidgwick and his wife Eleanor, Myers, and Lodge; Flournoy came from Geneva, and Schrenck-Notzing from Munich. They were joined by a certain Dr J. Ochorowicz from Warsaw, an expert on hypnotism. Richet had enlisted Eusapia Paladino, the most famous materializing medium of the age, to demonstrate her powers.[14]

Paladino was born in Puglia, in southern Italy, in 1854, so she was around 40 at the height of her psychic feats. She was a small, square-jawed woman with 'piercing eyes, and the true head of a Roman empress', wrote Richet.[15] She did not speak much French or English, but the messages came through in a mixture of the two; she could not read or write. She had been orphaned when a child (her father was reputedly killed by brigands), and then employed as a servant in the household of an aristocratic Neapolitan family devoted to Spiritualism. Her patron wrote to the forensic specialist Cesare Lombroso in Milan, vaunting her powers, and she was tested by Lombroso himself in 1891. He pronounced her psychic abilities inexplicable and—with that curious hubristic complacency of the times— consequently genuine. Lombroso was an important support in a later lustrous career.

Her specialities also included table-turning, tambourines and guitars playing by themselves as they floated through the air, bells ringing, sprinkles of water, and 'the conveyance of a vase full of jonquils from a table at the far end of the room . . . and its being held in turn under each face to enable us to inhale the highly increased perfume of the flowers'.[16] Above all, she was able to form spirit limbs and structures. The company were assembled to witness her powers.

By the end of his life, Charles Richet would have held around 200 sessions with Paladino, and in 1895, he was enchanted by the results. It was Richet who annexed the biological term 'ectoplasm' to describe her feats: 'Even if there were no other medium in the world,' he wrote, 'her manifestations would suffice to establish scientifically the reality of tele- kinesis and ectoplasmic forms.'[17] Later, he exclaimed, 'It is very absurd; if a truth can be absurd. Yes, it is absurd. But no matter, it is true.'[18]

After sessions with Paladino, the Sidgwicks also felt able to write to their colleague and brother-in-law, the Cambridge physicist Lord Rayleigh, 'Practically, we are convinced that there is something supernormal.'[19] But they were keen to experiment further. So they took Eusapia back with them to Cambridge to continue the experiments, and lodged her with the Myerses at their house. During a further gruelling sequence of nineteen seances, held daily or every other day from 1 August to 12 September for several hours at a time, they put Eusapia through her paces to determine the nature of the wonders she conjured.

Sidgwick and Myers were unlikely perpetrators of this dubious phase of scientific inquiry, and their fellow sitters at one or more of the Cambridge seances included other men and women of the highest intellectual and social respectability—Eleanor Sidgwick and Eveleen Myers, Professor W. S. Verrall and his wife, Lord Rayleigh and his wife, as well as several others, and of course Richet himself. At one session, the famous escapologists and conjurors, the Maskelyne brothers, joined the party. Yet in its determination to find out what the medium was doing, this highly placed group of people flouted every notion of decorum obtaining in their society in order to achieve their end.

The minutes of seances conducted in Cambridge in 1895 were mostly written up by the punctilious Alice Johnson, the secretary of the SPR, as in this example from the first evening, written on scrap paper from the Cambridge Examinations:

Aug 1 1895

[With Mr and Mrs Myers, Prof. and Mrs. Sidgwick], Mrs Verrall, Mr. Rogers, Mr. Dixon and Miss Johnson.

Mr F. Myers lay down on the floor again so that he could see her knees.

7.40 Eu[sapia] begins to laugh; indicating the arrival of John King [her spirit guide]. Then moans & becomes quiet again. Dr Rogers remarks that her eyeballs are turned up.

[As table rises] Mr Rogers holding her knees states that there are no movements of the muscles in them.

8.14 Medium comes out of trance asks who is holding her legs & is told. Prof. Sidgwick comes out from under table.

8.20 trance returning: Prof Sidgwick goes in again.

. . .

8.30 Mrs Myers said she saw something white. Mrs. Verrall also saw it.

. . .

8.33 Mr Dixon calls out 'Who's moving my chair?' Prof Sidgwick is again under the table & holds Eu's feet & knees, Mr Dixon holds one hand & Mrs Sidgwick the other, Mr Myers has his hands on side of Eu's head.

8.55 . . . Mrs Sidgwick sees a hand, foreshortened, between her & the window; first thinks it is Eu's but Mr Myers says Eu's hand was (held by him) on her lap at the time.

. . .

9.2 . . . Eu says she wishes her feet to be left alone, & Prof Sidgwick comes out from under the table. Mr Myers says 'My chair is being dragged from under me & I am being gently dug in the ribs.' Here Prof. Sidgwick goes under the table again & holds Eu.'s feet . . .

. . . Mrs Sidgwick says she feels J. K. [John King] stroking her face & chin. J. K. laughs.

. . .

9.08 Eu's head is on Mr Myers' shoulder.

. . .

9.12 Mr Myers says 'her head is on my shoulder.' Mrs Verrall says 'I saw a great white thing appear behind Mr Myers, perhaps the cushion.' . . . Mr Dixon grabbed at it & touched it; then it drew back. He said it felt like a hand or at all events something more solid than a cushion.

9.22 S under the table again.

9.50 . . . Mr Myers: 'I have got the shoe put in my lap by a hand which pressed my thigh first.'

. . .

Mr Myers: 'Look at the curtain, it is swelling up against me, a hard thing is pressed against me.' Mrs Myers has got both Eu's feet as well.

Mrs Myers undressed her after 10.20.[20]

The Sidgwicks remained hopeful that Paladino was not a 'humbug', one of their favourite words, but they had to admit that the evidence pointed to fraud. Nevertheless, they explained away her sleight of hand as a character defect, separate from her genuine powers, hence the urgency of 'control': the bonds, gags, and other obstacles they devised with feverish ingenuity to monitor her movements, and to prevent her propensity to play tricks. This obsessive pursuit of 'scientific control' led to these antics under the table: there are photographs in the SPR archive of Eusapia's little Victorian boots gripped by a pair of male hands. This evidence of rigour now reads of course rather differently; shown without explanation, most viewers would think they were looking at a still from a Surrealist film exploring Victorian fetishism: Luis Buñuel's *Diary of a Chambermaid,* for example. But then, it looked like objective circumspection, and William James singled out the SPR's methods as original, courageous, and necessary.

Even after Eusapia's conjuring exploits were imitated, and thereby exposed, several members of the Society, led by Oliver Lodge and Frederic Myers, loyally continued to hold 'that (however antecedently improbable) there is here, besides adroit trickery, an admixture of genuine phenomena'.[21] When they continued to maintain that any tricks were her personal doing, whereas the spirits that moved through her were genuine and true, and her psychic phenomena genuine, they simply disclose how profoundly desire leads understanding and shapes the stories people tell themselves. The huge amounts of energy spent on these questions in pages and pages of the annals of the SPR and other groups show the urgency and the intensity of feelings that consumed these questors. For example, Eleanor, one of the most assiduous chroniclers of their efforts, would write later in evident disappointment, only very rarely were Eusapia's materialisations said to develop into fully-formed phantoms. . . . Morselli [author of a book about Paladino] tied her to a campbed inside the cabinet . . . and thereafter, in fairly good light, six phantoms, it is alleged, presented themselves in succession in the opening of the cabinet curtains—the last one being a woman with a baby in her arms! . . . Normally, however, the appearance of 'hands' and the so called 'heads' and similar pseudopods (as they are called) are E's most advanced materializations.[22]

Though Eusapia herself would not be able to meet the wistful implications of these comments, other mediums would soon make the attempt.

She died in 1918, and around ten years after her heyday, her innovations were continued by the medium 'Eva C.', the centre of Schrenck-Notzing's experiments in Munich from 1911 to 1913. As we saw, Eva produced miraculous images—ideoplasts—but she also starred in the photographs taken of the phenomena: thus she acted as a developer of other-worldly images, while she herself inspired remarkable records of her trance productions. Schrenck-Notzing took the photographs, setting up several cameras at different angles and distances, and in his book he claims total amazement at what ensued. He acted as archivist of a wide range of ectoplasmic pods, strings, veils, and structures. The lurid commingling of female physical display, scientific language, and forensic, evidentiary process brings to a prurient culmination the labours of psychical investigators since the foundation of the Society for Psychical Research. But the seances which Juliette Bisson staged could also be included among the remarkable studio practices of the period, while the mediums could be numbered among extraordinary performance artists of the period, alongside Alice Adams and Claude Cahun. The *mises-en-scène* of those bizarre Munich seances often resemble the photographs of Bellocq or other specialists in clandestine erotica. The medium Stanislawa P., for example, performed in a black veil swathing her head, and was photographed spitting or leaking long viscous skeins of white stuff, which seem to pass as if miraculously through the fabric over her face. Sometimes wearing a blindfold, sometimes gagged, sometimes undressed, Eva C. and Stanislawa P. make disturbingly fetishized and erotic figures (Figure 24, p. 286).

The developments of the Twenties changed the symbolism of spirit, moving away from airy and combustible ether towards effluvia, more akin to Stoic concepts of semen. Unlike any of the preceding vehicles of spirit, ectoplasm's affinities verge on the category of bodily wastes, palpable and tangible, emphatically not sublimed matter: it leaked and bubbled and flowed from the medium's innards. There is nothing more startlingly incongruous than photographs of heavily furnished and furbelowed domestic interiors, in which everything and everyone is draped, swirled, tied, and bundled, while the body of the medium oozes and dribbles shapeless blobby stuff—offal was indeed used by Margery Crandon, instead of the cheesecloth or other fabrics of her predecessors.[23]

The metaphors for soul and spirit at work in these scenes allot ectoplasm to the category of symbols of generation: the foam, or *aphros*, of semen and spittle that can generate, as in creation myths, and heal, as when Jesus performs his miracle cure of a blind man by spitting in his ears, and another, by anointing his tongue with his own saliva. The child as the 'spit' of his father comes into use only in the early nineteenth century, however, and the now familiar phrase 'spitting image' for an uncanny likeness, for the 'fetch' or double of someone, first appears in 1859, according to the *OED*; both these figures of speech shadow an equivalence between the different bodily fluids, though it remains puzzling why they should enter the language long after the biology on which they depend had been superseded. This cluster of somatic, even abject images then shifts back into the zone of spirit thought, because in Aristotelian biology, as alluded to earlier, seed was immaterial and only stamped out the form of the material body.

Oliver Lodge, discussing the form of human survival after death, explicitly had recourse to the image of larvae: 'the change [from life to afterlife] appears to be a liberation from matter, accompanied by a retention of our ethereal connection . . . of something which we already possess, though here and now its possession is only known to us by inference from indistinct phenomena—by, as it were, larval indications.'[24]

The word 'larva', used in English for the early stage of a caterpillar, meant 'ghost' or 'spectre' in Latin, but is also used by Horace to designate a mask, such as might frighten an observer, while the verb *larvo* meant to bewitch or enchant. Ectoplasmic masks and limbs are indeed larval: they promise the emergence of forms, but do not deliver them. The term 'pseudopods', used for some of the 'structures', catches this relationship with the embryonic— and relates to the fundamental ideas about spirit imprinting matter as in Aristotle's comparison of body and soul to wax and the seal that impresses and shapes it.

At a rather less exalted level, the Surrealists' *Critical Dictionary*, edited and written by Georges Bataille and others in the late Twenties, includes an entry on ectoplasm, written with characteristic sly humour by Jacques Brunius, film-maker and art critic. It defined ectoplasm as

part of the human body, external to it, unstable, sometimes soft, occasionally hard, from time to time vaporous, variable in volume, visible only in semi-darkness, making an impression on photographic emulsion, presents to the sense of touch a humid and slippery sensation, leaving in the hand a residue which, when dry, has under microscopic examination the appearance of epithelial cells, without odour or definite taste, in other respects fleeting and transient, whether projected or otherwise, of uncertain temperature, fond of music.

It added, knowingly, 'Fish- and game-birds' intestines, even inflated with a bicycle-pump, are not ectoplasms.'[25] In the same volume, the Surrealist and anthropologist Marcel Griaule also meditated on spittle—at once balm and filth; he concluded its tour of oral symbolism in a paroxysm of rhetoric: 'It is the limp and sticky stumbling block shattering more efficiently than any stone all undertakings that presuppose man to be something—something other than a flabby, bald animal, something other than a raving demiurge, splitting his sides at having expectorated such a conceited larva: a comical tadpole puffing itself up into meat insufflated by a demigod.'[26]

He could have been invoking ectoplasm: the stuff which offered the self-portrait of the human species for a bewildered rational age.

Ectoplasmic phenomena remained formless and in some sense unidentified: by analogy with ether, they more often figured the original protoplasm of the world, the materialization of spirit, rather than ghosts with personal identities. In many ways the psychic researchers' endeavours constitute the last stand of the strong materialists, for the discoveries of waves, particles, and quantum mechanics have redrafted the nature of matter in such subtle and complex ways that the distinction between materiality and immateriality is dissolving, especially in the realms opened by new technologies.

Sir Arthur Conan Doyle, an unswerving supporter of
Spiritualism, appears after his death in 1930, with an
unidentified sitter, in an image taken by the popular
psychic photographer, William Hope.

23

Materializing Mediums

Under 'Duncan Helen, Mrs.' in the catalogue of the archives of the Society for Psychical Research, the entry appears: 'Sample of Ectoplasm, Material alleged to have been captured from Mrs Helen Duncan, materialising medium, at a seance in 1939'. I asked to see 'the sample of ectoplasm'. The librarian asked me, 'Are you sure? It's very nasty.' My instant reaction was, 'Would you prefer me to look at it somewhere else?' I thought there might be a desk of shame, where I could be supervised and other readers would not be disturbed. He said, 'No, but be discreet.'

There was nothing corporeal about it when it arrived, in the strict sense of human or animal tissue. Inside an acid-free archive box, there was a folded heap of dressmakers' lining silk, the cheapest kind of fabric, a man-made fibre, once white but yellowed by age. About four yards had been cut straight from the bolt, left unhemmed, the selvedge plain. It had been washed and ironed, but the creases where it had been crumpled were still marked; the pattern of these showed that it had been tightly wadded. There were traces of old blood that the laundry had not erased (the cloth had been secreted in her stomach, it was alleged). The volume of it was astonishing to me. Remembering Thomas Browne and others who attempted to weigh souls,[1] I went over to the librarian and asked him if he had any scales. The librarian agreed that it would be a good idea to weigh the sample; he suggested the post room, where there would be scales. We put it on the tray; Mrs Duncan's ectoplasm weighed 236 grams—less than expected, for the material felt slumpy and heavy to the touch. Lighter, diaphanous stuff, such as muslin, or white of egg, looks like the mediums' preferred substances in earlier photographs.[2]

Ectoplasm appeared in certain very special conditions; then vanished, re-absorbed, the theory goes, into the body of the medium. So the specimen from Helen Duncan's seance is rare: it was lent to the SPR for analysis. Dissident sitters who wanted to expose the mediums as frauds would attend a seance and then snatch at the ectoplasmic phantoms and bear them away in triumph: another such spoil was given to Harry Price to analyse in 1931. Gleefully, he pronounced this sample cheesecloth, and Duncan a charlatan.[3]

The very subject of ectoplasm now tends to provoke involuntary laughter, shivers, and, on closer look, real horror; the documentary images of the mediums, often in considerable physical distress, strike us now as foolish, crazy, embarrassing, prurient, repellent. The disparities in class, wealth, and education—and, above all, gender—between the researchers and the mediums remained shamefully ignored, it seems, at the time. But ecto-plasm is an important chapter in the story of spirit: it represents the final shake of the pieces that make up the traditional picture of ethereality. It offered its believers a wonderful proof of the existence of other states of matter, and as such, embodies a transition in the history of scientific inquiry between Christian metaphysics and quantum theory: it also, with regard to the argument of this book, materializes long enduring metaphor at the most literal level, demonstrating the power of language in shaping experience.

Like the materializing mediums who preceded her—Paladino, Carrière—Helen Duncan presented her body as a porous vehicle for the phenomena, which exuded from all orifices—nose, breast, ears, navel, vagina. She occupied the role of transmitter, in an analogous fashion to the wireless receiver, catching cosmic rays whose vibrations produced intelli-gible phantoms and presences. Photographs that were taken of Mrs Duncan in trance, with her spirit control 'Peggy'—a hideous, garish mask wrapped in a sheet looming behind her—provoke incredulity.

Many such photographs were taken, and they evidently do not catch the communal experience that led so many participants to feel that they had been in touch with the other world, seen their loved ones again, and been consoled and enriched. The photographs themselves cannot convey any of this at all. But they themselves looked different to participants as well, transfigured by the trust placed in them as true pictures of the spirits. The spirit photograph portrayed the 'extras' as benignly static, and the medium itself could not convey the necessary animate, motile, tactile, and dynamic character expected of spirit beings. In this respect, psychic portraits, however popular they remained—well into the twentieth cen-tury—still gave a very poor account of a seance, which could be highly dramatic, noisy, with tables jumping, trumpets sailing through the air, flowers and other gifts from the ghosts arriving with sudden impact, and, throughout, the groans, moans, grunts, remarks, and laughter of the medium in trance and the chatter of the spirits speaking through her. All this turmoil produced a new group of psychic images: dramatic records of the ectoplasmic seance that furnished proofs—it was believed—of the manifestations that took place under its tensions.[4] Seance photographs represent an elaborate, dramatic, protracted, and highly peculiar collabora-tive effort to raise spectral phenomena; they record what took place, but, unlike an 'ideoplast' or 'psychograph' or 'psychicon', they are no longer the phenomenon itself. In a Julia Margaret Cameron image of an angel, only her photograph exists to make the angel appear before us, just as Hippolyte Baraduc's tiny pictures capture his soul states of anger and sorrow; but in the work of the materializing mediums who emanated ectoplasms, teleplasms, pseudopods, apports, and various other prodigies, they happened, according to their participants, regardless of their verification by photography.

This is not a hard and fast distinction, however. The processes that bring ectoplasm into the world are often reproductive, modelled by extended analogy on photography: they cause impressions on wax, as casts from the energy or vibrations of spirits. Sometimes, even more alarmingly, the metaphor of giving birth shades into the image of generating a copy, as the spirit takes form as ectoplasm.

Photography, as well as offering a deep metaphor for the relation between external matter and immaterial thought, also played an inestimable role in disseminating the *mise-en-scène* and conduct of mediums, from country to country, The mediums themselves were nomadic: a cross between the peripatetic conférenciers of today's academe and international artists, performers, and entertainers. Also, whereas the sitter sat quietly and often alone in front of the camera in Miss Houghton's sitting-room or Mrs Deane's studio, ectoplasmic seances from the 1880s onwards were group happenings, and they made heavy demands of the mediums. Trances became ever more dramatic and physically strenuous, often painful.

The craze for such experiences did not abate after numerous exposés of the mediums' claims. Ectoplasm continued to act as the prime kind of developing agent for the other side, its adherents believed. It made possible the impression, as in a print or cast, of the presence of impalpable, imponderable, light and other immaterial forms from the mind of the medium. Or so maintained Sir Arthur Conan Doyle (Figure 25, p. 298). The inventor of that hero of deductive reasoning, Sherlock Holmes, declared in 1923 that he was completely convinced by the spirit hand formed from one of the paraffin gloves 'obtained by Dr Geley, Prof. Richet and Count de Grammont from an ectoplasmic figure under the mediumship of M. Kluski'. He continued, 'the ectoplasmic form was clearly visible, as it dipped its hand into the bucket of hot liquid paraffin. I have actually seen the thin paraffin gloves which came from the dematerialized hand . . . (in Paris). The experiment was absolutely final.'[5] Conan Doyle was responding to a fierce attack on his gullibility: 'Mr Rinn twits me for only having seen ectoplasm twice. Ectoplasm in solid form is a rare substance and I have been very fortunate to see it twice.' He cites photographers (Schrenck-Notzing, Mme Bisson, *et al.*) 'who have published several hundred photographs of this extraordinary substance. . . . For Mr Rinn or any other conjuror to deny its existence is simply to show that he is ignorant of recent scientific developments and is behind the times.' Three years later, Sir Arthur was still resolute: 'The ectoplasm pictures photographed by Madame Bisson and Dr. Schrenk-Notzing . . . may in their first forms be ascribed to the *medium's thoughts or memories taking visible shape in ectoplasm.*'[6]

Another medium practising sensationally during this period was Margery Crandon, who was married to a prominent society gynaecologist in Boston; her husband's social standing helped attract sitters when she first began performing under the significant name 'Psyche'.[7] This had been a popular *nom de plume* for clairvoyants on the entertainment circuits where the occult touched the freak show.[8]

Margery Crandon was born in 1897; her brother Walter had died in a railway accident when she was 14, and he then became Psyche's 'spirit control', a character who turned up at her seances, often whistling loudly, breaking out into the Wedding March, 'his theme song', ribbing the participants, and even taunting them. At one session, a spirit 'rattled on, saying the Lord's prayer in German rapidly, ending up with "Go to hell". Considerable cheering was given this act. Dr Crandon explained that his wife didn't know a word of German.'[9]

Among her most admired phenomena were Walter's thumbprints, which appeared in the course of a seance in England in 1929, imprinted on dental wax: the spirit coming over from the other side with enough substance and weight to leave his unique seal (Figures 4a, 25a, pp. 44, 307).[10] Here wax, the classical sympathetic correlative of spirit, makes a literal return on the otherworldly map. But Margery/Psyche surpassed even this remarkable spirit signature when Walter began to form teleplasmic hands and heads, and even, most significantly, promised to deliver an ectoplasmic foetus.

A sitter reported:

The physical phenomena of the evening were obvious progressive steps in the production of the promised speaking head. Psychic light, bigger than have ever been seen before, by us, appeared over Psyche's chest . . . The luminous hand was seen on the table and after a long upright light almost suggesting a phantom. Walter said: 'Those are my shining skin [*sic*] outlining my form but it has no bones. That is what a phantom is. Tomorrow bring a thermometer to put in my mouth and have a notebook . . . This head I am making will be a real head, bones and all features. You people will get the shock of your lives!' . . . He liked Dr R.'s idea of putting the cigarette in the mouth of the head. 'This stuff I am using tonight is like macaroni. It is not transparent.'[11]

Lady [Florence] Barrett, wife of the SPR founding member, and eminent physician Sir William Barrett examined Margery Crandon before the sitting, and explained afterwards that she did indeed conclude that 'the ectoplasmic rods had been formed by a kind of birth process'.[12] It has to be said as well that all the notes to these sessions, with their crude voyeurism and credulity, make sordid and dismaying reading, while the photographs taken, showing Margery with her legs spread and amorphous sludge heaped on her tummy dangling down, are shockingly squalid. William MacDougall, Professor of Psychology at Harvard, was one of a group of scientists called in to examine the photographs of Margery's spirit forms; in one case, he gave the opinion that 'Margery's emanations were composed of an animal's lung tissue cut to resemble a human hand'.[13]

Another contemporary showed enough sympathy to speculate on Margery's motives. Crandon was well connected in Boston through his medical practice, and a widower twice over when Margery married him; she was also twenty-five years younger than him, and less securely placed in Boston society. She had arrived without family from Canada. One of the scientists called in to examine her activities suggested that 'her husband was tired of her and it was with the hope of regaining his confidence and affection that she had invented the mediumship'.[14] If this was the case, it would resemble somewhat George Hyde Lees' intuitive response to her husband W. B. Yeats, also a highly established and older man, when she turned herself into his most fertile and indispensable medium.

When mediums wrote their memoirs, they never—as far as I have discovered—complain, or indeed disclose anything except unswerving fidelity to the psychic gift they inherited, and the phenomena they were consequently able to summon. But in many cases, their stories are muffled, compared to the sitters' assiduous records. Whereas all the sitters are given their titles, Prof., Dr, Mrs, and so forth, the mediums' first names are commonly used. Lord Rayleigh, after examining the founder of Spiritualism, Katy (ex-Fox) Jencken, came to the comforting conclusion, 'Mr Jencken seems to me to be rather a fool, and if this be so the phenomen[a are] genuine, as no fool could do them as tricks.'[15]

Such lack of curiosity about the mediums strikes the reader now as baffling. Margery left one exchange of letters with the secretary of the SPR in the Twenties, E. J. Dingwall. She complains about pains in her nose—hardly surprising when she was expelling so much stuff from her nostrils during the seances. Nor does any of the surviving correspondence in the archives illuminate the *interior* life and thinking of the mediums themselves, women like Eva Carrière, Eusapia Paladino, or Margery Crandon, from their point of view.

Nobody seems to connect Margery's physical distress, which caused her to cancel quite often, with her production of ectoplasm. Her spirit control

Walter once commented, a participant recalled, 'Pay no attention to her. Let her groan. She hasn't any pain. Blow your nose, Kid. I'm like an octopus, I can attach myself anywhere and then put life into it. She must sit very tight. Don't ask her how she feels.'[16] The same indifference to Helen Duncan's welfare also prevailed, even when Duncan was suffering serious health difficulties brought on by diabetes, overweight, and the exactions of her ectoplasmic feats.

Serious and high-minded as the Sidgwicks and their colleagues and successors were, these travellers into the unknown were precisely attracted by the mediums' near-death states, in which they lost their self-possession. The trances, fits, numbness, and transports which the mediums experienced opened them up as channels for others. Perhaps because the people involved in psychic and Spiritualist research show such earnest application to the task, there is something ghastly and shameful, and, at the same time, inadvertently hilarious about their shenanigans; it is also a cause for profound dismay to all who believe in intellectual effort at all that thoughtful men and women should have colluded with such deceptions and, all unconsciously, in the synergy of their interests, brought about a spiral of ever-increasing duplicity, while inciting an exhibition of trance mediums at their most abject: mediums were not only for the most part female, but were clearly subordinate in social status and economic power to the psychic investigators. For all these emotional reasons, the extent and influence of the psychic enterprise have only recently been paid serious attention, and the legitimate contexts in which it arose, the resonance of the questions it put, and the depths of its effect on ideas of the self in psychology and literature are only now beginning to be assessed. This psycho-sexual story, about unconscious gratifications, can be explored more fully, as Alex Owen has done in a fine study, *The Darkened Room*.[17]

Psychic happenings like Margery Crandon's 'spirit forms' do not develop, as the idea of the revenant does, the Christian idea of the unique individual soul. In this, and in other areas of psychic research, an influence of Theosophy and its adaptation of Hindu ideas plays on the concepts. Ectoplasmic manifestations are not phantoms or ghosts, although in their symbolic repertory (white, shapeless, animate) they conform to an ancient vocabulary of spirit, and ectoplasm as spirit-made-matter also stretches from ethereal, phantasmic whiteness, exemplified by Helen Duncan's yards of white satin, to a state of emergent being, typified by the cold, formless lumps of some sort of tissue, as produced by Eva Carrière and Margery Crandon.

But these poles correspond to two classes of phenomena, conflated under the single idea of ectoplasm. As we have seen, Myers and others in the SPR posited, on the one hand, spirit controls who were 'projections of the double'—namely, the spirit of a person—and, on the other, talked about 'precipitations of the *akās*'—the non-personal, universal energy that flows through and unites creation. The ectoplasmic effluvia and pseudopods that Carrière and Crandon also spewed do not body forth the mediums' own vital spirits, or even the spirit of their spirit controls. They are phantasmic templates on which the conjured spirit—the 'incorporeal personal agent'— makes his or her mark—using touch to guarantee presence. Someone dead was still someone in the Christian sense, but was also dispersed into a generalized energy of the cosmos—a concept opposed to humanist individualism.

Elizabeth d'Espérance vividly reflects the sense of disorientation that a medium in trance experienced as she channelled a spirit, 'Anna':

Am I the white figure or am I the one in the chair? Certainly they are my lips that are being kissed. Is it my face that is wet with the tears which these good women are shedding so plentifully? Yet how can it be? It is a horrible feeling, this losing hold of one's identity. I long to put out one of these hands that are lying so helplessly, and touch someone just to know if I am myself or only a dream—if 'Anna' be I, and I am lost as it were, in her identity . . . I wonder in an agony of suspense and bewilderment, how long will there be two of us . . .?[18]

Mediums were habitually treated as mere instruments, through whom the participants access the supernatural: they themselves have the power to contact the uncanny, but this uncanny is then transmitted to the others. On account of this necessary, but somehow disparaged position of the medium, she seems to me to take the place of the sacrificial victim, with the sitters as the hierophants of the rite. The ordeal, the self-exposure of mediums like Eusapia Paladino and Margery Crandon when producing ectoplasm, also reverses the process of ritual sacrifice in one respect: animal tissue is not oblated, offered to the powers above, destroyed by fire in order to be metamorphosed into the rising smoke of the holocaust on an altar, but is produced from insubstantial lights and breezes and wispy vapours to take form down below as living matter—temporarily. The medium is desecrated in an act of psychological abjection in order to recuperate, from the other side, lost flesh, consumed creatures. She turns smoke back into live cinders, to return—and reverse—Mallarmé's metaphor for the soul, and she thereby offers proof of the existence of matter beyond the known material conditions, and consequently, of life after death.

The spiritualist seance does not replicate a blood offering to the gods—it recasts sacrifice in the context of an industrial and scientific age, just as the medium, uttering messages from spirit controls, or marking gnomic phrases at the promptings of voices, harks back to the sibyl and Delphic oracles which Myers had studied, while also reproducing the action of nineteenth-century progressive industrial technology. The high Victorian commitment to processes of scientific objectivity led the explorers of seance phenomena down a blind alley, but in this they were men and women of their time, when unexplained natural forces required ordering and harnessing to be converted into material—and spiritual—goods.

While Myers' metaphysics of telepathic and subliminal selves shadow forth a strong psychological tendency this century, the astral language of spirit that he and his peers deployed has been denatured by the same decades' deepest experiences. The yearnings of Myers and Sidgwick, and, later, Oliver Lodge or Mrs Duncan's clients for an immortal and metaphysical dimension to human life—not survival in others' memories, but survival itself, as a wraith, as a spirit—presents us with the final, doomed twist in the religious wager that Darwin and Freud had closed down. Adam Phillips has remarked: 'Darwin and Freud, that is to say, in their quite different ways are persuading us to become good losers. . . . It is as though, they suggest, we have added to the ordinary suffering of biological life the extraordinary suffering of our immortal longings, of our will to permanence.'[19] Late Victorians in the SPR and their many faithful followers later were not prepared to be losers. One of the recurrent events in the lives of all the SPR members is prize-winning: these men were stars at school, in college, and expected to master a world which would not offer them the kind of contest they had expected. They did indeed suffer from immortal longings, for a will to permanence. It is almost too apt, though it shows the punning agility of dreams, that for a time they even tried to turn spirit solid, to grasp a cloud, to capture the ether as ectoplasm. Their experiments denatured the language of spirit they were adapting when they forced metaphorical axioms into literal realizations. However, it is a profound paradox that, while Myers' psychology encloses lasting ideas about human consciousness, the methods he and his successors applied to demonstrating their conjectures reveal only human yearnings.

The story of ectoplasm—from Eusapia Paladino to Helen Duncan and her sample of cheap satin—embodies the bankruptcy of a long chapter of spiritual questing. But the quest also reveals how far signs, under pressure from history, can move. It is not known exactly how Paladino and Carrière and the others produced the various phenomena, and all the struggles of the SPR never did discover their methods; but of course it was folly to imagine that because a cause could not be established, there must be a paranormal or psychic origin. William James touched the heart of the process that made possible this chapter of inquiry and the direction it took when he warned how belief helps create fact. Many of his contemporaries and colleagues were looking through a telescope from the wrong end, questing proof of the spirit when they could have attended more closely to the psyche.

While members of the SPR struggled to do with spirit and spirits, a concurrent tendency was carrying many others to question consciousness itself. The defining human capacity for reflexivity led these artists, writers, and thinkers to ponder their own processes of cognition and interpretation. The crucial next step after the positivist methods of the SPR becomes an inquiry into reflexivity: to understand consciousness itself by questioning the way we understand ourselves as thinking, perceiving selves. In this complex and tentative fashion, many questors after spirit undertook the unfinished, long journey inwards.

Around 1855, Justinus Koerner, poet and doctor, began adding fanciful interpretations to the popular game of imagining devils and monsters in ink blots.

24

The Rorschach Test; or, Dirty Pictures

Visible things always hide other visible things.

René Magritte

The artists' practice of dreaming into stains and marks in order to invent new compositions took a psychological turn in Romantic literary circles in Germany, when the doctor and poet Justinus Koerner (1786–1862) began transforming smudges and blots on his letters to friends by doodling figures he divined in the shapes; later, he spattered ink on to paper on purpose, and then took the further step of folding it to produce a symmetrical image (Figure 26, p. 307). He enhanced his fantasia by adding brushmarks—of eyes or other features. Skeletons, ghosts, imps, bats, and moths predominated, and he wrote whimsical verses to accompany them. Koerner suffered from very poor eyesight, so this was his way of transforming incapacitating blurs into aesthetic 'creatures of chance'.[1] The practice caught on, he reported in 1857, after some of his works were 'joyfully taken up in lotteries in Stuttgart and Dresden, which had been organised for the poor by charitable women'.[2] As a new parlour game, blots were genial successors of silhouettes: they offered a different kind of portrait, closer to fortune-telling, and just as Lavater had claimed seriously to diagnose character from his shadow play, so Koerner's entertainment was destined to become an instrument of clinical psychology.

After studying medicine at Tübingen, Koerner became friends with several writers among the German Romantics who were interested in fairy-tales and the new scientific psychology, including Adelbert von Chamisso. His first published volume of poems was called *Reiseschatten* ('Shadows of Voyages'). He explored dream states, somnambulism, Spiritualism, and the occult, as well as healing magic in several studies, including a biography published in 1857 of Anton Mesmer, the discoverer of 'animal magnetism'. He was intrigued that his *Klecksographien*, from the German *Klecks*, meaning splodge or blotch, produced figures that harked back to ancient figures of idols, mummies, and pagan gods, and he linked this to the very make-up of the human mind, thus interpreting fantasy as psychological revelation, and grounding the occult in physiology.

The practice that became the official psychological test in effect began as a parlour game, played by philanthropic ladies running blotting bees and an English dentist ('to the King of Belgium', no less) who created an autograph album that he called *The Ghosts of My Friends* (1910). He asked friends to sign their names along the fold of a page and then closed it to blot it: the 'ghost' then emerged on both sides of the gutter.[3]

These ways of tapping the unconscious remained unofficial and per-sonal—and playful. By contrast, in 1921 the Swiss psychologist Hermann Rorschach (1884–1922) began conducting interviews with schizophrenic patients using a series of ten picture-cards, five in colour and five in black and white, to stimulate their responses and recognition (Plate 7).[4] As every-one knows, the Rorschach test entails precisely finding meanings where there is nothing represented, only abstract and random symmetries, and it applied the results to the diagnosis of character. In many ways, Rorschach was continuing the age-old methods of fortune-telling. From antiquity, divination of every kind—from the quivering of a sacrificed animal's innards to the casting of coins or sticks or the flight of ravens or the scrutiny of tea leaves or coffee grounds or indeed the reading of any set of unintelli-gible and accidental marks—could establish a meaningful link between happenstance and someone's personal character and destiny: in a sense all mantic and oracular methods aim at a form of psychological illumination. The Rorschach test adapted Leonardo-esque ideas of fantasia and Cozens' uses of blots to psychological purposes. Numerous techniques of unravelling nature's riddles and reconstituting its secret patterns to become intelligible show a riotous imagination in play with curiosity, desire, and the longing for consolation.

Rorschach was inspired, he said, by *Klecksen*, as well as by the children's game of gazing at clouds and finding phenomena floating therein. He had decided against a career as an artist like his father, to become instead a psychiatrist. In Zurich, also the birthplace of his contemporary Carl Jung (b. 1875), he famously developed his instrument of psychological analysis, by transferring the primary burden of interpretation to the client/patient or subject, and then reinterpreting the responses to reveal the person's character. This process extended the interchange between soothsayer and petitioner, but made it open and transactional, whereas in fortune-telling (crystal-gazing, palm-reading) it remains unspoken, subliminal. In this way, he medicalized age-old methods of divination from the promptings of random and inchoate ciphers, and claimed for scientific psychology a pro-cess of imaginative decryption: this was a crucial, as well as a symptomatic, step in the delineation of unique personhood.

Rorschach died in 1922 at the young age of 37, the year after the pub-lication of his book *Psychodiagnostik*. His test has remained famous, and was very widely used as a diagnostic tool throughout the Fifties and Sixties in different parts of the world, with real consequences for many patients involved.

In 1945, Rorschach tests were administered to Nazi leaders and their collaborators (twenty-one were tested during the Nuremberg trials, and 209 in Copenhagen). The experiments were not conducted for official purposes of the court, but out of curiosity for what they might reveal. The results were not used as evidence, and were published only recently, in 1995.[5] Eichmann was also tested, in 1961, before his trial in Jerusalem. No single profile of a Nazi psychology crystallized from their responses, which was disappointing to those who wished to define it in order to contain it in the future: in this sense again, the motive behind Rorschach testing echoes the ambition of fortune-telling to peer into the unknown and ward off impending danger.

The tests have remained in clinical use, though the secrecy that kept the original set of cards from public view has been breached, and their adherents are losing ground and have recently come under scrutiny and serious criticism. Yet some still value the method, the psychologist Eric Zillmer, for example, maintaining that 'the Rorschach is not an X-ray of the mind or of the soul as is often the popular opinion, but it can project a picture of the psychology of the person, when administered and interpreted correctly'.[6] Its principal drawbacks, in his opinion, are the time it takes to administer and the complexity of collating the responses: in a high-pressure epoch of dwindling resources, multiple-choice questionnaires are quicker, standard-ized, and therefore preferred. It is also the case that in the intervening years since 1921, Rorschach's butterfly patterns have become so popular and so familiar that few people, taking the test, could respond to the cards in all innocence.

In 1984 Andy Warhol carefully reproduced on huge canvases (some as large as 164 × 115 inches) a series of Rorschach patterns, some in stark black and white, some in sumptuous gold on white, some in muddied layers of colour. By magnifying them to these dramatic proportions, turning any smears and runs and stains into formal marks, Warhol brought out the abstract, hieratic power and even Zen-like intensity of the patterns' aesthetic of randomness-in-symmetry. But this paradox is closely shadowed by another: a non-figurative sequence of forms, intentionally meaningless and openly inviting attributed significance, appears to be verging on obscenity, as it were speaking a language that is not quite intelligible but sounds suspiciously filthy: Rorschachs really can look very like office party jokes, xeroxes of bottoms pressed to the glass of the photocopier.

Warhol adroitly achieves a state of suspension between a kind of apathetic, affectless autism and sensational, explosive even, material in a great number of his works in all media. In his Rorschach paintings, Warhol shows that 'no

form is so "innocent" (or abstract) that it can ever   he corruption of a
projective interpretation, a "seeing-in" or a "seein   [7]

The intrinsically organic suggestiveness of the   which must often
provoke tension in psychiatric patients asked to res   ith their fantasies,
swells in Warhol's paintings to flaunt a kind of pornographic brinkmanship.
Made by pressing two sides together and stroking them down, the patterns
intrinsically stir thoughts of contact, of privy touch, of orifices. (There is a
joke about the test which describes how a doctor exclaims at the thoughts
the patient reveals, only to have the patient protesting, 'But it's your fault for
showing me such dirty pictures!') The contemporary British artist Cornelia
Parker went straight to the heart of this question with a recent print of a
Rorschach image; she called it 'Pornographic Drawing' and made the blot
with ink ground from videotapes which had been seized and destroyed by
British customs authorities. But the title also invites a 'reading' of the image
as the imprint of female genitals—a chance occurrence of the hard-core
shot known as 'split beaver'.[8]

While painting his Rorschachs, Warhol was still involved in his lifelong
adventures in portraiture: after the famous sequences of icons of pop idols,
the extraordinary slow-motion film studies of individuals alone under the
camera's scrutiny, the *Interview* magazine paparazzi encounters, he explored
body art ('Piss Paintings') as autographic display. The Rorschach pictures
are not abstracts, not exactly, but an extension of his abiding obsession with
dissolving the boundary between private and public domains, and achieving
maximum exposure for every object of his curiosity. The very concept of
the standard Rorschach cards epitomizes yet another, Warholian paradox,
that an identical mark can still be saturated with personal difference: every
card becomes different according to the beholder's fantasy, just as every
Brillo Box or Marilyn that Warhol made to look the same is also different.

Neither Rorschach himself nor any of his precursors considered isolating
the particular perceptual phenomenon that sees faces in the clouds and
castles in the air; but the faculty of deciphering figures in random marks
has recently been given a technical name by psychologists: *pareidolia*.
This neologism, coined from Greek *para* (beside, with a suggestion of amiss)
and *eidolon*, arises from strong interest in subjective perception as a prime
part of the workings of consciousness—a return to *fantasia*. Questions about
the origins of such phenomena now probe the mysteries of the human
mind, and find there the undecidability that used to wrap heavenly portents:
from that inward turn of the uncanny at the end of the eighteenth century,
the challenge no longer consists in distinguishing devil from divinity, but
madness from sanity. By the nineteenth century, wide research into cognition and states of mind had developed the strong idea that Freud made
familiar as the unconscious, and powers of apprehension were turned back

from God to the individual, and grounded in the psyche. For Freud this was shaped by the singular childhood experiences of a person; whereas for Jung this unconscious was a pool in which every human bathed (the collective unconscious).

Since then, and continuing into the present time, the problem undergoes another shape shift: the chief sticking point now concerns the status of the subject *qua* subject: am I experiencing this, or is something or someone experiencing it through me? Or can I know if this is or is not the case? Could I be the mere object of the phenomenon, its instrument and not its perceiver?

The term 'pareidolia', coined in psychological circles, has not yet been defined in print dictionaries like the *OED*. It has been posted for discussion on the Web—mostly on self-professed sceptics' sites—since around 1999, and it defines a perceived image which occurs spontaneously as an illusion—the profile of the devil in smoke rising from the World Trade Center in that now famous photograph would be an example of an illusion, but distinct from a delusion, since any observer can see it. Or, as in Leonardo's and Botticelli's mental exercises and in Rorschach tests, pareidolia can be consciously adopted and fostered by the perceiver. Another neologism, *apophenia*, was made up in 1958 to describe specifically crazy delusions, which are not recognized as illusions by the beholder, as in visions. These can inspire great horror and pain: so many forms of madness drive sufferers to see significant and ominous patterns in sounds, numbers, dates, as well as visual impressions.[9] Examples are too numerous to relate: but Martin Luther threw an ink bottle at the devil, while Judge Schreber, when he was undergoing his bouts of madness, wrote that 'the sun has for years spoken with me in human words and thereby reveals herself [Schreber is writing in German] as a living being'.[10] And there is Freud's analysis of Leonardo's painting of St Anne with the Madonna and Child in the Louvre, in which he draws attention to the outline of a vulture descried, as 'an unconscious picture-puzzle', in the drapery wound round the Virgin Mary's knees. Freud links this with Leonardo's nursling memories: 'when I was in my cradle, a vulture came down to me, and opened my mouth with its tail, and struck me many times with its tail against my lips.'[11] The shape of the drapery coincides exactly, Freud reports, with this visionary configuration: the tail feathers touching the Christ-child's mouth in the picture.

At one level, pareidolia extends into psychotic and paranoid territory powers of pattern recognition intrinsic to many widespread practices in circulation among completely sane people (unless belief in such automatically disqualifies you): astrology, for example, or any number of fortune-telling methods. But at another level, such extremes of imposing intelligibility only continue the ordinary cognitive processes that gave us the beauty and order of the constellations in the heavens, hermeneutics in art appreciation (as in Freud's excited comments on Leonardo), or even meaning in music.

Pareidolia casts the observer as the medium of the message, and throws doubt on the message's autonomous existence apart from that observer, let alone its veracity. Struggle between these contradictory points of view, between design and chance, between the objective and the subjective, the physical and the metaphysical, continues to fuel intense discussion and activity around the quest for the nature and character of spirit, late in the Victorian period and into the twentieth century. For when God departed, another first cause was sought: it is one of the sharpest contradictions that the rational resistance to subjectivity undergirds the paranormal search for external explanations; that the very rejection of significance in visions such as *fata morgana* and pareidolia powered the quest for impersonal and objective forces that would explain random patterns, chaotic formlessness, and other phenomena that eluded full understanding. The psychic researcher F. W. H. Myers explicitly fingered the heavenly portent as a test case, when he told an anecdote about the philosopher Henry Sidgwick meeting the Italian revolutionary Mazzini at a dinner party. Mazzini had come upon a crowd who were gazing at a cross in the sky. Mazzini could not see it, but the people around him insisted that he must be able to. Eventually, he found someone, 'one gazer who looked rather more intelligent than the rest. . . . Mazzini took hold of his arm, gave him a slight shake, and said to him, "There is not any cross at all." A change came over the gazer's face. . . . "No, as you say, there is no cross at all." '[12]

Henry Sidgwick was very impressed by this anecdote, and stressed its relevance to the issue of evidence in all inquiries into unexplained, divine or metaphysical happenings. There may have been a light effect, a parting in the clouds, a luminous cross-shape; but can that be ascribed to external agency, and what external agency could that be, when Anglican Christianity had decided that all miracles had ceased since New Testament times?

A vast and enlightened body of theology and philosophy—not least the opposition to witch-hunters—has issued warnings through history about discovering in the products of fantasia anything more solid or indeed truthful than a subjective reflection of a person's mind. Yet, as we have seen, the Rorschach test has been used as a diagnostic tool for personality since the 1920s in Zurich, and remains in clinical use, giving results that affect patients' destinies, establishing their guilt in crimes and their mental condition. Rorschachs represent a prime modern example of the shift away from external portraiture to internal imaging and the corresponding rise in the value of the subjective mind's vagaries in the search for what it means to be somebody.[13]

Day-dreaming and sky-gazing are quintessentially human capacities, and it was the mark of Modernism that its writers—Proust, Henry James, James Joyce—finally transmuted the holy terror of multiplicity and plurality, of inconstancy and amorphousness, into a passionate curiosity about complexity. 'My name is Legion' became not the devil's banner, but the proud device of the self, the proof that an autonomous being was alive and able to receive impressions actively. The colossus of French Romanticism, Victor Hugo, pointed the way into the fractured consciousness of the twentieth century, when in self-chosen exile in Guernsey from 1851 to 1870, he improvised paintings from blots and smudges.

Hugo brought his own inner turbulence to the making of blots, marks, and spills. He experimented with *Tache*, or stain paintings, in which he discerned a whole Gothic phantasmagoria of ruined castles, leaning towers, abysses, crags, shipwrecks, gallows, crooked and winding stairs, and many sea creatures and monsters, including a colossal toadstool, all plunged in moody chiaroscuro and velvety washes of sepia and sable.[14] Mostly, the poet metamorphosed chance marks into recognizable if imaginary scenes, but sometimes he simply called the resulting picture 'Abstract Composition'; he transformed his own name into a giant octopus, crumbling towers, ragged storm-tossed clouds, or looming apocalyptic spectres.[15] Dramatically depicting his own psyche through these improvised, accidental marks, he placed himself back into the image they make through the letters that make up his identity, as well as recognizing in them the turmoil of his feelings. Yet the poet's impassioned, moody watercolours do convey his sense of another world, beyond the physical senses and reached through concentrated fantasy. He also made some wonderfully inventive *Pliages*, or 'foldings', to produce elaborate crustaceous traceries of symmetrical diaperings—another prophecy of a coming aesthetic, but in this case of the Rorschach test. An eloquent, fluent, sensuous watercolourist, he often strikes a boldly Expressionist note, as if he were hailing Pollock or Cy Twombly from the other side of the twentieth century. Hans Arp, the artist, commented that 'Chance art, as expressive of modernity, is therefore uniquely and *necessarily* modern.'[16]

In the case of Victor Hugo, intellectual curiosity fostered commitment to magic and the occult. After the death of his much loved daughter Léopoldine in a drowning accident, Victor Hugo became very involved in table-turning, planchette or Ouija board experiments, and other means of contacting spirits. Léopoldine frequently spoke to him. But he also began receiving copious messages from all kinds of visitors, including Dante, Galileo, and Voltaire, and even 'the Ocean', who held forth to the company in an astonishing outpouring of rhetorical bombast scattered with furious expletives. Some of the communications passed straight into print. As someone observed at the time, 'Victor Hugo was channelling Victor Hugo.'[17]

In the essay *On Being Ill*, when Virginia Woolf lay in bed staring out of the window at the 'gigantic cinema' in the sky, she reflected on the eddies and currents of her own attention as it figures out the drama of the nothing unfurling under her gaze: the stir up in the clouds mimics her 'endless activity' of thinking, and of that special human act—reflexivity. Her reverie wanders over the multiplicity of consciousness, her own and others', and she connects the process with the development of her self. She drifts back in time, and considers 'those embryo lives which attend about us in early youth until "I" suppressed them'.[18] That note of regret that Woolf sounds, with its slight Freudian ring, does not contain the shadow that was starting to spread over the concept of the dreaming 'I', or eye: Victor Hugo was filled with Romantic confidence in his personal mastery; Rorschach did not question that patients would disclose their inner selves in response to his 'blots'; and Virginia Woolf was nostalgic for the polymorphousness of lost youthful selves, easily stirred to projective fantasy.

Gradually, by contrast, another question was gathering force: was this dreaming self in control? Or, as Lewis Carroll had teased in the last chapter of *Through the Looking Glass*, was the Red King in Alice's dream, or was she in his? ' "This is a serious question, my dear," ' Alice tells Kitty. ' ". . . He was part of my dream, of course—but then I was part of his dream, too!" ' The closing words of the book turn to the reader: 'Which do *you* think it was?'[19] Jorge Luis Borges consciously responded to this many times in his writing, but it is his story 'The Circular Ruins', first published in 1941, that crystallizes for contemporaries the full disturbing potential of Carroll's playful challenge: is the dreamer being dreamed?[20] This was no mere shivery-pleasurable Chinese box of a literary conceit. It fingered a crucial instability at the centre of ideas about the uses of fantasy, especially, as Carroll had intimated and Borges echoes, in the infinite duplication of images of self that new media brought about.

Part X

Film

George Meliès, showman and pioneer film-maker,
delighted in photography's powers of illusion, comic and
macabre: his wife, Jeanne d'Alcy, appears as a victim of
the guillotine.

25
Nice Life, an Extra's

> We must reveal an individual reflected in the glass who persists in his illusory country ... and who feels the shame of being only a simulacrum obliterated by the night, existing only in glimpses.
>
> Jorge Luis Borges

Edgar Allan Poe's tale 'The Domain of Arnheim' (1847) features a vastly wealthy aesthete, Mr Ellison, of a cynical, materialist, misanthropic tendency, who scorns natural scenery: every view or picturesque scene is marred by some error or infelicity that needs to be moved or removed. Then Ellison suggests another explanation for the lack of pleasing aesthetic in nature: 'There *may* be a class of beings, human once, but now invisible to humanity, to whom, from afar, our disorder may seem order—our unpicturesqueness picturesque; in a word, the earth-angels, for whose scrutiny more especially than our own, and for whose death-refined appreciation of the beautiful, may have been set in array by God the wide landscape-gardens of the hemispheres.'[1]

Poe's tale was prescient in ways he could not have consciously known, for it announces a world of disincarnate intelligences at work organizing the world and human experience. For the Gothic fantasist Edgar Allan Poe, the idea that an Other was governing the workings of chance and ruling human experience of nature's sights issued another challenge to creative imagination. Ellison's idea of earth-angels who have past beyond death and been 'refined' in the process, proposes a relationship between art and nature that differs from Albertian mimesis or Leonardoesque fantasia or later Romantic or Surrealist views of the imagination's role. After God and the hand of Providence, after *Natura Pictrix*, Poe brings into play another set of organizing powers, spirits who assemble and reassemble meaning in the world as they see fit, practising their own unknowable processes of pareidolia. Nature itself, as we experience it, might itself be a *fata morgana* of hidden patterns and harmonious order deployed for the satisfaction of some other, higher gaze. It projects the significance of random arrangements on this plane beyond human recognition altogether into the minds of impersonal powers.

With this eerie, elliptical proposal, Poe foresees the coming of the post-human age, when human beings will no longer control the organizing intelligence of the planet, but be subordinate to other principles. 'The Domain of Arnheim' thus becomes a prophetic allegory of cyberspace and its influence on consciousness now.[2]

Mr Ellison will not, however, accept our subordination to the imaginative aesthetic of some intangible otherworldly beings. He rebels against the earth-angels, and like his predecessors among such spirit rebellions, he aspires to become like them. He dedicates himself to disposing of nature according to his desires, reorganizing the scenery of the domain of Arnheim in order to adapt it for the human gaze, to please 'the eyes which were to behold it *on earth*' (emphasis added). Helped by the inheritance of an even more fabulous fortune, the aesthete sets about this task, and 'The Domain of Arnheim' ends with a dream voyage into an artificial paradise of Ellison's devising. A canoe takes the voyager gliding down a river and through a gorge, and the tale then climaxes in a truly entrancing finale:

Meantime the whole Paradise of Arnheim bursts upon the view. There is a gush of entrancing melody; there is an oppressive sense of strange sweet odor;—there is a dream-like intermingling to the eye of tall slender Eastern trees—bosky shrubberies—flocks of golden and crimson birds—lily-fringed lakes—meadows of violets, tulips, poppies, hyacinths and tuberoses—long intertangled lines of silver streamlets—and, upspringing confusedly from amid all, a mass of semi-Gothic, semi-Saracenic architecture, sustaining itself as if by a miracle in mid-air, glittering in the red sunlight with a hundred oriels, minarets, and pinnacles; and seeming the phantom handiwork, conjointly, of the Sylphs, of the Fairies, of the Genii, and of the Gnomes.

This is a truly enchanted vision of *fata morgana*: castles in the air. Significantly, Poe's poetic imagination carries him beyond the figure of Mr Ellison, the supreme landscape gardener, on to more ethereal makers—those fairies and genii and gnomes.

Mr Ellison was modelled perhaps on William Beckford, the fabulously rich English dandy, proprietor of Fonthill Abbey, where Alexander Cozens, of the 'blot' theory of picture-making, tutored the young Beckford, and Philippe de Loutherbourg staged his *son-et-lumière* spectaculars. The Sultan Vathek, hero of Beckford's novel, written in 1782 and read by Poe, also plunges into a phantasmagoric, Faustian quest for all knowledge and power. (Borges called *Vathek* 'the first truly atrocious Hell in literature', which takes the reader into 'the tunnels of a nightmare.')[3] His annihilation in the abyss for his depravity becomes an aesthetic self-immolation in Poe's vision: a hero turned into image.

René Magritte read Poe's tale in Baudelaire's highly wrought translation,[4] and it inspired several pictures, some called 'The Domain of

Arnheim', others 'L'Appel des Cimes', made over more than twenty years after 1936 (Plate 8).[5] Magritte refused to expound his own riddles, and it is beside the point to try and unpick them, though not entirely redundant to loosen at least the many knots he ties in the eye-strings of ordinary perception.

Magritte was in dispute with the Surrealists and their leader André Breton, and became opposed to Surrealist obscurity, to reeling flights of fancy, as he saw it. In a spirit of contradiction, he liked to shatter illusions by calling attention to the tricks and devices he used to create them. Whereas Breton is a conjuror who lets nothing slip, and revels in his abstruse linkages and metaphorical inventions, Magritte makes plain his sleights of hand, forcing us to see his riddles as riddles, and never taking pity and allowing a solution. His deadpan mysteries resolutely remain exteriors; the interiors he exposes only serve to deepen the sense of vacancy: there is nothing and nobody there except paint. This muteness turns into a kind of existential autism, in stark contrast to Breton's rapturous multiplicity of selves.[6]

Many objects in Magritte's art—bowler hats, street lamps, harness bells, clouds—insistently present blank solid inexpressiveness as part of this rejection; they discountenance orthodox Surrealist hopes for fruitful significance, so much in evidence in Breton's apocalyptic poem of 1940, *Fata Morgana*. Whereas Breton avowedly aimed at applying analogy with loquacious ebullience in order to seed more and more meanings, Magritte likes to baffle and to silence and to conceal. His cloudscapes—his 'intrusive skies' in David Sylvester's phrase—first appear in the late Twenties, most compellingly in *The False Mirror*, a painting of a huge Cyclopean eye with the iris swimming with clouds around the disturbingly blank spot of the pupil.[7] Typical Magritte clouds float above this vision; fleecy white trooping cushions, against an uninflected azure sky, such conventionally idlyllic etheric heavens, bland and placid vehicles bringing *calme et volupté*, provide the signature motif in the music of the banal Magrittean uncanny. The artist was also struck by an essay that Poe had written, in which he comments that the word 'infinity' conceals meanings like a cloud.

Clouds also play a significant part in the series of paintings after Poe's tale: so, when Magritte represents 'The Domain of Arnheim', what does he show us of the earth-angels' vision of the world?

In one variation on the Poe story painted in 1938, two eggs lie on a window sill, while the mountain range behind rises to a bird's head with spread wings, as if the eggs had been laid by the figure in the rock. In another, of eleven years later, the bird-mountain rears up in the landscape, while its true reflection (not reversed) reappears in the shattered pieces of the window pane—as if the pane were a two-way mirror. 'The outside is brought inside in a devastating way,' writes David Sylvester, 'the painting giving the impression of that claustrophobic moment of terror when a bird hurtles into a window.'[8] But this impact cannot quite have happened in this manner, as the artist contrives his favourite confusion between reality and image, and the snowy stone bird remains in and of the mountain. So it is Magritte, and through him, *we* who configure the mountain as a bird, in the same way as plains or valley dwellers give anthropomorphic or zoomorphic names to landmarks and peaks. Furthermore, the broken shards of mirror, as in other pictures by Magritte, retain the image that had appeared through the window, and endow it with painted materiality, adding to the puzzle-ment. The mirror then comes to command, within the limits of Magritte's painting, a condition of material illusion which could make sense only in a different perceptual universe, one that could exist from another, unseen category of perceptive beings. The vision of the eagle presents a variety of the earth-angels in Poe's tale, one of that class of invisible beings whom Poe imagined holding the unseen order of nature in their gaze.

Magritte's brain-teasers are called 'The Domain of Arnheim' after Poe's story, because it is not possible for us to know, or even to imagine, what might be the harmonious arrangements devised by nature to satisfy hypo-thetical earth-angels. Magritte responds to the Paris Surrealists' doctrinal trust in the powers of the unconscious to pattern vision, writing, life, and destiny, by offering a dead end to interpretation: there is no way out of his visual riddle.

The clouds sail into view in such a picture as ciphers that encipher nothing: no phantom images lurk in their fluffy pillows, no *fata morganas* or haloes of glory fill their vacuity. Magritte was bad-temperedly resistant to human and imaginative imposition of meaning: he protested against the desire for understanding: 'our gaze always wants to penetrate further so as to see at last the object, the reason for our existence',[9] and in enigmatic picture after picture of blank skies and inscrutable clouds, of the sky as 'a screen over a void', he rejected both cognition and fantasy. Only the earth-angels would ever know what might be visible.

How does this relate to spirits and spirit today? Poe's story and Magritte's response hold the key, it seems to me, to understanding the change that has occurred since Victorian scientific speculation brought communications media into the search for explanations of the unexplained, including human quiddity. Just as the angle of view shifted from the Albertian and Newtonian observer to the Romantic, Kantian, subjective percipient, so now it has shifted again: Poe's earth-angels, disembodied, their consciousness inaccess-ible to humans, present a rich allegory of twentieth- and twenty-first-century cyber-dwellers.

Invisible seers who recompose human languages of sign and vision postulate another form of subjectivity, a perceiving subject who is indeed

Other and outside our frame of reference. This seer or earth-angel of Edgar Allen Poe is a cyborg before the concept was invented—occupying a similar instrumental space to the proliferating processes and instruments that have been invented to penetrate the mysteries of invisible, hidden worlds, both inner and outer, and to look back at ourselves.

In medicine, optical and other probes now include, besides the veteran telescope and microscope, an ever-growing variety of body-imaging techniques. EEG scans (electroencepholography) were invented in 1875; a hundred years later, CAT scans (Computerised Axial Tomography) were discovered—they use multiple X-rays to build up a complete picture. Ultrasound scans, PET (Positron Emission Topography), fMRI (functional Magnetic Resonance Imaging), and nuclear imaging all provide pictures of inaccessible organs and processes. For forensic purposes, when the need to establish the identity of victims and perpetrators unites medical requirements and the comfort of the bereaved (after catastrophes such as earthquakes and floods) with the demands and interests of the law, digitized analyses are increasingly applied. In Britain, the government in 2005 presented a Bill to Parliament requiring all residents to carry identity cards with digitized data.

The fields of medicine, security, and surveillance join the extensive area of communications, especially in the growing use of tagging prisoners on remand, or paedophiles or other individuals on lists of dangerous persons. Orienting satellites—also used in computerized car maps—are among the many processes which connect us ethereally with one another—through the mobile phone, through the digital photograph dispatched from the phone. They make available in all these different ways an alternative knowledge of ourselves as bodies in the world, and in consequence a way of seeing ourselves from outside ourselves. They enhance reflexiv: institute a changed self-consciousness.

These are not the only instruments of mediated consciousness: fictive and virtual media expand the range further. Once human perception is dethroned from its traditional role as observer and interpreter, the possibilities of what lie beyond the threshold of the sensory—inwardly and outwardly—became tantalizingly vast. The new media have become intertwined with a freshly imagined, Other consciousness, not divine, not perhaps omnipotent, but endowed with the ethereal intelligence of earth-angels and capable of discovering coherence and cogency where they appear to be absent and of establishing another order of experience, itself a form of light, the contemporary phantoms of moving and acoustic media.

In 1847, when Poe was writing, they were just beginning; by the end of the century, radio and cinema had arrived, and television, while still remote, was in the offing. Thinking about the changes in self-consciousness that the new earth-angels brought about, Walter Benjamin noted: 'The feeling of strangeness that overcomes the actor before the apparatus . . . is basically of the same kind as the estrangement felt before one's own image in the mirror. But now the reflected image has become separable, transportable. And where is it transported? Before the public.'[10] What happens to that stranger has added a dimension to experience which has changed our sense of who we are.

In his first novel *Mashen'ka* (1926), Vladimir Nabokov envisaged the afterlife in the language of film, and imagined the continued existence of the soul as an extra: 'As he walked he thought how his shade would wander from city to city, from screen to screen, how he would never know what sort of people would see it or how long it would roam in the world.'[11] The extra participates in the action in the background or from the sidelines, and performs an identity that is of its nature contingent, almost but not quite superfluous. A 'figurant' in French, the extra is chosen for qualities that lend him to blending into the scene without becoming too visible: Nabokov's character has gained a kind of perpetual anonymity of the modern man in the crowd.

A lesser-known fiction writer than Nabokov who takes up spectral presence and new identities in the medium of film was the amanuensis, inspiration, and friend of Jorge Luis Borges, and a fellow Argentinian— Adolfo Bioy Casares. Bioy's novella, *The Invention of Morel* (1940) is a strange, compressed, enthralling fable, written in the form of a diary by a fugitive from justice. He has escaped to an island, which seems abandoned, and is struggling for survival among the ruins. But every day at the same time he encounters a mysterious group of elegant party-goers who walk to a certain place to view the sunset, and he begins to fall in love with a woman, Faustine, though she never appears to see him, or indeed, as he finds out, the space-time in which he exists. Gradually he pieces together that the inventor, Morel, has created machines—hydraulic machines worked by the tides—that project the island's former inhabitants as they were in life, doing and saying the things they said, in the places where they were, thus preserving them eternally. In the process of granting them this uncanny immortality and perpetuity, bound to their memories, his machines steal their souls. Gradually, the narrator decides to operate the machines on himself; he begins to feel himself disappearing and becoming one of Morel's undead: 'I have scarcely felt the progression of my death; it began in the tissues of my left hand; it has advanced greatly and yet it is so gradual, so continuous, that I do not notice it. I am losing my sight. My sense of touch has gone; my skin is falling off . . . My soul has not yet passed to the image.'[12] He welcomes the state, as he believes he will find Faustine in the phantasmic realm created by the invention of Morel.

The novella is inspired: highly evocative, eerie, comic, genuinely enchanted, a personal apocalypse both romantic and bleak. Bioy was the source of several of Borges's plot lines, as the latter was quick to acknowledge. Borges's darkly smiling shadow falls across Morel's island, and his recursive fables about doubles, dreams, labyrinths, copies—'The Circular Ruins', as cited before, but also 'The Garden of the Forking Paths' and 'Pierre Menard, Author of Don Quixote', are closely related to Bioy's delicate and enticing fantasy about the palimpsestic contiguity of reality and illusion. Bioy, however, ties his invention more closely to contemporary, technological experience than does Borges in his more fabulist, metaphysical ironies, and the title of his novella nods in the direction of H. G. Wells, and another extreme inventor on an island—Dr Moreau. But whereas Wells, the biologist, was concerned with eugenics and evolution and the metamorphosis of humans into hybrid animals and monsters, Bioy couches his reflections very precisely in images of film projection, and worries at the specific issue of enfleshment and consciousness: ' "The images are not alive," ' the narrator tells us. ' "But since his [Morel's] invention has blazed the trail, as it were, another machine should be invented to find out whether the images think and feel (or at least if they have the thoughts and feelings that the people themselves had when the picture was made; or course the relationship between their consciousness and these thoughts and feelings cannot be determined). . . . Someday there will be a more complete machine." '[13]

This visionary novella inspired the cult movie of the Sixties, *Last Year in Marienbad*, not altogether unexpectedly, since the eternity in which Faustine and her friends have their existence resembles cinematic reality so closely.[14] While their copies, forged by Morel, survive eternally, the original selves wither and die—a situation that has become altogether commonplace, as we are now familiar with the lingering vitality of stars and heroes, who abide as images—light in celluloid.[15]

This is the other key difference between the subjective projective imagination of Romanticism and the modern, public spectacles of earth-angel infotainment. Cinema has been implicated in haunted and magical psychology from its beginnings. Key early works—from the funny 'trick' films about apparitions and ghosts made by Georges Meliès and others (Figure 27a, p. 332), to the haunted fantasies of Expressionist German films, *Nosferatu* and *The Cabinet of Dr Caligari*. Later, intense exchanges between psychoanalysis and Hollywood, as most vividly expressed in Hitchcock's *œuvre*, confirmed this closeness. Different narrative techniques used in film have increased the ever more popular skewing of the real and the fictive, the warping of imaginary into actual, and vice versa. Invented memories correspond to the fabricated images of the movies. Vanishings and shinings, ghosts incarnate, angels on earth, beings who can fly—or teleport—from one place to another, telepathic communications—all these spirit motifs have naturalized through the big screen and the home monitor. Uncanny mental states, ranging from second sight to amnesia, are necessary to the many plots turning on disembodied identities and metamorphic possibilities; such stories move thoughts from one body into another. Deeply and more threateningly, individuals can absorb transmitted feelings and perceptions from outside their own personal borders, which then effect changes to their core, and mould their identities. These exchanges between outside and inside, between time past and time present—granulated temporal rhythms, volatile proximities, spatial vaulting, metamorphic compression and expansion— have become the stock-in-trade of the blockbuster movie, popular television, video and computer games (*The Matrix, Star Trek, Buffy the Vampire, The X Files, Lara Croft*), while, increasingly, they figure at the heart of the concerns of contemporary writers and artists.[16] The influences on this cyber-fantasy strain in entertainment remain the Old Masters of the Gothic macabre, Poe, H. P. Lovecraft, and Philip K. Dick, as Victoria Nelson has discussed in her study *The Secret Life of Puppets*. They have led the development of a new, pleasurable, psychological techno-paranoia, verging on mysticism, and its runs a live current connecting nineteenth-century psychical research to contemporary culture and states of disorientation.

As mentioned in Chapter 20 in relation to Judge Schreber, sufferers from mental disturbance began identifying their persecutors with the new media. The ideas that the psychoanalyst Victor Tausk put forward in his paper on 'The Influencing Machine'[17] inspired the contemporary American artist, Tony Oursler, to re-create a phantasmagoric *son-et-lumière* spectacle, first in Madison Square Garden, New York, and then in Soho Square, London. He called his installation after Tausk's paper, and it featured rappings and spectral voices beamed through the television, as reported by many witnesses. By this means, the artist voiced his own ideas:

Telecommunication systems such as the internet are the end product of a long drive towards the current paradox of mind/body separation. . . . This paradox of the discorporative impulse, the shedding of the physical body for the ethereal utopian virtual presence and the promises of ultimate interconnectivity is at once linked to the fear of the void, isolation, and disassociative conditions. . . . Today when the average person finds themselves increasingly engaged with mimetic systems, as they move from telephone to television to internet, and back again, the metaphor of the uncanny technological equation between life and death is all the more relevant.

Television, his art implies, has become the influencing machine on all our minds. It also sets the scene for a new afterlife, where the past meets the future and turns into an ever repeating, eternal present: 'Television archives store millions of images of the dead, which wait to be broadcas[t]   to the living. . . . at this point, the dead come back to life to have an in[fluence] on the living. . . . Television is, then, truly the spirit world of our age. it preserves images of the dead which then can continue to haunt us. . . . it also gives us the phenomenon of living ghosts, or stars as we like to call them.'[18]

Tony Oursler does not claim to be a medium or a magus. He is simply a child of the Seventies, of the television age, the same age as systems such as cable and satellite and the Web. The polyphonic aural universe fascinates Oursler as deeply as visual signals. In his art, he listens in and collects evidence of the senses in the altered conditions of consciousness that now obtain.

In his 2003 novel *Elizabeth Costello*, J. M. Coetzee also addresses the disembodied states of existence in cyberspace. In the book's closing pages, the protagonist—a famous woman writer, a manifest *alter ego* of the author as well as a kind of antagonist or doppelgänger—is waiting to pass through a gate. She does not know where she is, but she wants to travel through and onwards, and to do that, she has to pass the gatekeepers, who are asking for a statement of belief from her. We, the readers, understand, as she does not, that she has died and has become a modern version of a ghost. She is on the threshold of eternity, in that antechamber where the Egyptians first imagined the eternal judges reckoning the sum of one's life, but Coetzee pictures it as a disorientating setting which she cannot quite identify, nor can she place, the other people she sees there. Her personal apocalypse is numb and arid and empty, described with typical Coetzee parsimony of affect. She senses that it is some kind of resort, perhaps in Italy, but then it begins to feel like a detention centre of some kind, a Nazi camp, even. She finds money in her purse—'play money' it appears to her, which she has not seen before—and she wonders if the various minders and guards and waiters are in fact actors, and if the setting is in fact some kind of set. She sits at a café table, trying to compose her confession.

The couple at the next table have their little fingers hooked together. Laughingly they tug at each other; they bump foreheads, whisper. They do not seem to have confessions to write. But perhaps they are not actors, full actors . . . perhaps they are just extras, instructed to do what they do every day of their lives in order to fill out the bustle of the square, to give it verisimilitude, the reality effect. It must be a nice life, the life of an extra.

As she sits in her eerie underworld, Coetzee's *alter ego* has been pondering rather drily and weightily, as is her wont, the nature of reality and the writer's relations with it: ' "There used to be a time when we knew," ' she says in the course of one of the lectures she gives. ' "We used to believe that when the text said, 'On the table stood a glass of water,' there was indeed a table, and a glass of water on it, and we had only to look in the word-mirror of the text to see them. But all that has ended." ' Drawing attention to his own sleight of hand in writing, Coetzee has his character continue, ' "The word-mirror is broken, irreparably, it seems. About what is really going on in the lecture hall your guess is as good as mine." '

As Elizabeth Costello wanders about the antechamber of the other world, still incapable of drafting the statement demanded by the judges, she exclaims, ' "How beautiful it is, this world, even if it is only a simulacrum!" ' But to end this suspended life and be released from the camp/resort/film, Costello the writer has to surrender her doubting, sceptical mind and show that she believes in something: by a ferocious paradox, this eerie realm of unreality exacts a suspension of disbelief: ' "We can't afford unbelief," ' a woman tells her, laughing disconcertingly. ' "Only the light soul hangs in the air." '[19]

The features of Coetzee's eschatology are banal, not visionary, far more banal than Morel's desert island. But his limbo is also eerie, and that eeriness arises from the unreality of the conditions; they possess only semblance, not substance. They double the real, but turn it spectral. Reality here has been absorbed into representation, and belongs here to photography, to movies, in analog duplicity, as well as in digital virtuality. Even the language Costello hears spoken is a universal language; she wonders if it might be Esperanto. But this is, like the extras, like the scene setting, the condition of global cinema, where film characters can be beamed anywhere and understood everywhere: it is one of the common experiences of travelling great distances today that you go into a café and there is . . . the news reader from the telly at home just as you left him a few hours before but thousands of miles away, and there is Jack Nicholson and/or Julia Roberts speaking fluent Tagalog, or Gujarati. The word 'dubbing' carries a trace of doubling in English, but in French and Italian this reference becomes explicit (*doubler*, *doppiare*).

Elizabeth Costello is finally able to squeeze out of her withered heart a statement to the tribunal that she believes in something—in the survival instinct of frogs stuck in mud for the long dry season, who come to life again and dig their way out of the caked mud-flats of the Dulgannon River in rural Victoria, Australia and 'soon their voices resound again in joyous exultation beneath the vault of the heavens'.[20]

It is a complicated conclusion, and Coetzee is always opaque, with his retentive ironies and cold, autistic manner. The critic James Wood, reviewing the Coetzee novel, praised Mrs Costello's pinched *auto-da-fé*, commenting that it amounts to trusting in the life of a fiction. He writes: 'To enter the frog's life is like entering a fictional character's life . . . And this is a kind of religion, akin to the worship of a God who gives us nothing back. If it represents the paganisation of belief in God, it also represents the sacralisation of belief in fiction. Because, like suffering and death, fiction, too, is not an idea.'[21]

But Coetzee has not given up stringent irony, and he is voicing the statement about frogs and hope and the life spark through a figure who is presented in a very equivocal light and with a great deal of self-disgust. In the frogs' case, she is also given to write some repellent fulsome prose. But, far more importantly, Wood's notion of belief in fiction does not fully analyse or help us live with the spectral and false character of cinematic, digital, and virtual representations in themselves; it does not explore the differences between the varieties of phantasms haunting us now, from both mental images, on the one hand, and on the other the creatures themselves living and being, regardless of any other to observe them or utter their name—the contrast caught by Marianne Moore's 'real toads in imaginary gardens'.

Coetzee allows the writer Costello to leave the ersatz, pasteboard ante-chamber to the afterlife after she has honoured the frogs and declared her belief in them precisely because they are not inventions. They hang on to life without understanding anything; and their doing so is noble, because it is not a result of reflection or fantasy or irony, or pretence—all those human capacities that arise from our ability to tell stories to ourselves. Their act is real, not fiction. Their life cycle, she says, 'to the frogs themselves [it] is no allegory, it is the thing itself, the only thing'.[22] By contrast, fiction *is* an idea—in all its forms; the glass of water is never on the table in a book. But whereas language always allowed the imagination its place, visual technologies give it no room: through their perfect fabrications, the glass of water does appear. In this sense, Mrs Costello's surroundings are as real—or not—as the environment of film or the domain of Arnheim disposed by invisible earth-angels.

Humans differ from frogs, despite Coetzee's gloomy and abject identification with animals, because they experience life of a degree and quality that frogs do not (as far as we can tell). Humans have the kind of minds that make things up and can be persuaded to lend credence to them. Recovering the existence of that imagination has become urgent business; by a further twist, it has fallen to imagination to do the necessary work now of distinguishing spectres and resisting the new turn of the uncanny that, in the twentieth and twenty-first centuries, it looks just like home.

If real-life stories on television and in the papers communicate experiences of altered identity and lost selves, these 'true reports', like those from exotic lands during the first European voyages, are deeply entangled with imaginary materials: the agents of soul-theft number in their unappeasable company those dark and bloody ghouls, vampires, Frankenstein monsters, angels, and engines, all of them cult figures with box office clout who first materialized in eighteenth-century Gothic. At this point in the history of media and consciousness, they are the dominant spectres, and the stories which they inhabit dramatize current threats to humanity: processes of unselving and desouling.

The new species of phantasms evolving intrinsically within film have found another chronicler in the French artist Pierre Huyghe. Oursler has immersed himself in the problems of cyberspace, but, by contrast to Oursler's chilled-out, affectless acceptance, Huyghe has worked with a group of artists loosely connected under the banner of 'Relational Aesthetics', the name given their approach by the French curator Nicolas Bourriaud.[23] They oppose the spectral celluloid and digital regime, and by operating on film's illusionism, reassert the claims of the world, matter and time.

Huyghe has created a series of film works to inquire into the nature of film itself and to expose the power of the medium to fashion experience.[24] In 1996, he made a two-hour-long video called *Doublures* ('Doublings'/ 'Dubbings'), in which he turns the camera on interpreters working on film subtitles. We watch them reacting to a film we cannot see, dubbing the dialogue as it unfolds: not by accident the film is the 1982 Steven Spielberg horror film *Poltergeist*, about a nasty case of haunting, and the specifically acoustic possession of a house and its occupants. The dubbers at work supplant the actors' voices, but they have no presence: self-possession becomes endangered for everyone.[25] Dubbing/doubling another's identity has not been contained in the fictions of the movies—in call centres in India and elsewhere, employees are trained to speak the language of the customer, even allotted new American personae, names, and profiles. They have been dubbed: 'cybercoolies'.[26]

In 1999, under the title *The Third Memory*, Pierre Huyghe continued his investigation of cinematic reality. This film features the bank robber John Woytowicz, whose story inspired the classic thriller *Dog Day Afternoon*, directed by Sidney Lumet in 1972. In the film, Woytowicz was played by Al Pacino, and when Huyghe traced him after his release from prison and took him back nearly three decades later to the scene of his crime to recall it, it becomes clear that the feature film has become totally interfused with his own recollection. Woytowicz became a folk hero because he held up the bank to get money for his lover's sex-change operation, so his story itself concerns the difference of outside and inside, and involves masquerade, disguise, one self hidden inside another, a body that one feels does not belong to one. This kind of physical alteration or metamorphosis also belongs among the cluster of psychological possibilities that film has excited. On the one hand, in cinematic space-time, Nicole Kidman has a different nose in one film from another, and Al Pacino a protean body; these are then multiplied, dispersed, magnified, miniaturized, and stretched over skied billboards or captured in miniature airplane monitors or digital screens. They in turn offer a pattern for imitation by we who gaze at them and long to slough our own carcasses and adopt their faces—by cosmetic surgery, transplants, and treatments.

Huyghe went on to ask, can we arrange the form our haunting takes—even by our own past experiences? In two ways his critical challenges to cinematic 'image-flesh' demand, first, embodied consciousness—someone has to be at home, and their condition not only image-flesh. Secondly, the temporal order must be restored, time must pass. The first requires addressing the status of the image; the second demands rejoining the flux of time. His most eerie and compelling art piece, 'No Ghost Just a Shell' (2003) focuses on Annlee, a Japanese manga cartoon character (Figure 27a, p. 332). In collaboration with Philippe Parreno, Huyghe bought her from a standard catalogue produced for the animated film industry. The cost of such figures rises with the levels of complexity in the virtual character; Annlee was at the lowest end—a simple line drawing of no special distinction. Having bought her, Huyghe and Parreno brought her to life, giving her a part to play and a voice, a new kind of Olympia automaton for our times. In a short cartoon, 'Two Minutes Out of Time', she speaks of herself in a combination of first person and third person: 'She is a passer-by, an extra. She was designed just like that,' says the voice. Then, switching to the first person she appeals to the viewer:

My name, my name is Annlee. Annlee. I've a common name.
I was a frozen picture, an evidence submitted to you.
I have become animated however not by a story with a plot, no . . .
I'm haunted by your imagination . . . and that's what I want from you. . . . See,
I am not here for your amusement . . . You are here for mine![27]

Several things are happening here: Annlee's large child eyes and touching utterance provoke the kind of emotions associated with sincerity, that index of truthfulness, and so she shows up very uncomfortably the disjunction between that truthfulness freighted by affect—and truth, objective reality. This fissure has gaped wide in contemporary society and psychology, with higher value accorded to the truthfulness of emotional response, not accuracy or weight of evidence.[28] But she also changes the direction of the current between perceiver and perceived: she is haunted by us because without us, she has no existence. Annlee never did have a soul—and her body possesses only appearance. She is 'No Ghost Just a Shell'.

Fantasy characters in virtual worlds, like Annlee, now have a value in the counterpart symbolic realm of circulating money. Players in chat rooms cum computer games are engaged on interminable quests, and exchange goods and services for sums of real money, some of them very large. The new generation of computer games, called MMORPGs (massively multi-player online role-playing games) ascribe a novice an 'avatar', an *alter ego* in the phantasmic universe of the game. In 2004, 'Lineage', a new virtual world, numbered more than half a million inhabitants, all of them questing and killing with wands, ray guns, knobkerries—you name it—in search of phantom treasure and virtual power. One economist calculated that in 'Norrath', another virtual megalopolis on the Net, the real-world GNP per imaginary denizen outstripped those of India and China.[29]

In relation to the inhabitants of virtual worlds, Pierre Huyghe has asked, 'Is there a narrative for the "ghost" coming from the future?' In the case of Annlee, he supplied an answer. With his collaborator, he copyrighted her *in her own name*—thus liberating her from the market in which she originated as a commodity which could be owned by a purchaser; instead, in an elaborate charade, he legally assigned her rights over the use of her own image, thus effectively closing her participation in further art ventures. These legal and economic manœuvres resonate with the formal emancipation of slaves.[30]

By adding to our perplexities about the truth status of all representations, Annlee focuses attention on a new kind of ghost who haunts us. In their hundreds of thousands, in their millions, these new ghosts are figments in the sense that Andy Warhol, who was so invested in photographic doubling, in specular celebrity, meant when he said, 'I always thought I'd like my own tombstone to be blank. No epitaph, and no name. Well, actually, I'd like it to say "figment".'[31] Warhol was brought up in the cult of icons, in a Polish Catholic community in Pittsburgh which observed the Orthodox rite, and the worship of images permeates his twentieth-century fascination with spectral fame, outlasting mortality, inhering in the image-flesh of idols—stars like Jackie Kennedy and Marilyn Monroe, especially if they have suffered an early or violent, sacrificial death. In his desire to live and die as a figment, Warhol touched the soul stuff of modern times.

Even in monochrome, Durer communicates the
seductiveness of the Whore of Babylon on the scarlet
beast with 'a golden cup in her hand full of
abominations and filthiness of her fornication . . .'
(Rev. 17:3–4).

26

Disembodied Eyes: The Culture of Apocalypse

> How simply the fictive hero becomes the real;
> How gladly with proper words the soldier dies,
> If he must, or lives on the bread of faithful speech.
>
> Wallace Stevens

Spirits are still active, if not in the sense that a believer in Marlowe's audience or a participant in a Spiritualist seance would have meant. Angels and spectres have changed character, and meaning and impact, but they are visible and powerful through entertainment media in ways that cohere with their past appearances. Shaping the forms that new memories take and the degree of intensity with which they impinge, technologies of reproduction and representation act as the chief catalysts of a new phantasmagoria masquerading as empiricism. They wrap us in illusions, and have installed a new supernatural at the heart of personal and social imagination. This dynamic impels contemporary experience, especially politics. A difference has developed from the Fifties, when Roland Barthes first probed the concealed ideology of modern mythic vehicles, and now: this inheres in the illusory powers of mass communications, and their relation to time and reality, and the way they impress on the mind and imagination. Politics and entertainment are not always clearly distinguishable any more, since their principal vehicles have shifted from distinct forums, parliaments, and theatres, or other platforms for live performance, to the same entertainment media: movies, television, and newspapers.

The wars of our time represented in highly popular story cycles are not easy to keep apart in the mind's eye from the conflicts conducted in reality and on news channels, and this is not just because *The Lord of* or *Star Wars* or the *Narnia* books or the Harry Potter series are allegories. A recent poll found that a terrifying number of people in the UK thought that Hitler was a figment and believed that the Orcs' defeat at Helms Deep in *The Two Towers* actually took place. (This is not to mention headline news about the last episode of *Friends*, or the unfolding of *The Office* or *Eastenders*.) The reasons for this confusion lie deep, and to understand this disturbing situation, we could look at medieval witchcraft beliefs, which similarly set up an imaginary reality. As Stuart Clark points out at the start of his book *Thinking with Demons*, medieval belief in devils was often found among the most learned theologians of the Church, not among the ignorant peasantry alone, as easily supposed. 'To make any kind of sense of the witchcraft beliefs of the past,' he writes, 'we need to begin with ⎯⎯e. By this I mean not only the terms in which [beliefs in devils] were ⎯d, and the general systems of meanings they presupposed, but the n of how language authorizes any kind of belief at all.'[1]

Today we can include, under the rubric of language, mass communications media: the new means of representing the world have complicated the question, for they have realized things that could not have been made possible before except in fantasies—the voice of the beloved in one's ear from a mobile phone on a faraway country, the doubling of a child who can see himself in a home video as he was four years earlier, thus experiencing 'granulated time' (that useful term of the literary critic Ato Quayson).[2] These technical processes, which include virtual reality simulations, animations, and digitized processes of image-making, reproduce—approximately but uncannily—the generative, image-producing faculties of mind, according to the model that some researchers into consciousness propose. The consequences are complex and very little understood, but the argument of this book has been that they need to be attended to more closely.

Our present magic writings do not represent the world as we think it operates—not altogether. That would exceed even today's credulity. But they do process the ways we live our thoughts in our daily experiences of images and voices, and the new realization of mental picturing and its powers has been made possible because we now inhabit forms of disembodiment all the time, from the family album to the CCTV monitor. Recalling our children, we are likely to remember a photograph. ('Memories at risk', runs a current advertising slogan for digital cameras.) Our phantasmata— the mental picturing of thought—are imprinted by received representations, not direct experience, and it is often hard to retrieve the personal memory from the welter of representations around us. The Greek word *eidolon*, used of a spectre or a simulacrum, denoted something not incarnate or real. Our 'idols' now are indeed phantasmatic: long-dead figures from history, stars and athletes, survive in their spectral incarnations on celluloid. Suicide bombers project themselves into eternity by enshrining their last hours in ritual videos: turning themselves into lasting ghosts. Even in less terrible, ordinary day-to-day existence, the deepest sense of the self has been altered by the experience of seeing ourselves familiarly move and talk on screen and monitor. The predicament of Narcissus, who did not know that he was beholding his own image in the pool, has been turned upside down: we now know ourselves in our mind's eye mostly by projecting internally a camera's eye view.

The spectral self of contemporary mass media belongs in the same current as the popular rise of apocalypse, through the uses of imagery that evoke both, and the attendant disregard for the reality of flesh, mortality, and pain. This is a crucial development in representation, deeply affecting audiences' emotional intelligence of audiences.

Apocalyptic plots have begun to seem natural, the deepest narrative grand design inevitable, even biological. This is just what action-packed stories do. J. R. R. Tolkien dramatized an epic struggle to cast out the power of evil, and J. K. Rowling's Harry Potter faces another Sauron in the guise of Lord Voldemort, whose name parses as Wish for Death. Many other writers face the question, Is it possible to turn apocalypticism's characteristic vehicles in a different direction, or even halt them? Philip Pullman, with *His Dark Materials*, has added his imagination to the anarchic, radical, and Blakean New Jerusalem of English apocalypticism; other authors, with a different kind of readership—for example, Margaret Atwood (*Oryx and Crake*)—have taken up apocalypse again as political allegory, and struggled with this master plot.

The Book of Revelation, or the Apocalypse, where angels appear in strength, has acquired new influence in the contemporary world, and refreshed the existence of spirits with unforeseen consequences. The development depends greatly on public storytelling today, especially film spectaculars about catastrophe and war. Blockbuster movies, on the one hand, and political prophecy, on the other, constantly aspire to the dynamic rush of a newly invigorated apocalyptic sublime.

The return of religious thinking—and intense conflict—has been one of the strongest surprises of the twenty-first century, and it has brought with it a return to supernatural writings, of which the Book of Revelation is one of the most influential and controversial. As a book of revelation, the work has not lost its prophetic mission, and not only historically. It anticipates—inaugurates, even—modern genres: it is a monster comic, a horror video, and a sci-fi fantasy. I am not by any means the first to see an affinity between angels and engines: the philosopher Michel Serres, in his book on angels, included jets in his survey (his study was published before September 11, 2001) [3] And H. G. Wells, pioneer of science fiction, took the bold, utterly modern step of imagining the angels of Revelation as engines from Mars, and in *The War of the Worlds*, written at the end of the nineteenth century, describes megadeath visited on earthlings in suburban Surrey and central London, Martians wielding heat ray guns and chemical miasma taking the place of the angels of the seven vials in the Apocalypse. This was before the First World War saw the use of gas in the trenches, before the Second World War and the Bomb, and before the new generation of devices—WMD, long-range surveillance media, smart bombs, and other forms of disembodied intelligence systems.

English literature would be different without the figures, tropes, and cadences of Revelation in the King James Authorized Version; metaphorical phrases too numerous to recount have passed into common speech. But familiarity and scriptural aura have clouded the literal story which the [...] and it is from this perspective (the Schoolmen themselves [...]ed this first level of meaning) that trouble has become acute in [...]es. The trouble has become intertissued with contemporary technologies—with the possibilities of weapons and of entertainment media, and how these modern technologies have altered the nature of the literal, by uncoupling act from representation, the event as performed from image as perceived. Plato's anxiety about the mendacity of verbal and visual representations has attained a new, acute truth value—which can be seen, from many different angles, in the questions raised by the photographs taken of Iraqi prisoners being tortured (see below). There is a sinister fusion here: a literal reading of Scripture reacts with photographic communication technologies to produce an apocalyptic of dissociation.

This closing book of the Bible has been given a thousand and more readings, divined to promise a thousand and more Jerusalems on Earth, including the Third Reich, unfortunately. Exegesis has endowed it with mystical depths of great historical importance. Its riddling story, hiding its subjects under cipher, prosopopeia, anathemata, and other linguistic devices, ensured that it was and remained ambiguous, as well as acutely controversial from the start. It has now emerged to new prominence: this inaugural document of hallucinated triumphalism can illuminate the present dimensions of fantastic realities because its vision of righteous war now informs world leaders' outlook and strategy. The present, disturbing diffusion of this biblical book has a new, unexamined moral force, a redundant nastiness, the kind that many centuries of thought about justice and humanity have striven to put aside. But we can no longer mock it out of meaning, as Shaw did in *The Adventures of the Black Girl in her Search for God* (1932), describing it as 'a curious record of the visions of a drug addict which was absurdly admitted to the canon under the title of *Revelation*'. Shaw rightly draws attention to the title, for the Greek word *apocalypse* ('to unveil'), does not make quite the same claim to a true vision as the less frenzied and less triumphant 'Revelation' of the Authorized Version and other subsequent versions. While 'Apocalypse' promises violence in the act of disclosure, and implies a frenzied, subjective vision (as in W. B. Yeats' convulsive apocalyptic about Ireland, for example), the word 'Revelation' conveys a more calm and cogent realization of something true and objectively applicable. The political uses of the book today have shifted from personal illumination to religious 'revelation' as a warranty for state violence, a remodelled concept of retributive justice and the just war.

Apocalyptic visions of the End tear aside the veil on a vision of a new beginning—for some. The final book of the Bible does not end like the Oedipus trilogy, with the recognition and chastening of the hero by his terrible fate, or like *Hamlet* or *Macbeth*, with almost everyone, including the heroes, dead on the stage. It is, if you like, *Hamlet* retold from the point of view of the survivor and victor Fortinbras, and that is not the tragedy of the Prince of Denmark. The Book of Revelation solicits its audience to identify with the blessed ones, and does not show much pity, or invite us to feel it either, for those cast into outer darkness; it excites us into a storm of hope; in the words of Bernard McGinn, the leading scholar of the book, it 'offers the prospect of a fresh start, *for a remnant*' (added emphasis).[4]

If tragedy is written in the historic present of existential intelligence, such things happen; if the preferred tense of psychoanalysis is the poignant conditional perfect, the paths that might have opened, the way not taken, then apocalypse takes place in the optative mood and the wishful tenses, the jussive or the imperative, that this may happen, let it happen, so be it, to them, not to us, not to me. The text is in this sense performative: it builds its effects from figures of speech that present desiderata as acts; the words have meaning as allegory, as oracle, intricating an enigmatic tissue of symbols.

The author of Revelation gives his name at the beginning as John, and he was identified fairly soon with the Beloved Disciple, and with the author of the Gospel of St John.[5] These overlapping personae halo the author of Revelation with lustre, and add considerable weight to the book's claims to truth telling. But set aside the appealing image of St John the Divine, and the Apocalypse then resembles many, minor works of fevered and frenzied numerological and visionary invective produced in the turmoil of the Judaeo–Hellenistic world: dream almanacs, *grimoires* or books of spells, esoterica deemed apocryphal such as the Book of Enoch, and many other visions of the afterlife sometimes ascribed to Mary, sometimes to Paul, or to other apostles. This type of communication from the future was flourishing in the Mediterranean basin and Near East in the first and second centuries, and it exhibits a similar taste for magic and miracles, charged with a will to power, a belief in curses, a drive for mastery, and a thirst for revenge. Of all the material in the New Testament, it most resembles the Old, resonating with 'little apocalypses' in the Book of Daniel, the vision of Ezekiel, and other passages in which railing, burning, smiting, make up the business of heaven.

Structured as in a tree-like stemma, the narrative branches into clusters: seven letters, seven trumpets, seven vials, and so forth. The episodes fork furiously, drawing power from magical practices used in oral performance, such as chanting, repetition, and accumulation. The book possesses a kind of self-pleasuring thrust and vehemence and rhythm; its harsh music makes itself heard down the centuries in works as diverse as John Bunyan and Andrea Dworkin, Toni Morrison and Stephen King. In the Authorized Version, the English punches out the curses, moving to the rhythm of a heavyweight placing blows: on the Whore of Babylon, phrases land again and again ('. . . hate the whore . . . eat her flesh, and burn her with fire' (17: 16)).

No one who reads it soon forgets its famous visions: the blazing presence with a great voice as of a trumpet; the Lamb of God with seven horns and seven eyes; the great book with seven seals, and the four horsemen, who include Death on 'a pale horse'; the cascading disasters—famine, plague, wild beasts, earthquakes—on 'the great day of his wrath'; the huge falling star, called Wormwood; the locusts 'with hair like the hair of women . . . the teeth of lions . . . and . . . breastplates of iron . . . and tails like scorpions with stings' (9: 7–10); more angels with 'breastplates of fire, and of jacinth, and brimstone' mounted on horses with lion's heads (9: 17); the angel who gives John a little book, which he eats in order to read it; the woman clothed with the sun, who is attacked by 'a great red dragon', so huge and all encompassing, he sweeps down the third part of the stars of heaven with his tail (12: 3–4). 'War in heaven' ensues, and Michael the archangel overcomes the dragon, 'that old serpent, called the devil and Satan' (12: 7–9). (This is the all-important crux in the Bible, when Satan is identified with the tempter in Eden, the rebel angel who fell from heaven' (Luke 10: 18), and with the 'sons of God' who descend on earth to couple (Gen. 6: 1–4).) He makes his appearance just past midpoint.

The second half of the book keeps up the storm of massacres, carnage, and revenge, to evoke the war between another beast and the saints: 'If any man worship the beast . . . the same shall drink the wine of the wrath of God . . . he shall be tormented with fire and brimstone . . . the smoke of their torture ascendeth up for ever and ever' (14: 10–11). An avenging angel harvests the wrongdoers and throws them into the winepress of the wrath of God, 'and the blood . . . came out . . . even unto the horse bridles, by the space of a thousand and six hundred furlongs' (14: 19–20). Seven plagues ensue; then the seven bowls of God's wrath, visiting more bloody death on all creatures in the sea, and dropping demon spirits that look like frogs. The plain of Armageddon sees the outpouring of the last of these seven vials— accompanied by a great voice, announcing, 'It is done.' The great cities of the nations fall. 'And every island fled away, and the mountains were not found' (16: 20). The Whore of Babylon appears (Figure 28, p. 334), seated on a scarlet beast with seven heads and ten horns, with written on her forehead her titles 'MYSTERY, BABYLON THE GREAT, THE MOTHER OF HARLOTS AND ABOMINATIONS OF THE EARTH' ([sic] 17: 5). '[S]he shall be utterly burned with fire,' promises the angel; 'they shall see the smoke of her burning' (18: 8, 9). Over several verses—some quoted before—she becomes a live holocaust, a burnt offering, and eventually her seductive body is dashed to pieces and eaten. As the theologian Tina Pippin writes, somewhat drily, 'The Apocalypse is not a safe place for women.'[6]

More prophecies of struggle, battle, death, and mayhem follow, all promising the comfort of ultimate vindication, which will wring glory from tribulation in the ecstatic vision of the New Jerusalem in bridal array, the glittering city of precious stones, and the wedding feast of the Lamb. This turns out to be no gentle repast: the guests will 'eat the flesh of kings, and the flesh of captains, and the flesh of mighty men, and the flesh of horses' (19: 18)—something not usually represented in artists' visual renderings. The wedding ends curses and pain and strife for the Lamb's servants, the blessed. The dragon is hurled into the abyss and chained for a thousand years, and the servants of God are placed in safety, in the heavenly city.

The last chapter opens, 'And he shewed me a pure river of water of life, clear as crystal'; it then describes the tree of life 'which bare twelve manner of fruits' and promises that 'there shall be no night there . . . and they shall reign for ever and ever'. In these closing verses, which undoubtedly cast a serene spell of hope, the Godhead repeats the promise, 'I come quickly': the pact for the elect will culminate in the Parousia, otherwise called, especially in evangelical circles, 'The Rapture'. Nevertheless, the last verse of the book—before the final greetings and blessings—returns to the stand of harsh denunciation, antagonism, and ostracism. These constitute in effect the closing thoughts of the entire Christian Bible, and they are: 'For without are dogs, and sorcerers, and whoremongers, and murderers, and idolaters, and whosoever loveth and maketh a lie' (22: 15).

So, after punishment has been meted out to the errant churches, and the seals have been opened and the trumpets blasted, after the loosing on Earth of plagues and flames, torrents, earthquakes, stinging and lashing monsters, after multitudinous angels and engines have blasted the sinful world, and another angel has loudly cried 'Woe', and horsemen have ridden down the sky, thousands of them in monstrous armour, the book's violence at last winds down, and it ends with a vision of coming victory for a few, the remnant, the chosen survivors. Armageddon does not engulf us all in this book: it holds out the hope that it will engulf all of *them*—Satan, the Beast, the Dragon, the Whore of Babylon, the unchaste and the lukewarm, dogs and sorcerers, and all those other famous antagonists and embodiments of evil—*they* will be swept away, while we, the elect, will survive.

The language of intolerance, intemperateness, the anathema on the enemy amounts to this: a spell of exclusion.

But who are the others who must be destroyed? Who are we? Who is speaking?

Apocalypse has invited a myriad arcane readings, but each one allows another to grow, as is characteristic of magic babel. Metaphor and meaning jostle in the listener's or reader's mind, fomenting one referent, then another, and bubbling up with this perception, and then that, in an over-stimulated superfluity of effects. The writer seems to be mounting vivid word-pictures, but they do not always make it possible to envisage the wonders and portents he describes; allegory and figures of speech struggle to compose coherent pictures, and we are undoubtedly helped by artists such as Dürer and Blake, and in the cinema Ingmar Bergman (and the epics, *Apocalypse Now, The Day After Tomorrow*). Movies, above all, have found in the Book of Revelation a quasi-organic iconology for its own kind of storytelling, not in content only, but in the very nature of Apoca-lypse's cast of characters: monsters and war, angels and engines, populate any number of visions of the end of days, and on the whole, the theme has become the staple of the most popular spectaculars. These even begin to echo the repetitions in Revelation itself: remakes, sequels, prequels (the *Star Wars* series; *King Kong* revisited by Peter Jackson, director of *Lord of the Rings*).

But at the same time, the very persuasiveness and cogency bequeathed to the visions by some of the art they have inspired (and movies' simu-lated realities above all) conceal the irrational core of the apocalyptic narrative: the huge disjunctions of scale, the arbitrary numbers, both too neat and too huge, the demented and skewed relationships among all the narrative elements—the time period, the characters, the impact of the violence. An audience feels what is happening with fear and trembling, indeed; but it is a fundamental misconception to receive it as something that is taking place, or could do so, even in the perspective of eternity. Dante's apocalyptic journey silently corrects its forerunner, the medieval poet taking meticulous care with the spatial and temporal co-ordinates, and with the embodied and personified cast of supernatural beings (angelic and diabolical) in order to realize persuasively within them the visionary adventure that John experienced. Similarly, if Dürer did not command our respect through his preternatural dexterity with the burin, we might baulk at the grotesques he combines and the scenarios he deploys (Figure 28, p. 334). The listener or reader has to overcome the awkwardness of imagining angels with pillars for legs, and how John ate the little book.

The poor fit of drama and meaning, in respect of a dead lamb opening a very large book, and later marrying 144,000 virgins, boggles the logic of the imaginary—with incongruities that Dante and Milton dazzlingly avoid. (Dürer compresses several episodes together, and diplomatically edits out extremes of phantasmagoria, while Blake presses out the metaphors in his own personal, highly embodied mythology.) This might appear far too literal a reading of a mystical text central to the Christian doctrine of redemption, but forcing the mind to think about the cogency of narrative is useful, because the surface meanings are so confused. Hence the many code-breakers, the many messages discovered in it, the stream of prophecies that fail and fail again. Believers do not lose confidence: they simply return to the task of finding another secret message, which this time they will read correctly. The rebarbative incongruities of the patent narrative, the abundance of unstable and efflorescing latent messages, have a parallel in the incoherence and excess of simulation in contemporary culture. But this very difficulty can illuminate an ethical aspect missing in representations today and, by extension, in experience itself.

The hyperbolic realism achieved in contemporary film culture presents an analogy to the grotesque surplus of the Apocalypse, but the difference is perhaps that the illusion of cosmic mayhem was just that for early receivers of the Bible, whereas for over a hundred years, today, dreams of revenge and victory can turn into history. It is significant that the very word 'Armageddon', with its odd phonetic associations with armies and monsters, only began to figure a historical cataclysm, a real 'final conflict', in the nineteenth century. The first citation for this meaning in the *OED* does not give Hobbes or Blake, as I would have guessed, but Shelley in 1811, and then a long gap before the proverbial use becomes ingrained. Armageddon as an image of mass slaughter in the battle to end all battles keeps pace with the rise of modern armaments, total warfare, and mega-death from the Great War to the years of the atomic blasts and to current phantasmagoric scenes, such as Star Wars and the Terrorist attacks unfolding on screens in every home—the metaphors of Revelation turned active. But the nub of the problem of apocalyptic today arises not only from armaments themselves, but from the loss of meaning incurred in the illusions and spectacle of apocalyptic vision.

The Book of Revelation was written rather late—around 95 CE or per-haps even later—and was included in the canon only after fierce debate; it was the last text to be admitted into the Bible, after a struggle with another contender, *The Shepherd of Hermas*. The *Shepherd* is the first Christian allegory extant, and was written, by Hermas, in the first century CE, soon after the Apostolic era. It opens with a scene between the visionary and his muse, a woman called Rhoda, to whom, Hermas writes, he was sold as a slave. In its intense illumination, this relationship announces Dante's initi-ation through his adored, stringent Beatrice. Hermas' eyes opened, he then sees the Church personified as an old woman, whom at first he takes to be the pagan Sibyl; the female—and old at that—does not here signify corrup-tion, or helplessness. She issues ten commandments and some penalties for failing to keep them, but her general outlook is lenient, so much so that her laxity in connection to fidelity in marriage caused outrage, and helped block *Hermas'* way into the canon. The vision continues with thoughts on angels—also heretical, it was later decided—and some very fine symbolic passages using allegorical motifs, such as that of the Shepherd himself, which strongly recall Jesus's most bucolic and homely parables. What happens, for example, when our hero Hermas meets a ferocious beast illustrates the difference between the canonical Book of Revelation and the interdicted allegory: 'there shone out a glimpse of sun, and, lo, I beheld a vast monster like to a whale, and from its mouth issued fiery locusts, and it was in size, as it were, an hundred feet long, and it had a head like an earthen vessel. And I began to weep, and to ask the Lord to deliver me from it.' So far, recognizable as apocaplytic. But Hermas then hears a voice urging him not to lose faith, and 'I boldly gave myself up unto the beast. It came on with such a rushing noise, that it could evidently have destroyed the city.' But instead, this is what occurs: 'I came near it, and the huge reptile stretched itself on the ground, and did nothing but put out its tongue, and did not move at all until I had passed by.'[7]

This episode might lack spectacular colour and drama compared to the sound and fury of Revelation, but it certainly expresses a different psychology in handling hostility. The approach might also seem preeminently Christian according to at least one strand in the religion. Had Hermas gone on the attack, the monster might have done more than loll its tongue. As the Chinese sage Li Kuan put it, 'War is like a fire. If you do not put it out, it will burn itself out.'[8]

Indeed, until the fifth century, the churches of Syria, Cappadocia, and even Palestine did not accept Revelation. Luther considered removing Revelation from his translation of the Bible, as 'Christ is not taught or known in it,' he wrote.[9] Its subsequent history since has made it even more inflammatory than it was when, in the aftermath of the destruction of the Temple in Jerusalem, it first denounced the Roman Empire as the work of the devil. The final solution it evokes—those smitten, smoking, charred victims—summon up uneasily the work of a more recent creed: Nazi mythology was influenced by the prophetic interpretations of Revelation offered by the medieval abbot Joachim of Fiore, who had indeed foretold the coming of a Third Reign.

From the 1960s to the 1970s, studies of apocalyptic thought by Christopher Hill and E. P. Thompson chiefly engaged with radical millenarianists who had invoked the persecuted, heroic survivors of Revelation. These analyses looked to the seventeenth-century revolutionaries, and to Blake and to Abolitionist religious zeal in both America and England, and conjured the impassioned resistance of world-turned-upside-down movements. Inspired by the desire to lift the dead weight of history as tradition from post-war society, these historians looked to the eternal horizon of Apocalypse, where the past is abolished and the future has become the longed-for present. In doing so, they showed little concern for the often deep connection of apocalypticism with authority.

Bernard McGinn, who has revised those post-war historians, reminds us that the influence of the Book of Revelation originated with 'the well-educated and well-situated clerical intelligentsia ... potent political figures.'[10] He goes on to declare that apocalypticism was adduced 'in support of the political and social order' both retrospectively—by reviewing the past in its light, and prospectively, by prophesying conflict to come. The last book of the Bible may have blazed in the Diggers' and Levellers' minds, lit up Blake's imagination, and lived in the pockets of the ragged-trousered philanthropists who came after him, but it also stood open on the desks of clerks and scholars who worked for the interests of reigning authorities who in the past (when Dante was descending into Hell and meting out justice on his foes, and Milton was revisiting the Fall) were emperors and kings—and sometimes, queens. Something of this still resounds in the characterization of acts of war and terror in the present time, in the ceaseless fight advocated by George W. Bush and Tony Blair, their passionate self-justifications, and their rationale for their new concept of a just war. Revelation now resounds in the discourse of war on the lips of the most powerful and most dangerous world leaders.

The present strands of the Book of Revelation in the contemporary imaginary are bound by memories of both World Wars, but the lessons of Nazi applications of its vision have not been absorbed. Rather, the contrary. The plot, the images, the language of the Bible's closing vision permeate the speeches of Bush and Blair, and structure the very premiss of 'the war on terror' that the destruction of the World Trade Center inaugurated a new time, a cataclysmic break with the past.[11]

Prophecies of retributive justice also strike again and again in the US administration's proclamations, and through the alliance of evangelical Christians and Zionists resonate with explicit biblical images in the general US politics of the Middle East, most notoriously in the 'Axis of Evil' speech of 29 January 2002, in which Bush tellingly phrased his apocalypticism in semi-archaisms that move from ordinary American speech habits to portentous uses of full auxiliary verbs.[12] The President's continued fondness for calling his term of office his 'watch' echoes Revelation, which exhorts, 'Be watchful' (3: 2); and constantly warns that the unwary will be taken by the enemy. The speech writer behind the speech disclosed, in his memoirs, that Bible study classes are held in the White House and speech-writers and aides are expected to attend.[13]

The apocalyptic perspective permeates political consciousness more widely, far from the White House's inner council chambers, quite independently of the government. Congregations of evangelical Christians everywhere read the Bible as docu-drama, with literal application to world affairs, and in North America, more millions—some of them the same people, but not all—have also responded to a poll saying that they believe in angels. As Bernard McGinn also commented, himself prophetically, in 1987: 'most of those who ponder the book today see it . . . as the divinely given plan for the coming armageddon.'[14]

Glorious Appearing: The End of Days, the eleventh of the best-selling *Left Behind* books, continues to unfold a present-day apocalyptic final battle. The series' authors are Tim LaHaye, an evangelical pastor, and Jerry B. Jenkins, a professional ghost writer for celebrities (including Billy Graham). *Armageddon*, the tenth in the series, was the first to appear on the *New York Times* bestseller list, in April 2003, the month after the war in Iraq began.[15] The story unfolds a paranoid plot featuring international conspiracies of all kinds, financial, military, religious, terrorist, and so forth, led by the Antichrist who, as in the Apocalypse, will falsely promise peace instead of a holy war.[16] The vengeful rhetoric of Christian fundamentalism makes common cause with hardliner Israeli Zionism; Islamic calls for jihad use mirror-image apocalyptic language: Hamas prophesying rivers of blood, Sharon announcing retaliation no less bloodthirstily.

J. R. R. Tolkien's fantasy epic was created during the same post-war decades as the utopian histories of E. P. Thompson and Christopher Hill, and it too conjures a myth of struggle and deliverance, revolutionary energy and hope, carried by little people against tyrannical might and unharnessed destruction. The Hobbits from the Shire, furry, small, and tubby, had first appeared in Tolkien's 1937 book *The Hobbit*, which was imbued with the Arcadian and English nostalgia that pervaded that era, bringing Toad and Rabbit and Winnie the Pooh and other teddy bears into polite, comforting nursery literature, and culminating in Aloysius, the talismanic soft toy of *Brideshead Revisited* (1945). Tolkien had been invalided out of the trenches, but he lost his family and most of his friends from his university days in that war, and his experience can be descried in the endless combat of *The Lord of the Rings*. The book became a secular bible for the hippy generation, and traces of their brand of anarchism—individualist, hedonist, pacific, antinomian—linger in the medieval and Celtic nostalgia that envelops the book's afterlife as a touchstone of the New Age. But its present incarnation, as a film, projects into our here and now a vision of one small, beleaguered tribe and its allies overthrowing a mighty imperium in altogether changed political circumstances and a different imaginary climate, without much thought of transformation, negotiation, organic exchange, and development.

Some other filaments of past and present apocalypticism are worth teasing out, in order to grasp why its myth has regained moral force and reinvigorated the Counter-Enlightenment reign of spirit forces in our time. An Anglo-Saxon epic, such as *Beowulf*, were established as the Ur-text of English Literature by Tolkien at Oxford, where one of the students in the Sixties was Philip Pullman, the latest epode to emerge from the homegrown Christian tradition. Pullman read English—unhappily—and then started out as a schoolteacher in Oxford during the first peak phase of the Tolkien cult and, as he often recalls with some asperity, the popular ascendancy of another Oxford children's visionary, C. S. Lewis and the *Narnia* cycle. Pullman's highly ambitious trilogy, *His Dark Materials*, consciously defies both those precursors: he challenges the archaic savagery and the apocalyptic vision of Tolkien's invented Englishness and Lewis's Anglican piety. He draws on a parallel, dialectical literary tradition, taking on Milton, speaking with Blake (who has, for these purposes, become an angelic presence, constantly there), shadowing Bunyan, and surpassing certainly Milton and even Blake in his defiance of Christian dualism, his rejection of the doctrine of original sin, and his championing of women, children, and their energies of curiosity, sex, and love. He stages several topoi of apocalyptic struggle, but in each case, makes a knight's move in another direction.

The scandalous, worldly, beautiful, Lilith-like anti-heroine, Mrs Coulter, is a wicked mother, but with a difference, and her seductiveness works its spell on the reader as well as on Lyra and many other victims. His Satan, the towering explorer and magus Lord Asriel, radiates rebellion in Miltonic fashion, but he too is a complex case, as in intrepid pursuit of knowledge, he defies the control and interests of the Authority's prelates, who wish to steal, hoard, and pervert any results he obtains. The concept of Dust, which streams through the book, symbolizes the life force of particle physics, on the one hand, and on the other, more defiantly, the energy and vitality of carnal knowledge.

Taking a cue from Blake's Urizen, the divine power who strangles the infant joy in his grip, Pullman performs a supreme act of delinquent, topsy-turvy imagination, when the child heroes Lyra and Will meet the Ancient of Days, the Authority himself: he was so old, and he was terrified, crying like a baby and cowering away into the lowest corner. ' "He must be so old—I've never seen anyone suffering like that—oh, Will, can't we let him out?" '

The once supreme ruler of heaven and earth, creator of the world, is lying in a crystal casket, like a victim of Alzheimer's on a geriatric ward, and Lyra is moved to pity, and with Will, assists the decrepit creature out of his casket:

'it wasn't hard, for he was light as paper, and he would have followed them anywhere, having no will of his own, and responding to simple kindness like a flower in the sun. But in the open air there was nothing to stop the wind from damaging him, and to their dismay his form began to loosen and dissolve. Only a few moment later he had vanished completely.'[17]

In this bizarre tableau of the death of God, Pullman inverts the deposition and pietà motifs of Christianity, and cradles the crumbling, cowardly, abject old man in the arms of two children, so that, in front of the power who has visited his harsh justice on the world, we witness two rough, ignorant kids applying the different medicine of mercy.

Finally, Lord Asriel and Mrs Coulter sacrifice themselves to bring to an end the rule of the usurping angel Metatron, and to allow Lyra and Will to return to enfleshed, ordinary human existence in unfolding time. As Lord Asriel exclaims, angels are jealous of human beings, because ' "They haven't got *this*!" ', and he pinches the arm of his companion, ' "They haven't got *flesh.*" '[18] So *His Dark Materials* resists apocalypse in favour of what Gerald Manley Hopkins called *haeccitas*, the thisness of things, the phenomenon of the here and now, the flesh you can pinch and that feels pain, the base, raw material of life. Pullman has in many ways dramatized—for children!—an epic claim that resounds to Blake's antinomian axiom, 'Everything that lives is holy.' This is to make large claims for Pullman, but it is important to note his swerves and soarings away from the usual apocalyptic script.[19]

The Italian philosopher and Catholic Gianni Vattimo, in *his* apocalyptic book, *After Christianity* (2002), offers a similar insight. He too lambasts the Church for dishonestly invoking a concept of nature and natural law in the service of its own violence, against women and homosexuals especially. Nature has been changed into an unassailable grand truth. So sex has to be 'natural' (no use of contraception and so on).[20] Vattimo is by no means the only prominent Christian to grasp at the Blakean legacy: while the Association for Christian Teachers has denounced the blasphemies of Philip Pullman, and American fundamentalists have anathematized him as well, the Archbishop of Canterbury flabbergasted *Guardian* readers when he praised the vision of the books and the production at the National. Without addressing apocalypticism directly, Rowan Williams nevertheless issued a challenge which implies a strong critique of it: '[But] what kind of a church is it', he asked, 'that lives in perpetual and murderous anxiety about the fate of its God? What the story makes you see is that if you believe in a mortal God, who can win and lose his power, your religion will be saturated with anxiety—and so with violence.'[21]

In the years of the Bomb, of the Cold War, of the Cuban missile crisis, the first wave of Tolkien-mania and *Narnia's* success, Frank Kermode was also thinking about apocalypse. In his influential book, *The Sense of an Ending*

(1967), Kermode develops a powerful argument about the differences between myth and fiction through a meditation on the vision of the end of the world in Revelation. Kermode agreed with Roland Barthes' polemic in *Mythologies* that myth communicates ideology—static, traditional, conservative, bound to the past, and antithetical to the true enterprise of literature. Kermode distinguished *chronos*, the flow of time, from *kairos*, the moment of being; fiction bundles *kairoi* to form the timeless aeon of redemptive order, saturated with revisionary, not reactionary meaning. This space of *kairoi*, created by the religious vision of the significant end, sets up the symbolic order established by fiction. Kermode puts great emphasis on the immanent meaning of fiction, which, like apocalypse, imbues the foretime with meaning and endows it with a rationale, to render it bearable: this is the salvific promise of art.[22]

Malcolm Bull, an astute critic of millennial themes, has pointed out that moments of being have a purpose, in literature as in life, and that this is not always to be found in their ends: 'human time is not made of chronological time but is, as in Ecclesiastes, "a time for this, and a time for that".'[23] We experience time for its significance as it happens and as it swells and subsides according to its import: we do not inhabit endings, and much of the literature of the last hundred years has striven to imitate what Proust called the intermittences of the heart. The deep difference between inter-mittences (processes), and *teloi* (ultimate ends) illuminates the way in which apocalypticism in its new historic form endangers democratic negotiation and incremental compromises. Revelation's vision of future time is predi-cated on lost time past, on nostalgia for a Golden Age: Alpha is Omega—an ourobouros, not biting, but sucking its own tail in infantile plenitude. Jerusa-lem is forfeit, but the New Jerusalem will step down from heaven in grace and beauty and pour her blessings on us. The visionary formula stubbornly resists the attrition of the present or the possibility of small gains in favour of the radiant conviction about the past and the future. To understand more about radical apocalypticism in the twenty-first century, we can look to developments in storytelling over the last fifty years, and see certain formative changes taking hold.

The handling of time in recent movies and their cognates (television, computer imaging, digital photography) throws into question the ancient trust in art and literature's fictive temporal order. Wallace Stevens' vision of this order of art, from which Kermode derived his inspiration, the *aevum*, or perduring era composed of *kairoi*, or bundled moments of being, the other space-time of imagination, has been recast through current media enactments. Propelled into the real through current brilliant techniques of illusion, the space of fiction fulfils aspects of apocalyptic prophecy at its most obscurantist. (In some ways those informants who thought that the battle of

Helms Deep took place were right: it did take place—for the filming, and in the movie.) Ultimately, it is not, perhaps, the violence in entertainment that does the deepest damage, but the promise of possible gratification by these means: the performance of the action, projected into an eternal present, lasts ...ed, repeated again and again, and so becomes a real event, a real act ...g in an ever present actual time.

The status of reality within movies is, of course, too complex to unfold completely here,[24] but one aspect provokes immediate scrutiny: how technical wizardry alters experience. False semblance in mirroring techniques of realism has been richly analysed by Rosalie Colie in her book on reflexive paradox, where she writes, for example: 'all artistic illusionism . . . risked focusing too much on its own artifice and on the weakness of the human eye. By aiming totally to deceive, it pointed to the relativities of perception. . . . the more faithful the likeness, the greater the falsity of the picture, the greater its isolation from any reference point outside of the creating, re-creating self.'[25] The tumults of apocalyptic visions today raise this acute problem. The awesome illusionism of *The Lord of the Rings*, as filmed by Peter Jackson and his host of technicians, puts any audience into an amazement, drawing attention to itself as virtuoso performance, detaching us from the events unfolding. Through computer-generated imagery (CGI) and more than *700* different modes or types of special effects (animation, bluescreen, mattes, models, etc.), the film summoned realities that are not there. In interviews, the horde of designers all testify to their fidelity to reality, to historical methods of forging armour, brewing mead, raising elvish castles in the air, cloning Orcs in mud. The computer simulations of the battles were so fine-tuned, so the story goes, that when the programmers began to run the software, some of the soldiers did not take part in the strategies as scripted, but took to their heels and ran away.

But this film refuses those laws of the flesh in which experience is grounded: that carnal condition which Blake attempted to proclaim, that praise of dust and of flesh that Philip Pullman has sung.

Bodies crash down a mountain side on to jagged bare splinters of lava, and then show a mere charming cosmetic scratch. Nobody ever holds their nose or gags at the reek of corpses, as they do in medieval paintings of the Raising of Lazarus. Film passionately strives for authenticity and verisimilitude—think of *The Passion of the Christ, Troy,* and *Alexander*—especially where violent clashes are concerned, and the spectacle of physical ordeals and pain. But this new kind of realism never admits what blows or blades really inflict or the consequences of violence (Jesus could not have survived the scourging that Gibson stages). When Frodo, at the end of the trilogy, still feels the wound in his shoulder, it is a genuine and even exceptional moment, which calls for unusual empathy: he has been transformed by the ordeals he has undergone. More commonly, the person on screen, dematerialized into photons and as ethereal as a shade in Homer's under-world, necessarily feeds only an illusion of physicality. Film-makers pile on the carnage and the gore, but unlike the ghosts in Homer's underworld who can speak with Odysseus after they have drunk the black blood of a sacrificed ox, cinematic spectres simulate but never attain the human condition—that pinch on real flesh that Lord Asriel tells us the angels envy.

More even than the visual sleight of hand, sound effects pack impressions with the force of events taking place for real. The elusiveness of embodi-ment and material being is hidden under the quadrophonic sensorama of crashing, roaring, squelching, splitting, slicing, hewing, flogging—the soundscape stands in for the physical act of the horrors depicted and acts directly on the audience's viscera. So, faced with the awesome techniques of illusion of film today, the spectator grasps at the reprieve of disbelief—twice over: this is only happening on screen, and it is not happening at all to the actors and participants. Otherwise the scenes of Armageddon on film would become as unbearable as the fighting on the Somme which originally blasted Tolkien's nerves. (It is interesting that in watching filmed Armageddon, the horses focus the sharpest worries, at least for me, because they can perform, they can be trained to make mock battle, but performance is not the same for them, and in some important way, it is always happening for real for them.)

Even in the most stirring scenes of torment and damage, something twists and directs the audience towards unfeeling. This effectively denatures viewers, disconnecting them—us—from fellow feeling. Hence the rise in 'reality' entertainment, from the sadism of *Big Brother* to the return of savage spectacles that were thought banished from civilization.[26] In the light of the mounting appetite, traditional ideas about aesthetic responses need revising: Aristotelian catharsis does not meet the present situation; nor does Coleridge's 'willing suspension of disbelief'.

Wallace Stevens offered a most perceptive discrimination when he wrote, in one of his many poems that meditates on the reality of art, the truth of language, and the status of fiction:

> Yet to speak of the whole world as metaphor
> Is still to stick to the contents of the mind
>
> And the desire to believe in a metaphor.
> It is to stick to the nicer knowledge of
> Belief, that what it believes in is not true.[27]

But the poet did not foresee how this 'nicer' state would become the only refuge from the torments so vividly realized on film screens, and that the disjunction between embodied and disembodied realism would lead to faithless speech. The consequent disengagement grows and spreads by analogy, even when the fictive and the fantastic are not at issue. In a sense this is the apocalyptic condition: in the vision of the end, the flesh is resurrected not as flesh but as image-flesh, a form of angelic *apatheia*, or non-feeling, cyber-matter, which feels nothing and occupies nowhere but the screen, no time except the present of its unfolding through whatever medium of communication it is assuming as its vehicle. This is angelic disembodiment: the pale and trembling existence of Humphrey Bogart and Lauren Bacall, James Dean and Marilyn Monroe, for ever and ever here and now, of Hugh Grant and Catherine Zeta-Jones for ever in the future as they are now. These lives that are not lives, presences that are not presences, penetrate and change our own conditions of reality, and have altered consciousness of self and embodied being.

The state of overwrought fictive sensation, comparable to the metaphorical excess and narrative hyperbole of the Book of Revelation, demands that the audience/reader either thrills to the bloodshed or takes refuge in numbness. Imaginary battle spectaculars become a kind of training in resisting fear, in stopping the springs of empathy. Huge arrays of weapons, soldiery, monstrous animals, siege machinery from every epoch of warmongering, are deployed in vast spectaculars of terrifying carnage from horizon to horizon, but you are asked to sit tight and watch; a squashed fly in Shakespeare can produce more pity.

Such apocalyptic scenarios also pose the disturbing question, Who are the Orcs? Who are these *untermenschen* who have become the enemy now? The writer Edgardo Cozarinsky expresses this anxiety well in *The Bride from Odessa*, when in a story a character wonders about 'the Third Reich's theatrical passion for creating a real life apocalypse. A sort of Oberammergau passion in reverse? . . . Were Auschwitz, Maidanek and Treblinka the other side of some shining souvenir medallion from Oberammergau?'[28]

Consider the shocking photographs of prisoners from Abu Ghraib and elsewhere in Iraq. These came in a variety of levels of veracity: some were staged for the camera as *tableaux vivants* of punishments and degradation; some of them were posed to intimidate and threaten; some of them have been faked in the UK to recall what happened. Some were indeed neither staged, nor imitations. Several could not be easily categorized: real atrocities and torture were play-acted, as if for a bondage scene filmed for S & M cultists; such images were then transmitted by pornography's new native element, the internet, to amuse the folks back home. Perpetrators defended themselves by saying that they were 'only posing'—it wasn't for real.

One cause for this dissociation lies with the uses of cinematic realism. For a start, with all its dazzling computer-generated images, it does not include understanding of suffering, neither of bodies and enfleshed fragility, nor of human beings and psychological vulnerability. The production values of contemporary films strive for authenticity in communicating a visceral experience of ordeals and pain. Whereas when we *read* about pain and suffering and death, we empathize, and the victims' existence coheres with the entire imaginative projection of the text, in films of c~~~~~' scenes cannot be veridical: the image turns everything into a g; pretend.

Happily, public revulsion against the Iraqi material showed that affectless dissociation has not altogether triumphed. The photographs made a difference, and the disavowals did not find acceptance. The outcry also revealed that images have huge power to shock us into thought. But—though the photographs have indeed stirred widespread dismay and shame—their making also conveyed how the consumption of fantasy can denature us. They reveal the disappearance of act into image. In these trophy pictures, the subject's existence as a person vaporizes—he becomes a phantasmic enemy, his degradation a symbolic ritual designed to deliver pleasure and triumph to the viewer.

The suicide bombers also create icons of a different kind for the *aevum* when they make their farewells on video: these grim and sacramental memorials are then broadcast to keep their martyrdom present and of lasting significance: they too are weapons of what the historian of science Bruno Latour has called 'Iconoclash'—the battle for control of images.[29]

The hot and unremitting violence of cinematic visions of angels and engines may even communicate revolt against the very conditions of disembodiment, of not being involved, both in film and in warfare for audiences out of the war zones. Smart bombs, robot disposal units, stealth planes, missiles, all disengage attackers from their victims. Hand-to-hand combat ennobles battle: a cavalry charge into a horde of Orcs or a phalanx of Persians is heroic in a way that a radar-controlled missile is not. Resistance to showing real-life carnage, in Iraq or elsewhere, on news channels reveals how deeply violence has become an entertainment opportunity, so that its reality cannot be owned up to or grasped. As fantasy, it can be borne, but not as reality, just as the thirst for revenge and restitution powers the prose of the Apocalypse, driving meaning out of history into the torrid zone of dream and desire.

Can we perceive another meaning in angels and engines, an alternative to the spectral effect on sense of self, identity, and politics today? Grasping the present extent of apocalyptic today can only be a start. But language and imagination govern ways of thinking, and from that work of cognition follow ways of doing. New means of representing the world have 'realized' things that were not possible before except in fantasies. Besides the spectacular Armageddons of contemporary experience, for real in the case of terrorist attacks and invasions, for fun in the case of special effects cinema and virtual media, the new conditions of reality that have been brought to bear on our lives by the angels and engines of now must give rise to scrutiny, not acquiescence. Significantly, one kind of spectre has emerged strongly from the very heart of apocalyptic popular culture: the zombie. Since the early decades of the twentieth century, zombies have grown ever more popular as pre-eminent figures of the dissociated and denatured self.

The spellbound victim of voodoo sleepwalks in the Val
Newton-Jacques Tourneur film, *I Walked with a Zombie*,
1943.

27
Our Zombies, Our Selves

Back to back, belly to belly,
Don't give a damn
'Cos I'm stone dead already.
'The Zombie Jamboree', c.1950

Among the spectral host conjured in contemporary culture, one sort of spirit above all has come to haunt popular imagination: zombies. Alongside vampires, zombies are the most familiar inhabitants of the supernatural realm, but their form of living death differs in original personality and meaning. A zombie is someone whose soul has been stolen, whose body has not exactly died but passed into the power of a magician or owner who uses it for his (rarely her) own purposes. By contrast, a vampire is a corpse that has been reanimated; both are ghosts with a difference. Unlike phantoms, who have a soul but no body, zombies and vampires are all body—but unlike the vampire who has will and desire and an appetite for life (literally), a zombie is a body which has been hollowed out, emptied of selfhood. The word 'zombie' derives from 'jumbie', one of the most common words for 'spirit' in the Caribbean, appearing frequently in ghost stories, folk-tales, and documentary accounts of the archipelago throughout the last century.

But zombies, in contrast to the generic group of jumbies, embody a vision of human existence that was precipitated by a chemical fusion of slavery, its abolition and its reinstatement, excited and fired in the kiln of poisoned power relations. Slave culture formed the concept, out of Africa and in the Caribbean, to describe the way in which slavery stripped someone of personhood. The invention has since grown to describe individuals in a world of wealth and power that, to say the least, offers each of us a very different horizon of possibilities, yet for all its insistence on choice and access and enablement strategies and empowerment, manages to communicate to many of its members a feeling of numbing and volitionless vacancy. Zombies embody the principal ghostly condition of our time, the successor of waxworks, shades, ghosts, apparitions, and the host of paranormal spirits who have figured the dead in public since the eighteenth century. Soul-theft is a master plot that readers began to recognize in the nineteenth century, but which has inspired, since the Twenties, ever waxing enthusiasm among a far larger public than the literary-minded. Zombies can shed light on the concept of soul now—and of soullessness.

This penultimate chapter will offer a very brief genealogy of the zombie, with some fragments of prehistory for this potent imagining of a post-human—indeed, posthumous—state of existence. Zombies have come to typify a modern personality, to convey vividly a danger to individuality and the self in figurative terms.

It is odd, at first look, that such an idea of a person should take a hold when ideas of soul have weakened. But in many ways the cult following of the zombie embraces the disappearance of the soul, rejoices with dark and hollow laughter at the terminal sentence that the living dead represent. For, unlike the spirit or spirits that this book has been invoking, a zombie is embodied and material, walks and bleeds and sweats.

Vampires can speak—they have even dictated their autobiographies[1]— whereas zombies are condemned to silence, as if their tongues had been cut out (one of the penalties inflicted on slaves). Fantastic monsters are often singled out by the peculiar noises they make: grunts, shrieks, the incongruous whimper of a kitten that Ovid describes Scylla uttering, the Jabberwock whiffling and burbling; but zombies are mute. They are more silent even than ghosts, but they resemble them in that they are revenants, forced to live suspended in time, neither fully alive nor fully dead, in a state of anomie degree zero, disaffection to the point of numbness. But they are all too living in their living death, yet absent in presence, and they figure the elusiveness of meaning itself.

The 'Philosopher's Zombie', for example, has become a measure by which what we mean by human consciousness can be tested, in the work of David J. Chalmers.[2] Jacques Derrida was also interested in the zombie's state of undecidability and made it a figure of language itself, which in his view is both there in text, as it were embodied, but fugitive, unstable, not-there. Slavoj Žižek has also adopted this new kind of ghost, as belonging to the 'forbidden domain of the Thing', from which human beings recoil.[3] Funerary rituals in every culture attempt to overcome resistance to the fact of death and the thingness of the corpse: obsequies lay the ghost so that it will agree to depart. But they are not always efficacious: zombies are the most recent of these troops of the unquiet dead.

The concept of the living dead surfaces, without a name, in scattered myths and terrors: Dante, for example, meets in the frozen depths of Cocytus in the pit of hell the shade of Fra Alberigo, who explains that traitors like him can pre-decease their bodies, and fall into the lowest circle of hell to start their eternity of torments, eyes sealed shut by the ice, wholly entombed in permafrost—a kind of cryogenesis—while they are still in the world. Dante exclaims in horror, for he has seen one of the sinners around and about in the world above, recently, eating and drinking and wearing clothes. The friar then explains that this sinner was so wicked that before even his murder victims had arrived in the afterlife, the devil had taken possession of his soul; Dante had effectively beheld a zombie, and the idea repels him so profoundly that he refuses the man's plea to melt his frozen eyes with his touch.[4] Dante imagined the possibility, but he did not have a word for the soulless, hollow man left in the world above; his traitors remain exceptional cases in medieval thought, and the suggestion that Dante makes is even heretical. Shakespeare also invokes 'a living dead man' in *The Comedy of Errors* (v. i. 242), significantly a play about sorcery, uncanny switched personality, and the perilous loss of identity: this walking corpse is Dr Pinch, described in the dramatis personae as 'a conjuring doctor'.

So in some sense the concept of a zombie was waiting for a name. It would take the full impact of economic forces of imperial industrial power to effect its emergence into consciousness and popular usage. Its first use in the English language, by Robert Southey in his *History of Brazil* (1810–19), designates a very different concept: 'Zombi' appears in the book as the name of a liberation martyr-hero, an early exemplar of elected ruler, the chieftain of a free band of rebels against Portuguese rule in Brazil, who dies heroically rather than resume a life in chains. He is a vital spirit, a daimon of honour and valour.[5] But, just as Zombi the Brazilian hero suffers the inversion of the meaning of his name, so when it comes to designate the enslaved living dead, the Romantic dream of enfranchisement, which Southey and his peers, including Coleridge his brother-in-law and Wordsworth, was itself hollowed out of hope—for a complex set of historical, political, and personal reasons.[6]

Since then, the word 'zombie' has dramatically and significantly fallen from grace. If it first acquired its new, abject, and terrifying meaning within the context of slavery as an image of the uttermost condition of cancelled selfhood, zombification increasingly now threatens well outside the circuits of voodoo cults or the supernatural: it has become an existential term, about mental and physical enslavement. For children, to be called a zombie is an insult, traded in the playground; for adults, zombies offer the chance for a rueful, gallows humour joke against ourselves.

The zombie has been robbed of all the qualities that make up personhood—feelings, sentience, reflexivity, memories—but survives under a sentence of immortality (like a vampire). Unlike angels and daimons, pagan shades or Christian ghosts, the zombie is a spectre still tormented by the carnal condition of being, especially toil. It has much in common with the robot, a figure that enters popular culture around the time that zombie movies are becoming successful; but the robot is a machine, a direct descendant of E. T. A. Hoffmann's doll Olympia and the automata of the showmen in the eighteenth century (the Czech brothers Karel and Josef Capek invented the word—from 'robota', Czech for drudgery; and Karel dramatized the concept in the play *R.U.R.* (*Rossum's Universal Robots*) in 1920). In stark contrast, a zombie once was someone like you and me. In this sense zombies are closer kin with the Creature from Frankenstein, who was pieced and patched from exhumed body parts.

Zombies also have counterparts in another species of soulless victims, the smilingly perfect protagonists of the brilliant suburban horror film, *The Stepford Wives* (1974).[7] Like them, the figure of the replicant, immortalized in the film *Blade Runner* and inspired by the techno-paranoid inventions of Philip K. Dick, has also been voided of personal qualia and filled instead with techno-stuff—a machine consciousness, including memories which do not belong to their own lives, in so far as they can be said to have lives.[8] Both Stepford Wives, replicants, and 'simulos' are close cousins to the clone in popular perception, for beneath the clone beats the terror of losing uniqueness of personal identity.[9] In *A Number* by Caryl Churchill, the word 'clone' was never mentioned, but the 'numbers' in the play were the children who feared that they were indeed clones. This new category of a person, classified as a non-person, is literally unspeakable and unnameable, a thing, a copy, but still someone 'not very like but very something terrible', whose consciousness of self can only stir an agony of contradictions.[10]

With ideas of the soul growing ever weaker, what it means to be you, what is the thing inside me that makes me me, has become the sharpest and most resistant of questions.

Yet identical twins, who are true clones, never grow up to be inter-changeable as people, and even defy genetic fatalists. In the complex, human scale of things, there is no such thing as a clone.[11] But the clone and the replicant express a dread of losing the self and being substituted without knowing it: a fear that has deepened with modern instruments of communication and reproduction. These anxieties flourish in recent fiction: in *Never Let Me Go* (2005), Kazuo Ishiguro projects these fears into an imaginary, recent past, when clones are farmed to provide spare organs, while in *The Secret* (2001), Eva Hoffman imagines a daughter's horror and despair at finding she is her mother's clone.

Like the interest in astral bodies, the story of zombies' entrance belongs in the history of psychic Orientalism in the stir around empire; their adventures in Western fantasy keep pace with the increase of world trade and exchanges of labour and commodities. Part of this story has been told in several studies (including one of my own),[12] so in this book, I am going to focus on their evolving character in twentieth-century culture, and in particular, their affinity with spirits summoned on film: zombies can help illuminate the combined lifelikeness and unreality that the medium succeeds in conveying. Their incarnate but numb and vacant condition reproduces the state of someone captured on film forever: materially present but also entirely absent.

The plot of Pullman's sequence *His Dark Materials* turns on loss of soul, figured in these richly imaginative books as a personal daemon. The daemons of children have powers of metamorphosis, and the heroine's beautiful and wicked mother, Mrs Coulter, plans to split child daemons from their owners in order to obtain their powers, especially of metamorphosis: 'a human being with no daemon was like someone without a face, or with their ribs laid open and their heart torn out; something unnatural and uncanny that belonged to the world of night-ghasts, not the waking world of sense.'[13] Children who suffer from Mrs Coulter's designs on their powers of metamorphosis become zombies: Pullman uses the word, and in the course of his epic bravely declares the materialist grounds of his own beliefs, as we saw, and resistance to a metaphysical account of individual essence.

Although Philip K. Dick and Philip Pullman have made the threat of soul-theft and all its consequences the mainspring of their memorable plots, and J. K. Rowling has created terrifying Dementors, who also void their victims of selfhood, it is film, not books, that has spread replicants and zombies, through film media's instrinsic sympathy with states of doubling, conjured absence, and captured time past.

Like Florence Cook's Katie King, W. B. Yeats's Leo Africanus, Eva C.'s Bien Boa, and even Hélène Smith's Martians, zombies travelled on the new communications systems, probes, and cables, bringing with them news from the far reaches of European nations' colonial ambitions. Through popular B-movies, such as *White Zombie* (1932), *The Revenge of the Zombies* (1943), and *I Walked with a Zombie* (1943), reports brought back by travellers, missionaries, and anthropologists (Mary Kingsley from West Africa at the turn of the century, Zora Neale Hurston from Jamaica and Haiti in the Thirties) disseminated a vision of primitive trance rituals, possession, and magic spells, at once seductive and horrifying.[14] Among the beliefs they retold, the Haitian fear that a magician—a 'voodoo master'—could suck out his victims' souls and then put them to work for them forever in his mines and sugar mills seems to have struck a ringing chord in the early twentieth-century public. The sources claimed factual and objective status, of course, but they were tossed into the cauldron of Gothic fantasy to produce the authentic *frisson* of psychic Orientalism for mass consumption.

Zombie B-movies from the start convey a seething mass of anxieties, political and personal. In *White Zombie*, Bela Lugosi plays the zombie master, known as 'Murder' Legendre; this was the year after he had embodied Dracula, to great acclaim, and he again hammed it up, in tremendous diabolical make-up—widow's peak wig, beetling brows, goatee—with sinister close-ups of his magical, Freemason's hand clasps and his needle-spotlit, hypnotic eyes, through which he bends his victims to his desires. The critics sneered, but it was a hit with the public, one of the most successful films in economic terms of the decade.[15]

A first-person account of voodoo rituals in a book called *The Magic Island* (1929) influenced the script. William B. Seabrook, an Englishman resident in New York who went to live in Haiti for two years, was on the whole sympathetic to the islanders' culture, and though frequently salacious in tone, he does give valuable eyewitness descriptions of voodoo trance rituals on an island that had been one of the richest imperial possessions of the French.[16] His account had an impact in two very different worlds: on the one hand, the Surrealist circle in Paris, which took up Seabrook with enthusiasm (especially the photographer Man Ray), fascinated by his experiments with drugs, sado-masochism, altered states, and cannibalism; on the other, American B-movies, in which the lurid vision of Afro-Caribbean magic psychology excited thrills and shivers with racist overtones (it is sobering how imaginative struggles to reconsider axioms of personal liberty relate to acutely problematic areas of twentieth-century exploitation, sexually and racially).

When Seabrook's book came out in New York, it inspired a playwright, Kenneth Webb, to write a drama entitled simply *Zombie*, which was staged in New York in 1932. The word for this kind of victim was so little known at that date, that Webb sued the film-makers Edward Halperin and Victor Hugo Halperin after they announced their new production, *White Zombie*, later the same year. He claimed the idea was his. He was unsuccessful, and his suit was thrown out, the law deciding that by this date, the word 'zombie' had entered the public domain.

White Zombie: the film's concerns lies with its white protagonists, not with the few black figures seen fleetingly in the background and in a spectral sugar mill where slaves tread and trudge, zombies enslaved to Murder Legendre's will: at one point one falls into the grindstone, but the zombies plod on, regardless, working the treadmill. The protagonists are Americans and English, both patrician—a plantation owner and his butler, a young couple arriving on the Caribbean island to get married. The film was shot night-for-night in strongly atmospheric chiaroscuro on old sets created for *Dracula* and *The Hunchback of Notre Dame*, and the story plot plays out an allegorical fable about new world innocence and *ancien régime*, European decadence, but the plotting operates a kind of wishful inversion of political realities in the Caribbean region. The young bride becomes the victim of voodoo, a catatonic walking shell, the direct inheritor of spellbound hero-ines of Romantic poetry and opera, and of Victorian poetry, fiction—and medicine. Her desouled state both conveys sexual possession, as evoked in

Gothic horror, but in this context also mimics the loss of selfhood entailed by slavery—legally and experientially.

Haiti was still under American occupation at the time of the film's making—as it had been since 1918. This regime lasted until 1934—land had been seized by foreign owners, and forced labour was used to build the 'protectorate' and its amenities. As one critic has suggested, 'Murder' Legendre represents a distorted projection of American guilt about the occupation.[17] So the plot directs its sympathies towards the white visitors, portraying them as vulnerable to the soul-theft and enslavement practised on the island, and in doing so, it deflects guilt from the audience at best, or, at worst, obscures the issue of exploitation: whose liberty is being lost, whose is being gained? Some kind of profound self-interest compels the makers of *White Zombie* to meditate on slavery and its afterlife, while conspicuously avoiding the historical facts of the subject as such. However, while at the patent level of the story, the spellbound bride is the innocent victim of sinister black magic, at a latent level, she loses herself when she comes into contact with the forces that govern the island's activities: she loses her wits rather than grasp and accept that knowledge of oppression. It is as if the film is saying, 'Don't look now. Don't ask where your money is coming from: you will not be able to bear it if you find out.'

During the same period, when audiences were flocking to the movie, and Hurston began visiting the Caribbean to carry out her own ethnographical research, the Depression was vitiating relations between work and production, and undoing obligations between workers and bosses, labourers and proprietors. This implied meaning of zombie—the counterpart of the robot, who, when redundant, is unplugged and thrown away—returned with a vengeance, literally, in the film *The Night of the Living Dead*, as we shall see below.

Eight years after Hurston's remarkable account of her field trips, another B-movie destined for cult status, *I Walked with a Zombie* (1943), became the next popular hit after *White Zombie* to feature the legend of the living dead in Caribbean magic,[18] and to repeat the inversion and focus again on an elite, female, victim of enchantment. Directed by Jacques Tourneur and produced by Val Lewton (the same team responsible for the psychological spookiness of *Cat People*), the film commands a different form of attention more than sixty years after its making, because its deep concerns have with time revealed their contours, in rather the same way as erosion can uncover a buried site.[19] The very attempt to control anxieties about colonial conflict, to turn different beliefs into cathartic stories, led this film-making team into contradictions and *non sequiturs* that betray unresolved anxieties in the marrow of the plot.

A cynical and worldly English plantation owner, Paul Holland, hires a Canadian nurse, Betsy Connell, to look after his wife, who has been afflicted with a strange, mute, automaton existence. He accompanies her to his island, Saint Sebastian, on board ship, and when she reaches it, she finds an unhappy house, filled with twisted relationships, haunted by the living, the dead, and the living dead.

The film's source was a short story written by a reporter, Inez Wallace, who had visited Haiti,[20] and the plot openly re-visions *Jane Eyre*, with the 'madwoman in the attic' played as another white victim, the beautiful dumb blonde wife of the plantation owner, and her mother-in-law standing in here for Grace Poole and the hired nurse for Bronte's heroine, the governess. The connection between the craziness of Bertha Mason, the first Mrs Rochester, who came from the West Indies, and the soul-stealing powers of voodoo was made explicit in this film for the first time. Wallace writes of 'her first zombie': 'he was the colour of caviar, a sort of greyish-black. He walked with a stiff-legged shuffle and his eyes looked out at me—but did not see me. I knew immediately he was a zombie.'[21] This description, not given in the film script itself, was followed by the imposing actor playing Carrefour, keeper of the crossroads, whom the heroine encounters when she takes her patient to be cured by the voodoo priest, the 'houngan'. His part in the film is purely theatrical—he stalks the action and inspires dread, but belongs nowhere in the plot. At night, he prowls the plantation house, his stiff, corpse-like silhouette looming in the room where Betsy is keeping vigil over her patient, among the interlaced shadows of Caribbean wrought iron and louvres. As in Seabrook's study, *The Magic Island*, white consciousness comes face to face with black magic under its own compulsion, and the potential dangers of zombification grow in the confrontations. Like the ghost of Beloved, in Toni Morrison's novel (1987), who personifies the history of slavery's cruelty and bloodshed, the zombies in Tourneur and Lewton's spooky film visit the sins of the past on the present.

I Walked with a Zombie takes the question of female catalepsy deeper than does *White Zombie*, and the later film may lie behind the ingenious reverse angle view of *Wide Sargasso Sea*, Jean Rhys's famous reworking of *Jane Eyre* in her 1967 novel.[22] The film bundles a whole sheaf of causes for the loss of the wife's wits, and none of them is compatible with any other. Each competes in the film's unresolved quest for the key to the mystery of life, embodied by the zombie's life-in-death state of being. The entranced wife is described as 'a sleepwalker who can never be awakened', a 'ghost', 'the living dead'. Her state arose, originally, we are told in a calypso, after she violated sexual codes of conduct, and slept with her husband's brother. She never speaks, does not appear to see anything or anyone, and moves automatically to the summons of conflicting masters—and mistresses—and their spells. The film is far too anxious to cover all possibilities to reach a conclusion, and in this incapacity, it partakes oddly of the vacancy of zombies itself.

The magic rites of the drumming, chanting, entranced voodoo cultists up in the 'houmfort', or voodoo shrine, on the mountain turn out to be controlled by Mrs Rand, a missionary's widow and the mother-in law of the zombie wife: she confesses her guilt, but her confession is rejected by the medical doctor on the case as 'a mere trick of the imaginative fancy of a woman'. Other explanations circle the victim, but, in the end, the power of spells over the mind is never entirely gainsaid. It is, however, detached from a single individual's control—be it by a voodoo priest, or missionary widow—on to the larger horizon of history: the zombie's heart is pierced, and her plight ended with an arrow taken from the figure of Saint Sebastian, who gives the island its name. This statue is the figurehead of the slave ship that brought the plantation workers from Africa, and it is known to them as Ti-Misery—that is, Little Misery. So in this story, the zombie sucks into itself the wrongs of the past, performs their dehumanizing, death-dealing effects over a prolonged, even unending existence which, like memory itself, will not die, until in the again wishful denouement, the victim is impaled through the heart and drowned at sea. The last words of the film are: 'Lord who knowest the secrets of all hearts, yea, Lord, pity them that are dead and give peace and happiness to the living.' The waters close, and oblivion, it is implicitly and devoutly desired, can bring about its own magic. This must include us, watching in the dark. *I Walked with a Zombie* dramatically conveys a new twist on the idea of collective guilt and psychological possession, or loss of self.

The concept of this new, voided, numb person spreads through the fictions of the Sixties: Sylvia Plath's narrator in her pitiless novel about breakdown, *The Bell Jar* (1963), cannot escape out of the walls of glass that have descended to enclose her and command conscious and active being: Plath reaches for sheaves of metaphorical identities, populating her story with forms of diminished life—germs, mosquitoes, slaves. Esther sees herself taken over, first by a dybbuk (a demon from Judaic legend), then by a zombie.[23]

A generation after the film *I Walked with a Zombie*, another oddity also became a cult movie, and sealed the appropriation of the zombie for white consciousness of its own haunted predicament: *The Night of the Living Dead*, made in 1968 by the independent producer George A. Romero and the screenwriter and director John A. Russo, in Pittsburgh, once the great steel capital of America, with a strong white labour tradition. The mills were closing, and Pittsburgh was facing utter decline, and Romero took the bold step of relocating the zombie, out of Africa or the West Indies, to the United

States. He reconfigured zombies as 'living dead', and crossed them with another ghost from early cinema, the vampire. His zombies have been reanimated in their graves by a nuclear disaster, and have risen as undead ghouls, ravening to devour human flesh. Like vampires, their bite contaminates victims with the same raging hunger, and so zombiedom spreads, ineluctably, at contact. The film's horde of zombies, shuffling unstoppably towards their prey, appear vacant and bestial, but also somehow torpid as blocks of stone; they were cast from local citizens of Pittsburgh and wear their own working clothes: they are recognizably the labour force of contemporary industrial America, threatened with unemployment in the decaying capital of steel. They joined this apocalyptic vision, becoming extras in a story of their own destiny and in many senses playing themselves.[24]

Capital and the proletariat, long vested in metaphors of consumption and cannibalism, here savagely return as ravening workers, bent on devouring the living, and, in the process of consuming bodies, converting the consumed into more mindless engines of decay. Romero is 'almost entirely responsible for the familiar incarnation of the zombie as a ghoulish cannibal', for giving the figure 'extra bite', as one critic aptly put it.[25]

In this potent dystopic allegory, the hero Ben defends the small group of the besieged in a house where they have taken refuge. Ben was played by a black actor, Duane Jones—the background material on *The Night of the Living Dead* maintains that he was simply the best actor who auditioned for the role, and was given the part for this reason. It is true that the script never alludes to his being black: an aspect that the *Cahiers du Cinéma* critic at the time found utterly absurd and also reprehensibly and oppressively colourblind—as if Ben was somehow not present materially, and his being the only black made no difference. But the effect, to a viewer today, surely deepens the politics of *The Night of the Living Dead* in a most eloquent fashion, especially in the closing sequence, when this most sympathetic hero, who has proved so cool under fire, so resourceful and uncompromising, is callously picked out by the sheriff's sharpshooter and gunned down. The flames of the posse's torches and the seething shadow of the night-time conflict recall—in a clear tribute to the victims—the lynchings of those years in the civil rights struggle.[26]

In this film, the posse can shoot to kill: zombies are not immortal. In other vehicles, different ways of escape are offered: in the Caribbean, zombies can find release from their endless labour by eating salt, whereupon they can fly back to their lost homelands in Africa (Earl Lovelace, the Trinidadian writer, explored this folklore in his novel *Salt* (1998)).

Zombies have global presence: the word is now adopted or has been revived in many languages and cultures. Fela Kuti sang about the 1976 *coup* in Nigeria in his biting satirical number 'Zombie', describing conscripts in a dictator's army sent into fight and kill for him, as 'Zombie no go go unless you tell am to go | Zombie no go think unless you tell am to think . . . Go and kill . . . Go and die.' Zombies swarm in the urban crowd at rush hour, as another blazing song, the calypso known as 'The Zombie Jamboree', which to the bounciest beat and gayest tune, sings out defiance: 'Back to back, belly to belly, | Don't give a damn | 'Cos I'm stone dead already.' The calypso won the Carnival prize in 1955 at the height of the Cold War, and it focused on the atomic bomb as the death masters' instrument of choice; Harry Belafonte later recorded it, and introduced freshly cutting political references, including an image of the towers of the World Trade Center the year after they were built:

> There's a high-wire zombie 'tween the World Trades
> A King Kong zombie on the Empire State
> But the biggest zombies Tokyo to Rome
> The zombies who call the city home.
> (Hah! What they do! Huh!)[27]

The Simpsons have parodied the zombie movie, in an episode which includes a lofty rebuke from Bart to Lisa that zombies do not like being called that, and she should say instead, 'living impaired'. In gift shops and at toy counters you can now buy 'In-Crowd Zombies', small role-playing figurines who have overtaken smurfs and wombles and other cuddly monsters in the imaginary and its commercial vehicles. The rock musician who directed the Goth horror film *The Devil's Rejects* (2005) has adopted the name Rob Zombie. Children's games draw increasingly on the repertory of magic, in an eclectic amalgam that certainly relishes the *frissons* of voodoo.

The zombie was uprooted from its origins in the African diaspora of the Caribbean, and the slave condition which it embodied has shifted ground, from its historical and actual relation to economic conditions of labour, to a broader psychological description of human existential diminishment. Yet the concept of the zombie crystallized a state of being that does still remain in play between holders of different levels of power—masters and slaves, men and women, owners and employees.

A film critic writing in 1967 about *I Walked with a Zombie* commented: 'The world does not remain unexplained if its story is told. Concomitantly, when it is not explained, as here, the world's story cannot be told.'[28] Zombies have become figures of the world's unspeakableness; in their speechlessness they speak of this. They embody that nullity and disaffection that makes the untellable story of the world possible to bear. Their nature recalls V. S. Naipaul's bitter rage against the history of his native region, when he wrote: 'The history of the islands can never be satisfactorily told.

Brutality is not the only difficulty. History is built around achievement and creation; and nothing was created in the West Indies.'[29] This is of course untrue, not least because among its creations, the zombie figures as a most acute, symptomatic and pervasive symbol of the living death inflicted by humans on one another. The term's meanings keep twisting and turning in the utterance of different parties, now a weapon to put distance between us and them, an insult, an estranging label, a joke, a bond to draw us closer together, and finally a mirror of a certain common fear of numbness and loss. If the eighteenth century set up the concept of self-possession as a psychological and ethical ideal, the present time is haunted by threats to that happy state: 'agency' and 'empowerment' are buzz words continually shadowed by their doubles, their 'duppy', their zombie.

The paranoid model of a subject doomed to lose all self-possession also suffuses the plot of the *Matrix* films, much indebted to Dick's paranoid imagination, where the reality of existence all around human beings is a computer-generated illusion. 'Welcome to the desert of the real!,' says Morpheus, leader of the resistance, gesturing to the desolate wastes of Chicago, the old world of being that has been effaced by the new world of appearances.[30] Apocalyptic in its vision, the film struck a strong chord of sympathy: the public recognized something they knew, and responded.

While the quest for human spirit has engendered a train of spirits—from angels to ectoplasms—in modernity, soul is now chiefly figured by its absence.

On the Western Front during the First World War, gas
was used as a lethal weapon; here, in a photograph that
announces the poison clouds of the future, German fog
apparatus is being tested.

Conclusion

> Of course the night left empty-handed.
> Worse, it swept the streets for litter
> as you slept—intact—your soul as
> heavy as your self; sleek, seal-like,
> made of light, love, marrow,
> milk and honey, made of body.
>
> Michael Symmons Roberts, 'Attempts on Your Life'

In response to the first question raised at the start of this book—'What is soul stuff?'—doomed scientific quests mined the materials of the symbolic imagination and speculated about ether, magnetic light, radiant matter, and, eventually, ectoplasm, as they searched for an answer. The historical record is one of failure. But it also reveals how history can inform our future endeavours, if only to warn of excessive confidence in answers presented by each successive generation. The other question—'What is the psyche?—touches us as human beings even more closely today. The age of databanks, mechanical reproduction, and instantly accessible digital archiving has unravelled the Genome, with the full combinatory codes of human DNA, giving us spectrography of the iris of the eye and of a strand of hair in order to identify and track individuals.[1] But the two questions are coupled, because consciousness is part of the body, and questions about the workings of consciousness raise questions about its constitutive elements, and these lead straight back to the complex problem of individual being.

The logic of the imaginary furnished materials for thinking about spirits—wax, air, light, and shadow. But it turns out that however deeply rooted in the imagination's forms, these metaphors are contingent, shaped in relation to time and experience—and can be superseded. So one of the most tried vehicles of the sublime—the cloud stuff of heaven—has changed meaning; while its power to communicate terror remains, it has fallen into the sump of the impure in any vision of metaphysical realities. The classical and baroque ether was fiery, and the radiant clouds that filled heaven were made of this fiery element, as we saw (Chapter 6). Today, combustion announces pollution and poison, for industrial progress gradually abolished the gambolling cloud-babies, the underlit vortices of the empyrean, the radiant nimbuses that sheathe angels in vaporous light. Once upon a time, Raphael painted the Madonna of Foligno upwafted by curling surf of blue-grey angel-clouds, Correggio depicted the ravishing approach of a god as a mass of blue-grey smoke (Plate 1), Titian invited us to believe in the Assumption of the Virgin taking place within and upon a roiling mass of shadowy cumulus, and Poussin caught Mary up to heaven on a roll and blast of thundercloud (Plate 3). But we live now as successors to the splitting of the atom and to the nuclear-powered ascension of the mushroom cloud at he Second World War and during the hydrogen bomb tests in cific.

Photography made the crucial difference in adulterating the materials of this airy family of symbols. The Crimean War was the first to be documented by the camera, but Roger Fenton's famous images show a hushed and still desolation, for the camera speeds in the 1860s were simply too slow to capture action or explosions as they were happening. The first images of shells bursting, of bomb blasts and billowing gusts of smoke in warfare, seem to have been taken in the First World War. The photographs are military records, made in a spirit of discovery of new weapons, presented in the archive of the Imperial War Museum as evidence, historical and scientific (Figure 30, p. 370). Black-and-white photographs show the effect of mines exploding, of shells' impact, of gas canisters spewing out their poisons, of rifle fire igniting: boiling plumes of grey smog, or solid walls of smoke and debris, sometimes soft, miasmic bodies of cloud floating above the ground, apparently the purest shade of white, all innocence and ethereality.[2] Poison gas filled the landscape of the trenches with light, spiralling heads of cloud, and brought Darth Vader muzzles to the troops—and their horses—for protection against the evil; infantry smokescreens raised tall, impenetrable barriers. The new horrors of chemical warfare proved parts of the invisible air materially present and undeniably tangible, while the contamination of industrial emissions added to the new experience of air, to the newly malignant character of the fiery aether.[3]

The American photographer Michael Light recently published a quiet, relentless archive of nuclear tests between 1945 and 1962. *100 Suns* presents an overwhelming photographic record, and it communicates its deadly burden of meaning all the more eloquently for the reticence of its author's commentary.[4] The book also inspires a turmoil of mixed feelings: the design is aesthetically beautiful, and the photographs thrilling and utterly horrifying at one and the same time. They were taken at a time when their meaning for us now was not yet formed: they are saturated with dramatic irony of a truly terrifying intensity. US sailors stand to attention, in the desert or on battleships in the vicinity, to watch the tests, protected by little more than sunglasses; the inhabitants of the regions where the tests took place are altogether effaced, of course. But this disregard of the very conditions of human existence was itself rooted in incomprehension of the energy and nature of fire and air.

Photographs of such blasts and devastation—from atomic bombs to the records of the burning World Trade Center—produce a twisted effect, and I do not think I am alone when the power and terror of the firebursts deliver a hit, a rush. These images are sublime—in the strict sense that they open up visions of the abyss. The very complexity of this response encapsulates a pervasive cultural dilemma, about the relations of pleasure and representation, of symbolism and experience. However, assaying signs such as clouds and cloudiness, learning their history and modifications over time, can at least help one analyse the effect that such images of bombs and bombing have on us now. For as signs of dream and possibility, clouds still float through our world: as the default setting of the Windows screensaver, in numerous ads for future investments, insurances, fortunes. Clouds are still buoyed by ancient exhalations of ethereal paradises, divine power, immortal longings.

The Virgin Mary, when she appears in modern visions, say at Fatima, or in Medjugorje in present-day Croatia, still favours ethereal modes of transport: holy pictures issued from the shrines as souvenirs, with special prayers for Mary's intercession on the other side, show her aloft and aureoled in glowing light, standing on a small, radiantly pure white cloud which is carrying her in the same manner as the *Bodhisattvas* of the Buddhists. But no religious image-maker today would paint the murky turmoil that buoys some ascending saints, or wraps inky Jupiter, or wreathes smoky haloes round the sphere of divinity in High Renaissance art. Holy cloud transports now are washed whiter than white.

But apart from weaponry of death and terrorism, there are the billowing plumes of cooling towers, the smog of car-choked cities, the leaching of the ozone layer, the melting of the icecaps, the growing asthmatic problems of children and older people. And so we need another constellation of metaphor to convey the unpolluted, uncontaminated zone of spirit. The language of the ether opened casements on to the realm of the u   h..t it depended on conditions and on aspirations that have since been new kind of cloud; we breathe a different air now.

While the imagery conveying soul, spirit, and ghosts has been shape-shifting, the study of human consciousness has been moving over from one discipline to another: from theology to philosophy, from biology to neuroscience, where an array of scientists, from different backgrounds, are industriously experimenting, researching, speculating, and writing to meet the avid curiosity of the public as well as the esteem of their peers. Bookstores are bulging with studies of *Homo sapiens* as a neurophysiological specimen. What sins were to the Christian philosopher, or teeth and bones to the palaeontologist, dendrites, axons, neurons, and synapses have become to the questors after consciousness. The brain, together with its genetic inheritance, has emerged as the prime vehicle of selfhood—after the soul and the psyche. Memories stored in the brain carry the plot of a person through a lifetime; by tracking the brain's complexities, a new kind of story about consciousness emerges, which dislimns supreme human ego in favour of exchanges at the level of the cell, the species, the animal condition, and reveals human resemblance and sympathies to the rest of the natural world.

There is much disagreement and great expanses still of *terra incognita*, in spite of the apparent fullness and conviction of the writers. The leading thinkers and popularizers in the field—such as Roger Penrose, John Searle, Steven Pinker, Daniel Dennett, Antonio Damasio, Gerald Edelman—mostly contend. Edelman declares that he wants to 'disenthrall' the subject from mystery and metaphysics, and the neuroscientist Semir Zeki, aiming to develop a neurological account of aesthetic pleasure, pinpoints the exact location in the brain of responses to colour and form.

Although it does not lie entirely beyond the bounds of possibility that you and I—like the doctors deciphering the data or biologists working on the Genome—could be trained to read genetic strings of code and (more certainly) to interpret computer records of them, these tokens of a person's individuality give little insight into what makes them who they are experientially or psychologically. The forensic particularity of DNA only sharpens the mystery of a person's quiddity as experienced in relations between people. In most of the ways that matter—unless you are searching for a criminal, a biological relative, or a genetic trait—it can tell you little. Even if you are looking for a tendency to a congenital illness, it will not reveal the person (no two diabetics are any more alike as people than two decathlon athletes).

Typing people by digital means goes hand in hand with surveillance systems, automatically queued telephone help lines, electronic vocal responses, and other cybernetic presences that populate the social body with replications of the self of varying degrees of permanence. This development relates to the story about spirits that *Phantasmagoria* has been telling. The history that runs from waxworks to DNA databanks reveals the gradual process of disembodiment rather neatly: the attempt to grasp the singularity of a person moves from portraying their outward appearance as faithfully as possible, to capturing their inalienable self in a barcode legible only—so far—by algorithms set up in computer program. When the murderer Joseph Paul Jernigan donated his body to science, it was frozen, sliced into 1871 sections, uploaded on to the World Wide Web to become the cyber-Everyman or Adam, for study as a generic human.[5] This zenith of forensic investigation thus dematerializes the cadaver—and abrogates all individuality of the person. It is a paradox of the twenty-first century that the most secure and detailed identifying methods ever devised remain at a personal level bluntly anonymous.

Slavoj Žižek, discussing the growing dominance of biology and genetics in thinking about consciousness, the brain, and individuals, recently quoted a quip made by Tom Wolfe—'Sorry, but your soul has just died.' He warned that 'the biogenetic threat is a much more radical version of "the end of history", one that has the potential to render the free autonomous subject of liberal democracy obsolete'. Illustrating the dangers he foresees, he gave an example of a rat implanted with a chip in its brain which allows it to be controlled remotely: 'what was new in the case of the rat was that, for the first time the "will" of a living agent, its "spontaneous" decisions about its movements, were taken over by an external agency.' Mounting a defence of social and psychological theories of mind, Žižek concluded a little shakily; but in this very shakiness, he reveals how stubbornly metaphysics remain part of human consciousness, or at least of those parts that were defined as 'imagination' and make up language and adopt it as a tool of communication with others. He recommends squaring up to the neuro-scientific threat as a training ground for opposition: 'Reducing my being to the genome forces me to traverse the phantasmal stuff of which my ego is made, and only in this way can my subjectivity properly emerge.'[6] Neuroscience has given ancient *fantasia* a new guise under the rubric 'fictionality', and this aspect of consciousness—the power to make phantasms rise in the mind's eye—remains a defining, and possibly unique, human capacity and a central characteristic of the human spirit.

At the same time as these changes in the metaphors for spirit and the concept of the conscious person, new media have also modified self-consciousness, as this book has been discussing. A familiar, inescapable and sought-after part of enveloping reality has become the record of our presence now, and in the past. Communication media, generated by the scientific tapping of electricity and other forces, rays, and waves, have wrapped us in spectral contacts with the time before this time, with events that have taken place and their opposite. Nobody before the Victorians knew what they looked like at different stages of their development—unless they were kings or queens, and even then, they had not watched themselves moving and speaking and laughing in years long gone. This development has changed ideas of self, and it has also wrought a total metamorphosis on memory: children, loved ones, public figures, stars of stage and screen, icons with cult followings, live on as they were at a certain time through their moving images. Watch a group of family or friends taking pictures of one another: the image in the tiny screen of the digital camera is spellbinding to a degree that eclipses the reality, as one person after another looks in enchanted absorption at the miniature picture, where life looks alive to a degree it somehow does not attain in reality. Is it the novelty that fascinates us? Do the frame and the miniaturization condense the circumstances with the intensity of made representations, and so make life itself more vital? Like the fortune-teller's balls or magic mirrors, like Lyra's alethiometer in *His Dark Materials*, Google Earth tracks my exact position in my study as I write this; by beaming up to its satellite, I guarantee my presence by a magic of doubling that is vertiginous and thrilling, just as that tiny moving picture in the screen of a mobile phone seems to crystallize meaning in some magical, keyed-up way.

Great events are also captured as future memories: the flash of cameras accompanies—and alters—them as they happen. Experiences increasingly take place through the lens, on screen, to pluck them out of time and hold them fast in the parallel space-time continuum where the event is repeated unchanged again and again. In that haunting, poignant fashion of the home movie, everyone stays as they once were—then. Yet the proportion of video recordings—of birthdays, weddings, great historic moments (the Pope's lying in state, a football win)—that the maker plays more than once has remained small. The point seems to be to translate reality into representation and fix and store it, at the moment that it happens. Something about the relationship of our inner world to lived actuality makes the flowing image in the monitor utterly compelling. The mobile phone photograph has made victims of accidents and bombings witnesses of their own ordeals and trans-formed the meaning of Faust's desire to stay this moment. For the first time, in some new technological alchemy, the moment in which I find myself, the place where I stand, the presences around me, including my own, are instantly translated into a flow of communications out of time, out of place, *in absentia*.

The invented Orphic media of modernity imitated the movements of the mind—of memory's phantasms and desire's fantasies—when they uncoupled visions from natural law and gave them the boundless and weightless elements of dream reality. But since their discovery and diffusion, they have refashioned the map of human consciousness and fostered spirits to suit the times; these phantoms are interwoven with developing ideas about the person. This conjunction presents one of the principal reasons for the return of magical imagination today. In the same way that photography could capture the spirit of a person, and radio and the telegraph communi-cate the acoustic and disembodied presence of another, so colour movies, television, digital media, and, even more recently, the virtual reality of the internet have forged a new narrative of spirits and spectres. Contemporary media of representation—including above all digitization—convey a plural and labile theory of consciousness that installs virtual presences, phantoms, hauntings, and doubles in the ordinary way of things. They wrap us in illusions of phantoms and phantasms, turning reality into dream, dream into act, and myths into realities. But there is a difference between the Fifties, when Roland Barthes first probed the constrictive ideology of modern myth, and the media's uses now: leakage between simulated and actual reality is not trapped inside the cinema or the gameboy, does not keep safely within the boundaries of *The Truman Show*, in which the protagonist does not realize he is a character in a soap opera and that his life is unfolding in front of an audience of millions. It is funny when actors receive letters of condolence about a bereavement, or wedding presents arrive—for events taking place in the life of the character they play in a fiction. But it is less funny that television news need to label an interview 'Live' to in viewers that it is really taking place at that moment, and that, con warning may appear across footage of bombings or other events vision announcing 'Metaphorical Images' or 'Fake News'—to distinguish these images from 'Live' ones. Metaphorical—not fictional, not simulated, not untrue: we are being asked to receive this faithless speech as somehow truthful. A new generation of video games incorporates documentary footage and mixes it up with virtual scenarios, emptying meaning from the damage caught on film and denaturing responses to its truth.

Genetic coding, outward resemblance, and media reproduction are hardly the only places to look for answers to the mystery of human singularity at the individual level of animate vitality: physical particularity is not the same as psychological identity, even when you do not scan a supernatural horizon for understanding consciousness, individuality, and metamorphoses of the body–soul difference. Singularity is not subjectivity. Becoming a subject— becoming ensouled as a person—means becoming someone who constitutes experience through thinking and imagining in relation to experience, rather than taking up position as an object of observation. Finding a way to communicate this singular interiority offers a ground of resistance to de-souling—zombification—which many works of writing and art struggle to establish. Margaret Atwood has even declared, 'not just some, but all writing of the narrative kind, and perhaps all writing, is motivated, deep down, by a fear of and a fascination with mortality—by a desire to make the risky trip to the Underworld, and to bring something or someone back from the dead.'[7]

'The burning question, then, becomes this,' wrote Félix Guattari, 'Why have the immense processual potentials brought forth by the revolutions in information processing, telematics, robotics, office automation, bio-technology and so on up to now led only to a monstrous reinforcement of earlier systems of alienation, an oppressive mass-media culture and an infantilizing politics of consensus?' The trouble he diagnosed a decade ago has grown more acute, and many have joined their voices to the cry against simulacra, virtual realities, and the flux of images that contribute to the general destabilization of reality. Guattari's burning question asks for more than inveighing against spectral disembodiment. It goes to the heart of the theme of this book because, as he continued, 'My wish is that all those who remain attached to the idea of social progress—all those for whom the social has not become an illusion or a "simulacrum"—look seriously into these questions of subjectivity production.'[8] 'Subjectivity production' is a clumsy phrase, with a dead ring. 'Ensouling' would be a better term to convey this dream, just as new metaphorical constellations need to be discovered in the skies that language and imagination unfurl before our mind's eye.

We are cast as extras at the spectacle, and one of the ways of re-naturing this soulless state is to take charge ourselves of the counterfeit in relation to one another—by making its portrait at the very least, or even disfiguring its features. For knowing I am a zombie or—since it is not possible for a zombie to judge—realizing that at best I am fast moving towards zombiedom, demands an act of self-consciousness which in itself means that the state is not yet highly advanced in my case, not yet properly terminal. In contemporary accounts and works of art, fictional and otherwise, that confront this condition, various forms of metamorphosis have gained over those long-held principles of the self—mind–body unity and integrity of memory, embodiment, and consistency over time. A non-Christian, classical, mythical idea about individual potential and polyvalence has set aside a traditional concept of soul.

Hearing voices, experiencing hauntings, slipping between reality and imagination, and dislocating in time and space, characters and their authors are in different ways projecting a new model of subjectivity. Harold Pinter, in his speech accepting the Nobel Prize in 2005, described his method of creating a play from single words overheard and dim shapes forming in his mind: he portrayed himself as a passive and unknowing receiver of his writings, and used the phrase 'almost hallucinatory'. In the footsteps of Yeats, James Merrill's long, incantatory lyric meditation, *The Changing Light at Sandover*, was produced by himself and his friend and lover in communication with another exotic visitor, the spirit of 'Ephraim', who dictated via Ouija board, while his fellow American, the endlessly productive and innovatory John Ashbery, produced a book-length poem, *Girls on the Run*, in which he does not use the first person at all, dissolving self into the alternative self of a gang of little girls. Likewise, the French writer Franck Venaille forgoes the use of the pronouns *je* and *moi* in his poetry.[9]

If self-awareness is altering its nature, the boundary between the real and the imagined has also weakened—though it has never been as distinct, in my view, as commonly believed. In some unprecedented way, the various operating dynamics of magic stories—time shifts, ubiquity, hypnosis, possession, metamorphosis itself—now charge the currents of popular culture more densely than at any time since the first high wave of the Gothic in the late eighteenth century. Magical psychology, unstable, metamorphic, telepathic, and deracinated, permeates many of the most enjoyed stories being written and read and performed, far beyond the fantasy literature originally caught under the Latin American terms 'magic realism' and 'lo real maravilloso' ('marvellous reality'). Interest in persons as no longer unified, but split, doubled, or even multiple—haunted by an evil genius or illuminated by a familiar daimon—have combined with new instruments of perception and knowledge, and inspired new psychological investigations into such little understood aspects of personal consciousness as well as human interaction: these include, for example, crowd psychosis, mass illusions, the role of mimicry in learning, traumatic memory, and 'the transmission of affect'. These approaches to the individual posit a person who is not a singleton, but a node in a web of connections. Many of these connections are imperceptible, or at least little noticed and hardly understood.[10]

Many artists working today with images and with words and stories are unsettling the foundational principles of personal identity along these lines, performing metamorphoses on themselves and their subjects. Some project themselves into animal changes of shape, or imagine sci-fi alien mutations, or even dramatize new visions of monsters, and thereby transvalue hitherto abhorrent and abominable phenomena. Others are concerned with consciousness itself, with its mutability, its proneness to possession, and its multiple potential. The self splits, is usurped by *alter egos*, and becomes disunited and free-floating. This newly developed consciousness of the personal subject operates as an extension of contemporary media, and of the potential and virtual universes they have opened. In other words, for this new kind of protagonist, the faculties of what used to be called soul— fantasy, memory, sensation, emotions—exist in symbiosis with televisual communications and the laws that organize them. These warps of memory and perception, the proleptic energy of fantasy, various forms of disembodiment such as celebrity images and dream displacements, psychic travel, altered states of consciousness, and, above all, the bewildering inter-sheaving of actuality and imaginings, of dream and reality—all these themes recur in literature from Jorge Luis Borges to Philip Pullman, as well as in popular entertainment media for all ages.

A storyteller such as Borges can institute through 'reasoned imagination'—his phrase—a metaphysical and poetic dimension of reality, and help re-position us as we confront our selves and our identities. The Spanish novelist Javier Marias, clearly a close reader of Borges, has explored with savage comic inventiveness the bewildering interplay between his own fictions and experience, and has created a vivid, and indeed cogent, picture of their shifting and palimpsestic layerings. Marias grounds his characters and their stories securely within horizons of material reality, and does not introduce Gothic effects or invoke a supernatural dimension. James Lasdun, in his novel *The Horned Man*, similarly stages a protagonist who cannot distinguish his imaginings from his experience, and does not allow his readers to discern the boundaries either; the queering of reality in this story of breakdown in Manhattan includes a weird and terrifying and absurd metamorphosis—into a stag, in what is both a homage to Ovid's cruel story of Actaeon and a bitter, double allusion to Falstaff cozened at the end of *Merry Wives* and to the perennial cuckold.

More usually, however, when poets and novelists project metamorphing personalities and destabilized identities, they have recourse to the venerable languages of ghost possession and the supernatural, and then attempt—with varying degrees of success—to refashion them to appeal to contemporary readers and resonate with their experience.

Setting aside mandarin Modernists on the one hand and the avid readers of Stephen King and other supernatural horror writers on the other, it is striking how the public responds strongly to fictions of possession and unstable identity: in *Beloved* by Toni Morrison, the title character is a child murdered by her mother, who returns as a poltergeist; in *The Famished Road* by Ben Okri the narrator is an *abiku* or spirit child speaking from another, parallel world; *Alias Grace* by Margaret Atwood tells the story of a woman possessed by the ghost of her dead friend who commits murder to avenge her. In J. K. Rowling's celebrated books, Harry Potter finds his evil enemy Voldemort leaking into his mind, breaking through his defences, taking up occupation like a recovered traumatic memory, and then, like Tolkien's Frodo under assault from Sauron's magnetic attraction for the ring and its bearer, Harry and his chums in the Order of the Phoenix battle against the universal conspiracies of Voldemort and his Death Eaters, who have infiltrated the now proto-fascist Ministry of Magic.[11] They retaliate with magic: through translocation and invisibility under Harry's special wizard cloak; through doublings, metamorphosis, clairvoyance, flight, and the dream transmission of information and defences. Metaphors of such psychological assaults echo the suspected actions of a smart bomb or a stealth plane or a chemical weapon.

Fear of soul-theft also still takes hold of many imaginations beyond the screen or the page: alien abduction reports tell of creatures from another world or even another dimension, scooping the essence of their prey and replacing it with their own in order to propagate their own species.[12] Sarah Kember, in her study *Virtual Anxiety*, diagnoses how the fears excited by global power, technological invasion, and contamination inspire conflicting stratagems: 'The subject responds defensively with fantasies o boundary reinforcement, or alternatively disembodiment.'[13]

The inquiry into individuality and mutual interaction needs to deepen; the biological and neuroscientific line of analysis needs languages to think with. Such an undertaking becomes political, analytical, and constructive, and artists, performers, and writers who are grasping the imaginary fabric that swathes and freights our consciousness today are sometimes answering the call to grasp technologies as the prime shaper of human identity now and recognize their effects, engage with social issues, and revision the seductiveness of illusions as a first step towards dreaming them differently. They can help—and they often mean to—reorientate readers' and audiences' perceptions, and shape subjectivity within a mesh of reciprocal and social relations. Those working in this vein rough-hew inherited phantasms, not only mining their undoubted pleasure and power. In a material sense, spirits are indeed channelled, and the media are here, now.

Notes

Prologue

1. Santa Caterina da Bologna, *Le Sette Armi Spirituali*.
2. Votive picture with prayer given to the author at the shrine.
3. In Montefiascone, in central Italy, for example, the shrine of S. Lucia Filippini (1672–1732) centres on her incorrupt body, displayed in the centre of the church in a glass casket: she has been embalmed, and her white face appears cast in pale wax. Its girlish smoothness contrasts with the characterful portrait of her hanging in the nearby convent of the order of Maestre Pie, which she founded to teach girls in free schools.
4. The craftsmen-artists who worked on the shrine from 1684 to 1695 were Giuseppe Mazza, Enrico Haffner, and Marcantonio Francheschini.
5. Freud, 'The Uncanny', in *The Uncanny*, 123–63.
6. Galvani, *De viribus electricitatis in motu musculari*. It was part of the advanced, enlightened character of Bolognese learning that he was assisted by Lucia Galeazzi, his wife, as he described in his account of the experiment. Galvani wrote a eulogy to her when she died in 1790; he is buried in the side chapel beside her: Galvani, *Elogio della Moglie Lucia Galeazzi Galvani*. Laura Bassi Veratti (d. 1778) is also buried in the church; she was a pioneering teacher of physics at the Institute of Sciences.
7. The word 'galvanize' has at least two meanings: applied to metals, it means coating iron or steel with zinc through an electrolytic process in order to protect it from corrosion; figuratively, it means something closer to Galvani's work, the revitalization of a moribund or torpid organism: 'I was galvanized into action.'
8. He was interested in the nervous system and its invisible transmission of signals throughout the body, and proposed that the effect arose from the electrical charge of the external muscle (positive) and the internal nerve (negative); he had in point of fact introduced an electrical current through the body, but this was thought at the time to be a kind of animal electricity, and was called 'galvanism'. Alessandro Volta (1745–1827), in Pavia, showed that galvanism has no connection to animals, and realized that in Galvani's experiments, the body merely acted as a conductor.
9. Mary Shelley, *Frankenstein*, ch. 4.
10. Ibid., preface.
11. Ibid. ch. 5.
12. Henry Wellcome, the voracious Victorian collector of all things pertaining to

the history of medicine, acquired a section of Bentham's skin, which was
included in the exhibition *Medicine Man*, BM, 2003.

Introduction: The Logic of the Imaginary

1. *A Catechism of Christian Doctrine* (1889), 3.
2. The literature on these questions is dauntingly vast and varied. I have found
   specially helpful: Crabbe, *From Soul to Self*; Riley, *The Words of Selves*; Seigel,
   The Idea of the Self; Taylor, *Sources of the Self*; Wierzbicka, 'Soul, Ame, Seele,
   Dusha'.
3. See D. P. Walker, 'Medical *Spirits* and God and the Soul'.
4. See Berlin, *Against the Current* 1–24.
5. Focillon, *Life of Forms in Art*, 15.
6. Angela Leighton, 'Wallace Stevens's Eccentric Souvenirs', from work in
   progress kindly shown to the author, 2005; forthcoming in *On Form: Poetry,
   Aesthetics, and the Idea of the Literary* (Oxford, 2007).
7. Focillon, *Life of Forms in Art*, 34–5.
8. Caillois, *La Pieuvre*, 230. Caillois (1913–78) founded with Georges Bataille and
   Michel Leiris the Collège de Sociologie in 1938 to study the presence of the
   sacred in ordinary life.
9. The repertory of ancient religions and philosophy, especially those founded on
   reincarnation, includes many symbols which I am not exploring: see Bettini,
   Kinship, Time, Images of the Soul, 197–246, for a fine account of 'The Bee, the
   Moth, and the Bat; Natural Symbols and Representations of the Soul';
   Osmond, *Imagining the Soul, passim*; also Warner, *Fantastic Metamorphoses*, 90–1,
   for the symbol of the butterfly.
10. Cf. S. Clark, *Thinking with Demons*, p. 3.
11. David Summers uses the terms 'force' and 'counterforce' for the difference
    between the seer and the seen. He writes: 'the emergence of imagination and
    representation in their modern forms is the first instance of the transformation
    of the traditional faculties of the soul according to the modern conviction that
    force is a final principle. If the external world is a theatre of forces in inter-
    action, the internal world, the experienced world of the subject, arises from a
    counterforce, somehow like force in being susceptible to it, but different. . . .
    Force and counterforce have provided an armature for two vast, ongoing
    modern projects: natural science and technology, and the correlative definition
    and institutionalization of the "subject" and "subjectivity".' Summers,
    '*Cogito* Embodied', in Meyer (ed.), *Representing the Passions*, 13–36.
12. Benjamin uses it in the first version (1935) of his celebrated essay, 'The Work of
    Art in the Age of Mechanical Reproduction'; see Krauss, *Optical Consciousness*,
    179–80.
13. I have been greatly inspired in these thoughts by Snyder, 'Picturing Vision'; see
    also Cantwell Smith.
14. Noakes, 'Cranks and Visionaries', 10.
15. Burwick, 'Romantic Drama', 182.
16. See Crews, 'Out, Damned Blot!'.

17. *Le Radical*, 1895, from Noel Burch, *Life to Those Shadows*, 20, quoted by the performance artist Zoe Beloff, 'Two Women Visionaries', <www.zoebeloff.com>.

18. Wallace Stevens, 'Imagination as Value', in *The Necessary Angel*, 153ff.; cf. Tiffany, *Toy Medium*, in which he explores how poetic language can play 'a more substantial role . . . in the *institution* of material substance' (p. 15).

Chapter 1   Living Likenesses, Death Masks

1. Angeletti, *Gerformtes Wachs*, plate 207.
2. See, e.g., Francesco Solimena, 'Sic Transit Gloria Mundi', in *Vanitas*, 280–1. The iconography of penitence is also related, as adapted in Georges de La Tour's Wrightsman Magdalen, in which she is contemplating a guttering candle, symbolizing earthly vanity. There even exists a miniature wax relief by Johann Christof Rauschner of Emma Hamilton as the Penitent Magdalene, making histrionic lamentation, VAM.
3. The waxworks sculptor Mark Richards informed me that flash photographs, as taken by visitors, cannot capture this quality of translucency because light does not bounce off the waxy surface, as off oil paint, but sinks into it. Personal communication, 13 June 1993.
4. e.g., *Youth Pierced by the Arrows of Love*, by Joseph Pertot of Berne, *c.*1692, shows the waxen flesh of Cupid and his victim studded with seed pearls to give an analogous sheen, VAM.
5. Aristotle, *De Anima* II, 1. 412b, trans. Hett, 68–9.
6. The late John Skeaping, personal communication; more recently, the artist Kiki Smith confirmed this intrinsic problem of 'life-casting'; see Warner, 'Wolf-girl, Soul-bird', in *Kiki Smith*, exh. cat.
7. Fenton, 'The Mummy's Secret'.
8. Pliny the Elder, *Natural History*, bk. XXXV, 153.
9. Verschaffel, 'Where There's a Voice, There's a Body'. 'On Death Masks', from *The Lectures 1991*, Witte de With, Rotterdam (1992), 89.
10. Diderot, 'L'Histoire et le secret de la peinture en cire', in *Œuvres complètes*, ii. 822, my trans.
11. At San Carmine Maggiore, Naples.
12. Walker Art Gallery, Liverpool. <http://www.liverpoolmuseums.org.uk/walker/collections/19c/gibson.asp>.
13. Weekes, *Lectures in Art*, 159.
14. Ibid. 169.

Chapter 2   Anatomies and Heroes: Madame Tussaud's

1. For Zumbo's wax pictures in VAM, see <www.vam.ac.uk>; see also Jordanova, *Sexual Visions*, 43–65; Lightbown, 'Le cere artistiche del '500'.
2. They were displayed in the Human Biology Department until 2001, when they were moved to the Palazzo Poggi, a resplendent baroque building owned by the university.

3. The new museum has assembled celebrated cabinets of curiosities and scientific materials, including Ulisse Aldrovandi's collections of minerals and natural wonders, the remarkable models of human reproduction from the School of Obstetrics and mementoes of the work of Galvani and other Bolognese scientists. See *Palazzo Poggi Museum*, guide ed. Tega.

4. A. Muzzi, 'Il laboratorio di Galvani', shows Galvani making the demonstration, assisted by his wife Lucia Galeazzi and his nephew Camillo. Museo Palazzo Poggi, <http://www.unibo.it/musei/palazzopoggi/poggi_eng/palazzo/collez. htm>.

5. Uglow, 'In the chamber of miracles'.

6. The artist Helen Chadwick was working on a 'Cameo' depicting her, part of a series inspired by the Hunterian, but died in 1996 before she completed it. It was destroyed in the warehouse fire at Leyton in 2004.

7. Hilloowala *et al.*, *The Anatomical Waxes of La Specola*, 48.

8. Ibid. 51.

9. Table in Musée de l'École de Médecine made by Efisio Marini.

10. Waxworks, file, JJC.

11. Butterfield, review of *Jean-Antoine Houdon: Sculptor of the Enlightenment*.

12. Abbé de Véri, quoted in Bailey, *Patriotic Taste*, 108 and in Butterfield, review, 8.

13. Butterfield, review, 9.

14. Benjamin, *Illuminations*, 217–52.

15. Angeletti, *Geformtes Wachs*, plate 56. The display shows Jerry Hall being modelled by Mark Richards, her blue eyes matched for colour with a glass set.

16. See Freedberg, *The Power of Images*, 192–245.

17. See Pamela Pilbeam, *Madame Tussaud and the History of Waxworks*, pp. xiii, 32.

18. There is no corroborating evidence for this phase of her career, however, and it may have been conveniently 'remembered'.

19. As still takes place all over the Catholic world, including Little Italy, New York, on the feast of San Gennaro.

20. Tussaud, *The Romance of Madame Tussaud's*, 52. (The author is Madame Tussaud's respectable—and English—grandson.)

21. She is depicted at work in a complex tableau in the museum, next to the scene of Marat's death, beneath shelves filled with death's heads of heroes past and present.

22. Gatacre and Dru, 'Portraiture in *Le Cabinet de Cire* de Curtius and its Successors'; Hinman, 'Jacques-Louis David and Madame Tussaud'.

23. Gavin Turk, a contemporary Britart sculptor who frequently explores the waxworks tradition, made another replica of 'The Death of Marat', after David's painting (1998).

24. Henry Wellcome, later in the century, bought another for his collection; see *Medicine Man*, exh. cat., 322; also <http://www.thebritishmuseum.ac.uk/med-icineman/>.

25. 'Waxworks', 1/20, JJC.

26. The museum bought it from the accused, M. F. Pearcey, who killed her lover's wife and baby, with all her effects, for £25 in 1891.

27. See During, M.v. and Poggesi, *Encyclopaedia Anatomica*.

28. Jordanova and Sawday, *The Body Emblazoned*.

29. See Lemire, 'Fortunés et infortunés de l'anatomie et des préparations anatomiques, naturelles et artificielles', in *L'Âme au corps*, 70–100.

30. See Latour, 'What is Iconoclash? Or is there a world beyond the image wars?' in *Iconoclash*, exh. cat, 14–37; *Apocalypse Now*, exh. cat., 94–7.

31. See Rose, 'The Cult of Celebrity' in *On Not Being Able to Sleep*, 201–15.

32. Aristotle, *The Poetics* 4a, trans. Potts, 20.

33. The Musée Grévin opened in 1882; the décor of the dark, labyrinthine entrance hall was devised by the caricaturist Alfred Grévin, working with a journalist, Arthur Meyer.

34. Ondine Concannon, conversation with the author.

35. *The Dawn of Photography*, exh. cat.

Chapter 3 On the Threshold: Sleeping Beauties

1. Aristotle, *Nicomachaean Ethics*, 1139ª1, quoted in 'Commentary on Aristotle's "De Anima"', in D'Arcy (ed.), *Aquinas: Selected Writings*, 60.

2. So the label in Madame Tussaud's said, in 1995, when I began this research.

3. This elaborate tableau was devised by the stage designer Julia Trevelyan Oman.

4. Marie-Thérèse Louise de Savoie-Carignan (b. Turin 1749, d. Paris 1792). The Princesse de Lamballe was one of the ghost figures seen walking at Versailles by the visitors from England. See Castle, *Apparitional Lesbian*, 112–16, 127–30, 133–4, 263 n. 94; Chantal Thomas, in her novel *Les Adieux à la reine*, dramatizes vividly the intensity of their relationship.

5. Fleischmann, *La Guillotine en 1793*, 290.

6. Emilie Desmier d'Archiac (1773–94), who died with her mother, is the likely subject of the waxwork.

7. *Biographical and Descriptive Sketches of the Distinguished Characters which Compose the Unrivalled Exhibition of Madame Tussaud's and Sons.*

8. Ruggeri, 'Il Museo dell'Istituto de Anatomia Umana Normale'.

9. Jordanova, *Sexual Visions*, 43–65.

10. Waxworks 3/61, JJC.

11. Martinotti, *Le Cere anatomiche della Specola*; for the history of the museum of La Specola, see *La Ceroplastica nella Scienza e nell'arte*, 1–135; see also Bronfen, *Over Her Dead Body*, 100–1.

12. See Detroit Institute of Fine Art, <http://www.artchive.com/artchive/F/fussli/fuseli_nightmare.jpg.html>.

13. The affinity between mortal remains and waxworks can be seen in the macabre tableau of Saint Bernadette's death, staged in the Musée Grévin in Paris. Meanwhile, in the convent at Nevers where she died in 1879, the visionary of Lourdes is laid out, embalmed—and reputed to be incorrupt by special privilege: two different kinds of effigy, but very like. Again, a religious drama presses out the shape of the secular theatre of fame.

14. John Adams Whipple, 'Hypnotism', *c.*1845, in *The Waking Dream*, exh. cat., 125.
15. Hilgard and Hilgard, *Hypnotism and the Relief of Pain*; see also 'Hypnosis, Experimental', in Gregory and Zangwill (eds.), *Oxford Companion to the Mind*, 329–30.
16. Bronte, *Jane Eyre*, 14–15.
17. *Cornelia Parker*, exh. cat., 30–5, 37, 52, 54.
18. Freud, 'The Uncanny'.
19. Rilke, 'Some Reflections on Dolls—Occasioned by the Wax Dolls of Lotte Pritzel', in *Rodin and Other Prose Pieces*, 121–2; see Warner, 'Self-portrait in a Rear-view Mirror', in *Only Make-Believe*, exh. cat, 4–19.
20. *Ron Mueck: Making Sculpture*; see also *Sensation*, exh. cat., 33, 126–7, 203.

Chapter 4 The Breath of Life

1. Bushinski, 'Spirit (in the Bible)'.
2. Quoted by St Hippolytus, *Refutation of All Heresies*, quoted in Hamilton, *Christian Middle Ages*, 7.
3. There is even a semantic connection to 'fizz', via the seventeenth-century meaning of breaking wind!
4. See McNicholl, 'Spirit', and 'Spirit, Modern Philosophies of'.
5. Helen Chadwick adopted this device from the Vanitas tradition which she explored in numerous works; see Warner, 'In the Garden of Delights'; also Chadwick, *Enfleshings*. Tacita Dean, another highly original and thoughtful contemporary artist, created the work called 'A Bag of Air: Catching Cloud, Air and Dew Alchemical Piece' (1995), *Witte de Witt Cahier # 6* (July 1997), 115–17; see also Tacita Dean, *Complete Works and Filmography 1991–2003*, in *Tacita Dean*, exh. cat.
6. Aquinas, *Summa Theologiæ*, Pt. 1, q. 51, art. 2, quoted Mayr-Harting, *Perceptions of Angels in History*, 19.
7. In FMC.
8. Donne, 'A Sermon Preached at the Earl of Bridge-waters house in London at the marriage of his daughter, the Lady Mary, to the Eldest son of the Lord Herbert of Castle-iland', 19 Nov. 1627, in *The Sermons of John Donne*, viii. 94–109.
9. Donne, *Poems of John Donne*, i. 21–2. See Tillyard, *The Elizabethan World Picture*, 45–60.
10. Kirk, *Secret Commonwealth*, 49–50; (spelling modernized); see also Hunter (ed.), *Occult Laboratory*; Warner, intro. to Kirk, *Secret Commonwealth* (New York and London, forthcoming).
11. Some ballerinas may have started dancing on points before Taglioni: the *Encyclopaedia Britannica* cites a lithograph of Fanny Bias *en pointe* in 1821, and mentions the possibility of Geneviève Gosselin also doing so as early as 1815, but Taglioni established the method in the title role of her father's ballet *La Sylphide* in 1832.
12. Aristotle, *Generation of Animals*, 736B–737A, 166–73; D. P. Walker, 'Medical Spirits and God and the Soul', 226.

13. Aristotle, ibid. 729a, pp. 108–9, also offered a rather more vivid domestic metaphor, writing that fertilization happened in the same way as 'the fig-juice or the rennet contains the principle which causes [milk] to set—for the making of junket'. This second property of spirit, the impressing power to form matter, associates spirit with active agency.

14. Galen, *Opera Omnia*, ed. Kühn, V. 643, quoted in D. P. Walker, 'Medical *Spirits* and God and the Soul', 225.

15. See Walker's excellent discussion of Protestant philosophers, such as Melanchthon, Michael Servetus, and Henry More, and their divergence from Catholic dogma, ibid., 224 ff.

16. Locke, *Drafts for the Essay Concerning Human Understanding*, draft A, i. 10; cf.: 'The same thing happens concerning the Operations of the Mind, viz. Thinking, Reasoning, Fearing, etc., which we concluding not to subsist of themselves, nor apprehending how they can belong to Body, or be produced by it, we are apt to think these the Actions of some other Substance, which we call Spirit; whereby yet it is evident that, having no other Idea or Notion, of Matter, but something wherein those many sensible Qualities, which affect our Senses, do subsist; by supposing a Substance wherein Thinking, Knowing, Doubting, and a power of Moving, etc., do subsist, We have as clear a Notion of the Substance of Spirit, as we have of Body.' Walmsley, 'Locke's Natural Philosophy'.

17. See Brown and Corner.

18. John Dryden with William Davenant, *The Enchanted Island*, v. ii. 16–25, in *Works of John Dryden*, p. 75.

19. 'Of the Popular and received tenets concerning Man, which examined, prove true or false', in Browne, *Pseudoxia Epidemica*, 315–16.

20. See Stinson for the pioneering materialism of the surgeon William Lawrence.

21. Brumberg, *Fasting Girls*; 64–73. After reviewing this study, I was inspired to write a short story, 'The Food of Angels', which appeared in *Mermaids in the Basement* (1994).

22. 'Notes on the Experiment between Dr. Baurieux and the criminal Languille (Montpellier, 1905)', in *Archives d'Anthropologie Criminelle*, quoted by the artist Douglas Gordon in his piece '30 Seconds Test', in *Seele*, exh. cat., 42–3.

23. Quoted in Bloom, *Omens of Millennium*, 3.

24. Ibid. 83–8.

25. Ibid. 227.

26. Wallace Stevens, *Collected Poems*, 496–7; idem, *Necessary Angel*, 131–56.

Chapter 5 Winged Spirits and Sweet Airs

1. Plato, *Phaedrus*, 51; see Hart, *Images of Flight*, *passim*, for an exploration of flying as a hope.

2. Calvino, *Six Memos*, 26–7.

3. Virgil, *Georgics*, Bk. IV, ll. 471–4, in *The Eclogues, The Georgics*, 124.

4. e.g., on a Greek vase, sixth century BCE, Pergamon Museum, Berlin, 1684, in Malcolm Davies and J. Kathirithamby, *Greek Insects*, 106–7, and a Roman gem, Thorvaldsen Museum (1929), no. 504, from Cook, *Zeus: A Study in Ancient Religion*, ii. 1., 645, fig. 563; see Warner, *Fantastic Metamorphoses*, fig. 20 and pp. 90–1.

5. e.g., fifth century relief, Coptic Museum, Cairo, in Kahil and de Bellefonds, Commentary, *Lexicon Iconographicum Mythologiae Classicae* (Zurich, 1992), vi, 1, 246; also Warner, *Fantastic Metamorphoses*, 113.

6. Hesiod, *Theogony*, ll. 116–20.

7. Ibid. ll. 194–7.

8. Brittain (ed.), *Penguin Book of Latin Verse*, 61; 'L'angelica farfalla' (the angelic butterfly') of Dante, *Purgatorio*, x. 125.

9. See, e.g., *Pélérinage de la vie humaine*, Bibliothèque Royale, Brussels, MSS. 10197–8, French c.1375–85, fol. 110.

10. In the Museo del Prado, Madrid. See <http://www.artcyclopedia.com/artists/patinir_joachim.html>.

11. In the Galleria Doria-Pamphili, Rome. See <http://www.doriapamphilj.it>; I owe the information about the eagle's wings to Ann Sutherland Harris, to whom, many thanks.

12. Gerard de Lairesse, *Hermes Ordering Calypso to Release Odysseus*, in The Cleveland Museum of Art. See <http://www.clevelandart.org/Explore/artistwork.asp?artistLetter=L&recNo=7&woRecNo=0>.

13. See Bettini, 197–246; Bown, *Fairies*, 125–68.

14. Jerusalem Bible; the KJAV gives: 'and, lo, the heavens were opened unto him, and he saw the Spirit of God descending like a dove, and lighting upon him.'

15. Gen. 8: 8–11; the biologist Rupert Sheldrake has remarked that the dove Noah releases is the first carrier pigeon mentioned in history. Sheldrake, 'How Do Pigeons Home?', in *Seven Experiments*, 32.

16. See, e.g., a Nottingham alabaster relief of the Annunciation, AMO; Anon., *Retable de Boulban*, c.1450, Provençal, Louvre, Paris.

17. The inclusion of the *Filioque* clause in the Creed became one of the issues that caused the schism with the Eastern church; the iconography of this embattled principle of Roman belief is known as 'the Throne of Grace'; Perella identifies the earliest example in 1100–1150, in a missal from Cambrai, Bibliothèque Municipale, MS 234, fol. 2, see Perella, *The Kiss*, fig. 22 and pp. 253–9.

18. One version is in the Galleria Nazionale di Arte Antica, Rome; see <http://www.wga.hu/frames-e.html?/html/s/saraceni/>. A later version is in Burghley House; see *Italian Paintings from Burghley House*, exh. cat., plate 48.

19. *Saint Gregory the Great with Saints Ignatius Loyola and Francis Xavier*, National Gallery, London; see <http://www.nationalgallery.org.uk/cgi-bin/WebObjects. dll/CollectionPublisher.woa/wa/work?workNumber=L603>, from the collection of Sir Denis Mahon.

20. Joyce, *Ulysses* [1937] (London, 1958), 186.

21. *Annunciation*, San Pietro, Bologna; see Freedberg, S.J., 114.
22. Aristotle, *De Anima*, II. viii. 420^{b}6, 30–5, trans. Hett, 114–19; Verschaffel, 'Where There's a Voice, There's a Body'.
23. The musicologist Dominique Fernandez has deplored the music of Verdi and Rossini precisely because their dramatic writing insisted on the maleness and femaleness of the voices and aligned them with the singers' sex.
24. Agastino Ciampelli, *God the Father with Music-Making Angel*, BM, reproduced in *Graceful and True*, exh. cat., 83; cf. painting by Francesco Albani, *The Trinity with the Virgin Mary and Musician Angels*, FMC.
25. Quoted in Deleuze and Guattari, '1730: Becoming-Intense, Becoming-Animal, Becoming Imperceptible', in *A Thousand Plateaus*, 304.

Chapter 6 Clouds of Glory

1. Leonardo da Vinci, *Treatise on Painting*, i. 109–10; ii. 33v, para 265.
2. Ovid, *Metamorphoses*, Bk. 1, ll. 599–606, trans. Humphries; see also Io in Aeschylus, *Prometheus Bound*, esp. ll. 561–8; Graves, *Greek Myths*, i. 190–3. Zeus/ Jupiter's cruelties and ingenuity include making a false Juno out of clouds and tempting Ixion with this vision; after Ixion rapes this *eidolon* of the goddess, he is condemned to burn on a wheel of fire in the underworld. The cloud phantom, Nephele, then bears a child, a centaur, who in turn becomes the progenitor of Chiron, the most wise of the centaurs and tutor to the young Achilles. Graves, *Greek Myths*, i. 208–10, 225–9.
3. Hughes, *Tales from Ovid*, 7.
4. Eksderdjian, *Corregio*, 284.
5. Mayakovsky, 'A Cloud in Trousers', in *The Bedbug and Selected Poetry*, 61–109. I am most grateful to Richard Hollis for lending me his copy.
6. Homer, *Iliad*, trans. Rieu, Bks. 16, 20.
7. Lessing, *Laocoön*, 50.
8. Graves, *Greek Myths*, i. 191.
9. I am aware that I diverge here from Hubert Damisch, who explicitly theorizes Correggio as a pioneer painter of optical subjectivity, arguing that his use of perspective posits a viewer's vantage-point below the tumultuous scene in the heavens.
10. In FMC.
11. <http://www.nationalgallery.org.uk/cgi-bin/WebObjects.dll/ CollectionPublisher.woa/wa/work?workNumber=L887>.
12. Deleuze, *The Fold*, 11.
13. As Esther da Costa Meyer commented in response to my Tanner Lectures at Yale, 1999, 'one might well ask . . . if the clouds' location in the ethereal realms does not come freighted with the hidden metaphysics of time.'
14. Hills, *Venetian Colour*, 45.
15. Cantor, 'The Theological Significance of Ethers', in Cantor and Hodge, *Conceptions of Ether*, 135–55.
16. Barrow, *Independent Spirits*, 73.
17. Virgil, *Eclogues* VI, ll. 31–5, trans. Day-Lewis, 26.

18. Ovid, *Metamorphoses*, trans. Innes, Bk. 1, ll. 52–3, p. 30.
19. See Hart, *Images of Flight*, 168–84.
20. Kircher, *Itinerarium Exstaticum*, Pt. 1, p. 205.
21. Eliot, *Collected Poems*, 11.
22. Kircher, *Itinerarium Exstaticum*, Pt. 1, p. 205.
23. Mary Douglas, 'The Eucharist, its Continuity with the Bread Sacrifice of Leviticus', paper given at Duke University, April 1998. My thanks to Mary Douglas for lending me this paper, which appears in a different form in Douglas, *Leviticus as Literature*, 59–65.
24. Kircher, *Mundus Subterraneus*, 193.
25. Kircher, *The Vulcano's*, 55 (emphasis added).
26. See the representation of the element 'Aer', e.g., from *Escalier des Sages* (1689) by Barent Coenders van Helpen, in Klossowski de Rola, *The Golden Game*, 298.
27. See, e.g., Sebastiano Ricci's highly volatile painting, *Apotheosis of a Saint*; <http://www.clevelandart.org/provenance/prov_search.asp?artist=R>.
28. Marlowe, *Doctor Faustus*, sc. xiv, ll. 92–6, p. 45.
29. C. Taylor, *The Landscape Magazine* (1793), 84–7; I am grateful to Anne Lyles for bringing this description to my attention.

Chapter 7 *Fata Morgana*; or, Castles in the Air

1. Keightley, *Fairy Mythology*, 433; see 'Mor-Rioghain' in O'Hogain, *Myth, Legend and Romance*, 307–10; also B. Walker, *Women's Encyclopaedia of Myths and Secrets*, 674–5.
2. See Giardina, *Discorso sopra la Fata Morgana di Messina, con alcune note dell'eruditis-simo Sig. Andrea Gallo*, in *Opuscoli di Autori Siciliani*, 117–48; Antonio Minasi, 'Dissertazione sopra un Fenomeno volgarmente detto Fata Morgana', in *Dissertazioni*, 1–104; Pindemonte, 'La Fata Morgana', in *Poemetti Italiani*, 144–67; Brewster, *Letters on Natural Magic*, 133–56.
3. Giardina, *Discorso*, 122.
4. Ibid. 125 ff.
5. See T. Neil Davis, 'Fata Morgana'; see also excellent analysis of the phenomenon and photograph by Jack Stephens, <http://www.islandnet.com/~see/weather/elements/infmrge.htm>.
6. *Anonymi gesta Francorum et aliorum Hierosolymitanorum*, ch. XXIX, 45–50, 67.
7. Lycosthenes, *Prodigiorum ac ostentorum chronicon*; see also Bondeson, *Feejee Mermaid*, 36–63.
8. Lycosthenes, *Prodigiorum, passim*, but esp. 158–453.
9. e.g. 'A True Relation of Strange and Wonderful Sights Seen in the Air' (London, 1656), ESTC.
10. See Paré, *Livre des monstres*, in *Les Œuvres*, 801 ff.
11. Boiastuau, *Histoires prodigieuses*, 140v; my translation.
12. Parshall, 'Albrecht Dürer's *Gedenckbuch* and the Rain of Crosses'.
13. Stuart Clark, personal communication, 23 Oct. 2000; his book *Vanities of the Eye* will be published in 2007 by Oxford University Press.

14. Victor Sage's term, from his forthcoming book *A Cultural History of European Gothic*.

15. Pomponatius, *De naturalium effectuum causis*, 62–3.

16. Pomponatius, *De naturalium effectuum causis*, 63–4.

17. Pomponatius, *De naturalium effectum causis*, 109–10, quoted in Daston, 'Material Powers', unpublished paper kindly lent me by the author.

18. Pomponatius, *De naturalium effectuum causis*, 63–4, quoted in Daston, 'Material Powers'.

19. Machen, 'The Bowmen', *London Evening News*, Aug. 1914. Machen then published *The Bowmen and Other Legends of the War*, see his Introduction, followed by the story itself, pp. 1–38.

20. Wolfgang Koeppen's devastating and hallucinatory novel, *Death in Rome*, (1954), trans. Michael Hofmann (London, 1992).

21. Breton, 'Fata Morgana', in *Signe ascendant*; also in *Poems of André Breton*, 130–55, 251–3.

22. Breton, *Signe ascendant*, 9.

23. Ibid. 12.

24. See O'Toole, ' "That Close Center of Things" (Werner Herzog Interviewed by Lawrence O'Toole)', 41–8; Cleere, 'Three Films by Werner Herzog; Lloyd, ' "Objectivity" as Irony: Werner Herzog's *Fata Morgana*'.

25. 'Satanic Cloud above the Statue of Liberty', taken in 1989 by Denise Allison or Clifford Scullion, exhibited in *The Inner Eye*, exh. cat., 83.

Chapter 8 'Very Like a Whale'

1. Ruspolo, *Musaeum Kircheranium*.

2. 'Gamahès', e.g., are 'healing talismans made of stones inscribed with natural astrological hieroglyphs'; see Gaffarel, *Curiosités inouïes sur la Sculpture talismanique des Persans*, (Gaffarel was librarian to Richelieu and chaplain to the King); see Caillois, *Writing of Stones*, passim; also Baltrušaitis, *Abérrations*, i. 87–149; Schefer, 'Pierres de rêve'; also *An Aside*, exh. cat., selected by Tacita Dean.

3. *OED* gives first use by Henry More, *A Modest Inquiry into the Mystery of Iniquity*, ll. 1. ix; I first heard the term in Douglas Trevor, 'Milton and the Thermoscope', at the conference 'Interior Temptation', Northwestern University, 5–7 Dec. 2003.

4. Thomas Carlyle, *The Life of John Sterling* (London, 1851) 1.viii.78; quoted in *OED*.

5. Freud, *Leonardo*, 155–63.

6. Burwick, 'Romantic Drama', 182.

7. Janson ' "The Image Made by Chance" ', 258, 265.

8. R. J. Dean, *Living Granite*, 32; Meaden, *Secrets of the Avebury Stones*, plates 98 and 206. The author and photographer does not rule out the possibility that these might be among the very earliest *intentional* figurative carvings (!).

9. Klee, *Diaries*, no. 27, quoted in Glaesemer, 'How Invention Derives from the Blot'.

10. Aveni, 'Astronomy in the Americas', in C. Walker (ed.), *Astronomy before the Telescope*, 277–300.

11. See Bompiani, 'The Chimera Herself', in Feher, Nadaff, and Tazi (eds.), *Fragments*, i. 364–569.

12. Janson, ' "The Image Made by Chance" ', 266.

13. Charles Edward Eaton, 'Cloud Pictures', *Sewanee Review*, 92, 4 (1984), 534.

14. Aristophanes, *Clouds*, trans. Rogers, ll. 340–8, pp. 294–7.

15. Lucretius, *Lucy Hutchinson's Translation*, Bk. 6, ll. 204–12, p. 184.

16. See *Minerva Driving out the Vices from the Garden of Virtues*, Louvre, Paris; <http://www.masterworksartgallery.com/cgi-bin/showpicture>; and his *Saint Sebastian*, Kunsthistorische Museum, Vienna; see Lightbown, *Mantegna*, 80, 408; Damisch, *Théorie du nuage*, 102–5.

17. Vasari, *Temple of Vasari: Lives of Painters*, 3, 254–64.

18. Da Vinci, *Treatise on Painting*, i. 59; ii. 33v, para. 93.

19. Ibid. i. 50–1; ii. 35v, para. 76.

20. Ibid.

21. Panofsky, *Life and Work of Albrecht Dürer*, 44.

22. John Ruskin, 'Of Truth of Clouds: First of the Region of the Cirrus', in *Modern Painters*, i., Part 2, 375; also *Modern Painters*, v, pt. 7, ch. 1; Robert Hewison, 'The Storm-Cloud of the Nineteenth Century', in *Ruskin, Turner, and the Pre-Raphaelites*, exh. cat., 265–9; see also John Walsh, 'Skies and Reality in Dutch Landscape'.

23. Damisch, *Théorie du nuage*, 257 ff., figs. 6a–6b.

24. Oppé, *Alexander and John Robert Cozens*; Damisch, *Théorie du nuage*, 255–6.

25. For the history of 'skying' and the explorations of other artists see *Constable's Clouds*, exh. cat., esp. John Gage, 'Clouds over Europe', 125–34.

26. Oppé, *Alexander and John Robert Cozens*, 44.

27. Ibid. 173. It is not likely that Cozens had come across Chinese watercolour theory of cloud paintings and dream stones, though his new method resembles it in many respects; see Damisch, *Théorie du nuage*, 277–311; also *Worlds within Worlds*, exh. cat.

28. 'Sundry Studies of Landscape Composition by Cozens the Elder', BM 198.a.2.

29. Adam Dant, exhibition at Adam Baumgold Gallery, New York, 2003; also numerous leaflets published by the artist, on subliminal images in the collections of the Louvre, the Tate, etc.: e.g., 'The Anecdotal Plan of Tate Britain', 2001.

30. See Gage, 'Clouds Over Europe'; also Anne Lyles, ' "That immense canopy": Studies of Sky and Cloud by British Artists *c*. 1700–1860', in *Constable's Clouds*, exh. cat., 135–50.

31. Erasmus Darwin, *The Botanic Garden*, in *The Loves of the Plants*, 53–4.

32. Howard, 'On the Modification of Clouds'; see also Hamblyn, *Invention of Clouds, passim*.

33. Warner, *Fantastic Metamorphoses*, 179.

34. Badt, *John Constable's Clouds*, 15–21.

35. Letter to John Fisher, 23 Oct. 1821, quoted in Walsh, 'Skies and Reality', 110. Cf. the German painter Caspar David Friedrich, writing: 'as a rule, they [clouds] show the effects of these causes with the same truth and clarity with which the physiognomy and the whole being of a person betray the feelings of his soul and the state of his health' (*Gilberts Annalen der Physik*, 1805, quoted by John Gage, 'Clouds over Europe', 133). I am most grateful to John Gage, University of Cambridge, for kindly lending me the article before publication.

36. Hogg, *Private Memoirs*, 40.

37. Hogg, 'Nature's Magic Lantern', in Hogg, *Works of the Ettrick Shepherd*, 459–60.

38. Burwick, 'Romantic Drama', 182.

39. Spender, *From a High Place*, 221.

Chapter 9 The Eye of the Imagination

1. Aristotle, *De Anima* III, vii. 15, pp. 176–7.

2. The literature of consciousness studies burgeons week by week, and I am not going to attempt to review it here. See a trenchant piece by Ian Hacking, 'Get Knitting', review of Steven Rose, *The 21st Century Brain*, in which Hacking cites Locke as the first person to use the term 'consciousness'.

3. Descartes, *Dioptrics*, Discourse VI, in *Philosophical Works*, ed. Haldane, 253.

4. Descartes, *La Dioptrique, Discours 1*, in *Œuvres Philosophiques*, ed. Alquié, i. 704 (contains the illustrations); see also Descartes, *The Passions of the Soul*, 31–6, ibid. pp. x, xx. See Summers, '*Cogito* Embodied: Force and Counterforce in René Descartes's *Les passions de l'âme*', in Meyer (ed.), *Representing the Passions*, 13–36.

5. John Pecham (Joannes Peckham), *Perspectiva communis*, Proposition 1, 46 (49), quoted in David L. Clark, 'Optics for Preachers', 341.

6. See Eco, 'Sugli Specchi', in *Sugli Specchi e altri saggi*, 93–7.

7. Hippolytus, *Refutation of All Heresies*, 103–8.

8. Jaensch, *Eidetic Imagery*, 16.

9. Stevenson, e.g., in an essay entitled 'A Chapter on Dreams', in *Across the Plains*, 229–52, 252.

10. See Kemp and Walker (eds.), *Leonardo on Painting*, 22–3, 222, 224; Clark, 'Optics for Preachers', 332–5, 337–41.

11. This engraving was published in *Trilogium animae* (*The Three Parts of the Soul*) by Ludwig of Prussia (Nuremberg, 1498); see Massing, 'From Manuscript to Engraving', 102; Swan, 'Eyes Wide Shut', 566; Carruthers, *Book of Memory*, 47 ff.

12. Swan, 'Eyes Wide Shut', 570.

13. Gesner, *Physicarum*, 194.

14. Maclean, 'Robert Fludd'; see also Yates, *Art of Memory*, 320–41.

15. Fludd, *Utriusque Cosmi*, ii. 17; among preceding, comparable models, see, e.g., Theodor Galle after Natale Bonifacio, *A Synoptic Table of the Microcosm–Macrocosm Analogy* (1596), reproduced in Swan, 'Eyes Wide Shut', 569; this print is a version of a design by Andrea Bacci of 1580.

16. Fludd, *Utriusque Cosmi*, 218.

17. Ibid. 3, 47.
18. Rorty, *Philosophy and the Mirror of Nature*, 49–50, quoted in Crary, *Techniques of the Observer*, 43.
19. Coleridge, *Biographia Literaria*, i. 304–5.
20. Baudelaire, 'Notes nouvelles sur Edgar Poe', in *Œuvres complètes*, 350.

Chapter 10 Fancy's Images, Insubstantial Pageants

1. Warner, 'Painted Devils and Aery Nothings'.
2. Origen, *Contra Celsum* 1. 68), ed. Chadwick (Cambridge, 1953), 62–3, quoted in Kieckhefer, *Forbidden Rites*, 44.
3. Clark, *Thinking with Demons*, 80 ff.
4. Wright, 'All Done With Mirrors'. S. During, *Modern Enchantments*, 9, 11–14, 84.
5. Marlowe, *Doctor Faustus*, sc. 13, ll. 104–10.
6. Ibid. sc. 14, l. 79.
7. Cf. Connor, 'Fascination, Skin and Screen'.
8. Merleau-Ponty, *Le Visible et l'invisible*, 189–204, 302–15.
9. Kirk, *Secret Commonwealth*, 53–5.
10. *The Tempest*, ed. Kermode (1958; repr. 1987), p. xl.
11. Clark, *Thinking with Demons*, 233–50.
12. Ibid. 459–71.
13. See Mannoni, *Great Art*, 136–75; S. During, *Modern Enchantments*, 101–5; Oursler, 'Timestream: I Hate the Dark. I Love the Light', in Oursler, *The Influence Machine*, exh. cat., 80–103; Mannoni, 'The Art of Deception', in *Eyes, Lies and Illusions*, exh. cat., 40–52, with numerous illustrations.
14. Quoted in Crompton *et al.* (eds.), *Magic Images*, 5; for Kircher, see Findlen, *Athanasius Kircher*; Godwin, *Athanasius Kircher*.
15. Giovanni da Fontana, 'Bellicorum instrumentorum liber cum figuris delineatis et fictitiis literis conscriptus', MS of 1420, includes a sketch of a cowled figure holding a lantern, which throws a huge shadow of a devil, with bat wings, clawed feet, and spear, captioned 'apparentia nocturna ad terrorem videntium' ('a nocturnal apparition for the terror of those who see it), reproduced in Mannoni, *Grand Art*, 40.
16. The famous engravings which appear in the 2nd edn. of Kircher, *Ars Magna* (1671) contain certain elementary errors that make it certain that Kircher himself did not oversee the artist at work: e.gs the painted slides would need to be upside down in the projector in order to appear the right way up on the wall, as illustrated clearly elsewhere in the 1st edition's many optical diagrams of camera obscura projections and other inversions.
17. See Hecht, 'The History of Projecting Phantoms, Ghosts and Apparitions', *NMLJ*, 3, no. 1 (Feb. 1984), 2–6; no. 2 (Dec. 1984), 2–6.
18. Giardina, *Opuscoli di autori Siciliani*, 140.
19. Carena, *Tractatus de Officio Sanctissimae Inquisitionis*, 217–18, quoted in Slawinski, 'Marino, le streghe, il cardinale'.
20. Kircher, *Ars Magna*. Responses to embryological anomalies such as 'Miss Atkinson, the pig-faced lady' (Wellcome Iconographic Collections, ICV 7184),

the Elephant Man, and Siamese twins have varied widely through history. Any human malformation or oddity which could be interpreted in terms of an animal resemblance was considered particularly meaningful, and was frequently ascribed to 'maternal impression', the process by which a mother who suffered a shock or unpleasant encounter during pregnancy was thought to inadvertently imprint its image on the body of the child. See Daston, 'Material Powers'.

21. Kircher, *Ars Magna*, 113.
22. Hobbes, *Leviathan*, 9: quoted in Castle, *Female Thermometer*, 163.
23. Kircher, *Ars Magna*, 152.
24. Deleuze, *The Fold*, 4.
25. Lange-Fuchs, 'On the Origin of Moving Slides', 10–14.

Chapter 11 Darkness Visible: The Phantasmagoria

1. Mannoni, *Great Art*, 136–75; Barber, 'Phantasmagorical Wonders'; see also S. During, Modern Enchantments, *passim*; Heard, 'Paul de Philipsthal & the Phantasmagoria in England, Scotland and Ireland', Part One: 'Boo!', Part Two: 'Shoo!'; Lange-Fuchs, 'On the Origin of Moving Slides'; also Crompton *et al.* (eds.), *Magic Images*.
2. Castle, *Female Thermometer*, 17; see also Warner, *No Go the Bogeyman*, 40 ff.
3. WNC; see also *Eyes, Lies and Illusions*, exh. cat.; Stafford, 'Revealing/Technologies/Magical Domains'.
4. E.-G. Robertson, *Mémoires récréatifs, scientifiques et anecdoctiques d'un physicien-aéronaute*, 1, 272–310. Mannoni, *Grand Art*, 32–3; Robinson, 'Robinson on Robertson'; *idem*, 'Shows and Slides', in Crompton *et al.* (eds.), *Servants of Light*; Ruffles, 'Phantasmagoria Ghost Shows'; Heard, 'Paul de Philipsthal' parts 1 and 2; Bartley, 'In Search of Robertson's *Fantasmagorie*'.
5. E.-G. Robertson, 1, 294–5.
6. Ibid., 1, 144–5, quoted in Robinson, 'Robinson on Robertson', 5.
7. Anon., Conversation No 4.
8. See *The Panorama Phenomenon*, exh. cat.
9. File 'Dioramas', JJC.
10. Burwick, 'Romantic Drama', 169.
11. Altick, *Shows of London*. I saw a working life-size replica of this device in the exhibition *Cloud Images: The Discovery of Heaven*, Jenisch Haus Museum, Hamburg, 2004; it is now permanently installed in the Landesmuseum, Altona.
12. Letter to Louisa Beckford, 1838, quoted in Oliver, *Life of William Beckford*, 89–91.
13. Brewster, *Letters on Natural Magic*, 63, 76 ff., 82–9.
14. Carroll, *Alice's Adventures in Wonderland*. See Warner, *Fantastic Metamorphoses*, 190, for Carroll's introduction of reverse action, jump-cuts, and other cinematic narrative techniques.
15. Robertson, *Mémoires récréatifs*, 1, 276–94.
16. See Bold, 'The Magic Lantern: Hogg and Science'; see also J. Carey, Introduction to Hogg, *Private Memoirs*, pp. ix–xxi.

17. See Warner, *Fantastic Metamorphoses*, 185.

18. Goethe, *Werke*, iv Abt., Bd. 31, 163–4, trans. and quoted in Burwick, 'Romantic Drama', 185.

19. Goethe, *Werke*, iv Abt., Bd. 45, 80, trans. and quoted in Burwick, 'Romantic Drama', 186.

20. Burwick, 'Romantic Drama', 188.

21. e.g. 'Icebergs', *c.*1860, and 'Aurora Borealis', *c.*1900, made by the firm of Carpenter and Wesley, London, WMS.

22. Jenness, *Maskelyne and Cooke*. See also <www.magiclanternshows.com/history.htm>.

23. Burwick, 'Romantic Drama', 171.

24. See Greenacre, *Magic Lanterns*.

Chapter 12 The Origin of Painting; or, The Corinthian Maid

1. Pliny the Elder, *Natural History*, Bks. xxxv, xliii, 370–3.

2. Rosenblum, 'The Origin of Painting'; Wille, *Die Erfindung der Zeichenkunst*; Newman, 'Marking Time: Memory and Matter in the Work of Avis Newman', in *Avis Newman*, exh. cat., 275; also Muecke, ' "Taught by Love": The Origin of Painting Again', *Art Bulletin*, June 1999, pp. 297–302.

3. See e.g. David Allan, *The Origin of Painting (The Corinthian Maid)*, 1775, NGS, also Joseph Wright, *The Corinthian Maid*, 1782–4, NGAW; <http://www.nga.gov/collection/gallery/gg61/gg61-61130.0-exhibit.html>.

4. Douglas R. Nickel, ' "Second sight": Julia Margaret Cameron and the Victorian Imagination', paper for symposium 'On a Portrait: The Aesthetic and Social Worlds of Julia Margaret Cameron' (1815–79), NMPFT.

5. Bertillon, *La Photographie judiciare* (Paris, 1890), see *L'Âme au corps*, exh. cat., 400, 402. His notorious 'anthropometry' was officially adopted in 1888 in France.

6. Similar educational aids were also disseminated, using photographs as primary evidence: e.g., 'Dr Rud. Martin's Wall Illustrations of all types in the most perfect style of photochrome . . . intended to serve as help to teachers in primary and middle schools', an English advertisement, issued by the Institute Orell Fussli, in Zurich. Photographic Collection, PRM; see also *Spectacular Bodies*, exh. cat, 122–3.

7. Plato, *Republic*, 602D, 523B, 365C, 583B; Philostratus, *Life of Apollonius of Tyana*, Bk. II, 22; see Padel, 'Making Space Speak', in Zeitlin and Winkler (eds.), *Nothing to Do with Dionysus?*, 350–1.

8. Heinrich Philipp Bossler from Speyer made *Schattenrisse*, or silhouette portraits of the Von Breuning family in 1782, and, two years later, of Mozart, Schubert, *et al.*; Beethoven House, Bonn (visited in May 2003); the Goethe House, Weimar, displays silhouette portraits of the poet and his circle (Fig. 14a, p. 166), as well as 'Scenes from *Faust*'.

9. In *L'Art de connaître les hommes par la physionomie*; see Lavater, *Essays on Physiognomy*, pl. XXV, 176–9.

10. I would like to thank Susanna Szanto for her dissertation, 'Features of the

Soul: The Aesthetic Appeal of Phrenology in Nineteenth-Century America', written for my seminar, 'Figuring the Soul', University of Pittsburgh, 1997.

11. See, e.g., Varnedoe, 'The Artifice of Candor' and 'The Ideology of Time'.

12. De Quincey, 'Suspiria de Profundis: Being a Sequel to the Confessions of an English Opium-Eater', in De Quincey, *Confessions*, 87.

13. See numerous examples in *The Dawn of Photography*, exh. DVD.; see also Haworth-Booth, *Things*, for T. R. Williams, *Articles of Vertu*, and *Mortality*, 76–7, 78–9.

14. Nadar, 'Balzac et le Daguerréotype', in *Quand j'étais photographe*, quoted in Bajac, *Invention of Photography*, 143; see also Sontag, *On Photography*, 158–60.

15. Lucretius, *The Way Things Are*, 120–1, quoted in Tiffany, *Toy Medium*, 202.

16. See Tiffany, *Toy Medium*, 200–7; Daston, 'Material Powers'.

17. See Coe and Haworth-Booth, *Guide to Early Photographic Processes, passim*.

18. *Julia Margaret Cameron: The Complete Photographs*, 64.

19. Lotte Reiniger, *The Adventures of Prince Achmed*, was superbly restored and reissued on DVD by the BFI, with accompanying notes, in 1999.

Chapter 13 The Danger in the Mirror

1. Ovid, *Metamorphoses*, Bk. III, ll. 339–510 (Narcissus's lament fills ll. 441–73); ed. Miller; trans. Humphries, 70.

2. Ibid. ll. 422–4, 70.

3. Coleridge, *Poems*, 163. In the note Coleridge quotes his own poem 'The Picture, or The Lover's Resolution', which evokes a similar Narcissus scene, ibid. 283–7.

4. Freud, 'On Narcissism: An Introduction', in *On Metapsychology*, 65–97.

5. 'Narziss' (two poems), in Rilke, *Werke*, ii: *Gedichte und Übertragungen*, 56–7.

6. It is likely that Freud knew the poems or at least knew *of* them, through Lou Andreas-Salomé, to whom at least one was written.

7. Lacan, 'The Mirror Stage as Formative of the I Function' [1949], in Lacan, *Écrits*, 75–81; see also Jacqueline Rose, Introduction, in Mitchell and Rose, 30, and 27–57.

8. It formed part of Sir John Soane's founding collection of the BM, and is now on show in the Enlightenment display in the Edward VII Galleries.

9. Dryden, *King Arthur* or *The British Worthy*, in *Dramatic Works*, VI, 267–8.

10. See Magee and Milligan, *On Blindness*.

11. Frazer, 'Taboo and Perils of the Soul', 94–6.

12. Kirk, *Secret Commonwealth*, 52–3; Hunter, *Occult Laboratory*, 80.

13. Kirk, *Secret Commonwealth*, 53; Hunter, *Occult Laboratory*, 81.

14. Walter Scott, *Letters on Demonology and Witchcraft*, 163–6.

15. Homer, *Odyssey* XI, ll. 495–0, ed. Murray; trans. Fagles, 256.

16. Virgil, *Georgics* IV, ll. 499–500, in *Eclogues*, trans. Day-Lewis, 125.

17. Dante, *Purgatorio* XXV, ll. 94–104, in *Divine Comedy*, trans. Sinclair, 328–9.

Chapter 14 Double Vision

1. Tennyson, 'The Lady of Shalott', in Gardner (ed.), *New Oxford Book of English Verse*, 636–41.
2. Spenser, *The Faerie Queene*, III, ii. 19.
3. Ibid. III. ii. 38, 45.
4. Her ending in the boat partly echoes Ophelia drowned for love, but it does also anticipate Arthur's last journey to Avalon, as pictured by Cameron in one of her most derided *tableaux vivants*, 'So like a shatter'd column lay the King', *Cameron Complete Photographs*, fig. 1193.
5. Chamisso, *Peter Schlemihl*, ch. 1.
6. Four times between 1861 and 1910, while other versions were also published at this time, three times in a popular series from the Clarendon Press, in Oxford, as well as school bilingual editions. There were many French translations too, and at least one Russian translation.
7. E. T. A. Hoffmann, 'A New Year's Eve Adventure', in *Best Tales of Hoffmann*, 111.
8. Hoffmann, 'The Story of the Lost Reflecton', ibid. 116–28.
9. Otto Rank, 'Der Doppelgänger', *Imago* (1914), 97, quoted in Heide Schlüpmann, 'The First German Art Film'.
10. Cf. Schlüpmann, 'The First German Art Film'.
11. See Miller, *Electric Shepherd*. I have written about Hogg's great novel in *Fantastic Metamorphoses*, 179–87.
12. The symbolism of skin as identity and the relation of this organ of sense to the making of art lie at the core of the horrific tale of the flaying of Marsyas, told by Ovid in *Metamorphoses*, Bk. VI, ll. 382 ff. and explored by Titian amongst others as an allegory of creativity. See 'A Conversation: Anish Kapoor and Donna De Salvo, in *Marsyas*, 60–5, and Warner, 'The Perforate Self'.
13. Hofmannsthal, *La Femme sans ombre*.
14. As the French translator of the book comments, Hofmannsthal proposes that 'The shadow here is this "good" shadow which reminds me of the external character of my own body which is a benign thing, which can be embraced, caressed or suffer violence at another's hands. This shadow stands in opposition to . . . the reflection, the narcissistic "evil double" . . . the dangerous fascination of the Selfsame.' Jean-Yves Masson, 'Postface', ibid. 151.
15. See Brassaï, *Marcel Proust*, *passim*.
16. Barrie, *Peter Pan*, 26.
17. Ibid. 29.

Chapter 15 The Camera Steals the Soul

1. See Silversides, *Face Pullers*, 6–9.
2. Needham, 'Little Black Boxes', 647. I am grateful to him for drawing my attention to his letter.
3. *Private Eye*, 7 Apr. 1995, clipped for me by Tim Marlow, to whom many thanks.
4. James O'Brien, *The New York Times*, 5 March 1995, sect. 13, p. 13.
5. Frazer, 'Taboo and the Perils of the Soul', 77–97.

6. Frazer, *Questions*, 38–42.
7. Thomson, *Images of China*, Introduction.
8. Frazer, *Taboo*, 96.
9. Dobson, 'On the Andamans and Andamanese', 464.
10. Simson, 'Notes on the Jivaros and Canelos Indians', *JAI*, ix (1880), 392, quoted in Frazer, *Taboo*, 97.
11. Maxime du Camp, 'Le Nil, Egypte, et Nubie', quoted in Flaubert, *Flaubert in Egypt*, 101–2.
12. In early photographs women appear to express reluctance in front of the camera rather more frequently than men; while not ignoring the enormous differences between cultures, women's faces often play a more important role in their social identity than men's, and are much more closely governed by rules of modesty and decorum. The English anthropologist Beatrice Blackwood, working in New Mexico in 1926, took photographs to support her anthropological research and concentrated on women, to whom she enjoyed more access than her male counterparts. In a special section of the Pitt Rivers Museum's collection of ethnographic photographs in Oxford, catalogued under the rubric 'Camera Shy', a sequence of three snapshots shows women of Acomita, sitting selling pottery, and then dashing for cover as Blackwood approached or covering their faces with their pagnes. Many of these subjects were Christian converts, living on a mission: this cultural change might bear on their relation to photography.
13. 53/Misc. 3, Photography Collection, PRM.
14. See Powers, 'Passion Play', review of Mari Sandoz, *Crazy Horse: The Strange Man of the Oglalas* (in 1930–1 the author interviewed several survivors among Crazy Horse's friends), and of Larry McMurtry, *Red Cloud: Warrior-Statesman of the Lakota Sioux* (1999); see also Dippie, 'Representing the Other: The North American Indian', in Edwards (ed.), *Anthropology & Photography*, 132–6.
15. See Fleming and Luskey, *Shadow Catchers*, 8, 10, 28, 45, 48, 120, 121; Barthes, *Camera Lucida*, 92.
16. Charles Guillain, no. 159, in *Dawn of Photography*.
17. For several reasons, not least because I have so few ways into the beliefs of Native Americans and other indigenous peoples, I am not going to speculate any more about their psychology in front of the camera, or about stories from their culture about the soul, the camera, and the settlers and soldiers who reconfigured the map of the Americas.
18. See Christian, Jr., *Apparitions, Late Medieval and Renaissance Spain*, *passim*.
19. LC. See <http://www.pbs.org/weta/thewest/resources/archives/eight/68_09. htm>.
20. Curtis Graybill and Boesen, *Edward Sheriff Curtis*, 4.
21. Ibid. 13.
22. He would remove clocks and lamps from their surroundings; see Sante, 'American Photography's Golden Age', 63.
23. See Cannadine, *Ornamentalism*, 85–100, for the memorialization of colonial grandeur.

24. Curtis, *Hidden Faces, passim*.
25. The photographer Joseph Kossuth Dixon gave the title to his book of photographs taken in 1908–17.
26. Curtis, *Visions of a Vanishing Race*; there is an earlier volume, however, which recognized the wishfulness of these titles: Lyman, *Vanishing Race and Other Illusions*.
27. Taken in 1907, Whyte Museum, Banff, Canada; see Lippard, 'Doubletake'.
28. Letter to the author, 20 Sept. 1993.
29. Joe Kane, 'Moi Goes to Washington', photograph by Richard Avedon, taken 8 Oct. 1993, *New Yorker*, 2 May 1994, 73–81; later published in Kane, *Savages* (London 1996).
30. I came across the phrase 'a future memory' for the first time in Calvino, 'Adventures of a Photographer', in *Difficult Loves*, 40–52. Since then, it has become commonplace: the company developing my films in New York, in the autumn of 2003, has the slogan 'Memories for the Future' printed on the wallet; it then started appearing in advertisements for cameras and photographs in London, 2004–5.
31. Andriopoulos, 'The Terror of Reproduction', paper kindly let to the author.
32. Kohler, *Das Eigenbild im Recht*, 5–6, quoted in Andriopoulos, 'Terror of Reproduction'.
33. See, e.g., the 'scotographs' transmitted by the chieftain Golden Cloud to Madge Donohue, *Le Troisième Oeil*, 98–101.
34. See, e.g., photograph of a tourist group with natives, Juan Belaieff Island in the Paraguay River near Asunción, in Lutz and Collins, *Reading National Geographic*, 212.
35. Hugh Tomlinson, 'Strasbourg privacy revolution', <http://www.carter-ruck.com/articles/090704_StrasbourgPrivacyRevolution.html>.
36. Maria Miesenberger, a Swedish photographer, has created a sequence of portraits of children playing, in which she blurs their features or silhouettes them to render them unrecognizable. She hangs these around sculptures showing children hiding their faces in their T-shirts, making a strong comment on 'poster children' and other child portraits in conventional media, and their pervasive eroticization. See also Kincaid, *Erotic Innocence, passim*.
37. Calvino, 'Adventure of a Photographer', 47.
38. Tournier, 'Les Suaires de Véronique', in *Le Coq des bruyères*, 139–58: 152.
39. I first became aware of the custom in Saigon in the early Seventies, when I saw that a photograph of a smiling soldier who had been killed in the Vietnam War had been placed on his bier in the funeral chapel.
40. The artist Christian Boltanski has made numerous installations using these funerary effects: e.g., his piece '174 Dead Swiss' (1990), resembles the chapel dedicated to the Italian Air Force in Santo Stefano, Bologna.
41. See Merewether, 'Naming Violence in the Work of Doris Salcedo', 36.
42. Barthes, *Camera Lucida*, 63–71.
43. Sontag, *On Photography*, 13–16.
44. Sontag, *Regarding the Pain of Others, passim*, but esp. 85–101.

Chapter 16 'Stay This moment': Julia Margaret Cameron and Charles Dodgson

1. Goethe, *Faust*, Pt. 1, ll. 101–2. As it happens, Faust does not repeat the phrase when Helen of Troy does appear, though her effect on him is similar, and precipitates his doom.
2. Virginia Woolf, Diary entry for 31 Dec. 1932; quoted in Lee, *Virginia Woolf*, 636.
3. Woolf, *To the Lighthouse*, 149–54.
4. *Cameron: Complete Photographs* (2003), figs. 279–323, 326–33.
5. Woolf, *Freshwater*, passim. Woolf has special fun with the coffins which Mrs Cameron ordered for her husband and herself in preparation for their journey to Ceylon (India in the play).
6. Woolf, 'Sketches of the Past', in *Moments of Being*, 78–160.
7. Taylor, ' "Some Other Occupation" ', in *Lewis Carroll*, exh. cat., 27–38; Gernsheim, *Lewis Carroll Photographer*, 27–38; Cohen, *Lewis Carroll*, 148–51.
8. Carroll, 'Hiawatha's Photographing' (1857), in *Phantasmagoria*, 66–77.
9. Carroll, *Through the Looking Glass*, 126–7.
10. See Atherton, 'Lewis Carroll', 128.
11. Cohen, *Lewis Carroll*, 89 n.
12. Ibid. 241.
13. Derrida, 'The Deaths of Roland Barthes', 281–2.
14. Nicky Bird's work, in her book *Tracing Echoes*, (Leeds: Wild Pansy Press, 2001), interprets Cameron's portraits of Isle of Wight neighbours through the lens of their descendants, actual and fancied—who resemble Cameron's models, thus inspiring an 'uncanny double take'. This genealogical research restores personal histories and identity to the models in allegories or fictions, and deepens the link of photography with archiving, rather than imagining—in spite of the uncanny inversion of time that also takes place, the movement forward into the future.
15. Hibbert, *Sketches of the Philosophy of Apparitions*.
16. See Wilson, 'Gastric Fantastic', *Fortean Times* (Feb. 2004), 180.
17. *Cornhill Magazine*, July 1862, cited by Flint, 'Painting Memory', 529.
18. In 'What Is the Fourth Dimension?' (1884), quoted in Flint, *The Victorians and the Imagination*, 280.
19. McDonagh, *De Quincey's Disciplines*, 38–42; and Frayling, *Fuseli's The Nightmare*, 9–20.
20. Frayling and Myrone, '*The Nightmare*' in Modern Culture'.
21. Warren, 'The Thunderstruck and the Boxer', in Morrison and Baldick (eds.), *Tales of Terror from Blackwood's Magazine*, 243–80.
22. See Charcot and Richer, *Les Démoniaques dans l'Art*.
23. Matthew Arnold, 'They sleep in shelter'd rest . . .', from 'Tristram and Iseult'; see <http://www.lib.rochester.edu/camelot/arnold.htm>.
24. Unexpectedly, Carroll writes that they use 'the gate of ivory', Homer's entrance for false dreams; it is not quite clear how he means his readers to understand this. However, this is also the gate through which Aeneas passes when he leaves the underworld, and Virgil also leaves his hero's choice a mystery.

25. e.g., 'Kate Keown Reading', Cat. no. 986, p. 376 and 'Marie Spartali' cat. nos. 465–85, pp. 260–4; no. 986, p. 412. *Julia Margaret Cameron: The Complete Photographs*.

26. See Rodier, *Clementina, Lady Hawarden*.

27. Haworth-Booth observes that Whistler's paintings of women in reverie were influenced by Hawarden.

28. Lady Hawarden was pregnant throughout her working life. The sequence breaks off when the two favourite models, Trotty (Isabella Grace) and Chukky (Clementina, like her mother) were 19 and 17; she herself died of pneumonia, at the age of 42.

29. The Cameron circle also included Anne Thackeray Ritchie, daughter of the writer, and sister of Minny, Leslie Stephen's first wife. Anne Thackeray translated Marie-Catherine d'Aulnoy (c. 1650–1705), the French writer of fairy-tales whose beast bridegrooms, monstrous and magical animal meta-morphoses—into serpents and dragons, hinds and parrots—inspired many of the dazzling pantomimes and fairy plays put on in London by the versatile impresario James Robinson Planché from the 1840s onwards (his own transla-tion was published in 1855). Anne Thackeray continued to explore the French enchanted terrain opened by Planché, rewriting the tradition in her *Bluebeard's Keys and Other Stories* of 1874. Cameron photographed, 'Anny' in 1868–70, and it is easy to imagine that Cameron and Anne Thackeray Ritchie stimulated each other's voyages into fairy worlds. See Garnett, *Anny*, 19–20, 52–4, 155; *Cameron: Complete Photographs*, cat. nos. 501–3, pp. 268–9.

30. Cameron did begin a sequence illustrating George Eliot's *Adam Bede* in 1874, but it did not develop.

31. Olsen, *From Life*, gives a remarkable account of the family's improvidence—their combination of generosity, borrowing, and hand-to-mouth existence.

32. Cameron, unpublished letter, quoted in Olsen, *From Life*, 227.

33. She photographed one of her child models, Freddy Gould, looking down, and called the image 'First Ideas', and she took her own grandchild while he was sleeping, isolating him and lighting him to draw attention to the paradoxical concentration of the state, its inwardness. The way Mary Hillier, her most versatile model of all, looks away, or looks down, lost in thought, in the early Cameron sequence 'Fruits of the Spirit' (*c.*1864) (VAM), draws the viewer into her state of mind, issuing an invitation to empathize with, not only to behold, the physical qualities of the group of mother and children.

34. *Cameron: Complete Photographs*, nos. 1163, 1164, pp. 472–3.

35. Kermode, *Sense of an Ending*, 70–89.

36. Joanne Lukitsch has written eloquently about Cameron's handling of shadows, and her effects of relief, and formulated a crisp axiom: 'For real think light, for idea think lens'. Conference on Cameron, NMPFT, 2004.

37. *Cameron: Complete Photographs*, 46.

38. Scarry, *Dreaming by the Book*, 24.

39. *Cameron: Complete Photographs*, nos. 335–6, pp. 226–7; nos. 310–11, p. 220.

40. *TLS*, 21 Mar. 2003.

41. Coleridge, 'On the Imagination', in *Biographia Literaria*, ed. James Engell and W. Jackson Bate, ch. 13 in *Collected Works*, vii. 304.

42. Cf. the film-maker Chris Marker, who, also alive to clunky literalism, has remarked, 'On entrevoit plus qu'on ne voit' ('You glimpse more than you see'), and added that 'the starting point is the subjectivity of the dream'. Werner Herzog also 'rejected fact in favour of imagery', and characterized photography as a creative and poetic medium, criticizing 'the embalming function that apparently self-justifying reportage exercised on its subject, and endorsing a vital link between material and perception'. See Lloyd, ' "Objectivity" as Irony: Werner Herzog's *Fata Morgana*', *Monogram*, 5 (1974), 8–9.

Chapter 17 Spectral Rappers, Psychic Photographers

1. Fort, *Wild Talents*.
2. Winter, *Mesmerized*, 15–31.
3. Metzger, *Select Strange and Sacred Sites*; Peter Lamborn Wilson, 'Burnt Over', in *Fantastic*, exh. cat. 21–5.
4. Wire transmission preceded the telephone by several decades, but the two media are symbiotic, not least because Western Union was the first to go into business with the new 'electric toy' in 1879. The principle of the telephone had been discovered thirty years before, by an Italian immigrant living on Staten Island, Antonio Meucci (d. 1889), who demonstrated his prototype to investors in 1860, but without success. He could not afford the patent fees, and in 1873, he failed to renew his 'notice of intent' to obtain a patent; in 1877 Alexander Graham Bell, who had sight of Meucci's ideas, established his company. Meucci sued, but unsuccessfully. In 2003, the US Congress formally acknowledged his primacy, with an apology. What is even more remarkable about this little-known inventor is that he was a friend of Garibaldi, who stayed with him on Staten Island and took a job in a candle-making factory, before returning to their country and helping to make it modern Italy. See Schiavo, *Antonio Meucci, Inventor of the Telephone*.
5. Wrixon, *Codes, Ciphers, and Secret Languages*, 119–21.
6. Solnit, *Eadweard Muybridge and the Technological Wild West*; Worthington, *A Study of Splashes*.
7. See Daston and Galison, 'The Image of Objectivity'; also Chaloner, 'The Most Wonderful Experiment in the World', 368.
8. ?Simon Marmion, 'The invisible spirit of Gui de Corvo', J. Paul Getty Museum, M531, fol. 7, in Schmitt, *Ghosts in the Middle Ages*, plate 9.
9. In Alfonso the Wise, *Cantigas de Santa Maria*, Escorial MS TI1, fol. 80; Ibid. plate 25, pp. 210–13.
10. Mumler, 'The Personal Experiences of W. H. Mumler in Spirit-Photography, written by himself. Boston, 1875'. See Ferris (ed.), *Disembodied Spirit*, exh. cat., no. 36. ; also Krauss, Rolf, 'The beginnings of ghost photography: William H. Mumler', in Krauss, *Beyond Light*, 125.
11. Mumler was not found guilty, but the trial took the shine off his claims: Gerry,

The Mumler 'Spirit' Photograph Case. New York, 1869. See Durant, 'Adrift in the Fluidium: Notes on Believing', in *The Blur of the Otherworldly*, 56–73.

12. Coulston Gillispie (ed.), *Dictionary of Scientific Biography*, 474 ff.

13. William Crookes, in *Chemical News*, 50 (1879), 130, quoted in Noakes, 'Cranks and Visionaries', 221.

14. See Barrow, *Independent Spirits*, for a finely researched study of the political involvement of Spiritualist and related movements, esp. pp. 67–95.

15. William Crookes, 'The Mediumship of Miss Florence Cook', and 'The Last of Katie King', *The Spiritualist*, 6 Feb. and 5 June 1874; repr. in Crookes, *Researches into the Phenomena of Modern Spiritualism*; see <http:// www.survivalafterdeath.org/books>. Crookes's trust was passionately defended: one scientist who witnessed Florence Cook at work in Berlin in 1899 was still taking up arms for the cause sixty years later. See Letter, June 1963, enclosing report on 'Summary, or The Sittings of the medium Florence Cook at Berlin in 1899', Dr Hans Gerloff to C. D. Broad, Broad Papers DI/14, WLTCC.

16. Letter from E. R. Dodds to C. D. Broad, 9 Nov. 1962, Broad Papers DI/14, WLTCC.

17. Dr Hans Gerloff, Broad Papers D1/14 189, WLTCC.

18. The apparition of the Morgans in the shape of King father and daughter is startling, given the blood-soaked derring-do of Henry Morgan, one of the most successful sackers and looters of early imperial history. He also does not seem to have had any children. See Zahedieh, 'Sir Henry Morgan', in *DNB*.

19. Luckhurst, *Invention of Telepathy*, 155.

20. Noakes, 'Cranks and Visionaries', 174.

21. Crookes, 'Some Possibilities of Electricity', *Fortnightly Review*, n. s. 51 (Feb. 1892), 174, quoted in Andriopoulos, 'Terror of Reproduction'.

22. Ibid. 176, quoted in Andriopoulos, 'Terror of Reproduction'.

23. Gunning, 'Phantom Images', 65–6.

24. I am grateful to Stephen Wilson, a descendant of Georgiana Houghton, for sending me copies of her art. Personal communication, 4 May 2004.

25. Kipling, 'When earth's last picture is painted . . .', in 'Envoi'. The 'Spiritual Crowns' which Miss Houghton devised as she channelled spirits for her friends echo the spare, pure drawings of Mother Ann Lee, the Shaker prophet, and show strong affinities with the concerns of Wassily Kandinsky when he wrote about the abstract language, line, stroke and colour in his celebrated essay, *Concerning the Spiritual in Art* (1910). While Houghton's paintings are virtually unknown, her photography gained a large and fervent public for the visitors from the other side crowding her albums.

26. Houghton collaborated with the photographer Frederick Hudson; see Houghton, *Chronicles of the Photographs of Spiritual Beings*, esp. Pl. 5.

27. Varley, *Report on Spiritualism*, quoted in Noakes, 'Cranks and Visionaries', 172.

28. Tarde, *The Laws of Imitation*, p. xiv, quoted in Leys, 'Mead's Voices', 279. Paladino is sometimes spelled Palladina, but the SPR uses the first version, so I have followed this. For her career, see Lodge, JSPR, 1894); Flammarion (1907),

104–5; Podmore (1911), 87–149; Carrington (1912); Dingwall, 'Eusapia Palladino: Queen of the Cabinet', in Dingwall, 178–217. The photographs of her materializations (anon.) are reproduced *Im Reich der Phantome*, exh.cat., figs. 93–4,

29. Flammarion, *Les Forces nouvelles inconnues*, 104–5.

30. 'Spectral Illusion', *Chambers' Miscellany* (1872), quoted in Castle, *Female Thermometer*, 179.

31. Anon. note to Album SP3 of Crewe-Warrick Circle, 1920–3, SPRA. Mr Warrick deposited his albums with the SPR in 1953 at the age of 94. He also left his money to the Perrot–Warrick Society, at his former college, Trinity College, Cambridge; the funds continue research into the paranormal.

32. Anderson, 'The Wood Nymph', in Anderson, *The Complete Fairy Tales and Stories*, 934–53, 951.

33. See Peterson; <http://www.virgendeguadalupe.org.mx/>.

34. W. D. H., 'Cameras: The Technique of Photographic Imaging', leaflet of an Exhibition at the Museum of the History of Science, Oxford, 20 May–13 Sept. 1997.

35. The photography historians Mike Weaver and Doug Nickel have dated the beginnings of photographing spirits as early as *c.*1867, produced by a German visiting speaker (Schrenck-Notzing?) to the British Spiritualist Alliance. His talk could help explain the oddity of Mr Sludge's name, given by Browning before any of the published manifestations of ectoplasm.

36. J. R. R. Tolkien calls one of the hobbits Sam Gamgee, perhaps in an allusion to his podginess? Gamgee had the idea from Mathias Mayor, *La Chirurgie simplifiée* (Brussels, 1842), but added antiseptic conditions in its making.

37. Letter from F. W. Warrick to a London business man, 5 Nov. 1923, file 'Psychic Photographs', SPRA.

38. The psychic researcher Fred Barlow, a member of the Crewe circle of Spiritualists, which included Warrick, made a rich collection of more than 500 psychic photographs during the Twenties and Thirties, and gave them to the BL. See under Collections: Barlow.

39. Now in the Conan Doyle Centre, Ransom Library, Austin, Texas.

40. Schrenck-Notzing's *Materialisations-Phaenomene* includes 275 photographs and 167 diagrams.

41. Report of H. Dennis Taylor, 'Eva C.', Box 1, SPRA.

42. Mavor, 'Photographs are Fairyish', BMPFT.

43. Cooper, 'Cottingley: At Last the Truth'; (see <www.lhup.edu/~dsimanek/cooper.htm>).

44. Correspondence of J. Arthur Hill with E. J. Dingwall, 30 Oct. 1922, 'Psychic Photography 8', SPRA.

45. E. L. Gardner, 'Fairy Photographs', *Strand Magazine*, Dec. 1920, cutting in 'Psychic Photography', 8, SPRA.

46. There have been two novels at least inspired by the events, and two films, *Fairy Tale. A True Story* (1997), dir. Charles Sturridge, and *Photographing Fairies* (1997), dir. Nick Willing. See also the artist Matt Collishaw's *Catching Fairies*, 1994, private collection.

47. Braude, *Radical Spirits*, 176–7.
48. See Owen, *Darkened Chamber; idem, Place of Enchantment.*
49. Colbert, 'Harriet Hosmer and Spiritualism'.
50. Further examples: Sophia De Morgan (née Frend), wife of the London mathematician Augustus De Morgan, published *From Matter to Spirit: The Result of Ten Years' Experience in Spirit Manifestations* (London, 1863); Annie Horniman, Yeats' patron and friend, was an active supporter of the Order of the Golden Dawn.
51. Castle, *Apparitional Lesbian*, 112–16, 124–6.
52. Myers, *Human Personality*, ii. 274. There is also an archive online of 'Art After Death', which comprises interviews with artists in the afterlife conducted by spirit mediums. The first CDs feature the Countess of Castiglione, Yves Klein, and Joseph Cornell. See <www.doublearchive.com>.

Chapter 18 Phantoms to the Test: The Society for Psychical Research

1. James, 'Frederic Myers's Service to Psychology' [1911], in *Essays in Psychical Research*, 196; quoted in Hayward, 'Popular Mysticism and the Origins of the New Psychology', 133.
2. Quoted by Evans-Wentz, *The Fairy-Faith in Celtic Countries*, 479, in Foster, *W. B. Yeats*, i. n. 156.
3. Noakes, 'Cranks and Visionaries'.
4. Ibid.
5. See Schultz, *Henry Sidgwick*. esp. ch. 5, 'Spirits', for a superb and detailed account of the Sidgwicks' psychic involvement.
6. Ibid. 483–508.
7. Myers, *Collected Poems* see Beer, *Providence and Love*, 143, for a most perceptive account.
8. Broad, 'F. W. H. Myers'.
9. Draft letter, from F. W. H. Myers to Mrs Lewes (George Eliot), 7 Dec. 1872, TCL MS Myers 11/118, quoted Beer, *Providence and Love*, 133.
10. Myers, 'Greek Oracles', in *Hellenica*, 426.
11. William James, 'Address by the President', *PSPR*, 12 (1894), 5.
12. The Combined Index to *JSPR* lists more than forty articles and notes by Mrs Henry Sidgwick.
13. Salter, 'Introduction to the Study of Scripts' (unpublished), 101. Salter Papers, WLTCC.
14. See Mrs. Henry Sidgwick, '"Spirit" Photographs: A Reply to Mr. A. R. Wallace', *PSPR*, 7, Suppl. 268–89.
15. Eleanor Sidgwick abridged it for a subsequent single-volume edn., published in 1918.
16. See Beer, 'Essaying the Heights'.
17. The 2-vol. 1st edn. was abridged twice, in 1907 by L. H. Myers, and in 1919 by S. B. and L. H. Myers. A new edition appeared in 1954.

18. Myers, *Human Personality and Its Survival*, 1, 11–19, 34–9; 2, 251–3, 270–4; see Broad, 'F. W. H. Myers'.
19. Hayward, 'Popular Mysticism', 157, 186.
20. Derrida, 'Telepathy', trans. Nicholas Royle, *Oxford Literary Review*, 10 (1988), 3–41, 14; see Luckhurst, ' "Something Tremendous, Something Elemental": The Ghostly Origins of Psychoanalysis', in Buse and Stott, *Ghosts*, 50–71.
21. Harry Price was a conjuror, self-publicist, and psychic investigator, who had broken with the SPR in 1923 in order to set up his own National Laboratory of Psychic Investigations, where he organized a relentless series of public experiments with international performers in such specialist arts as telepathy, telekinesis, apporting, teleplasmics, etc. He was one of the most prominent figures in occult circles before the Second World War, and his rich library of supernatural and conjuring books and ephemera is now housed in Senate House Library of the University of London. But he was also the scourge of all other claimants to spiritual powers, and intent on gleefully exposing everyone else besides himself as a fraud and a charlatan.
22. Myers, 'Note', First Report of the Committee of the SPR . . . [on] Marvellous Phenomena', *c.*1884–5, Myers Archive, HPL.
23. *Daily News*, 18 Jan. 1926, in file 'Psychic Photography: Mrs A. E. Deane', SPRA.
24. Myers, *Human Personality and Survival*, ch. 10; quoted in Lodge, *Christopher*, 60.
25. Letter of Winifred Coombe-Tennant, Christopher's mother, 23 Sep. 1917, quoted in Lodge, *Christopher*, 72, 78.
26. See Dyer, *Missing of the Somme*, 32–43.
27. Letter from Sir Oliver Lodge to E. J. Dingwall, 8 Apr. 1922, File 'Psychic Photography: Mrs A. E. Deane', SPRA.
28. See Gaskill, *Hellish Nell*, passim.
29. See esp. two fine studies: Thurschwell, *Literature, Technology and Magical Thinking*, and Luckhurst, *Invention of Telepathy*.
30. Myers, 'Note'; see n. 22.

Chapter 19 Soul Vibrations; or, The Fluidic Invisible

1. JJC; see S. During, *Modern Enchantments*, 90.
2. 'Tout vit, tout agit, tout se correspond: les rayons magnétiques émanés de moi-même ou des autres traversent sans obstacle la chaîne infinie des choses créées; c'est un réseau transparent qui couvre le monde, et dont les fils déliés se communiquent de proche en proche aux planètes et aux étoiles. Captif en ce moment sur la terre, je m'entretiens avec le chœur des astres, qui prend part à mes joies et à mes douleurs!' Nerval, *Aurélia*, my trans. See Vincent Gille, 'L'Etincelle: Le courant du rêve', in *Trajectoires du rêve*, exh. cat., ed. Gille, 194.
3. Leadbeater, *Clairvoyance*, 62.
4. Reichenbach, *Physico-Physiological Researches on the Dynamics of Magnetism*;

Farrar, 'Reichenbach', in Coulston Gillispie (ed.), *Dictionary of Scientific Biography*, 359–60.

5. See Elizabeth Barrett Browning, *Complete Works*, ed. Charlotte Porter and Helen A. Clarke, vi. 653–4. I am grateful to Margaret Reynolds for pointing out this connection.

6. Reichenbach, *Physico-Physiological Researches*, 573.

7. *OED*, quoting S. Blancard's *Physical Dictionary* (London, 1693).

8. The names Ramsay gave these gases are themselves revealing of the symbolic value attached to properties of air: argon is named after Argos, the many-eyed custodian appointed by Jupiter to watch over Io after he has changed her into a heifer: does Ramsay's train of thought suggest that this pervasive substance (1 per cent of the atmosphere) wraps us in its unseen gaze? Helium, which had been guessed at by Lockyer in 1868, is the lightest gas of all, and was called after the god of the sun, Helios; xenon means strange; neon, new; krypton, secret.

9. Solovoy, *JSPR*, 5 (1891), 158, quoted in Grove, 'Roentgen's Ghosts'.

10. Chaloner, 'Most Wonderful Experiment in the World', 357.

11. Ruskin, *The Queen of the Air*, 48.

12. Hopkins, in *Poems and Prose*, 54–8.

13. Ibid. 65–6.

14. Derrida, *Cinders*, 43.

15. He then modulates the metaphor of the rising smoke into a thought on writing and inspiration and the desirable state of vagueness, a higher form of expression than literalism (his own lines meanwhile adopting a kind of mimetic elusiveness of course):

> Ainsi le choeur des romances
> A la lèvre vole-t-il
> Exclus-en si tu commences
> Le réel parce que vil
>
> Le sens trop précis rature
> Ta vague littérature.'

('So the choir of romances flies to the lip; exclude from it, if you begin the real because it is base. Too precise a meaning erases your mysterious literature.') *Mallarmé*, 96.

16. 'What a difference between ash and smoke,' Derrida exclaims; 'smoke seems to lose itself, and better, without leaving a sensory residue, but rises, takes the air, becomes subtle and sublimates itself. Ash falls, weary, heavy . . . is very divisible.' *Cinders*, 73.

17. Connor, 'Machine in the Ghost'.

18. Baraduc, *L'Âme humaine*, followed by *Méthode de radiographie humaine*.

19. Baraduc, *L'Âme humaine*, 19.

20. The BL copy is dedicated in his hand to 'étudiantes Anglaises' (!).

21. Baraduc, *Vibrations de la Vitalité humaine*, 149.

22. e.g., Flammarion, *Les Forces nouvelles inconnues*, 104–5.

23. Andreas Fischer, ' "La Lune au front"; Remarques sur l'histoire de la photographie de la pensée', in *Le Troisième Oeil*, 139–51.

24. See Grove, 'Roentgen's Ghosts'.

25. Eisenbud, *The World of Ted Serios*; see Mark Alice Durant, 'Adrift in the Fluidium', in *The Blur of the Otherworldly*, exh. cat., 56–77; Stephen E. Braude, 'Les Psychographies de Ted Serios', *Le Troisième Oeil*, 155–65.

26. Leadbeater, *The Astral Plane; idem, Man Visible and Invisible; and idem, Thought-Forms.*

27. Ringbom, 'The Sounding Cosmos'.

28. See also Arnold Schoenberg, 'Materische Einflüsse' (1938), *Journal of the Arnold Schoenberg Institute*, 2, no. 3 (June 1978), 237; Esther da Costa Meyer, 'Schoenberg's Echo: The Composer as Painter', in *Schoenberg, Kandinsky, and the Blue Rider*, exh. cat., 37–61.

29. Daniell Cornell, 'Alfred Stieglitz and the Equivalent'.

30. See also the photographs of Robert J. Scott and Victor Adamenko in *Le Troisième Oeil*, exh. cat., 136–8. An object on a photographic plate creates an image of itself if exposed to high-voltage, low-current electricity, as was discovered *c.*1890 by Jacob Narkiewicz-Jodko in Russia, ibid. 67.

Chapter 20 Time Travel and Other Selves

1. Carroll, *Sylvie and Bruno*, chs. 21–3, in *Complete Sylvie and Bruno*, 146–71.

2. Ato Quayson, 'Fecundities of the Unexpected'.

3. Butler, *Life and Habit*, 78, 85.

4. Freud made the connection between these two newly revealed dimensions of mystery when he described the unconscious as 'the true psychical reality: in its innermost nature it is as much unknown to us as the reality of the external world, and it is as incompletely presented by the data of consciousness as is the external world by the communications of our sense organs.' Freud, *Interpretation of Dreams*, 615.

5. 'The Subliminal Self', *PSPR*, quoted in James, 'What Psychical Research Has Accomplished', in *The Will to Believe*, 315–16.

6. Thurschwell, *Literature, Technology and Magical Thinking*, 19.

7. Myers, 'Greek Oracles', 425–92; *idem, Human Personality and Its Survival*, 1, 119–20; 2, 189–277.

8. Myers, 'Greek Oracles', 461–2.

9. Charles Epheyre (Charles Richet), 'Soeur Marthe', in *Revue des Deux Mondes*, 1889, 384–431, quoted by Hacking in 'Telepathy'.

10. Hacking, 'Telepathy', 437.

11. See 'First Report on Thought-Reading', *PSPR*, 1 (1882–3), Second Report, etc. See Hacking, 'Telepathy'.

12. Luckhurst, *Invention of Telepathy*, 76–8.

13. See 'First Report on Thought-Reading', 15–16, quoted in Thurschwell, *Literature, Technology and Magical Thinking*, 29.

14. President's address, 25 Jan. 1889, *PSPR*, 5, 399–402.

15. Carl du Prel, *Die Entdeckung der Seele durch die Geheimwissenshaften*, 281, quoted in Andriopoulos, 'Psychic Television', 629.

16. Andriopoulos, 'Psychic Television', 629.

17. Ibid. 631.

18. Flammarion, 'Refluum Temporis', in *Lumen*, 64–105.

19. See Wells, *The Time Machine*, intro. Warner, xv.

20. See S. During, *Modern Enchantments*, 135–77; Beckman, *Vanishing Women*, 3–31; Frank Gray, 'George Albert Smith's Visions and Transformations: The Films of 1898', in Popple and Toulmin (eds.), *Visual Delights*, 170–80. I have not been lucky enough to see any of Smith's films, and my account is taken from Gray's invaluable article.

21. 'Brighton Kinematograph Factory—Its Wonders and Humours', 2, quoted in Gray, ibid., 178.

22. Wells, *Invisible Man*, 95.

23. Terry Ramsaye, 'Robert Paul and The Time Machine', in Geduld (ed.), *Definitive Time Machine*, 196–203.

24. Victor Tausk, 'On the Origin of the "Influencing Machine" in Schizophrenia', 521. I am most grateful to Mark Cousins for this reference. See Oursler, *The Influence Machine*, esp. ' "Smoke and Mirrors", *idem*, "Influence Machine": A Conversation between Tony Oursler and Louise Neri', 56–61, and Warner, ' "Ourself behind Ourself, Concealed": Ethereal Whispers from the Dark Side', 70–7; see also Mark S. Roberts, 'Wired: Schreber as Machine, Technophobe, and Virtualist', in Weiss (ed.), *Experimental Sound*, 27–41; and Turner, 'The Influencing Machine'.

25. Schreber, *Memoirs*, 54–5.

26. Museum of Pathological Art, Psychiatric University Hospital, Heidelberg; see *Beyond Reason*, exh. cat.

27. Thurschwell, *Literature, Technology and Magical Thinking*, 86–114, has written most perceptively on James's treatment of media and telepathy, and the channelling of his spirit by his secretary, Theodora Bosanquet, who took dictation from him in life, and death does not seem to have stopped the process. Luckhurst, *Invention of Telepathy*, also casts a penetrating and thoughtful light on psychic research in its social context and discusses its relations with Modernism, as both psychology and language, 234 ff.

28. Kipling, *Traffics and Discoveries*: 'Wireless', 181–99; 'They', 243–65; 'Mrs Bathurst', 268–89; see also introduction by Hermione Lee, 7–29.

29. Beer, 'Myers's Secret Message', in *Providence and Love*, 116–88, tells the story superbly well.

Chapter 21 Exotic Visitors, Multiple Lives

1. D'Espérance, *Shadow Land*, between pp. 398–9.

2. *Le Troisième Oeil*, exh. cat., 99–101.

3. Photograph in file Eva C., SPRA; see Luckhurst, *Invention of Telepathy*, 152–60.

4. Flournoy, *Des Indes à la planète Mars*; *From India to the Planet Mars*, pp. ix–x;

see review by Castle, 'Flournoy's Complaint', *LRB*, 23 May 1996; see also Rosenberg, 'Speaking Martian'.

5. Flournoy, *From India to the Planet Mars*, trans. Vermilye, 316, 326.
6. Jung, 'Foreword', in *Erinnerungen, Traume, Gedanken von C. G. Jung*, ed. Aniela Jaffé (Olten, 1988), trans. Sonu Shamdasani, in Flournoy, *From India to the Planet Mars*, ed. Shamdasani, pp. ix–x.
7. Foster, *W. B. Yeats*, i. 490.
8. Nevinson, quoted in Foster, *W.B. Yeats*, ii. 71.
9. Foster, *W. B. Yeats*, i. 614 n. 36.
10. ibid. ii. 73.
11. 'Anima Hominis', sect. V of *Per Amica Silentia Luna*, quoted in Foster, *W. B. Yeats*, ii. 79.
12. *Le Troisième Oeil*, exh. cat., 98–101.
13. Salter Papers, WLTCC; Salter, 'Introduction to the Study of the Scripts', unpublished, *c.*1948; deposited 1963; see PSPR vols. xvii and xx, and Podmore (1911), 225 ff., for ingenuity in deciphering hidden meanings. I am most grateful to Diana Chardin for her help with these materials, as well as her catalogue, compiled in 1996.
14. Beer, *Providence and Love*, 138–88.
15. Connor, 'Echo's Bones: Myth, Modernity and the Vocalic Uncanny'.
16. Doyle, *Wanderings of a Spiritualist*, 31.
17. His sister Eleanor Lodge was active, like Eleanor Sidgwick, in higher education for women, becoming Vice-Principal of Lady Margaret Hall, Oxford, and then Principal of Westfield College, London, 1921–31.
18. Lodge, *Ether and Reality*, 179.

Chapter 22 Touching the Unknown

1. In *Dramatis Personae*, 1864. In Robert Browning, *Complete Works*, v. 285–351.
2. Ibid. ll. 456 ff.
3. De Vane, *Browning Handbook*, 307–12.
4. Aristotle, *De Anima* II. ix. 421a, 20–5.
5. D'Espérance, *Shadow Land*, 259–65; the performance artist Zoe Beloff has created an elaborate tableau inspired by this medium's work; see 'Two Women Visionaries', <www.zoebeloff.com>.
6. Georgiana Houghton, quoted in Connor, 'Machine in the Ghost', 208.
7. It is worth noting that, in the late 1850s when Robert Browning was composing his long dramatic monologue 'Mr Sludge', he may have wanted his fraud's name to hint at ectoplasmic blobs, but he does not introduce such phenomena specifically into his plausible villain's weaselly rigmarole of self-justification.
8. Ady, *Knowledge*, 15 June 1883, 355/2.
9. Ibid.
10. Geley, *L'Ectoplasmie et la clairvoyance*, 15.

11. Ibid., planches XXI, XXX, 240–1.
12. Ibid. 199.
13. Of the 275 mediums listed in the Index to Mediums in SPRA, a full 190 are men, but the women made more of an impact and became the subjects of the most intense experiments and inquiries.
14. See Lodge, 'Experience of Unusual Phenomena'.
15. Charles Richet to Alice Johnson, Secretary of SPR, 1898, file on 'Eusapia Paladino', SPRA.
16. 'Hesperus', 'Eusapia Paladino', *Light*, 23 May 1896, 243–4.
17. Richet, *Thirty Years of Psychical Research*, 34. (Elsewhere, he says he only held 100 plus, p. 412.)
18. Ibid. 544.
19. Letter from Eleanor Sidgwick to Lord Rayleigh, 23 Aug. 1894, file 'Eusapia Paladino', SPRA.
20. From first of three notebooks of seances, file Eusapia Paladino, SPRA.
21. Myers, 'Letter to the editor of *The Westminster Gazette*', 10 Feb. 1899.
22. 'Eusapia Paladino', Box 1, article by Eleanor Sidgwick in SPRA, 21, 518 ff.
23. The ectoplasmic hands she produced were identified as animal lung tissue.
24. Lodge, *Christopher*, 72–3.
25. Brunius, 'Ectoplasm', originally from *The Encyclopaedia Da Costa* (1947), quoted in *Encyclopaedia Acephalica*, 110–11.
26. Marcel Griaule, 'Spittle', originally from *The Critical Dictionary*, ed. Georges Bataille, in *Encyclopaedia Acephalica*, 79–80.

Chapter 23 Materializing Mediums

1. 'Of the popular and received tenets concerning Man, which examined, prove true or false,' in Browne, *Pseudoxia Epidemica*, 315–16.
2. Malcolm Gaskill, author of *Hellish Nell*, has also enjoyed an interesting encounter with the Duncan cloth: 'I let it catch the air, and watched it billow and shimmer, only to be sternly reminded by one of the University Library staff that they preferred readers not to throw the manuscripts around the room' (personal communication).
3. Price, *Confessions*, 155,164. See also Gaskill, *Hellish Nell*, 124–40.
4. Schoonover, 'Ectoplasms, Evanescence, and Photography'.
5. Doyle, 'Why Spirit Photographs, Ectoplasm, and Ghost Gloves are Genuine', newspaper cutting in file, SPRA (emphasis added).
6. Doyle, *History of Spiritualism*, 1.v. 114 (emphasis added).
7. See 'Margery', PSPR, 36, Pt. 98 (Nov. 1925); B. K. Thorogood, ed., 'The Margery Mediumship', PSPR, 20, 21, 22 (1928), 1–228; also Tillyard and Evans, 'Four Seances with Margery in Boston, 1928', HPL; Tillyard, 'Records of Two Seances with "Margery" at 10, Lime Street, Boston, Mass., USA', BJPR, 1, 5 Jan.–Feb. 1927, 150–60; Hudson Hoagland, 'Science and the Medium: The Climax of a Famous Investigation', *Atlantic Monthly*, Nov. 1925, 666–81; all in HPL.

8. In the 1880s, in the Egyptian Hall, Piccadilly, e.g., one of the attractions was a fortune-telling automaton called 'Psyche'.

9. J. B. Rhine and Louisa E. Rhine, 'An evening's observations on the Margery Case', envelope 1, file 'Margery', SPRA.

10. William H. Button, 'The Margery Mediumship: A solus sitting for thumb print, March 11, 1931 under additional technique of control', *PSPR*, Feb. 1931. The impressions are kept in the SPRA.

11. Notes on seance of 26 Feb. 1925, file, 'Margery', SPRA.

12. Letter from Mowbray, to London Spiritualist Alliance, 13 June 1947, file, 'Margery', SPRA.

13. *Truth*, 3 Mar. 1926; *New York Times*, 28 Feb. 1926; cuttings in file, 'Margery', SPRA.

14. Edward Worcester to Sir William Barrett, 3 Dec. 1924, file 'Margery', SPRA.

15. Noakes, 'Cranks and Visionaries', 93.

16. *SPRP*, 36, pt. 98 (Nov. 1925) 44.

17. Owen, *Darkened Room*, esp. 202–35.

18. D'Espérance, *Shadow Land*, 346–7, quoted in Beloff, 'Two Women Visionaries', <www.zoebeloff.com>.

19. Phillips, *Darwin's Worms*, 127.

Chapter 24 The Rorschach Test; or, Dirty Pictures

1. J. L. Koerner, 'Bosch's Contingency', 249–50; see also Gamboni, *Potential Images*, for a wide-ranging study of the different types of such illusions.

2. A. J. Koerner, *Kleksographien*; Gamboni, *Potential Images*, 56–9.

3. Willie Davenport, 'The Ghosts of My Friends' (1910), MS in WNC.

4. Rorschach, *Psychodiagnostik*; Gombrich, *Art and Illusion*, 157; J. L. Koerner, 'Bosch's Contingency', 250–1; Klopfer and McGlashan Kelley, *Rorschach Technique*; Najafi, 'Bats and Dancing Bears: An Interview with Eric Zillmer'.

5. Zillmer, *Quest for the Nazi Personality*.

6. Najafi, 'Bats and Dancing Bears'.

7. Krauss, 'Carnal Knowledge', in *Andy Warhol: Rorschach Paintings*, exh. cat 7–8.

8. The lingerie chain Agent Provocateur has used such Rorschach butterflies in black on rose-tinted mirror glass for the décor of its boutiques, evoking lace underwear, as I saw at Terminal 4, Heathrow airport, Aug. 2005.

9. Peter Brugger, 'From Haunted Brain to Haunted Science: A Cognitive Neuro-science View of Paranormal and Pseudoscientific Thought', in Houran and R. Lange (eds.), *Hauntings and Poltergeists*, quoted in R. T. Carroll, *Skeptics' Dictionary*.

10. Schreber, *Memoirs of My Nervous Illness*, 32.

11. Freud, *Leonardo*, 159–61, 117.

12. Sidgwick and Sidgwick, *Memoir*, 165–6; see also Schultz, *Henry Sidgwick*, 306.

13. See Crews, 'Out, Damned Blot!'.

14. These and many other examples of the poet-artist's powerful, proto-Surrealist work can be seen at the Maison Victor Hugo in Paris, and at his house in

Guernsey, where he lived during his exile from 1851 to 1870. Rodari *et al.*, *Shadows of a Hand*.

15. Luc Sante, 'The Octopus Bearing the Initials VH', in Rodari *et al.*, *Shadows of a Hand*, 8–12.
16. Quoted by J. L. Koerner, 'Bosch's Contingency', 251.
17. Sante, 'Octopus', 11.
18. Woolf, *On Being Ill*, 19.
19. Carroll, *Through the Looking Glass*, 222–3.
20. Borges, 'Circular Ruins', in *Fictions*, 52–8.

Chapter 25 Nice Life, an Extra's

1. Poe, 'The Domain of Arnheim', in *Complete Tales*, 546–56.
2. See esp. Nelson, *Secret Life of Puppets*, 273–90.
3. Borges, 'On William Beckford's *Vathek*', in *Total Library*, 236–9.
4. As the eerie tale sets out the possibility of gaining happiness through art and power, and imagines the alteration of reality through one person's aesthetic will, it is not surprising that this was one of Poe's stories that Baudelaire chose to translate. When the French writer first came across Poe's work, he exclaimed that he was his very own *semblable*, his own double, casting a mimic shadow across his writing from an America twenty years before. See Poe, *Histoires grotesques et sérieuses*, 151–71.
5. See Sylvester, *Magritte* (1969), 52–3.
6. Verschaffel, 'Peinture vache, peinture métaphysique? René Magritte et le sublime', *Magritte* (1996), 67–80.
7. Sylvester, *Magritte* (1969), 9.
8. Sylvester, *Magritte* (1992), 302.
9. From Magritte, *Écrits*, quoted in Whitfield, *Magritte*, exh. cat. 1992.
10. Benjamin, 'Art in the Age of Mechanical Reproduction', in *Illuminations*, 230–1.
11. Nabokov, *Mary (Mashen'ka)*, 1926, quoted in Andriopoulos, 'Terror of Reproduction'.
12. Bioy Casares, *Invention of Morel*, 102–3.
13. Ibid. 82.
14. The Quay Brothers, visionary film-makers and puppeteers, also pay tribute to Bioy's story with their recent film about an island dominated by a maker of automata, *The Piano-Tuner of Earthquakes* (2005).
15. Christine Brooke-Rose, an English writer who has lived and worked in France all her life, wrote a blithely comic *jeu d'esprit* called *Textermination* (1991): here literature is under threat of annihilation, because nobody reads any more. The travesties of posterity, who, making films, cast one performer as a character completely out of character, fail to honour the figments of the word. So characters from many books and stories, along with authors, novelists, and poets, travel to an international conference on literature to make their views felt with the doyens and guardians of culture. Emma from *Emma* at the airport

finds herself in a taxi—a Flaubertian diligence—with . . . Goethe; another Emma, Emma Bovary, gets into another conveyance, and many join the journey—a whole host of ghosts of story, Mr Tulkinghorn and Clarissa Harlowe, Lucien and Fabrice, Robinson Crusoe, Dorothea, Mr Rochester, and Lotte from *Werther*. I could continue. Every reader can add the names of favourite characters, and register them at entry. Every one of them is on their way to the annual Convention of Prayer for Being in San Francisco. They want to become enfleshed. They want this, not only for the sweets of existence, but because they feel denatured by modern media.

16. Quayson, 'Fecundities of the Unexpected'.
17. Tausk, 'On the Origin of the "Influencing Machine" in Schizophrenia'.
18. Tony Oursler, manuscripts kindly lent by the artist, and adapted as 'Monologues', in *The Influence Machine*, 34–49.
19. Coetzee, *Elizabeth Costello*, 212–13.
20. Ibid. 216.
21. James Wood, 'A Frog's Life', *LRB*, 23 Oct. 2003.
22. Coetzee, *Elizabeth Costello*, 217.
23. Bourriaud, *Relational Aesthetics*.
24. See Jerome Sans, 'R. for Remake', interview with Pierre Huyghe, 'Demo Installation', Aarhus Kunstmuseum, 16 Mar.–5 Apr. 1999; <www.aarhuskunstmuseum.dk>.
25. Contemporary disjunctions of voice and body have also inspired Tacita Dean's film *Foley Artist* (1996), about two specialists in sound effects working at Shepperton Studios: see *Tacita Dean*, exh. cat. Gillian Wearing, the British video artist, has made some powerfully unsettling tapes in which she mixes and matches one character's voice with another's body and face (*2 into 1* (1997); *10–16* (1997)), the effect of this contradiction (old man's face, child's piping) is hilarious and deviant, often in a very disturbing way. The manœuvre, which extends the unnerving potential of communication devices to dissolve the integrated self, was swiftly adopted by advertisers—for a soft drink, I think— who added a lot of song and dance, but clearly focused on the same deeply unnerving disjunction between the usual reliable indicators of a person, present in person, mind and body united, voice and outward appearance; see Wearing, 20, 42, 74–80, 82–5.
26. These workers' existence out of time and place is the subject of an original mixed media theatre event, *Alladeen*, directed by Marianne Weems with the designer Keith Khan (London, New York, and other places, 2003–4). With regard to these new forms of displaced selves, Desmond Tutu, when asked (*c.* 2000) about the harrowing testimony that the Truth and Reconciliation Commission listened to day after day in South Africa, described the sense of anguish the commissioners felt in empathy with the victims telling their stories. But he then added that he felt the people who suffered most during the legal proceedings were the simultaneous interpreters in their booths, who repeated the words of the witnesses in the first person. Sometimes, these witnesses were describing torments they had undergone. In other cases, they were describing

torture and crimes they had themselves perpetrated. This act of dubbing another's experiences, Archbishop Tutu said, caused them terrible pain.

27. See Huyghe and Parreno, *No Ghost Just a Shell*, *passim*.
28. See B. Williams, *Truth and Truthfulness*, *passim*, esp. 1–12, 84–96. I was fortunate to attend a seminar that Bernard Williams gave on this theme, at the University of London, *c*.2002.
29. James Meek, quoting Edward Castronova, 'Get a Life', *Guardian 2* (3 Aug. 2004), 2–3.
30. Jan Verwoert, 'Copyright, Ghosts and Commodity Fetishism', in Huyghe and Parreno, op.cit., 184–92.
31. Andy Warhol, *America* (New York, 1985), 126–9.

Chapter 26 Disembodied Eyes: The Culture of Apocalypse

1. S. Clark, *Thinking with Demons*, 3.
2. Quayson, 'Fecundities', paper given at the 'Making Waves' conference in honour of Gillian Beer, 4–5 July 2003, Cambridge, published in Moretti *et al.*, *The Novel*, ii.
3. Serres, *Légende des anges*, 7–9.
4. B. McGinn, *Visions of the End*, 31–2; see also *idem*, 'The End of the World and the Beginning of Christendom', in Bull (ed.), *Apocalypse Theory*, 58–89.
5. Irenaeus, Clement of Alexandria, and Tertullian identified him as the evangelist and the apostle.
6. Pippin, *Death and Desire*, 80; see also Keller, *Apocalypse Now and Then*. Elaine Wainwright, Theology Faculty, University of Auckland, kindly lent me these books.
7. *Shepherd of Hermas*, 33.
8. Quoted in Kerrigan, *Revenge Tragedy*, 292.
9. B. McGinn, 'Revelation', in Alter and Kermode (eds.), *Literary Guide to the Bible*, 529.
10. B. McGinn, *Visions of the End*, 31–2.
11. In a speech made in March 2004, Blair invoked Armageddon by name, and cast his decision to go to war in Iraq in visionary terms: '. . . Here is where I feel so passionately that we are in mortal danger of mistaking the nature of the new world. If the 20th century scripted our conventional way of thinking, the 21st century is unconventional in almost every respect . . . it was defined by September 11.' September 11 was for me a revelation [*sic*]. The purpose was to cause such hatred between Muslims and the west that religious jihad became reality, and the world engulfed by it. The global threat to our security was clear. So was our duty: to act to eliminate it.' *Guardian*, 6 March 2004; <http://www.guardian.co.wk/print/0,3858,4874052–103550,00.html>.
12. 'We'll be deliberate, yet time is not on our side. I will not wait on events, while dangers gather. I will not stand by, as peril draws closer and closer. . . . Our war on terror is well begun, but it is only begun. This campaign may not be finished

on our watch—yet it must be and it will be waged on our watch.' State of the Union Address, 29 Jan. 2002. <http://www.whitehouse.gov/news/releases/2002/01>.

13. In his second inaugural speech Bush again adopted biblical turns of phrase, archaic imagery, and the cadences of the evangelical movement: 'For a half a century, America defended our own freedom by standing watch on distant borders. After the shipwreck of communism came years of relative quiet, years of repose, years of sabbatical—and then there came a day of fire . . .' Later, after resonating with references to Lincoln and American love of liberty, the apocalyptic rhetoric returned: 'By our efforts, we have lit a fire as well—a fire in the minds of men. It warms those who feel its power; it burns those who fight its progress, and one day this untamed fire of freedom will reach the darkest corners of our world.' 20 Jan. 2005; <www.whitehouse.gov/news/releases/2005/01/20050120-1.html>.

14. B. McGinn, 'Revelation', 539.

15. See Lawrence and Jewett, *Myth of the American Super-Hero*; the authors place the book's mission in the history of the national psyche and its individualist will-to-power.

16. See Joan Didion, 'Mr Bush and the Divine', *NYRB*, 6 Nov. 2003, 81–6.

17. Pullman, *Amber Spyglass*, 431–2.

18. Ibid. 394.

19. It is not so easy to keep faith with this theme. The play based on the books, in the first version written by Nicholas Wright for Nicholas Hytner's production at the National Theatre in London, 2002, showed the pressure of contemporary apocalypticism and allowed the reigning Manichaean combat myth to impose its dualism. The imagined ecological utopia in the third volume vanished, along with the benign older woman scientist, the good mother and ex-nun Mary Malone. This stage version was subsequently revised. Meanwhile, the film producers are fighting shy of his plot's assault on organized religion, or so it is reported—the book was bought for its success, not for its meanings, and present-day entertainment does not in effect permit such originality or liberties as Pullman proclaims.

20. Gianni Vattimo is a self-proclaimed devout Catholic, though he declares: 'The sexual morality long preached by the church, which sees sexuality mainly, or exclusively, as a means of reproduction, involves considerably less respect and attention for the other than the ludic, seductive, and aesthetic sexuality of Don Juan.' Vattimo, *After Christianity*, 114.

21. Rowan Williams, '"A Near-Miraculous Triumph"', *Guardian* 2, 10 Mar. 2004, 11.

22. Kermode, *Sense of an Ending, passim*, but esp. the first two lectures, 'The End' and 'Fictions', 3–64.

23. Malcolm Bull, 'Tick-Tock', *LRB*, 9 Dec. 1999; see also Bull, 'On Making Ends Meet', in Bull, 1–20.

24. See McKinnon, *Only Words*, for a powerful polemic that a rape performed on film is a rape.

25. Colie, *Paradoxica Epidemica*, 360, quoted in S. Clark, *Thinking with Demons*, 234.
26. A rise in fighting with animals has been reported; the nastier sides of the Net broadcast images of murders, executions, and so on. 'Bumfights', or fights set up for money between homeless and derelict people, have been filmed. These activities are illegal, and various moves are being made to tighten controls. That they occur at all is horrifying. See John Sutherland, 'How Rufus the Stunt Bum Offended the US Congress', *Guardian* G2, 22 Aug. 2005.
27. Stevens, 'The Pure Good of Theory', in *Collected Poems*, 329–333, 332.
28. Cozarinsky, *Bride from Odessa*, 136.
29. See Latour, 'What Is Iconoclash? Or Is There a World Beyond the Image Wars?', and Joseph Koerner, 'The Icon as Iconoclash', in *Iconoclash*, exh. cat., 14–37, 164–213.

Chapter 27 Our Zombies, Our Selves

1. See Anne Rice, *Interview with the Vampire* (1976), first of the cult books *The Vampire Chronicles*; cf. *Buffy the Vampire*, TV series.
2. I am grateful to Jonathan Lamb who, by asking me if zombies could speak, drew attention to their condition of muteness. See Blackburn, *Think*, 52–4; Warner, *Fantastic Metamorphoses*, 123–4; Dean W. Zimmerman, 'Dispatches from the zombie wars', *TLS*, 28 April 2006, 8–9.
3. Žižek, *Looking Awry*, 25.
4. Dante, *Inferno*, Canto XXXIII, ll. 109–50.
5. See Warner, *Fantastic Metamorphoses*, 119–20.
6. See, e.g., Fulford, *Landscape, Liberty and Authority*, and Roe, *John Keats and the Culture of Dissent*.
7. From the novel by Ira Levin, directed by Bryan Forbes.
8. Dick, *Do Androids Dream of Electric Sheep?*
9. e.g., Michael Cunningham, *Specimen Days* (2005), also imagines a future in which 'Simulos', or androids, have been manufactured to serve humans: these are closer descendants of robots and automata.
10. Churchill, *A Number* (2004).
11. e.g., if one identical twin begins to suffer mental illness, the other's vulnerability to developing it is by no means certain; the smallest differences in emotional histories and life circumstances will foster distinctions. See Segal, *Indivisible by Two*.
12. Warner, *Fantastic Metamorphoses*, 119–32.
13. Pullman, *Northern Lights*, 215.
14. Hurston, *Tell My Horse*; Deren, *Divine Horsemen*, and the film made from the footage she shot from 1947 to 1951), ed. Chevel and Teiji Ito, *Divine Horsemen: The Living Gods of Haiti* (1985).
15. '[It] remains one of the haunting and interesting films of its time.' Michael Price and George Turner, '*White Zombie*: Ugly Duckling Becomes a Swan'.

16. Seabrook, *Magic Island*; Michel Leiris wrote about the book in *Documents* 6, 1929. See *Undercover Surrealism*, exh. cat., 146–7.

17. Tony Williams, '*White Zombie*—Haitian Horror', *Jump Cut*, no. 28 (Apr. 1983), 18–20.

18. J. P. Teldte, 'Narration and Incarnation: *I Walked with a Zombie*', *Film Criticism*, 6, 3 (Spring 1982), 18–31; Gwenda Young, 'Shadows: Jacques Tourneur's Cinema of Ambiguity', *Film Ireland*, 83 (Oct./Nov. 2001), 42–4.

19. O'Brien, 'He Walked . . .', 30–2.

20. I have not been able to trace the story, but see related material, Inez Wallace, 'I Walked with a Zombie', in Haining, 95–102.

21. Interview with Inez Wallace, in press folder of *I Walked with a Zombie*, BFI.

22. See Romita Choudhury, ' "Is there a ghost, a zombie there?" Postcolonial intertextuality and Jean Rhys' *Wide Sargasso Sea*', *Textual Practice*, 10, 2 (1996), 315–27.

23. Plath, *Bell Jar*, 81, 92, 96, 121.

24. John A. Marmysz, 'From Night to Day: Nihilism and the Walking Dead', *Film and Philosophy*, (1996), 138–44.

25. Steve Beard, 'No Particular Place to Go', *Sight and Sound*, 3, 4 (Apr. 1993), 30–1.

26. Romero followed with *Dawn of the Dead* (1979), *Day of the Dead* (1985), and, in 2005, *Land of the Dead*. The thirtieth anniversary edition (1989) of *Night of the Living Dead*, made by Romero and his team, frames the original plot in a new context of fundamentalist preaching, Satanist sympathies, and child murder— weakening, in my view, the political overtones of the original.

27. 'Zombie Jamboree', written by Conrad Eugene Mauge, Jr., or by Lord Invader (a Tobagan a.k.a. Lord Intruder, Rupert Westmore Grant), was first recorded in the 1950s in the USA, and performed later the same decade by the Kingston Trio. (See 3-CD set 'The Kingston Trio–36 All Time-Favorites', CEMA Special Products; a Division of Capitol Records, Inc., S23–17653). Also per- formed several times by Belafonte during the Sixties and Seventies, by Bob Marley, and by Rockapella, on Spike & Co., *Do It A Cappella*, Elektra 60953–2.

28. Sylvie Pierre, review *of I Walked with a Zombie, Cahiers du Cinéma* no. 195 (1967) 68–9 (my translation).

29. Naipaul, *Middle Passage*, 28.

30. Žižek took this line for the title of his essay on 9/11, published in 2002.

Conclusion

1. Anne Joseph and Alison Winter, 'Making the Match: Human Traces, Forensic Experts and the Public Imagination', in Spufford and Uglow (eds.), *Cultural Babbage*, 193 ff.

2. e.g., 'Chemical warfare. The bursting of a Livens bomb at the objective.' ('It will be noticed what a dense cloud is formed. A slight idea may be gathered of the concentration of gas developed on an enemy's position'); 'Making a smoke screen to conceal batteries Passchendaele, Sept 1917'; 'An Impact of liquid fire and smoke from a W.P. rifle grenade. Gas Headquarters First Army

Corps Rarecourt, Meuse, 6 October 1918'; 'American chemical war service starting a smoke screen, near Beauchamp, October 1918', all from the IWM.

3. The contemporary artist Craig McPherson. in his powerful sooty mezzotints of the surviving steel works in Pittsburgh, has memorably captured the inferno of heavy industrial wastelands and the contamination of their surroundings, through a medium that itself began to communicate the phantasmagorias of the Gothic Romantics. See *McPherson: Darkness into Light*, exh. cat.

4. Only in the concluding pages does Light give some background, setting out a simple list of the code names used for the hundred projects, their dimensions, tonnage, and 'fusion yield': Moth (1955, Nevada), Trinity (1945, New Mexico), and numerous tests in the Bikini Atoll with names like Bravo, Romeo, Yankee. Bravo, e.g., was 'the largest US nuclear device ever exploded', the fireball swelling to nearly 4 miles wide within a second of detonating, 'the top of the debris cloud carrying the vaporised reef would ultimately reach 130,000' and a diameter of 66 miles'. The flash reached Okinawa, 2,600 miles away. Local islanders were irradiated and fell sick. The atoll was evacuated and continues to be too far radioactive for anyone to return. Light, *100 Suns*.

5. The artist Marilène Oliver has adapted the process to create portraits of living individuals; by Magnetic Resonance Imaging, she takes sections through their body, screenprints them on to acrylic, and then reassembles them in a stack to form a three-dimensional standing figure—who looks like a phantom. *Self-Portrait*, from *Family Portrait* series, 2002, stands in the Prints and Drawings Room of the VAM. My thanks to Gill Saunders for her notes on the work, 22 June 2005; see Gill Saunders and Rosie Miles, *Prints Now: Directions and Definitions*, forthcoming.

6. Žižek, 'Bring Me My Philips Mental Jacket', *LRB*, 22 May 2003, 3–5.

7. Atwood, *Negotiating with the Dead*, 156.

8. Guattari, 'Régimes, Pathways, Subjects', in Crary and Zwinter, *Incorporations*, 29, 35.

9. After I heard Jamme read, in Cambridge in 1997, I asked him about this choice, and he answered 'I simply cannot speak in the first person'. I pointed out that he had just done so, whereupon he exclaimed, indignant, 'I am not pathological, quand-même!' By coincidence, as I was checking these references, I discovered that John Ashbery has translated Jamme's 1986 collection *Récitation de l'oubli*.

10. Brennan, *Transmission of Affect*, was left unfinished when the author was tragically killed in a road accident, but the book contains some bold lines of questioning about what it means to say that you can sense the mood in a room, or take the pulse of a group, or feel 'in tune' with another person.

11. Rowling, *Harry Potter and the Order of the Phoenix*.

12. The terror resembles legends of fairies stealing babies from their cradles and substituting changelings, or even beliefs that fairies can swarm out of the fairy hill and take possession of a grown woman and switch everything about her except her outward appearance. As recently as 1895, Bridget Cleary's husband

and some of their family, friends, and neighbours together rolled her in the fire to release the fetch who had stolen her away, and bring back the real Bridget Cleary; she died of her injuries. See Bourke, *Burning of Bridget Cleary, passim*.

13. Kember, *Virtual Anxiety*, p. viii.

Bibliography

Collections

Barlow, Fred, *A Collection of Psychic Photographs*, ed. E. J. Dingwall, *c.* 1930 (BL PIX).
Harry Price Library: Scrapbooks, various boxes (uncatalogued) (HPL).
Imperial War Museum (IWM).
John Johnson Collection, Bodleian Library, Oxford (JJC).
Society for Psychical Research Archive, Cambridge University Library (SPRA).
Wellcome Iconographic Collections (WIC).
Wellcome Library, London (WLL).
Werner Nekes Collection, <www.http://wernernekes.de> (WNC).
Wren Library, Trinity College, Cambridge (WLTC).

Catalogues

L'Âme au Corps: Arts et Sciences 1793–1993, ed. Jean Clair (Paris, 1994).
An Aside, selected by Tacita Dean, SBT, 2004–5.
Apocalypse: Beauty and Horror in Contemporary Art, ed. Norman Rosenthal (London, 2000).
The Apocalypse: The Shape of Things to Come, ed. Frances Carey with essays by Frank Kermode *et al.* BM, 1999.
ARCHIVE, <www.doublearchive.com>, works by Anne Walsh and Chris Kubick.
Art Spirite Mediumnique Visionnaire Messages d'Outre-Monde, with essays by Roger Cardinal, Roger and Martine Lusardy, La Halle St Pierre (Hoëbeke, 1999).
Beyond Reason: Art and Psychosis: Works From the Prinzhorn Collection, HGL 1996.
The Blur of the Otherworldly: Contemporary Art, Technology, and the Paranormal, selected with essays by Mark Alice Durant *et al.* (Baltimore, 2005).
Cameron, Julia Margaret, *The Complete Photographs*, by Julian Cox and Colin Ford, with contributions by Joanne Lukitsh and Philippa Wright, J. Paul Getty Museum (Los Angeles, 2003).
—— *19th-Century Photographer of Genius*, by Colin Ford, NPG, 2003.
—— *Photographs from the J. Paul Getty Museum* (Malibu, Calif., 1996).
—— *The Whisper of the Muse: The World of Julia Margaret Cameron*, ed. Jeremy Howard, Colnaghi (London, 1990).
Lewis Carroll, with essays by Marina Warner, Michael Bakewell, and Roger Taylor, British Council touring exhibition, 1998.
Le Cere Anatomiche Della Specola, ed. G. Martinotti (Florence, 1979).
Helen Chadwick, ed. Mark Sladen, Barbican Art Gallery, London, 2004.

Constable's Clouds: Paintings and Cloud Studies by John Constable, ed. Edward Morris, with essays by John Gage and Anne Lyles, NGS, and National Museums and Galleries on Merseyside, 2000.

The Dawn of Photography: French Daguerreotypes, 1839–1855, MMA, 2003; CD-rom, 0–300–10189–9;   <http://www.metinuspum.org/special/French_Daguerro-types/dawn-images.htm>.

Tacita Dean: Selected Writings et al., 8 vols., MAMVP (Paris and Göttingen, 2004).

Devices of Wonder: From the World in a Box to Images on the Screen, ed. Barbara Maria Stafford and Frances Terpak, Getty Research Institute (Los Angeles, 2001).

The Disembodied Spirit, ed. Alison Ferris, Bowdoin College Museum of Art, Brunswick, Maine, and Austin Museum of Art (Austin, Tex., 2004).

Dream Machines, selected by Susan Hiller, SBT, 2000.

Embodied Spaces (Montreal, 1993).

Eyes, Lies, and Illusions: The Werner Nekes Collection, with essays by Marina Warner and Laurent Mannoni, HGL, 2004–5.

Fantastic, with essay by Peter Lamborn Wilson, MassMOCA, 2003–4.

Der Geraubte Schatten Photographie als ethnographisches Dokument, ed. Thomas Theye, Stadtmuseum, Munich, and Haus der Kulturen der Welt (Berlin, 1989).

Gothic Nightmares: Fuseli, Blake and the Romantic Imagination, by Martin Myrone, with essays by Christopher Frayling and Marina Warner (London, 2005).

Graceful and True: Drawing in Florence c.1600, by Julian Brooks with essay by Catherine Whistler (Oxford, 2003).

Hiller, Susan, *Wild Talents*, Galeria Foksal, Warsaw, 1997, Institute of Contemporary Art, University of Pennsylvania (Philadelphia, 1998).

Hugo, Victor, *Shadows of a Hand: The Drawings of Victor Hugo*, ed. Florian Rodari et al. (New York, 1998).

Ich Sehe Was, Was Du Nicht Siehst! Sehmaschinen und Bilderwelten: Die Sammlung Werner Nekes Museum Ludwig, Cologne, 27 Sept.–24 Nov. 2002 (Göttingen, 2002).

Iconoclash: Beyond the Image Wars in Science, Religion and Art, ed. Bruno Latour and Peter Weibel, Zentrum Kunst Museum, Center for Art and Media (Karlsruhe, 2002).

Identity and Alterity: Figures of the Body 1895–1995, selected by Jean Clair, Venice Biennale 46, 1995.

Im Reich der Phantome Fotografie des Unsichtbaren, with essays by Veit Loers, Carl Aigner, Urs Stahel, Mönchengladbach – Krems-Winterthur, 1997.

The Inner Eye: Art Beyond the Visible, selected with essay by Marina Warner, SBT, 1996.

Inside the Visible: An Elliptical Traverse of Twentieth Century Art: In, Of, and From the Feminine, by Catherine De Zegher (Cambridge, Mass., 1996).

Italian Paintings from Burghley House, by Hugh Brigstocke and John Somerville, touring exhibition (Alexandria, Va., 1995).

Anish Kapoor: Marsyas, TGL 2002.

Kiki Smith: A Gathering, 1980–2005, by Siri Engberg, with essays by Linda Nochlin, Lynne Tillman, and Marina Warner, Walker Art Center (Minneapolis, 2006).

Körperwelten: A Guide to the Exhibition, by Gunther von Hagens, Atlantis Gallery (London, 2001).

Darkness into Light and the Art of the Mezzotint: Craig McPherson, FMC, 1998.

Madame Tussaud's, *Biographical and Descriptive Sketches of the Distinguished Characters which Compose the Unrivalled Exhibition of Madame Tussaud's and Sons* (London, 1850).

Magritte, TGL, 1969, curated, with essay by David Sylvester.

Magritte, HGL, 1992, curated with essay by Sarah Whitfield.

Magritte, ed. D. Ottinger, Musée des Beaux-Arts, Montreal, 1996.

Magritte, ed. Daniel Abadie, Galerie National du Jeu de Paume (Paris, 2003).

Ron Mueck: Making Sculpture at the National Gallery, by Colin Wiggins and Susanna Greeves, NGL, 2003; <http://www.nationalgallery.org.uk/exhibitions/past/mueck.htm>

Medicine Man: The Forgotten Museum of Henry Wellcome, by Ken Arnold and Danielle Olsen (London, 2003).

Avis Newman, with essay by Michael Newman, Camden Arts Centre (London, 1995).

Noise, by Simon Shaffer and Adam Lowe, Kettle's Yard (Cambridge, 2000).

Only Make-Believe: Ways of Playing, by Marina Warner, with essays by Marina Warner and Mary Jacobus (Compton Verney, Warwickshire, 2004–5).

Oursler, Tony, *The Influence Machine*, Artangel exhibition (London, 2001).

Palazzo Poggi Museum: Science and Art, by Walter Tega (Bologna, 2002).

The Panorama Phenomenon, eds. Evelyn J. Fruitema and Paul A. Zoetmulder (The Hague, 1981).

Cornelia Parker, with essay by Jessica Morgan (Boston, 2000).

Photography: An Independent Art: Photographs from the Victoria and Albert Museum 1839–1996, by Mark Haworth-Booth (London, 1993).

The Quick and the Dead, selected by Deanna Petherbridge, SBT, 1997.

Registration Marks: Images by Adam Lowe, with essays by Adrian Cussins, Bruno Latour, Brian Smith, Pomeroy Purdy Gallery (London, 1992).

Ruskin, Turner, and the Pre-Raphaelites, with essays by Robert Hewison *et al.*, TGL, 2000.

Schoenberg, Kandinsky, and the Blue Rider, by Esther da Costa Meyer and Fred Wasserman, Jewish Museum (New York, 2003).

Seele: Konstruktionen des innerlichenin der Kunst, ed. Johannes Bilstein and Matthias Winzen, Kunsthalle (Baden-Baden, 2004).

Sensation: Young British Artists from the Saatchi Collection, Royal Academy (London, 1997).

Signs and Wonders: Nikos Pirosmani (1862–1918) and Recent Art, by Bice Curiger, with essay by Tobia Bezzola (Zurich, 1995).

Spectacular Bodies: The Art and Science of the Human Body from Leonardo to Now, by Martin Kemp and Marina Wallace, HGL (London, 2000–1).

The Spiritual in Art: Abstract Painting 1890–1985, selected with essay by Maurice Tuchman, Los Angeles County Music of Art (Los Angeles, 1986).

Stieglitz, Alfred, *Alfred Stieglitz and the Equivalent Reinvented: The Nature of Photography*, selected with essay by Daniell Cornell (New Haven, 1999).

Things: A Spectrum of Photography 1850–2001, by Mark Haworth-Booth (London, 2005).

Trajectoires du rêve: Du Romantisme au surréalisme, by Vincent Gille, Pavillon des Arts (Paris, 2003).

Le Troisième Oeil: la photographie et l'occulte, ed. Clément Chéroux, Andreas Fischer, Pierre Apraxine, *et al.*, Maison Européenne de la Photographie (Paris, 2004–5); trans., as *The Perfect Medium*, MMA (New York, 2005).

The Waking Dream: Photography's First Century, selected by Pierre Apraxine, MMA (New York, 1993).

Andy Warhol: Rorschach Paintings, with essay by Rosalind Krauss (New York, 1996).

Worlds within Worlds: The Richard Rosenblum Collection of Chinese Scholars' Rocks, Asia House, New York, and Sackler Museum (Cambridge, Mass., 1997).

Undercover Surrealism: Georges Bataille and Documents, HGL (London, 2006).

Vanishing Race and Other Illusions: Photographs of Indians by Edward S. Curtis, by Christopher M. Lyman (Washington, DC, 1982).

Vanitas: II Simbolismo del tempo, by Alberto Vaca, Galleria Lorenzelli (Bergamo, 1981).

Wunderblock: Eine Geschichte der modernen Seele, by Jean Clair, Cathrin Pichler, and Wolfgang Pircher (Vienna, 1989).

Books and Articles

Abbott, Evelyn (ed.), *Hellenica: A Collection of Essays* (Oxford and Cambridge, 1880).

Ackerman, Diane, *An Alchemy of Mind: The Marvel and Mystery of the Brain* (New York, 2004).

Adorno, Theodor W., *The Stars Down to Earth and Other Essays on the Irrational in Culture*, ed. Stephen Crook (London, 1994).

Aeschylus, *Prometheus Bound*, etc., ed. and trans. Philip Vellacott (Harmondsworth, 1983).

Aldrovandi, Ulisse, *Monstrorum Historia* (Bologna, 1642).

Alter, Robert, and Kermode, Frank (eds.), *The Literary Guide to the Bible* (London, 1987).

Altick, Richard, *The Shows of London* (Cambridge, Mass., 1978).

Anderson, J. C., *The Complete Fairy Tales and Stories*, trans. Erik Haugaard (London, 1979).

Andriopoulos, Stefan, 'The Terror of Reproduction: Early Cinema's Ghostly Doubles and the Right To One's Own image' (forthcoming in *New German Critique*, 2006).

—— 'Psychic Television', *CI* 31 (Spring 2005), 618–37.

Angeletti, Charlotte, *Geformtes Wachs : Kerzen, Votive, Wachsfiguren* (Munich, 1980).

Anon., 'Conversation No 4: "The Red Woman of Berlin" ', *The Portfolio*, 5 Feb. 1825.

Anonymi gesta Francorum et aliorum Hierosolymitanorum, ed. B. A. Lees (Oxford, 1924).

D'Arcy, M. C. (ed.), *Aquinas, Thomas Selected Writings* (London, 1939).

Aristophanes, *The Clouds*, trans. Benjamin Bickley Rogers (Cambridge, Mass., and London, 1960).

Aristotle, *Generation of Animals*, ed. and trans. A. L. Peck (Cambridge, Mass., and London, [1942] 2000).

—— *De Anima*, trans. W. S. Hett (Cambridge, Mass., and London, [1936], 1995).

—— *Meteorologica*, trans. H. D. P. Lee (Cambridge, Mass., and London [1952], 1978).

—— 'On the Art of Poetry' in *Classical Literary Criticism*, trans. T. S. Dorsch (London, 1965).

Armstrong, Isobel, 'Transparency: Towards a Poetics of Glass in the 19th Century', in Spufford and Uglow, *Cultural Babbage*.

Ashbery, John, *Girls on the Run* (Manchester, 1999).

Astronomy before the Telescope, ed. Christopher Walker (London, 1996).

Atherton, James, 'Lewis Carroll: The Unforeseen Precursor', in *The Books at the Wake* (London, 1959).

Atwood, Margaret, *Negotiating with the Dead: A Writer on Writing* (Cambridge, 2002).

—— *Alias Grace* (London, 1996).

Bachelard, Gaston, *La Poétique de la rêverie* (Paris, 1960).

—— *L'Air et les songes: Essai sur l'imagination du mouvement* (Paris, 1959).

Badt, Karl, *John Constable's Clouds* (London, 1950).

Bajac, Quentin, *The Invention of Photography*, trans. Ruth Taylor (New York, 2001).

Baltrušaitis, Jurgis, *Abérrations: Essai sur la légende des formes, i: Les Perspectives Depravés* (Paris, 1995).

—— *Le Miroir: Essai sur une légende scientifique; Révélations, science-fiction et fallacies* (Paris, 1978).

—— *Anamorphic Art*, trans. W. J. Strachan (Cambridge, 1976).

Balzer, Richard, *Peepshows: A Visual History* (New York, 1998).

Baraduc, Hippolyte, *Les Vibrations de la vitalité: humaine méthode biométrique appliqué aux sensitifs et aux névrosés* (Paris, 1904).

—— *Méthode de radiographie humaine . . . des vibrations de l'éther* (Paris, 1897).

—— *L'Âme humaine: ses mouvements, ses lumières* (Paris, 1896).

Barber, X. Theodore, 'Phantasmagorical Wonders: The Magic Lantern Ghost Show in Nineteenth-Century America', *Film History*, 3, 2 (1989), 73–86.

Barrie, J. M., *Peter Pan and Wendy* [1911] (London, [1921] 1979).

Barrow, Logie, *Independent Spirits, Spiritualism and English Plebeians, 1850—1910* (London, 1986).

Barthes, Roland, *Camera Lucida*, trans. Richard Howard (London, 1982).

Bartley, Mike, 'In Search of Robertson's Fantasmagorie', *OLJ* 7, no. 1, 1–5.

Batchen, Geoffrey, *Burning with Desire. The Conception of Photography* (Cambridge, Mass., and London, 1999).

Baudelaire, Charles, *Œuvres complètes*, ed. Marcel A. Ruff (Paris, 1968).

Bauman, Zygmunt, *Liquid Love* (Cambridge, 2003).

Baxandall, Michael, *Shadows and Enlightenment* (New Haven, 1995).

Beckford, William, *Vathek*, ed. Roger Lonsdale (Oxford, 1998).

Beckman, Karen, *Vanishing Women: Magic, Film, and Feminism* (Durham, N C, 2000).

Beer, John, 'Essaying the Heights: Sounding the Depths of Being: F. W. H. Myers and Edmund Gurney', in *Post-Romantic Consciousness: Dickens to Plath* (London, 2003), 44–76.

—— *Providence and Love: Studies in Wordsworth, Channing, Myers, George Eliot and Ruskin* (Oxford, 1998).

Beloff, Zoë, 'Two Women Visionaries', <www.zoebeloff.com>.

Benjamin, Walter, *Illuminations*, ed. Hannah Arendt, trans. Harry Zohn (New York, 1969).

Bergson, Henri, *Dreams*, trans. Edwin E. Slosson (London, 1914).

—— *Matter and Memory*, trans. N. M. Paul and W. S. Palmer (New York, [1911] 1991).

Berlin, Isaiah, *Against the Current: Essays in the History of Ideas*, ed. Henry Hardie (Oxford, 1991).

Besant, A., and Leadbeater, C. W., *Thought-Forms* (London and Benares, 1905).

Bettini, Maurizio, *Anthropology and Roman Culture: Kinship, Time, Images of the Soul* (Baltimore, 1991).

Bezzola, Tobia, 'Signs and Wonders', trans. David Brett, in *Signs and Wonders*, exh. cat., 165–7.

Binski, Paul, *Medieval Death: Ritual and Representation* (London, 1996).

Bioy Casares, Adolfo, *The Invention of Morel*, trans. Ruth L. C. Simms [1964] (New York, 2003).

Blackburn, Simon, *Think: A Compelling Introduction to Philosophy* (Oxford, 1999).

Bloom, Harold, *Omens of Millennium: The Gnosis of Angels, Dreams, and Resurrection* (London, 1996).

Boaistuau, Pierre, *Certaine Secrete Wonders of Nature*, trans. E. Fenton (London, 1569).

—— *Histoires prodigieuses*, WL MS 136 (Paris, 1560).

Bold, Valentine, 'The Magic Lantern: Hogg and Science', in *Studies of Hogg and His World*, no. 7 (Sterling, 1996), 5–17.

Bobik, J., 'Soul'; 'Soul, Human: 4. Philosophical Analysis', in *NCE*.

Bondeson, Jan, *The Feejee Mermaid* (New York, 1999).

Bonnefoy, Yves, '*Igitur* and the Photographer', trans. Mary Ann Caws, *PMLA*, 114, 3 (May 1999, 329–45).

Borges, Jorge Luis, *The Total Library, Non-Fiction 1922–1986*, ed. Eliot Weinberger, trans. Esther Allen, Suzanne Jill Levine, and Eliot Weinberger (London, 1999).

—— *Labyrinths: Short Stories and Other Writings*, ed. Donald A. Yates and James E. Irby (Harmondsworth, 1970).

—— *Fictions*, ed. Anthony Kerrigan (London, 1965).

Bourke, Angela, *The Burning of Bridget Cleary* (London, 1999).

Bourriaud, Nicolas, *Relational Aesthetics*, trans. Simon Pleasance and Fronza Woods (Paris, 2002).

Bown, Nicola, *Fairies in Nineteenth-Century Art and Literature* (Cambridge, 2001).

Brady, I. C., 'Soul, Human: 1. Oriental and Greek Conceptions: 2: Patristic and Medieval Writers', in *NCE*.

'The Brain', *Daedalus JAAAS*, 127, no. 2 (Spring 1998).

Brandon, Ruth, *The Spiritualists: The Passion for the Occult in the Nineteenth and Twentieth Centuries* (New York, 1983).

Brannigan, John Robbins, Ruth, and Wolfreys, Julian (eds.), *Applying: To Derrida* (Basingstoke, 1996).

Brassaï, Georges, *Marcel Proust sous l'empire de la photographie* (Paris, 1997).

Braude, Ann, *Radical Spirits. Spiritualism and Women's Rights in Nineteenth-Century America* (Boston, 1989).

Brennan, Teresa, *The Transmission of Affect* (Ithaca, NY, 2004).

Breton, André, *The Poems of André Breton: A Bilingual Anthology*, trans. and ed. Jean-Pierre Cauvin and Mary Ann Caws (Austin, Tex., 1982).

—— *Signe Ascendant* (Paris, 1949).

—— Eluard, Paul, and Soupault, Philippe, *The Automatic Message, The Magnetic Fields, The Immaculate Conception*, trans. David Gascoyne, Anthony Melville, and Jon Graham (London, 1997).

Brewster, Sir David, *Letters on Natural Magic, Addressed to Sir Walter Scott* (Edinburgh, 1832).

Brittain, Frederick (ed. and trans.), *The Penguin Book of Latin Verse* (Harmondsworth, 1962).

Britton, Donald, 'The Dark Side of Disneyland', in Welt, *Mythomania*, 113–26.

Broad, C. D., 'F. W. H. Myers', in *Man, Myth & Magic*, 68 (London, 1971), 1918–20.

Bronfen, Elisabeth, *Over Her Dead Body: Death, Femininity, and the Aesthetic* (Manchester, 1999).

Brontë, Charlotte, *Jane Eyre*, ed. Michael Mason (London, 1996).

Brooke-Rose, Christine, *A Grammar of Metaphor* (London, 1965).

—— *Textermination* (Manchester, 1991).

Brooks, Peter, *Realist Vision* (New Haven, 2005).

Brown, Horace M., 'The Anatomical Habitat of the Soul', AMH, 5, 1 (Spring 1923), 1–22.

Browne, Thomas, *Pseudoxia Epidemica*, ed. Robin Robbins (Oxford, 1981).

Browning, Robert, *The Complete Works*, v, ed. John C. Berkey, Allan C. Dooley, and Susan E. Dooley (Waco, Tex., and Athens, Oh., 1996).

Brumberg, Joan Jacobs, *Fasting Girls: The Emergence of Anorexia Nervosa as a Modern Disease* (Cambridge and London, 1988).

Bruno, Giuliana, *Atlas of Emotion: Journeys in Art, Architecture and Film* (London, . 2002).

—— *Walking on a Ruined Map: Cultural Theory and the City Films of Elvira Notari* (Princeton, 1993).

Bull, Malcolm, ed., *Apocalypse Theory and the Ends of the World* (Oxford, 1995).

Burwick, Frederick, 'Romantic Drama: From Optics to Illusion', in Stuart Peterfreund (ed.), *Literature and Science: Theory and Practice* (Boston, 1990), 167–208.

Buse, Peter, and Stott, Andrew (eds.), *Ghosts: Deconstruction, Psychoanalysis, History* (London, 1999).

Bushinski, L. A., 'Spirit (in The Bible)', in *NCE*.

Butler, Samuel, *Life and Habit* [1877] (London, 1910).

Butterfield, Andrew, review of exh. *Jean-Antoine Houdon: Sculptor of the Enlightenment*, *NYRB*, 17 July 2003, pp. 7–10.

Caillois, Roger, *La Pieuvre* (Paris, 1973).

Caillois, Roger, *The Writing of Stones* [*L'Ecriture des pierres*, 1970], trans. Barbara Bray, intro. by Marguerite Yourcenar (Charlottesville, Va., 1985).

Calvino, Italo, *Six Memos for the Next Millennium*, trans. Patrick Creagh (London, 1992).

—— *Difficult Loves*, trans. William Weaver (London, 1983).

Cameron, Julia Margaret, *Annals of My Glass House* (London, 1874).

Cannadine, David, *Ornamentalism: How the British Saw the Empire* (London, 2001).

Cantor, G. N., and Hodge, M. J. S. (eds.), *Conceptions of Ether: Studies in the History of Ether Theories 1740–1900* (Cambridge, 1981).

Cantwell Smith, Brian, 'From Imagination to Technology and Back Again: Catching Our Concepts Up with Our Creations', from *The Architecture of the Future: Rethinking Technology and Values from Gutenberg to AOL/Time Warner*, Symposium in Honour of Kimberley J. Jenkins, 15 Feb. 2002.

Cardinal, Roger, 'André Breton and the Automatic Message', in Ramond Fotiade (ed.), *André Breton: The Power of Language* (Exeter, 2000), 23–36.

Carey, Frances, 'The Apocalyptic Imagination: Between Tradition and Modernity', in *The Apocalypse*, exh. cat., 270–97.

Carrington, Hereward, *Personal Experiences in Spiritualism* '(*including The Official Account and Record of the American Palladino Seances*)' (London, 1912).

Carroll, Lewis, *Alice's Adventures in Wonderland* and *Through the Looking Glass*, ed. Hugh Haughton (London, 1998).

—— *Lettres à ses amies-enfants*, ed. Jean-Jacques Mayoux, trans. Henri Parisot (Paris, 1977).

—— *Phantasmagoria and Other Poems* [1869], (London, 1911).

—— *The Complete Sylvie and Bruno* (San Francisco, 1893).

Carroll, Robert Todd, *The Skeptics' Dictionary*, <http://skeptic.com>.

Carruthers, Mary, *The Book of Memory: A Study of Memory in Medieval Culture* (Cambridge, 1990).

Castle, Terry, *The Female Thermometer, Eighteenth-Century Culture and the Invention of the Uncanny* (New York and Oxford, 1995).

—— *The Apparitional Lesbian: Female Homosexuality and Modern Culture* (New York, 1993).

A Catechism of Christian Doctrine [1889] (London, 1971).

[Dei Vigri], Santa Caterina da Bologna, *Le Sette Armi Spirituali*, ed. Sr M. Giovanna Lo Bianco (Bologna, l998).

La Ceroplastica nella Scienza e nell'Arte: Atti del 1 Congresso internazionale. Florence, 3–7 June 1975, 2 vols.

Chaloner, Clinton, 'The Most Wonderful Experiment in the World: A History of the Cloud Chamber', *BJHS*, 1997, 357–74.

Chamisso, A., *Peter Schlemihl*, trans. Sir John Bowring (London, [1824] 1861).

Charcot, Jean-Michel, and Richer, Paul, *Les Démoniaques dans l'Art* (Paris, 1887).

Charney, Leo, and Schwartz, Vanessa R. (eds.), *Cinema and the Invention of Modern Life* (Berkeley and London, 1995).

Christian, William, A., Jr., *Visionaries* (New York, 1996).

—— *Apparitions in Late Medieval and Renaissance Spain* (Princeton, 1981).

Christie, Ian, 'Celluloid Apocalypse', in *The Apocalypse*, exh. cat., 320–40.

Churchill, Caryl, *A Number* (London, 2002).

Clark, David L., 'Optics for Preachers: The *De Oculo Morali* by Peter of Limoges', *Michigan Academician*, 9, 3 (Winter 1977), 329–43.

Clark, Stuart, 'Demons, Natural Magic, and the Virtually Real: Visual Paradox in Early Modern Europe', in Gerhid Scholz Williams and Charles D. Gunnoe, Jr. (eds.), *Paracelsian Moments: Science, Medicine, and Astrology in Early Modern Europe* (Kirksville, Md, 2003), 223–46.

—— *Thinking with Demons: The Idea of Witchcraft in Early Modern Europe* (Oxford, 1999).

Classen, Constance, *The Color of Angels: Cosmology, Gender and the Aesthetic Imagination* (London and New York, 1998).

Cleere, Elisabeth, 'Three Films by Werner Herzog: Seen in the Light of the Grotesque', *Wide Angle*, 3 no. 4 (1980), 12–19.

Clifford, James, *The Predicament of Culture: Twentieth-Century Ethnography, Literature and Art* (Cambridge, Mass., and London, 1988).

Coe, Brian, and Haworth-Booth, Mark, *A Guide to Early Photographic Processes* (London: Victoria and Albert Museum, 1983).

Coetzee, J. M., *Elizabeth Costello: Eight Lessons* (London, 2003).

—— 'Confession and Double Thoughts: Tolstoy, Rousseau, Dostoevsky', *Comparative Literature*, Summer 1985: 7, 3, 193–232.

Cohen, Morton N., *Lewis Carroll: A Biography* (London, 1995).

Colbert, Charles, 'Harriet Hosmer and Spiritualism', *American Art*, 10, 3 (1996), 28–49.

Coleridge, S. T., *Biographia Literaria*, ed. J. Shawcross, 2 vols. (Oxford, 1970).

—— *The Collected Works of S. T. Coleridge*, ed. Kathleen Coburn and Bart Winer (London, c.1983).

—— *Poems*, ed. J. B. Beer (London, 1963).

—— *Samuel Taylor Coleridge*, ed. M. J. Jackson (Oxford, 1985).

Connor, Steven, 'A Dim Capacity for Wings: Angels, Flies and the Material Imagination', paper given at University of Stirling 10 Nov. 2004, <http://www.bbk.ac.uk/english/skc/atmospheres.htm>.

—— 'Transported Shiver of Bodies: Weighing the Victorian Ether', paper given at conference British Association of Victorian Studies, University of Keele, 3 Sept. 2004, <http://www.bbk.ac.uk/english/skc/atmospheres.htm>.

—— *Dumbstruck: A Cultural History of Ventriloquism* (Oxford, 2000).

—— 'Voice, Technology and the Victorian Ear', in Luckhurst and McDonagh (eds.) (2000), *Transactions*, 16–29.

—— 'The Machine in the Ghost: Spiritualism, Technology, and the "Direct Voice" ', in Buse and Stott (eds.) (1997), *Ghosts* 203–25.

—— 'Echo's Bones: Myth, Modernity and the Vocalic Uncanny', in Michael Bell and Peter Poellner (eds.), *Myth and the Making of Modernity: The Problem of*

Grounding in Early Twentieth-Century Literature (Amsterdam and Atlanta, Ga, 1998), 213–35.

—— 'Fascination, Skin and Screen', *Critical Quarterly*, 40, 1 (1998), 9–24.

Cooper, Joe, 'Cottingley: At Last the Truth', *The Unexplained*, 117 (1982) 238–40.

Corner, George W., 'Anatomists in Search of the Soul', *AMH*, 2, 1 (Spring 1919), 1–7.

Coulston Gillispie, Charles (ed.), *Dictionary of Scientific Biography* (New York, 1973).

Cozarinsky, Edgardo, *The Bride from Odessa*, trans. Nick Caistor (London, 2004).

Crabbe, M. James C. (ed.), *From Soul to Self* (London, 1999).

Crary, Jonathan, *Suspensions of Perception: Attention, Spectacle, and Modern Culture* (Boston, 1999).

—— *Techniques of the Observer: On Vision and Modernity in the Nineteenth Century* (Cambridge, Mass., and London, 1990).

—— and Kwinter, Sanford (eds.), *Incorporations: Zone 6* (New York, 1992).

Crews, Frederick, 'Out, Damned Blot!', *NYRB*, 15 July 2004, 23–5.

Crompton, Dennis, Franklin, Richard, and Herbert, Stephen (eds.), *Servants of the Light: The Book of the Lantern* (Kirk by Malgcard, 1997).

Crompton, Dennis, Henry, David, and Herbert, Stephen (eds.), *Magic Images: The Art of Hand-Painted and Photographic Lantern Slides* (Ripon, 1990).

Crookes, William, *Researches in the Phenomena of Spiritualism* (London, 1874).

Curtis, Edward S., *Edward S. Curtis: Hidden Faces*, ed. Christopher Cardozo (Boston, 1996).

—— Graybill, Florence, and Boesen, Victor, *Edward Sheriff Curtis: Visions of a Vanishing Race*, photographs prepared by Jean-Antony du Lac (New York, 1976).

Cussans, John, 'Tracking the Zombie Diaspora: From Subhuman Haiti to Posthuman Tuscon', 'Zombie Diaspora', paper given at 'Monsters and the Monstrous: Myths and Metaphors of Enduring Evil', Budapest, 2004; eBook form ed. Paul Yoder and Peter Mario Kreuter. See <http://www.interdisciplinary.net/publishing/idp/eBooks/mammme.htm>.

D'Avenant, Sir William, *The Dramatic Works* (Edinburgh and London, 1873).

Da Costa Meyer, Esther, 'Schoenberg's Echo: The Composer as Painter', in *Schoenberg*, exh. cat., 2003.

Da Vinci, Leonardo, *Treatise On Painting*, ed. and trans. Philip McMahon (Princeton, 1956).

Damasio, Antonio, *The Feeling of What Happens: Body and Emotion in the Making of Consciousness* (London, 2000).

Damisch, Hubert, *La Théorie du nuage pour une histoire de la peinture* (Paris, 1972).

Dante Alighieri, *The Divine Comedy*, trans. John D. Sinclair, 3 vols. (London, 1958).

Darrieussecq, Marie, *La Naissance des fantômes* (Paris, 1998).

Darwin, Erasmus, *The Botanic Garden: A Poem in Two Parts* (London, 1791).

Daston, Lorraine, 'Material Powers of Imagination in Early Modern Europe: Impressions of Subtle Effluvia', Northwestern University Conference on 'Interior Temptation', 5 Dec. 2003, forthcoming, kindly lent by the author.

—— and Galison, P., 'The Image of Objectivity', *Representations* (1992), 11, 81–128.

Davis, Erik, *Techgnosis: Myth, Magic and Mysticism in the Age of Information* (New York and London, 1998).

Davis, T. Neil, 'Fata Morgana', article no. 261, *Alaska Science Forum*, 1 Sept. 1978, <www.gi.alaska.edu>.

Dayan, Joan, *Haiti, History, and the Gods* (Berkeley and London, 1998).

De Quincey, *Confessions of an English Opium-Eater and Other Writings*, ed. Grevel Lindop (Oxford, 1996).

De Vane, William Clyde, *A Browning Handbook* (New York, 1955).

Dean, Robert J., *Living Granite: The Story of Borglum and the Mount Rushmore Memorial* (New York, 1949).

Deleuze, Gilles, *The Fold: 'Leibniz and the Baroque'* [1988], trans. Tom Conley (Minneapolis, 1993).

—— and Guattari, Félix, *A Thousand Plateaus: Capitalism and Schizophrenia*, trans. Brian Massumi (London, 2003).

Deren, Maya, *Divine Horsemen: The Living Gods of Haiti* (New York, 1953).

Derrida, Jacques, *Spectres of Marx: The State of the Debt, the Work of Mourning and the New International*, trans. Peggy Kamuf (London, 1994).

—— 'The Deaths of Roland Barthes', trans. P.-A. Brault and M. Naas, in Hugh J. Silverman, *Philosophy and Non-Philosophy since Merleau-Ponty* (London, 1988), 259–96.

—— *Psyché: L'Invention de l'Autre* (Paris, 1987).

—— *Cinders*, trans. Ned Lukacher (Lincoln, Nebr., 1984).

Descartes, René, *Œuvres Philosophiques*, ed. Ferdinand Alquié (Paris, 1963).

—— *Philosophical Works*, ed. E. Haldane (Cambridge, 1911).

Dick, Philip K., *Do Androids Dream of Electric Sheep?* (New York, 1968).

Diderot, Denis, *Œuvres Complètes*, 15 vols. (Paris: Herman, 1969–73).

Dingwall, E. J., *Very Peculiar People: Portrait Studies in the Queer, the Abnormal and the Uncanny* (London, 1950).

Dobson, G. E., 'On the Andamans and Andamanese', *JAI*, 6 (1875).

Doniger, Wendy, *The Woman Who Pretended To Be Herself* (Chicago, 2005).

—— *The Bedtrick: Tales of Sex and Masquerade* (Chicago, 2000).

—— *Splitting the Difference: Gender and Myth in Ancient Greece and India* (Chicago, 1999).

Doniger O'Flaherty, Wendy, *Dreams, Illusions and Other Realities* (Chicago, 1986).

Donne, John, *Poems of John Donne*, ed. E. K. Chambers (London, 1896).

—— *The Sermons of John Donne*, ed. Evelyn M. Simpson and George R. Potter, 10 vols. (Berkeley and Los Angeles, 1956).

Douglas, Mary, *Leviticus as Literature* (Oxford, 1999).

—— 'The Cloud-God and the Shadow Self', *Social Anthropology*, 3, 2 (1995), 83–94.

Douglas-Fairhurst, Robert, *Victorian Afterlives: The Shaping of Influence in Nineteenth-Century Literature* (Oxford, 2002).

Doyle, Arthur Conan, *History of Spiritualism* (London, 1926).

—— *The Coming of the Fairies* (London, 1922).

—— *Wanderings of a Spiritualist* (London, 1921).

Draaisma, Douwe, *Metaphors of Memory: A History of Ideas about the Mind* (Cambridge, 2000).

Dreams, ed. Francesco Bonami and Hans Ulrich Obrist (Castelvecchio, 1999).

Dryden, John, *The Works of John Dryden* (Berkeley and London, 1970).

—— *The Dramatic Works*, ed. Montague Summers, 6 vols. (London, 1932).

Duffy, Maureen, *The Erotic World of Faery* (London, 1989).

Durant, Mark Alice, 'The Blur of the Otherworldly', *Art Journal* (Fall 2003), 6–15.

During, Monika von, and Poggesi, Marta, *Encyclopaedia Anatomica*, with photographs by Saulo Bambi (Cologne and London, 1999).

During, Simon, *Modern Enchantments: The Cultural Power of Secular Magic* (Cambridge, Mass., and London, 2002).

Dyer, Geoff, *The Missing of the Somme* (London, 1994).

Ebert, John David, *Celluloid Heroes and Mechanical Dragons: Film as the Mythology of Electronic Society* (Christ Church, New Zealand, 2005).

Eco, Umberto, *Sugli Specchi e altri saggi* (Milan, 1985).

Edelman, Gerald M., 'Building a Picture of the Brain', *Daedalus* (Spring, 1998), 37–69.

Edwards, Elizabeth (ed.), *Anthropology & Photography 1860–1920* (London and New Haven, 1992).

Ekserdjian, David, *Correggio* (New Haven and London, 1997).

Eliade, Mircea, *Images and Symbols: Studies in Religious Symbolism*, trans. Philippe Mairet (New York, 1969).

Eliot, T. S., *Collected Poems 1909–1935* (London, 1956).

Elkins, James, *The Object Stares Back: On the Nature of Seeing* (New York, 1996).

Elster, Jon (ed.), *The Multiple Self* (Cambridge, 1985).

Encyclopaedia Acephalica, ed. Alastair Brotchie, *Comprising the Critical Dictionary and Related Texts*, ed. Georges Bataille, and *The Encyclopaedia Da Costa*, ed. Robert Lebel and Isabelle Waldberg, trans. Iain White (London, 1995).

Endo, Shusaku, *Deep River*, trans. Van C. Gessel (London, 1994).

Enright, D. J. (ed.), *The Oxford Book of the Supernatural* (Oxford, 1995).

Ernst, Max, *Une Semaine de bonté ou les sept éléments capitaux* (Paris, 1934).

—— *Au delà de la Peinture* (Paris, 1925).

D'Espérance, Elisabeth, *Shadow Land, Or Light from the Other Side* (London, 1894).

Ewing, William A., *Inside Information Imaging the Human Body* (London, 1996).

Fantasmagoria, on recueil d'histoires d'apparitions de spectres, revenants, fantômes, etc., trans. J. B. B. Eyrie, 2 vols. (Paris, 1812).

Fattori, M., and Bianchi, M. (eds.), *Spiritus*, IV Colloquio Internazionale Roma 7–9 January 1983 (Rome, 1984).

Feher, Michael, with Naddaff, Ramona, and Tazi, Nadia (eds.), *Fragments for a History of the Human Body, Zone* 3, 4, 5 (New York, 1989).

Fenton, James, 'The Mummy's Secret', *NYRB*, 44, 12, 14 July 1997.

Ferguson, Frances, 'Pornography: The Theory', CI, 21, 3 (Spring 1995), 670–95.

Ferris, Alison (ed.) 'The Disembodied Spirit', in *The Disembodied Spirit*, exh. cat.

Findlen, Paula (ed.), *Athanasius Kircher: The Last Man Who Knew Everything* (New York and London, 2004).

Flammarion, Camille, *Les Forces nouvelles inconnues* (Paris, 1907).

—— *Récits de l'infini. Lumen: Histoire d'un Comète: Dans l'infini* (Paris, 1873); *Lumen*, trans. A. A. and R. M. (London, 1897).

Flaubert, Gustave, *Flaubert in Egypt: A Sensibility on Tour*, trans. and ed. F. Steegmuller (London, 1972).

Fleischmann, Hector, *La Guillotine en 1793 d'après des documents inédits des Archives Nationales* (Paris, 1908).

Fleming, Paula Richardson, and Luskey, Judith Lynn, *The Shadow Catchers: Images of the American Indian* (Hong Kong, 1993).

Flint, Kate, 'Painting Memory', *Textual Practice*, 17 (3) 2003, 527–42.

—— *The Victorians and the Visual Imagination* (Cambridge, 2000).

Flournoy, Théodore, *From India to the Planet Mars: A Case of Multiple Personality with Imaginary Languages*, ed. Sonu Shamdasani (Princeton, 1996).

—— *From India to the Planet Mars: A Study of A Case of Somnambulism with Glosso-lalia*, trans. Daniel B. Vermilye (New York, 1900).

—— *Des Indes à la planète mars: Étude sur un cas de somnambulisme* (Geneva, 1899).

Fludd, Robert, *Utriusque Cosmi* . . . (Oppenheim, 1617–19).

Focillon, Henri, *The Life of Forms in Art*, intro. Jean Molino, trans. Charles B. Hogan and George Kubler (New York, 1989).

Ford, Jennifer, *Coleridge on Dreaming: Romanticism, Dreams and the Medical Imagination* (Cambridge, 1998).

Fort, Charles Hoy, *Wild Talents*, revised by 'X', intro. by Michel Meurger (London, 1998).

Foster, Roy, *W. B. Yeats, ii: The Arch-Poet* (Oxford, 2003).

—— *W. B. Yeats, i: The Apprentice Mage* (Oxford, 1997).

Frayling, Christopher, 'Fuseli's *The Nightmare*: Somewhere Between the Sublime and the Ridiculous', in *Gothic Nightmares*, exh. cat., 9–20.

—— and Myrone, Martin, '*The Nightmare* in Modern Culture', in *Gothic Nightmares*, exh. cat., 207–12.

Frazer, J. G., *Questions on the Customs, Beliefs, and Language of Savages* (Cambridge, 1907).

—— 'Taboo and the Perils of the Soul,' in *The Golden Bough*, 3rd edn. (London, 1938).

Freedberg, David, *The Power of Images: Studies in the History and Theory of Response* (Chicago, 1989).

—— and Jan de Vries (eds.), *Art in History/History in Art: Studies in Seventeenth Century Dutch Culture*, (Santa Monica, Calif., 1991).

Freedberg, S. J., *Circa 1600: A Revolution of Style in Italian Painting* (Cambridge, Mass., 1983).

Freud, Sigmund, *The Uncanny*, trans. David McClintock, intro. by Hugh Haughton (London: 2003).

—— *On Metapsychology: The Theory of Psychoanalysis*, trans. James Strachey, ed. Angela Richards (London, [1984], 1991).

Freud, Sigmund, *The Interpretation of Dreams* (trans. and ed. James Strachey (Harmondsworth: 1967).

—— *Leonardo and a Memory of his Childhood*, trans. Alan Tyson, intro. Brian Farrell (Harmondsworth: 1966).

Fulford, Tim, *Landscape, Liberty and Authority: Poetry, Criticism and Politics from Thomson to Wordsworth* (Cambridge, 1996).

Gaffarel, M. I., *Curiosités inouïes sur la sculpture talismanique des Persans: Horoscopes des patriarches et lectures des étoiles* (Paris, 1629).

Gage, John, 'Clouds Over Europe', in *Constable's Clouds: Paintings and Cloud Studies by John Constable*, exh. cat., 125–34.

Galvani, Luigi, *Elogio della moglie Lucia Galeazzi Galvani* (repr. Bologna, 1937).

—— *De viribus electricitatis in motu musculari* (Bologna, 1791).

Gamboni, Dario, *Potential Images: Ambiguity and Indeterminacy in Modern Art* (London, 2005).

Gardner, Helen (ed.), *The New Oxford Book of English Verse* (Oxford, 1972).

Garnett, Henrietta, *Anny: A Life of Anne Thackeray Ritchie* (London, 2004).

Gaskill, Malcolm, *Hellish Nell, Last of Britain's Witches* (London, 2000).

Gatacre, Edward V., and Dru, Laura, 'Portraiture in *Le Cabinet de Cire de Curtius* and its Successors', in *La Ceroplastica nella Scienza e nell'Arte Atti del 1 Congresso internazionale* (Florence, 1977), ii. 617–38.

Gauld, Alan, *The Founders of Psychical Research* (London, 1968).

Geduld, Harry M. (ed.), *The Definitive Time Machine* (Bloomington, Ind., 1987).

Geley, Gustave, *L'Ectoplasmie et la clairvoyance: observations et expériences personelles* (Paris, 1924).

Gernsheim, Helmut, *Lewis Carroll: Photographs* (London, 1969).

—— *Lewis Carroll Photographer* [1949].

—— and Gernsheim, Alison, *L. J. M. Daguerre: The History of the Diorama and the Daguerreotype* (New York, 1968).

Gerry, Elbridge Thomas, *The Mumler 'Spirit' Photograph Case* (New York, 1869).

Gesner, Conrad, *Physicarum Meditationum Annotatiorum et Scholiorum* (Zurich, 1586).

Giardina, Domenico, 'Discorso sopra la Fata morgana di Messina, in *Opuscoli di autori Siciliani*, i (Catania, 1758).

Glaesemer, Jürgen, 'How Invention Derives from the Blot', *Parkett*, 8 (1986), 76–80.

Godwin, Joscelyn, *Athanasius Kircher: A Renaissance Man and the Quest for Lost Knowledge* (London, 1979).

—— *Robert Fludd, Hermetic Philosopher and Surveyor of Two Worlds* (London, 1979).

Goethe, *Faust: A Tragedy in Two Parts* (Stuttgart, 1959).

Gombrich, E. H., *Shadows: The Depiction of Cast Shadows in Western Art* (London and New Haven, 1995).

—— *The Sense of Order* (London, 1979).

—— *Art and Illusion: A Study in the Psychology of Pictorial Representation* (London, 1962).

Goodfield-Toulmin, June, 'Blasphemy and Biology', *The Rockefeller University Review*, Sept–Oct. 1966, 9–18.

Gorman, M., 'Soul, Human: 3. Modern and Contemporary Thought', in *NCE*.

Graves, Robert, *The Greek Myths*, 2 vols. (Harmondsworth [1955] 1966).

Green, David (ed.), *Where is the Photograph?* (Brighton, 2003).

Greenacre, Derek, *Magic Lanterns* (Haverfordwest, 1986).

Greenler, Robert, *Rainbows, Halos, and Glories* (Cambridge, 1980).

Gregory, Richard, *Mirrors in Mind* (New York and Basingstoke, 1997).

—— and Zangwill, O. (eds.), *The Oxford Companion to the Mind* (Oxford, 1988).

Grove, Allen W., 'Roentgen's Ghosts: Photography, X-Rays, and the Victorian Imagination', *Literature and Medicine*, 16, 2 (Fall 1997), 141–73.

Gunning, Tom, 'The Cinema of Attractions: Early Cinema, its Spectator and the Avant-Garde', in Thomas Elsaesser and Adam Barker (eds.), *Early Cinema: Space-Frame-Narrative* (London, 1989).

—— 'Phantom Images and Modern Manifestations: Spirit Photography, Magic Theater, Trick Films, and Photography's Uncanny', in Petro, *Fugitive Images*, 42–71.

—— 'Haunting Images: Ghosts, Photography and the Modern Body', in *Disembodied Spirit*, exh. cat.

Gurney, Edmund, with F. W. H. Myers and Frank Podmore, *Phantasms of the Living* (London, 1886).

Hacking, Ian, 'Get Knitting': Review of Steven Rose, *The 21st Century Brain*, *LRB*, 27, 16 (18 Aug. 2005).

——, *Rewriting the Soul: Multiple Personality and the Sciences of Memory* (Princeton, 1995).

—— 'Telepathy: Origins of Randomization in Experimental Design', *Isis*, 79, 3 (Sept. 1988), 427–51.

Haining, Peter, ed., *Zombie! Stories of the Walking Dead* (London, 1986).

Hamblyn, Richard, *The Invention of Clouds: How An Amateur Meteorologist Forged the Language of the Skies* (London, 2002).

Hamilton, Bernard, *The Christian Middle Ages* (London, 2003).

Hankins, Thomas J., and Silverman, Robert J., *Instruments and the Imagination* (Princeton, 1995).

Hart, Clive, *Images of Flight* (Berkeley and Los Angeles, 1988).

Hayward, Rhodri, 'Popular Mysticism and the Origins of the New Psychology, 1880–1910' (Ph.D. University of Lancaster, 1995); forthcoming as *Resisting History: Religions Transcendence and the Inventions of the Unconscious* (Manchester, 2007).

Heard, Mervyn, 'Paul de Philipsthal & the Phantasmagoria in England, Scotland and Ireland', Part One: 'Boo!', *NMLJ*, 8, 1 (Oct. 1996), 2–7; Part Two: 'Shoo!', *NMLJ*, 8, 1–2 (Oct., 1997), 11–16.

Hecht, Herman, 'The History of Projecting Phantoms, Ghosts and Apparition's', *NMLJ* 3, no. 1 (Feb. 1984), 2–6; 3, no. 2 (Dec. 1984), 2–6.

Henkel, Kathryn, *The Apocalypse* (Baltimore, 1973).

Hermas, *The Shepherd of Hermas*, trans. and ed. Charles H. Hoole (London, 1870).

Hesiod [and Theognis], *Theogony* and *Works and Days*, trans. with introductions by Dorothea Wender (Harmondsworth, 1973).

Hibbert, Samuel, *Sketches of the Philosophy of Apparitions*, 2nd edn. (Edinburgh and London, 1825).

Hilgard, E. R., and Hilgard, J. R., *Hypnotism and the Relief of Pain* (New York, 1975).

Hiller, Susan, and Coxhead, David, *Dreams: Visions of the Night* (London, 1976).

Hilloowala, Rumy, *et al.*, *The Anatomical Waxes of La Specola*, trans. and ed. Joseph Renahan, Julianne Hilawala, *et al.* (Florence, 1995).

Hills, Paul, *Venetian Colour: Marble, Mosaic, Glass, 1250–1550* (New Haven and London, 1999).

Hinman, Helen H., 'Jacques-Louis David and Madame Tussaud', *Gazette des Beaux Arts*, XLVI 1965, 231–8.

Hippolytus, St, *The Refutation of All Heresies*, trans. Revd J. H. MacMahon, Ante-Nicene Christian Library, 6 (Edinburgh, 1867).

Hobbes, Thomas, *Leviathan*, ed. C. B. Macpherson (Hermondsworth, 1968).

Hobson, J. Allan, *Dreaming: An Introduction to the Science of Sleep* (Oxford, 2002).

Hoffman, Donald D., *Visual Intelligence: How We Create What We See* (New York and London, 1998).

Hoffman, Eva, *The Secret: A Fable for Our Time* (London, 2001).

Hoffmann, E. T. A., *The Best Tales of Hoffmann*, ed. E. F. Bleiler, trans. Alfred Packer (New York, 1967).

Hofmannsthal, Hugo von, *La Femme sans ombre*, trans. and ed. Jean-Yves Masson (Paris, 1992).

Hofstadter, Douglas R. and Dennett, Daniel C. (eds.), *The Mind's I: Fantasies and Reflections on Self and Soul* (Brighton, 1981).

Hogg, James, *The Private Memoirs and Confessions of a Justified Sinner*, ed. John Carey (London [1969], 1999).

—— *The Works of the Ettrick Shepherd: Tales and Sketches*, ed. Thomas Thomson (London, 1973).

Homer, *The Odyssey*, trans. Robert Fagles (New York, 1996).

—— *The Iliad*, trans. E. V. Rieu (Harmondsworth, 1976).

—— *The Odyssey*, ed. and trans. A. T. Murray (Cambridge, Mass., and London, 1919).

Hopkins, Gerard Manley, *Poems and Prose*, ed. W. H. Gardner (London, [1983] 1985).

Hopkinson, Amanda, *Julia Margaret Cameron* (London, 1986).

Houghton, Georgiana, *Chronicles of the Photographs of Spiritual Beings and Phenomena Invisible to the Material Eye* (London, 1882).

Houran, J., and Lange, R. (eds.), *Hauntings and Poltergeists: Multidisciplinary Perspectives* (Jefferson, N.C., 2001).

Howard, Luke, 'On the Modifications of Clouds, and on the Principles of their Production, Suspension, and Destruction . . .', *Philosophical Magazine* (1802) 97–107; 17 (1803) 5–11.

Hughes, Ted, *Tales from Ovid* (London, 1996).

Hume, David, 'Of Miracles', from *An Enquiry Concerning Human Understanding*, in *Dialogues Concerning Natural Religion*, ed. Richard H. Popkin (Indianapolis and Cambridge, 1998).

Hunter, Michael (ed. and intro.), *The Occult Laboratory: Magic, Science and Second Sight in Late 17th Century Scotland* (Bury St Edmunds, 2001).

Hurston, Zora Neale, *Tell My Horse: Voodoo and Life in Haiti and Jamaica* [1938] (New York, 1990).

Huyghe, Pierre, and Parreno, Philippe, *No Ghost Just a Shell* (New York, 2003).

Ishiguro, Kazuo, *Never Let Me Go* (London, 2005).

Jacobson-Widding, Anita, 'The Encounter in the Water-Mirror', in *Body and Space: Symbolic Models of Unity and Division in African Cosmology and Experience*, ed. Anita Jacobson-Widding, Uppsala Studies in Cultural Anthropology, 16 (Uppsala, 1991).

—— 'The Shadow as Expression of Individuality in Congolese Conceptions of Personhood', in Michael Jackson and Ivan Karp (eds.), *Personhood and Agency. The Experience of Self and Other in African Cultures*, Uppsala Studies in Cultural Anthropology (Washington, DC, 1990), 31–58.

Jaensch, E. R., *Eidetic Imagery and Typological Methods of Investigation*, trans. Oscar Oeser [1930] (Westport, Conn., 1970).

James, William, *Essays in Psychical Research* (Cambridge, Mass., 1986).

—— *The Varieties of Religious Experience: A Study in Human Nature* [1901–2] (London, 1960).

—— *The Will to Believe and Other Essays in Popular Philosophy* (New York, 1897).

Jamme, Franck André, *Extracts from the Life of a Beetle*, trans. Michael Tweed (New York, 2000).

Janson, H. W. ' "The Image Made by Chance" in Renaissance Thought', in Millard Meiss (ed.), *Essays in Honour of Erwin Panofsky*, De artibus opuscula, 40.1 (New York, 1961), 254–66.

Jay, Martin, *Downcast Eyes: The Denigration of Vision in Twentieth-Century French Thought* (Berkeley and London, 1993).

Jenness, George A., *Maskelyne and Cooke: The Egyptian Hall, London, 1873–1904: A Chronological Record of the Old-Time Magic Shows* (Enfield, 1967).

Johnson, George, *Fire in the Mind: Science, Faith and the Search for Order* (London, 1995).

Jordanova, Ludmila, *Sexual Visions: Images of Gender in Science and Medicine between the Eighteenth and Twentieth Centuries* (London, 1989).

—— and Sawday, Jonathan, *The Body Emblazoned: Dissection and the Human Body in Renaissance Culture* (London, 1995).

Kandinsky, Wassily, *Concerning the Spiritual in Art* (1914), trans. M. T. H. Sadler (New York, 1977).

Keightley, Thomas, *The Fairy Mythology* (London, 1910).

Keller, Catherine, *Apocalypse Now and Then: A Feminist Guide to the End of the World* (Boston, 1996).

Kember, Sarah, *Virtual Anxiety: Photography, New Technologies and Subjectivity* (Manchester, 1998).

Kemp, Martin, *Science of Art: Optical Themes in Western Art from Brunelleschi to Seurat* (New Haven and London, 1990).

Kemp, Martin, and Walker, Margaret (eds.), *Leonardo on Painting: An Anthology of Writings by Leonardo Da Vinci* (New Haven, 1989).

—— *Leonardo Da Vinci: The Marvelous Works of Nature and Man* (Cambridge, Mass., 1981).

Kermode, Frank, 'Millennium and Apocalypse', in *The Apocalypse*, exh. cat., 11–27.

—— *The Sense of an Ending: Studies in the Theory of Fiction with a New Epilogue* [1967] (Oxford, 2000).

—— Introduction to William Shakespeare, *The Tempest* [1958], (London, 1987).

Kerrigan, John, *Revenge Tragedy, Aeschylus to Armageddon* (Oxford, 1996).

Kieckhefer, Richard, *Forbidden Rites: A Necromancer's Manual of the Fifteenth Century* (London, 1997).

Kincaid, James R., *Erotic Innocence: The Culture of Child Molesting* (Durham, NC, 1998).

Kipling, Rudyard, *Traffics and Discoveries* [1904], ed. Hermione Lee (London, 1992).

Kircher, Athanasius, *Ars Magna Lucis et Umbrae* (Amsterdam, 1671).

—— *The Vulcanos, Or, Burning and Fire-Vomiting Mountains, Famous in the World: With their Remarkables, Collected for the Most Part Out of Kircher's Subterranenous World*, anon. trans. (London, 1669).

—— *Mundus Subterraneus* (Amsterdam, 1665).

—— *Itinerarium Exstaticum Quo Mundo Opificium* (Rome, 1656).

Kirk, Robert, *The Secret Commonwealth*, ed. Stewart Sanderson (Cambridge, 1976) (see also under Michael Hunter).

Klein, Robert, 'Spirito Peregrino', in *Form and Meaning: Essays on the Renaissance and Modern Art*, trans. Madeline Jay and Leon Wieseltier (New York, 1979).

Klopfer, Bruno, and McGlashan Kelley, Douglas, *The Rorschach Technique: A Manual for a Projective Method of Personality Diagnosis* (New York, 1942).

Klossowski de Rola, Stanislas, *The Golden Game: Alchemical Engravings of the Seventeenth Century* (London, 1988).

Koeppen, Wolfgang, *Death in Rome*, trans. with an introduction by Michael Hofmann (London, 1992).

Koerner, Joseph L., 'Bosch's Contingency', in Lerhart v. Graevenitz and Odo Marquard (eds.), *Poetik und Hermeneutik*, xvii (Munich, 1998), 240–74.

Koerner, Justinus, *Kleksografien* (Stuttgart, 1890).

Kohler, Josef, *Das Eigenbild im Recht* (Berlin, 1903).

Krauss, Rosalind, *The Optical Unconscious* (Cambridge, Mass., 1993).

Krauss, Rolf H., *Beyond Light and Shadow: The Role of Photography in Certain Paranormal Phenomena, An Historical Survey*, trans. Timothy Bill and John Gledhill (Munich, 1993).

Lacan, Jacques, *Écrits: The First Complete Edition in English*, trans. Bruce Fink, with Héloïse Fink and Russell Grigg (New York, 2006).

Lakoff, George, and Johnson, Mark, *Metaphors We Live By* (Chicago, 1980).

Lange-Fuchs, Hauke, 'On the Origin of Moving Slides', *OLJ*, 7, 3, 10–14.

Lasdun, James, *The Horned Man* (London, 2002).

Lavater, Gaspard, *Essays on Physiognomy*, trans. Thomas Holcroft (London, 1844).

Lavater, Lewes, *Of Ghostes and Spirites Walking by Night* [1572], ed. J. Dover Wilson and May Yardley (Oxford, 1929).

Lawrence, John Shelton, and Jewett, Robert, *The Myth of the American Super-Hero* (Grand Rapids, Mich., 2002).

Leadbeater, C. W., *Clairvoyance* (London, 1917).

—— *Thought-Forms* (London, 1905).

—— *Man Visible and Invisible: Examples of Different Types of Men as Seen by Trained Clairvoyance* [1902] (Wheaton, Ill., 1987).

—— *The Astral Plane: Its Scenery, Inhabitants, and Phenomena* (London, 1895).

Lear, Jonathan, *Open-Minded: Working Out the Logic of the Soul* (Cambridge, Mass., 1998).

Lee, Hermione, *Virginia Woolf: A Working Life* (London, 1996) (see under Besant).

Lessing, G. E., *Laocoön; or, The Limits of Painting and Poetry*, trans. Edward Allen McCormick (Baltimore, 1984).

Lewis, I. M., *Ecstatic Religion: An Anthropological Study of Spirit Possession and Shamanism* (Harmondsworth, 1971).

Leys, Ruth, 'Mead's Voices: Imitation as Foundation, or, the Struggle against Mimesis', CI, 19 (Winter 1993), 277–307.

Light, Michael, *100 Suns* (London, 2003).

Lightbown, R. W., *Mantegna* (Oxford, 1986).

—— 'Le Cere artistiche del '500, *Le Arte illustrate*, 3, 30–3 (1970), 46–55; 34–6 (1970), 30–9.

Lippard, Lucy, 'Doubletake: The Diary of a Relationship with an Image', *Third Text*, 16/17 (Autumn/Winter 1991), 134–44.

—— (ed.), *Partial Recall with Essays on Photographs of Native North Americans* (New York, 1992).

Lloyd, Peter, ' "Objectivity as Irony: Werner Herzog's *Fata Morgana*', *Monogram*, 5 (1974), 8–9.

Locke, John, *Drafts for the 'Essay Concerning Human Understanding', and other Philosophical Writings*, ed. Peter H. Nidditeh and G. A. J. Rogers, 3 vols. (Oxford, 1990).

Lodge, Sir Oliver J., *Ether and Reality* (London, 1922).

—— *Christopher: A Study in Human Personality* (New York, 1919).

—— 'Experience of Unusual Phenomena Occurring in the Presence of an Entranced Person (Eusapia Paladino)', JSPR, Nov. 1894, 306–60.

Luckhurst, Roger, *The Invention of Telepathy 1870–1901* (Oxford, 2002).

—— 'Passages in the Invention of the Psyche: Mind-Reading in London, 1881–84', in Luckhurst and McDonagh, *Transactions*, 117–50.

—— and Jo McDonagh (eds.), *Transactions and Encounters: Science and Culture in the Nineteenth Century* (Manchester, 2002).

Lucretius, *Lucy Hutchinson's Translation of 'De rerum natura'*, ed. Hugh de Qulhem (London, 1996).

—— *The Way Things Are* [*De Rerum Natura*], trans. Rolfe Humphries (Bloomington, Ind., 1968).

Ludwig of Prussia, *Trilogium animae* (The Three Parts of the Soul) (Nuremberg, 1498).

Lutz, Catherine A., and Collins, Jane K., *Reading National Geographic* (Chicago, 1993).

Lycosthenes, Conrad, *Prodigiorum ac ostentorum chronicon* (Basle, 1557).

Lynch, W. E., 'Soul (in the Bible)', in *NCE*.

Machen, Arthur, *The Bowmen and Other Legends of the War* (London, 1915).

Maclean, Ian, 'Robert Fludd', in *DNB* <http://www.oxforddnb.com/view/article/9776>.

Magee, Bryan, and Milligan, Martin, *On Blindness* (Oxford, 1995).

Mallarmé, Stéphane, *For Anatole's Tomb: A Parallel Text Edition*, trans. with introduction by Patrick McGuinness (Manchester, 2003).

Mallarmé, ed. and trans. Anthony Hartley (Harmondsworth, 1965).

Mannoni, Laurent, *Le grand Art de la lumière et de l'ombre: Archaéologie du cinéma* (Paris, 1994), trans. Richard Crangle as *The Great Art of Light and Shadow: Archaeology of the Cinema* (Exeter, 2000).

—— 'Christiaan Huygens et la lanterne de peur', *1895: Revue de l'Association Française de Recherche sur l'histoire du cinéma*, no. 11, 49–78.

Mantel, Hilary, *Beyond Black* (London, 2005).

Marias, Javier, *Dark Back of Time*, trans. Esther Allen (London, 2003).

Marlowe, Christopher, *The Tragical History of Doctor Faustus*, ed. A. H. Sleight (Cambridge, 1961).

Martinotti, G., *Le Cere anatomiche della Specola* (Florence, 1979).

Massing, Jean-Michel, 'Dürer's Dreams', JWCI XLIX, 238–44.

—— 'From Manuscript to Engravings: Late Medieval Mnemonic Bibles', in J. J. Berns and Wolfgang Neuber (eds.), *Ars Memorativa* (Tübingen, 1993), 101–15.

Mavor, Carol, *Pleasures Taken: Performances of Sexuality and Loss in Victorian Photography* (Durham, N.C., 1995).

—— 'Photographs Are Fairyish', *Archive*, NMPFT, Feb. 2004, 24–9.

Mayakovsky, Vladimir, *The Bedbug and Selected Poetry*, trans. Max Hayward and George Reavey, ed. Patricia Blake (London, 1961).

Mayr-Harting, Henry, *Perceptions of Angels in History* (Oxford, 1998).

McDonagh, Jo, *De Quincey's Disciplines* (Oxford, 1994).

McGinn, Bernard, *Visions of the End: Apocalyptic Tradition in the Middle Ages* (New York, 1979)

McGinn, Colin, *Mindsight: Image, Dream, Meaning* (Cambridge, Mass., and London, 2004).

McKinnon, Catherine, *Only Words* (London, 1994).

McLuhan, Marshall, *The Mechanical Bride* (London, 1951).

McNeillie, Andrew, *Slower* (Manchester, 2006).

McNicholl, A. J., 'Spirit', and 'Spirit, Modern Philosophies of', in *NCE*.

Meaden, Terence, *The Secrets of the Avebury Stones: Britain's Greatest Megalithic Temple* (London, 1999).

Meltzer, Françoise, 'The Uncanny Rendered Canny: Freud's Blind Spot in Reading Hoffmann's "Sandman"', in *Introducing Psychoanalytic Theory*, ed. S. Gilman (Berlin, 1982), 218–39.

Merewether, Charles, 'Naming Violence in the Work of Doris Salcedo', *Third Text*, 24 (Autumn 1993).

Merleau-Ponty, Maurice, *Le Visible et l'invisible*, ed. Claude Lefort (Paris, 1964); trans. Alphonso Lingis as *The Visible and the Invisible, followed by Working Notes* (Evanston, Ill., 1968).

Meyer, Richard (ed.), *Representing the Passions: Histories, Bodies, Visions* (Los Angeles, 2003).

Miller, Karl, *Electric Shepherd: A Likeness of James Hogg* (London, 2003).

—— *Doubles: Studies in Literary History* (Oxford, 1985).

Minasi, Antonio, *Dissertazioni Sopra diversi fatti meno ovvii della Storia Naturale* (Rome, 1773).

Mitchell, Juliet, and Rose, Jacqueline, *Jacques Lacan and the École Freudienne* (London, 1986).

Moretti, Franco (ed.), *The Novel*, 2 vols. (Princeton, 2006).

Morrison, Robert, and Baldick, Chris (eds.), *Tales of Terror from Blackwood's Magazine* (Oxford, 1995).

Morrison, Toni, *Love* (London, 2005).

—— *Jazz* (London, 1992).

—— *Beloved* (London, 1987).

Muecke, Frances, ' "Taught by Love": The Origin of Painting Again', *AB*, June 1999, vol. 71, no. 2, 297–302.

Muldoon, Sylvan J., and Carrington, Hereward, *The Projection of the Astral Body* [1929] (London, 1939).

Mulvey, Laura, 'The "Pensive Spectator" Revisited: Time and its Passing in the Still and Moving Image', in Green (ed.), *Where is the Photograph?*, 113–22.

Myers, F. W. H., *Collected Poems, with Autobiographical and Critical Fragments*, ed. Eveleen Myers (London, 1921).

—— *Human Personality and Its Survival of Bodily Death*, 2 vols. (London, 1903).

—— *Hellenica: A Collection of Essays*, ed. Evelyn Abbott (Oxford and Cambridge, 1880).

Nadar, Félix Tournachon, *Quand j'étais photographe* (Paris, 1899); trans. Thomas Repensek as *My Life As A Photographer*, October, 5 (Summer 1978).

Najafi, Sina, 'Bats and Dancing Bears: An Interview with Eric Zillmer', *Cabinet*, 5 (Winter, 2001), 84–90.

Naipaul, V. S., *The Middle Passage* (London, 1962).

Nead, Lynda, *Victorian Babylon: People, Streets and Images in Nineteenth-Century London* (London and New Haven, 2000).

Needham, Rodney, 'Little Black Boxes', *TLS*, 28 May 1967, 647.

Neidich, Warren, *Blow-Up: Photography, Cinema and the Brain* (Riverside, Calif., 2003).

Nelson, Victoria, *The Secret Life of Puppets* (Cambridge, Mass., 2001).

Nerval, Gérard de, *Aurélia* (Paris, 1959).

Nickel, Douglas R., ' "Second Sight": Julia Margaret Cameron and the Victorian Imagination', forthcoming.

Noakes, Richard, ' "Cranks and Visionaries": Science, Spiritualism and Transgression in Victorian Britain' (Ph.D. thesis, Cambridge University, June 1998).

O'Brien, Geoffrey, 'He Walked with a Zombie', *NYRB*, 9 March 2006, 30–2.

O'Hogain, Daithi, *Myth, Legend and Romance* (New York, 1991).

Oliver, J. W., *The Life of William Beckford* (London, 1932).

Olsen, Victoria, *From Life: Julia Margaret Cameron and Victorian Photography* (London, 2003).

Oppé, A. P., *Alexander and John Robert Cozens* (London, 1952).

Osmond, Rosalie, *Imagining the Soul: A History* (Thrupp, Gloucestershire, 2003).

O'Toole, Lawrence, ' "That Close Center of Things": Werner Herzog Interviewed', *Film Comment*, 156 (Nov.–Dec. 1979), 41–8.

Ovid, *Metamorphoses*, trans. Rolfe Humphries (Bloomington, Ind. [1955], 1983).

—— *Metamorphoses*, trans. by Mary M. Innes (Harmondsworth, 1954).

—— *Metamorphoses*, trans. Frank Justus Miller (Cambridge, Mass., and London, 1916).

Owen, Alex, *The Place of Enchantment: British Occultism and the Culture of the Modern* (Chicago and London, 2004).

—— *The Darkened Room: Women, Power and Spiritualism in Late Victorian England* (London, 1989).

Packer, Alison, Beddoe, Stella, and Jarrett, Lianne, *Fairies in Legend* (London, 1980).

Paley, Morton, *The Apocalyptic Sublime* (New Haven, 1986).

Panofsky, Erwin, *The Life and Work of Albrecht Dürer* (Princeton, 1995).

Paré, Ambroise, *Livre des Monstres* (Paris, 1575).

Parrinder, Patrick, *Shadows of the Future: H. G. Wells, Science Fiction, and Prophecy* (Liverpool, 1995).

Parshall, Peter, 'Albrecht Dürer's *Gedenckbuch* and the Rain of Crosses', paper given 1999–2004 at the BM and the NGA, forthcoming.

Pecham, John (Joannes Peckham), *Perspectiva Communis*, ed. and trans. David C. Lindberg (Madison, 1970).

Pélérinage de la vie humaine, Bibliothèque Royale, Brussels, MS 10197–8.

Penrose, Roger, *Shadows of the Mind: A Search for the Missing Science of Consciousness* (London, 1993).

Perella, Nicolas James, *The Kiss Sacred and Profane: An Interpretative History of Kiss Symbolism and Related Religio-Erotic Themes* (Berkeley and Los Angeles, 1969).

Peterson, Jeanette Favrot, 'Creating the Virgin of Guadalupe: The Cloth, the Artist, and Sources in Sixteenth-century New Spain,' *The Americas*, Vol. 61, No. 4, April 2005, 571–610.

Petro, Patrice (ed.), *Fugitive Images: From Photography to Video* (Bloomington, Ind., 1995).

Phillips, Adam, *Houdini's Box: On the Arts of Escape* (London, 2001).

—— *Darwin's Worms* (London, 1999).

Philostratus, Flavius, *The Life of Apollonius of Tyana*, trans. Christopher P. Jones (Cambridge, Mass., 1912).

Pilbeam, Pamela, *Madame Tussaud and the History of Waxworks* (London, 2002).

Pindemonte, Ippolito, *Poemetti italiani* (Turin, 1797).

Pippin, Tina, *Death and Desire: The Rhetoric of Gender in the Apocalypse of John* (Louisville, Ky., 1992).

Plath, Sylvia, *The Bell Jar* (London, 1966).

Plato, *Phaedrus*, trans. Walter Hamilton (Harmondsworth, 1973).

—— *The Republic*, trans. and ed. Sir Desmond Lee (Harmondsworth, 1973).

Pliny the Elder, *Natural History*, trans. W. H. S. Jones (London and Cambridge, Mass., 1963).

Podmore, Frank, *The Newer Spiritualism* (London, 1911).

—— *Telepathic Hallucinations: The New View of Ghosts* (London, 1909).

Poe, Edgar Allan, *The Complete Tales*, ed. Alix Perry (New York, 1981).

—— *Histoires grotesques et sérieuses*, trans. Charles Baudelaire (Paris, 1966).

Pomponatius, Petrus, *De naturalium Effectuum Causis: Sive de Incantationibus* [Basel, 1556].

Popple, Simon, and Toulmin, Vanessa (eds.), *Visual Delights: Essays on the Popular and Projected Image in the Nineteenth Century* (Trowbridge, 2000).

Price, Harry, *Confessions of a Ghost Hunter* [London, 1936] (London, 1993).

—— *Rudi Schneider: A Scientific Examination of his Mediumship* (London, 1930).

Price, Michael, and Turner, George, '*White Zombie*: Ugly Duckling Becomes a Swan', *American Cinematographer*, 69 (Feb. 1988), 40.

Pullman, Philip, *His Dark Materials*, 3 vols.: *Northern Lights* (London, 1995), *The Subtle Knife* (1997), and *The Amber Spyglass* (2000).

Quayson, Ato, 'Fecundities of the Unexpected: Magical Realism, Narrative and History', in Moretti, vol. 1 (Princeton, 2006).

Rainey, Lawrence, 'Taking Dictation: Collage Poetics, Pathology, and Politics', *Modernism/Modernity*, 5, 2 (1998), 123–53.

Reichenbach, Charles von, *Physico-Physiological Researches on the Dynamics of Magnetism, Electricity, Heat, Light, Crystallization, and Chemism* [*sic*], trans. John Ashburner, 2 vols. (London and Paris, 1850–1).

Rice, Anne, *Interview with the Vampire* (London, 1976).

Richet, Charles, *Thirty Years of Psychical Research*, trans. S. de Brath (London, 1923).

Rickard, Bob, and Michell, John, *Unexplained Phenomena: A Rough Guide Special* (London, 2000).

Riley, Denise, *The Words of Selves: Identification, Solidarity, Irony* (Stanford, Calif., 2000).

Rilke, Rainer Maria, *Rodin and Other Prose Pieces*, trans. G. Craig Houston, intro. William Tucker (London, 1986).

—— *The Duino Elegies*, trans. Patrick Bridgwater (London, 1966).

—— *Werke in Drei Bänden* (Frankfurt, 1966).

Ringbom, Sixten, 'The Sounding Cosmos: A Study in the Spiritualism of Kandinsky and the Genesis of Abstract Painting', *Acta Academiae Abiensis*, Ser. A, 38, 2 (1970), 80–4.

Roberts, Gareth, *The Mirror of Alchemy: Alchemical Ideas and Images in Manuscripts and Books from Antiquity to the Seventeenth Century* (London, 1994).

Roberts, Michael Symmons, *Corpus* (London, 2004).

Roberts, Michèle, *In the Red Kitchen* (London, 1990).

Robertson, Etienne-Gaspard, *Mémoires récréatifs, scientifiques et anecdoctiques du physicien-aéronaute*, 2 vols. (Paris, 1830).

Robertson, Robin, 'Camera Obscura', in *A Painted Field* (London, 1997).

Robinson, David, 'Robinson on Robertson', *NMLJ*, 4 (1986), 4–13.

Rodier, Virginia, *Clementina, Lady Hawarden; Studies from Life 1857–1864*, intro. by Marina Warner, 'The Shadow of Young Girls in Flower' (New York, 1999).

Roe, Nicholas, *John Keats and the Culture of Dissent* (Oxford, 1996).

Rorschach, Hermann, *Psychodiagnostik* (Berlin, 1920).

Rorty, Richard, *Philosophy and the Mirror of Nature* (Princeton, 1979).

Rosenblum, Robert, 'The Origin of Painting: A Problem in the Iconography of Romantic Classicism', *AB* 39, 4 (Dec. 1957), 278–90.

Roth, Michael, 'Hysterical Remembering', *Modernism/Modernity*, 3, 2 (1996), 1–30.

Rouch, Jean, 'On the Vicissitudes of the Self: The Possessed Dancer, the Magician, the Sorcerer, the Film-maker and the Ethnographer', trans. Steve Feld and Shari Robertson, *Studies in the Anthropology of Visual Communication*, 15, 1 (1978), 2–8.

Rowling, J. K., *Harry Potter and the Order of the Phoenix* (London, 2003).

Royle, Nicholas, *The Uncanny: An Introduction* (Manchester, 2002).

—— *Telepathy and Literature: Essays on the Reading Mind* (Oxford, 1991).

Ruffles, Tom, 'Phantasmagoria Ghost Shows', *Udolpho*, 30 (Autumn 1997), 21–3.

Rugg, Linda, *Picturing Ourselves: Photography and Autobiography* (Chicago, 1997).

Ruggeri, Franco, 'Il Museo dell'Istituto di Anatomia Umana Normale', in *I Luoghi del Conoscere (La Città del sapere*, ii) (Milan, 1988).

Ruskin, John, *Modern Painters*, ed. David Barrie (London, 1987).

—— *The Queen of the Air* [1869] (London, 1907).

Ruspolo, Francisco Mariae, *Musaeum Kircheranium* (Rome, 1709).

Salter, W. H., 'Introduction to the Study of the Scripts', unpublished. *c*.1948. Deposited WLTCC, 1963.

Ryle, Gilbert, *The Concept of Mind* (London, 1949).

Sante, Luc, 'American Photography's Golden Age', *NYRB* 4 Apr. 1996, 62–7.

Sass, Louis, *Madness and Modernism: Insanity in the Light of Modern Art, Literature and Thought* (Cambridge, Mass., 1992).

Scarry, Elaine, *Dreaming by the Book* (New York, 1999).

Schefer, Olivier, 'Les Pierres de rêve: minéralogie visionnaire', in *Trajectoires de rêves*, exh. cat., 202–17.

Schiavo, Giovanni E., *Antonio Meucci, Inventor of the Telephone* (New York, 1958).

Schiff, Richard, 'Photographic Soul', in Green (ed.), *Where is the Photograph?*, 95–111.

Schlüpmann, Heide, 'The First German Art Film: Rye's *The Student of Prague*' (1913), in Eric Reutschler (ed.), *German Film and Literature: Adaptations and Transformations* (New York, 1986), 9–24.

Schmitt, Jean-Claude, *Ghosts in the Middle Ages*, trans. Theresa Lavender Fagan (Chicago, 1998).

Schoonover, Karl, 'Ectoplasms, Evanescence, and Photography', *Art Journal*, 62, 3 (Fall 2003), 30–41.

Schreber, Daniel Paul, *Memoirs of My Nervous Illness*, intro. by Rosemary Dinnage, trans. Ida McAlpine and Richard A. Hunter [1955] (New York, 2000).

Schrenck-Notzing, Albert von, *Materialisations-Phaenomene ein Beitrag zur Erforschung der Mediumistischen Teleplastie* (Munich, 1923).

Schultz, Bart, *Henry Sidgwick: Eye of the Universe—An Intellectual Biography* (Cambridge, 2004).

Schwartz, Vanessa R., *Spectacular Realities: Early Mass Culture in Fin-de-Siècle Paris* (Berkeley and Los Angeles, 1998).

—— and Charney, Leo (eds.), *Cinema and the Invention of Modern Life* (Berkeley and Los Angeles, 1995).

Sconce, Jeffrey, *Haunted Media: Electronic Presence from Telegraphy to Television* (Durham, N.C., 2000).

Scott, Sir Walter, *Letters on Demonology and Witchcraft* (London, 1830).

Seabrook, William, *The Magic Island* (New York, 1929, 1936).

Segal, Nancy L., *Indivisible by Two: Lives of Extraordinary Twins* (Cambridge, Mass., 2005).

Seigel, Jerrold, *The Idea of the Self: Thought and Experience in Western Europe since the Seventeenth Century* (Cambridge, 2005).

Sepper, Dennis L., *Descartes's Imagination: Proportion, Images, and the Activity of Thinking* (Berkeley and London, 1996).

—— *Newton's Optical Writings: A Guided Study* (New Brunswick, N. J., 1994).

Serres, Michel, *La Légende des anges* (Paris, 1993).

Sheldrake, Rupert, *Seven Experiments that Could Change the World: A Do-it-Yourself Guide to Revolutionary Science* (London, 1994).

—— *The Presence of the Past* (London, 1988).

—— with Fox, Matthew, *Natural Grace: Dialogues on Science and Spirituality* (London, 1997).

Shelley, Mary, *Frankenstein, or The Modern Prometheus*, ed. Maurice Hindle (London, 1992).

Shelley, P. B., *Poetry and Prose*, ed. Donald H. Reiman and Sharon B. Powers (New York and London, 1977).

Sidgwick, Eleanor, and Sidgwick, Arthur (eds.), *Henry Sidgwick: A Memoir* (London, 1906).

Silversides, Brock V., *The Face Pullers: Photographing Native Canadians 1871–1939* (Saskatoon, Canada, 1994).

Simcock, A. W., *Photography 150: Images from the First Generation*, Museum of the History of Science (Oxford, 1989).

Sinclair, Mary Craig, *Southern Belle* (Phoenix, Ariz., 1957).

Slawinski, Maurice, 'Marino, le streghe, il cardinale', *Italian Studies*, 54 (1999), 52–84.

Smith, Lindsay, *The Politics of Focus: Women, Children and Nineteenth-Century photography* (Manchester, 1998).

Smithson, Robert, *The Collected Writings*, ed. Jack Flam (Berkeley, 1996).

Snyder, Joel, 'Picturing Vision', *Critical Quarterly*, 6 (1980), 499–526.

Solnit, Rebecca, *Motion Studies: Eadwueard Muybridge and the Technological Wild West* (London, 2003).

Sontag, Susan, *Regarding the Pain of Others* (London, 2004).

—— *On Photography* (London, 1978).

Spender, Matthew, *From a High Place: A Life of Arshile Gorky* (New York, 1999).

Spenser, Edmund, *The Faerie Queene*, ed. J. W. Hales, 2 vols. (London [1910], 1969).

Spufford, Francis, and Uglow, Jenny (eds.), *Cultural Babbage: Technology, Time and Invention* (London, 1996).

Stafford, Barbara Maria, *Body Criticism: Imaging the Unseen in Enlightenment Art and Medicine* (Cambridge, Mass., 1993).

—— 'Revealing/Technologies/Magical Domains', in *Devices of Wonder*, exh. cat., 1–109.

Steiner, Rudolf, *The Anthroposophical Movement*, trans. Christian von Arnim (Bristol, 1993).

Stevens, Anthony, *Private Myths: Dreams and Dreaming* (London, 1995).

Stevens, Wallace, *The Collected Poems* (New York, 1982).

—— *The Necessary Angel: Essays on Reality and the Imagination* (New York [1942], 1951).

Stevenson, R. L., *The Strange Case of Dr Jekyll and Mr Hyde*, ed. Jenni Calder (London, 1979).

—— *Across the Plains with other Memories and Essays* (London, 1900).

Stewart, Susan, *Columbarium* (Chicago and London, 2003).

Stinson, Daniel T., *The Role of Sir William Lawrence in 19th Century English Surgery* (Zurich, 1969).

Stoichita, Victor, *A Short History of the Shadow* (London, 1997).

Summers, David, '*Cogito* Embodied: Force & Counterforce in René Descartes's *Les Passions de l'áme*', in Meyer (ed.), *Representing the Passions*, 13–36.

Swan, Claudia, 'Eyes Wide Shut: Early Modern Imagination, Demonology, and the Visual Arts', *Zeitsprunge*, 2003, 560–81.

Talbot, W. H. Fox, *Some Account of the Art of Photogenic Drawing* (London, 1839).

Tausk, Victor, 'On the origin of the "Influencing Machine" in Schizophrenia', *PQ* 2 (1933), 519–56.

Taussig, Michael, *Mimesis and Alterity* (New York, 1993).

Taylor, Charles, *Sources of the Self: The Making of Modern Identity* (Cambridge, 1989).

Terpak, Frances, 'Objects and Contexts', in Stafford and Terpak (eds.), *Devices of Wonder*, exh. cat., 143–364.

Thomas, Chantal, *Les Adieux à la reine* (Paris, 2002).

Thomson, John, *Illustrations of China and its People* [1843–4] (London, 1982).

Thurschwell, Pamela, *Literature, Technology and Magical Thinking, 1880–1920* (Cambridge, 2001).

—— 'Refusing to Give up the Ghost: Some Thoughts on the Afterlife from Spirit Photography', in *Disembodied Spirit*, exh. cat.

Tiffany, Daniel, *Toy Medium: Materialism and Modern Lyric* (Berkeley, 2000).

Tillyard, E. M. W., *The Elizabethan World Picture* ([1943], Harmondsworth, 1981).

Tolkien, J. R. R., *The Lord of the Rings*, 3 vols. (London, 1966).

Tournier, Michel, *Le Coq des bruyères* (Paris, 1978).

Trotter, David, *Cooking with Mud: The Idea of Mess in Nineteenth-Century Art and Fiction* (Oxford, 2001).

Turner, Christopher, 'The Influencing Machine', *Cabinet*, 14, Summer, 2004, 52–5.

Tussaud, John Theodore, *The Romance of Madame Tussaud's* (London, 1920).

Uglow, Jenny, 'In the Chamber of Miracles', review of Philipp Blom, *To Have and to Hold: An Intimate History of Collectors and Collecting* (London, 2002), *TLS*, 26 July 2002.

—— (ed.), *The Chatto Book of Ghosts* (London, 1994).

Varnedoe, Kirk, 'The Artifice of Candor: Impressionism and Photography Reconsidered', *Art in America*, vol. 66, Jan. 1980, 66–78.

—— 'The Ideology of Time: Degas and Photography', *Art in America*, vol. 66, June 1980, 96–110.

Vasari, Giorgio, *The Temple of Vasari: Lives of Painters, Sculptors and Architects*, trans. A. B. Hinds, 8 vols. (London, 1800).

Vattimo, Gianni, *After Christianity*, trans. Luca D'Isanto (New York, 2002).

Verschaffel, Bart, 'On Death Masks', in *The Lectures 1991*, Witte de With (Rotterdam, 1992), 75–91.

—— 'Where There's a Voice, There's a body', *Theologschrift*, 9 'Theater and Music' (Brussels, Berlin, Dresden, Vienna, 1995).

Virgil, *The Eclogues, The Georgics*, trans. Cecil Day-Lewis, ed. R. O. A. M. Lyne, (Oxford, 1983).

Vitebsky, Piers, *The Shaman Voyages of the Soul: Trance, Ecstasy and Healing from Siberia to the Amazon* (London, 1995).

Waldberg, Patrick, *Surrealism* (London, 1965).

Walker, Barbara, *Women's Encyclopaedia of Myths and Secrets* (London, 1983).

Walker, Christopher (ed.), *Astronomy before the Telescope* (London, 1996).

Walker, D. P., 'Medical *Spirits* and God and the Soul', in M. Fattori and M. Bianchi (eds.), *Spiritus*, IV Colloquio internazionale Roma, 7–9 January 1983 (Rome, 1984), 223–44.

Walmsley, Jonathan, 'Locke's Natural Philosophy in Draft A of the Essay on Human Understanding', *JHI* 65, no. 1 (Jan. 2004), 15–37.

Walsh, John, 'Skies and Reality in Dutch Landscape', in D. Freedberg and J. de Vries (eds.), *Art in History/History in Art* (Santa Monica, 1991), 95–117.

Warhol, Andy, *America* (New York, 1985).

Warner, Marina, *Fantastic Metamorphoses, Other Worlds: Ways of Telling the Self* (Oxford, 2002).

—— *No Go the Bogeyman: On Scaring, Lulling and Making Mock* (London, 1998).

—— 'Painted Devils and Aery Nothings: Metamorphoses and Magic Arts', in Tom Clayton, Susan Brock, and Vicente Forés (eds.), *Shakespeare and the Mediterranean*, PISA, 2004, 308–31.

—— 'The Perforate Self, or Nought is Not Naught', *Parkett*, 63 (2003).

—— 'Self-Portrait in a Rear-View Mirror', in *Only Make-Believe*, exh. cat., 4–19.

—— 'Wolf-girl, Soul-bird: The Mortal Art of Kiki Smith', in *Kiki Smith*, exh. cat., 42–53.

Warnock, Mary, *Imagination and Time* (Oxford and Cambridge, 1994).

Washington, Peter, *Madame Blavatsky's Baboon: A History of the Mystics, Mediums and Misfits Who Brought Spiritualism to America* (New York, 1995).

Gillian Wearing, by Russell Ferguson, Donna De Salvo, John Slyce (London, 1999).

Weekes, Henry, *Lectures in Art* (London, 1880).

Weiss, Allan S. (ed.), *Experimental Sound and Music* (New York, 2001).

Wells, H. G., *The Invisible Man*, ed. Patrick Parrinder, intro. by Christopher Priest (London, 2005).

—— *The Time Machine*, ed. Patrick Parrinder, intro. by Marina Warner (London, 2005).

—— *The Definitive Time Machine*, ed. Henry M. Geduld (Bloomington, Ind., 1987).

—— *The Short Stories of H. G. Wells* (London [1927], 1952).

Welt, Bernard, *Mythomania: Fantasies, Fables, and Sheer Lies in Contemporary American Popular Art* (Los Angeles, 1996).

Wierzbicka, Anna, 'Soul, Âme, Seele, Dusha', in *Semantics, Culture, and Cognition: Universal Human Concepts in Culture-Specific Configurations* (Oxford and New York, 1992), 31–63.

Williams, Bernard, *Truth and Truthfulness: An Essay in Genealogy* (Princeton, 2002).

Wilson, Peter Lamborn, *Angels* (London, 1980).

Winter, Alison, *Mesmerized: Powers of Mind in Victorian Britain* (Chicago, 1998).

Wood, Gaby, *Living Dolls: A Magical History of the Quest for Mechanical Life* (London, 2002).

Wood, James, 'A Frog's Life', *LRB*, 23 Oct. 2003.

Wood, Michael, 'Productive Mischief', review of Jorge Luis Borges, *Collected Fictions*, trans. Andrew Hurley, *LRB*, 4 Feb. 1999.

Woolf, Virginia, *Moments of Being: Autobiographical Writings*, ed. Jeanne Schulkind (London, 2002).

—— *On Being Ill* [1926], intro. by Hermione Lee (Ashfield, Mass., 2002).

—— *To the Lighthouse* [1927] (London, 1990).

—— *Freshwater* [?1923/1935], ed. Lucio P. Ruotolo (London, 1976).

Wordsworth, William, *Selected Prose*, ed. John O. Hayden (London, 1998).

Worthington, A. M., *A Study of Splashes* (London, 1908).

Wright, Iain, 'All Done with Mirrors: Politics, Magic and Theatrical Illusion in *Macbeth*', paper given HRC ANU, 2001; published in a different version, *Heat*, Dec. 2005, 179–200.

Wrixon, Fred B., *Codes, Ciphers, and Secret Languages: A Comprehensive Guide to their History and Use* (London, 1989).

Yarnall, Judith, *Transformations of Circe: The History of an Enchantress* (Chicago, 1994).

Yates, Frances, *The Art of Memory* (London, 1966).

Zahedich, Nuala, 'Sir Henry Morgan', in *DNB*.

Zamora, Lois Parkinson, and Faris, Wendy B. (eds.), *Magical Realism Theory, History, Community* (Durham, N.C., and London, 1995).

Zeitlin, Froma, and Winkler, J. (eds.), *Nothing to Do with Dionysus?* (Princeton, 1990).

Zillmer, Eric, *The Quest for the Nazi Personality* (Hove, 1995).

Žižek, Slavoj, *Looking Awry: An Introduction to Jacques Lacan through Popular Culture* (Cambridge, Mass., 1991).

Index

Augustine of Hippo, St 63, 72, 122, 123
aura and auras 64, 71, 261–2, 262–3, 290
aurora borealis 97, 255
automata 53, 54, 126, 152, 359–60
automatic writing 237, 282
Avedon, Richard 198

Bacon, Roger 164
Balfour, Arthur 238, 240
ballet 388 n. 11, *Gisèle* 64
balloonists 113–14
Balzac, Honoré de 164, 194, 200
Baraduc, Doctor Hippolyte 259–60,
        261, 301
Barker, Robert 150
baroque 74, 76, 77, 78–9, 87, 91
Barrett, Sir William 235, 237–8, 268,
        302
Barrett Browning, Elizabeth 234, 255,
        287
Barrie, J. M. 186, 227
Barry, Madame Du 47–8, 49
Barthes, Roland 193, 201, 335, 349,
        377
Bassermann, Albert 198–9
Bataille, Georges 296
Baudelaire, Charles 129, 320
Bauhaus school 261–2
Beckett, Samuel 283
Beckford, William 111, 152, 320
Belafonte, Harry 367
Bell, Charles Milton 193
Benedict XIV, Pope 31, 33, 34
Benjamin, Walter 35–6, 323–4
Bentham, Jeremy 5, 6
Bergman, Ingmar 342
Bernadette, St 51–2, 387 n. 13
Bertillon, Alphonse 160
Besant, Annie 261–2 *see* Pl. 6
Bible 74, 76, 97, 98, 175
    Book of Revelation 337–45, 349
Bioy Casares, Adolfo 324–5
Bisson, Juliette 231–2, 295, 302;
        Figs. 21, 24
black magic 139, 364

Blair, Tony 345
Blake, William 228, 342, 343, 347, 350
Blavatsky, Madame 227
Bloom, Harold 67–8
blots:
    Alexander Cozens 104, 111–13, 309,
        320; Fig. 10
    Andy Warhol 311–12
    Rorschach test 309–12; Pl 7
    Victor Hugo 315
Boaistuau, Pierre 99; Pl. 2b.
Bologna xx, 1–2, 3, 5–6, 26, 31–2, 33–4,
        48–9, 201
Borges, Jorge Luis 316, 324, 325, 379–80
Borglum, Guzton 107
Botticelli, Sandro 109, 113
Bourriaud, Nicolas 330
breath 12, 57, 61–8, 78, 87, 89
Breton, André 101, 321
Breuer, Marcel 52
Brewster, Sir David 113, 152–3
Broad, C. D. 226, 239
Brocken spectre 105, 114, 115
Brooke-Rose, Christine, 416 n. 15
Browne, Thomas 66–7, 299
Browning, Robert 287–8
Brunius, Jacques 297
Bry, Theodore de 126; Figs. 11, 12a
Bull, Malcolm 349
Bunyan, John 340, 347
Burwick, Frederick 154
Bush, George W. 345
Butler, Samuel 266

Cabbalists 67
The Cabinet of Dr Caligari (1919) 52,
        147–8, 212, 325
cadavers 32–3, 41, 42, 374
Caillois, Roger xiii, 12
Calvino, Italo 71, 200, 402 n. 30
Cambiaso, Luca 70, 86–7; Fig. 7
Cambridge University 238, 239, 293
cameos 159, 162, 165
camera obscura 137–8, 141, 147, 151,
        208, 230

cloud(s) – *Cont.*
  modernity 373
  photographs 262
  portents 100
Coetzee, J. M. 327–9
Coleridge, Samuel Taylor 10, 114, 208,
    211, 351, 359, 365
  fancy and imagination 128–9, 170,
    218
  and Henry More 106, 282
Colie, Rosalie 350
communications technology 222, 225,
    228, 248, 254, 258–9, 271, 273,
    274, 323, 336, 375–6
conjurors, 123–4, 156, 293
    Home, Daniel Dunglas 227, 287–8
    'Dr Pepper's Ghost' trick 153, 154
    see magicians
computers
    computer imaging 54, 349–350
    cyberspace 322–32
    digitization 54, 323, 336, 349,
      375–6
    games 332
    internet 326, 332, 374, 376
consciousness 10, 41–2, 47, 52, 67, 78,
    242, 266–7, 273, 373–4, 379
  brain 125, 374
  day-dreaming 52, 315
    déjà vu 54, 210, 241
  subliminal self 242, 266–7, 306
  see Butler; Freud ; Myers; self-
    consciousness; unconscious
Constable, John 111, 114
contemporary art 42–3, 53, 107, 262,
    326
  Relational Aesthetics 330–2
  Rorschach patterns 311–12; Pl. 7
  sculptures 55–6
  see also art, and names of artists
Cook, Florence 225, 226–7, 277, 286
Coombe-Tennant, Christopher 244
copyright 198, 199
Corbin, Henri 67
Correggio 84, 86–7, 372; Pls. 1, 2a.

Cosimo, Piero di 109
cotton wool 217, 230–1, 290
Cozarinsky, Edgardo 352
Cozens, Alexander 104, 111–13, 309,
    320; Fig. 10
Crandon, Margery 230, 296, 302–3, 304,
    305; Figs. 25a
Crookes, William 224–5, 226–8, 237,
    241, 254, 255, 256, 269, 277,
    286–7, 291; Fig. 19
Cruikshank, George 178, 181; Fig. 16
Curtis, Edward S. 195, 196, 197
Curtius, Philippe 24, 36–9, 46–8, 49;
    Fig. 5

Dadd, Richard 233
daemons 10, 282, 361
Daguerre, Louis 44, 154
daguerreotypes 44, 163–4, 194, 216
Damasio, Antonio 374
Dant, Adam 112
Dante Alighieri 122, 175, 176–7, 342,
    358–9
Darget, Louis 260; Fig. 21a
Darwin, Charles 306
Darwin, Erasmus 113–14
Davenant, William 65
David, Jacques-Louis 36, 38, 39
Davy, Humphry 255
De Mille, Cecil B. 100
De Quincey, Thomas 163, 211
Dean, Tacita 417 n. 25
Deane, Mrs. (Ada) 229, 243, 244, 245
death masks 23, 24–5, 35, 38–9, 41, 160,
    229
Dee, John 172, 283
Deleuze, Gilles 87–8, 141, 272
Dennett, Daniel 374
Derrida, Jacques 209, 242, 257, 358
Descartes, René 9, 62, 87, 121, 171;
    Fig. 11a
devil(s) 115, 123, 131, 133, 139, 142, 149,
    335–6
Dibutades 158–9, 161, 163, 184, 200;
    Fig. 14

Hagens, Gunther von 42
Hall, Radclyffe 234
hallucinations 139, 148, 210, 212, 241, 272
Halperin, Edward and Victor Hugo 362
Harry Potter books (Rowling) 208, 337, 361, 380
Harvey, William 87
Hauksbee, Francis 272
Hawarden, Clementina, Lady 168, 213–14; Fig. 15
Haynes, Frank Jay 188; Fig. 17
Hayward, Rhodri 242
Helmont, J. B. van 255
Herschel, Sir John 165, 217
Herzog, Werner 98, 101–2, 189
Hesiod *Theogony* 73
Hibbert, Dr Samuel 210
Hill, Christopher 344, 346
Hillier, Mary 165, 209, 218
Hills, Paul 88
Hinduism 247, 261, 304
Hinton, Charles H. 210
Hippolytus 123–4
Hirst, Damien 42
Hoban, Russell 208
Hobbes, Thomas 140, 343
Hodgson Burnett, Frances 208
Hoffmann, E. T. A. 54, 181, 359
Hofmannsthal, Hugo von 184–5
Hogarth, William 32–3
Hogg, James 115, 153, 175
Holy Spirit (Holy Ghost) 60, 61, 76; Fig. 6
Home, Daniel Dunglas 227, 287–8
Homer 84, 176, 351
Hone, William 142
Hooke, Robert 123
Hope, William 220, 231, 243; Fig. 25
Horace 125
Hornor, Thomas 150–1
Hosmer, Harriet 234
Houdini, Harry 246, 287
Houdon, Jean-Antoine 35

Houghton, Georgiana 228, 243
Howard, Luke 114
Hugo, Victor 315
Hurston, Zora Neale 361, 363
Hutchinson, Lucy 109
Huygens, Christiaan 137
Huyghe, Pierre 330–2; Fig. 29a
hypnosis 51, 210, 211, 269
 hypnotized chicken 143; Fig. 12c

IBLS (Investigative Bureau into the Location of the Soul) ii
I Walked with a Zombie (1943) 356, 361, 363–5, 367; Fig. 29
icasm 106, 149
iconodulia 133
iconography 49–50, 75
idolatry 97
Ignatius, St 77
illusion/illusionism 43, 54, 381
 apophenia 313
 chimera 108
 dioramas 29, 44, 150, 164
 of life 46–57
 magical 123–4
 meteorology 114–15
 movie 270–1, 350
 optical 94–103
 pareidolia 313
 of sleep 47–53
 stagecraft 132–7
 see special effects; waxworks
image(s) 12, 72, 122, 138, 170
 eidetic 124–5
 in nature 106–8; *see* endpapers;
  tailpieces 20, 57, 93, 117, 177,
   186, 316, 354, 381, 419, 450
 photographic 352–3
 see death masks;
imagination 11, 52, 68, 91, 125, 213, 329
 cognitive psychology 100
 fantasy 121–9
 and photography 218
 logic of the 12–13, 371
 magic lanterns 137–43

reality and myth 377, 379
time travel 273, *see also* cinema; radio;
    television
medical dissection 32–3
mediums 221, 225, 228–9, 230, 231–2,
    234, 242, 268, 381
  channelling Frederic Myers 282–3
  haloes 255
  incarnations 277–80
  Incorporeal Personal Agent 247–8
  materializing 245, 268, 299–307
  as modifier/transformer 280
  payment of 291
  as performance artists 295, *see also*
    under individual names
melancholia 140–1, 142, 163, 201
Meliès, Georges 156, 271, 318, 325;
    Fig. 27
memorabilia 40, 53
memory 136, 142, 242, 336
  brain 374
  historical reconstruction 195
  and imagination 126–7
  metamorphosis 375
  monochrome and 163
  photography 186, 265–6
  and recognition 159–60, 161
  unconscious 266
Mendelssohn, Felix 79
mental illness 212, 272, 326
Merrill, James 377
Mesmer, Franz Anton 4, 10, 51, 211,
    221, 309
mesmerism 51, 210, 211–12, 253, 268
Messina, Straits of 95
metamorphosis 88, 92, 139, 258, 361,
    375, 380
metaphors 54, 366
  apocalyptic 342, 343
  breath 61, 63
  inner eye 128
  lucidity 123
  mirror 122, 172
  optical 124, 140, 141
  photography 164, 194, 243, 301

physics 258
shadow 184
soul 305
spirit 12, 13, 62–5, 71–80, 83–103,
    296, 375, *see also* light; wax
metaphysics 62–3, 66, 96, 128, 306, 375
meteorology 65, 93, 94–103, 114–15
Meucci, Antonio 405 n. 4
miasma 84, 337
Michaux, Henri 211
Michelangelo 4, 107
microscopes 115, 123, 136, 137, 279
millennarianism 344, 349, *see also*
    Revelation, Book of
Milton, John 342, 347
mimesis 107, 108, 116
mimics 123
mind's eye 128, 131, 139, 141, 165, 218,
    375, *see also* imagination
mirages 98, 101, see *fata morgana*
mirrors 96, 97, 100, 115, 122, 138, 140,
    141, 142, 151, 171–2, 324
  children's literature 207, 208–9
  'Dr Pepper's Ghost' trick 153, 154
  Magritte's paintings 322; Pl. 8
  mortality and 173–4
  in poetry 179–81
Moberly, Charlotte Anne 234
Modernism 261–2, 315–16
monochrome 161, 162–5, 181, 210,
    243
Morandi, Anna 32
More, Henry 106, 128, 282
Morgan, Henry Owen 227, 406 n.18,
    see King, John
Mormons 222
Morrison, Toni 380
Morse code 222, 258
mortality 23, 31, 174, 244, 257
mourning 197, 200, 206, 209, 228,
    244
Mueck, Ron 55–6
Muller, Catherine-Elise (Hélène
    Smith) 278–80; Fig. 23
Mumler, William H. 224, 243

photography/photographs – *Cont.*
  'Cottingley Fairy' 233–4
  death mask realism 24–5
  digital 323, 349, 375
  early printing processes 164–5
  famous portraiture 215–16, 217–18
  fictional 206, 209, 212–18; Fig. 18
  Kirlian 262–3
  Lewis Carroll's 207–8
  memory and 265–6
  monochrome 162–5, 181, 210, 243
  mourning/commemoration 201,
    204, 206, 244
  portraiture 35, 162–5, 174, 181, 189,
    191–202, 206, 215–18, 244
  of prisoners in Iraq 352–3
  psychic 77, 220, 222–5, 228–35,
    241–6, 294, 295, 296, 300
  scotographs 282
  seances 300–1, 303
  self-knowledge 185
  sleep 212–13
  soul-stealing 174, 189, 191–202
  subject-ego/object ego 198–9
  spoof ghost 233
  spontaneous 102
  thought projection 259–61, *see*
    Baraduc; Darget; Donohue;
    Paladina
  war 370, 372–3
  women 401 n. 12, *see also under*
    individual photographers
phrenology 35, 160
physics 88–9, 96, 113, 138, 221, 253–5
physiognomy 35
Piero della Francesca 78
pilgrimages 26, 27
Pinker, Steven 374
Pinter, Harold 378
Pippin, Tina 341
Plath, Sylvia 365
Plato 71, 72, 122, 138, 141, 161,
  338
Platonism 91, 125
Pliny the Elder 24, 66, 159

pneuma 61, 62, 89
Podmore, Frank 241
Poe, Edgar Allan 52, 129, 319–20, 321,
  322, 326
poetry:
  clouds 84–5
  ether 256–7
  mediums 287–8
  metamorphing personalities 379–80
  mirrors 179
  narcissism 170
  portents 101, 321
  reality of art 351
politics, Book of Revelation and 338,
  345
Pollock, Jackson 112, 315
Pomponazzi, Pietro 100, 122
pornography 42
portents 98–100, 114–15, 132, 134, 142,
  154, 267, 312, 314; Figs. 9a, 9c
portraiture 24, 312
  photography 35, 162–5, 174, 181,
    189, 191–202, 206, 215–18, 244
  waxworks 35, 36–40
Poussin, Nicolas 39, 92, 372; Pl. 3
Powell, Michael 181
Prel, Carl du 269
Price, Harry 243, 299, 409 n. 21
Prinzhorn, Hans 273
projection 131–6, 243, 259–61, 304, 324,
  325
projective imagination 115, 231, 280–1,
  325
prophecy 106, 337, 340, 341, 343, 345
Protestantism 115
Proust, Marcel 124, 185, 217, 266, 315
psyche 10, 71, 121, 175, 176, 211, 242,
  267, 313, 371, *see also* self; soul
psychic research 67, 88, 272
  Crookes 226
  ectoplasm 299
  Flournoy 278–80
  reality of experiences 288–95
  SPR 234–49, 268–9, 304–6, 326
psychoanalysis 272, 339

and spirit distinction 66–7
stolen 174, 183–4, 189–202, 357, 358, 361, 380–1
as infant 75
transmigration of 13, 247
uncanny 54, 305
winged 71
Southey, Robert 359
special effects 156, 183, 270–1, 350–2
spectres 10, 133, 134, 153, 173, 223, 224
Spender, Matthew 116
sperm 64–5, 73, 296
Spielberg, Steven 163, 330
spirit(s) 9–10, 13, 52, 56
    as breath 61–8
    contacting 222–35
    cyberspace 322–32
    Native American 194, 199, 282
    and soul distinction 66–7
    winged 71–80
    zombies 10, 356, 357–68, *see also* angels; ghosts; spectres
Spiritualism 67, 88, 221–2, 225–6, 228–32, 234, 237, 242, 255, 268
    aftermath of First World War 244–5
    ectoplasm 91, 243, 245, 278, 290–307
spitting images 296
spittle 296, 297
SPR (Society for Psychical Research) 226, 234–42, 244, 248, 260, 268, 283, 288, 292, 299, 303, 304, 306
sprites 62, 71, 72, 75, 224
Stanislawa P. (medium) 295, 298; Fig. 24
Statius 176
Stein, Gertrude 247
Stephen, Leslie 206
stereoscopes 113
Stevens, Wallace 11, 68, 349, 351
Stevenson, Robert Louis 124, 175, 183, 227, 247, 268
Stieglitz, Alfred 262
Stoicism 89
Strachey, Lytton 238
Strauss, Richard 184

stream of consciousness 242, 267, 273
Strutt, F. W. *see* Rayleigh, Lord
subjectivity 378–81
suicide bombers 353
supernatural 87, 106, 110, 122, 139, 142
superstition 99–100
Surrealism 101, 107, 109, 297, 320–1, 322, 362
surveillance 323, 374
Susini, Clemente 34, 42, 48–9; Fig. 4
suspended animation 51–2, 56
Suvée, Joseph 159; Fig. 14
Swan, Claudia 125
Swinton, Tilda 53
symbolism
    birds 75–9, 140; Fig. 7a
    insects 64
    see also children; foam and froth
Sylvester, David 321

tableaux 39, 149, 212, 214, 216
Taglioni, Marie 64, 388 n. 11
Tarde, Gabriel 229
Tausk, Victor 272, 326
taxidermy 33, 41, 42
technology 13, 241, 242, 254, 273, 323
telecommunications 323, 326
telegraphy 222, 225, 228, 254, 258, 269
telepathy 211, 234, 238, 241, 242, 254, 267, 268–9
telescopes 115, 123, 136, 137, 138, 151
television 225, 241, 269–70, 326–7, 349, 351, 367
Tennyson, Alfred Lord 179–81, 206, 214, 215, 217
terrorism 345, 373
thanksgiving offerings 23, 27–8, 29
theatre 132–7, 152–6, 253, 362
Theosophy 227, 241, 246, 254, 261, 304
Thérèse of Lisieux, St 26
Thompson, E. P. 344, 346
Thompson, S. P. 113
Thomson, John 191

Warren, Samuel 211
Warrick, F. W. 229, 231, 407 nn. 31, 38
Washington, George 29
Watts, G. F. 217–18
wax/waxworks 11, 12, 14, 46–57, 150, 384 n.2–4
    anatomical 29–44, 48–9; Fig. 4
    ideoplasts 229, 260, 295
    religious 23–30, 50
    spectral casts 291
    spirit imprints 291, 301, 302; Figs. 4a, 25a
Wearing, Gillian 417 n. 25
Webb, Kenneth 362
Wedgwood, Josiah 35, 159
Weekes, Henry 29
Wegener, Paul 183
Wells, H. G. 270, 271, 278, 280, 325, 337; Fig. 22
White Zombie (1932) 361–3
Wiene, Robert 147, 212
Wilde, Oscar 184
Williams, Rowan 348
Wilson, C. T. R. 256
wings 68, 71–80
wireless 273, see also radio
witch-hunts 99, 134
witchcraft 133, 194, 245, 336
Wolfe, Tom 375
women:
    altered states 211–12

photography 225
'sensitives' 254–5
spiritualism 225–6, 227, 228, 234, 282–3
university education 238
Wood, James 328–9
Woolf, Virginia 205–6, 247, 283, 316
Wordsworth, William 34–5, 114, 359
Worthington, A. M. 223
Woytowicz, John 330
Wright, Elsie 233
Wright, Joseph 159
Wright, Patience 39–40
Wyld's Monster Globe 151
Wynfield, David Wilkie 217

X-rays 136, 225, 256, 323

Yeats, W. B. 277, 280–2, 303, 338

zeitgeist 62
Zeki, Semir 374
Zillmer, Eric 311
Zionism 346
Žižek, Slavoj 358, 375
zombies 10, 356, 357–68
Zulu warriors 196
Zumbo, Giulio Gaetano 31, 384 n.1